D1130061

Understanding Popular Violence in the English Revolution

This is a critical re-evaluation of one of the best-known episodes of crowd action in the English Revolution, in which crowds in their thousands invaded and plundered the houses of the landed classes.

The so-called Stour Valley riots have become accepted as the paradigm of class hostility, determining plebeian behaviour within the Revolution. An exercise in micro-history, the book questions this dominant reading by trying to understand the interrelated contexts of local responses to the political and religious counter-revolution of the 1630s and the confessional politics of the early 1640s. It explains both the outbreak of popular 'violence' and its ultimate containment in terms of a popular (and Parliamentary) political culture that legitimised attacks on the political, but not the social order.

In seeking to understand the immediate event, the book advances a series of arguments of more general importance for the enterprise of reading crowd actions. As well as being a contribution to the history of the English Revolution, the book also questions how that history has been written. Exposing the genealogy of the Stour Valley riots, the study offers a critical reflection on how the history of the popular role within the Revolution has been, and might be, constructed.

JOHN WALTER is Reader in History and Director of the Local History Centre, University of Essex

Past and Present Publications

General Editor: JOANNA INNES, *Somerville College, Oxford*

Past and Present Publications comprise books similar in character to the articles in the journal *Past and Present*. Whether the volumes in the series are collections of essays – some previously published, others new studies – or monographs, they encompass a wide variety of scholarly and original works primarily concerned with social, economic and cultural changes, and their causes and consequences. They will appeal to both specialists and non-specialists and will endeavour to communicate the results of historical and allied research in the most readable and lively form.

For a list of titles in Past and Present Publications, see end of book.

Understanding Popular Violence in the English Revolution

The Colchester Plunderers

JOHN WALTER

CAMBRIDGE
UNIVERSITY PRESS

PUBLISHED BY THE PRESS SYNDICATE OF THE UNIVERSITY OF CAMBRIDGE
The Pitt Building, Trumpington Street, Cambridge CB2 1RP, United Kingdom

CAMBRIDGE UNIVERSITY PRESS
The Edinburgh Building, Cambridge, CB2 2RU, UK http://www.cup.cam.ac.uk
40 West 20th Street, New York, NY 10011–4211, USA http://www.cup.org
10 Stamford Road, Oakleigh, Melbourne 3166, Australia

First published 1999

Printed in the United Kingdom at the University Press, Cambridge

Typeset in Times 10/12 pt   [CE]

A catalogue record for this book is available from the British Library

Library of Congress Cataloguing in Publication data

Walter, John, 1948–
    Understanding popular violence in the English Revolution: the Colchester plunderers / John Walter.
        p.   cm. – (Past and present publications)
Includes index.
ISBN 0 521 65186 7 (hardback)
1. Great Britain – History – Puritan Revolution, 1642–1660 –
Destruction and pillage. 2. Political violence – England –
Colchester Region – History – 17th century. 3. Social conflict –
England – Colchester Region – History – 17th century. 4. Pillage –
England – Colchester Region – History – 17th century. 5. Riots –
England – Colchester Region – History – 17th century. 6. Stour Valley
(Essex and Suffolk, England) – History. 7. Colchester Region
(England) – History.   I. Title.
DA406.W35 1999   942.06′2 – dc21   98–39338   CIP

ISBN 0 521 65186 7 hardback

It being my lot to be fixed in the Town of COLCHESTER, and finding that it abounds with many curious Materials, which, if digested, might be of use to present and future generations, I thought I could not better employ my leisure hours than in compiling this Book, which I now offer to the Reader.

Philip Morant, *The History and Antiquities of the most ancient Town and Borough of Colchester* (1748), Preface.

Contents

Acknowledgements

This book has been many years in the research and writing and I have, in consequence, incurred a large number of obligations. Space does not allow me to acknowledge them all here, but they can be found in the footnotes to the volume. The research for this book has taken me to many libraries and archives. If I sometimes groaned as the trail led me on, the consistently friendly welcome and helpful service I received helped to ease the extra mile(s). I would like especially to thank the staff at the Essex Record Office – in particular, at Chelmsford Vic Gray, and later Ken Hall and Janet Smith and at Colchester Paul Coverley and Jane Bedford – who have provided unfailing support. I would also like to thank the staff at the Bedfordshire, Hertfordshire, Leicestershire, Northamptonshire and Suffolk Record Offices, the British Library Manuscripts Room, Public Record Office, Cambridge University Library Manuscripts and Rare Books Rooms, Bodleian Library and the Albert Sloman Library at the University of Essex. At the Department of Historiography and Archives, English Province of the Society of Jesus, J. G. Holt, S. J. and Tom McCoog, S. J. helped me to locate important sources. The depth of analysis attempted in what follows would not have been possible without the advantage of the many excellent unpublished dissertations on early modern Essex; I would like to thank in particular Mark Byford, Bill Cliftlands, Robin Clifton, Frances Condick, James Davies, Nigel Goose and Richard Dean Smith. Local historians in both Essex and Suffolk have been generous in sharing their knowledge with me. I would like to thank in particular Gordon Blackwood, Peter Northeast, Lyn Boothman and Arthur Teece of the Long Melford Historical Research Group, Frank Grace and Janet Gyford, the historians respectively of early modern Ipswich and Witham. Drs Janet Cooper and Chris Thornton of the Victoria County History of Essex generously allowed me to consult their Colchester files. Fellow students of seventeenth-century England helped with references. I would like to thank in

particular Tim Wales, Tom Webster and Mike Braddick. Christopher
Thompson, with whom I have enjoyed many conversations, generously
shared with me information and sources from his own unrivalled
knowledge of the Earl of Warwick and the county community of Essex.
At Essex, my colleague Steve Smith brought his specialist knowledge to a
reading of part of the manuscript, and stimulating exchanges with him
helped me in my clumsy efforts to rethink the validity of class as an
explanatory category for early modern societies, while my fellow early
modernist, Joan Davies, helped me to find parallels with her own and
others' work on confessional politics in early modern France. I am
grateful for having been given the opportunity to give preliminary
sketches of the project as papers at seminars at the Universities of
Bristol, Cambridge and Manchester and the 1996 Symposium on Religious Dissent in East Anglia and would like to thank participants for
their comments. Teaching students in the University of Essex Local
History Centre and the Department of History allowed me first to think
through and refine many of the arguments here; I have learnt from them
all. Mike Braddick, Anthony Fletcher, John Morrill and Keith
Wrightson each read a draft of the manuscript. I would like to thank in
particular Keith Wrightson for the characteristically close reading he
gave the manuscript and John Morrill for his willingness to answer my
many queries about (sometimes obscure) aspects of the period; if he
sometimes wondered whether the questions would ever cease, it never
showed. Their consistent encouragement while I stripped away layers of
interpretation and wondered where (and whether) the research would
end was vital. Bill Cliftlands, whose 1987 doctoral dissertation on the
'well-affected' and the 'country' in the English Revolution I supervised,
helped to educate me in the possible sources for this project; exploring
them renewed my admiration for the energy and imagination he brought
to his research. I would like to record my gratitude for the award by the
Humanities Research Board of the British Academy under its Research
Leave Scheme which, together with generous study leave from the
University of Essex, made possible the final writing of the book. G. I.
Morrison provided inspiration while I wrote. Since this project was
conceived in the bed, and nourished at the board, of Pat and Arthur
Brown, whose encyclopaedic knowledge of Essex and its histories
provided a source of inspiration, I hope they will accept this as partial
repayment for their friendship. Bron, Ben and Angharad had absolutely
nothing to do with the research and writing, but everything to do with its
eventual completion. I thank them for their love.

Abbreviations

APC	*Acts of the Privy Council of England*, ed. J. Dasent et al. (London, 1890–1964)
BL	British Library
Bodl. Lib.	Bodleian Library
CCC	M. A. E. Green, ed., *Calendar of the Proceedings of the Committee for Compounding, etc., 1643–1660* (5 vols., London, 1889–92)
CJ	*Journals of the House of Commons*
CRO	Essex Record Office, Colchester branch
CSPD	*Calendar of State Papers, Domestic Series*
CSPV	*Calendar of the State Papers and Manuscripts, Relating to English Affairs, Existing in the Archives and Collections of Venice, and in other Libraries of Northern Italy*, ed. R. Brown and A. B. Hinds (38 vols., London, 1804–1947)
CUL	Cambridge University Library
DNB	*Dictionary of National Biography*, ed. Sir L. Stephen and Sir S. Lee (London, 1917–)
EA	*Essex Archaeology and History*
EHR	*English Historical Review*
EJ	*Essex Journal*
ER	*Essex Review*
ERec	*Essex Recusant*
ERO	Essex Record Office
ESRO	East Suffolk Record Office, Ipswich
HJ	*Historical Journal*
HLRO	Houses of Lords Record Office
HMC	Historical Manuscripts Commission
JBS	*Journal British Studies*
MR	*Mercurius Rusticus, or The Countries Complaint of the Murthers, Robberies, Plundrings, and other Outrages,*

	Committed by the Rebels on his Majesties faithfull Subjects (Oxford, 1643), repr. in P. Thomas (ed.). *The English Revolution 3. Oxford Royalists* (4 vols., London, 1971)
LJ	*Journals of the House of Lords*
PJ	*Private Journals of the Long Parliament*, ed. W. H. Coates, V. F. Snow and A. Steele Young (New Haven and London, 1982–97)
P&P	*Past and Present*
PRO	Public Record Office
PSIA	*Proceedings of the Suffolk Institute of Archaeology*
RecHist	*Recusant History*
RO	Record Office
SR	*Suffolk Review*
TEAS	*Transactions of the Essex Archaeological Society*
TRHS	*Transactions of the Royal History Society*
VCH	Victoria County History
WP	*Winthrop Papers*
WR	*Walker Revised*
WSRO	West Suffolk Record Office, Bury St Edmunds

Introduction

An event is a portentous outcome ... It is not just a happening there to be narrated but a happening to which cultural significance has successfully been assigned. And its identity and significance are established primarily in terms of its location in time, in relation to a course or chain of other happenings. Both their internal design and their assigned significance mark events as in the first instance matters of sequence, of the organisation and meaning of action in time. Events, indeed, are our principal points of access to the structuring of social action in time ... Events, however detailed, are constructed not observed.

Philip Abrams, 'Explaining Events: A Problem of Method'[1]

When the Colchester gentleman, Sir John Lucas, stepped out of his back gate shortly after midnight on 22 August 1642, he stepped almost immediately into the pages of history: his secret attempt to take aid to Charles I on the eve of civil war aroused the hostility of the townsfolk and raised crowds numbered, it was said, in their thousands. These crowds plundered and vandalised his house and subjected Sir John and his family to a series of indignities that transgressed boundaries of status and gender in early modern society. Thereafter attacks on noble and gentry households spread out into the counties of Essex and Suffolk. The scale of popular 'violence' ensured that the episode figured prominently in the contemporary record and secured for Sir John a place in the hagiography of the Revolution's victims. In turn, the prominence of the event in contemporary print culture ensured its writing into the later historiography of the English Revolution. When historians of the English

---

Place of publication is London unless otherwise stated.
[1] P. Abrams, *Historical Sociology* (Shepton Mallet, 1988), p. 191

1

Revolution talk of class conflict being a determinant of plebeian political behaviour, it is almost always to the 'Stour Valley riots' to which they turn in support of their argument. The case of the Colchester Plunderers is now taken to be *the* example of class hostility as the determinant of a popular role in the English Revolution. This study – an exercise in micro-history – offers a critical re-evaluation of the episode, the uses to which it has been put in the historiography of early modern England and the uses to which it can be put in recovering evidence of a popular political culture in early modern England.

The scale of the attacks and the level of destruction in the summer of 1642 was unprecedented. Not even in the rebellions of the sixteenth century had the gentry been the targets of such popular fury. The attacks represented a decisive break with the pre-revolutionary tradition of protest. In that tradition, early modern crowds, operating within a culture of obedience which placed a premium on securing legitimacy for their actions, had sought to defend their rights and to seek justice by negotiating with, rather than challenging, authority. They deliberately fashioned their protest to assert the legitimacy of their actions and demands. In so doing, they often mimicked the role required of the local magistracy by the English Crown. Food rioters 'confiscated' grain being illegally transported or traded and either returned it to the authorities in pointed criticism of their inactivity or sold it at a 'just price'. Protestors against enclosure took direct action by pulling down hedges *and* sought to embarrass both encloser and authority by a (selective) appropriation of laws designed to regulate enclosure and by appeals to a moral economy, in the early modern period as much that of the Crown (and church) as crowd. Riot was the last, rather than first, resort. While protestors employed on occasion a rhetoric of violence, violence, where it occurred, was directed against property, not persons, or displaced symbolically through the use of proxies, such as effigies of enclosers.[2]

While studies of the early modern crowd have challenged earlier stereotypes and established that there was a politics informing and shaping the protest, they have seen that politics as generally limited and largely instrumental. Thus in recent and well-received studies of agrarian protests in the fens of the east and forests of the west that began during the Personal Rule and extended into the English Revolution we are told that the riots were essentially defensive and conservative. Rioters in the

---

[2] J. Walter, 'Crown and crowd: popular culture and popular protest in early modern England (sixteenth and seventeenth centuries)' in *Sotsial'naia istoriia: problemy sinteza* (Moscow, 1994), pp. 235–48. This article develops some of the subsequent comments made here at greater length.

fens did not give expression to political feelings, but contented themselves with drawing attention to specific grievances of immediate concern; there was little to suggest any generalised political stance. Similarly, protestors in the western forests manifested positive political indifference. Rural disorders there were 'essentially non-ideological and non-revolutionary' in character.[3] These judgements were endorsed in a general study of 'village revolts' from the early sixteenth to mid-seventeenth centuries. While acknowledging the sophistication with which protest could be organised, a consistent (and troubling) refrain in Professor R. B. Manning's study is that protestors are 'devoid of political consciousness and their writings or utterances do not employ a political vocabulary'; in effect riots displayed 'primitive or pre-political behaviour because they failed to develop into some modern form of protest or participation in the political nation'.[4] Inasmuch then as riots could be said to represent a form of popular political action this was 'traditional', 'customary' or even 'reactionary'. David Underdown's most recent work offers a sensitive analysis of popular politics and a convincing demonstration of the spread of political consciousness beyond the political nation, narrowly conceived. But Underdown too sees this politics as conservative, if not universally deferential. It was grounded in a normative (and mythical) conception of a just society. Popular protest reflected a localist orientation and drew on the legitimising force of custom.[5]

In 1642 violence was directed against the property and persons of the landed class and in so doing threatened to turn the world upside down. What then explains the seemingly sharp disjuncture between the Stour Valley attacks and the preceding pattern of protest? David Underdown has suggested that there have been three models by which historians have sought to explain the popular role in the English Revolution: deference (which has been largely used to explain royalist success in acquiring an army), localism, and class (which has been used to explain popular Parliamentarianism). Of these, it is the last which has been held to explain the turn of events in Essex and Suffolk in the summer of 1642. It was, in Underdown's words, 'class hatred of the gentry' that prompted popular violence.[6] This has for a long time been the commonly accepted

---

[3] B. Sharp, *In Contempt of All Authority: Rural Artisans and Riot in the West of England, 1586–1660* (Berkeley and London, 1980); K. Lindley, *Fenland Riots and the English Revolution* (1982).

[4] R. B. Manning, *Village Revolts: Social Protest and Popular Disturbances in England, 1509–1640* (Oxford, 1988), pp. 2–3, 309–11, 318–19.

[5] D. Underdown, *A Freeborn People: Politics and the Nation in Seventeenth-Century England* (Oxford, 1996), pp. vii, ix, 59.

[6] D. Underdown, *Revel, Riot, and Rebellion: Popular Politics and Culture in England 1603–1660* (Oxford, 1985), ch. 1 and p. 169.

interpretation. Most firmly developed by Marxist historians of the English Revolution, and in particular in the work of Brian Manning, this consensus represents a rare point of historiographical agreement amongst revisionists and post-revisionists alike.[7] This study questions that orthodoxy. It does so by subjecting the consensus on both the 'politics' of the early modern crowd and the role of class in explaining the exceptionalism of the Stour Valley attacks to a critical re-examination.

The emphasis on a backward-looking politics is a common trope in studies of primitive and 'pre-political' protest in European and other societies. Undoubtedly, protestors drew on the image of a normative past to defend their rights. But the interpretation of this in terms of custom and conservatism is unnecessarily constraining. It is not always appreciated that appeals to an often imagined past could produce radical, not conservative, protest when used to confront change. Indeed work on the ability of peasants to selectively appropriate, even to invent, custom suggests the dangers of conflating custom with conservatism.[8] Fracturing crowd actions by classifying them according to a typology of riot (food, enclosure, etc.) almost inevitably produces an analysis which emphasises their limited and instrumental nature. Similarly, labelling protests non-political is accomplished by a questionable reference to their failure to engage with 'high politics'. But if we abandon the typologies by which protest has been dissected, and replace the teleological hierarchies implicit in defining the political with a focus on how power was constituted and contested in early modern society, then we can begin to uncover the often complex politics behind crowd actions.

It is possible to suggest a reading of popular protest in early modern England that offers a more integrated and dynamic reading of popular politics. English monarchs, all too aware of the limited forces of repression at their control, sought to police social and economic change in order to minimise the threat of popular disorder. They did so within the terms of a public discourse that repeatedly stressed that the rationale for royal policies was to protect their subjects and, in particular, the weak and poor. By so doing, they sought to transmute power into authority and thereby secure popular consent to their rule. A provincial magistracy, drawn from a landed class with attenuated seigneurial powers,

---

[7] B. Manning, *The English People and the English Revolution* (1976), pp. 171–83.

[8] See, for example, R. Faith, '"The Great Rumour" of 1377 and Peasant Ideology' in R. Hilton (ed.), *The English Rising of 1381* (Cambridge, 1984), pp. 43–73; Faith, 'The class struggle in fourteenth-century England' in R. Samuel (ed.), *People's History and Socialist Theory* (1981), pp. 50–60; R. M. Smith, 'Some thoughts on "hereditary" and "proprietary" rights in land under customary law in thirteenth- and fourteenth-century England', *Law and History Review*, 1 (1983), pp. 60–82. I am grateful to Richard Smith for discussion on this point.

needed also to secure their authority by a visible attentiveness to popular grievances. Thus, the formal weakness of the state's repressive force, coupled with an acute awareness (even moral panic) about increasing social tensions, made authority ready to respond to popular grievances. In turn, the dependence of power holders from monarch to magistrates on the maintenance of respect for their authority placed a premium on rule by law, and through the law courts. At the same time, lacking a professional bureaucracy, royal government sought to enlist popular support by publicising its policies to police economic change, even inviting the people's co-operation in the detection of wrongdoing. Out of this was created a strong sense of legitimation for those who engaged in protest. Central then to popular political culture was a set of expectations about the proper exercise of authority. Central to these was the idea of a just king whose rule, by definition, could not tolerate oppression of his people since monarchy existed to deliver justice to all its subjects. protestors invoked, rather than challenged, royal authority; protest was studded with expressions of loyalty to the monarch.

Parallel to the politics of subsistence represented by opposition to enclosure and defence of the priorities of poorer consumers, there was another strand of popular politics. This saw a more formal engagement with the political and religious policies of the English Crown. Both the politics of subsistence and this more formal politics could be comprehended within a broader popular political culture. This was not a recent creation, but the demands of the Tudor state and the confessional consequences of the Reformation had increased both its depth and the level of political consciousness. This development could also be partly located in the structural weaknesses of the English monarchy. The Crown's lack of professional bureaucracy or a standing army led in part to the communal and associative character of a political rule that required, as well as promoted, a high degree of semi-autonomous government.[9] Thus, crowds that expressed a belief in their right to police the grain market could also advance claims to police confessional boundaries.

A popular political culture that had at its core a series of expectations about the responsibilities of the good king (or good lord) carried with it the possibility of a rejection of respect for that authority. To label popular politics conservative underestimates its capacity for critical analysis. The 1630s saw Charles I pursuing policies, not least in forest and fen, which challenged his image as a just king and transgressed this

---

[9] P. Collinson, *De Republica Anglorum: or History with the Politics Put Back* (Cambridge, 1990).

broader sense of popular rights. The popular experience of the 1630s as a period when religious and political liberties were also challenged, mediated from 1640 by denunciations in Parliament, pulpit and press, of the *ancien régime* of Charles I's Personal Rule, threatened a challenge to the earlier tradition of loyalty to the king. There was, therefore, the possibility that the new political space represented by the criticism and collapse of authority at the onset of the English Revolution would see a realisation of the potentially radical critique inherent within this tradition of popular political culture. The events of the summer of 1642 might have been taken as the start of just such a process. But if so, that potential was not realised. This study seeks to explain the outbreak of popular violence, and its ultimate containment, in the critical early months of the Revolution in terms of a popular (and Parliamentary) political culture that legitimised attacks on the political, but not the social, order.

This study did not start life as a book. It was to be one of a number of discrete article-length studies of the various forms of crowd action in early modern England that were intended to be, and remain, preliminary statements to a larger study of popular political culture in early modern England.[10] Each of these studies was designed to support an argument for the importance of contextualising crowd actions. This was to be a double contextualisation. The first was to be a contextualisation of the social dramas represented by crowd action within the immediate context of local social, economic and political structures and relationships. This represented an attempt to get behind the impoverishing and power-saturated records of authority that labelled protest as riot in order to recover the fuller meaning of the actions so stereotyped. The second was to be an examination of the political meaning of crowd action within the broader context of a political culture characterised both by popular participation therein and knowledge thereof. This was a culture which formally proscribed riot, but acknowledged the responsibilities of power within a public discourse in such a way that it could be appropriated to legitimise independent popular action.

Crowd actions, these studies argued, have too often been ripped from their immediate integument, and used to support (sometimes merely to

---

[10] J. Walter, 'Grain riots and popular attitudes to the law: Maldon and the crisis of 1629' in J. Brewer and J. Styles (eds.), *An Ungovernable People: The English and their Law in the Seventeenth and Eighteenth Centuries* (1980), pp. 47–84; 'A "Rising of the People"? The Oxfordshire Rising of 1596', *P&P*, 107 (1985), pp. 90–143. A further study re-examining the late sixteenth-century disorders over food, presented as a paper to the 1985 Medieval and Tudor London seminar, Institute of Historical Research, has not yet been published.

decorate) macro-historical analyses and their master narratives in ways that misread the complexity of their meanings. The case studies were designed to show that an insensitivity to these contexts had led to misunderstandings of the individual episodes that were their subject. This too was the case with the attack on Sir John Lucas. Once begun, work on the episode recovered a larger roll-call of attacks than had previously been known and added complex layers of meaning to that conflict. The 'Stour Valley riots' were not restricted to the Stour Valley. Nor were the 'riots' largely spontaneous attacks in which class hostility masqueraded as anti-popery. The crowd actions were not unexpected and they involved either directly or indirectly an alliance which brought together political figures like the Earl of Warwick and ministers and the middling sort, who in turn had links with the godly radicals of London. All this suggested the need for a deeper contextualisation, one that not only located the attacks within the micro-politics of local and regional society but which also traced important developments over a longer time span and engaged more directly with the dense political developments of the 1630s and early 1640s. Thus this book grew from the chrysalis of an article (though not I hope like Topsy).

Writing the history of an event and eventful history have attracted recently a more theoretically informed discussion.[11] This study uses the immediate event represented by the attacks to examine the interplay between structure and process and within that the role of popular agency in early modern England. The analysis operates at several levels and within various time spans to offer a 'braided narrative'.[12] An exercise in micro-history, it offers a thickened description of the event. That micro-history is paralleled by a concern with broader historical trends in the period and with the interrelationships between the local and 'national', particularly in the political and religious history of the 1630s. Thus, in order fully to comprehend the meanings of the attacks it draws on, and in its turn contributes to, the analysis of a large number of specific themes in the history of early modern England and the English Revolution; among these, the social relationships of production in rural

---

[11] L. Stone, 'The revival of narrative', *P&P*, 85 (1979), pp. 3–24; P. Burke, 'History of events and the revival of narrative' in Burke (ed.), *New Perspectives on Historical Writing* (Oxford, 1992), pp. 233–48; W. H. Sewell, 'Three temporalities: towards an eventful sociology' in T. J. McDonald (ed.), *The Historical Turn in the Human Sciences* (Ann Arbor, 1996), pp. 245–80; L. J. Griffin, 'Temporalities, events and explanation in historical sociology: an introduction', *Sociological Methods and Research*, 20 (1992), pp. 403–27. P. Abrams, 'Explaining events: a problem of method' in his *Historical Sociology*, pp. 190–226, remains one of the most incisive discussions of the potentialities of eventful history.

[12] The phrase is Peter Burke's: Burke, 'History of events', p. 163.

industrialisation; the dissemination of news through a developing communications infrastructure and the growth of a political public; the resistance of reformed religion to the challenge of Arminianism and ceremonialism and the conflicts this produced at the level of the parish; the provincial politics of Personal Rule in the 1630s and the impact of the collapse of the *ancien régime* in the early 1640s. In doing so, the micro-history marries the concerns of the political historian with the techniques and sources of the social historian to present a more detailed picture at a more intimate level of the impact of the events of the 1630s and early 1640s.

It is not just in the large number of topics that the study covers, nor in the rich detail that it permits, that the advantage of micro-history can be seen. The power of historical analysis has been significantly advanced by the specialised sub-disciplines that have proliferated. But these advances have not been without cost. The heuristic abstractions practised by these 'adjectival histories' carry with them the danger of failing to recognise the interrelatedness of the past, sometimes in ways that threaten the value of their analyses.[13] The book argues that to understand the attacks in terms of their causation and meaning we need to recognise the ways in which for contemporaries the discrete abstractions of history's sub-disciplines – economic, religious, political, cultural history – were experienced not as discrete subjects. A contextualised analysis allows us to pay attention to how their meanings converged with, and contaminated, each other.

One other powerful gain offered by micro-historical analysis is that it restores to history, and a role in its making, those groups whose marginality and subordinate status threaten their exclusion.[14] A contextualised micro-history allows us to reconstruct the lived experience of the actors in the narrative. It also allows us to see not only how they experienced the larger historical processes and events, but how their understandings (and misunderstandings) influenced how they responded to, and participated in, them. If contemporary perception played an important part in determining what form their agency would take, then the tighter focus of micro-history makes it possible to grasp the interrelatedness of factors in lived experience that informed contemporary perception. As the example of the Colchester Plunderers makes clear, popular 'violence' was neither

---

[13] For the phrase 'adjectival histories', see A. Wilson, *Re-Thinking Social History: English Society 1570–1920 and its Interpretation* (Manchester, 1993), p. 20. For a discussion of the dangers of narrow specialisation in a mature social history, see K. Wrightson, 'The enclosure of English social history', *Rural History*, 1 (1990), pp. 73–81.

[14] See the collection of essays in E. Muir and G. Ruggiero (eds.), *Micro-history and the Lost People of Europe* (Baltimore and London, 1991); G. Levi, 'On microhistory', in Burke (ed.), *New Perspectives*, pp. 93–113.

simply reactive nor narrowly instrumental. The shape of the crowds' actions and their choice of targets were informed by their construction of the crisis of the early 1640s, a crisis simultaneously experienced as a threat to both livelihoods and liberties. Their understanding of the crisis drew on their recent experience of the impact of the period of Personal Rule and its collapse, experience mediated (for some) by a classed reading of those events and by a cultural inheritance of anti-popery, a tradition of political participation, and the discourses of an emerging Parliamentary political culture.

This study, then, uses local knowledge to address larger historical issues. Central to these is an attempt to understand the meaning of popular violence in early modern England. The book advances a series of arguments as to how we should read crowd actions. In turn, central to this is an emphasis upon the existence of a popular political culture, a political culture which the book reconstructs within the specific conjunctures of the early 1640s. It was this political culture, I argue, and the identities it underwrote, that informed the crowds' actions in the attacks of the summer of 1642. The book offers a critical reflection on the relative roles of the languages of class and anti-popery in constructing those identities and prompting the attacks. At the same time, as well as being a contribution to writing the history of the English Revolution, this study is also intended to be a critical contribution to how that history has been written. It examines how the definition of what happened in the event, and why, became the focus of political struggle within contemporary polemic, and how in turn the interpretations this created were absorbed uncritically into later historical narratives. Exposing the genealogy of the narratives of the Colchester Plunderers, the study uses this to offer a wider critical reflection on how the history of the popular role within the English Revolution has been, and might be, constructed.

Part 1

The event

1. *An event and its history*

And that their loss of liberty might not be all their punishment, it was the usual course (and very few scaped it,) after any man was committed as a *notorious malignant*, (which was the brand,) that his estate and goods were seized or plundered, by an order from the House of Commons or some committee, or [by] the soldiers, (who in their march they took the goods of all catholics and eminent malignants as lawful prize), or by the fury and licence of the common people, who were in all places grown to that barbarity and rage against the nobility and gentry, (under the style of *cavaliers*,) that it was not safe for any to live at their houses who were taken notice of as no votaries to the Parliament.

So the common people (no doubt by the advice of their superiors) in Essex on a sudden beset the house of Sir John Lucas, one of the best gentleman of that county, and one of the most eminent affection to the King, being a gentleman of the privy chamber to the Prince of Wales; and upon pretence that he was going to the King, possessed themselves of all his horses and arms, seized upon his arms, seized upon his person, and used him with all possible indignities, not without some threats to murder him: and when the mayor of Colchester, whither he was brought, with more humanity than the rest, offered to keep him prisoner in his own house till the pleasure of the Parliament should be farther known, they compelled him, (for he was willing to be compelled,) to send him to the common gaol; where he remained, glad of that security, till the House of Commons removed him to another prison, (without ever charging him with any crime).

Edward Hyde, Earl of Clarendon,
The History of the Rebellion and Civil Wars in England Begun in the Year 1641, book 6, pp. 36–7
(published in 1702, but written *c.* 1647).

Shortly after midnight on 22 August 1642 the Essex gentleman Sir John Lucas attempted to leave his house at St John's Abbey near Colchester to join Charles I.[1] His intention was to take with him men, horse and arms to support the king in the coming civil war. His plans, however, had been betrayed. As he attempted to slip through the back gate of his house, he was detected by a night-watch set by the mayor of Colchester. A musket was fired and word carried into the town. There the alarm was taken up. Drums were beaten and the beacon fired to alert the inhabitants of the surrounding villages. Reports that there were a hundred men in arms at St John's put the town in an uproar. Colchester's trained bands and the Parliamentary volunteers, some five hundred of whom had assembled in the town, besieged the Abbey and brought up two pieces of ordinance to make a battery. Rumours of men in arms within St John's then brought men, women and children who gathered in groups, altogether some two-thousand strong, around the house.

At daybreak, the crowds rushed into the house. There they seized Thomas Newcomen, a minister in the town, who was to have acted as Lucas's chaplain. 'They tease his clothes of his back, beat him with their Cudgels and Halberts, & with infinite exclamations, carry him in triumph through the chief streets of the Town, by the way ent[e]ring into a wild but very serious consideration, not whether he should dye (for that they had resolved at first) but to what death to put him; one votes drowning, another stoning, another bids him beat out his braines.' But after consulting one of the aldermen of the town, the crowd carried Newcomen to the town's gaol, promising to return and take order with him later.

Back at the house, a search uncovered 'much armor and a great many of new pistolls and carbines ready charged, new greate sadle and other warlike furniture'. These, together with Sir John's horses, were seized and taken away. The crowd imprisoned all the servants of Sir John they could find. One old retainer was seized and bound to a tree and interrogated with a musket to his breast and lighted matches between his fingers: What were his master's intentions? Had Mr Newcomen sworn them to an oath of secrecy? Some twenty of the invaders rushed into the 'Ladies chamber'. There they lay hands on Sir John's mother, his wife and sister. They too were interrogated at swordpoint as to the where-abouts of the 'Cavaliers' and arms. Sir John's wife and sister were then marched off under armed guard. His mother, led through the town 'with the like or greater insolency', narrowly escaped being struck down by a sword blow aimed at her by a man on horseback. 'Faint and breathlesse',

---

[1] The account that follows is derived from B. Ryves, *Mercurius Rusticus, or The Countries Complaint of the Murthers, Robberies, Plundrings, and other Outrages, Committed by the Rebels on his Majesties faithfull Subjects* (1643), pp. 1–5.

she was allowed with ill grace to pause at a shop, 'yet this leave was no sooner obtained but the rest of that rude rabble, threatened to pull downe the house unlesse they thrust her out'. Two other gentlewomen from the household who had managed to escape found no refuge. Neighbours dared not take them in since threats were made to burn their houses if they did so.

Sir John and his arms secured, the crowds turned their attention back to St John's. 'Having secured the M[aste]r they now beginne to plunder the house. All is prize that comes to hand, mony, plate, jewells, linnen, wollen, brasse, pewter, etc. A few houres disroabe the house of that Rich furniture that had adorned it for many yeares'. By early afternoon, fresh rumours were circulating: 200 armed horsemen had been discovered hiding in the vault of the Abbey; they have killed nine men and were about to descend on the town.[2] Shops were shut up 'on the instant' and crowds again streamed to St John's. Discovering no cavaliers, they proceeded to batter down doors, windows and walls and to 'tear his [Sir John's] evidences'. The house wrecked, the crowds began on his walks and gardens, for whose beauty Sir John had been praised by no less than Charles I's mother-in-law, Marie de Medici. From there they moved on to his park. Here they killed the deer and chased away the cattle. Finally, 'to shew that their rage will know no bounds, and that nothing is sacred or venerable which they dare to violate, they breake into St *Giles* his Church' and break open the family vault.

The attack on Sir John Lucas was only the first and best known of a series of such attacks in the counties of Essex and Suffolk in the year 1642. It proved the starting point for a whole string of crowd actions in which the houses of catholics and supporters of Charles I were attacked, their contents stripped, and their owners hounded out of the region. These attacks took place mainly within the clothmaking region of the two counties. They have come to be known to historians as the Stour Valley riots, somewhat inaccurately since they were by no means restricted to the Stour Valley and, as will be seen, 'riot' is an impoverishing label with which to describe the complexity of events in the summer of 1642. The attacks feature prominently in accounts of the role of the people within the English Revolution, especially those which see that role as an expression of class conflict. Indeed, such is the frequency with which they are cited in both monograph and textbook, that they

---

[2] In one of the first printed accounts to appear within a week of the action rumours of the discovery of 200 men had been turned into a 'fact': BL, E114(30), *A Message sent to the Parliament.*

have come to be taken as a paradigm for crowd actions in the early stages of the Revolution.

Why has this episode come to enjoy such prominence? In the early stages of the civil war such instances of popular actions were by no means restricted to the eastern counties. Although we lack as yet a systematic study to establish their incidence and geography, there is already sufficient evidence of other such popular actions to support Richard Baxter's claim that 'the Warre was begun in our streets before the King or Parliament had any Armies'. In other regions, notably the west of England, there were attacks on catholics or those seeking to raise military support for the king under the commission of the array.[3] But do the attacks in Essex and Suffolk enjoy their prominence because they represent the most serious example of this form of action? To some extent, their prominence must certainly lie in their geographical spread, in their duration (there were fears of further outbreaks as late as December, when some smaller incidents did in fact occur) and, above all, in the level of destruction inflicted by the crowds. Although detailed local research might unearth similar events elsewhere, the attacks were very widespread throughout the two counties, indeed more widespread than even the most detailed accounts have hitherto suggested.

But there is another compelling reason for the 'popularity' of the attacks. It was the threat posed by their timing, almost as much by their actions, that brought them notoriety. They occurred on the very cusp of the civil war at a time when the pace of the move towards armed conflict by committed minorities confronted the gentry with choices they had sought to avoid behind masks of localism or neutralism. In so doing, the attacks seemed to offer confirmation of the widespread fear that the growing conflict between the supporters of Parliament and Charles I would sever the links between public peace and private security. They offered royal propagandists a sensational example with which to make their case. Thus, their timing ensured that they would receive widespread attention and this, in turn, guaranteed them a prominent place in the historical record.

From the outset, the end of Charles I's Personal Rule and the start of negotiations between the king and the Parliamentary leadership had been marked by what contemporaries saw as popular disorder by the 'many-headed monster'. The range of grievances prompting crowd actions meant that disorder was more widespread and frequent than gentlemen had previously experienced. In many counties enclosures were thrown

[3] Richard Baxter, *The Holy Commonwealth*, p. 457, quoted in R. Macgillivray, *Restoration Historians and the English Civil War* (Hague, 1974), p. 155 and n.; B. Manning, *The English People and the English Revolution* (1976), ch. 7.

down, in churches altar rails and images were destroyed, and in boroughs and market towns the elections to both the Short and Long Parliaments were marked by enthusiastic, in places tumultuous, popular participation. Such levels of disorder had not been experienced since the mid-sixteenth century rebellions, and their appearance in the capital in the 1640s was a particularly unwelcome novelty. Gentlemen feared that the disorder that exploited the collapse of the political order presaged a more direct challenge to the social order – the pulling down of social hierarchies along with hedges and altar rails. 'We must take care', declared one MP in a speech subsequently printed, 'that the Common-people may not carve themselves out Justice, by their Multitudes. Of this we have too frequent experience, by their breaking downe Inclosures, and by raising other tumults, to as ill purposes. Which if they be not suddenly supprest, to how desperate an Issue, this may grow, I'll leave to your better judgements.'[4]

This was an old fear of ruling elites, fed by memories of earlier rebellions and given added menace in an English polity where the absence of a standing army or police meant that gentry authority rested heavily on acceptance by their inferiors of their right to rule. But in the period between 1640 and 1642 it seems to have reached a new intensity. Sir Simonds D'Ewes voiced these fears in a speech, recorded in his Parliamentary journal for June 1642, in which he reminded his audience of past English rebellions as well as the German Peasants War. He went on to prophesise that, 'there is no doubt but that all right & propertie all *meum* and *tuum* must cease in civill warrs: & wee know not what advantage the meaner sorte alsoe may take to divide the spoiles of the rich & noble amongst them'. D'Ewes rightly merits the epithet of the English Cassandra, but the fears he articulated were more widespread. Many others feared 'the danger that poverty and want can bring will come on too fast'. The correspondence of the Verney family in Buckinghamshire contain a series of letters written through the summer of 1642 in which Sir Edmund Verney urged the family steward to look to the defences of Claydon, 'for I feare a time maye come when Roag[ue]s maye looke for booty in such houses'.[5]

In part, this rising anxiety was a reflection of the sheer level of disorder, affecting as it did so many regions and communities – capital as well as counties, towns as well as villages. It was also because the collapse

---

[4] BL, E199(8), *An Honourable And Worthy Speech: Spoken in the High Court of Parliament By Mr Smith of the Middle Temple, 28 October 1641.*
[5] BL Harleian MS 163, fol. 153 v; C. Holmes, *The Eastern Association in the English Civil War* (Cambridge, 1974), p. 43; F. P. Verney, *Memoirs of the Verney Family during the Civil War*, 2 vols. (1892), vol. 2, p. 94; HMC, Cowper MSS, ii, 312–13.

of authority, and with it censorship, seemed to threaten a radicalisation of the ideologies shaping crowd actions which might offer a more direct threat to the social order. But perhaps as important was the greater publicity given to outbreaks of disorder, in particular by the rapid emergence of an active press following the collapse of censorship. This novel development saw also the misreporting of crowd actions, translating rumours into the reality of riot and attributing to rioters reported speeches that perhaps had their origins in the disturbed psyches of the landed classes. It was as much this shift in the reporting and representation of 'riot', as any change in the aims and actions of crowds, that raised levels of anxiety amongst the gentry.

It was surely not coincidence that 'Comparative histories' began to appear in this period, which drew pointed comparisons with the bloody deeds of the Anabaptists in the German Revolution of 1525; nor that references began to multiply in print, and political, culture to earlier English rebels, memories of whose misdeeds were anyway preserved in civic rituals and in the chronicles that were a common item in many gentlemen's libraries.[6] For example, in February 1642, the London bookseller George Thomason acquired *The iust reward of Rebels, or The Life and Death of Iack Straw, and disobedience to their King and Country*. This was a not unsympathetic history of the 1381 Rising which nevertheless drew the uncomfortable conclusion that 'the mechanicks and the meaner sort of people ... are always apt to envie their superiors, and are therefore prone to any Innovation favouring the cause of the seditious Commons.' D'Ewes' words about the collapse of *meum* and *tuum* were echoed in a sermon at St Paul's Cross at the end of July 1642 which warned that in war there 'is no distinction betweene the *Magistrate* and people, but *Cade, and Straw, and Tyler* will beard the King, and give all Iudgements out of their lawlesse lips'. Preachers in the region of the attacks were making similar observations.[7] This revival in public discourse of narratives of earlier examples of popular upheaval doubtless helped to fashion responses to events in the early 1640s. The tumultuous

---

[6] BL, E136(33), *A Warning for England Especially for London in the Famous History of the Frantic Anabaptists their wild Preachings & Practices in Germany* (1642); F. J. Levy, 'How information spread among the gentry, 1550–1640', *JBS*, 36 (1982), pp. 25–30; C. L. Kingsford (ed.), *Chronicles of London* (Oxford, 1905), pp. 15–16, 158–62.

[7] BL, E136(1), A3 r. See also R. Yarlott, 'The Long Parliament and the fear of popular pressure, 1640–1646' (M.A. thesis, University of Leeds, 1963), pp. 20–1; BL, E113(16), E. Udall, *The Good of Peace & Ill of Warre set forth in a sermon preached by Ephrain Udall* (1642), p. 20; H. Ferne, *The Resolving of Conscience upon this question*, (1642), p. 18; D. Whitby, *The Vindication of a true PROTESTANT and faithfull Servant to his Church, Daniel Whitby, Rector of Theydon-Mount in Essex From Articles exhibited against him in the Exchequer-Chamber at Westminster, By a few Schismaticall, tempestuous, illiterate heedlesse People* (Oxford, 1644), p. 7.

presentation of petitions to Parliament in January 1642, for example, had led one MP to enter in his journal a discussion of the 1381 Rising. The Earl of Dorset's wish that 'my children had never been borne, to live under the dominion of soe many Cades and Ketts, as threaten by their multitudes and insurrections to drowne all memory of monarchy, nobility, gentry, in this land' may well have been directly occasioned by reports of the attacks on Sir John Lucas and others.[8]

Thus, fear of the people as a 'many-headed monster' had become an important strand in the political discourse of 1642. As evidence of disorder multiplied, Charles and his advisors sought deliberately to play on such fears. By the summer of 1642 it was royalist propaganda that was best able to exploit an emphasis on the rule of law and to deliver the accusation that it was their opponents whose actions threatened both law and property by teaching the people to disobey authority. Thus, the king's pronouncements put increasing stress on the interrelationship between Parliament's challenge to royal authority and popular disorder. Through the spring and early summer of 1642 printed royal proclamations and declarations invoked the names of 'Wat Tyler, Jack Cade and Kett the Tanner' and the spectre of the Anabaptists to accuse Parliament of unleashing the 'many-headed monster'.[9] The king's *Answer to the Nineteen Propositions*, issued on the 18 June 1642, which accused Parliament of countenancing riots and disorder, thrust home this association:

> at last the common people (who in the meantime must be flattered, and to whom licence must be given in all their wild humours, how contrary soever to established law, or their own real good) discover the *arcanum imperii*, that all this was done by them, but not for them, and grow weary of journey-work, and set up for themselves, call parity and independence liberty, devour that estate which had devoured the rest, destroy all rights and proprieties, all distinctions of families and merit, and by this means this splendid and excellently distinguished form of

---

[8] *PJ*, 1, p. 128; D. L. Smith, 'Catholic, Anglican or Puritan? Edward Sackville, fourth Earl of Dorset and the ambiguities of religion in early Stuart England', *TRHS*, 6th ser., 2 (1992), p. 119.

[9] Edward Hyde, Earl of Clarendon, *The History of the Rebellion and Civil Wars in England Begun in the Year 1641*, ed. W. D. Macray, 6 vols. (Oxford, 1888), vol. 2, pp. 9–12; BL, E241(1), *An Exact Declaration of all the Remonstrances, Declarations, Ordinances, and other passages betweene the King's Majesty and his Parliament, beginning at his Majesties return from Scotland, December 1641, and continuing until 21 March, 1643* (London, 1643), pp. 283 [vere 5]–6, 311–19, 322; *Stuart Royal Proclamations 2, Royal Proclamations of King Charles I, 1625–46*, ed. J. F. Larkin (Oxford, 1983), no. 339, pp. 770–75; M. Hartman, 'Contemporary explanations of the English Revolution 1640–1660' (Ph.D. thesis, University of Cambridge, 1978), p. 29.

government end in a dark, equal chaos of confusion, and the long line of our many noble ancestors in a Jack Cade or a Wat Tyler.[10]

Shortly before the August attacks, the king had sought to give the widest possible publicity to this line of attack. The judges, going on their Assize circuits through the provinces in late July, were instructed to stress in the Charge delivered at the beginning of each Assize the king's intention to 'take care for the suppressing of all insurrecions if any such should happen, and of all riottes and unlawfull assemblies under any pretence whatsoever not warranted by the lawes of this land'. They were to ensure that a strict watch be kept for rogues and vagabonds, the gentry's traditional bogies. At the same time there was a concerted campaign to promote loyalist petitions at the Assizes which echoed the accusation that Parliament's leaders were deliberately promoting riot. For example, the Declaration of the county of Hereford of mid-July 1642, attacked 'the private, if not publique mutinous rabble, which ill spirit was ready at all times to be raised by a whisper from any of those worthy Members'.[11]

This then was the context for reactions to the attacks. Occurring as they did at a critical time in the deteriorating relationship between Crown and Parliament, when men were trying to decide where their allegiances lay, it was inevitable that the attacks would become the focus of political propaganda. Parliamentary propaganda had also sought to manipulate the threat of popular disorder through petitions and speeches, to try to persuade both king and political nation of the need to secure a swift settlement. In the face of the greater success of royalist propaganda, Parliament sought to portray the attacks as the actions of loyal protestants, whose zeal was directed against popish and malignant forces, in the service of king and Parliament and which were therefore quickly brought under control.[12] But the attacks were especially valuable to the royalists for they confirmed that the Parliament was acting in revolutionary ways, unleashing the people and threatening the rule of gentlemen as well as kings.

It was then their timing, as much as their scale and intensity, that ensured the notoriety of the Colchester Plunderers.[13] In turn, it was this

---

[10] J. Kenyon (ed.), *The Stuart Constitution 1603–1688: Documents and Commentary* (Cambridge, 1966), pp. 21–3.

[11] Bodl. Lib., Tanner MS 63, fols. 1–2, 110; PRO, SP, 16/491/52; A. Fletcher, *The Outbreak of the English Civil War* (1985), pp. 298–321; J. Webb, *Memorials of the Civil War between King Charles I and the Parliament of England As it Affected Herefordshire and the Adjacent Counties*, 2 vols. (1879), vol. 2, pp. 343–4.

[12] BL, E55(2), *The Parliament's Vindication of John Pym Esquire*, p. 4; J. Vicars, *Jehovah-Jireh: God in the Mount OR, England's Parliamentarie-Chronicle* (1644), pp. 144–5.

[13] The phrase is first used some months after the original attacks by Colchester's MPs to refer to the crowd who had sought to revive the attacks at the end of 1642: CRO, D/Y 2/7, p. 69.

notoriety that ensured their writing into modern accounts of the episode. As a consequence much of the evidence upon which these narratives are based is distorted either deliberately, as a product of royalist propaganda, or unconsciously, by the panic engendered both by the attacks and the broader political context. This should have produced caution in the way this evidence has been used, but for the most part it has not. Most historians have allowed themselves to be seduced by such easily accessible and richly vivid contemporary (although not necessarily eyewitness) accounts of the Stour Valley episode. The brief and colourful narrative that opened this chapter is itself deliberately drawn from just these sources. Re-evaluation of the event must begin therefore with the re-evaluation of the sources from which its history has been written.

The first published accounts of the attack on Sir John Lucas appeared in the Parliamentary newsbooks. Then, as now, the attacks represented sensational copy for the writers and publishers for whom accurate reporting was a novelty. We still know too little of how the publishers of these early newsbooks obtained their information.[14] Where accounts of the attacks were not merely lifted from other journals (already an honourable journalistic practice), they drew on reports to the Commons, in particular letters to the Speaker, speeches therein and the measures Parliament took. Where the newsbooks were able to gain access to letters sent to the Commons or reports of the day's proceedings, then their information could be valuable. In the case of the August attacks, there were several occasions when the newsbooks were able to draw on first-hand evidence in the reporting of events. In particular, the letter sent by the mayor of Colchester to the Speaker provided copy whose detail (with insufficient recognition of the problems its provenance suggests) was to prove important in subsequent narratives.[15] But competition amongst the newsbooks meant that they could also be wildly inaccurate, passing

---

[14] But see, J. Frank, *The Beginnings of the English Newspaper 1620–1660* (Cambridge, Mass., 1961); A. Cotton, 'London Newsbooks in the Civil War: their political attitudes and sources of life' (D.Phil. thesis, University of Oxford, 1971); J. Raymond, *Making the News: An Anthology of the Newsbooks of Revolutionary England 1641–1660* (Moreton-in-the-Marsh, 1993).

[15] The mayor's letter forms the main source for the accounts in several pamphlets and newsbooks: Colchester Public Library, Local Studies Collection, *The Parliament's Resolution Concerning the Sending of Sir Thomas Barrington and M. Grimston to Colchester for the pacification of an uproare of 2000 men, gathered together upon the discovery and apprehending of Sir John Lucas, with two hundred men, twelve warre-horse, and great store of Ammunition, with many Muskets, Pistols and Carbines ready charged, and by him provided to be sent to his Maiesty the day following*; BL, E114(30), *A Message*; E114(36), *Special Passages And certain Informations from severall places, Collected for the use of all that desire to bee truely Informed*.

off rumour as fact. For example, one newsbook – *An exact and true Diurnall* (*sic*) – informed its readers that letters from Essex reported that on the Tuesday after the attack on Lucas, there was 'a great tumult raised at Hadley and Ipswich of divers ill affected and desperate persons doing much mischiefe to the inhabitants of the said Townes, pretending they were for the King, and would not be governed by a few Puritans'. Local sources provide no confirmation of these incidents, no other newsbook carries such a report, and there is no record of Parliament's supposed deliberations and orders on being informed of the attacks. This report of letters from Essex purporting to carry information about incidents in Suffolk towns was probably a piece of creative invention by a newsbook which had failed to report the attack on Lucas.[16]

It was not, however, the newsbooks that have provided the core of most historical narratives. This was provided by a pamphlet published a year later in the royalist 'newsbook', *Mercurius Rusticus*. Most narratives rely on this the most detailed account of the attacks on Lucas and the Countess of Rivers. The narrative which began this chapter is constructed by paraphrasing *Mercurius Rusticus*. Its complete title, rarely given, immediately suggests something of the problems inherent in its use: *Mercurius Rusticus, or The Countries Complaint of the Murthers, Robberies, Plundrings, and other Outrages, Committed by the Rebels on his Majesties faithfull Subjects*. As the title makes abundantly clear one of the most important and frequently cited accounts of the attacks was a piece of royalist polemic. But this is seldom acknowledged by those who use it, and there has been little critical discussion of such a seductively rich source. Indeed, although its subject matter ensured successive reprintings into the eighteenth century, we still know too little about *Mercurius Rusticus'* genesis and production.[17]

The author of *Mercurius Rusticus* was Bruno Ryves. Ryves was a royalist clergyman, who had himself experienced the type of disorder about which he was to write, having been thrust out of his living by the godly of the parish and, as he claimed, forced to spend a dark and wet night sheltering under a hedge.[18] Before the civil war Ryves had held

---

[16] BL, E202(39), *An exact and true Diurnall of the Proceedings in Parliament* (22–29 Aug 1642), *sub.* 26 Aug. Another newsbook reported the crowds at Colchester as going on to attack the house of Lady Riche there, mangling reports of the attack on the Countess of Rivers at St Osyth and confusion of her family with that of the Parliamentarian Earl of Warwick's family of Rich: E114(34) *A Continuation of certaine Speciall and remarkable passages from both Houses of Parliament* (25–30 August 1642), p. 3.

[17] F. Madan, *Oxford Books: A Bibliography of Printed Works Relating to the University and City of Oxford or Printed or Published There*, 3 vols. (Oxford, 1895–1931), vol. 2 (1912), pp. 430–3. Lois Potter, *Secret Rites and Secret Writing: Royalist Literature 1641–1660* (Cambridge, 1989) makes no reference either to Ryves or to *Mercurius Rusticus*.

[18] *DNB*, *sub* Bruno Ryves; J. Rouse Bloxham, *A Register of the Presidents, Fellows, . . . of*

livings at Stanwell, Middlesex and in the City, and he had been appointed a chaplain to Charles I. The strength of Ryves' royalism is brought out in the petition of the inhabitants of Stanwell which complained of his preaching against Parliament. Ryves, it was alleged, had told his parishioners that:

we oft [ought] to obay the king in al[l] his commands, that there were some Brownists and Anabaptists in these times that did command contrary to the King's commands, but we oft [ought] not to obey their commands, for they seek to shake off all obedience to lawful authority, al[l]edging some skriptures, that we were damned if we persist in it.[19]

Joining the king in Oxford, Ryves began publication of *Mercurius Rusticus*. Ryves wrote with some verve, showing a sense of drama and turn of phrase that perhaps helps to explain a contemporary's character-isation of his preaching as 'florid', as well as something of his appeal to later historians.[20] So rich was the copy that the Colchester Plunderers offered that Ryves devoted much of the first three issues of his newsbook to their misdeeds. That Ryves began the first weekly issue, issued some nine months after the original event and reprinted some weeks later in Shrewsbury, with the stale news of the attack on Sir John Lucas, questions *Mercurius Rusticus*'s status as a 'newsbook'.[21] It was clearly intended to be a contribution to the royalist war effort, and the knowledge that Ryves was a member of the king's Council of War offers powerful evidence of the politics behind its publication.[22] In the first issue, Ryves ends his address *To the Reader* with the following declaration:

I shall promise in the sight of God and Remembring that Lyers are in the number of those against whom the gates of the new *Ierusalem* shall be shut, to deale with all Candor and Ingenuity, not out of a desire to render them odious, abuse the Reader either with falsehoods or uncertainties, but to report nothing but what hath been examined and attested by men of knowne truth and Integrity; and if anything shall chance to passe which upon better Information shall appeare false, I shall not blush to Retract it by an Ingenuous acknowledgement.[23]

St Mary Magdalene College, 7 vols. (Oxford, 1853–81), vol. 2, pp. 51–7; A. G. Matthews (ed.), *Walker Revised. Being a Revision of John Walker's Sufferings of the Clergy during the Grand Rebellion 1642–60* (Oxford, 1948), pp. 56–7.

[19] H. J. Todd, *Memoirs of the Life and Writings of the Right Reverent Brian Walton*, 2 vols. (1821), vol. 1, p. 307.

[20] *DNB*, *sub* Ryves.

[21] P. W. Thomas, *Sir John Berkenhead 1617–1679* (Oxford, 1969), pp. 50, 255.

[22] *WR*, pp. 56–7. For evidence of the seriousness with which the royalists approached the dissemination of 'news', see Thomas, *Berkenhead*, ch. 2.

[23] [Bruno Ryves], *MR*, week 1, 20 May 1643, A4v, repr. in P. Thomas (ed.), *The English Revolution 3, Newsbooks 1, Oxford Royalist*, 4 vols. (London, 1971), vol. 4, p. 124.

Such a declaration might be thought a little disingenuous since the preceding pages had been devoted to an attack on Parliamentary tyranny and inflammatory puritan preachers. Ryves was a member of the king's Council of War, writing from the heart of the royal cause, and published by the king's printer. It is more than probable that he shared the maxim of the early eighteenth-century work, du Fresnay's *A New Method of Studying History*, that 'the Rising of a People against their lawful Prince' was a case in which the historian was obliged not to be impartial.[24] Ryves clearly intended to use the atrocities he catalogued in *Mercurius Rusticus* to smear Parliament and its supporters with the responsibility for popular violence and radicalism.

We might have expected those who have used Ryves' account of events at least to have declared him *parti pris* and to have exercised some caution before accepting his version of events. Nevertheless, it would be wrong to dismiss out of hand Ryves' narrative or his claims for candour as an author. In the case of the Lucas episode he certainly had access to the Mayor of Colchester's account from which he quoted, although this probably came at second-hand from the newsbooks it can be shown he consulted.[25] It is also most probable that he had more direct and first-hand evidence from which to construct his narrative. Based in Oxford, Ryves was well placed to gather information of atrocities from his fellow refugees. For example, it has been shown that he was able to provide a detailed account of the disorder in another Essex town, Chelmsford, because he received information directly from, among others, the minister who was the main victim of popular violence there.[26] In the case of the Colchester Plunderers possible Oxford informants would have included both members of the Lucas family and Thomas Newcomen. As we will see later there is in fact evidence to suggest that Newcomen was one, perhaps the main, source for Ryves' Colchester narrative. While it remains impossible to winnow out Ryves' embellishments, a knowledge

---

(Quotations hereafter from *Mercurius Rusticus* are from this edition of the original weekly issue.)

[24] P. N. Lenglet du Fresnay, *A New Method of Studying History, trans. and improved by R. Rawlinson*, 2 vols. (1728), vol. 1, p. 282, cited in Macgillivray, *Restoration Historians*, pp. 7–8.

[25] BL, E114(36), *Special Passages And certain Informations from severall places, Collected for the use of all that desire to bee truely Informed* (23–30 August 1642). Ryves referring to the discovery of cavaliers at Lucas's house gives exactly the same number as that in the earlier account, BL, E114(30), *A Message*.

[26] H. Grieve, *The Sleepers and the Shadows. Chelmsford: a Town, its People and its Past 2: From Market Town to Chartered Borough 1608–1888* (Chelmsford, 1994), pp. 60, 62. Sir John Berkenhead, editor of the royalist newsbook, *Mercurius Aulicus*, has been shown to have drawn on similar sources of information in Oxford: Thomas, *Berkenhead*, pp. 37–9.

of the preceding relationship between the Lucas family and Colchester offers some confirmation of his account.

But despite Ryves' claim to truth-telling, a closer reading of his text reveals something of the deliberate fashioning in its production. Colchester's rulers were identified by their occupations – John Langley, 'Grocer and Captaine of the Train Band', Henry Barrington, 'Brewer and Alderman' – in an appeal to the shared contempt of his gentle readers. Ryves shaped his narrative of the atrocities he reported to maximise the sense of shock in his readership. In the narrative of the Colchester attacks alone, he highlights violence against exactly those groups that the codes of conduct in civil war decreed should be protected: women, ministers, the old and the dead. Discussing the attack on the Countess of Rivers, Ryves informs his readers, 'And that you may guesse what spirituall men they were, and likewise in what danger this honorable Person was in, they express themselves in this rude unchristian Language, *That if they found her they would try what flesh she had.*' His account of the attack on Sir John Lucas's house included the vignette of the invasion of the Lucas's 'Ladies Chamber' where a naked sword was set to Sir John's wife's breast. We cannot know whether this ever happened, nor whether the words against the Countess of Rivers were ever spoken. It hardly matters. The threat to the female body was being used to symbolise the threat to the social and moral order. These transgressions, of an inner space heavily inscribed with the hierarchies of gender and class in the Lucas case, illustrated perfectly the threat to the social order of the 'many-headed monster' let loose by Parliament.[27]

By contrast, there are silences in the text that need exposing. Ryves mentions only two of the many attacks on catholic households that we know to have occurred, and in neither case does he reveal that these were in fact catholic families. Instead, his narrative of the attack on the Countess of Rivers is constructed in such a way as to offer the reader only plunder as the motive for the attack. Despite the space he devoted to the Colchester Plunderers and events in the Stour Valley, he fails to mention any of the many other attacks on catholics. It seems unlikely that these silences reflected his ignorance. Nor does it seem likely that the attention he devoted by contrast to attacks on protestant ministers was to be explained simply by fellow feeling or by the networks of information offered by patterns of clerical sociability among the ejected clergy corralled in royalist Oxford. Ryves deliberately sought to exaggerate the

---

[27] B. Donagan, 'Atrocity, war crime and treason in the English civil war', *American Historical Review*, 99 (1994), p. 1142; Donagan, 'Codes and conduct in the English civil war', *P&P*, 118 (1988), pp. 65–95; Donagan, 'Did ministers matter? War and religion in England, 1642–1649', *JBS*, 33 (1994), pp. 119–56; *MR*, pp. 2, 11.

sense of offence in his reader by suppressing evidence of the confessional identity of his catholic victims and ignoring the others because he wished to represent the episode as an attack on fellow protestants by, as he termed the attackers at one point in his text, 'the *Essex* schismatics'. This has the curious consequence that the main text upon which historians have drawn in their reconstruction of the attack offers no support for the widely held argument that anti-popery was one of the main causes of the attacks.

The success of *Mercurius Rusticus* – it was reprinted in the same year as its first appearance, and in 1646, 1648, 1685, 1723, 1732 and, finally, in 1971[28] – has provided historians with a printed and readily accessible source. It also helped to ensure the incorporation of the Colchester episode into the local history of the period, a tradition of historical writing not usually sensitive to such 'histories'. It was its inclusion in his mid-eighteenth-century history of Colchester by Philip Morant, loyal clergyman (and himself a plunderer – of other people's archives) that ensured its subsequent incorporation into the local history of town and county. It would be interesting to know whether Morant had first learnt of the Colchester Plunderers from stories in a town that certainly kept alive the memory of the martyrs of the 1648 siege of Colchester, one of whom was Charles Lucas, Sir John's younger brother. But despite the fact that he worked extensively among the borough's records, sticking several letters relating to the attacks into one of his 'scrapbooks', it is clear that Morant derived his account from *Mercurius Rusticus*, a book he can be shown to have possessed.[29] Thus, it was Bruno Ryves' version of events which passed into local history via Morant and that venerable historical tradition of plagiarism which for a long while after Morant's original researches passed for local history.[30]

Ryves represented one major source of transmission. There was another, again in print and even more readily accessible, whose fame helps to explain the prominence of the episode in later discussions of the role of the people in the English Revolution. This is *The History Of The Rebellion and Civil Wars in England* by the Earl of Clarendon, formerly

---

[28] Thomas (ed.), *The English Revolution 3, Newsbooks 1, Oxford Royalists*, vol. 4, pp. 1–3; Frank, *English Newspapers*, p. 309.

[29] P. Morant, *The History and Antiquities of the most ancient Town and Borough of Colchester*, 2 vols. (1748), vol. 1, p. 54. Morant's copy of the 1723 edition of *Mercurius Rusticus* is in the Essex Record Office: ERO, Acc. 5157. It would appear that Morant owed his knowledge of this account to a transcription of it by another cleric, John Newton, to whose antiquarian labours he paid tribute: CRO, D/DRg 1/226, pp. 272–5.

[30] [P. Muilman], *A New and Complete History of Essex From a Late Survey ... By a Gentleman* 6 vols. (Chelmsford, 1769–72), vol. 1, p. 36; E. L. Cutts, *Colchester* (1888), p. 177; E. Stokes and J. H. Round, 'Political History', *VCH Essex*, ed. W. Page and J. H. Round, vol. 2 (1907), p. 231.

Edward Hyde, Charles I's chief political adviser and propagandist, whose account in book VI of his *History* opens this chapter. Clarendon's account too was retrospective, being written while he was in exile in Jersey between June and October 1647, when the emergence of a popular third force, in the shape of the Levellers, gave added bite to fears of the 'many-headed monster'. Moreover, there is a further resemblance to *Mercurius Rusticus* in that Clarendon also relied on printed reports of the attacks. As he himself observed in December 1647 of this period of the composition of his *History*, he wrote 'upon the stock of an ill memory, refreshed only with some few pamphlets and diurnals'.[31] Analysis of his text shows that one of those was most likely the same newsbook recounting the Mayor of Colchester's letter to the Speaker of the Commons that Bruno Ryves had used. The figure he gives for the Countess of Rivers's losses suggests that he also drew upon at least one other pamphlet account.[32]

Clarendon in his *History* may have sought to create 'the impression of authorial detachment and objectivity'.[33] But he wrote also as a man who had acted as one of the king's most important and subtlest polemicists in the midst of a world turned upside down. He wrote to deter English gentlemen from ever repeating the mistake of unleashing the common people who had, 'in all places grown to that barbarity and rage against the nobility and gentry, (under the style of *cavaliers*,) that it was not safe for any to live at their houses who were taken notice of as no votaries to the Parliament'. This explains both his choice of the examples of attacks on Sir John Lucas and the Countess of Rivers and, like Bruno Ryves, his shaping of the evidence to emphasise the violence and to implicate Parliament in its occurrence. Clarendon devoted some space to these events because they provided a telling example of his thesis that it was Parliament, and not the king, who threatened the rule of law and confirmed the link between Parliamentary innovation and popular radicalism. As he concluded his account, 'these and many other instances of the same kind in London and the parts adjacent, gave sufficient

---

[31] *State Papers Collected by Edward, Earl of Clarendon*, 3 vols. (Oxford, 1767–86), vol. 2, p. 385; cf. p. 288. For details of the circumstances under which Clarendon wrote his history, see C. H. Firth, 'Clarendon's "History of the Rebellion": part 1, the original "History"', *EHR*, 19 (1904), pp. 26–54. Clarendon may also have had other connections with the events of 1642, evidence of which has not survived. For example, he was visited in October 1646 by the sequestered Essex rector of Fobbing: O. Ogle, W. H. Bliss and W. D. Macray (eds.), *Calendar of the Clarendon State Papers*, 3 vols. (Oxford 1869–76), vol. 3, p. 338.

[32] BL, E114(30), *A Message*. This account also draws on the Mayor of Colchester's letter.

[33] M. W. Brownley, *Clarendon and the Rhetoric of Historical Form* (Philadelphia, 1985), p. 42. But see the more critical comments in R. Hutton, 'Clarendon's "History of the Rebellion"', *EHR*, 47 (1982), esp. p. 87.

evidence to all men how little else they were to keep who meant to preserve their allegiance [to the king] and integrity in the full vigour.'[34]

The accounts then from which historians have created a narrative of the Stour Valley attacks and sought to analyse popular behaviour within them are polemical accounts in the 'paper skirmishes'[35] which Parliamentarian and royalist writers fought for the allegiances of the propertied classes. The royalists' use of the episode to illustrate their thesis that Parliament's attack on the king threatened to let loose the 'many-headed monster' ensured the availability of accessible and vivid accounts of the attacks for later historians to draw on. From the very earliest histories of the rebellion, it was the case of the Colchester Plunderers, drawn from the accounts of either Ryves or Clarendon, that were used as an example of popular violence.[36] When from the later nineteenth century onwards, successive intellectual shifts in the writing of the history of the period – democratic, populist and Marxist – brought a renewed interest in the role of the people in the English Revolution, the example was there to be drawn upon, its availability advertised by its inclusion in the opening chapter of that foundation text for students of the civil war, Samuel Rawson Gardiner's *History of the Great Civil War*.[37]

By the latter-half of the twentieth century references to the Colchester Plunderers had become near standard in works dealing with the popular role in the English Revolution, and the episode had even made it into textbooks on the period.[38] And it is this notoriety that has ensured the attacks' fame. Most accounts have drawn on the example precisely to support arguments that the people exhibited marked class hostility towards their superiors and that it is this that characterises their involvement in the conflict, especially in its early stages. Not surprisingly,

---

[34] B. H. G. Wormald, *Clarendon: Politics, History and Religion 1640–1660* (Cambridge, 1951), pp. 89–92; Clarendon, *History*, vol. 2, pp. 318–9.

[35] Firth, 'Clarendon's "History"', p. 40.

[36] D. Lloyd, *Memoires of the Lives, Actions, Sufferings and Deaths of Those Noble, Reverend, and Excellent personages That Suffered . . . in the late Intestine Wars* (1668), pp. 474, 688, whose list of victims makes clear his debt to Bruno Ryves' account; Lawrence Echard, *The History of England. From the Beginning of the Reign of King Charles the first, to the Restoration of King Charles the Second* (1718), p. 342, which plagiarises Clarendon and cites Ryves.

[37] R. Samuel, 'British Marxist historians, 1880–1980: part one', *New Left Review*, 120 (1980), pp. 21–96; B. Schwarz, 'The people in history: the Communist Party historians group, 1946–56' in R. Johnson, G. McLennan, B. Schwarz, D. Sutton (eds.), *Making Histories: Studies in History-Writing and Politics* (1982), pp. 44–95; S. R. Gardiner, *History of the Great Civil War 1642–1649*, 3 vols. (1886–1891), vol. 1, p. 14. Gardiner cites neither Clarendon's *History* nor *Mercurius Rusticus* as his authorities, but draws on the account of the Mayor of Colchester's letter provided by the contemporary pamphlet, *A Message*.

[38] D. Hirst, *Authority and Conflict: England 1603–1658* (1986), pp. 51, 79, 230.

this has been most marked within the works of those writing within the populist-Marxist tradition. For example, in Christopher Hill's various works references to the Stour Valley riots support discussions of the animus that the 'many-headed monster' felt for its masters and rulers. They also feature prominently in Brian Manning's discussions of their role in the Revolution in various of his works. In *The English People and the English Revolution* Manning, after giving a detailed narrative of the attack on Sir John Lucas and the Countess of Rivers, writes that the 'popular attacks on the royalist nobility and gentry veered out of control of the Parliamentarian nobility and gentry, and revealed an underlying rebelliousness against the ruling order.'[39]

More intriguingly, this interpretation has become common to both Marxist and non-Marxist accounts of the episode. Clive Holmes, whose *Eastern Association in the English Civil War* is one of the best studies of the region in the 1640s, concluded that,

the riots looked ominously like the 'inundation of the vulgar' ... The element of class conflict in the August riots was partly concealed by the political and religious motivation claimed by some of the participants ... But those present during the riots, even Parliamentary supporters, had no illusions about 'honest inhabitants' with 'peaceable intentions'. The Mayor of Colchester was scared out of his wits by the violence of the 'rude people'.[40]

More recently, Anthony Fletcher has written that, 'for a short time in the latter stages of the Stour Valley panic the countrymen became less discriminating in their targets and a bitter vein of class hostility emerged.' Such is the consensus on this reading of the attacks that even general discussions of the social structure of early modern England have been able to advance this reading of the attacks in support of the argument that early modern society registered class conflict.[41]

What all these accounts have in common is that the attacks on which they draw are not analysed in their own right. With varying degrees of acknowledgement of their context – depression in the cloth industry, the strength of puritanism and anti-catholicism in the region – they have been used to substantiate larger theses. However, knowledge of the genealogy of the earliest accounts of the attacks counsels caution in such

---

[39] C. Hill, 'Lord Clarendon and the puritan revolution' in his *Puritanism and Revolution* (1958), p. 203; 'The many-headed monster' in his *Change and Continuity in Seventeenth Century England* (1974), p. 195; *The World Turned Upside Down: Radical Ideas during the English Revolution* (1972), pp. 18–20; Manning, *English People*, p. 180.

[40] Holmes, *Eastern Association*, p. 43.

[41] A. Fletcher, *The Outbreak of the English Civil War* (1981), p. 378; J. Sharpe, *Crime in Early Modern England 1550–1750* (1984), pp. 138–9; Sharpe, *Crime in Seventeenth-Century England: A County Study* (Cambridge, 1983), p. 208.

approporiation. But until recently there has been little attempt to establish the accuracy of such accounts, nor to acknowledge the fashioning that political interest might have dictated. As Ronald Hutton has noted in another context, 'those concerned to represent the war as a social conflict have quoted Clarendon without any attempt to establish the accuracy of the statements in question'.[42]

This study seeks to do so. It offers a 'braided narrative'[43] of the event, grounding an understanding of the processes it contained within the structures of both regional society and economy and early modern political culture. Its purpose is to place the attacks into those contexts from which they have become detached. Having established the highly politicised context out of which the early accounts of the event arose, it attempts a close reading – a 'thick description'[44] – of the social drama of the attacks firmly situated within the double context of the more immediate local and regional environment and the wider context of the interrelationships between popular political culture and the political history of the period. Contextualising the Colchester Plunderers offers a more complex reading of the events of the summer of 1642. In its turn, this analysis raises important questions about how we should read, and what we should label, crowd actions in the world we have lost. Central to this critical exercise are questions of how we can recover evidence of the political behaviour and beliefs of those whom the inequalities of the past render too frequently historically inarticulate and of the appropriate theoretical framework within which to interpret that evidence. This study seeks to suggest that, freed of the evidence of pejorative and polemical accounts, one of the dominant meanings of the crowd actions in the summer of 1642 can be found in popular, and Parliamentarian, political culture.

[42] Hutton, 'Clarendon's "History"', p. 70.
[43] The phrase comes from Peter Burke, *History and Social Theory* (1992), p. 163.
[44] C. Geertz, 'Thick description: towards an interpretive theory of culture' in his *The Interpretation of Cultures* (New York, 1973), pp. 3–30. For critical discussion of Geertz's concept of 'thick description' see, R. G. Walters, 'Signs of the times: Clifford Geertz and the historians', *Social Research*, 47 (1980), pp. 537–56; P. Shankman, 'The thick and the thin: on the interpretive theoretical program of Clifford Geertz', *Current Anthropology*, 25 (1984), p. 261–70.

2. *The Attacks*

The rude multitude in divers counties tooke advantage by these civill
& intestine broales to plunder & pillage the Houses of the Nobilitie
gentrie & others who weere either knowen Papists or being protestants had sent or provided horses monie or plate to send to the
King, or such as being rich they would make malignant that soe they
might have some couler to robb & spoile them. Thus were Sir John
Lucas & other protestants the Countess of Rivers the Ladie Audley
and other papists plundered in Essex not onlie their goods or
household stuffe taken away & spoiled, but their verie houses
defaced & made unhabitable.

> Sir Simonds D'Ewes' Parliamentary Journal, entry for
> 9 September 1642 (BL, Harleian MS 163, fol. 324)

The attack on Sir John Lucas was the starting point for a string of
attacks, whose roll call was longer, and geographical spread greater, than
previously suspected. Over the next week the crowds gathered at
Colchester fanned out into the surrounding countryside to attack a
whole series of other targets. They doubtless recruited support on their
procession, their passage promoted other attacks. In yet other communities, news of their actions prompted independent attacks. The attacks
were to continue on into September and to flare up again in the winter of
1642. This chapter offers a fuller account of the attack on Sir John Lucas
and reconstructs the series of attacks in the counties of Essex and Suffolk
that followed as a necessary preliminary to uncovering the meaning of
these crowd actions. Any analysis of the progress of the attacks will
doubtless impose a pattern that belies the confusion that characterised
events at the time. But since the crowds' victims were not chosen at
random, there is a pattern to be recovered.

Sir John Lucas's planned march to the king was not unexpected. Given the close proximity of his 'country' seat to Colchester – little more than a stone's throw from the town walls – it would have been difficult to have kept his preparations secret. Certainly, the town had knowledge of his intentions for at least a few days before. The delivery of arms to Sir John Lucas by the town carrier on the 19th of August had become the subject of 'a greate report' about the town and presumably, since this was market day, within Colchester's hinterland. According to the Mayor, Thomas Wade, the reports 'bred in our common people such feares and Jealousise as that they wanted but an opportunitie to search his house'. As will be seen later, there had been even earlier signs that when it came to civil war Lucas, a committed supporter in the 1630s of the king's Personal Rule, would offer Charles I his support.

A letter from the Mayor to Harbottle Grimston, the town's Recorder and MP, written even as the town's rulers were trying to pacify the crowds, provides a first-hand account of the events at Colchester.[1] On Sunday 21 August, the Mayor had been informed by John Langley, one of the aldermen of the town, captain of the Parliamentary volunteers and a man we shall meet again, 'that he was credibly informed that Sir John Lucas intended to send away divers horses as this day to the King', information which was repeated by the High Constable that evening. In response, the Mayor had ordered a watch to be set about Sir John's house. At about midnight, the watch had detected an attempt to send some horse out of the back gate of the house and across the fields – if the town knew of Sir John's intentions, then he too knew of their actions. The watch stayed the horse and sent word into the town, 'that there were a hundred men in armes' at Sir John's, a figure which subsequently proved wildly exaggerated, but which testifies to the state of panic in the town. Drums were beaten and the town put in an uproar. The trained bands and the Parliamentary volunteers, then being assembled in the town, proceeded to besiege the house. The inhabitants of the town – men, women and children to the number of 5,000 according to the mayor – also flocked to St John's. Fearing that the crowds 'might doe some hurte', the Mayor with other of the justices and aldermen, made an unsuccessful attempt to persuade the crowds to disperse. They processed around the house from one in the morning, and made repeated proclamation throughout the night for the crowds circling it to depart.

Failing to disperse the crowds, the Mayor gave orders for the trained bands to guard St John's. But at daylight, 'the rude sort of people' broke into the house. They seized some eight or nine more horses and discovered 'much armor and a great many of new pistolls and carbines

[1] HLRO, Braye-Teeling MS, no 11.

ready charged, newe greate sadle and other warlike furniture', part of which they carried off to the town hall. One of Sir John's servants, captured by the crowds, confessed that Sir John and ten of his servants had intended to ride to the king, and that the minister Thomas Newcomen, who was to have gone with them as Lucas's chaplain had given them an 'oath of service', 'and nothing would satisfie these tumultuous people but that Sir John Lucas, his mother and servants must be committed'. That knowledge of the oath of secrecy seems to have particularly incensed the crowds offers evidence of the latent fears and anxieties present in the town. Was Sir John's intention to support the king by riding to him or by slaughtering his opponents within the town?

The mayor therefore requested Sir John, together with his mother and sister, to accompany him to his house. 'But when the people knew they were not committed but were at my house, they came in great numbers and tell me to my face they would downe my house, upon my heade.' To save the Mayor's house, Sir John and the others, including Thomas Newcomen, were taken willingly to the town's Moot Hall, though whether they were held in the town gaol, as the account in *Mercurius Rusticus* claimed, is not made clear. While this was happening, others had proceeded to attack the house itself. 'The rude people doe much abuse themselves and Sir John also in Riflinge his house, spoylinge his goods, and carrieing awaie of his plate, money, bookes, boxes, wrightinges and all sorts of household stuffe and furniture', reported the Mayor. (We will return to the matter of Sir John's 'wrightinges' and why they should have been a prize trophy.) Signing himself 'your distressed friend', the Mayor appealed to Grimston to send him, 'with all speede', advice about what to do with Lucas and Newcomen and their confiscated horse and arms.

Like Ryves' text, the Mayor's letter, while written in the heat of the moment, constructed a narrative with its own purpose. The repeated emphasis on the social composition of the crowds – 'common people', 'rude people' – distanced the town's rulers from the attack. Any affronts suffered by the Lucas entourage at his hands were the direct result of popular coercion. While the Mayor was careful to detail the actions he and his colleagues had taken to try to disperse the crowds, to guard the house and to afford Sir John and his family the protection their status demanded, his letter sought to suggest that the situation in the town had gone beyond their control. Despite attempts to disperse the crowds, 'they regarded us not, noe more than they doe a child'. The Mayor's letter and its tone are readily explained by his alarm at events and by his need to justify the apparent disregard for social niceties involved in locking up a powerful landed family. But whether he was scared out of his wits by the

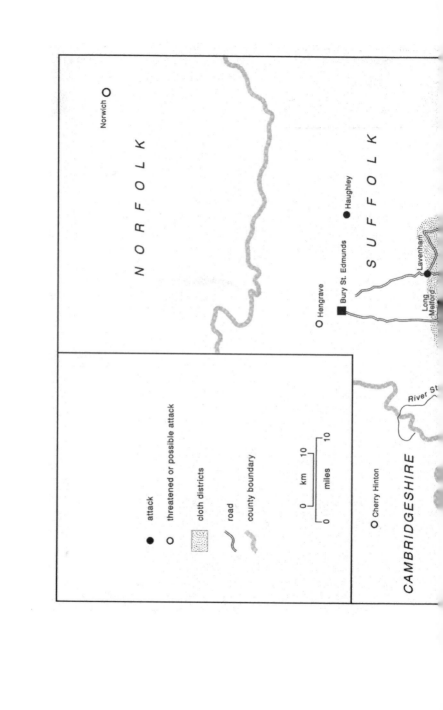

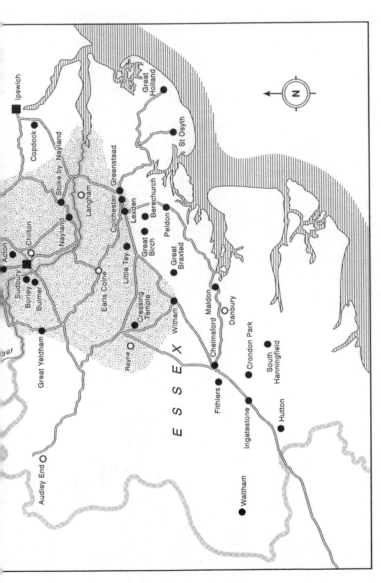

The distribution of the attacks in Essex and Suffolk, August–December 1642

rude people, as has been claimed, or by the fear of the fallout from the attack remains to be seen. As will later become clear, Colchester's authorities had good reasons to attempt to distance themselves from a possible accusation of complicity in the attacks.

By contrast, Bruno Ryves' account in *Mercurius Rusticus*, written months later, specifically attributed the violence to the deliberate licence afforded the people by the town's rulers.[2] According to him, Sir John's plans had been betrayed by one of his servants to John Langley, one of the town's rulers. Grocer Langley together with brewer Barrington had spent Sunday 'in riding to *Coggeshall, Bocking, B[r]ayntree, Halsteed*, and other Townes of their owne Faction', calling on them to set armed watches to intercept Sir John on his intended journey. With the assistance of the Mayor, it was they who had set a guard of the town's trained band to watch the house. When Lucas was detected leaving, it was another alderman, Daniel Cole, christened the '*Fulk of Colchester*' by Ryves, who ordered the beacon to be fired in order to bring up the volunteers. The interrogation of the old family servant had been conducted by 'a young pragmaticall boy', John Furley, the son of another aldermanic family noted, as Ryves' epithet suggests, for its religious nonconformity. Ryves draws no distinction, as did the Mayor, between guards and attackers. In his opinion, the guard the Mayor set to protect the prisoners should have had 'some honest men to guard them from those guardians, who were as forward as the People to drinke their blood.' It was only after the large-scale destruction, claims Ryves, that the Mayor took action to protect the house. 'And now the Major's care begins to shew it selfe, he sets a guard upon the house', but this was a guard that allows some £100 worth of grain to be carried away, 'and the most of it, to their own houses'. Nor does Ryves make any mention of the Mayor's attempt first to lodge Sir John and his family in his own house. Throughout his account Ryves was at pains to stress the scale and extent of the destruction and the level of popular hostility and violence against the family. Even the nearby church of St Giles was invaded and an attack made upon the family tombs. That Ryves was not exaggerating the scale of destruction is suggested by an observation made in 1648 that nothing remained of St John's but 'bare walls'.[3]

The alarm caused by Lucas's attempted flight to the king had both attracted very large numbers into the town and had sent out ripples of

[2] *MR*, pp. 1–8.
[3] MS account of the siege of Colchester, MSS of the Duke of Beaufort at Badminton House, Gloucester. I am grateful to Margaret Richards, the archivist at Badminton House, for providing me with a copy of the relevant pages of this MS.

panic into the surrounding communities. The letter from Colchester's Mayor had ended by informing Grimston:

> they are come to such a head (beinge a mixte company of towne and country) that we knowe not howe to quiet them, and I ver[il]y beleive if we had five trayned bands we could not suppresse them, unles they bee killed, they are so resolute, and resolved to goe on in their course. And we are afraide these rude people haveinge gotten such a company together will not staye heere, for they give out speeches, they will goe to the Lady Savage's at Saint Osith, and to some other places about the towne.

Rumour and panic came to focus almost immediately on the activities of the catholics who lived in the region and it was they who became the crowds' main victims. One report of the attack on Lucas has the Colchester crowd crying, 'that now they were met together, the Parliament and Country expected it of them to deale in the same manner with the Papists'.[4] On 23 August, a day after the attack on Sir John Lucas, a large section of the Colchester crowds had set off, as the town's Mayor had feared, to St Osyth, some nine miles south-east of Colchester, seat of Lady Elizabeth Savage, from 1641 the Countess of Rivers.[5] The Rivers' catholicism had made them in the past the object of rumours and suspicion on the streets of Colchester. According to *Mercurius Rusticus*, the Colchester attackers began a game of cat and mouse with the countess. They reached St Osyth only a few hours after the countess had made her escape. There, joined by sailors and what one catholic called 'the whole country rout', 'they enter the house, and being entered, they pull downe, cut in pieces, and carry away her costly hangings, Bedds, Couches, Chaires, and the whole furniture of her house, robbe her of Plate and Monies: they teare downe her Wainscote, Leads, and Windowes; they leave not a doore, nor so much as a barre of a Window behind them.' According to the countess herself, they ransacked the house, carrying away her 'furniture, hangeings, plate, mony, apparrell, linnen and other household stuffe, even to ye least parcell'. Her corn was carted off, her cattle driven away, and her gardens destroyed. 'In a fewe hours [they] disfurnished it of all the goods which [she] had been many years with great curiosity providing.' Although the countess was not attacked, her servants were. The evidence suggests that crowds, recruiting

---

[4] Stoneyhurst College, Stoneyhurst MSS, MSS Angliae, 7, fol. 122 (xerox, Department of Historiography and Archives, English Province of the Society of Jesus).

[5] Elizabeth, Countess of Rivers was the daughter of Thomas, Earl Rivers who had died in 1639, leaving her all his estate. She was by then a widow, her husband Lord Savage having died in 1635: Cambridge University Library, Hengrave MSS 2, fol. 253; L. Dow, 'The Savage hatchment at Long Melford', *PSIA*, 26 (1955), pp. 214–9.

further support from the local area, continued to be active there for several days afterwards.[6]

Forewarned, according to *Mercurius Rusticus*, the countess herself had fled with her family to her other house at Long Melford in Suffolk. This was a journey little short of thirty miles, but the crowds followed her there, gathering further support en route, 'the *Essex* Schismatics' meeting in Suffolk with 'some that are as madde as themselves'. Grimston singled out seamen from among those joining the attackers. Theirs was a significant presence, for as we shall see they were as a group noted for the strength of their anti-popery.[7] On Wednesday 24 August,[8] 'a multitude of like disposed persons, threatening [according to the countess] her death' nearly caught up with her. They entered the house 'before she had fully escaped their sight' (doubtless declining to use on this occasion the 'back-gate for beggars and the meaner sort of swains to come in at' that had charmed the essayist James Howell when he was a tutor to the family). Once again, the crowds ransacked the house. According to the entry in the diary of John Rous, a clergyman living in the north of the county, 'the lady Savage's house was defaced; all glasse broken, all iron pulled out, all household stuffe gone, all sielings [ceilings] rent downe or spoiled, all likely places digged where mon[e]y might be hidden. The gardens defaced, Beere & wine consumed & let out (to knee deepe in the cellar). The deere killed and chased out.'[9] According to *Mercurius Rusticus*, the countess 'hardly escapes with her life: she abandons her house, and leaves it to the mercy of these new ministers of justice, who not only rifle and deface the house, but make strict search for her person'. Other evidence suggests that she was helped to escape by a neighbouring gentleman, Sir Robert Crane. On the move again, the countess sought sanctuary some thirteen miles away at Bury St Edmunds, by then the second town in the county.[10] Bury seems also to have been in a state of agitation. The newsbook *Speciall Passages* reported that the town had 'beene in greate feares a long time' because the magazine for the western half of the county was in an inconvenient place with the key in the hand of those not pleasing to the inhabitants

---

[6] *MR*, p. 11; Stoneyhurst MSS, MSS Angliae, 7, fol. 122; HLRO, MP HL 29 August 1642; Edward Hyde, Earl of Clarendon, *The History Of the Rebellion And Civil Wars in England Begun in the year 1641*, ed. W. D. Macray, 6 vols. (Oxford, 1888), vol. 2, p. 319; ERO, Q/S Ba 2/48 (exam. Mary Hoy), 5/1/3; PRO, ASSI 35/85/5, m. 58.

[7] BL, Harleian MS 163, fol. 308 r.

[8] Given the distances involved, this dating might be questioned. According to Ryves (*MR*, p. 11) it was 'within a day or two' that the crowds pursued her to Long Melford.

[9] J. Howell, *Familiar Letters or Epistola Ho-Elianne*, 10th edn (Aberdeen, 1753), p. 76; BL Additional MS 22,959, fols. 85 v–86 r.

[10] F. Grace, 'A historical survey of Suffolk towns', *SR*, 5 (1982), pp. 105–13.

(i.e. supporters of the king).[11] At first the countess found the gates shut against her. Allowed into the town, she was forced to flee to London the next day.

Once again, the reports stressed the wholesale nature of the plunder and destruction. Both St Osyth and Melford Hall, one of the largest houses in Suffolk, had been made uninhabitable. Visiting Long Melford in 1649, the Essex minister Ralph Josselin noted in his diary, 'I saw the ruines of that great [house] plundered out and desolate without inhabitant'. According to a much later report her house at St Osyth remained uninhabited for the next seventy years. Some idea of the destruction can be gauged from the estimates of the countess's losses. Harbottle Grimston, sent down by the Commons to St Osyth, put the losses there at some £40,000. The countess herself in a petition to the House of Lords put her losses at £50,000, besides the destruction of her houses. Writing later, Bruno Ryves estimated her losses at £100,000 and told his readers that he had heard others suggest a figure of £150,000.[12] In her own subsequent petition, the Countess claimed that the attacks had left her without 'so much as a change of apparell'. Whatever the true figure, these were prodigious losses.

The next set of targets were those within the town or within close striking distance of Colchester. These were probably attacked before or at the same time as the attack on the Countess of Rivers as the crowds began to move outwards from St John's. The Audleys were a catholic family who lived at Berechurch, which was outside the town's walls but within its liberties. The presence of this catholic household on the borders of the town had long been a source of tension and conflict. In Whitsun 1640, wild rumours about catholics assembling there had produced a panic in the streets of Colchester and had prompted a botched attempt by some of the young men of the town to search the house. The attack on Lucas now made possible the ransacking of Berechurch. Once again the house was subjected to a wholesale attack and, according to *Mercurius Rusticus*, the attackers plundered the family's cattle as well as their house. Sir Henry Audley, the head of the household, was not there, having sought and obtained permission to travel abroad in 1641, a decision probably not unrelated to the earlier panic and the increasing anti-popery of the period. But his family was. In her petition to the Commons in early September, Lady Audley com-

---

[11] BL, E114(36), p. 22.
[12] BL, Harleian MS 163, fol. 308 r; *MR*, p. 11; HLRO, MP HL, 29 August 1642. Even after the destruction of 1642, Melford Hall was second only to Hengrave Hall in the 1674 Hearth tax assessment: D. Dymond and E. Martin, eds., *An Historical Atlas of Suffolk* (Ipswich, 1989), p. 146.

plained of being 'herselfe & her children affrighted, having lost in monie, plate, goods & household stuffe above the value of 800li'. At a later date, Sir Henry himself claimed that, 'his whole per[so]nall estate was plundred and taken away by the rude people that rose in Essex in the yere 1641 or 1642 & they then pulled down his house & made it altogether [un]inhabitable to his damage 3000li.'[13]

These statements need to be treated with some caution; that detailing the losses came from evidence placed before the Committee for Compounding to support the Audleys' petition for a more reasonable composition fine. However, first-hand evidence in support of these claims comes indirectly from a 1647 case in Chancery. The case had a curious origin. A Colchester attorney, who had given a bond on behalf of a client prosecuted by Audley's agent for allegedly taking part in the attack, later found himself being prosecuted by Audley when his client became bankrupt. The original action had arisen out of the aftermath of the attack at Berechurch. William Lawrence, a Colchester grocer, had been prosecuted for taking part in the attack. One of Audley's trustees seeing him with the crowds had brought a successful action of trespass against him for taking away a copper and a large amount of rye valued at £40. However, Lawrence claimed that he was not there as one of the attackers. When 'the Comon rude people resorting to the dwelling house of the said Sir Henrie ... deemeing him then to be a roman catholic ... did deface part of his said house & dispoyled & wasted some of his said goods', he had gone with others from Colchester to rescue Sir Henry's property. But, 'seeing the rude multitude to be soe great, [they] were not able to repell them'. What is clear is that the attack here, as at St John's, had been marked by widespread destruction. On the funeral monument which Sir Henry had erected in 1648, he had written, 'Non aedes (Belli Civilis furore diructas) [He did not rebuild his house, destroyed by the fury of the Civil War]'.[14]

Catholics were not, however, the only targets of the Colchester crowds. Sir Thomas Lucas, Sir John's brother, who later complained of having had his records plundered, was probably among those first attacked.[15] Some of those assembled at Colchester had gone on to attack unpopular local ministers in Colchester and the surrounding area. According to *Mercurius Rusticus* Gabriel Honeyfold, a minister with a

---

[13] *PJ*, 3, p. 337; PRO, SP, 19A/95, fol. 85. In her petition Lady Audley stated that her husband had left the country. Having received a licence from the king to travel abroad in July 1641, he had probably been abroad for over a year: PRO, SP, 16/482/2 and 40.

[14] PRO, C2/Chas I/L21/5; *MR*, p. 9; PRO, SP, 19A/95, fol. 85; K. Mabbitt, 'The Audley chapel in Berechurch Church', *TEAS*, 22 (1940), p. 93.

[15] PRO, SP, 23/198, p. 607.

living in Colchester and another at the nearby village of Ardleigh, was one of those attacked.[16] He had his 'Bonds, Billes and Evidences' taken from him and his house stripped of all its furniture, leaving 'not a shelfe behind them, nor a pin to hang a hat on'. When he went to the Mayor to request his help to recover his property, Alderman Cole, whom we have already seen implicated in the attack on Lucas, had told him that 'he wond[e]red he would offer to come abroad, being a man so much hated'. Finding himself turned away, Honeyfold was then mobbed in the streets. 'A multitude of boyes and rude people throng about him, and prosequute [sic] him through the streetes with exclamations and outcries; nor doe they stay there, their hands second their tongues, throwing stones and dirt at him.' When a kinsman took him into his house, the crowd threatened to pull down the house, until at last Honeyfold too was forced to take 'sanctuary' in the town's gaol. Ryves also describes an attack on the same day by a crowd from Colchester on the minister Erasmus Laud at his parish of Little Tey, some six or seven miles to the west of the town. There the attackers spoiled his goods, drove away his cattle, robbed him of £20 and of his and his wife's clothes.

Once again, Ryves was anxious in his account to emphasise the violence of the attackers and the failure of the authorities to take action to protect the crowds' victims. The codes of war made attacks on the elderly and ministers especially shocking. That Honeyfold was both old and a minister made his case a particularly telling one for Ryves to use. Ryves was also concerned to emphasise the irrationality of the violence. In the case of the attack on Laud, he suggested that he owed his fate to the mere fact of sharing the same surname as the unpopular Archbishop of Canterbury, William Laud. The minister's 'very name with these men was a crime and reason enough to expose him to their rage'.

Several of those involved in the attacks on the ministers were among the very few attackers subsequently indicted. One of those indicted at the Essex Quarter Sessions for the attack on the Little Tey minister was also indicted for breaking into the house of William Collingwood, the minister at Great Birch, some four miles from Tey, on the morning of the same day and stealing a pistol, brass pot and five shillings in money.[17] Five miles to the south of Colchester at the village of Peldon, a living to which the Rivers family held the right of presentation, a crowd attacked and robbed the house of the minister on the 24 August and would appear to have done so again the following day. At Great Holland, further towards the coast and some fourteen miles or so from Colchester, the minister at another Rivers' living, Edward Cherry, was forced to

[16] *MR*, p. 11.   [17] ERO, Q/SR 319/ 13, 15, 16.

abandon his rectory.[18] The incident at Great Braxted, recalled later in the century, in which the minister, Thomas Meighan, 'was taken out of his house by a Multitude and carried away as a Prisoner' may provide evidence of a further attack, given the parish's proximity to the centres of the attacks. *Mercurius Rusticus* reported that 'a hundred men from *Cogshall* and *Colchester* side (some of that crew that plundered Sir *John Lucas's* his house)' had also planned to attack Edward Symmonds, the minister at Rayne, some twenty-three and eleven miles respectively west of Colchester and Coggeshall. Although there is no supporting evidence, Ryves' dating of this threatened attack to after Symmond's return from being examined before the Commons would place it shortly after the beginning of the attacks, Symmonds' release having being ordered on the 18th of August.[19] The dating of offences in indictments is sometimes inaccurate, but if the dating is here correct it suggests that in the days after the attack on Lucas smaller crowds were touring Colchester's neighbouring villages and settling scores. Little Tey, Great Birch and Peldon were in an arc to the south-west of Colchester. At least some of those who attacked the minister at Peldon came from Colchester and had also been involved in the attack on the Countess of Rivers' house at St Osyth.

By 24 August both Parliament and the local authorities had begun to take action to try to prevent the attacks developing any further. But what had begun as a local action quickly spread beyond Colchester to involve a whole series of communities in Essex and Suffolk. The rapidity with which such attacks spread is a reflection of the pre-existing tensions and anxieties that the deteriorating relationship between king and Parliament and news of the attacks on protestants in the Irish rebellion had created. Arthur Wilson, steward to the Earl of Warwick, provides an eye-witness account (albeit one only some time later committed to paper) of the panic that both prompted and fed on the attack on Lucas.[20] Wilson had been sent to Melford with the earl's coach in response to a plea from the countess to rescue her. His account paints a vivid picture of the problems he faced in trying to navigate a way to Long Melford through a region where, 'even the better sort behaved themselves as if their [*sic*] had beene a dissolution of all gouerment [and] no man could remaine in his owne

---

[18] ERO, Q/S Ba 2/48. This is probably what Cherry refers to in his petition of 1660, when he talks of 'the violence of the late Warre': HLRO, MP HL, 21 June 1660.

[19] Bodl. Lib., J Walker MS, c. 2, fol. 102; *MR*, week 2, p. 14: CJ/ii/698, 709, 727.

[20] CUL, Additional MS 33, fols. 19–21. Although described as a diary, internal evidence suggests that Wilson wrote up at least part of the diary as late as the 1650s. It should be noted that Wilson's emphasis on the threat he faced from crowds described variously as 'the Beast' and 'Guidie Multitude' served to frame his narrative as exemplifying God's particular goodness towards him, a trope repeated throughout his account of his life.

house w[i]thout feare, nor bee abroad w[i]th safetie'. Progress was slow. Wilson recalled that it was 'with difficultie I past through litle villages of Essex, where their black bills and course [coarse] Examinations put us to divers demurs, and but that they had some knowledge both of mee and the Coach I had not past w[i]th safetie'. When he eventually managed to get to Sudbury, two miles from Long Melford:

not a man appeared till wee were w[i]thin the Chaine, and then they began to run to their Weapons, and before wee could get to the Marketplace the Streets swarmed w[i]th people ... The Mouth cried out this Coach belongs to the Ladie Rivers, and they are going to her Cave ... and some that pretended to be more wise and knowing then the rest said that I was the Lord River, and they swarmed about mee, and were so kind as to lay hold on mee. I told them I was Steward to the Earle of Warwick, a lover of his Countrie, & now in the Parliam[en]t's imployment ... And that I had lett[e]rs in my pocketts, if they would lett any of the Magistrates see them, that would make me appeare to be a friend & an honest man. This said, the Mouth cried out letters, letters; the tops of the trees, & all the windowes were throng[e]d with people, who cri[e]d the same. At last the Maior came Crowding in with his Officers ... The Maior's wisedome said hee knew not my lords hand, it might be and it might not, and away he went, not knowing what to doe to mee, nor I what to say to them.

Although Wilson was eventually able to get away, he was forced to abandon the attempt to reach Melford, 'for I heard from all hands there was so great a Confusion at Milford that no man appeared like a Gentleman, but was made a prey to that ravenous Crew'. His rescue attempt finally faltered little more than a mile away at Sir Robert Crane's house at Chilton. According to Wilson, Sir Robert himself had been 'forced to retaine a train'd band in his house (although hee was a Parliament man) to secure himself from the fury of that Rable, who threat[e]ned him' for his part in helping the countess to escape.

Wilson's account doubtless needs to be read as that of a gentleman writing about his inferiors (and some time after the event) with all the stereotypical assumptions that might imply. However, it conjures up the confusion and panic that reports of the initial attacks and rumours of worse had created. Writing from Suffolk a week after the attacks had started, a correspondent of Sir Simonds D'Ewes noted it was hard to say what was true, 'for wee heare of a 100 lyes in a day'. Such panics were not confined to the immediate region of the attacks. Bishop Wren, the bogey of the godly in the region and the object of rumours in an earlier 1640 panic at Colchester, was the subject of similar alarums. From south Essex, it was reported that, 'the County were much afraid of him ... he hath given out threat[e]ning speeches that hee would set fire of some Town in the Country, and burnt [*sic*] downe *Waltham Abbey* of which hee is owner'. As D'Ewes' correspondent noted, 'these [attacks] have mayde such a broyle in the Co[u]ntry that now in every Place People are afaryd of one another and know not hee to trust'. Similar rumours may just excuse the false report in a London newsbook of disorders at Hadleigh and Ipswich in which pro-royalist crowds declared their intention not to be 'governed by a few Puritans'.[21]

Sir Thomas Barrington and Harbottle Grimston, despatched by Parliament, reached Colchester on August 24th. They estimated the crowds still assembled there to be some four to five thousand strong. But by then crowds had hived off to attack other targets. Grimston reported that they had found, 'those unruely people dispersed in great multitudes throughout severall p[ar]tes of the County, having rifled many houses and almost ruinated the houses themselves.'[22] Those who attacked Sir John Lucas were said to have been responsible for attacking and plundering the house of Thomas Bayles, on 24 August at Witham, some thirteen miles to the south-west of Colchester, causing losses later put at £1,600. Bayles was a lawyer and a JP with suspiciously close links with local catholic families.[23] While the original Colchester crowd provided a nucleus for other attacks – the Countess of Rivers described her attackers as a 'rude multitude (raysed for the most part in and about Colchester)' – it seems certain that they were joined by those who shared their fears and that their actions were the signal for both combined and independent attacks. The warrants sent out by the authorities in Suffolk called on the parish constables to prevent crowds moving through their parish and the parish's own poor from leaving the parish. In his recollections of the attack that took place at Copdock, Henry Forster spoke of his family's 'fellow catholic neighbours who complained more of the insolence of their own parishioners than of those who came afar off'. Ralph Josselin, the minister at Earls Colne, some ten miles to the west of Colchester, noted in his diary, 'our poore people in Tumults arose and plundered divers Houses, papists and others and threatened to go farther'.[24]

---

[21] BL, Harleian MS. 385, fol. 209; MS 365, fol. 209; BL, E202(42), *Exact and True Diurnall*, p. 2; BL, E202(39) *Exact and true Diurnall*, *sub* 26 August 1642.

[22] BL, Harleian MS 163, fol. 307 v; Warwickshire RO CR 2017/C9/2 (I am grateful to Monica Ory of the Warwickshire Record Office for making a copy of this available).

[23] PRO, SP, 16/491/128; SP, 29/295/73; P. R. Knell, 'Essex recusants sequestered during the civil war and Interregnum: part 4', *ERec*, 12 (1970), pp. 17, 19. W. Hunt, *The Puritan Moment: the Coming of Revolution in an English County* (Cambridge, Mass., 1983), p. 306, mistakes Bayles for the minister of Witham.

[24] HLRO, MP HL, 29 August 1642; ESRO, FB, 19/I2/2 [18]; H. Foley, *Records of the English Province of the Society of Jesus*, 6 vols. (1875–80), vol. 2, p. 450; *The Diary of*

Geography suggests that they might have been among those whom Barrington and Grimston encountered when, en route to Colchester and Long Melford, they had come across 'divers houses in pillaging' at Great Yeldham, some eighteen miles down the Colne valley from Colchester and eight from Long Melford.

Long Melford too seems to have served as a satellite centre for a further series of attacks. Crowds numbering three to four thousand were said to have assembled there and at Lavenham. Within Melford itself, the house of the Martins, a landed catholic family, was attacked. Their chapel must have provided an obvious provocation for their godly neighbours. The Melford house of Mistress Carey, another catholic, whose husband had been steward on the Rivers' estate, was also attacked. So too was the minister at Long Melford, Robert Warren. His house was searched, some said it was pulled down, his papers destroyed (including the manorial records for the rectory manor of which he was lord), his household goods and five horse taken from him. Warren was reported to have been 'huffed and shuffed about, but (as is said) hurt not otherwise'. He himself claimed that he was only released after he had handed over money to his tormentors.[25]

Thereafter, as in Essex, crowds spread into neighbouring parishes. The evidence for these other attacks is more scanty – Ryves, for example, provides details for Suffolk of only the attack on the Countess of Rivers – and other sources usually provide no more than a reference to the fact of there having been an attack. As a result it is not always possible to say for certain whether the crowds that assembled at Long Melford were responsible. But it seems likely that the very large crowds that assembled at Melford went on to attack other houses in the neighbourhood, gathering support on their procession. The panic that Arthur Wilson encountered at Sudbury, as well as the geography of the attacks, would suggest that the town's inhabitants were prominent both at Melford and in the subsequent actions attacking catholic families in the town's hinterland. A letter, appearing under the date August 24th in a London newsbook, which noted that, 'the people in those parts begin to take

Ralph Josselin 1616–1683, ed. A. Macfarlane (British Academy, Records of Social and Economic History, NS 3, 1976), p. 13.

[25] BL, Harleian MS 365, fol. 209; Wall, *Long Melford*, pp. 82–8; *Diary John Rouse*, pp. 121–2; Stoneyhurst MSS, MSS Angliae, vii, fos. 122–3 (I am grateful to Lyn Boothman for information about John Carey); BL, Harleian MS. 85, fol. 209; WSRO, FL, 509/3/15, pp. 1, 5; J. Walker, *An Attempt Towards Recovering An Account of the Numbers and Sufferings of the Clergy of the Church of England, Heads of Colleges, Fellows, Scholars, etc. who were Sequestered, Harass'd etc. in the late Times of the Grand Rebellion* (1714), p. 395 (which misdates the event to August 1641).

example by the insurrection at *Colchester*, and rescue prisoners, [and] plunder houses', was written from Sudbury.[26]

Acton Place, the home of the catholic Daniels family, was probably one of the first places to be attacked after the attack on the Countess, since Acton was the neighbouring parish to Long Melford. The Daniels were linked both by ties of kinship and neighbourliness to the Rivers. Another branch of the Daniel family at Bulmer, four miles to the south of Long Melford, was also attacked. According to Nicholas Daniel his mansion house was 'plundered and ruined by rude people' and rendered uninhabitable. The house of Thomas Wright, a yeoman and catholic, at Borley, midway between Bulmer and Long Melford, was attacked at the same time and 'much defaced and ruined by rude people'. Another of his houses in Suffolk may also have been attacked.[27] Since Yeldham, where Barrington and Grimston had encountered crowds on 24 August, was only four miles from Bulmer it would seem likely that these attacks were part of the same episode.

Frances Weston, the dowager countess of Portland, another victim, was probably attacked as part of the same sequence. According to her son, the second earl, whose own house at Chiswick had been the intended target of Parliamentary troops in early August, his mother was 'turned out of doores, the bed where she lay taken from her, and the poore people's houses who offered to receive her threatened to be pulled downe'. The family had several estates in the region; this attack most likely took place at either the house of her own family, the catholic Waldegraves at Borley, or at the Weston manor of Nayland.[28] At nearby Stoke by Nayland, Gifford Hall, the home of the recusant Sir Francis Mannock, was attacked. According to John Rous, the house 'was pillaged of all goods (and, as is said, not his writings spared, which he craved, but were torne, nor his dogs)'.[29] Since the Naylands were midway between Colchester and Long Melford it is probable that these attacks were sparked by the crowds on either their outward or return journey to Colchester.

Lavenham, another important cloth centre four miles to the north of

---

[26] BL, E114(36), *Special Passages and Certain Informations*, 23–30 August 1642, p. 22.

[27] PRO, SP, 23/79/194, /134/465; ASSI, 35/85/5.

[28] PRO, SP, 16/491/119; HLRO, MP HL, 6 September 1642. The earl's petition of 6 September mentions only Essex as the place where the attack occurred. One of Portland's daughters had married Richard White. If his mother was living with them then she could have been one of those attacked at Hutton: R. E. Chester Waters, *Genealogical Memoirs of the Extinct Family of Chester of Chicheley, Their Ancestors and Descendants*, 2 vols. (1878), vol. 1, p. 101; M. Van Cleave Alexander, *Charles I's Lord Treasurer: Sir Richard Weston, Earl of Portland*, (1975), pp. 30–4.

[29] *Diary of John Rouse*, ed. M. A. E. Green (1856), vol. 66, p. 122.

Long Melford, also registered attacks. On 29 August, Sir Simonds
D'Ewes' agent wrote from Suffolk, 'we are troubled with tumultuous
People ... there is they say 3 or 4 thousand gathered and have done
much hurt about Melford and Lavenham [and] other places, but it is
most to the Papyst houses ... and these have mayde such a broyle in the
Co[u]ntry that now in every Place People are afaryd [i.e. afeared] of one
another and know not hee to trust'. Although there is no other evidence
for what occurred at Lavenham, the landed family of the Skinners,
whose catholicism had brought them some notoriety, were probably
victims there.[30]

While the original epicentres at Colchester and Long Melford may
have provided the critical mass for all these attacks, it is clear that there
were also separate nuclei from which other attacks were launched. The
evidence of these attacks places a further question mark over the title –
the Stour Valley riots – by which this episode is commonly known. In
Essex, there were attacks further south in the county. Maldon, a small
port and borough with a population of about a thousand, was a separate
centre from which mobile crowds mounted attacks on catholic households. According to a letter written in early September to a chaplain to
the catholic Petre family, 'those of Maldon side rise also, some 50, or 60
saylers made head [and] resolved to doe as the Colchester men had
taught them'.[31] At Maldon itself, Edmund Church, a catholic landowner
with lands throughout Essex (including Colchester) and other counties,
was the victim of an attack. Given his surname, Church's misfortune
provided a fellow catholic and poet, Thomas Wilford, with the perfect
pun: 'What Sacriligious Synod durst/Presume to plunder Churches first?/
Was it by the ffuries consent?/Or what is worse the Parliament?' Church
had been already the victim of an earlier episode. At the time of the
petitioning in the county against the popish threat in January 1642 his
barn and two stacks of rye at Mucking in the very south of the county
had been attacked by a crowd of a hundred artisans and labourers. Now
in August 1642, 'ye poore people of ye neighbourhead [*sic*]' pulled down
and carried away a barn and an oxhouse, declaring that 'Edmond
Church was a papist' and that they would pull down his house if any

---

[30] BL, Harleian MS. 385, fol. 209. In 1637 the godly of the region had been shocked by
tales of the eldest son's alehouse bragging of his desire to kill the king and go to Rome:
The Registrum Vagum of Anthony Harison (Norfolk Record Society, 32, 1963), p. 182;
WP, III, 1631–1637, p. 386.

[31] Stoneyhurst College, Stoneyhurst MSS, MSS Angliae 7, fols. 122–3. For the argument
that Mr Talman, the name of the recipient, was a pseudonym of Henry Moore, chaplain
to Lord Petre, see G. Holt, *St Omer and Bruges Colleges 1593–1733. A Biographical
Dictionary* (1979), p. 183.

opposed them.[32] Ministers may also have been attacked in this region. Bruno Ryves reports an attack on one. Mr Stevens, the minister at the Petre living of South Hanningfield, six miles west of Ingatestone, was plundered. He managed to escape, leaving his children to hide the family's plate before the plunderers arrived. However, *Mercurius Rusticus's* account claims that the poor woman with whom they hid their plate was killed by the plunderers, being struck 'on the head with a Club with such violence, that her brains came out at her nostrills'. (If this was so, then this is the only recorded death throughout the whole episode of the attacks.)[33]

The main target for the crowds' attention in this area of Essex was the Petre family and those associated with it. The Petres were the leading catholic landowners in the county with extensive estates and a remarkable number of cadet branches. There had been at least one earlier incident on the Petre estates – a large-scale attack on the family's fishponds at West Thorndon and enclosures at Stock and Butsberry in the spring and summer of 1641 – and both during and after the August actions there were to be invasions of the family's deer parks. In August 1642 several Petre houses were attacked. Sailors from Maldon attacked Crondon Park, nine miles to the south-west of the town, and tore down all the hangings, broke open trunks in the house and carried away some linen and silver. Thereafter another crowd, this time composed of the Parliamentary volunteers assembled in that area, attacked the Petre house of Fithlers. Others went to Hutton where they attacked and robbed some tenants of the Petre family of their cattle and goods, leaving so it was reported, 'neither shelf, bed stoole nor any utensell'. It is probable that at the same time the house of another catholic Sir Richard White at Hutton was also attacked. Finally, a crowd of over one hundred, again made up of Parliamentary volunteers, went to the Lady Petre's at Ingatestone and attempted unsuccessfully to raise the local inhabitants, telling them 'that if it might be done with her own safety, she would poyson, or cut theyr throates'. The soldiers were persuaded to depart with three or four pieces of gold, but the next day a smaller group of twenty accompa-

---

[32] *To all the ROYALISTS That Suffered for His MAJESTY and to the rest of the Good People of England. The Humble APOLOGY of the English CATHOLICS* (n.p., 1666), p. 14; *APC 1615–1616*, p. 87, *1616–1617*, p. 327; R. Lee, *Law and Local Society in the time of Charles I: Bedfordshire and the Civil War* (Bedfordshire Historical Record Society, 65, 1986), p. 9; BL, Additional MS 5541, p. 221; *CCC*, 4, pp. 2402–3; ERO, Q/SR, 316/24; PRO, SP, 23/113, pp. 125–6.

[33] The parish registers for South Hanningfield do not survive before 1660: F. G. Emmison, *Catalogue of the Essex Parish Records 1240–1894* (Chelmsford, 1966), p. 128.

nied by two officers returned and subjected the house to a thorough search for arms.[34]

It would seem probable that known catholics in communities where attacks were known to have been made, would also have been victims. For example, the crowd that attacked Thomas Bayles at Witham were scarcely likely to have left the house of the Southcotts, a more prominent catholic family living there, unscathed. If the later complaint of having been plundered made by Francis Wright, the unpopular minister at Witham, was not coded royalist language for his sequestration, then he too may have been attacked then.[35] The event, undated but before Christmas 1642, to which John Wenlock of Langham in north Essex later referred in which he 'was threatened to have my house pulled down, and all my goods taken away by Riflers' may just have occurred at the same time that crowds were attacking the Mannocks at nearby Stoke by Nayland.[36] References in the Commons' Journal to horse, plate and arms of unnamed catholics stayed in the region may hint at other episodes of popular action.[37] Since most of the catholics within this region and the region of the Colne and Stour valleys to the north were attacked, it is possible that there may have been incidents for which evidence has not survived in the other area where there was a clustering of catholics, over to the west of the county. On 25 August two Essex JPs had reported that, 'those riotous people w[hi]ch are nowe assembled in a riotous tumultuous & rebellious mann[e]r ... are likewise resolved to goe in that riotous mann[e]r to Audley End ... and there to plunder & rifle the howse of the right ho[nourab]le the Earle of Suff[olk] & by the way to plunder & rifle div[er]se howses'. Suffolk was not himself a catholic. There is, however, evidence to suggest that his actions as a large

---

[34] ERO, D/DP, L36/2; Alexander, *Lord Treasurer*, p. 32. Sir Richard and his wife fled to the continent in 1642: Stoneyhurst MSS, MSS Angliae, 7, fols. 122–3. In a later petition, undated but probably from the 1650s, Lord Petre complains of the loss of the furniture from his three houses and of a large sum of money from his London house, but does not specify whether this was the result of action by the crowds or by sequestrators: ERO, D/P, E60.

[35] T. B. Trappes-Lomax, 'The Southcotes of Witham Place and their contribution to the survival of catholicism in Essex', *ERec*, 3 (1961), pp. 105–15; HLRO, MP HL, 23 June 1660 (petit. of Fras. Wright). Wright complained that 'his house [was] Plundred, and his estate sequestred'. In May 1643 he was said not to have preached at Witham in the last twelve months: HLRO, MP HL, 6 May 1643.

[36] J. Wenlock, *To the most illustrious, High and Mighty majesty of Charles II ... the Humble Declaration of JOHN WENLOCK, Langham* (1662), p. 24. The events Wenlock describes may have come later in response to instructions in December 1642 to raise the trained bands and enter the houses of those that had not contributed to the militia: BL, Additional MS 18,777, fol. 90a.

[37] See, for example, *CJ/ii/799*.

landowner had excited popular hostility.[38] There was a large concentration of catholics at nearby Saffron Walden which served also as a social centre for the catholic families living in north-west Essex. There had been earlier attacks on at least two of these families in the summer of 1640 by the troops assembled for the Scottish war. Edward Greene of Little Sampford in Essex had been one of the victims of an earlier attack in which fifty or more of the soldiers assembled in the county for Scotland were encouraged to pull down his house. If there were no further attacks in the summer of 1642 this may have been because the authorities were successful in intercepting the crowds.[39]

Similarly, we have little evidence for Suffolk of the fate of the catholic families in the other areas of the county where they were clustered.[40] We know that Henry Forster and his family were attacked at Copdock. The account of the attack by one of the sons of the family claimed that their house was the fourth to be attacked by crowds drawn from both Essex and Suffolk. This account, though first-hand, is not without its own characteristic trope since the attack is rendered as an example of the testing of faith by religious persecution over which his father successfully triumphs by resignation to the will of God. Nevertheless it is valuable in providing evidence of the tensions that lay behind such attacks.[41] As was the case with the Audleys at Colchester, the family's activities had for some time been the occasion of rumour and fear on the streets of the nearby town of Ipswich. Rumours of a secret army kept underground in the day and trained at night, of the preparation of very large amounts of food and of the arrival of armour had resulted in the house being beset for three nights in a row by men sent by the 'chief of Ipswich'. In turn, 'the rabble of Ipswich was so incensed thereby that they could scarce be kept from gathering into a head to come and pull our house down over our heads, lest we should cut their throats with the hidden army'. There

[38] HLRO, MP HL, 28 April 1643.
[39] PRO, SP, 16/491/128; N. C. Elliott, 'The Roman Catholic community in Essex 1625–1701', *ERec*, 25/6 (1983/4), pp. 8–9; PRO, SP, 16/463/27; PCR, 2/52, p. 634; ERO, Q/SR 311/15. A surviving gaol calendar shows that the JPs who raised the alarm about the crowds' intentions to go to Audley End, and whose houses stood between the crowd and its objective, were responsible for arresting several of the attackers: ERO, Q/SR 319/46.
[40] The well-informed account of the attacks includes one name, Sir Henry Sudyes, whom it has not been possible to identify: Stoneyhurst College, Stoneyhurst MSS, MSS Angliae, 7, fol. 122.
[41] Foley, *Society*, vol. 2, pp. 450–1. The account was clearly written some time after the event, since it describes the attackers being drawn from the 'associated counties'. I have failed to locate the original from which Foley transcribed this account and which might allow it to be dated. A note in the manuscript volumes of his published work indicates that the original was transcribed from the Jesuit archives in Belgium, much of which have since been destroyed.

are striking parallels here with the attack on Sir John Lucas. Rumour of armies and arming had led to official action by the rulers of Ipswich, which in turn, had only increased popular anxieties and anger. It was probably rumours such as this, transmitted through the many links that tied communities together in the region, which attracted there crowds who had already attacked Sir John Lucas and the Countess of Rivers. The account is also valuable in giving a glimpse of the processes that more abbreviated accounts render simply as an event. Knowledge of the earlier attacks arrived at least a day before the crowds themselves, allowing Forster time to send his children and servants to protestant families and to hide some of his goods in his neighbours' houses. When the rest of the family was at prayer in the chapel – an understandable action, but one hardly designed to lessen the crowd's hostility – news was brought 'that the rabble began to appear in troops, and were overheard to say, that if they could catch ... Mr Forster they would lock him into some chamber, and set fire to the house'. This forced the family to fly, abandoning the house to the crowds. Here as elsewhere the attack was notable for the destruction caused, sufficient according to the account to move a protestant neighbour, 'Squire Bloisse', to tears.

Rumour and panic spread to other counties in the region. *A true and exact relation of the present estate of the City of Norwich*, appearing on 27 August, claimed that because of the trade depression 'we can scarce keep the poor from mutiny, and [it] filleth us with fears, such as hasten on apace even to desperation, and make many people to mutter, and speak it out'. A troop of 'well-affected horsemen' – the description leaves it uncertain whether these horsemen were officially in the service of Parliament – had met outside Cambridge in late August with the intention of searching all the papists' houses and had announced their resolution to go to the Isle of Ely to search Bishop Wren's house which they suspected had been made a magazine for the catholics. In early September Parliament was informed, 'that many of the Inhabitants of the County of *Cambridge* and the Isle of *Elye*, are desirous that the Captains of the Trained Bands within the said County ... may be enabled to assemble their Companies, for the Suppression of riotous Insurrections within the said County (if any shall be)'. Further north, there were reports from Lincolnshire of fears of plundering prompted by rumours in late August of landings in the county by cavaliers.[42] Lincoln-

---

[42] BL, E114(27), *A true and exact relation of the present estate of the City of Norwich, made known to the High and Honorable Court of Parliament, by way of Petition, for the speedy prevention of eminent dangers, which from other Counties and places examples hath bin too apparently seen*; E127(6), *An Extract of Severall Letters which came by the last Post, or otherwise, from all parts of the Kingdome, since the fifth of November to this present*

shire, like Essex, felt itself to have been left defenceless by the failure to return arms which had been taken for the king's Scottish campaign. Detailed local research might uncover evidence of further attacks in these regions.

The response of the Parliamentary authorities to these unprecedented attacks on members of the landed class was immediate, but curiously muted. Parliament had received the Mayor's letter informing them of the attack on Lucas on the same day that he had written it, 23 August. Recent experience might have prepared them for the news. Writing in early August Sir Robert Crane, MP for Sudbury in Suffolk, had noted that 'the soldiers doe some times mistake a protestant house for a papist', and the Commons had therefore decided to take action. Accordingly, the Lords and Commons had issued a flurry of orders on 17 and 18 August to prevent any further disorders by the troops being raised for Parliament. Indeed, on 17 August, the Commons had instructed the MPs for Essex to write a letter to the county's JPs requiring them, 'to punish such as have or shall pillage any House of any Inhabitant in the County'. Did this order suggest that rumours of threatened action by the people against their enemies had already reached Parliament or was it designed to anticipate action by the troops there? We cannot tell.[43] Nevertheless the majority in the Commons, if not the Lords, clearly welcomed the action in preventing Lucas from taking support to the king. The attackers were to be thanked for their zeal. However, even the Commons were anxious. As we have seen, Colchester's two MPs, Sir Thomas Barrington and Harbottle Grimston, were dispatched to Colchester, 'to appease the Tumults' and to send up Lucas and Newcomen. They were also to search the Countess of Rivers' house and to free the house and its inhabitants from 'any Tumults'.[44]

Barrington and Grimston had wanted to set off immediately, but they were unable to leave until mid-afternoon. They later claimed that the House's delay lost some further £40,000 in goods. That night they rode some thirty miles to Chelmsford, the county town. The next day they arrived at Colchester, their unusual route suggesting that they had ridden there via the Stour Valley in an attempt to stop further attacks of which

November the twelfth, pp. 5–6; BL, E114(27), A2v; LJ/v/341–2; BL, E115(9), *Joyfull News from the Isle of Ely, Declaring the Manner of apprehending Bishop Wren*, pp. 2–3; Bodl. Lib., MS Dep. c. 153,60, fol. 116. Parliament had ordered several MPs into Cambridgeshire to see the militia ordinance put into effect on the 29th: CJ/ii/743.

[43] Bodl. Lib., Tanner MS. 63, fol. 125; LJ/v/300; CJ/ii/725, 727; Husbands, *An Exact Collection of all Remonstrances* (1643), p. 565.

[44] LJ/v/318, 319; CJ/ii/732–4; BL, Harleian MS. 163, fol. 297v; BL, E114(36), *Special Passages*, p. 18.

they may have gained knowledge once in the county. Grimston then went on to the Countess of Rivers' house at St Osyth. On the 25th the Commons received a letter from Barrington and Grimston. They reported that they had found, 'a body of 5 or 6 thowsand men, who upon their telling them of how displeasing the rifling and pillaging of S[i]r John Lucas his howse was to the Parliament, they all expressed much sorrow for what they had done ... and ... they did thereupon disperse themselves and made restitution of divers of those goods that they had taken'.[45] On the same day, Grimston wrote privately to Lord Fielding that though he and Barrington were, 'armed with noe other authoritie but faier p[er]swasions to worke uppon them with ... God hath blessed us soe farre as yett in all places where wee have bene, to pr[e]vaile with them and to appease them'. Nonetheless, Barrington and Grimston asked Parliament to set up a committee to send down instructions 'for the appeasing of the present tumults & the prevention of them for the future'. The House of Commons responded the same day by ordering the Essex MPs in the House to write to the county authorities to assist Barrington and Grimston. At the same time they expressed a wish that the Lords would join with them in desiring the Earl of Warwick, the Lord Lieutenant and real power in the county, 'for a few Days to come into the County of *Essex*, for the better Preservation of the Peace of that County'. Both measures suggest a developing anxiety about the spread of the attacks. On the same day the Commons had received a letter from Sir Robert Crane in Suffolk giving details of the tumults around Sudbury.[46]

Still on the 25th, the county authorities had begun to take action. Late in the day the Sheriff for Suffolk, Sir William Castleton, had sent out warrants for the trained bands and other able men to muster near Bury St Edmunds the following day. However, when the trained bands did assemble they refused to accompany the sheriff, for reasons the source does not specify. It was not until Friday the 27th, under the acceptable leadership of Mr North, that they apprehended some of the attackers. Warrants were also sent out to raise horse and to assemble them closer to the centre of the attacks at Great Waldingfield, a village both close to Sudbury and Long Melford. By then magistrates in the county had begun to send out warrants to the parish constables ordering them to mount double watch and ward 'of honest and able men' to prevent any passing 'in a tumultuous or hostile mann[er]' and to apprehend any unknown or suspicious men passing through their parish. Orders were

---

[45] BL, Harleian MS 163, fols. 307 v–r. Hunt, *Puritan Moment*, p. 304, in having Barrington not leave London until the 24th underestimates the speed, and hence seriousness, with which Parliament responded.

[46] *CJ*/ii/736–7; Warwickshire RO, CR, 2017/C9/2; BL, Harleian MS. 163, fols. 298 v, 307 v.

also given for searching the houses of those suspected to have stolen goods. These measures were said to have prompted some to make voluntary restitution. A similar attempt was made to raise the trained bands in Essex. On the 25th two JPs ordered the sheriff to raise the trained bands to prevent the attacks spreading. Two days later the Commons ordered the sheriff to preserve the Mildmays' house at Danbury 'and other Houses in that County'.[47]

Parliament's swift dispatch of Colchester's MPs showed its concern to prevent the disorders spreading. But the ambivalence inscribed within the message the MPs were charged to deliver also reflected Parliament's concern with the threat of a possible royalist rising within the region.[48] Thus the 'honest Inhabitants' – not a usual term of address for rioters who had attacked their betters – were to be told that they had done 'a very acceptable Service to the Commonwealth, and such a one as doth express a great Zeal to their Religion and Liberties'. Nevertheless, 'lest the gathering together of so many Persons might seem to give some Occasion to Persons ill-affected, of misconstruing their peaceable Intentions, they are farther to signify unto them, that it is thought fit they should for the present disperse'.[49] Parliament was caught between its concern to snuff out a possible royalist rising and its awareness that if the very means of so doing appeared to the gentry as an eruption of the 'many-headed monster' then crowd action could recruit more support for the king.[50] Parliament and its supporters in the region clearly feared however that the cure might be worse than the cause, since the need to suppress the disorders might provide the pretext for an attempt to raise forces for the king under the commission of array. Continuing worries over the potential royalist threat in the region help to explain Parliament's muted response to attempts locally to apprehend the attackers. As Sir Nathaniel Barnardiston informed Suffolk's sheriff, he was not to raise the county to suppress the attacks, since this was 'dangerous in these Turbulent times, and hath begott much feares & Jelosyes in the harts of many good men, how they may be imployed when they come into yo[u]r p[ar]ts for the furthering the execution of the Com[m]ission of Ar[r]ay, or otherwise against the Parliam[en]t'. Thus, when Barrington

---

[47] *Diary*, p. 121; ESRO, FB, 19/I2/1, 2 [12]; BL, Harleian MS 163, fol. 325; 385, fol. 209; PRO, SP, 16/491/128; *CJ*/ii/740.

[48] BL, Harleian M 163, fol. 307 v.

[49] *LJ*/v/318, 319; *CJ*/ii/732–4; BL, Harleian MS 163, fol. 297 v; BL, E114(36), *Special Passages*, p. 18.

[50] The attacks made on Parliament and its local supporters by one Essex minister probably drew on the example of the attacks: BL, E240(19), *A Perfect Diurnall of the Passages in Parliament*, 26 September–3 October 1642, p. 2; BL, Additional MS 18,777, fols. 11b–12a.

reported again to the House of Commons on 29 August he told them, that although some had advised him to raise the trained bands, he had not done so since this might have 'set the whole countrie into a combustion'. When the Sheriff of Essex had received the JPs' warrant to raise the power of the county, he had appeared before the Commons instead to enquire whether he should in fact do so. The House ordered him not to, 'but to labour to quiett the Country with as little force as possible'. As Sir Nathaniel Barnardiston had informed the Suffolk sheriff, 'though the Parliament doe utterly dislike the rude & barbarous Cariage & behaviour of the Tumultious people, [they] yet hould it fitt to forbeare to trouble & execute Justice upon them until the Kingdom be settled & at quiett againe, least it make the cure more dangerous.'[51] Nevertheless, the Commons quickly took action to purchase arms from the Netherlands to remedy their lack in Essex, a deficiency about which the county had long complained.[52]

Parliament's handling of the crowds' victims betrayed a similar ambiguity. The Lords' order had promised that the victims of the attacks should have redress in the courts of law. But as we have seen few of the attackers were prosecuted, even fewer convicted. A note in the assize files declares that those committed to Colchester castle to await the Assizes broke out of jail and were not recaptured, an event about which we would like to know a good deal more. Ironically, as we have seen, the attempt by one Colchester resident to protect the goods of the Audleys landed him in court several years later when the family sought by an action in Chancery against him to force others to compound for the goods they had taken.[53] Thanks to aristocratic solidarities the Countess of Rivers did secure a Parliamentary order for the restitution of her goods and, subsequently, for the payment of her rents in the face of a rent strike by her tenants. The order was printed and copies published in the region of the attacks. But William Bowyer, one of those caught selling her goods in London and committed to Newgate, was discharged by the House of Commons with an order to have the goods restored him, an incident of which Bruno Ryves predictably made much. According to one, possibly suspect, account the countess did recover a great part of her goods, if little of her money. However, her subsequent descent into poverty does not suggest that the order was particularly effective.[54]

[51] BL, Additional MS 18,777, fol. 134; Harleian MS 163, fol. 308 r; *CJ*/ii/747; Bodl. Lib., Tanner MS. 63, fol. 146.
[52] *CJ*/ii/745.
[53] PRO, C2/Charles I/ L21/52. Equity court records might hide other examples of victims trying to recover their property.
[54] BL, Egerton MS 2646, fol. 197; HLRO, MP HL, 29 August, 9 September 1642; *LJ*/v/331, 345; BL, E239(14), *A Perfect Diurnall of the Passages in Parliament*, 29 August–5

Despite this swift response, the attacks did not immediately stop. With reports of attacks elsewhere by troops on the houses of catholic gentry and threats of further plundering, Parliament, with the Lords to the fore, became more anxious to prevent a recurrence of events. Four days after receiving information about the attack on Lucas, Parliament had published a general order to prevent its troops breaking into houses on the pretence that their owners were catholics or disaffected. A committee was also to be established to draw up a Declaration 'for Restraining the Riots and Tumults in *Essex*'. Printed in at least two versions, the Declaration was published on 3 September and copies distributed to the authorities throughout Essex and Suffolk. Parliament again sought publicly to gloss the crowds' actions and willingness to cease 'as testimonie of that dutifull affection which they beare to the Parliament, and the present service of the Kingdom'. However, the Declaration also betrayed a concern that the attacks should not continue. It declared 'that the severall violent Actions by some of them unwarrantably committed, are extremely disallowed' and it ordered the restitution of stolen property and the cessation of unauthorised searches and plundering of houses on pain of punishment. But at the same time the Declaration renewed Parliament's pledge to disarm recusants and other enemies, ordered the trial of Lucas, Newcomen and any others who like them should disturb the peace of the kingdom, and promised to take special steps for the security of Essex. Thus even this document carried an ambiguous message. While threatening with punishment any who refused to return plundered property, the Declaration confirmed the confiscation of Sir John Lucas's horse for Parliament's use and thanked those who had prevented his escape. Moreover, the Declaration did not entirely ban further searches by the people, ordering only that hereafter they should assist those in authority.[55] Indeed, Parliament coninued to thank local communities for their actions in disarming its enemies.[56] These contradictory messages

September 1642; *CJ*/ii/753; ERO, Q/SBa 2/47; ESRO, B105/2/1, fol. 52; *CJ*/ii/789; *MR*, p. 11. The report of the recovery of her goods comes from the newsbook, BL, E119(2), *Speciall Passages*, 20–27 September 1642, p. 30. That Harbottle Grimston had acted as the countess's legal advisor doubtless helped her case: CUL, Hengrave MSS 1, vol. 3, fol. 240; MSS 88, vol. 2, nos. 151, 159, 162; vol. 3, nos. 56, 240.

[55] BL, M636(4), Dorothy Leeke to Lady Verney, 27 August 1642; *LJ*/v/321, 328, 335; *CJ*/ii/738, 740, 741, 749, 751; BL, E243(1), *An Exact Collection of all Remonstrances*, pp. 590–1; BL, E115(15), *A declaration of the Lords and Commons Assembled in Parliament Concerning the Abuses lately done by several persons in the County of Essex* (cf. E1380); ESRO, C9/11/61a; BL, E202(41), *A Perfect Diurnall of the Passages in Parliament*, 29 August–5 September 1642, pp. 6–7.

[56] On the 30 August it commended Brackley in Northamptonshire for its action in disarming papists. Since this was said to involve the townsmen and people, this is an action about whose shape we would like to know a lot more: BL, E202(43), *A True and*

were in part the product of a disagreement between Lords and Commons over the wording of the Declaration – the Lords initially having drawn up their own, more stringent, order which had not secured the Commons' approval.[57] However, the ambiguity continued to reflect a Parliament caught between concern to disown popular disorder and continuing anxieties over the royalist and popish threat. As late as the turn of the year Parliament was hearing reports of the boast of one (unnamed) Essex knight, 'that the County shewed not themselves for the kinge as others but yf the Commission of Array were executed in that County they should see what they would doe'.

These measures had some success in stopping the attacks. Copies of the Declaration reached Ipswich on 6 September. This was perhaps the Parliamentary warrant whose reading 'in the court' at nearby Copdock persuaded the Forsters' neighbours to fight off the plunderers. Parliament's Declaration was doubtless backed by attempts from the pulpit to pacify the people. When, for example, the poor at Earls Colne threatened to go further the minister Ralph Josselin 'endeavoured to suppresse [it] by publique and private meanes'.[58] Harbottle Grimston, returning to London on September the 8th with both volunteers and £30,000 raised on the Propositions, could report 'in what Distemper he found it [Essex], and how he left it in calm'.[59] The reality was however somewhat different. Continuing disorder encouraged Parliament to take more direct measures to address popular fears about the threat posed by catholics in the region. Grimston's report to the House occasioned yet another order, this time to the committee entrusted with drawing up the 3 September declaration, to consider instructions for disarming recusants and other ill-affected persons. According to the Parliamentary newsbook, *A Perfect Diurnall*, Parliament had received letters from Barrington and Grimston on 8 September informing them that 'many Recusants' houses are daily searched, and their Arms, Money & plate seized upon for the use of King & Parliament'. In early September the London newsbooks

Perfect Diurnall of the passages in Parliament, from Nottingham, Ashby and Leicester and other parts.

[57] *LJ/v/327*; S. Lambert, *Printing for Parliament, 1641–1700* (List and Indexes, special series, 20, 1984), p. 33.

[58] Foley, *Society*, vol. 2, pp. 450–1; *Diary*, p. 13.

[59] *CJ/ii/758*. Some reports date this to the 7th: BL, E116(26), *A Continuation of certain speciall and remarkable passages from both Houses of Parliament*, pp. 4–5 (which also reports incorrectly that Grimston brought with him Lucas – Sir John had been in London since 9 August); E239(16), *A Perfect Diurnall of the Passages in Parliament*; E239(17), *A Perfect Diurnall of the Proceedings in Parliament*; E239(18), *A Perfect Diurnall of the Passages in Parliament ... more fully and exactly taken*, pp. 4–5; E239(30), *A Perfect Diurnall of the Passages in Parliament*, 7 September 1642; CUL, Additional MS 89, fol. 39 r.

reported that the house of William Sams at Rivenhall, between Cogge-shall and Witham, had been searched by the trained bands. Sams was 'suspected to have much Ammunition therein for no good purpose'. The searchers had found ammunition for 60 men, 6 horse and £800 in plate and money. On 5 September, there was a further report that the Commons had received letters from Billericay and a number of other places in south Essex informing them that the trained bands had searched the houses of several catholics and other suspected persons and had seized money and plate which had been sent up to London. Late September brought news of further searches by the trained bands in South Essex, this time in the area around Rochford, which had uncov-ered arms for 40 men and £150 in money and plate.[60] It may have been significant that most of these reports came from areas where there had been no earlier report of popular attacks.

These measures were intended to reassure the people and thus to prevent further popular attacks. However, it is not clear that they did entirely put an end to popular searches. It would be wrong to draw too clear a line between unofficial and official searches; after all the attack on Sir John Lucas had involved both elements of the trained bands and Parliamentary volunteers. For example, in later September there was an attempt by a crowd to search the house of Henry Nevill, who was by then in arms with the King, at Cressing Temple to the south of the Essex cloth district. Earlier in the month the trained bands of nearby Witham were said to have arrested three men (at least one of whom was to be a signatory on the early 1643 Essex royalist peace petition), 'upon suspition of buying and conveying Armes to Cressing Temple'. In the belief that 'there was Armes and Ammuntion in his house, to be imployed against the Parliament, a great number of persons agreed together to search it', but they were prevented by Neville's servants' defence of the house. It was not until mid-October that Nevill's arms and a large number of horse, some of which belonged to the Petre family, were successfully impounded. This was also the case with those of another catholic family the Whites, at either their house at Mountnessing or Hutton.[61] Still in

---

[60] BL, E239(18); E 202(42), *An Exact and True Diurnall of the Proceedings of Parliament*, 29 August–3 September 1642, p. 6; E202(43), *A True and Perfect Diurnall of the passages in Parliament, from Nottingham, Ashby and Leicester and other parts*, 29 August–6 September 1642, pp. 6–7; E 202(44), *Remarkable passages or a perfect Diurnall*, A1 r; *A Perfect Diurnall of the Passages in Parliament 19th to 26 Sept 1642*, Q2.

[61] BL, E202(42), *An exact and True Diurnall Of The Proceedings in Parliament, from the 29. of August, to the 5. of Septemb. 1642*, p. 1; BL, E119(2), *Special Passages*, 20–27 September 1642; BL, Additional MS 18,777, fol. 33b. I am grateful to Janet Gyford, the historian of early modern Witham, for additional information about the identity of those involved in the buying of arms.

late September the royalist Earl of Carlisle, who had earlier attempted to raise the commission of array in the south of the county, informed the House of Lords that the people threatened to pull down his house at Waltham Abbey. By the end of the year much of the earl's deer had been slaughtered by poaching crowds.[62]

In both Essex and Suffolk then popular attacks continued into September and beyond. On 1 September, the sheriff of Suffolk wrote to the JPs in the areas of the earlier attacks informing them that he had been 'advertised yt great multitudes of such disordered people in many places w[i]thin ye ffranchise of Bury and other parts of ye County doe still gather together'. On the same day warrants were sent out to the parish constables renewing the orders for day and night watches, commanding the trained bands to be ready at an hour's warning to march to suppress any gatherings and ordering the constables not to allow any 'poore people or p[er]sons of meane Condicon ... to goe forth out of yo[u]r towne w[i]thout good cause'. A meeting of the JPs for the affected areas was held at Bury St Edmunds on 6 September. From there, the JPs informed the Commons that, though the 'first Tumult' had been suppressed, the attackers had reassembled. They were threatening to rescue the plundered goods now in the hands of the parish constables and they were menacing the magistrates. The JPs warned that unless those whom they had captured received exemplary punishment 'to secure them from further violence', 'they should be enforced to leave their severall habitations and to retire to other places of better security and soe the Countrey would be exposed to the rage and rapine of that unrulye multitude'.[63] Such rhetoric should be read with care. It may be explained in part a forthright response to the earlier order from the Parliamentary leadership to the sheriff not to actively pursue the apprehension and punishment of the attackers. But, even making allowance for the attempt by the Justices to bounce Parliament into taking tougher measures, the letter reflects the continuing instability within the county. Though the attacks began in Essex, they seem to have caused greater problems for the authorities in Suffolk.

Actions by the authorities, intended to neutralise the popish threat, may have had the opposite effect. When, for example, the Neville arms at Cressing Temple were finally seized, counter-threats were uttered that

---

[62] HLRO, MP HL, 4 January 1642/3; *LJ*/v/366, 373; R. E. Schreiber, *The First Carlisle. Sir James Hay, First Earl of Carlisle as Courtier, Diplomat and Entrepreneur 1580–1636* (Transactions of the American Philosophical Society, 74, pt 7, 1984), p. 182; ERO, Q/SR -318/34–42.

[63] Bodl. Lib., Tanner MS 63, fols. 146, 149; ESRO, FB 19/I2/2 [18]; BL, Harleian MS 163, fol. 325.

'two of his oxen taken from him should be deare oxen and that they had 300 armes att Mr White's house', another catholic household. From Suffolk in mid-October there came reports of anxieties about the great store of arms kept in Sir Thomas Jermyn's house coupled with rumours that the king intended to march into the county. Later in the month, the Commons received a report from the deputy lieutenants in Suffolk that 'the baser people are fomented and growe to a head', linked with a request that they might retain part of the monies collected there for Parliament to allow them to purchase 300 carbines. The parish authorities in the county were informed that, 'div[er]se lewde & disorderly people have assembled themselves in a tumultuous & Riotuous mann[e]r intendinge as is iustly feared to enter into some desparate actions'. Orders in Essex may reflect similar anxieties. At the same time, to judge from the records of one Suffolk town, Sudbury, in the heart of the earlier attacks, fears also persisted 'of the eminent danger of ffireing or other crime to be done' by papists, malignants and, now, cavaliers.[64] As this report makes clear the actual outbreak of fighting heightened anxieties in the region and added a further level of instability. Sir Dudley North later recalled that when he was sent down by the Commons to neighbouring Cambridgeshire he,

> found all full of terror, the common people generally apprehending, that the Cavaliers (as the Royalists were then called) were coming to plunder them. This fear was artificially put into them, as I could easily perceive: for the Country was full of strange fictions of their inhuman carriage in other countreys ... These allarms generated strange, wild, and indigested propositions, such as were not to be hearkened unto by any person of Judgement and experience.[65]

Sir Dudley's dismissal of the reality of the fears, delivered with all the benefit of hindsight and the lofty disdain of the gentleman for his inferiors, offers a poor guide to the prevailing realities. For Essex, the diary of Sir Humphrey Mildmay, former ship money sheriff and a loyal, if passive supporter of the Crown, paints a vivid picture of the continuing fears there. Fearing that their house at Danbury, five miles to the west of Maldon, was threatened, Lady Mildmay had obtained an order from the Commons in late August to prevent its plundering. At the beginning of September while Mildmay was at his other estate in Somerset he had

---

[64] BL, Additional MS 18,777, fols. 33b, 45; *CJ*/ii/807; BL, E240(40), *Perfect Diurnall*, 10–17 October 1642, *sub* 13 October; ESRO, FB, 19/I2/1, 2[9]; *CJ*/ii/820; WSRO, Sudbury Borough Records, Sextus Book, 25 October 1642.

[65] *A Narrative of Some Passages In or Relating to The Long Parliament* (1670), pp. 36–7. North refers to being sent into Cambridgeshire sometime before the 'Brentford encounter' (12 November); the Commons' Journal records an order for him to go into the county on 29 August: *CJ*/ii/743.

received 'a letter of Mischief from Danbury'. He clearly continued to expect trouble. Still in Somerset, he concluded his diary entry for 15 September with, '& noe ill Newes from Danbury'. Back home at Danbury, Sir Humphrey records his nearly daily fears of being visited by 'the plunderers':

> 3rd [November]: . . . Home by Newes of the bruets [?brutes] abroad, a Plunderinge . . . 4th: . . . att home all the day Expectinge the Barringtons & Plunderers . . . 5th: . . . in all fears
> 6th: . . . Early upp, but not Preparing for Church by Cause of feares of Roagues . . . 7th: Expected the Roagues but they came not . . . 9th: . . . late in bed this Morneinge full of fear & Troubles, but wee remained all the day in Peace I blesse god. 10th: . . . much Company att dynner, they all in Armes for the roagues. . . 11th: . . . all as yet quiet I blesse God . . . good Newes of the roagues . . . 13th: I was not to the Church for my Attention att Home. 14th: . . . in Peace as yett.[66]

In April 1643 Mildmay records returning again to his 'poor and dismembered house'. It is not clear whether the damage Mildmay's house suffered was as a result of popular action. But if so, it might reflect popular suspicions about his religious affiliations. While Sir Humphrey made no secret of his detestation for 'puritans', he appears to have enjoyed the company of catholics.[67]

As Mildmay's example vividly shows fears and rumours of further attacks persisted into November. From Norfolk in that month there was a report of 'the great companies of the poorer sort of people which pillageth and have gotten weapons as well as the CAVALEIRS [*sic*] and stand upon their owne guard neither for the King nor Parliament'. Whether there was any basis to such reports is unclear, but there appears to be independent evidence of popular attacks in Norfolk in both November and December. Norfolk's authorities when issuing orders for the disarming of Parliament's opponents gave instructions to 'leave fit weapons for defence . . . against any rude or pilf[e]ring people'.[68] Later in

---

[66] BL, Harleian MS 454, fols. 53, 54 v. That Mildmay at one point yokes together the plunderers and the Barringtons suggests that he did not discriminate between popular and Parliamentary 'disorder'.

[67] P. Lee Ralph, *Sir Humphrey Mildmay: Royalist Gentleman. Glimpses of the English Scene 1633–1652* (New Brunswick, 1947), pp. 161, 164; *CJ*/ii/740; BL, Harleian MS, fols. 53, 54 v. Mildmay appears to have enjoyed the company of catholics in London and Somerset, as well as in Essex. Several of the victims of 1642 were his dining companions (including in London the sister of the Countess of Rivers). The 'political' preferences that Mildmay showed in his dining make it clear that this was not just the accidental product of gentry sociability. Mildmay was a frequent purchaser of 'popish books' and heard at least one catholic sermon: *ibid.*, pp. 24, 32, 33, 39, 99, 206, 214.

[68] BL, E127(6), *An Extract of Severall Letters which came by the last Post, or otherwise, from all parts of the Kingdome, since the fifth of November to this present November the*

the same month, the Suffolk authorities in the area of the earlier attacks were writing to the parish constables of the 'disorders and distempers in the County ... & evill affected p[er]sons who hunger after Rapines & spoyleing & plunder of men's houses'. As a result, the Deputy Lieutenants had thought fit to raise a troop of horse in that area to be ready to 'suppresse any ill attempt'.[69] An explanation for the authorities' continuing anxieties is to be found in the report from a London newsbook on December 1st:

> Out of *Suffolke* it is reported, that there are a great number of unruly people that gather together, and are very hardly appeased, but would very faine plunder the Papists and malignants as being the cause of these present distractions, which stop all trading that the poorer people cannot be able to subsist, and therefore they begin to argue the case, whether in this great necessity it be not lawfull, for to take something from those that have bin the cause to deprive them of all manner of livelyhood as to perish for hunger.[70]

The continuing problems in the cloth trade that led to reports of popular disorder from other cloth regions help to explain the renewed threats. But the revival of fears of plundering may also be linked to renewed concerns in Suffolk about the threat from royalists and papists. Celebrations of the 5th November – the day on which Sir Henry Mildmay recorded his household being 'in all fears' – must once more have focussed on the popish threat and may help to explain the timing of the renewed threat of attacks. It was perhaps in response to such fears that the Commons on 1 December authorised the Deputy Lieutenants to disarm recusants in Suffolk. Whether there were further disorders in Suffolk is not clear, given the lack of relevant records. There may well have been. Plain reports of the seizing of horse belonging to catholics, as at Sudbury where horses being sent by Sir Robert Rookwood to Lady Petre's house were stayed, may conceal popular initiative or popular pressure.[71] There was certainly renewed disorder in Essex. According to Simonds D'Ewes, speaking in December, Harbottle Grimston had lately told him that the plundered goods freely handed in had been 'all againe forceably and violently taken away by those very people who had before brought it in'. Indeed we can show that in early December 1642 a 'greate

---

twelfth, pp. 5–6; C. Holmes, *The Eastern Association in the English Civil War* (Cambridge, 1974), n. 115, p. 253; Bodl. Lib., Tanner MS. 64, fol. 111.

[69] ESRO, HD53/2786, p. 1.

[70] BL, E242(31) *A Continuation of certaine Speciall and Remarkable Passages from both Houses of* PARLIAMENT, *and other Parts of the Kingdome*, 24 November–1 December 1642, *sub* 1 December.

[71] BL, E127(6), *An Extract of Severall Letters, Which came by the last Post*, p. 4; BL, Additional MS 18,777, fols. 73a, 78a; *CJ*/ii/833.

companey of People' (including sailors once more) set out from Colchester to attack the minister at Peldon, one of the crowds' victims in the summer. Others, attacked in the summer of 1642, may have found themselves revisited in the winter.[72] Sites of earlier disorder may have experienced new attacks.[73] Nor was this the end of such attacks. In the first week of the new year a crowd led by an Epping draper, with the nickname Prince Robert [?Rupert], finally made good the threat to attack the Earl of Carlisle's house at Waltham. In Suffolk a man was bound over as late as March 1643 at Ipswich 'for threatninge to plunder Mr Dade's house'. The choice of Dade, whose role as comissary for the archdeaconry of Suffolk and Laud's informant on the godly in and around Ipswich had made many enemies, suggests a strong strand of continuity with the earlier attacks.[74]

Despite their probable welcome for the initial attacks, Parliament's leaders did not welcome their continuation. The outbreak of civil war saw Parliament finally take effective action against those groups whose presence had occasioned popular anxieties, thus removing the pretext for further popular action.[75] The attempt to revive the attacks at the end of 1642, when Parliament was being told that the clothworkers were saying that they cared not about further depression in the trade 'for they hoped to live better then ever they had done', brought a swift and very different response from those in authority. Whereas earlier appeals for justice against the attackers had fallen on deaf ears, there was now immediate action from the authorities. When an attempt was made to relaunch the attack on the minister at Peldon, Colchester's rulers took a long series of statements from those involved, bound the perpetrators over, and wrote to inform the town's MP, Harbottle Grimston. In turn, Grimston

---

[72] BL, Harleian MS 164, fol. 272; CRO, D/B5 Sb 2/7, fols. 300 v–302 v. Does the Commons' order of 8 December 1642 (*CJ*/ii/881) for the restitution of Thomas Bayles' goods, victim of an attack at Witham in August, suggest a further attack or the sluggishness of Parliamentary procedure?

[73] The same day as the attack at Peldon 'divers lewde people' at Little Yeldham broke into the house of a yeoman and took away a large amount of wheat and cheese. The legal evidence however does not make it possible to establish whether this was more than burglary: PRO, ASSI, 35/85/5/3 and 61.

[74] *LJ*/v/526; ESRO, C8/4/7 (3 March 1642/3).

[75] From 1642 the responsibility to police catholics in the region was written into successive orders, culminating in the Eastern Association, the rationale for whose formation was to defend the region from the 'Spoylings of Papists': BL, E121(1), *Instructions Agreed upon by the Lords and Commons ... For members of the House of Commons, and Deputie-Lieutenants for the County of Essex, and Committees to be sent into the same County* (5 October 1642); E88(15), *A Declaration and Ordinance of the Lords and Commons Assembled in Parliament, For the Associating of the severall Counties of Norfolk, Suffolk, Essex, Cambridge, Isle of Ely, Hertford and the County of the City of Norwich* (3 February 1642/3); *LJ*/v/506–7; CRO, D/Y 2/5, p. 113.

quickly informed Parliament, dismissing any political identity for the revival by terming it simply 'the Plunderinge busines'. Parliament ordered those arrested to be brought to London and imprisoned. Despite the entreaties of Colchester's rulers on their behalf and several attempts by the town's MPs to secure them a hearing, they remained prisoners for several months. This show of activity by both the local and central authorities contrasts markedly with their inactivity when faced with the larger disorders of the summer. With the catholic threat neutralised, the renewed stirrings of a peace movement in the region, and fears of further disorders by the clothworkers, Parliament was eager to demonstrate to its propertied supporters its ability to maintain order.[76]

The picture that emerges from this accumulation of evidence suggests that the attacks which extended beyond the summer of 1642 were far wider than the focus on their most famous victims, Sir John Lucas and the Countess of Rivers, might suggest. There were almost certainly other attacks for which evidence has not survived or not yet come to light. For example, Lady Penelope Gage, sister to the Countess of Rivers, had written to her mother at the very beginning of 1642 from Hengrave Hall, to the north of Bury St Edmunds, informing her that 'we are dayly thre[a]t[e]ned by the com[m]on sort of people'. An undated letter from one of her servants, describing himself as 'noe ill member to that house 33 yeares especially in these miserable distractine tymes', talks cryptically of 'my service w[hi]ch I performed in suppressing many noxious occurrences by my owne pollicy, or giveing notice to avoyde the dangers, the p[ar]ticulers wheirof I will not comitt to paper'.[77] Just how widespread the attacks were may never be recoverable. The collapse of royal authority led to an absence at the centre of those institutions, among them the Privy Council, whose papers would normally have reported and recorded disorder. In the localities, this black hole was deepened by the collapse of the criminal courts. More intriguingly, the almost complete absence of prosecutions among those courts that did continue to function and whose records survive suggest that this gap in our knowledge may be the result, in part at least, of deliberate inactivity on the part of the authorities.

What is also striking is not only the scale of the attacks, but the mobility and persistence the crowds showed in attacking targets at some

---

[76] BL, Harleian MS 164, fol. 272 r; CRO, D/B5 Sb 2/7, fols. 300–3; CRO, D/Y 2/7, p. 69; 2/8, pp. 23, 27; 2/9, p. 99; *CJ*/ii/889; HLRO, MP HL, 30 December 1642, 4 January 1642/3; BL, E242(31), *A Continuation of certaine Speciall and Remarkable Passages*, 24 November–1 December 1642, p. 6; *LJ*/v/529.

[77] CUL, Hengrave MSS 88, vol. 2, nos. 150, 168.

distance. The role played by roving crowds aligned them more with the rebels of the sixteenth century, than with the localism of the typical early modern crowd. Crowds originally assembled in Colchester to attack Sir John Lucas clearly played an important role in a whole series of attacks in both Essex and Suffolk. As the leading town in the region with a population of some ten thousand or so inhabitants, an important market and the centre of the cloth industry, Colchester was at the heart of a series of networks. Its role as a market town, attracting both suppliers and customers from a wider region, was duplicated by other towns in the area of the attacks. Indeed, the care with which market days were staggered between towns in the region must have helped to spread rumours as well as to assemble crowds at the time of the attacks. We have seen that Colchester's Saturday market on 20 August was the occasion of the circulation of rumours about Sir John Lucas's attempts. From the 20 to the 26 of August the weekly round saw successive markets in Sudbury and Ipswich (20), Hadleigh and Bury St Edmunds (22), Lavenham (23), Needham Market (24), Stowmarket (25) and Clare (Friday, 26). That 24 August was also the occasion of St Bartholomew's fair at Sudbury may help to explain the numbers Arthur Wilson encountered there.[78] It was doubtless links such as these that made it possible to assemble so quickly such large numbers, initially in Colchester to prevent Lucas's escape to the king and thereafter to attack the other houses. Bruno Ryves' account suggests that the Colchester authorities had called in support from the surrounding clothing townships, while the Mayor of Colchester described those who attacked Lucas as 'a mixte companey of towne and country'. Thus, the geography of the attacks was woven out of the strands of cloth production that produced an unusually dense set of connections between some communities. Once assembled, segments of these crowds then left the town to attack a series of targets within a radius of up to some twenty miles. The Colchester crowds might well have travelled further – Audley End was thirty miles or more away on the county's western border. Geography might suggest that the attack on the Forster family at Copdock which lay outside the Stour Valley, some thirteen miles from Colchester and sixteen miles from Long Melford, was a separate episode. Since the village was only three miles from the godly town of Ipswich it might be thought that the attack originated there. However, while some from Ipswich must have joined in the attack and helped to swell the numbers to the six or seven thousand reported to have been present, the 'rabble' were said by the son of the

[78] ESRO, HD 474/1, pp. 35–7.

family who witnessed the attack to be those from Essex and Suffolk who had already pulled down the other houses.

The pattern of attacks raises a number of important questions. Essex and Suffolk were not the only counties in which proto-royalists and catholics were attacked. Catholics were attacked throughout England. According to the Venetian ambassador writing earlier in May 1641, 'in the country the peasants attack the houses of catholics, and even in the city they are not safe from serious injury'.[79] There is no comprehensive treatment of this subject and it may be significant that when general studies talk about the attacks it is usually to the 'Stour Valley' that they refer. More research then is needed before we have a complete picture, but the evidence of other regional studies suggests that these attacks do not seem to have been as comprehensive as in the Essex-Suffolk region. Neither apparently were they the work of the roving crowds that distinguish this episode, nor the product of a single series of attacks extended over some months. Where they come closest to this pattern, they were the work of troops raised to fight for Parliament. For example, troops raised in London in the summer of 1642 showed their godliness by combining anti-popery with iconoclasm as they marched westwards through Middlesex. They pillaged the houses of catholics and pulled down and burnt altar rails, defaced images and destroyed surplices and common prayer books in actions that ridiculed the rituals of the Laudian church. It may well be that more intensive local study would furnish further examples of similar attacks in other regions, but in our present state of knowledge the intensity of the attacks in Essex and Suffolk distinguish them from other regions in England. The broader comparison raises the question of why attacks were so widespread in the region of Essex and Suffolk in 1642.

The pattern of the attacks suggests that the title of the Stour Valley by which the episode has come to be described is something of a misnomer. Colchester and much of the Essex cloth industry were not themselves located within the Stour Valley. There were attacks beyond the wider area of the cloth industry. Nonetheless, the patterning of the episode suggests that it was the populous cloth communities, above all Colchester, that served as the epicentres of the attacks and the near co-habitation of catholics and clothworkers that explains much (but not all) of the geography of the episode. If the failure of the intended march on the Earl of Suffolk was not to be explained by intervention by the authorities, then it suggests that there were limits to the mobility of the crowds. Those attacks that took place beyond the cloth districts were to

[79] *CSPV, 1640–2*, p. 152.

be explained by the presence of other centres of contagion, the large urban centres like Ipswich and Maldon. The designation of the episode as the Stour Valley riots and the close fit thereby suggested with the cloth industry has encouraged historians to accord the clothworkers a leading role in the staging of the attacks and to look to the evident problems of the cloth industry to explain their involvement. But if cloth and catholicism were at the core of most of the attacks, the question of whether it was the clothworkers' reputation for protest occasioned by poverty or a political identity founded on their reputed puritanism that best explains their actions in 1642 needs more careful consideration.

Historians have emphasised the anti-catholic nature of the attack. But this emphasis on anti-popery is not without its problems. Contemporary reports stressed that the attackers threatened 'to plunder all the Papists'.[80] But it seems unlikely that all catholics in the region were victims of attacks. While the attacks on catholics were more widespread in Essex, the evidence suggests that in Suffolk few catholics beyond the Stour Valley were victims. If there had been attacks on other clusterings of catholics, for example that on the Suffolk-Norfolk border, it seems doubtful that they would have left no record. In contrast, the reconstruction of the attacks reveals that there were a wider variety of targets. Some historians have accepted the anti-catholic nature of the attack to the point that they have rechristened Sir John Lucas a catholic. But Lucas was a protestant. So too were the ministers attacked.

In 1642 the obligations of deference were decisively slighted. Both the scale of destruction and the size of the crowds single out these incidents from others both before and during the civil war. It is not just the fact that the gentry were attacked in their houses, though this in itself marks out these crowd actions from what had been customary in the earlier period. What followed would have been equally unimaginable before. In many cases there was a systematic destruction of the houses, as though the crowds sought not just to drive away their owners, but also to obliterate the physical signs of their presence. Historians who have recognised that catholics were not the crowds' only targets have drawn on the evidence of reports of attacks on 'both protestants and Papists' to

---

[80] BL, E114(30), *A Message*, p. 2 (although this newsbook reports the attack on the Countess of Rivers as having taken place at Colchester). For the misidentification of Lucas as a catholic, see P. R. Newman, 'Roman Catholic Royalists: papist commanders under Charles I and Charles II, 1642–1660', *Rec. Hist* 15 (1981), p. 403 (who in another reference to the episode translates the attack on Lucas to his house at Shenfield from which he took his title on entering the peerage: Newman, *The Old Service: Royalist Regimental Colonels and the Civil War 1642–46* (Manchester, 1993), p. 224); J. Lee Malcom, *Caesar's Due: Loyalty and King Charles 1642–1646* (1983), p. 25.

emphasise that the episode should be read as a challenge to the landed class. But, despite the fears of contemporaries, very few gentlemen in the region were attacked. Some, for example Barrington and Grimston, continued to command the respect that gentlemen assumed was their due. The most important point about the crowds in the summer and autumn of 1642 was that they were *selective* in their targets. It is this selectivity that holds the key to understanding the causes and meanings of crowd actions in 1642. Contextualisation of the event that was the signal for the wider attacks – the attack on Sir John Lucas – will reveal the complex inner histories that could lie behind that selection.

Part 2

Contextualising the crowd

3. The micro-politics of the attack on Sir John Lucas

> For Corporations, I see no re[a]son whye ther shoulde bee so manye
> for whye shoulde Tan[n]ers, & shooe-makers nott be contented to
> bee Governed by the same waye thatt Lordes Gentlemen, & good
> yeomen & freeholders are ... Butt these Townsmen muste bee
> Exsemted by their Charter. The truth Is thatt Everye Corporation Is
> a pettye free state agaynste monarkeye, and theye have don[e] your
> Matie more mischeefe In these late disorders with their Lecterors
> then anye thinge Else hath don.
>
> The Duke of Newcastle (brother-in-law of Sir John Lucas).[1]

In the Visitation of Essex in 1634 the Lucas family were described as 'of
St Johns neere Colchester'.[2] 'Too near Colchester' would be a better
description of their location. In March 1640, Sir John Lucas wrote a
characteristic letter of complaint about the activities of the saltpetremen
in his house which lay just outside the town walls at Colchester. Their
actions in breaking open the main gates to the house had meant that 'the
house lies exposed to the spoile and rapine of unruly people whereof that
towne is very full'.[3] It was the misfortune of the Lucas family that,
although landed gentry, they lived little more than a stone's throw from
one of the largest towns in provincial England, an industrial centre
notorious for its levels of contention and disorder. Contextualising
Lucas's relations, in this chapter with the Corporation and commons of
Colchester, and in the following chapter with the county community,

---

[1] S. A. Strong, *A Catalogue of Letters And Other Historical Documents Exhibited in The Library at Welbeck* (1903), p. 206.
[2] W. Metcalfe (ed.), *The Visitations of Essex*, vols. 13–14 (Harleian Society, 1878–9), vol. 1, p. 437.
[3] PRO, SP, 16/449/25.

reveals depths of conflict that help to explain the precipitating event in the attacks in the summer of 1642.

Bruno Ryves' account sought to implicate Colchester's rulers in the attack on the Lucas family and their minister, Thomas Newcomen. Given Ryves' role in the royalist propaganda campaign, it might be felt that little credence should be given to his account (although as we have seen this knowledge has not prevented historians making his account a primary source for the events in the summer of 1642). However, I want to suggest that Ryves' account both deserves to be taken more seriously and to be read more critically. His ability to name Sir John's leading opponents among the Corporation, names not mentioned in other news-book accounts, suggests that he had access to somebody with detailed local knowledge. The most likely candidates would seem to have been either Lucas himself, who had eventually escaped to Oxford, or a member of his family or household. Writing in 1714, John Walker noted of Newcomen under his entry in his *Sufferings of the Clergy*, ''tis Reported by some of his *Relations*, that he was the author of *Mercurius Rusticus*, which is Doubtless a Mistake, for Wood expressly Ascribes it to Dr *Bruno Ryves*, without the least Doubt, or Hesitation'.[4] If, however, we read these claims not as applying to authorship of the whole work, but to the account of events in Colchester then they would seem to lend weight to the argument that Newcomen was the first-hand source on which Ryves drew. Since Newcomen had intimate knowledge of the politics and personnel of Colchester we should look more carefully at the micro-politics hinted at by Bruno Ryves which helped to determine Sir John Lucas's fate. Colchester's scale and urban identity provides a depth of documentation not matched by the records for the other smaller and rural communities caught up in the attacks. Ironically, the story these records reveal offers some confirmation of Bruno Ryves' reading of the politics behind events at Colchester in the summer of 1642.

'There are few townes in England, that can more truly glory, in an honorable and antient pedigree and descent, then this towne', Harbottle Grimston told the listeners to his speech as Recorder of Colchester at election day in July 1642.[5] His audience must have listened with growing approval when he went on to tell them that Colchester, in a county with 414 villages and 20 market towns, far exceeded these other communities, 'like the Cipresse tree, amongst small twiggs'. With a population of some

---

[4] J. Walker, *An Attempt Towards Recovering An Account of the Numbers and Sufferings of the Clergy of the Church of England, Heads of Colleges, Fellows, Scholars, etc. who were Sequestered, Harass'd etc. in the Late Times of Grand Rebellion* (1714), p. 318.
[5] Hertfordshire RO, Gorhambury MSS ix, A9, unfol.

ten or eleven thousand inhabitants Colchester was not only the largest town in seventeenth-century Essex, but one of the largest provincial centres within the national urban hierarchy. As a major port for the export of agricultural produce, much of which went to feed the growth of London, Colchester was able to take advantage of expanding east-coast trade with the capital, the north-east and the Netherlands, as well as developing an active interest in fishing. 'This place is the Granary of the County, and Fish-Market of these Eastern parts' declared a letter-writer in 1648.[6] The town also served as a market centre, holding three markets a week as well as a number of fairs through the year, and as a service centre for its hinterland. But of greatest importance in explaining Colchester's growth was its role as the leading centre of textile pro-duction in the region. It was this that most shaped Colchester's economy and society and in this reflected the wider experience of the region at the heart of the attacks in the summer of 1642. It was the misfortune of Sir John Lucas that he lived not only too near a town whose size precluded any hope of his exerting control over it, but also to a town whose (unstable) industrial base produced high levels of volatile poverty.

Colchester's population had doubled over less than a hundred years, much of this growth coming in the fifty years between the 1570s and 1620s when its population may have peaked at some 11,000. In a 1630s Exchequer court case, several of the town's inhabitants testified to this expansion. One thought the population had trebled since 1603, another that the population had grown by some 10,000.[7] These depositions have little value as an accurate demographic record, but they do offer an important insight into contemporaries' awareness of growth – and of the problems growth posed. Colchester's demographic and economic growth took place against a background of conflicts. Some of these conflicts involved groupings internal to Colchester, others cast the town or groups within it against external forces. It is important to grasp the nature of these conflicts since they were important both in explaining the events of the summer of 1642 and in determining the form those events took.

[6] *A Letter From a Gentleman in Colchester, to his Friend in London* (1648); N. Goose, 'Economic and social aspects of provincial towns: a comparative study of Cambridge, Colchester and Reading, *c.* 1500–1700' (Ph.D. thesis, University of Cambridge, 1984); Goose, 'Tudor and Stuart Colchester: economic history', *VCH Essex*, vol. 9, pp. 76–86.

[7] Colchester's population in the 1520s has been estimated at some five and a half thousand; by the early to mid-seventeenth century it had grown to ten or eleven thousand: R. Britnell, *Growth and Decline in Colchester, 1300–1525* (Cambridge, 1986), pp. 95, 201; I. Doolittle, 'The effects of the plague on a provincial town in the sixteenth and seventeenth centuries', *Medical History*, 19 (1975), p. 334; Goose, 'Provincial towns', pp. ii, 248–9; Goose, 'Tudor and Stuart Colchester', p. 81.

Neither cause nor grouping were constant, nor were they discrete. It was the misfortune of Sir John Lucas that the developments of the 1630s and his role therein served to simplify conflict, both internal and external, and to solidify groupings in opposition to him.

Early modern Colchester had a reputation for conflict. In 1595, the bishop of London, had reported to Sir Robert Cecil that he found, 'great quarrels and contentions, both in their civil bodies and among the ministers, the people divided and the priests taking part on both sides, and at war with themselves, as well in matter of popular quarrels as points of doctrine.' In 1646 the minister Giles Firmin told John Winthrop that, 'Providence hath placed mee in one of the worst places in the kingdome for opinions'. In 1662, the neighbouring clergyman Ralph Josselin, invited to preach at Colchester, confessed himself, 'allways afraid of that towne as not fitt to deale with their wrangling spirits.'[8] The premium that the rulers of early modern towns put on harmony and unity means that the Corporation records give only a partial (in a double sense) glimpse of internal conflict. Conflict was not always recorded, the causes of that conflict almost never, in official urban records. Doubtless something of this conflict in Colchester was to be explained by factional differences (common in early modern urban politics) and the familiar politics of 'ins' versus 'outs' which cut across the simple divide between oligarchy and freemen.[9] Nevertheless, the main political fault line within Colchester was between the town's rulers and those in whose interests supposedly they exercised power.

At the root of this conflict were overlapping disputes about the exercise of power and, in particular, its economic consequences. Early modern Colchester, like other boroughs, had experienced a drive towards greater oligarchy. By the end of the fifteenth century Colchester was governed by a 'self-perpetuating oligarchy'.[10] The charter of 1462 had established the form by which the town was to be governed until the 1630s: two bailiffs ruled the town and were joined by eight aldermen and a first and second council, each composed of sixteen members. Under this system, the town's freemen electors, numbering somewhere between a thousand and

---

[8] HMC, Salisbury MSS, 5, pp. 394–5; *WP, 5, 1645–1649*, pp. 88–9; *Diary of John Rous*, ed. M. A. E. Green (1856), p. 494.

[9] Factional conflict must have been marked in 1639; the Recorder's speech at the mayoral election in 1640 is much devoted to the perils of factionalism (with a further page and a half on the theme excised): Hertfordshire RO, Gorhambury MSS, 9, A.9, unfol.

[10] G. Martin, *The Story of Colchester from Roman Times to the Present Day* (Colchester, 1959), p. 37; R. H. Britnell, 'Bailiffs and burgesses in Colchester 1400–1525', *EAH*, 21 (1990), pp. 103–9.

five hundred,[11] exercised their franchise via an electoral college in a most indirect fashion designed to render their numerical advantage nearly nugatory.[12] The elected council had been enlarged between 1519 and 1525, but this was done only to secure wider support among the town's more prosperous families, and at the same time the rights of the electoral juries to change the borough office holders had been 'tightly circumscribed'. They were forbidden to change the body of aldermen without the aldermen's own consent. By 1524 the Corporation's members were drawn from only just over the top ten per cent of Colchester society.[13] Regulations later in the century reduced yet further the rights of the freemen in the election of their rulers.

Oligarchy may have been, as has been argued for Colchester, a means of attaching the rich to the interests of the town, but it was also a cause of increasing conflict between the town's ruling group and the larger body of freemen in the early modern period. Trouble in the early sixteenth century had spilled over into riot and under Elizabeth there was further trouble, culminating in the outright refusal of the freemen to elect the Corporation in 1595.[14] The seventeenth century saw an intensification of this conflict. In 1612, following what the Corporation described as great disorders and tumultuous assemblies over the elections, an unsuccessful attempt was made to introduce new regulations.[15] Further orders drawn up at the end of the year confirmed that the lines of conflict

---

[11] No annual list of freeburgesses survives. When the Corporation scrapped the election day feast in 1624, they allocated a sum of £8 suggesting a figure of 160 freeburgesses; in 1643 the chamberlain's accounts claimed for the diet of 285 electors, although this figure may have included some 40 or more of the Corporation members. In 1654 there were said to be 200 freeburgess electors, while a politically motivated purge of 1655 of those freeburgesses not entitled to vote produced a figure of 140: CRO, D/B5/Gb3, fols. 39 v–40; Vb3, 1642–43; J. H. Round, 'Colchester during the Commonwealth', *EHR*, 15 (1900), pp. 641–64. For higher estimates of *c.* 450 in 1619 and *c.* 900 in 1646, see J. Cooper, 'Tudor and Stuart Colchester: borough government', *VCH Essex*, vol. 9, p. 111.

[12] Martin, *Colchester*, p. 37; R. H. Britnell, 'Bailiffs and burgesses in Colchester 1400–1525', *EAH*, 21 (1990), pp. 103–9. The town was divided into four wards, each electing a headman who chose four others (each of whom had to be property owners with an annual income of at least forty shillings a year) and this body chose the bailiffs, aldermen and chamberlain. These officers then chose the first council of sixteen, which joined them in choosing the second, common council. Candidates for each tier of government were also restricted by a *cursus honorum* which ensured that candidates could only be drawn from the preceding tier.

[13] Cooper, 'Borough government', pp. 111–15; CRO, D/B 5/Gb1, fols. 50 r–3 v; Martin, *Colchester*, pp. 37–8; Britnell, *Growth*, p. 263; Britnell, 'Bailiffs and burgesses', pp. 103–9.

[14] Britnell, *Growth*, pp. 225–8, 231; M. S. Byford, 'The price of Protestantism: assessing the impact of religious change on Elizabethan Essex: the cases of Heydon and Colchester, 1558–1594' (D.Phil thesis, University of Oxford, 1988), ch. 3.

[15] CRO, D/B5, Gb2, fols. 109 v–12 v.

were drawn between the freemen and an oligarchic Corporation. Claiming that 'disorders and inconveniencies have increased within this Towne by the meanes of smalle estates and abilityes about the Choice of ... the Bailiffes and other officers', the Corporation sought to introduce yet more restrictive property qualifications for the right to vote and intricate forms of even more indirect election for the other posts. But at the next election day these were rejected by the freemen who went on to deselect several members of the Corporation, because 'they went aboute to take awaye their ancient lib[er]ties & customs'. In 1624 there was further conflict over a Parliamentary bill for the election of the bailiffs, aldermen and other officers by the common council.[16]

There was a parallel conflict between commonalty and Corporation over the election of the borough's two Parliamentary representatives. The freeburgesses had earlier had the right to elect the MPs, but the Corporation had come to claim the sole voice.[17] In 1627 an attempt was made by the Corporation, assembling in an upper room in presumably the Moot Hall where the writ was privately read, to select Sir Thomas Cheke and Edward Alford as the two members, 'according to the use & custome tyme out of memorye of man' as the entry in the Assembly Book claimed. But at the same time the 'common sort of burgesses in general', gathered in the lower room, had endorsed Cheke but rejected Edward Alford, replacing him with Sir William Masham. The bailiffs returned Cheke and Alford as the MPs, but the freemen successfully petitioned the House of Commons who overturned the Corporation's claim of a prescriptive right to choose the MPs, ruled that the freemen had a voice in Parliamentary elections, and ordered the Corporation to return Masham.[18] This conflict over Parliamentary representation provided an opening for the Earl of Warwick, the leading political figure in

---

[16] CRO, D/B5, Gb2, fols. 109 v–12 v, 115 v–18 v, 146; D/Y, 2/7, pp. 23–4, 241.

[17] The freeburgesses, however, seem to have played some part in the 1625 election when the Earl of Sussex's attempt to exercise electoral patronage was denied by the 'whole community ... consisting of a multitude': J. K. Gruenfelder, *Influence in Early Stuart Elections 1604–1640* (Columbus, Ohio, 1981), p. 11. As the town's Recorder and MP made clear in a debate about borough franchises in the Commons in 1640 commonalty at Colchester extended only to freemen: W. Notestein (ed.), *The Journal of Sir Simonds D'Ewes From the Beginning of the Long Parliament To the Opening of the Trial of the Earl of Strafford* (New Haven and London, 1923), pp. 542–3.

[18] CRO, D/B5, Gb3, fols. 68 v, 70; *Commons Debates in 1628*, ed. R. C. Johnson, M. F. Keeler, M. Jannson Cole and W. B. Bidwell, 4 vols. (New Haven and London, 1977–8), vol. 2, pp. 28, 31, 37, 162–3, 169, 171, 177–8, 182. Masham wrote to the bailiffs and aldermen in 1628 hoping that the controversies between them and the burgesses could be ended without public contest: CRO, D/Y, 2/8, p. 233. For the political symbolism of the groups that made up early modern corporations assembling in separate rooms, see R. Tittler, *Architecture and Power: The Town Hall and the English Urban Community c. 1500–1640* (Oxford, 1991), p. 110.

the county who had been extending his electoral influence over county and corporations, to influence thereafter the selection of Colchester's MPs. Both Cheke and Masham were allies of Warwick. The forging of a link between the Earl of Warwick and the town was to have a bearing on events there in the summer of 1642.

This image of a divided town – the Corporation in one room, the freeburgesses in another below – was only one of several in the period. In 1599 the Corporation had decided to replace the feast held with the freemen on mayoral election day with a private feast for the Corporation and their guests. The symbolism of this exclusion in a period which valued commensality would not have been lost on freemen given only a few pence each in compensation. That the Corporation had to renew the order, and chose to do so in the year of the disputed Parliamentary election, suggests the potential for conflict in this further symbolic exclusion. But it is evidence of more substantial conflicts which lends weight to the thesis of a developing conflict between Corporation and commonalty. Of these, the most important was the running struggle over common rights. It was this that was to bring the town's commoners into direct conflict with Sir John Lucas.

Colchester, a walled town, was surrounded by a patchwork of lands belonging to the Crown, to neighbouring lords of the manor or to the town itself. These last consisted of two sorts, the town fields, mainly given over to arable, and extensive heath and woodland used for pasture. While the heaths covered several thousand acres, the town fields had been reduced from the thousand or so acres at the time of Domesday to about 600 acres in the late sixteenth century. They were to be subject to further reduction in the first half of the seventeenth century.[19] Colchester's lands were important to the town's freeburgesses, giving as they did right of common over what were termed the 'whole year' (largely heath or woodland) or 'half-year lands' from Lammas to Candlemas (1

---

[19] *VCH Essex*, vol. 9, p. 256. Philip Morant, Colchester's eighteenth-century historian thought the town fields contained some 500 acres by the mid-eighteenth century: P. Morant, *The History and Antiquities of the most ancient Town and Borough of Colchester*, 2 vols. (1748), vol. 1, pp. 88–91. He was however hardly the impartial historian. He had interested himself on behalf of Lord Hardwick in his dispute with the burgesses in the 1750s, giving him the benefit of his antiquarian researches in the borough's archives and his hostile opinion of the commoners (while begging him not to say from whom the information came): CRO, D/Y, 2/2, pp. 351–6. It should be noted that nineteenth-century accounts of the town lands put them close again to the Domesday figure: B. Strutt, *A Plan for Regulating, Improving and Rendring More Beneficial The Common or Half-Year Land, Belonging to the Borough of Colchester, With The Form of a New Constitution, Calculated to Effect The Above Purposes* (Colchester, 1807); D. White, 'The lost lands of the freemen in Colchester', *EJ*, 20 (1985), pp. 31–3; Thomas Cromwell, *The History and Description of the Ancient Town and Borough of Colchester in Essex*, 2 vols. (1825), vol. 2, p. 261.

August–2 February). As their names suggest, common rights of pasture could be claimed for the whole year on the heaths and on the town fields between the harvesting and sowing of the spring cereal crops. The right to run a few sheep or cattle on the lands provided a valuable income supplement, particularly to those in the cloth trade where employment was increasingly uncertain and vulnerable to sudden crises. The town's unenfranchised poor might also benefit, legally or illegally, from the commons.

Enclosure in the urban context of Colchester was perhaps never an uncontentious issue, but considerable enclosure had taken place in the period of little or no population growth, much of it in the fifteenth century. However when piecemeal enclosure, licensed by the Corporation, continued into the sixteenth century, renewed population growth made it a source of obvious conflict. An ambitious attempt in 1538 to enclose and rent out of all the half-year lands encountered opposition and, as elsewhere in 1549, enclosure of the town lands may have played some part in what appears to have been a hitherto unremarked echo of the 1549 rebellions. In the mid-sixteenth century, conflict between the commonalty and the Corporation over the town lands led to an attempted bill in Parliament, followed by arbitration which ruled that the Corporation should not sell or enclose any of the commons without the consent of the majority of the common council.[20] Despite this, the regulation and enclosure of the commons remained a source of conflict between Corporation and commonalty.

Between the late sixteenth century and the 1630s a further 100 acres of the town fields was lost to the freeburgesses through enclosure. Despite some attempt by the Corporation to meet popular criticism, first assigning the rents to the relief of the town's poor and later using the revenue to set up a hospital, enclosure led to renewed complaints from the freeburgesses. Pressure on the town lands also brought attempts to restrict rights of common, especially over the half-year lands. Significantly, the dating of these orders coincided with the period of most rapid population growth in the town, the first stint restricting the number of animals a commoner could pasture coming in 1573.[21] However, court records suggest that illegal pasturing on the commons remained a problem. In 1627 further orders repeated the stint, allowed the appointment of burgesses to police the commons (who were however to be chosen by the bailiffs) and ordered that fines on those breaking the stint

[20] Morant, *History*, vol. 1, p. 90 n.; Byford, 'Price of Protestantism', pp. 109–10; BL, Stowe MS 829, fols. 24–32 r; *VCH Essex*, vol. 9, p. 257.
[21] *VCH Essex*, vol. 9, pp. 256–7; Goose, 'Tudor and Stuart Colchester', p. 248; Morant, *History*, vol. 1, pp. 88–91.

or wrongly claiming common, both perennial problems, should be used for the benefit of the town's poor.[22] But there was clearly some disagreement over these. The Corporation's Assembly Book recorded a decision in 1628 to send a deputation to London in order to inform the town's MPs what had been offered the free burgesses regarding the common lands and to counter an anticipated petition to Parliament from the burgesses.[23] 1629, a year of industrial depression and dearth, seems to have witnessed a temporary resolution of the controversy. Previous orders had been made by the Corporation alone, but in that year all orders relating to the half-year lands were cancelled and, with the 'mutual consent' of the most part of the freeburgesses and commonalty, a comprehensive scheme drawn up for their regulation. This introduced a new stint and schedule of fines and made arrangements for the annual election of four treasurers to administer the income from fines exclusively in favour of the families of poor freeburgesses.[24]

These same orders declared that there should be no further enclosure hereafter and – revealingly – that new leases to the town lands should be granted only with the express consent of an assembly of the commonalty and freeburgesses in the Moot Hall. Clearly the freeburgesses believed that, as in other towns, members of the Corporation had been rewarding themselves from their control of the town's lands, claiming that the half-year lands had been leased to aldermen of the Corporation who had allowed their enclosure and misappropriation.[25] In drawing up heads for a new charter for the town, the Privy Council in 1634 ruled that the freeburgesses should enjoy their right to all the commons without interruption or enclosure. Despite this the freeburgesses seem to have faced suits against them at the Assizes, and in 1638 they had to petition

---

[22] CRO, Colchester Court Rolls, trans. W. G. Benham, vol. 25, fols. 4ff.; D/B5, Sr 10, rot. 3, 24; D/B5, Ac. 29, 30; D/B5, Gb3, fols. 62 v-3. The Corporation also sought to prevent hogs wandering on the commons and streets, something that may most have affected the poorer freemen, given the importance of the pig in the plebeian household economy: fol. 64.

[23] CRO, D/B5, Gb3, fol. 73; CRO, D/Y, 2/10, p. 95. The conflict over the town lands is probably what Sir William Masham alluded to when he wrote in August 1628 that he hoped to hear an end to the controversies without it coming to a public contest: CRO, D/Y, 2/8, p. 233.

[24] Elections were to be indirect. In 1633 the number of herdsmen was reduced to four, to be chosen by the bailiffs out of eight names put forward by the freeburgesses; after 1635 the treasurers were to name the four herdsmen: CRO, D/B5, Gb3, fols. 81–3, 124 v, 139 v. For the problems in 1629, see J. Walter, 'Grain riots and popular attitudes to the law: Maldon and the crisis of 1629' in J. Brewer and J. Styles (eds.), *An Ungovernable People: the English and their Law in the Seventeenth and Eighteenth Centuries* (1980), pp. 47–84.

[25] CRO, D/B5, Gb3, fol. 73. For an example of the Corporation exonerating arable from claims of common right in 1611 (and the burgesses continuing to claim common rights), see CRO, D/Y, 2/10, p. 95.

the Privy Council for enforcement of the 1634 ruling, claiming again that the half-year lands were in the possession of several aldermen who had prevented their right of common 'by sinister ways' (including joining the half-year land to their 'year land', a trick formerly used by the unpopular abbots of St John's), and by vexing them with a multiplicity of legal actions.[26]

In the same petition the freeburgesses had raised the issue of the lease of Kingswood Heath. This was another area of contention. Kingswood Heath had been part of the considerable estate of King's Wood granted to the borough by Edward the Confessor and over which the free-burgesses had enjoyed the right to common their cattle and to collect wood. But upon renewal of this grant by Henry VIII, the Corporation had taken the decision to enclose 1,000 acres and in 1576 this had been leased to the Elizabethan courtier, Sir Thomas Heneage for a period of sixty years. This grant, which perhaps represented an attempt to secure friends at Court in order to counter a challenge to the town from the Lucas family, was greatly resented by the commonalty of Colchester. The 'poore of Colchester' petitioned the queen claiming that they were very much 'enjured by a [h]e[a]the wrongfull taking away from us and inclosed of our townesmen unto their own profit and commodity by the which [h]eathe being inclosed we ... be utterly spoyled and undone by reason of the covettes [covetous] desyre of our townesmen'.[27] Since this lease was coming to an end in the 1630s, it provided another source of dispute between Corporation and freeburgesses. The freeburgesses claimed that Sir Thomas had spoiled the woods, that the Corporation had leased the land at too low a rent which they had then pocketed for themselves, and that they were attempting to secure a renewal of the lease to their own advantage. The reversion to the enclosed portion of Kingswood Heath had been made to four aldermen in October 1638 who took possession in September 1639. A petition from the freeburgesses to the Privy Council with a counter-petition from the Corporation were referred to the Lord Chief Justice of the King's Bench. In 1639 Chief Justice Bramston found

---

[26] The Privy Council again found for the freemen and instructed the judges to allow no further actions to be brought against them: PRO, PCR, 2/49, pp. 140, 249, 283. There may also have been litigation in the Exchequer: CRO, Colchester MSS VII.6*, fol. 2.

[27] R. Britnell, 'The fields and pastures of Colchester, 1280–1350', *EAH*, 19 (1988), p. 162; W. G. Benham (ed.), *The Red Paper Book of Colchester* (Colchester, 1902), p. 166; Cromwell, *Colchester*, vol. 2, p. 242; Byford, 'Price of Protestantism', p. 108; PRO, SP, 12/240/115. Both hand and orthography make this a difficult document to read, but suggest that it may have come from a scribe numbered among Colchester's poorer sort. The undated petition is assigned by the editor of the *Calendar of State Papers, Domestic* to 1591, but the reference to dearth and to being encumbered with the Dutch for sixteen years suggests a date of *c*. 1585/6, when an official census found the Dutch to number 1,291. The census may well have been a direct response to this petition.

for the Corporation, but he also ordered that a commission of local gentlemen should examine the freeburgesses' complaints about the misemployment of the rents from the lease of Kingswood Heath. By the consent of both parties, the dispute over the half-year lands was left to the adjudication of the borough's Recorder, Harbottle Grimston. It is doubtful whether he was able to effect a settlement, resolution of the town's internal dispute being probably lost in the broader political disputes. Rights of common certainly remained a point of conflict between Corporation and freeburgesses through the Interregnum and on into the Restoration.[28] As we shall see the conflict over common rights was to resurface with a vengeance in the conflict with Sir John Lucas. It was Sir John who would reap the bitterness that earlier disputes had sown.

When Harbottle Grimston praised Colchester as the leading town in Essex, he reminded his listeners that, 'this place in antient tyme was the seate of many of our Brittish and English kings, who invested and endow'd this towne with many honorable and proffitable previledges and immunitys ... There are few townes in England, that can more truly glory, in an honorable and antient pedigree and descent, then this towne'. 'What made it so', he concluded, 'but your government'. But in this speech Grimston preached an ambiguous message. He yoked together Colchester's civic independence with its source in a grant from the Crown, a conjunction doubtless symbolised by the presence at this gathering of that symbol of the Corporation's authority, the great mace – emblazoned with the royal coat of arms.[29] Paradoxically, Colchester's independence as a borough was grounded on its dependence on the Crown. As a borough Colchester jealously guarded its independence from gentry rule and, less successfully, from the church. But it found it harder to do so against the Crown. The period before the events of 1642 saw Colchester in conflict with all three. As a consequence of the active part they played in the enforcement of the policies of Personal Rule in both secular and religious spheres, the local expression of these tensions was conflict with John Lucas (and with his chaplain). This provides another layer of explanation for the actions and alignments in the attacks of August 1642.

[28] CRO, Colchester MSS VII.6*, fol. 2; CRO, D/B5, Gb3, fols. 184 v, 186, 188; D/Y, 2/10, pp. 94–5; CRO, P2/1–3; PRO, PCR, 2/49, fol. 249, 2/50, pp. 82–3. The freeburgesses' complaints in 1654 about the half-year lands were almost identical to those of the 1630s, and there were further problems in 1660: CRO, D/B5, Gb4, fols. 127 v, 214 v; D/Y, 2/10, p. 96.
[29] Hertfordshire RO, Gorhambury MSS, ix, A.9, unfol.; CRO, D/Y, 2/10, p. 74.

Charles I's reign brought a sharp reminder of the limits to the town's independence – and in the most brutal fashion possible. After an earlier unsuccessful attempt, the Attorney General had called in Colchester's charter in 1633 and, after a good deal of wrangling, the borough had received a new charter in 1635. The issuing of a new charter drawn up 'as may best stand w[i]th [the] good govern[men]te of ye s[ai]d Towne and ye maintenance of such fitting and auncient privileges, *as are not inconvenient for his Ma[jes]ty's service*' was a reminder to the Corporation of the source of its power.[30] The surviving records do not make it possible to uncover the precise reasons for this challenging of the town's 'ur-text' – sadly, a note by Attorney General Noye 'of what they are questioned for' has not survived – but conflicts between the Corporation (or at least a section of it) and the freeburgesses seem to have played a role.[31] The inclusion in a draft of the Charter of clauses confirming the freemen's rights in their commons without enclosure and prohibiting the public stock from being put to 'great purses' might suggest that the freeburgesses had sought to take advantage of the questioning of the charter to have their grievances aired. But it may also be significant that the first of these clauses, relating to common rights, was missing from the new Charter.[32]

Internal conflict may only have been the opportunity for the Crown to achieve its own objectives in Colchester. Although it has been argued that there was no consistent or comprehensive policy by the Crown in the 1630s towards the boroughs that might parallel the attempted remodel-

---

[30] *VCH Essex*, vol. 9, p. 115; PRO, SP, 16/251/27; /252/8; PCR 2/44, pp. 222, 230–1. The 1612 dispute over Corporation elections had led the Attorney General to threaten to question their 'pretended liberties' by *quo warranto*: CRO, D/Y, 2/7, pp. 23–4; CRO, D/B5, Gb2, fol. 142 r; PRO, PCR, 2/43, pp. 365 (my emphasis), 366.

[31] PRO, SP, 16/252/8. It has been suggested that the new charter may have been the result of a drive by the Crown to reassert admiralty jurisdiction over boroughs. If this was the case then it has interesting implications for the town's relationship with the Earl of Warwick, who was then Vice-Admiral for the county. Colchester's charter was stopped at the Great Seal by the Lord Commisioners of the Admiralty to check that it contained nothing prejudicial to their jurisdiction: PRO, PCR, 2/45, p. 41. However the continuing conflict between Corporation and freemen probably played a role in bringing its charter into question. The register of the Privy Council refers to a hearing of 'both sides'(PRO, PCR, 2/44, pp. 230–1) and in its final order about the new charter the Council recommended the reinstatement of those aldermen who had been put out of their places. The Assembly Book shows only one possible exclusion: in October 1634 Robert Talcott had been demoted to the first council which he headed until his re-appointment as an alderman in October 1639: CRO d/B5, Gb3, fols. 132 r–196 v. For a helpful discussion of the process by which charters were issued, see S. Bond and N. Evans, 'The process of granting charters to English boroughs, 1547–1649', *EHR*, 91 (1976), pp. 102–20.

[32] PRO, PCR, 2/44, pp. 230–1; SP, 16/355/36; 356/21 and 21.i; *Borough of Colchester: The Charters and Letters Patent Granted to the Borough By Richard I. and succeeding Sovereigns* (Colchester, 1903), pp. 81–103; CRO, D/B5, Gb3, fols. 126 v, 133, 169 v.

ling of the 1660s or 1680s, there is evidence to suggest that the move against Colchester was part of a more general move against corporations. Judged by results, Colchester's new, more oligarchic charter could be seen as the product of a Caroline political culture that favoured hierarchy and authority against 'popularity' and which prompted the alteration of other boroughs' charters to limit the power of the 'rascality'.[33] Colchester's dignity was perhaps enhanced by the replacement of the bailiffs by the office of a mayor; its oligarchy was certainly strengthened. The charter, while abolishing indirect election by the electoral college, limited yet further the freeburgesses' ability to change their rulers.[34] It did not, however, bring an end to the questioning of the town's rights and privileges.[35]

The 1635 Charter expressed the hope, 'that if the Burgesses of the borough ... and their successors shall be able to enjoy from our grant fuller liberties and privileges, then they should feel themselves the more strongly obliged to perform the services which they could to us, our heirs and successors, as well from affection as from obedience'. In reality, the town had a long tradition of standing upon its privileges when confronted by the demands of the Crown. As Robert Aylett, the bishop of London's commissary had reported, 'I find ye people at Colchester like them of Ephesus, their Diana is their Liberty ...'.[36] There had been opposition to the Forced Loan, and the attempt in early 1629 to collect customs not formally granted by Parliament had met with resistance from Colchester's merchant community.[37] In the following years Col-

---

[33] W. A. H. Schilling, 'The central government and the municipal corporations in England, 1642–1663' (Ph.D. thesis, Vanderbilt, 1970), p. 26. (Contrast the comments of Henry Dade, a Suffolk official of the Admiralty, on the *quo warranto* against Ipswich, also in 1633: 'as hath likewise byn sued out against other corporations nowe': PRO, SP, 16/250/5); R. Cust and A. Hughes, 'Introduction: after revisionism' in Cust and Hughes, eds., *Conflict in Early Stuart England: Studies in Religion and Politics 1603–1642* (1989), pp. 1–46; A. Foster, 'Church policies of the 1630s' in Cust and Hughes, *Conflict*, p. 208; R. Cust, 'Anti-puritanism and urban politics: Charles I and Great Yarmouth', *Historical Journal*, 35 (1992), pp. 22–23; PRO, SP, 16/366/48; H. Owen and J. B. Blakeway, *A History of Shrewsbury*, 2 vols. (1825), vol. 1, pp. 406–12.

[34] Hertfordshire RO, Gorhambury MSS, ix. A.9, unfol. (speeches on election day 1639, 1640). By the charter appointment to all offices but the mayoralty was for life, and the 1635 arrangements for the election of the new Corporation replaced a third of the freeburgess electors with members of the old Corporation: CRO, D/B5, Gb3, fols. 141 v–2; *Charters*, pp. 81–103.

[35] In the later 1630s the courtier Archibald Hay was seeking to re-examine the charter in pursuit of his propertied interests in Colchester Castle and its lands: CRO, D/DRe, Z1.

[36] PRO, SP, 16/223/4; *Charters*, p. 82; The most frequent occasions for disputes were the fiscal and military levies which were the product of the late Elizabethan and Stuart war monarchy: *APC 1617–1619*, pp. 123, 164–5; *CSPD, 1611–1618*, pp. 535, 537; *1623–1625*, p. 113; *1627–1628*, pp. 74, 128, 156; *1635–1636*, p. 13; CRO, D/Y, 2/6, pp. 33, 41, 45.

[37] PRO, SP, 16/44/7; SP, 16/139/41. It is uncertain how widespread opposition in Colchester

chester showed itself no less willing to drag its feet over royal demands; if anything, its opposition became more marked. Not surprisingly, it was the demand for ship money that generated most trouble. Ship money raised all the potentially difficult issues about the relationship between town and county. Colchester's response to the first levy of the 1630s – it had protested about the earlier levy of 1627 – had been to refuse to carry out an assessment and then to complain that the sum of £1,000 laid on them by the sheriff represented a massive overassessment. Despite the fact that by the time of the 1635 writ Colchester's assessment had been reduced to £400, the town only collected the money under protest. It then objected to handing the sum collected over to the sheriff, claiming it was a breach of its privileges. In both 1636 and 1637 the town was successful in having its assessment reduced. But in May 1638 the Privy Council was again forced to write to the Mayor, now Henry Barrington, since the reduced assessment had not been paid and they had not received any report of progress in collecting the levy. Only £100 had been paid a month later. Finally, in December 1639 the Corporation took the decision to petition the Privy Council to be excused any payment at all that year 'in regard of the deadness of trading within this towne'. Of course it is possible that such procedural objections masked more politically motivated opposition from a Corporation, most of whose members were to show their opposition to Personal Rule in the changed circumstances after 1639. It was not until 1656 that the Corporation took the decision to remove the royal arms from the great seal, but concern for its liberties had led it well before then to challenge and, by 1642 at least, to defy royal authority.[38] This brought the town into direct conflict with Sir John Lucas, a zealous servant of the Crown.

Disputes between boroughs and neighbouring gentry were not un-common in early modern England, but that between Colchester and the Lucas family proved both long-running and particularly bitter. Colches-ter's relationships with the county's gentry were marked by an insistence on its privileges, especially when negotiating demands from the county magistracy.[39] The town was 'a great, and ancient corporation, the

was; Richard Cust omits Colchester from his case study of Essex: *The Forced Loan and English Politics 1626–1628* (Oxford, 1987).

[38] PRO, SP, 16/61/79; /282/51; /301/95; /392/49; PCR, 2/46, pp. 177–8, 2/48, fol. 182; Morant, *History*, vol. 1, p. 54 and n.; *CSPD 1635–1636*, p. 435; *1636–1637*, p. 381; V. A. Rowe, 'Robert second earl of Warwick and the payment of ship money in Essex', *TEAS*, 3rd ser., 1 (1963), p. 160; PRO, PCR, 2/49, fol. 87 v; CRO, D/B5, Gb3, fol. 200.

[39] For examples of the town's refusal to contribute to the county's charges or to allow its trained bands to be mustered with those of the county, see ERO Q/SR 261A/4; CRO, D/Y, 2/6, pp. 33, 41, 45.

liberties whereof have never heretofore been infringed as they now are likely to be'. This ringing declaration was occasioned by an order to the town's maltsters to appear before a commission of county JPs who were to sit at Colchester. In such a context the rhetoric may seem overblown, but it reflects Colchester's construction of a political identity centred on strongly held notions of civic independence. As the town clerk was said to have told a local gentleman who had objected to his rating for poor relief, 'what care we for the order of the Judges. They have nothing to do within our Corporacion and we have power here to do whatsoever we please.'[40] Conflict with a town which was jealous of, and quick to detect threats to, its power was almost inevitable for the Lucas family. Indeed the family was heir to a conflict started by the previous owners of its estate, St John's Abbey, which stretched back beyond the English Rising of 1381. But the Lucas family's, and in particular Sir John's, aggressive desire to defend their name and interests both deepened and enlarged the conflict.[41]

The Lucases could claim descent from a fifteenth-century Suffolk gentry family, but they owed their position to a less glamorous history of service as Colchester's town clerk and marriage within the mercantile elite of the town. It was a younger son of Thomas Lucas, Esq. of Saxham in Suffolk, who had established the family. Appointed town clerk of Colchester in the 1530s, this John contracted successive marriages with daughters of two of Colchester's wealthiest merchant families which brought him a landed estate around Colchester. As was the case with many gentry dynasties of the sixteenth century, it was the property market created by the Dissolution that gave the Lucases the land with which to buttress their claim to gentle status. John's purchase in 1548 of the manors and site of the abbey of St John's, upon which he built a 'noble mansion', founded the family's fortune.[42] This purchase simultaneously moved the family solidly into the ranks of the landed gentry, while physically removing it from urban society.

This was not, however, a straightforward move from urban to rural society. Described in documents as near to Colchester, St John's lay just outside the Roman walls of the town and, as the Corporation claimed repeatedly, within their jurisdiction. Moreover, the Abbey's estates were

---

[40] PRO, SP, 16/335/18; PRO, ASSI, 35/84/10/44.

[41] For examples of town-gentry conflict, often rooted in gentry purchases of monastic lands at the Dissolution, see P. Clark and P. Slack, *English Towns in Transition 1500–1700* (Oxford, 1976), ch. 9; D. MacCulloch, *Suffolk Under the Tudors: Politics and Religion in an English County 1500–1600* (Oxford, 1986), pp. 322–9; A. Hughes, 'Religion and society in Stratford-upon-Avon, 1619–1638', *Midland History*, 19 (1994), p. 61.

[42] Morant, *History*, vol. 1, pp. 19–21; G. Rickword, 'Members of Parliament for Colchester, 1547–1558', *Essex Review*, 4 (1895), pp. 110–22.

promiscuously intermingled with the town's lands and fell within the liberties of Colchester, an extensive area that lay outside the town walls but over which the Corporation exercised authority. In purchasing the Abbey and its lands, the Lucas family also inherited the conflicts that had characterised relationships between the monks of St John's and the burgesses of Colchester. The complex patchwork of intermingled manorial and town lands invited disputes over intercommoning, but the situation had been exacerbated by the policy pursued by successive abbots of an aggressive expansion of the demesne by buying up tenures and by enclosure. This had prompted riots by the townsfolk and helps to explain the invasion, theft and threatened destruction of the Abbey's estate records during the 1381 revolt.[43] Conflict between the town and the Lucas family as the Abbey's successors was therefore almost inevitable.

Open conflict, however, did not come until the later sixteenth century. John Lucas, who had links with the town through office and family, served as its MP in the Parliaments of 1548 and 1553. Thomas Lucas, his son, also represented the borough and in 1575 was elected Recorder of Colchester. It was Thomas who established the family both at the level of the county and the Court. He served as sheriff in 1578, was knighted and entertained Queen Elizabeth on her progresses of 1561 and 1579. He also added to the family's property and, in particular, ecclesiastical patronage, controlling at least eight livings, mostly in and around Colchester. The monument erected after his death by his wife in the family church of St Giles attributed to him 'prudencia, Justice & Hospitalitis' – wisdom, justice and hospitality. It was, however, during his life that relationships with the town deteriorated.[44]

In the 1570s Colchester's ruling group had been the target of a litter of libels.[45] Thomas Lucas's role as an ally of the bailiffs in the detection and

---

[43] D. Stephenson, *The Book of Colchester* (Chesham, 1978), pp. 55–6; R. H. Britnell, 'Colchester and the countryside in the fourteenth century: a search for interdependence between urban and rural economies' (Ph.D. thesis, University of Cambridge, 1969), pp. 59–60 and 420–30; Britnell, *Growth*, pp. 29–31; Britnell, 'Fields and pastures', pp. 159–65; *VCH Essex*, vol. 9, pp. 255–9; BL, Stowe MS 839, fols. 31 v–32 v; *The Red Paper Book of Colchester* (Colchester, 1902), *passim*; CRO, D/Y, 2/10, pp. 163, 189. D. Stephenson ('Urban participation in the English peasants' rising of 1381: the case of Colchester', *Revue Romaine D'Histoire*, 26 (1987), pp. 335–43), argues that the attack may have come primarily from peasants belonging to the Abbey's rural manors.

[44] Rickword, 'Members of Parliament', pp. 114–121; *List of the Sheriffs for England and Wales. From the Earliest Times to AD 1831 compiled from Documents in the Public Record Office*, List and Indexes, 9 (London, 1898; repr. New York, 1963), p. 45; Martin, *Colchester*, p. 51; D. Grant, *Margaret the First: A Biography of Margaret Cavendish, Duchess of Newcastle* (1957), p. 29; CRO, D/Y, 2/10, fol. 168; D/DRg, 1/226, p. 113.

[45] The issues behind the dispute are hard to disentangle, but on one level the libels

punishment of the author of the libels saw two further libels being cast around the town,

> chiefly agenst Sir Thomas Lucas and ... Thomas Upcher [one of the bailiffs], with the most fowle and unseamely wordes and tearmes sett out in their libelles in writinge, resembling him the said Sir Thomas Lucas and the said Thomas Upcher to Minos and Radmanthus, namyng the Two Infernall Judges to gyve sentence against libellors and Namyng the said Sir Thomas Lucas Kt pallyard [vagrant] and viper and other the vilest and most shameful and sclanderous wordes and names they could Devise.

Only one year after his appointment as Recorder, Sir Thomas Lucas and the offending bailiff were removed from office by the freeburgesses. That they chose to replace the bailiff with Thomas Hunwick, a wealthy clothier who had been the subject of a riotous attack by Lucas's servants in 1571, suggests where their allegiances lay. Sir Thomas seems not to have served as JP for the town after these events.[46] In 1584 Sir Thomas Heneage wrote to the bailiffs of Colchester about their dispute with his friend Sir Thomas Lucas:

> so neere a neighbor and so sufficient a gentleman, whose goodwill might stand you in farr better steade, as heretofore it hath donne, then your dissencons and quarrelles can be any waies comodious or quiet unto you. And if you wold receave the advice of a man that loves you you shold rather in time take up theire unkyndnesses then by opposite dealinge uppon every occasion leave causes of stomach in either of you, w[hi]ch will prove to be but the seedes of evill to you both.[47]

This advice went unheeded. The 1580s brought a series of conflicts with the town which seem to have permanently damaged relationships between family and borough. 'Nor will men serve him [Sir Thomas Lucas] if he be hanged at his gate', was how one gentleman summed up the depth of feelings in the town against the family.[48]

In 1577 the Privy Council had written to Sir Thomas about his choosing to muster 'some of the hooding of that towne which seemeth to savour of partialitie'. In the year after the humiliation of being rejected as Recorder, it would seem that Lucas was trying to

---

represented an attack on one of the bailiffs for his role in the Marian persecutions: Byford, 'Price of Protestantism', pp. 211–41.

[46] *APC 1571–1575*, pp. 41, 61; Byford, 'Price of Protestantism', pp. 253–6 and p. 298 n. Might the suggestion that Lucas, marrying into the Northamptonshire family of Fermor, had catholic sympathies (Grant, *Margaret the First*, p. 29) help to explain the attack on him?

[47] CRO, D/Y, 2/8, p. 85.

[48] CRO, D/Y, 2/10, fol. 172 v. Lucas was also accused of being a murderer: L. C. Sier, 'A rental of Greenstead manor, Colchester', *ER*, 27 (1918), p. 142.

use his powers within the county to get revenge within the town by forcing members of the Corporation to muster under his command. When Sir Thomas was once more sheriff for the county in 1584, he again sought to use his authority to lord it over the town, summoning several aldermen and other members of the Corporation to serve as jurymen at the Assizes and at Westminster. The muster also proved a potent area for further conflict. Having received a separate commission, the town's bailiffs had entrusted the training of their men to Mr Tey, a gentleman whose earlier dispute with Sir Thomas Lucas must have recommended him to them. Both Lucas and Tey had originally been given authority to oversee the mustering of the trained bands within the Colchester division of the county but Lucas, whose earlier action at the muster had led to his imprisonment by the Privy Council, had subsequently been dropped. Sir Thomas attempted to suborn Colchester men to train at the muster under his authority, promising one that he should 'weare hys lyverye duering hys lyffe'. Despite the Council's decision, Lucas still sought to disrupt the actual muster and to deny the bailiffs' attempts to exercise authority, refusing for example to deliver up a townsman he had recruited or to allow a search of St John's for him. When Tey and the bailiffs were exercising the trained bands in the grounds of Colchester Castle, Sir Thomas Lucas's men crowded in. Ordered to depart by the bailiffs, they refused and scuffles broke out. As a provocative symbol of this clash of authority, Sir Thomas's men refused to remove their hats in the bailiffs' presence, saying they would do so for Sir Thomas's friends, but not for his enemies.[49]

Behind these seemingly trivial episodes lurked larger issues of power and status. Sir Thomas's actions were intended as a direct threat to Colchester's status as a borough and its independence from the power of landed gentry. Indeed, there is evidence to suggest they may have been part of a more general challenge to the Corporation by the gentry of the surrounding area. In its turn, the borough's claim to exercise authority in the liberties was a snub to the local gentry. The volume of the surviving correspondence and papers relating to these disputes among the borough records testifies to how seriously the Corporation took these challenges to their authority. The Corporation mobilised all their connections in London and the Court to defend their liberties, and they seem to have

---

49 *APC 1577–1578*, p. 69; CRO, D/Y, 2/3, pp. 117, 125, 127; 2/9, pp. 211, 213, 217; PRO, SP, 12/170/76, /171/6, 7 and 7a, 37; CRO, D/B5, Sb2/4, fol. 39, 41; *APC 1580–1581*, pp. 51, 126–7, 131. Lucas seems to have been imprisoned briefly for conniving at an attack on one of the queen's footmen: *APC 1578–1580*, pp. 450–1; *1580–1581*, p. 9. The earlier attack on Hunwicke had also resulted in Sir Thomas having to appear several times before the Privy Council: *APC 1571–1575*, p. 61.

come off best. These slights to Sir Thomas may have led the family to⌐
abandon Colchester, for we learn from a Jacobean tithe dispute between
his son and a local minister that around 1585 Sir Thomas 'brake up
house keeping and lay at London 3 yeares'.[50]

Sir Thomas's return to Colchester saw renewed conflict with the
Corporation, once more over issues of rating behind which lurked larger
conflicts over power and jurisdiction.[51] 1603 brought further troubles,
revealing another area of conflict which would earn the Lucas family the
hostility of the commons as well as the Corporation of the town. In that
year, Sir Thomas was thought to have ordered the pulling down of
enclosures on St John's Green, another piece of disputed ground which
lay between the house of St John's and the town. A crowd, said to
number over one hundred, armed with axes and accompanied by many
children, pulled down and carried away rails and posts. The wife of one
of the victims, Thomas Fowlie, was the target for some typically black
humour. Set upon by two women, she was told, 'that though she were a
fowle they would pluck her fethers of[f] her back'. The causes of the riot
were complex and involved in-fighting between Colchester townsfolk,
but the depositions as taken down, with their various claims that it was
at Sir Thomas Lucas's 'pleasuer', 'will' and 'command' that the enclosures were pulled down suggest that Colchester's rulers were as interested
in finding an opportunity to score against their rival as in prosecuting the
rioters. When a constable of the town arrived and 'told the company that
they might as well have taken the Crowne from of the King's head as
have done that which they did', the rioters were said to have retorted that
Sir Thomas Lucas had willed the enclosures down by next Saturday and
that now was as good a time as any.[52]

It is clear that under Sir Thomas Lucas relations between the family
and the town had become marked by conflict over a potentially wide
range of issues. There is less evidence of overt conflict with Colchester
during the headship of Sir Thomas's son, another Thomas, who
succeeded his father in 1611. This was perhaps because of the family's
weakened position. This Thomas, having killed a courtier in a duel in
1597, had been outlawed and fled to France. In 1603 James I had had to
issue a warrant for a bill in Parliament to restore Thomas to 'his blood

---

[50] CRO, D/Y, 2/3, pp. 121–33; /5, p. 37; /7, pp. 213, 221, 225, 230, 235; /9, fol. 303.

[51] CRO, D/DRe, Z9/5. Sir Thomas denied that his lands in Colchester were liable to
assessment by the town for payment of 'composition service'. The Corporation's decision
to take legal advice about the agreement between the town and St John's Abbey points
to the earlier origins of this dispute: CRO, D/B5, Gb1, fol. 130 r.

[52] CRO, D/B5, Sb2/7, fols. 92 v–6 v. It may be significant that the only rioter to be bound
over to appear at the Quarter Sessions was clearly identified as claiming authority from
Sir Thomas.

and gentry'. Restored to his estates, Thomas, who unlike his father was not knighted, seems to have played small part in the affairs of the county.[53] However, it was as a direct result of his actions, that conflict was renewed. Sir John Lucas as second son would not have headed the family, but his father's outlawry and exile had meant that the eldest son, another Thomas, was born illegitimate.

When his father died in 1625, John, aged 18, was still a minor. If his mother is to be believed, the Corporation was quick to take advantage of this period of perceived weakness to re-open conflict with the family. In a petition of 1628 to the Privy Council, she claimed that since her husband's death she had been rated twice what he had paid in poor relief. But this was only the occasion of her complaint. She then went on to detail the ways that her son's inheritance was being damaged by the inaction of Colchester's rulers. In the woods and lands which formed the bulk of the estates, 'the poor people of the said Towne being without goverm[en]t doe make such spoile and destruction therein, & committ such other insolencies about [?] the dwellinge house of yo[u]r pet[ione]r as are not sufferable'. As the reference to lack of government makes clear she sought to lay the real blame for these problems upon the Corporation: 'complaint having bene severall tymes made as well by yor pet[itione]r's late husband & herselfe to the Bayliffs of the said Towne no relief hath bene given therein'. We do not know the outcome of this dispute, but we can be sure that Elizabeth Lucas's success in getting the case referred to Lord Maynard, Lord Lieutenant of the county, cannot have pleased Colchester's rulers whose relationship with the county was, as we have seen, marked by an irritable concern to defend the town's independence from outside interference.[54] Her success may also mark another important development: the restoration of the family to court favour. After the death of Thomas Lucas, Samuel Harsnet, a Colcestrian, for whom the Lucases were probably his first patrons, and by then Bishop of Norwich, had acted in effect as the family's guardian, bringing success in negotiations over marriage and the wardship of John Lucas. From at least 1625 the family had also secured the powerful friendship of the Duke of Buckingham, the 'much service and respect' they had shown him in his entertainment at St John's occasioning the promise that 'hee would be glad of any occasion to oblige them'.[55] This alignment of the

[53] W. P. W. Phillimore, *An Index to Bills of Privy Signet, Commonly called Signet Bills, 1584 to 1591 and 1603 to 1624* (British Record Society, Index Library, 4, 1890), p. 60; *Statutes of the Realm*, 4, ii (1819), p. 1016.

[54] PRO, SP, 16/89/53 (*CSPD* dates this to 1627, but a reference in *APC 1628–1629*, p. 8 supplies the date of 1628). In 1629 Elizabeth Lucas was presented to the church courts for failing to pay the church rate, 'being indifferently rated': ERO D/ACA/47, fol. 6 v.

[55] PRO, SP, 16/6/105; 7/27; 10/63.

family with the Court, and the uses to which they sought to put this relationship in their dispute with Colchester's rulers, was also to play an important part in the politics of the attack upon Sir John Lucas.

Sir John Lucas's inheritance included a bitter and long-running conflict with the town of Colchester and therefore brought with it a responsibility to defend the family's name and interests. To this duty he brought his own heightened and aggressive sense of honour. A concern for reputation was of course the duty of every gentleman, but in the case of Lucas this took on an exaggerated form. There is reason to suggest that this trait in Lucas's character owed much to the experiences of his family and his own upbringing. Lucas could trace his lineage back to fifteenth-century gentry stock, and he had inherited a substantial estate from his father described in the year of his death as 'of good qualitie, a man of 4m li in land'. The careful bequest by his grandmother to him, literally of the best of the family silver, gives an oblique indicator of how John as heir was marked out as the bearer of the family's inheritance.[56] But in reality it was only since the time of his grandfather that the family could claim gentry status. Compared to established county families like the Barringtons of Hatfield Broad Oak, they were relative latecomers. Moreover, the family's passage into solid county status had been interrupted. Both his grandfather and father had served as sheriff, an office losing its earlier pre-eminence and which was increasingly seen as the stepping stone for more junior families into the ranks of the county magistracy. But only his grandfather had been appointed a JP. None since the mid-sixteenth century had served as an MP, even for a borough (and certainly not for Colchester). That the family owed its fortune to the successes of John's great-grandfather as town clerk to the Corporation and much of its initial wealth to his marriages into the town's clothier families may have made John more anxious to defend his status as gentleman and, after 1638, knight. With wealthy clothiers as neighbours, Lucas would have believed with William Segar 'that riches (being of their owne nature vile) cannot make men Noble'.[57]

The disgrace of his father's outlawry, and consequent need for a private bill for his restitution 'in Blood', must help to explain this check to the family's progress into county society. But its importance may also lie in what it suggests of the character of Lucas's father. The duel was of

---

[56] *Visitations of Essex*, vol. 1, pp. 235–6, 437; G. E. Cockayne, *The Complete Peerage*, 13 vols. (1932–40), vol. 8, pp. 244–6; PRO, SP, 16/10/63; ERO, D/ACW 6/40. However, John's father left insufficient money – his inventory amounted to no more than £4,700 – to cover the £8,000 he bequeathed to John's sisters: ERO, D/DC, 20/9.

[57] W. A. Shaw, *The Knights of England: A Complete Record*, 2 vols. (1906), vol. 1, p. 205; J. G. Marston, 'Gentry honour and royalism in Stuart England', *JBS*, 13 (1973), p. 26.

course seen as the appropriate ritual in the defence of honour, but in a period where it excited royal displeasure and proscription, one that fewer actually underwent. Perhaps Lucas inherited something of his aggressive defence of honour from the family's history and, more immediately, from his father. If the Earl of Clarendon can be believed this was a trait that was shared by his brothers. Clarendon described his younger brother Charles, the royalist martyr, as brave in battle, 'but at all other times and places of a nature not to be lived with ... of a rough and proud nature'.[58] It may also be the case that the disgrace of his father's temporary loss of gentle status may have made his son more assertive in defence of the family's reputation. The biographer of John Bastwick, Colchester physician and puritan martyr, has suggested that John Lucas was the unnamed 'lord' whom Bastwick thought responsible for denouncing him to the authorities. If this identification is correct, then Bastwick's reference to this lord as one 'whose father stunk among hoes and ploughshares and belched black chaff ... this worthy, who by luxury, greed and lust is common talk in the neighbourhood' would suggest something of the talk against which John Lucas had to defend the family's reputation.[59]

Fortunately, we have been left an account of the upbringing of Lucas and his siblings which helps us to understand his making as a landed gentleman acutely aware of his status and of the need to defend it. That prolific author Margaret, Duchess of Newcastle, was John Lucas's younger sister. While we should be careful not to take as gospel truth her carefully fashioned *True Relation of my Birth, Breeding and Life*, it can certainly be read for the valuable light it throws on the values that the Lucas children were expected to absorb. Significantly, the account begins with a description of their father which stresses lineage: 'My father was a gentleman, which title is grounded and given by merit, not by princes; and it is the act of the time, not favour: and though my father was not a peer of the realm, yet there were few peers who had much greater estates, or lived more noble therewith.' Does the grounding of gentle status in lineage at a time when Renaissance thinking had put a greater emphasis

---

[58] Clarendon, *The History of the Rebellion And Civil Wars in England Begun in the year 1641*, ed. W. D. Macray, 6 vols. (Oxford, 1888), vol. 6, 108. Lucas was of course one of those military men of whom it has been suggested that Clarendon was less than objective in his judgement: Hutton, 'Clarendon's "History of the Rebellion"', *EHR*, 47 (1982), pp. 70–88.

[59] Frances Condon argues that the active role of John Danet, Lucas's attorney, and Thomas Newcomen, his chaplain, in entrapping Bastwick suggests that Lucas was the unnamed lord: 'The life and works of Dr John Bastwick (1595–1654) (Ph.D. thesis, University of London, 1982), *passim*. Lucas's political and religious affiliations would make him an ideal candidate for the role, but in the absence of firmer evidence the verdict must be returned as unproven.

on virtue hark back to the competitive and independent honour culture grounded in lineage described by Mervyn James. Whether this was the intention or not, the stress on lineage could certainly be used to deny the claims of mercantile wealth to gentle status. It also served to counter the claims of godliness as the true determinant of worth, competing claims that would have circulated among Sir John's wealthy and godly mercantile neighbours.[60]

According to the duchess, Sir John and his brothers and sisters 'were bred virtuously, modestly, civilly, honourably'. Throughout her account there is an emphasis on the inculcation of a sense of their status and of the appropriate behaviour this imposed in relations with their social inferiors. The Lucas children were brought up to receive and expect deference:

we were bred with respectful attendance, every one being severally waited upon, and all her servants in general used the same respect to her children (even those that were very young) as they did to herself; for she suffered not her servants, either to be rude before us, or to domineer over us ... Neither were we suffered to have any familiarity with the vulgar servants, or conversation: yet caused us to demean ourselves with an humble civility towards them, as they with a dutiful respect to us. Not because they were servants were we so reserved; for many noble persons are forced to serve through necessity; but by reason the vulgar sort of servants are as ill bred as meanly born, giving children ill examples and worse counsel.

Their mother, Elizabeth Lucas, set the children an example of appropriate behaviour, inculcating in them that 'rhetoric of status' which has been seen to be part and parcel of the new Renaissance emphasis on body and personality as the representation to others of gentle status. 'She was of a grand behaviour, and had such a majestic grandeur, as it were continually hung about her, that it would strike a kind of an awe to the beholders, and command respect from the rudest. (I mean the rudest of civilised people ...)'. Interestingly, this pattern of upbringing, with its marked concern for observing social boundaries, paralleled that shown by Charles I in his own household and court.[61]

---

[60] *The Life of the Duke of Newcastle To which is added The True Relation of My Birth, Breeding and Life By Margaret, Duchess of Newcastle*, ed. C. H. Firth (1886), pp. 275–98; M. James, 'English politics and the concept of honour, 1485–1642' (*P&P* supplement, 3, 1978); R. Kelso, 'The doctrine of the English gentleman in the sixteenth century', *University of Illinois Studies in Language and Literature* 14(i) (1929); A. Fletcher, 'Honour, reputation and local officeholding in Elizabethan and Stuart England' in Fletcher and J. Stevenson, *Order and Disorder in Early Modern England* (Cambridge, 1985), pp. 92–115; Marston, 'Gentry honour'; F. Heal and C. Holmes, *The Gentry in England and Wales 1500–1700* (1994), pp. 20–47 (esp. pp. 30–1).

[61] A. Bryson, 'The rhetoric of status: gesture, demeanour and the image of the gentleman in sixteenth- and seventeenth-century England' in L. Gent and N. Llewellyn (eds.),

After the death of her husband, Elizabeth Lucas had acted as his executrix. She also negotiated successfully for the wardship of John to be granted her.[62] Even when John came into his inheritance two years later, his mother continued to live at St John's and to play an active role in managing the family's affairs. It may well be that as the daughter of a London gentleman, John Leighton, Elizabeth Lucas passed on to her son a keen eye for estate management. Her daughter noted of her that, 'she was very skilful in leases, and setting of lands, and court keeping, ordering of stewards and the like affairs'. Certainly, Sir John was to prove extremely sensitive to any perceived threats to the family's estates in and around Colchester.

John Lucas, then, was nurtured in that culture of honour that was considered to be the validating birthmark of the gentleman and which, contemporaneously, was being given renewed emphasis in the court of Charles I. Schooled by his mother, he doubtless exhibited the civility that was part of the rhetoric by which gentlemen asserted and legitimised their status, for example initiating negotiations to purchase the horse and coach that were becoming an essential part of that status as soon he came into his inheritance.[63] That John Lucas held to a marked degree the self-assertiveness that was the necessary corollary of this obligation helps to explain his readiness to detect a threat to his status. Family and lineage were the matrix of this culture of honour and they had to be defended. In Lucas's case the peculiar proximity of the Lucas's 'country house' to the urban society of Colchester, with its Corporation of wealthy clothiers and merchants and commonalty of 'unruly people', as well as the inheritance of the conflict between Corporation and Abbey, made this defence both more necessary and more difficult. It was with a belief in his own innate superiority and the consequent need to defend his reputation that he conducted such relations as he had with his too-close neighbours who were able to amass both wealth and land from their position in a prospering urban economy.

The quintessential expression of the culture of honour was the duel, but in the changed circumstances of the early modern period it was becoming more often combat in the courts. Sir John Lucas proved very ready to resort to the law. His fondness for the law was later to be gently mocked in some verses by Sir John Denham when they shared a prison in

---

Renaissance Bodies: The Human Figures in English Culture c.1540–1660 (1990), pp. 136–53; J. Davies, The Caroline Captivity of the Church: Charles I and the Remoulding of Anglicanism 1625–1641 (Oxford, 1992), pp. 22–3.

[62] She employed the good offices of Peter Killigrew, suitor to one of her daughters: PRO, SP, 16/6/105;/10/63; CSPD 1625–1626, pp. 102, 111, 117.

[63] Bryson, 'Rhetoric of status'. Interestingly, Lucas was negotiating their purchase from his fellow victim, the Countess of Rivers: CUL Hengrave Hall MSS/88, vol. 2, no. 129.

the 1650s.[64] The result was a series of disputes that exceeded even the record of his grandfather. Both in their number and length, these disputes suggest John Lucas's particular litigiousness. For example, the single year of 1633 witnessed a number of unrelated cases brought by him in various courts. Lucas brought a case in Exchequer over damage caused by the cutting of his millpond. In the same year Lucas was also a defendant in the Exchequer in a case over the disputed lordship of an area of the heath outside Colchester and enclosures made by him there. 1633 also saw him involved in a dispute over his assessment for purveyance. Some of these appear on the surface to be the run-of-the-mill litigation that many landowners faced, but it can be shown that they attracted hostility which would later surface in the events of the early 1640s.[65] The dispute at Canwick mill, for example, had the potential to be more than a squall in a millpond. The defendant in the case, who claimed that the rebuilding of the mill had flooded his lands, was none other than Henry Barrington, a leading member of the Corporation, an ardent supporter of Parliament, and one of those to feature prominently in the account of the 1642 attack in *Mercurius Rusticus*.[66]

Three disputes in particular revealed the tendency for Lucas's taste for litigation to provoke wider conflict. The first again occurred in 1633. This arose from a complicated dispute over piping water to Colchester through land which he claimed as his, but which others claimed to be part of the lands over which the town exercised common rights.[67] In the early 1620s three contractors had piped water to provide a supply for the town. In order to reach the waterhouse they had built from the spring, the pipes had to cross a croft which belonged to one of the Lucas manors. The contractors therefore had had to make payment to Lucas's lessee. But in 1629 the lessee, Robert Talcott, claimed that the pipes damaged his crops. An attempt at arbitration failed and, following the deliberate cutting of the pipes by Lucas, the contractors petitioned the

---

[64] *Notes and Queries: A Medium of Inter-Communication For Literary Men, Artists, Antiquaries, Genealogists Etc.* (1850–), 7th ser., 10 (1890), pp. 41–2.

[65] PRO, E134/8 and 9 Charles I/ Hilary 21; PRO, E134/9 Charles I/Easter, 18; PRO, SP, 16/238/39. In 1629 Lucas was pursuing a Chancery law suit against the lessee of Canwick mill: PRO, C2/Charles, 1/L26/2; /L55/14. The defendant, William Gilson, may have been related to some of those who helped to pull down the Lucas enclosures in 1641; the list of those accused by Lucas includes one Colman Gilson as well a John Gibson whose occupation was a miller: HLRO, MP HL, 5 August 1641.

[66] Since Barrington had himself at one point held another mill at the Hythe which lay against Lucas meadowland, there may have other aspects to this conflict: PRO, E134/8, Chas I/Michaelmas 18; /8 and 9, Chas I/Hilary 21; CRO, D/B5, Gb2, fol. 182.

[67] The account of this dispute draws on the following sources: PRO, SP, 16/151/46; 247/22, 23; /248/4/418/4; /421/8; /422/119; /534/88; PCR, 2/43, pp. 256, 285–7; /50, fols. 134 v-5, 200 r–v, 278–9, 409–10; *APC 1629–1630*, pp. 84–5; HMC 4, House of Lords MSS, p. 91.

Privy Council in 1633. In doing so, they secured the support of Colchester's bailiffs and four aldermen, including again Lucas's opponent Henry Barrington.

The Privy Council at this stage thought that Talcott's 'indirect practices' 'and the averseness of John Lucas' were behind the dispute. They referred the dispute to the Earl Rivers – father to the Countess, Lucas's later fellow victim – for arbitration. Rivers reported that Talcott's lease of the croft, made by Thomas Lucas, had been surrendered to John Lucas and that whereas Lucas's father had given the contractors a hundred-year lease at a token annual rent of one shilling only, he was now demanding an annual rent of £3. Lucas claimed the higher figure in part because there was an alehouse at the waterhouse whose customers did much damage in the adjacent rabbit warren owned by his elder brother. The contractors countered that the land in dispute was in fact commonable and refused to pay the increased rent. Rivers was forced to refer the issue back to the Privy Council, who after questioning both parties found for the contractors. However, they laid the blame at Talcott's door, adding that 'hearing well of the said John Lucas otherwise' they 'doe conceive that he hath beene cheefely misled, and abused herein by the cunning and indirect practise' of Talcott. This was not the end of the dispute. Having once more referred the matter to local arbitration in 1639, the Privy Council again pronounced on the issue. But this time their decision favoured the Lucas family. The alehouse was to be suppressed and if the contractors refused to meet the new terms then the Lucas family were given the right to smash the pipes. What, if anything, the changed verdict owed to the relationship developing in the interim between the Crown and its loyal servant John Lucas can only be guessed at.

On one level this was no more than the sort of long-running dispute that contested property rights could give rise to in a litigious age. But on another level this squabble over a few shillings enables us to see how such disputes became an occasion for a further deterioration in relations between the Corporation and commonalty of Colchester and Sir John Lucas. It is easy to neglect the importance of access to water in early modern England and its cost, especially to the poorer sort. Seen in the context of a town whose hilltop location made water supply difficult, Lucas's actions become more than just a squabble over compensation. It was John Lucas who was seen as primarily responsible in getting the lease surrendered to him in order to extract more from the contractors; Talcott, it was pointed out, continued to farm the land. It was Lucas's bailiff who had gone to the workmen and asked in a jeering manner where to cut to do the most mischief. While the surviving sources reflect the contractors' case, which doubtless sought to blacken Lucas in order to strengthen their own position, there can be little doubt that there was a sympathetic audience within both Corporation and commonalty for this version of the dispute. Members of the Corporation (including Henry Barrington) supported the contractors. So did the townspeople. One man reported that, 'he cannot almost go in quiett upp & downe the streets, for people callinge after him to knowe when they shall have the water againe', the poor having been given previously free pots and pitchers of water. This was more than a storm in a water pitcher. The dispute was to run almost to the eve of the attacks against Lucas. Some idea of the hostility it created within Colchester is reflected in the fact that at the next election day Robert Talcott was displaced from the aldermanic bench and the town's freeburgesses continued to defy the Privy Council's order for his re-instatement until 1639.[68]

In the two years preceding the attack on his house, Lucas had become embroiled in two further disputes. Again these demonstrated both his highly developed sense of his rights and how hostility in Colchester towards him could spread right across the social spectrum. The first of these disputes ended with Lucas again in conflict with the town's rulers. Shortly before the Christmas of the previous year, his mother in his absence had agreed to allow the collectors of saltpetre access to St John's. However, Lucas complained that taking advantage of her absence in London they had insulted the servants, broken down doors and begun to dig where they had not been given permission to do so. Being 'civilly told' to desist, they had become 'more uncivill'. Arriving at the house with a cart, they had broken open the great double gates and announced their intention of digging in yet more places, including a barn where grain was stored. Finding the barn doors locked and 'to doe wrong a more Legall way they obtained a warrant from the Mayor of Colchester' – who in that year was John Langley, one of the other key names in Bruno Ryves' account of the 1642 attack. With the assistance of three of Colchester's constables, the collectors had proceeded to break open the doors and to dig up newly made floors, in doing so spoiling some of the grain. When Lucas wrote to complain to the Privy Council, the saltpetremen had been in the house for four months and still they continued to dig in new areas, 'and they go on in such a way that if some

---

[68] J. Mackworth Wood, 'The past and present history of Colchester Corporation Water Works with relation to underground water', *Essex Naturalist*, 17 (1913), pp. 21–36; CRO, D/B5, Cb1/10–11; PRO, SP, 16/248/4. Standard cost-of-living budgets make no allowance for the cost of water. Some idea of that cost is suggested by the claim that the poorer inhabitants of Colchester were able as a result of these waterworks to pay less than twenty shillings yearly for water.

speedy order be not taken Mrs Lucas shall not call any thing in her owne house her owne for even at this presente the barne doores & greate gates being broke ope[n] not only her corne but what ever else is in the house lies exposed to the spoile and rapine of unruly people whereof that towne is very full'.[69]

The saltpetremen gave a very different version of events. Lucas dismissed their account. 'I will not runne through their whole answers to make a general refutation of them; they are so full of impertinencies, that to take notice of them all were to fall into one my selfe'. What most concerned him was what he perceived as the slight to his family's house and status. As he protested, 'for them thus to trouble the house of a person of her qualitie there being many Innes & other houses in the towne fitt for their purpose where they have not bin is (as she conceives) neither faire nor equall dealing.' Predictably, it was the involvement of Colchester's Mayor and officers that angered Lucas most. 'They violated the privileges of the house the towne officers haveinge nothing to do there', Lucas complained. Given the history between family and Corporation, he had good cause to suspect their motives. That the deputy in charge of saltpetre operations shared the exact same name, John Langley, as the then Mayor has led at least one historian to think them one and the same person. They clearly were not. It has not been possible to establish whether the two Langleys were related, but if they were this can only have added to Lucas's belief that the town authorities were using the excuse of loyal service to the Crown to attack him and to renew their claim of jurisdiction over St John's.[70] Unless he could have an early hearing before the Privy Council, Lucas informed the secretary of state

> I shall be constrained to steere another course, and taking the opportunity of this terme to commence a suit in law against them: as for the Constables, I intend to sue them however; to this necessitie enforces me, to vindicate my right, and the privileges of my house; they are my inheritance, and as much mine as the house itselfe, and I must not, will not lose them.[71]

As we have seen, this stress on the need to defend his honour and reputation was a recurring theme in the disputes in which Lucas became

---

[69] PRO, SP, 16/449/25.

[70] PRO, SP, 16/450/36, 45; /451/25. Langley the Mayor would have relished the opportunity given him to invade Lucas's house. Nevertheless, they were not the same man as their signatures make clear: PRO, SP, 16/362/24 (Langley, mayor); /450/45 (Langley, salt-petreman). That the two men shared the same surname is intriguing, but I have been unable to establish if there was a family link.

[71] PRO, SP, 16/451/25.

embroiled. While the frequency and range of conflicts that Lucas engaged in help to explain his subsequent unpopularity, there was an additional element which Lucas himself brought to these conflicts and which was to help explain his fate in 1642 – his aggressive concern to defend himself against slights to his status. When the Earl Rivers had to explain his failure to secure agreement over the waterworks, even though no more than sixteen shillings divided the parties, he did so by reference to Lucas's character: 'the reason why Mr Lucas is more severe in this, I conceive to be, because he thinketh that by means of this Informac[i]on, they have made to your Lo[rdshi]pps, his credit lieth at stake, & therefore is desyerous, to Cleere himself, before yor Lo[rdshi]pps, before whom he hath byne thus traduced, as he thinketh.'[72]

The other major dispute in the run-up to the attack in the summer of 1642 also involved a serious challenge to Lucas's interests. Once more the nature of the dispute aligned both the Corporation and the commons against Lucas and the form their actions took foreshadowed events in 1642. The purchase of the Abbey and its manors had brought the Lucas family conflicts with the Corporation over issues of jurisdiction, status and power. It also had brought disputes over property. Since they involved issues of common rights in the lands surrounding the town, these had particular implications for both the freemen and the town's poor. We have already seen how rights of common had become a source of growing conflict within the town. This internal conflict was paralleled by conflict with the Lucas family both as heirs to the Abbey's property and as executors of its policy of enclosure. The Lucas family had lands scattered in the villages surrounding Colchester and elsewhere in Essex, but the bulk of the holdings were within the liberties of Colchester.[73] While attempts at enclosure by the family had led to conflict with both Corporation and commoners, the family in turn had to put up with the irritant of trespass and wood thefts, which they were unable to prevent, from a growing urban population. How far the family consciously sought to extend their holdings within Colchester cannot be discovered, but Lexden manor had been bought in 1613, the deer park at another Colchester manor, Greenstead, enlarged to some 230 acres, and there is incidental evidence of other smaller purchases.[74] Once again, it was John

[72] PRO, SP, 16/248/4.
[73] John Lucas's inheritance was described as consisting mainly of 600 acres and extensive woods within the liberties of Colchester, while his brother held at least one further manor – Lexden – also within the town's liberties: PRO, SP, 14/79 (Book of abstracts of inquisitions post-mortem), 8 November 1611; 16/89/53; CRO, D/Pa/[59].
[74] CRO, D/B5, Cb2/8, fol. 508 v; 'Book of sessions of peace 1630–1663', fols. 3, 3 v, 4 v; D/Pa/[59], p. 40; D/B5, Cb8, fol. 445 v; BL, Stowe MS 832, fol. 12.

Lucas who was by his actions to bring an earlier history of conflict to the boil.

Much of the town lands were still held in large and unenclosed fields, which ran into the lands of the neighbouring lords of the manor. Beyond these were areas of heath and waste lying mainly to the north and east of the town and interspersed with land over which neighbouring manorial lords claimed lordship. Forming as they did a complex mosaic, the town's lands had long provided an arena for conflict between townsmen and neighbouring lords.[75] In particular, the intermingling of Lucas and town lands in an area over which the Corporation claimed jurisdiction and the freemen common rights furnished a fertile ground for conflicts, as relations between Abbey and town had long shown.[76] The Lucas family also had lands in the extensive heaths to the north-east of the town. Lordship of the heaths had been in dispute between the Corporation and Sir Thomas Lucas.[77] This was again the continuation of a long-running controversy which had begun with the Abbey. It had led Sir Thomas to sue the Corporation at the Assizes and the Corporation to have the records at the Tower searched for a legal action of their own in defence of the commons and liberties of the town.[78] It seems also to have resulted in at least one townsman forfeiting his lands in the Lucas manor of Greenstead for 'some notorious and scandalous words spoken by him' against Sir Thomas.[79] In 1641 the dispute flared up again, this time in response to recent further enclosure by Sir John Lucas.[80]

On 13 May 1641 – the day after the execution of the Earl of Strafford

---

[75] Britnell, 'Fields and pastures', pp. 159–65; J. H. Round, 'The sphere of an archaeological society', *TEAS*, NS 14 (1915–17), pp. 200–04; *VCH Essex*, vol. 9, pp. 255–9. The dispersed nature of the town lands can be reconstructed from surveys of 1595 and 1599 (BL, Stowe MS 832, *passim*), from the Chamberlains' Accounts (e.g. CRO, D/B5, Aa1/19, Aa1/24); from early nineteenth-century maps of parish lands (e.g. CRO, CPL, 504, D/DR P17) and, most helpfully, from a nineteenth-century map of Colchester on which has been marked the then distribution of the half-year lands (Colchester Public Library, Local Studies Room). I am grateful to Dr Christopher Thornton of the Essex VCH for bringing this last item to my attention.

[76] Surveys of 1596 and 1599 drawn up by Colchester's authorities to assess purveyance give a vivid picture of the dispersal of Lucas holdings throughout the area of Colchester and its liberties (BL, Stowe MS 832, fols. 27–44), as does a later listing (CRO, 1649 Assessment).

[77] CRO, D/B5, Gb1, 13 July 1582; CRO, D/Y, 2/7, p. 205; CRO, D/B5, Sb2/4, fol. 184 v.

[78] It would appear that Sir Thomas had rejected an offer of arbitration and an attempt to get an intermediary to persuade him to accede to 'thys neygbourlye order': CRO, D/B5, Gb1, fol. 30 v; D/Y, 2/7, p. 205.

[79] CRO, Acc. C 47, GR 19, p. 3. Since this was the manor by which Lucas claimed rights over the disputed land the episodes may be related.

[80] The evidence in Sir John Lucas's account book of a sharp increase in the rental for the larger part of the disputed land at Lady Day 1641 suggests that the enclosure was very recent: Bedfordshire RO, L26/1457, pp. 7, 12, 16.

as several townspeople later dated it – a crowd of about a hundred
gathered in the streets of Colchester. They had been called together by
the blowing of a horn in Magdalene Street, a long street on which many
poor weavers lived, by a local miller, John Diglett. Diglett had gone from
house to house 'to gather company'. Thus assembled, they had processed
out of the town. The initial object of the crowd's attentions were
enclosures which Sir John Lucas had only lately erected on the heathland
at Rover's Tye. There the crowd pulled down and burnt hedges, rails,
posts and gates and spoiled and destroyed a great number of bricks,
faggots and a brickhill which had been made for Sir John. A little more
than two weeks later there was a further riot at Rover's Tye. According
to one witness, the crowd 'as soone as they had cryed out they had done,
called out lett us go to Parsons Heath', another area where Sir John
Lucas held enclosed land. They were dissuaded by a constable who had
been called to the scene, but on the 31 May another large crowd – some
said 200, others 400, strong – summoned again by the blowing of a horn,
did go to Parson's Heath. There they pulled down and burnt enclosures,
including those of Francis Bullock, a tenant of Sir John's in his Greenstead manor (who, incidentally, had taken Lucas's side in an earlier
dispute with his opponent Henry Barrington).[81] Witnesses talked of there
being so many fires that they could not count their number. These large
crowd actions were interspersed with actions on other days by smaller
groups who burnt posts and dug down mounds.

The identity of those assaulted reveals the real target for the crowd's
hostility. Of the three men attacked, one was a servant of Sir John Lucas,
one a brickmaker working for him who, together with the other victim,
was suspected of acting as his spy. This was violence by proxy. Some
rioters, it was claimed, had given out that they 'wished hartly that Sir
John Lucas had been there for they would have used him worse & would
have burnt him or ended him'. Others were alleged to have cried out, 'I
would Jack Lucas were here, they would burne him as they burned the
postes'. This public use of Jack to refer to Sir John Lucas was clearly
intended as a deliberate slight.[82]

The 31 May was Rogation Monday. Rogationtide was the point in the
year when parishes marked their physical boundaries. A ceremony that

[81] HLRO, MP HL, 27 July, 5 August 1641; CRO, D/B5, Sb2/7, fol. 286; T. C. Glines,
'Politics and government in the Borough of Colchester, 1660–1693' (Ph.D. thesis,
University of Wisconsin, 1974), p. 15; CRO, Acc. C47, GR 2; PRO, E134/8 and 9 Chas
I/Hilary 21.

[82] G. L. Apperson, *English Proverbs and Proverbial Phrases: A Historical Dictionary* (1927),
pp. 330–1; Morris Palmer Tilley, *A Dictionary of the Proverb in England in the Sixteenth
and Seventeenth Centuries* (Ann Arbor, 1950). Compare Bishop Wren's usage in speaking
of 'any upstart Jack gentleman in England': Heal and Holmes, *Gentry*, p. 343.

began with the minister pronouncing a biblical curse on those who had trespassed on their neighbours' lands and was followed by a procession around the parish frequently served in this period as the script for highly organised crowd actions against enclosure. Was this the case in 1641? The timing of the riot in Rogation Week is surely suggestive. The Rogationtide exhortation that 'it is the part of every good townsman to preserve as much as lieth in him, the liberties, franchises, bounds, and limits of his town and country' would have provided both text and occasion for this latest defence of common rights against the unneigh-bourly Lucas family.[83] As one of the rioters claimed, 'hee would shew as good evidence for the land as Sir John could'. That the Rogationtide ceremonies also served to mark out the moral boundaries of the local community would have added to its attraction as an occasion to denounce the unneighbourly behaviour of Jack Lucas.

The aftermath of the attack on the enclosures brought the running conflict between Sir John and the Corporation to a new intensity. The fact of the 'riot' now gave Lucas the opportunity to use the law to get back at his opponents. He immediately took the case to the House of Lords, forcing the accused to travel to London to answer his case against them.[84] This was in itself an affront to the Corporation's claim to exercise authority in the town and its liberties. But in seeking to have the action prosecuted before the Lords as riot, Lucas also sought to challenge the Corporation directly by implicating members of the Corporation in the destruction. Running through the depositions was the accusation that the plebeian crowd were set on work by their betters. John Theobalds deposed that as he sat with his wife by the door several weeks after the riots, she had accosted one Edward Byatt, a weaver, and told him that since Byatt had been at Parson's Heath he could tell who else was present. Byatt named John Rye as one who had given them sixpence and straw to kindle the fire, but said that 'before that hee would be punished hee would name other manner of men that sett them on worke then John Rye was or ever would be while he lived.' What Byatt's somewhat cryptic comment meant was made clear in other depositions. Several claimed that Thomas Lawrence, the chamberlain of Colchester, and Stephen King, a minor official, were present with their wives at the riot at Parson's Heath. The two men were seen to 'smile one upon the other' and Lawrence was heard to say to his wife, let us go 'for the game is now at his best'. King's wife was said also to have distributed money among some of the rioters.

[83] J. Griffiths (ed.), *The Two Books of Homilies Appointed to be Read in Churches* (Oxford, 1859), pp. 470–99; Walter, 'Crown and crowd', pp. 243–4.
[84] *LJ*/iv/272; HMC 4th, House of Lords MSS, p. 73.

Stephen King was himself a tenant of the Lucas manor of Greenstead. His presence suggests that there was opposition from some of the manor's tenants to the enclosures.[85] Since the Lucas family was the largest landowner in the immediate area around Colchester it was inevitable that members of the Corporation, as well as other townsmen, were tenants on their various manors. Several held land in the manors by which Lucas claimed the right to enclose the heathland. Both Henry Barrington and John Langley were tenants on Lucas manors. Mayor Wade and Alderman Daniel Cole, another of Bruno Ryves' 'conspirators' in the 1642 attack, also held Lucas land. The acknowledgement of their obligations to their lord may have proved irksome to men whose levels of wealth, landholding and standing in urban society accustomed them more often to acknowledge the deference of their dependants and inferiors. When that lord was the man with whom the Corporation had a running battle, then such feelings may have become even more pronounced. Much would have depended, of course, on Sir John's attitude to his role as lord of the manor. While the absence of detailed manorial records means that this is impossible to recover, the evidence of earlier conflict and his character suggests how he would have seen his role. It may well be significant that Barrington along with Stephen King were among those presented for default of view of frankpledge in 1639.[86] Lucas, however, was clearly trying to implicate those he had named as being behind the riots *as members of the town's rulers*. This claim is lent weight by the fact that the Corporation had a little over three months before sent a deputation to London to take legal advice, possibly in preparation for promoting a bill in Parliament, about the inclosures made by Sir John Lucas and others. (Who the other enclosers were is not known, but is it significant that only the Lucas enclosures appear to have been attacked?) Included in the deputation of four had been the Chamberlain, Thomas Lawrence.[87]

Whether or not the Corporation was involved in the attack on the

---

[85] CRO, Acc. C47, GR 2. Rye was a yeoman and previous church warden of Greenstead: ERO, D/ACV/5, fol. 24; BL, Additional MS 5505, fol. 61 r. However, the single allegation against John Rye needs to be set against the fact that he and his wife were also examined as witnesses on Lucas's behalf. Neither, however, list among those they saw at the riot the Edward Byatt who claimed to have received the money and straw from Rye.

[86] CRO, Acc. C47, GR 2; D/B5, Aa, 1/12; D/DRe Z1/2, fol. 6; D/Y, 2/10, pp. 71–2; D/Pa/[57], pp. 44–5; Acc. C47, GR 2; Bedfordshire RO, L26/1457, *passim*. King was a member of the frankpledge jury in October 1641.

[87] The reference to inclosures is tagged on to an order to send a committee to take councel about preferring a bill in Parliament for cutting a channel, repairing bridges and paving the streets. The manner of its insertion – following a full stop and being crammed in on top of the Mayor's signature – suggests that it was a late addition: CRO, D/B5, Gb3, fol. 211 v.

enclosures, the prosecution of the riot certainly became an occasion for continuing Lucas's conflict with both Corporation and commons. Lawrence and King, as well as several others accused of riot, were taken into custody, but not before the messenger sent from the House of Lords to bring up the accused was assaulted, together with a Lucas servant, in a 'broyle' in the streets of Colchester. Lawrence and King petitioned the Lords on 10 July, claiming that the Mayor had certified that they were not in town at the time of the riot and that they had had no hand in the riot. The ambiguities in the examinations taken locally suggest that the Corporation were prepared to bend the truth in their conflict with Lucas. Alderman Thomas Wade, mayor at the time of the 1641, as well as the 1642, attack, deposed that Lawrence had been at Norwich with him from 15 to 28 May (a statement which however did not exonerate Lawrence since the 'riot' at which he was said to have been present had taken place three days later).[88]

Lawrence and King's petition to the Lords brings out that underlying conflict was the familiar battle between Corporation and landed gentleman over power and jurisdiction. They alleged that indictments against the rioters had first been laid before the Colchester Quarter Sessions and that Sir John had promised to bring evidence before the local court but had failed to do so.[89] They wanted Sir John to be ordered to take his legal course by way of indictment before the local court, 'fforasmuch as all riots comitted in the Towne of Colchester are by the Charter of the towne graunted to them to enquire of, and to punishe'. Their intent was clear. Given the ill-feeling between Lucas and the town, a verdict delivered by a Colchester jury was hardly likely to find in his favour. Despite their petition, the Lords continued to hear the case and proceedings dragged on at least until August 1641, throwing up further occasions for conflict between Lucas and the Corporation.[90] Thus, a little over a year before the August attack Sir John Lucas's actions had angered both Corporation and commons. The resentments created by enclosure and the judicial aftermath in which Sir John had sought to use

---

[88] CRO, D/B5, Sb2/7, fol. 286; *LJ*/iv/293. Other witnesses deposed that King and Lawrence had only arrived after the destruction was over, that Lawrence had pulled away his wife and daughter when he found them there, and that King had reproved the crowd at Francis Bullock's for disturbing a sick man who was in the house.

[89] The relevant Quarter Session rolls which would permit a check on their claim do not survive. Is it significant that the form of words they chose did not necessarily imply that Sir John had initiated the indictments? The indictments may have been a pre-emptive move by the Corporation to head off action by Lucas.

[90] HLRO, MP HL, 10 July, 20 July, 5 August 1641; *LJ*/iv/293, 307, 312, 313, 317, 322. For a discussion of the Lords' attitude to cases involving enclosure riots, see J. S. Hart, *Justice Upon Petition: The House of Lords and the Reformation of Justice 1621–1675* (1991), pp. 164–9.

the opportunity to continue his conflict with the Corporation had their part to play in the later attack. The crowds in 1642 had good cause to 'teare his evidences'. The collision between Sir John's ambitions and the town's defence of its rights had produced exactly the alliance hinted at by *Mercurius Rusticus*.

A micro-history of relationships between the Lucas family and the town of Colchester suggests that there may indeed have been an inner-history to the attack on Lucas in 1642. Key members of the Corporation accused by Bruno Ryves in his account of the attack on St John's had a history of personal conflict with Sir John Lucas. In the two years before the August 1642 attack there had been an 'invasion' of St John's authorised by the then Mayor John Langley, and anger over enclosure had assembled crowds on the streets of Colchester who had proceeded to attack Lucas lands. It is likely that there were other sources of conflict for which evidence has not survived. Such was the relationship between the two parties that anything could become the occasion for continuation of the feud. But perhaps the most telling evidence about relations between family and town is the very silence at the heart of the records. Such a large household as that of the Lucas family[91] could not have avoided all contact with the town, but to judge by the evidence of the family's wills, as well as the Corporation's own records, the family had little to do with the town. Customary doles to the poor of the Lucas parishes apart, only clergymen appeared as beneficiaries from within the town in the Lucas wills.[92] It is possible that the Corporation granted Lucas freedom of the borough in 1636, the year that he was made sheriff.[93] But while other neighbouring gentlemen were careful to make presents of deer to the Corporation, the Lucases were noticeable by their absence from these ritual acknowledgements. Similarly, the Lucases did not receive those reciprocal gifts of sugar loaves which, as with corporations elsewhere, Colchester was careful to make to neighbouring gentry families like the Audleys of Berechurch or to county families like the Barringtons of Hatfield Broad Oak.[94] There was little sweetness and too much power in the relationship between Colchester and Sir John Lucas.

---

[91] In the survey of grain stocks taken by the town in 1608 the Lucas household numbered some thirty persons: in private possession, xerox copy CRO.

[92] Morant recorded an oral tradition attributing the building of almshouses in St Mary's parish to two sisters named Lucas, but as St Mary's was not the Lucas parish these may well have been of the family of the seventeenth-century town clerk of the same name: CRO, D/Y, 2/10, p. 4.

[93] CRO, Acc. C1, Index of Freeburgesses, book 1. Unfortunately the volume recording the admission has been lost since the compilation of this index.

[94] See, for example, the list for 1617: CRO, D/B5, Ab 1/8, rot. 20; Aa 1/12 (3 lbs sugar to

These fragments of evidence might then be taken to support Bruno Ryves' claim that Colchester's rulers were involved in stirring up the attack on St John's, and that in doing so they were seeking to settle scores, both personal and communal. As such they might also be taken to show that the politics of the attack on Sir John Lucas was local and personal – the politics of revenge. But to leave the analysis here would be extremely misleading. While the events of the summer of 1642 look like an example of familiar gentry-town conflict, there is yet another layer to the conflict that needs exposing. For the divisions of the 1642 attack can be mapped onto the broader religio-political conflicts. Sir John Lucas was an 'authoritarian royalist' and his conflicts with the Corporation and commons of Colchester were in part both an explanation for, and a consequence of, his political attitudes. Lucas's first-hand experience of the turbulence of urban and mercantile society doubtless made more attractive the Caroline image of the well-governed state which sought to elevate authority and order over 'popularity' and to bolster hierarchy in both church and society. Lucas's royalism was matched by the commitment of his opponents to the godly and Parliamentarian cause. The civil war was to reveal weighty support from within Colchester for the Parliamentary cause. As a royalist was to write of Colchester in 1648, 'this towne had beene long possest with the spirit of disobedience to the doctrine and discipline of the church'.[95] Colchester's reputation as a puritan citadel and the conflicts this created with royal and ecclesiastical administrations in the 1630s created another source of conflict with Lucas and his proxies, ministers appointed by Sir John to livings within the town. Since this confessional conflict came to focus on the role of Lucas's chaplain, Thomas Newcomen, it is dealt with separately in a later chapter.

In choosing to single out Barrington and Langley as most active in the attack against Lucas, Ryves chose well. They were two of the most important men among Colchester's rulers and it was they who led the godly Parliamentarian interest in the town in the 1640s and 1650s.[96] Their naming by Ryves points both to the role their histories suggest they might well have been expected to play in the August events and to the fact that Ryves was particularly well informed about Colchester's

---

Lady Audley, 5s. 6d.); F. W. Galpin, 'The household expenses of Sir Thomas Barrington', *TEAS*, NS, 12 (1913), p. 223; S. Mintz, *Sweetness and Power: the Place of Sugar in Modern History* (Harmondsworth, 1986), pp. 90–1.

[95] K. Sharpe, 'The Personal Rule of Charles I' in H. Tomlinson (ed.), *Before the English Civil War* (1983), pp. 53–78; Cust and Hughes, 'After revisionism', pp. 1–46; HMC MSS, Duke of Beaufort, pp. 19–30.

[96] C. Firth and R. S. Rait, *Acts and Ordinances of the Interregnum*, 3 vols. (1911), *sub* Barrington, H. and Langley, J.

politics. John Langley was a grocer, but that simple description, chosen by Ryves to appeal to the prejudices of his gentle readership, is a poor guide to Langley's wealth, power and status. His family may well have been of Flemish descent, but if so they had been integrated into Colchester society.[97] His father, Geoffrey, who died in 1624, had been a grocer and had held the highest office of bailiff in the borough. John inherited both calling and council membership, becoming an alderman in 1632, bailiff in 1633 and Mayor (the office replacing bailiff after the new charter of 1635) in 1640. Marriage cemented his links with his fellow rulers. He married three times, two of his three wives being daughters of fellow aldermen, Robert Talcott and William Mott. To the wealth trade as a grocer had brought his family, Langley had added landed interests in Colchester and elsewhere in the county. He had been among those forced to compound for not taking up a knighthood on the coronation of Charles I, and in the Visitation of 1634 Langley's claim to gentry status had been granted official recognition. Both his wealth and status were recognised in membership of the Colchester artillery company, a body whose leading hundred members at the time of the civil war were said to be worth some £100,000.[98]

Langley was also a member of Colchester's godly. His response when Mayor to the popish panic that broke out at Colchester in Whitsuntide 1640, discussed in detail in chapter six, suggests where his allegiances lay. According to an unnamed gentleman informant on those events, who criticised the Mayor for fomenting the panic, Langley was 'a man not long since in question before his M[ajes]ties Commissioners for Causes Ecclesiastical'.[99] Langley's religious commitment helps to explain his strong support from the outset for the Parliamentary cause. He was captain of the trained bands and shortly after the August events he led a group of Colchester volunteers to fight for Parliament. The letters he wrote to his fellow members of the Corporation reflect his zeal for the cause. Langley was undoubtedly one of Cromwell's 'men of spirit', 'a captain that knows what he fights for and loves what he

---

[97] Testamentary evidence makes clear that the John Langley who was one of the signatories of a letter in the name of the Dutch congregation (PRO, SP, 16/362/24) was not the same man, but it does not establish whether the two Johns were related: PRO, PROB, 11/219, fols. 336ff.

[98] CRO, D/B5, Cb1/7, fols. 208 v, 351; /9, fol. 153 v; *ibid.*, /10, fol. 546; *ibid.*, /11, fol. 112; F. Hull, 'Agriculture and rural society in Essex, 1560–1640' (Ph.D. thesis, University of London, 1950), appx 13, p. 629; *Visitations Essex*, 1, p. 433; CRO, Acc. C286, 112(a), p. 224; D/DRg1/226, p. 201; Sier, 'Greenstead Manor', p. 178; ERO, T/A 15, 18, 21, 22–3; Bodl. Lib., Rawlinson MS Top. Essex 1, fols. 116ff.

[99] PRO, SP, 16/458/13. This may explain why Langley's subsequent statement of events at Whitsuntide was described as an 'examination': 16/458/12. I have been unable to confirm Langley's appearance before the court of High Commission.

knows'.[100] A contemporary list of those in Colchester who subscribed to the expedition of the Earl of Essex in June 1643 included Langley, whose promise to contribute both himself and another man with horses for each was among the most generous of subscriptions. Throughout the 1640s and 1650s he combined his military role with holding office both within borough government (becoming Mayor again in 1646) and the Parliamentary regime.[101]

Langley's religious and political allegiances stretched beyond Colchester. His entry in the 1634 Visitation records the marriage of his daughter Margaret to a wealthy London trader in wool and silk. This was none other than John Venn, one of the leading London radicals in the events of the early 1640s. The links between Langley and Venn were reinforced by their common membership of the Artillery Company, an institution a later and hostile critic attacked as a meeting place for 'sectaries'. Venn was a Deputy President of the City of London Honourable Artillery Company; Langley had played an important role in the Colchester Artillery Company. If the identification is correct, John Langley became a member of the London Artillery Company in February 1640.[102] The links between Langley and Venn would have created channels of communication that throw fresh light on the events in Colchester and on Langley's part therein. For example, the close timing of popish panics in London and Colchester in 1640 may be explained by more than just Colchester's proximity to the capital. (Chance survivals reveal ties of kinship linking other members of Colchester's ruling group with London; there were probably more.)[103] Langley was known to be in London on several occasions in the early 1640s, including February 1641 when he was one of the deputation of

---

[100] CRO, D/Y, 2/8, p. 37; C. Hill, *God's Englishman: Oliver Cromwell and the English Revolution* (1970), pp. 65, 67.

[101] CRO, D/B5, Gb3, fol. 55v; D/Y, 2/8, p. 173; Bodl. Lib., Rawlinson MS Top. Essex 1, fol. 112; Firth and Rait, *Acts, sub* Langley, J.; J. G. A. Ive, 'The local dimensions of defence: the standing army and militia in Norfolk, Suffolk, and Essex 1649–1660' (Ph.D. thesis, University of Cambridge, 1987), p. 61.

[102] Anon., *Persecutio Undecima. The CHURCHES Eleventh Persecution. OR, A Briefe of the Puritan Persecution of the Protestant Clergy of the Church of England. Begun in Parliament, Ann. Dom. 1641* (1648), p. 56; G. A. Raikes, *The Ancient Vellum Book of the Honourable Artillery Company, Being the Roll of Members from 1611 to 1682* (1890), p. 57. It may however be that this was the London radical and sectarian of the same name: R. Brenner, *Merchants and Revolution: Commercial Change, Political Conflict, and London Overseas Trade, 1550–1653*, pp. 377, 539, 549, 630. If so, it has not been possible to establish whether there was a connection between the two Langleys.

[103] For example, in July 1640 Colchester's town clerk had contracted a marriage in London: G. J. Armytage (ed.), *Allegations for Marriage Licences Issued by the Bishop of London 1611–1828* (Harleian Society, 26, 1887), vol. 2, p. 252.

three sent to London by the Corporation to seek advice about Lucas's enclosures.[104]

The parallel between Venn's activities in London and Langley's actions in Colchester is very suggestive. Venn, a prominent member of the City's Common Council and an MP for the City in 1641, played an important role in helping to secure London for Parliament. In so doing, he had shown himself very willing to mobilise the London crowds to secure Parliament's objectives, playing a leading role in the circulation and presentation of petitions and in the organisation of political demonstrations in the City. The absence of any surviving correspondence for either Langley or Venn means we can only guess at what may have passed between them. However, given the shared political and religious identity it is possible to see Langley's role in Colchester mirroring that of Venn in London.[105] Both served as officers in Parliament's armies. Both were prominent members of the godly. Venn played a leading role in securing the City for Parliament and repeatedly mobilised the crowds and petitioners that allowed Parliament's leaders to push through their programme. Langley both in the Whitsuntide uproar and in the August attack seems to have been equally prepared to use popular pressure to secure godly and Parliamentarian interests.

This was not the full extent of John Langley's connections. Further evidence of his political and religious allegiances is provided by other of his family ties. His daughters Anne and Elizabeth both married Ipswich men. At least one of these, the clothier John Wade, seems to have moved in the same godly and well-affected circles. In 1637 he had acted as surety for an Ipswich clothworker who had been involved in the crowd who had attacked Bishop Wren's visitors in 1636 and had been accused of words against the bishop. The godly and Parliamentarian sympathies of members of Ipswich's ruling group like William Cage, Peter Fisher, Samuel and Robert Duncon paralleled those of Langley and Barrington. The regular links that existed between Colchester and Ipswich would have allowed for the exchange of information and views between the well-affected of the two towns. For example, the annual audit of the Colchester Hunwick charity by the Corporation of Ipswich entailed a formal meeting at either Colchester or Ipswich. One such meeting, taking

---

[104] HLRO, MP HL, 30 June, 5 July 1642; CRO, D/B5, Gb3, fol. 211 v. There may have been other links between the Langleys and London: John's great uncle, Christopher Langley, described as a merchant in his will, left bequests to three London friends, one of whom was John Wallington, citizen and ironmonger: F. G. Emmison, *Elizabethan Life 4: Wills of Essex Gentry and Merchants* (Chelmsford, 1978), pp. 294–5.

[105] V. Pearl, *London and the Outbreak of the Puritan Revolution: City Government and National Politics 1625–1643* (Oxford, 1961), pp. 126, 167, 175, 187–9, 216, 225–6, 234, 334; Brenner, *Merchants*, pp. 337, 356, 366, 370, 431, 484, 520, 548, 559, 605.

place in the August of 1640, would have allowed the two groups to exchange information about events in their respective areas, not least worries about the activities, real and rumoured, of catholics.[106]

Henry Barrington was also part of the godly Parliamentarian connection. A wealthy brewer and maltster, he also held land, some of it in the Lucas family manors. He came from one of the ruling families of Colchester – his father had twice been bailiff – and he in turn became one of the most important rulers of the town. A member of the first council in 1626, he became an alderman in 1628 and, like Langley, bailiff a year later. He was Mayor in 1637, 1641, 1648 and again in 1658. Barrington too played an important role in the local committees of the Parliamentary regime, serving also on the county committee and the committee for scandalous ministers. In the 1650s Barrington was the leader of the godly party in the borough and served as the town's MP in Barebone's Parliament. Like Langley, Barrington also had links with the godly elsewhere in the region. When Samuel Duncon, one of the leading supporters of the godly and Parliamentarian cause in Ipswich, wrote to the Mayor of Colchester in November 1642 advocating an association of the great towns in the region, he paid his respects to Henry Barrington. Barrington too was listed among those who subscribed to the Earl of Essex's expedition in June 1643. Thus whatever the nature of their personal conflicts, Barrington's political and religious allegiances placed him squarely in opposition to Sir John Lucas. While Lucas distinguished himself as a zealous collector of ship money in 1637, Barrington as Mayor in 1637–8 was in trouble with the government because of his failure to have paid in Colchester's ship money contribution.[107]

Other members of the Corporation implicated in Ryves' account had political and religious allegiances that placed them in opposition to Sir John Lucas's authoritarian royalism. The mayor at the time of the attack, Thomas Wade, was another active supporter of Parliament's military conflict with the king and an important member of the godly party in Interregnum Colchester. He had been in trouble with the ecclesiastical courts in the later 1630s for failing to receive Holy Commu-

---

[106] CRO, D/Y, 2/9, pp. 35, 129; F. Grace, '"Schismaticall and Factious Humours": opposition in Ipswich to Laudian Church Government in the 1630s' in D. Chadd (ed.), *Religious Dissent in East Anglia 3: Proceedings of the Third Symposium* (University of East Anglia, 1996), pp. 97–119.

[107] CRO, D/Pa/[57], pp. 44, 45; Acc. C47, GR2; D/B5, Cb1/8, fols. 194, 364, 439; /10, fol. 422; /11, fol. 400; Firth and Rait, *Acts*, sub Barrington, H.; BL, Additional MS 5829; G. Rickword, 'Members of Parliament for Colchester, 1603–1683', *ER*, 5 (1896), pp. 206–7; Round, 'Colchester and the Commonwealth', pp. 641–64; *ibid.*, *Register of the Scholars Admitted to Colchester School, 1637–1740* (Colchester, 1897), pp. 15, 43; CRO, D/Y, 2/7, pp. 221, 291; PRO, SP16/389/127.

nion, an action probably linked to the fierce dispute within the town over the Laudian policy of railing in the communion table.[108] John Furley junior, Ryves' 'young pragmatical boy', came from a large and wealthy Colchester family. Furley was the son of John senior, a linendraper and leading member of the Corporation, who had become alderman in 1635 and Mayor in 1638. The family's puritanism had brought it into conflict with the Laudian church and its local clerical supporter, Thomas Newcomen, and it doubtless earned John Furley his epithet from Bruno Ryves. Later, it led to strong support for Quakerism. John junior was another active supporter of Parliament. While his father subscribed for a fully equipped great horse and a dragoon with six weeks pay, John promised to go himself and to provide a man and musket with six week's pay on the Earl of Essex's expedition.[109] Finally, Daniel Cole, the man who was consulted by the crowd as to the fate of Thomas Newcomen in Ryves' account, had a similar, if less well-recorded, history. Cole was a member of the aldermanic bench and had served several times as bailiff and Mayor. He had extensive landed interests in Colchester and the surrounding villages, which on one occasion led ironically to his being a co-defendant with Lucas in a property dispute. He too had links by marriage with London. A bequest to the poor suggests that he and his family came originally from that centre of godly preaching, Dedham, a village in which he continued to hold land. In June 1638 he and his wife were presented to the archdeaconry court for not receiving communion above twice for the past two years and in the case of Cole himself refusing to kneel during divine service. Only his death, probably in 1643, prevented him from exhibiting the same commitment to the Parliamentarian cause as his fellow aldermen.[110]

Although the prior history of conflict did not determine political allegiances in the slide to civil war, the case study of Colchester does suggest how local and national divisions might come to be fused together. While Lucas hoped for personal gain from his allegiance to the king and expected access to the Privy Council and its backing in his various

---

[108] CRO, D/Y, 2/2, pp. 221, 230; Round, 'Colchester and the Commonwealth', pp. 647–8, 649n; ERO, D/ACA/52, fols. 234 v, 247; /53, fols. 9, 38 v.

[109] H. De B. Gibbins, 'The Furley family of Essex', *ER*, 8 (1899), pp. 86–95; Round, *Register*, pp. 12, 17, 43; Round, 'Colchester and the Commonwealth'; S. A. Golden, '*Bibliotheca Furliana* Revisited', *Journal of the Friends' Historical Society*, 50 (1962), pp. 72–6; C. R. Simpson, 'Benjamin Furley, Quaker merchant and his statesman friends', *Journal of the Friends' Historical Society*, 11 (1914), pp. 62–70; J. Besse, *A Collection of the Sufferings of the People called Quakers*, 2 vols. (1753), vol. 1, p. 194; CRO, D/Y, 2/2, p. 221.

[110] CRO, D/B5, Cb1/7–11; PRO, PROB 11/191, fols. 211ff.; E134/9, Car 1/E18; CRO, DRe Z1/2, fol. 6; ERO, D/ACA/53, fols. 17 v, 25.

disputes with the town, it was to Parliament that the Corporation turned when they sought to contest Lucas's enclosures. The necessarily incomplete histories of confessional identity and political allegiance suggest there were good grounds for Bruno Ryves to levy his accusations of involvement against Barrington, Langley and the others named in his account. For while these men had personal reasons to welcome the attack on Sir John Lucas, they also had important political and religious differences with him. It was their identity as members of the Parliamentary well-affected that made them obvious opponents of any attempt to raise royalist support. It was this that made it certain that they would oppose Sir John's attempted night ride.

David Rollison, in a study of a Gloucestershire clothing kin-coalition, has raised the deliberately provocative question of whether such groups 'expanded out, to colonise and interconnect in a genuinely national class in London in the decades before the civil wars?'[111] Bruno Ryves' account of the attack describes Barrington and Langley as riding to 'Townes of their owne Faction' to gather support to scotch Lucas's design.[112] Such shards of evidence as we do have suggest that there was in the eastern counties, as elsewhere in provincial England, a network of the well-affected that existed below, but connected with, the level of their better-recorded gentry counterparts. This network drew on ties of trade and kinship, but it also expressed 'new forms of community of "those that best rank with God"'. We can glimpse this in the example of the Essex preacher, Daniel Rogers, taking his Weathersfield congregation to hear sermons at Colchester and a whole series of other villages, in the circle of Essex and Suffolk gentry families represented in the dedication to one of the published works of John Rogers, preacher at Dedham, whose sermons were famous for their ability to draw the godly from a wide area, or in the clerical network that distributed the works of Prynne and other banned books in the 1630s.[113] A godly Parliamentarian connection ran through the towns and villages of the region. Correspondence around the elections to the Short Parliament provides evidence of the links – 'personal, mercantile and Puritan' – between the ruling group of a Suffolk town, Aldeburgh, and the merchant-landed circles around the Massachussets Bay Company. Such links might be found even below the level of the prosperous middling sort. The London woodturner Nehe-

---

[111] D. Rollison, *The Local Origins of Modern Society: Gloucestershire 1500–1800* (1992), p. 119.

[112] *MR*, p. 1

[113] James, 'Concept of honour', p. 92; T. Webster, *Godly Clergy in Early Stuart England: The Caroline Puritan Movement, c.1620–1643* (Cambridge, 1997), pp. 87, 269; J. T. Cliffe, *The Puritan Gentry: The Great Puritan Families of Early Stuart England* (1984), pp. 158–9.

miah Wallington had links with Essex and Suffolk, based partly on kinship and partly on trade and friendships with the godly of the region. Roger Thompson's work on the networks mobilised in migration to New England provides a wider glimpse of the potentialities of kinship and connection among the godly of East Anglia.[114]

Middling sort families like the Langleys and Barringtons lacked either the dynastic continuities or political visibility favouring the recording (and preservation of the record) of the behaviour and beliefs of the landed classes. This absence of records means that the motives and actions of even the wealthier middling sort in the politics of the period will be always under-represented. Nevertheless, the existence below the level of the gentry of those we might call well-affected 'honest radicals', and the multiplex links between them, suggest the need to qualify the judgement that the mobilisation of 1640–2 'derived mainly from the territorial influence of the country gentry'.[115]

There is then evidence to support Bruno Ryves' accusation that members of the Corporation were involved in the action against Lucas. It was not simply their own individual histories of conflict with Lucas and Newcomen that meant that they were ready to seize opportunistically on the chance to unleash the people on St Johns. It was both their individual religious and political beliefs and their collective experience as members of a Corporation locked into conflict with the aggressive Lucas that primed them to oppose Lucas's attempt to join the king. Moreover, there is evidence to suggest that they were not caught unawares by Lucas's attempted night flight. Amidst the uninformative entries of routine administrative matters that filled the Assembly Book of the Corporation, is an entry of an irregular meeting of a small number of aldermen on the 20 August 1642, the day we are told by the Mayor's letter that 'there was a greate report about our towne of some store of armes' sent to St John's. The entry noted the issue of one barrel of gunpowder and half a

---

[114] F. Grace, 'The elections at Aldeburgh to the Short Parliament of 1640', *SR*, 10 (1988), pp. 25–37; P. Seaver, *Wallington's World: A Puritan Artisan in Seventeenth-Century London* (1985), p. 191; R. Thompson, *Mobility and Migration: East Anglian Founders of New England 1629–1640* (Amherst, Mass., 1994).

[115] I use the phrase 'honest radicals' deliberately to echo the important earlier work of David Underdown (who is the author of the judgement cited here) in seeking out the supporters at the level of provincial and local society of the Revolution of 1648–9: ' "Honest" radicals in the counties 1642–1649' in D. Pennington and K. Thomas (eds.), *Puritans and Revolutionaries: Essays in Seventeenth-Century History Presented to Christopher Hill* (Oxford, 1978), pp. 186–205. Men like Duncon in Ipswich and Langley and Barrington were also part of Underdown's 'honest radicals' in 1648–9. For an important study that tries to uncover support for the Parliamentary regime at this level, see W. Cliftlands, 'The "Well-Affected" and the "Country": politics and religion in English provincial society, *c.* 1640–*c.* 1654' (Ph.D. thesis, University of Essex, 1987).

firkin of musket bullets for 'the public service of the town'. In the margin were the names of the eight aldermen who endorsed the action, among them Mr Wade, Mr Cole, Mr Barrington, Mr Langley and Mr Furley.[116]

This evidence suggests the need to revise existing accounts of the August attack. If, as seems likely, Bruno Ryves' detailed knowledge reflects information from Lucas or his circle, then of course his account with its attempt to blacken the name of leading Colchester inhabitants itself needs to be read as a continuation of the family's feud. But paradoxically independent evidence of the previous history of conflict between Lucas and the Corporation suggests that the account in *Mercurius Rusticus* may be closer to the truth than its partisan nature might suggest. By contrast, the emphasis on the unpredictable and uncontrollable role of the populace in the attack in Mayor Wade's letter (on which newsbooks and later historians have drawn) might be seen to have served to exculpate Colchester's rulers from precisely the accusation to which a knowledge of the bad blood between them and the Lucas family might have made them vulnerable. Pre-existing conflicts between Sir John Lucas and Colchester helped to fashion both the attack *and* its narrative. This does not of course rule out the possibility that events did turn into an uncontrolled attack, an issue which will we need to consider in a later chapter. But if this was the outcome, it may seriously misrepresent the origins, of events in Colchester in the summer of 1642.

[116] CRO, D/B5, Gb3, fol. 226 v.

4. The high politics of the attack on Sir John Lucas

A very great part of the Knights and Gentlemen of England in the several Counties (who were not Parliament Men) adhered to the King, except in *Middlesex, Essex, Suffolk, Norfolk, Cambridgeshire*, etc. where the King with his Army never came: And could he have got footing there, its like that it would have been there as it was in other places.

Richard Baxter.[1]

A kn[igh]t of Essex said that the County shewed not themselves for the kinge as others but yf the Commission of Array were executed in that County they should see what they would doe.

Walter Yonge's Long Parliament Diary.[2]

It has been customary to think of the counties of Essex and Suffolk as having been firmly in the Parliamentarian camp. As S. R. Gardiner could pronounce after briefly discussing the Stour Valley episode, 'in Essex Royalists were few'.[3] This assumption has deep roots and has caused not a few problems for those writing from within the region on its history, not least for Colchester's first historian, the loyal Tory parson, the Rev. Philip Morant.[4] But if we are to understand the full context for the

---

[1] *Reliquiae Baxterianae: Or, Mr Richard Baxter's Narrative of the Most Memorable Passages of His Life and Times*, ed. M. Sylvester (1696), p. 30.

[2] BL, Additional MS 18777, fol. 134a.

[3] Samuel Gardiner, *History of the Great Civil War* (1886), vol. 1, p. 12.

[4] P. Morant, *The History and Antiquities of the most ancient Town and Borough of Colchester*, 2 vols. (1748), vol. 1, p. 57: 'Thus from the whole course of History it appears that this Town, at least the Majority and the Governing part of it, were in the Parliament's Interests. So that they who, from the Resistance made by the town of Colchester against the Parliament's Forces should infer, that it was entirely loyal would be greatly mistaken'. Ironically, recent work suggests that there might have been a loyalist party within Colchester at the time of the second siege: G. Dann, S. Rowland and D. Wright, 'Civil war and political strife, 1642–48' in D. Stephenson (ed.), *Three Studies in Turbulence* (Colchester, 1976), pp. 7–9.

attack on Lucas we need to recognise that this identification owes too much to hindsight. Certainly, those charged with securing the region for Parliament in the difficult circumstances leading up to the clash of arms would not have shared this assumption. For the period from the late 1620s had revealed the existence of those in the region who were prepared to support actively the policies of the Crown in both church and state. Writing of the region later in the 1640s, Thomas May cautioned against assuming that the absence of military conflict in counties like Essex and Suffolk 'may be supposed to flow from the unanimity of their affections' for Parliament:

> for a great and considerable number of the Gentry, and those of the highest ranke among them were disaffected to the Parliament, and were not sparing in their utmost endeavours to promote the King's Cause, and assist his Force against it, which might have thrown those Countries (if not wholly carried them to the other side) into as much distraction, and sad calamity, as any other part of the Land hade felt.[5]

May's political sociology of allegiance in the eastern counties offers a clue which if pursued provides a deeper understanding the events of the late summer of 1642.

When Clarendon wrote of the attack on Sir John Lucas he implied that others were behind the attack. The 'common people' acted 'no doubt by the advice of their superiors'.[6] Since, as we have seen, Clarendon was following *Mercurius Rusticus*, he may have been doing no more than repeat his accusations. However, it is possible to suggest that there were indeed others besides Colchester's rulers who may have been sympathetic to the attack on Lucas. Lucas's strong identification with Charles I's ideal of authoritarian monarchy in the period of the Personal Rule, his role in a developing royalist movement in the region, and his public signs of support, made well before the aborted ride to Nottingham, for a military solution to the impasse with Parliament had all brought him enemies among the county's, as well as Colchester's, rulers. There were others, closely tied to Parliament in both the county and the capital, who had scores to settle with Sir John.

The collapse of Personal Rule apparently saw the region firmly in the control of those who would later support Parliament against the king. In Essex, the elections to the Short Parliament had seen the Warwick–Barrington connection emerge triumphant. In an election marked by

---

[5] T. May, *The History of the Parliament of England which began November the Third MDCXL with a short and necessary View of some precedent Years* (1647), bk 3, ch. 4, pp. 78–9.

[6] Clarendon, *History*, vol. 2, pp. 318–9.

heightened political tensions and a high level of popular participation,[7] Sir Thomas Barrington and Sir Harbottle Grimston had secured the seats for the county. In so doing they had defeated the Court candidate Henry Nevill, who had been part of the group of authoritarian royalists enforcing the unpopular policies of the 1630s. But their victory and the manner by which it had been achieved only served to expose divisions among the county's rulers.

Henry Nevill sent a detailed complaint to the Privy Council about the tactics used by the Earl of Warwick at the election.[8] Warwick, he alleged, had abused the powers of his Lieutenancy in ordering the captains of the trained bands to bring in support. Since they had power to charge people to supply arms none dared offend them, and by these means Warwick had gained many supporters. Similarly, Warwick had made good use of his extensive ecclesiastical patronage; 'those ministers who gave their voices for my lord of Warwick as Mr Marshall and others preached often out of theire own parishes before [the] ellection'. Finally, 'our Corporations of Essex Consistinge moste of puritans & haveing theire voyces' in electing their own MPs voted again in the county election. On the morning of the election itself, Barrington and Grimston had gone to the Earl of Warwick's lodgings which was surrounded by very large and exuberant crowds (in their thousands, Nevill claimed). In the midst of the acclamations of support, one man was applauded for reportedly saying, 'that if Nevill had the day they would teere the gentlemen to peeces', adding that 'there was a hundred more of his minde.' The man was apprehended, but even what to do with him became a cause of further division between the two groups. Lord Maynard entreated Sir Henry Mildmay of Chelmsford to take the man's bail since it was Maynard, with Lord Carlisle and their fellow gentry who were most affronted by the threatening speeches. However, Warwick (joined by two fellow JPs) took his bail 'to his great popular glorie'. The reference to Carlisle, the man later chosen by the king to head the royalist Commission of Array, gives a clear idea of the political divisions at issue here.[9]

It was precisely the greater political role events *and* Parliament's supporters allowed the people, and its growing association with disorder, that helps to explain the growth of a royalist party within the region. The

---

[7] The future royalist Sir Humphrey Mildmay noted in his diary that, 'there was such a Multitude of all sortes of people as I never before sawe': BL, Harleian MS 454, fol. 3.

[8] PRO, SP, 16/449/48. For evidence of Warwick's activism in the elections to the Long Parliament, see Anon., *Persecutio Undecima. The CHURCHES Eleventh Persecution. OR, A Briefe of the Puritan Persecution of the Protestant Clergy of the Church of England. Begun in Parliament, Ann. Dom. 1641* (1648), p. 56.

[9] Northamptonshire Record Office, Finch-Hatton MS 133 (I am grateful to Christopher Thompson for lending me a xerox copy of this reference).

reaction of Nevill, a man who like Lucas lived close to the cloth communities, suggests that in Essex, as has been argued for elsewhere, a royalist party of order recruited support from those industrial and wood-pasture areas where plebeian independence both before and after the climacteric of 1640 alarmed gentlemen.[10] What runs strongly through Nevill's account is his detestation of the role of the people in the election and of Warwick's acceptance of this. Discussing the double vote exercised by the inhabitants of the boroughs, Nevill splutters, 'itt is more then the greatest lord of England hath in theire burrowes [boroughs]. The multiplicetie of those people are meane Conditioned and most factious and few publique men and therefore noe waie conserned in the ellection'. Nevill's reference to 'publique men' makes explicit his belief that the people had no claim to share in the exercise of power. Nevill was descended from late fifteenth-century yeoman stock enriched by law and by marriage into the family of a London grocer (a fact the family hid with a claim to descent from Richard I's Standard Bearer). But unconscious of any irony, he objected to the way that inflation, having reduced the amount of land represented by the franchise qualification of the forty shilling freehold, had allowed those who were not even wealthy enough to feature in the subsidy lists to claim as great a voice as any [i.e. gentlemen] in the elections for the county.[11] If the qualification for a vote was raised to twenty pounds (supposedly the seventeenth-century equivalent of the original qualification) Nevill concluded, 'it were a great quiet to the state ... & then gentlemen woulde be looked uppon' and, he added sarcastically, 'itt would save the ministers a greate deale of paines in preacheing from their owne Churches'.

That Nevill's distaste for the people and popularity was more widely shared among the proto-royalist group is confirmed by the reaction of the group's leader, Lord Maynard, to the same set of events. In a letter written to the successful candidate, Sir Thomas Barrington, Maynard acknowledged the respect Barrington had shown him and all persons of quality throughout the election.[12] However, the rest of the letter was devoted to a diatribe against the role allowed Maynard's inferiors:

> when I found the rude vulgar people to grow to that insolencye of from striking of private men to fall to menacing of us all to pull us in peeces, I held it neither fitt in point of honor, nor safe to our persons to pass over in silence, but (being armed with authority) to express as well as my scorne & contempte thereof as my resolution to punish it

---

[10] A. Hughes, *The Causes of the English Civil War* (1991), p. 145.

[11] J. H. Round, *Peerage and Pedigree: Studies in Peerage Law and Family History*, 2 vols. (1910), vol. 2, pp. 202–13.

[12] BL, Egerton MS 2646, fol. 142.

severely w[i]thout respect to their multitudes. And besides when I found soe much undervaluing of my self in particular, not only from the inferior people, but from some whose outsides showed them to bee men of better breeding, as that they would neither soe much as make place for mee uppon the Bench nor shew any respect unto mee as I passed through the streets, I was constrained contrary to myn owne nature to teach them their dutyes not holding it fitting that my Mayster's honor [i.e. the king], and the place wherin I serve him should suffer through disrespect to my person ... I shall not easily suffer my self her[e]after uppon the perswasions of others to appeare in any popular assemblies whear fellowes without shirts challenge as good a voice as myself.

The tone of Maynard's letter is exactly that of Nevill's. Both objected to what they regarded as the slights they had received at the hustings – and elsewhere perhaps.[13] Both go on to generalise from this experience that politics was the prerogative of gentlemen. 'Fellows without shirts' should not be allowed to 'challenge as good a voice', people 'meane Conditioned and most factious' should not be permitted a say in the election of their betters.

For Maynard, Nevill, and their allies the unpleasant experience at Chelmsford represented an inversion of hierarchy. For these members of the county elite at least selection, not election remained the preferred process for choosing representatives.[14] And that process should be guided by due concern for the imperatives of honour and deference. While Maynard had to struggle to secure a place on the Bench – and not just any place, but one whose position signalled his precise placing within the pecking order of the county – his fellow Lord Lieutenant, the Earl of Warwick, as Nevill had observed, commanded room to be made in the Sessions Hall for Daniel Rogers, the silenced godly minister of Wethersfield. Warwick and Barrington were more prepared to acknowledge the right of the people to participate in the election and to accept therefore the need to canvass popular support. They may also have seen the

---

[13] Some time before mid-April, 'a notorious Scandall' had been raised against Maynard. Since the author was James Powley, the curate of Dunmow Priory and a Scot, who was ordered to make a public submission at the Assizes and to make a profession against the Covenant in Scotland, it seems probable that the scandal concerned Maynard's religio-political stance. No details survive of the libel, but given Maynard's Arminianism and chapel-building activities, it may not be too fanciful to wonder whether it included the smear of catholicism: PRO, PCR, 2/52, fol. 217 v; N. Tyacke, *Anti-Calvinists: The Rise of English Arminianism, c. 1590–1640* (Oxford, 1987), pp. 192–4. Nevill's religion had been the subject of popular speculation around the time of the electioneering, for which see below, p. 216.

[14] M. A. Kishlansky, *Parliamentary Selection: Social and Political Choice in Early Modern England* (Cambridge, 1986).

collapse of support for Maynard and others, a group perhaps more dependant on Crown patronage for their position in the county, as the restoration of a more 'natural' hierarchy. Perhaps not too much should be made of this difference. The letters of Maynard and Nevill need to be read as texts produced by a defeated party. Parliamentary selection, rather than election, may have been argued to be the norm, but even Maynard and the others would have recognised that already by 1640 in the county and its boroughs there was some discrepancy between normative order and political reality. On the other side, Warwick and Barrington were by no means democrats. Nonetheless, these caveats apart, there was a real difference here between the two groups. Barrington was the son of a man, Sir Francis, who had enjoyed electoral support among clothiers and minor gentry, and he himself enjoyed good relations with the burghers of Colchester. Warwick had been careful to treat the urban elite at Colchester with a show of consideration for their own claims to status, and he had also shown a willingness to ally himself with the town's freemen to secure his objectives.[15]

After the disorders of the election, the region was to experience at first-hand a whole series of disorders and, thanks to the collapse of censor-ship, to read or hear of others elsewhere, not least in the capital. The first of these were the mutinies among the troops assembled to fight the Scots. Essex was among those counties the Earl of Northumberland described, 'as so damnablie resti[v]e that I doubt we shall not gett neere our numbers of men from those places'. Trouble at the rendezvous in Chelmsford in the last week of June had led to fisticuffs between some of the soldiers and deputy lieutenants.[16] The troops may have been a notorious source of disorder, but here they were not simply defying authority. In striking the Deputy Lieutenants, they were flouting the respect for person which the English landed classes had used to secure acceptance of their rule over their inferiors. Worse yet, at the summer Assizes the county's rulers had seen the indictment (and acquital) of a husbandman for saying, 'if I were prest for a souldier the Kinge should be the first that I would ayme att'.[17] Problems of pay were a perennial

[15] R. Cust, 'Politics and the electorate in the 1620s' in R. Cust and A. Hughes (eds.), *Conflict in Early Stuart England: Studies in Religion and Politics, 1603–1642* (1989), p. 161. Among Barrington's expenses for the election was a payment of six shillings to the Colchester waits: Galpin, 'The household expenses of Sir Thomas Barrington', *TEAS*, NS, 12 (1913), p. 211.

[16] PRO, SP, 16/457/5; SP, 16/451/93; /459/36; /460/63; PC, 2/52, p. 616; BL, Harleian MS 383, fol. 176 v (I am indebted to Christopher Thompson for this last reference).

[17] PRO, SP, 16/451/93;/459/36; /460/63; /427/30, 35; PC, 2/52, p. 616; ERO, 'Calendar of Essex Assize Files', AF, 35/81/T/9. That this was an isolated case raises all the probems of extrapolating from single instances to more general popular attitudes, but the point here is that in the face of growing disorder early modern magistrates would surely have

source of protest, but dispersed to various towns the troops' actions displayed a novel (and hence worrying) ambition to intervene in the religio-politics of the period. As Lord Maynard informed the Privy Council, they have 'taken uppon them to reforme Churches'. The troops, many of them recruited locally, proceeded to process round the churches in the areas where they were stationed in the region. Altar rails were torn down and burned, images smashed, ministers menaced. Operating at the invitation of, or in tandem with, sections of the local parish, the troops set an example that was to be copied by others. A wave of iconoclasm in Essex and Suffolk continued into 1642.[18]

The differences in attitude apparent among the county's rulers in the elections were also apparent in differing reactions to these disorders. The Earl of Warwick's reports on the troop disorders reflect a confidence in his ability to control them, a confidence built on his power in the county and his popularity among the troops. When a group of soldiers were toasting Warwick's health, one soldier, William Bates, at his turn had cried, 'Here's a health to my lord of Warwick, King of Essex'. When later questioned, he justified it by saying that he 'would pledge it because he did heare that he was as a King in Essex'. When Warwick was forced to acknowledge the problem, there was a difference of tone from Maynard's anxious report. Warwick told the Privy Council, that 'although I use the best meanes I can to back their officers yet I find they have gott such a hand of them that they dare not displease them'. But he stressed, the soldiers 'had been reasonably quiet' until the rector of Bocking had sent them beer and money.[19] Drunkenness was often a pretext by which offenders in early modern England were allowed to escape the consequences of their otherwise criminal actions. Warwick, who had arrested his celebrant William Bates and the ringleader of the Bocking iconoclasts, took care to let the Privy Council know that the troops had told him that if any but he had arrested them they would have risen *en masse*. He also took the opportunity to report the troops' suspicions about the religion (i.e. possible popishness) of their officers.

It is of course likely that Warwick had some sympathy with the troops' iconoclasm.[20] But what was necessary reformation to the godly, was to

regarded any such statement with concern. That the husbandman was acquitted may be a further example of the 'Catch 22' that in monarchical cultures such statements were thought literally unthinkable.

[18] PRO, SP, 16/451/74; /453/48; /454/45–6; /456/42; /457/23, 104; 16/461/24; Bodl. Lib., Tanner MS 91, fol. 65; J. Walter, 'Abolishing superstition with sedition: iconoclasm in the early 1640s' (in preparation).

[19] PRO, SP, 16/459/27; PRO, SP, 16/461/25.i; PRO, SP, 16/461/24, 25.

[20] As early as 1626 Warwick had arranged for his former curate, Hugh Peter, to preach a sermon criticising the idolatry and superstition of the king's catholic wife. He later

others 'abolishing superstition with sedition'. By contrast, Maynard, an Arminian patron who counted Laud a close friend, had no sympathy with the troops' objectives. He was clearly frightened by the consequences of their actions, as his anxious correspondence with the Privy Council reveals. On the 22 July, Maynard wrote from the Assizes at Chelmsford to the Privy Council informing them of the complaints he had received, 'of many great Outcryes committed by the Soldiers in those places where they are billited, w[hi]ch doe daily increase the longer they stay'. Five days later, Maynard, though 'not a little ashamed that I am thus often troublesome unto your L[ordshi]ps about one and the same thing', felt compelled to write again about the soldier's disorders which 'doe every day increase by new attempts'. In late July Maynard had had to go to Saffron Walden in the north-west of the county to try to pacify the troops there. It had proved an unnerving experience. Amongst other troubles, a group of soldiers had struck down and robbed one of their officers. According to one report, 'My Lord Maynner [Maynard] when he was in Saffern walden to see ye Soulgers cotted, hee being afraid of the Soulgers because they came about him, Hee tooke out a handfull of mony and hurlled it one the ground & so set the Solgers a Scramelling for it and then set Spur to his Horsse and ride away with all the forse he could'.[21] Maynard had written again to the Privy Council in August, this time about the circulation among the Essex troops of a seditious pamphlet supporting the Scots, *Information from the Scottish Nation to all the true English*. The pamphlet was one of a number that had been shown to the troops by a Suffolk clothier, Edward Cole, who had obtained them from London, furnishing a further example of how the cloth industry's strong links with London made the dissemination of information from the capital so easy. Three days later, Maynard wrote again about the same incident, endorsing the letter, 'Hast[e], hast, hast post hast' and even noting on it the hour at which he had dispatched it.[22]

opposed the attempt of the Lords to moderate the Commons' order suppressing superstitious innovations in churches, while his allies in the Commons, Sir Henry Mildmay and Sir William Masham, had acted as tellers for those voting against the addition of a clause to prevent abuse of the prayer book and tumultuous disorders arising from the order: C. Thompson, 'Court and country: the Earl of Warwick and the government of Essex, 1619–1629', p. 24 (I am grateful to Christopher Thompson for allowing me to see this unpublished MS); S. Lambert, 'The beginning of printing for the House of Commons, 1640–42', *The Library*, 6th ser., 3 (1981), p. 50; Thompson, 'Committees, religion, and Parliamentary authority in early Stuart England', *EHR*, 40 (1990); *LJ*/iv/392; *CJ*/ii/279.

[21] Tyacke, *Anti-Calvinism*, p. 193; PRO, SP, 16/461/24; 463/27; BL, Additional MS, 21,935, fol. 89 v.

[22] PRO, SP, 16/464/79; /465/4. Another clothier with the same surname was in trouble at the same time. Samuel Cole and John Crosse, both clothiers of Dedham, had been involved in an argument in a London tavern which began with a military man asking

Perhaps the most intimate indicator of Maynard's fears is provided by his will. Before going to suppress the disorders Maynard had added a long codicil to his will in late June 1640, 'considering the late outrages, committed by insolent and disorderly persons uppon others' and in case he should 'come to an untymely end'. By the end of 1640 Maynard was dead. According to his wife, the injuries he had received while suppressing the troops, which had 'kindled all the summer in his blood', were the cause of 'his violent fever, and consequently of his soddaine death'.[23]

Suffolk's rulers were doubtless also polarised by their differing attitudes to popular interventions. There too the deputy lieutenants had first-hand experience of plebeian disregard for the respect hierarchy ought to command from the mustering troops, reporting that 'many mad pranks they have played which are not fitt to bee written'. Sir William Playter, who seems to have been the focus of an unsuccessful attempt to oppose the godly candidates, Sir Philip Parker and Sir Nathaniel Barnardiston, in the shire elections for the Short Parliament, had been 'much abused by these rogues'. In the fiercely contested elections to the Long Parliament, Henry North, the son of Sir Roger North who had also been active in the county during the Personal Rule, was defeated by Parker and Barnardiston. The Ipswich godly had been active in their cause. As in the case of the Essex elections, North and his supporters resented this plebeian role in their defeat. Sir Roger North had led a group of gentry up and down the town. Marching through the corn market to the cry of 'a North, a North', they had assaulted the sailors there, deriding them as 'water doggs'. After the election of Parker and Barnardiston, one hostile minister was reported, 'to scornefully say that none did chuse them but leathercoats, scarecrows and squirrel hunters'.[24]

Both the fact of popular violence and the knowledge that it asserted the right of the people to have a say in areas from which they had been excluded, generally in theory and largely in practice, worried sections of the gentry. Gentry worries were doubtless increased by the knowledge of popular disorders in the capital, for enjoying so many links with London

them 'if they were Puritans' and had ended with their arrest on an allegation of speaking words favourable to the Scots: PRO, SP, 16/466/93; /467/14–15.

[23] PRO PROB, 11/185, fol. 195 v; A. Kingsford, 'Essex and the civil war' in A. Clifton Kelway (ed.), *Memorials of Old Essex* (1908), p. 160 n.

[24] PRO, SP, 16/456/42, 77; /457/104; /459/95; Bodl. Lib, Tanner MS 65, fol. 124, MS 69, fol. 4, MS 115, fol. 131; Holmes, *Eastern Association*, pp. 22–3; T. Carlyle, 'An election to the Long Parliament' in his *English and Other Critical Essays* (1915), pp. 100–26; BL, Harleian MS 97, fols. 8 r–v, MS 158, fols. 286–94 r; P. Pinckney, 'The Suffolk elections to the Protectorate Parliaments' in C. Jones, M. Newitt and S. Roberts (eds.), *Politics and People in Revolutionary England* (Oxford, 1986), p. 205; C. Holmes, *The Suffolk Committees for Scandalous Ministers 1644–1646* (Suffolk Records Society, 13, 1970), p. 98.

knowledge of events in the capital were spread rapidly through the region, not least by the newsbooks appearing in number after the collapse of censorship. The example of a churchyard conversation in an Essex parish in early 1640 suggests the importance of proximity to the capital in raising the political temperature. Informing his fellow parishioners of the attack on Archbishop Laud's house, one man predicted, 'they would rise in the Country and yt there was no lawes now'.[25] The anxiety generated by such statements was in its turn to become a major factor in the way local elites responded to the unfolding of events in the early 1640s, responses to it increasingly determining political allegiances. Reactions to iconoclasm among the Essex magistracy provide one telling example of this. Dr Cliftlands has argued persuasively that it was their future political allegiances as royalist or Parliamentarian that determined the magistrates' sharply contrasting verdicts at the special sessions held in Essex to try those accused of pulling down altar rails.[26]

There were then important differences among the rulers of the region in their response to the interactions of heightened political and religious tensions and to the more active popular involvement these allowed. For example, the royalist Sir Humphrey Mildmay wrote in his diary of, 'the foolery and Impiety of the Earl of Warwick and his Rabble', his favoured phrase when talking of popular support for the Parliamentary cause.[27] Those like Maynard and Nevill, (and undoubtedly Sir John Lucas) who regarded honour and respect for hierarchy as the central values by which all political and social relationships should be governed looked on the involvement of the people in the political process as an unwelcome intrusion.[28] Lord Maynard's letter with its emphasis on his need to defend the yoked honour of himself and his master, Charles I, echoed Sir

---

[25] PRO, SP, 16/468/139.

[26] The troops that pulled down the rails at Kelvedon, Bradwell and Great Braxted were tried before the future royalists Sir Benjamin Ayloffe, Sir Thomas Wiseman and Sir William Maxey and found guilty. At the sessions which dealt with the incidents at Elmstead, Great Holland and Church St Osyth, presided over by the future Parliamentarians, Sir Harbottle Grimston and his eponymous son, all the indictments were dismissed. Cliftlands is careful to point out that other factors may have been involved – those indicted at the first inquest were soldiers and mostly not from the immediate locality, while those at the second were local men – but the contrast seems telling: W. Cliftlands, 'The "Well-Affected" and the "Country": politics and religion in English provincial society, c. 1640–c. 1654' (Ph.D. thesis, University of Essex, 1987), pp. 150–1.

[27] BL, Harleian MS 454, fol. 54; cf. P. Lee Ralph, *Sir Humphrey Mildmay: Royalist Gentleman, Glimpses of the English Scene 1633–1652* (New Brunswick, 1947), p. 152.

[28] In Maynard's case, it has been suggested that his experience of holding estate and authority in a region whose social structure favoured deferential relations, encouraged him to expect his authority to be obeyed more generally: R. Cust, *Forced Loan and English Politics 1626–1628* (Oxford, 1987), pp. 275–6. By contrast, for Lucas it may have been the very absence of such patterns of deference in a region dominated by the cloth industry that encouraged the emphasis he gave to honour and hierarchy.

John Lucas's assertion of this central value in his dealings with his social inferiors. In the case of Lucas, Maynard and Nevill their ideas seem to reflect that model of social and religio-political order identified with the Court culture of Charles I. This was a political culture which detested popularity and valued hierarchy and order.[29] Although these values might be said to be commonplace amongst the landed classes, the elevated emphasis they received under Charles I must have seemed all the more attractive to this group and others like them, especially when contrasted with the social and political inversions they now faced.

As both Maynard and Nevill's letters make clear they drew little distinction between the role of the people in the elections and in the troubles that began in 1640. They thought of both of them in terms of disorder. Nor from their position at the top of the county's social and political hierarchy did they seem to make much distinction between the groups which went to make up 'the people'. For them, the most important characteristic of wealthy clothier and humble artisan was that which they shared in common – lack of gentle status. But while their objections to the intrusion of the people was based in part on social prejudice, they were also based on real political and religious differences. Doubtless their hostility to an active role for the people encouraged a predisposition to exaggerate the seditious and disorderly nature of popular politics in the county. Reality for them however was bad enough. The late June mutiny at Chelmsford had seen the social distance between gentry and people breached in a way that few would have thought possible. A deputy lieutenant who had struck some of the mutineers for their insolent language had had his blows returned. This was perhaps the most worrying aspect of events and the one most difficult for historians to recover: the denial of the quotidian rituals in the social grammar of speech and behaviour by which the ruled acknowledged their rulers' 'superiority'. Contemporaries like Maynard and Lucas feared that such transgressions of bodily behaviour threatened popular transgression of the body politic.[30]

Thus, while Parliament's supporters had secured the county, they had done so at the cost of allowing their opponents to argue that it was achieved through a triumvirate of popular disorder, puritan preaching and political and social inversion. Ironically, the means and moment of

[29] Cust and Hughes, *Conflict*, pp. 21–4; J. Davies, *The Caroline Captivity of the Church: Charles I and the Remoulding of Anglicanism 1625–1641* (Oxford, 1992), pp. 18–23; K. Sharpe, 'The image of virtue: the court and household of Charles I, 1625–1642' in D. Starkey *et al.*, *The English Court from the Wars of the Roses to the Civil War* (1987), pp. 226–260.
[30] PRO, SP, 16/459/36; /457/104; BL, Harleian MS 383, fol. 176 r; PRO, SP, 16/459/36.

their victory had set in train a process that would persuade increasing numbers of the gentry of the region to turn to the king as the only guarantor of their property and status. While the supporters of Charles' Personal Rule had been defeated in the elections to Parliament, the swing of events thereafter, both at the centre and in the counties, offered them scope for renewed action. It afforded them the possibility of recruiting all those who were worried by the drift of Parliament's policies and by popular disorder, the two seemingly increasingly causally connected. This was to prove the Achilles' heel of Parliament's cause within the region. The months before the summer attacks saw a concerted drive by the royalists, building on the platform provided by those who had supported the period of Personal Rule, to recruit support. Sir John Lucas's night ride clearly came out of this movement. Responses to it therefore need to be set in the wider context of reactions to the larger royalist campaign.

Essex was among those counties close to London in which the activities of a proto-royalist movement caused concern to Parliament's leaders. In September 1641, Sir Thomas Barrington, back in Essex from the Commons, was worried by the opposition to Parliament's proceedings, 'by a Comixture of malcontents severally disaffected'.[31] When in April 1642 Parliament took action against the 'malignant and ill-affected Party' behind the Kentish petition, a move was made to empower the committee to consider any further such petitions from any county 'and especially of Essex (some intimation being given of that county ...)'. Since the Kentish petition, calling for the settling of the militia by agreement between king *and* Parliament and the restoration of order in the Church, had seen the emergence of a more obviously proto-royalist party, it might seem that something similar was afoot in Essex.[32]

The discovery among the papers of Henry Nevill of two drafts of an Essex petition to the king, dating probably from late 1641, casts new light on this movement. The first petition, in Nevill's own hand, served as a draft for the second.[33] It was described as being from, 'the justices of

---

[31] Beinecke Library, Yale University, Osborne Collection, Sir Thomas Barrington to Lord Howard of Escrike, 24 September 1641. (I am grateful to Christopher Thompson for lending me his transcript of this document.)

[32] *CJ*/ii/536–7; *PJ*, 2, pp. 198–9. For the Kentish petition, see A. Everitt, *The Community of Kent and the Great Rebellion 1640–1660* (Leicester, 1966), pp. 95–107. For the broader context of petitioning in defence of episcopacy, see A. Fletcher, *The Outbreak of the English Civil War* (1985), pp. 284–90.

[33] Leicestershire RO, DE 221/13/2/21 and /26. The heading to the first draft gives the date as No[vember] 1641. That the Quarter Sessions referred to in the petition took place on the 5 October 1641 and the reference to the destruction of church glass probably refers to

the peace & gentrie with divers of the inhabitants of the County of Essex both Clargy & layetie', but this comprehensive attribution had been changed on the more polished draft to 'divers Justices of the peace'. The change confirms that the petition was the work of a faction within the county magistracy and suggests that it had failed to attract the wider support claimed in the first draft. In the absence of signatures it is not possible to identify the group responsible, but the role of Nevill in its drafting as well as the tone of the petition makes it clear that it came from those who opposed the godly Parliamentarian leadership within the county. Nevill's first draft was full of phrases characteristic of his contempt for his inferiors, talking for example of the 'multitude whose minds are set uppon novelties rather than any set[t]led govermente'. The petitioners claimed that since a dispute at the county's Quarter Sessions amongst the Grand Jury had prevented the punishment of depravers of the prayer book, 'the unlimited conceite of the Com[m]on people doe[s] dayly increase & produce very ill effects both in the Church & civell govermente'. At the end of the first draft was a list giving specific examples of disorders in Essex churches. These ranged from attacks both verbal and physical on the prayer book, through acts of iconoclasm, to the practices of 'sedicious sectaries'. Although no copy of the petition appears to have survived, there appears to have been a near contemporaneous attempt to organise a petition 'in the behalfe of Episcopacy' in Suffolk.[34] Clearly, in a region that had witnessed a high-level of iconoclasm and attacks on ministers, those who sought to raise support for the king were seeking to emphasise the larger threat this disorder posed to state and society. The polemical purpose of the petitions was very clear, that from Essex calling for the settlement of 'that forme of worship w[hi]ch hath bene the Cement & Union of Church and state'.

Into 1642, these divisions became more apparent as king and Parliament sought more openly to recruit support. Royal intransigence and Parliament's need to embark on more radical measures made it easier still for Parliament's opponents in the region to accuse it of promoting policies prompting popular disorder. When Sir Thomas Barrington with other solidly Parliamentarian Essex MPs had been sent down to the county in early June to see the militia ordinance – Parliament's radical claim to sole military authority – put into effect, he had informed the House, that he 'understood from divers places in Essex that they were much staggered with the late proclamation which his majesty had set forth against the putting in execution the ordinance touching the militia'.

the iconoclasm at Chelmsford on the 5th of November suggests that the petition was drawn up late in 1641: ERO, Q/SR, 314; PRO, ASSI, 35/84/10/24.
[34] Bodl. Lib., Tanner MS 66, fol. 181.

But the concern Parliament's supporters in the county had shown – 'doubting their owne strength', according to one report – to get Parliament to release the Earl of Warwick from his duties with the Navy in order to allow him to return to the county, and the instructions given to the Essex MPs to report on any Deputy Lieutenant who refused to comply, reflect the anxieties these moves aroused. An Essex gentleman who had declared that all those who went to the militia muster were rebels was swiftly reported to the Commons, and Sir William Masham, brother-in-law of Sir Thomas Barrington and ally of Warwick, moved that the offender be summoned to answer before the Commons. When the militia ordinance was put into effect a petition promising their lives in support of the Parliament was subscribed by the assembled troops, circulated in the county the following week for wider subscription, and presented to the Commons by Sir Thomas Barrington. Ten-thousand were said to have signed and, it was claimed, more would have signed had there been sufficient time. This was clearly a deliberate exercise in political propaganda designed to gain doubters for Parliament and to silence potential support for the king. Parliament used its control of the presses to have the petition – with its denunciation of malignants and belief in a plot to subvert the subject's religion, laws and liberties – printed.[35]

These moves were an attempt to force as much as to represent public opinion in order to counter the activities of royalists in the region. It is clear that there were also organised movements afoot in the region to try to raise support for the king. Proclamation, pulpit and petition were all used as part of a concerted campaign to recruit royalist support.[36] In mid-June the Sheriff of Essex had presented to the Commons royal proclamations he had been ordered to publicise. The most worrying of these was that of 27 May prohibiting the raising of the militia under the militia ordinance. The Commons, with the Essex MPs active, carefully thanked the Sheriff and quickly secured a declaration forbidding the reading in the county of any proclamations against the militia ordinance. On the 7 July, the House heard from Sir Thomas Barrington that the

---

[35] *CJ*/ii/pp. 586, 588, 589, 597–8, 605, 628, 629–30; *LJ*/v/pp. 85, 141–3; *PJ*, 2, 368, 375, 380, 395, 398–9; *PJ*, 3, pp. 17–18, 89; Bodl. Lib., Tanner MS 63, fol. 43; HLRO, MP HL, 17 June 1642. Is it possible that a later hostile report, claiming that Warwick and Barrington, 'sent into Essex to raise the Country, told the people in publick meetings, that the Queene was landed with an Army of 13000 Papists', refers to this episode? If true, the attempt to mobilise anti-popery reflected anxieties over whether Parliament could carry opinion with it as it was forced to take measures which could no longer be legitimised as acts of restoration: *Persecutio Undecima*, p. 67.

[36] For the wider context to this attempt to gather support for the king, see Fletcher, *Outbreak*, ch. 9.

Mayor of Colchester had also received royal proclamations. (Might we detect the hand of Sir John Lucas here in their delivery to the town?) By then, these would have included that of 20 June, asserting the lawfulness of the royal Commission of Array and calling for obedience to its commissioners.[37]

These moves came to a head in the summer of 1642. As the London puritan and Parliamentary supporter, Nehemiah Wallington, noted, 'this month of July divers letters came out of many counties, concerning the papists and malignants [who] did strive to set the Commission of Array, and many Igips [sic], derideful words, mocks and scoffs, and reproachful terms by them, were cast upon the Honourable Court of Parliament, with many threats and great preparations to the ruin of them.[38] In that month, the king and his supporters sought to take advantage of the political platform provided by the holding of the summer Assizes. In his instructions to the judges, issued from York on 4 July and printed for wider dissemination, Charles had made it clear that he intended them to use the opportunity of the royal Charge, a speech delivered by the judges at the beginning of the Assizes, to recruit support. The judges were to stress the king's intentions to defend the church against the threat from both catholics and sectaries, to suppress riots and, 'because [of] ye distemp[er]s of the p[rese]nte tim[e]s, unhappily stirred up & fomented by some under specious but unjust pr[e]tencions and probablie to stirr up loose and ungou[er]ned p[er]sons under hope of impunity as farre as they dare to make a prey of our good subiects', to see the laws enforced against rogues and vagabonds, 'whereby the good and quiet people of our Kingdome may be secured, and the wicked and licentious may be suppressed'.[39] In other words, they were to play up the same themes of hierarchical inversion and popular disorder to be found in other royal pronouncements. By contrast, they were to represent monarchy as the only guarantor of the traditional hierarchies in church and society. The king was clearly seeking to play his strongest suit, law and order.

At the same time, the king had taken steps to remodel the Commission of Peace. A new commission had been issued for Essex on 15 July. This

---

[37] *Stuart Royal Proclamations, 2, Royal Proclamations of King Charles I, 1625–46*, ed. J. F. Larkin (Oxford, 1983), no. 339, pp. 767–9, 777–81; *CJ/ii/622*, 630–1, 646–7, 656. On the same day that the Essex sheriff informed the House of the sending of proclamations into the region, the Suffolk Quarter Sessions ordered that an able watch be set in Newmarket, 'on account of the danger arising from the continual travelling of passengers from Cambridge': 'Suffolk County Records', *PSIA*, 15 (1915), p. 168; *PJ*, 3, p. 183.

[38] R. Webb, ed., *Historical Notices of the Reign of Charles I, 1630–1646*, 2 vols. (1869), vol. 2, pp. 77–8.

[39] Bodl. Lib., Tanner MS 63, fols. 1–2; *CSPD 1641–1643*, pp. 349–50. It is of course probable that an attempt may have been made to use the Assize sermon for similar ends.

effected a radical (and pro-royalist) remodelling of the existing county Bench. Predictably, the Earl of Warwick, Sir Thomas Barrington and their allies, some eighteen in all, were excluded. They were replaced with obvious supporters of the king, headed by the Earl of Carlisle, who was appointed *custos rotulorum* in place of the Earl of Warwick. Carlisle had also been entrusted with the raising of the Commission of Array in Essex. Since it has been shown that remodelling elsewhere drew on detailed local knowledge, it would be interesting to know whether this was the case for Essex. Did John Lucas as former sheriff have a hand in the Essex purge? A similar purge seems also to have been attempted in Suffolk, as well as in other counties in the region.[40] This attempt by the king to secure a majority of his supporters on the influential county benches was a significant move, the more so given what was to occur at the summer Assizes. The king's charge to the Assize judges had ended with an invitation to the counties to petition the king and with a promise that the king would respond favourably to such entreaties. Clearly the king's supporters were to use the Assizes as a political forum at the heart of the region to publicise royal policy and solicit support.

Parliament was aware of the impending threat. There had been moves initiated by the Hertfordshire MPs to get an order to prevent Justice Malet, the judge riding the Home Counties circuit and who had played a leading role in the earlier Kentish petition, from using the occasion of the Assizes to speak against Parliament. On 14 July, Harbottle Grimston moved for a like order for Essex and Sir Simonds D'Ewes, one of the Suffolk MPs, for a more general order to restrain the Assize judges. On 20 July, the Commons issued their counter-orders to the Assize judges, requiring them to declare the Commission of Array illegal and to pronounce that, 'all those that are Actors in putting the same in Execution, shall be esteemed a Disturber of the Peace of the Kingdom, and Betrayer of the Liberty of the Subject'. In the case of Essex, however, this came too late. Justice Malet was reported to have openly attacked Parliament's proceedings at the Essex Assizes held at Chelmsford on 18 July. He had used the occasion to declare, 'that they ought to yeeld obedience to the king's demands' and that Parliament's ordinance [i.e. the militia] was against the law. He had then gone on to encourage the drawing up of a declaration of support for the king which was signed by some twenty-five of the Justices of the Peace and six members of the

---

[40] PRO, C231/5, p. 530; *PJ*, 3, pp. 274–5; Fletcher, *Outbreak*, p. 298; Bodl. Lib., Tanner MS 63, fol. 110; Bankes MS 52/30; *PJ*, 3, pp. 274–5. Whether Charles' attempts would have been successful remains doubtful; most of those put into the commission were courtiers and had little effective power in county society.

Grand Jury.[41] Largely re-iterating the royal promises in the king's charge and promising defence of Charles' person and prerogative, this Remonstrance and Declaration was a clarion call to the king's supporters. The list of signatories makes clear its partisan nature. Most would become firm supporters of the king in the civil war; ninth to sign was Sir John Lucas. That it represented a threat was recognised by Sir Thomas Barrington and others who drew up a counter-petition to the king urging his presence at Parliament to secure a settlement.[42]

The attempt by the king's supporters to use the Assizes as a political forum in Essex seems to have been part of a broader campaign in the region. The summer Assizes in Suffolk saw a virtual replay of events in Essex. In Suffolk, Parliament's supporters had shown none of the dynamism of their Essex counterparts and little had been done to enforce the Militia Ordinance.[43] This was, in part, a reflection of the uncertainty of Sir Nathaniel Barnardiston and others as to whether they could carry the county with them and consequently of a desire to try to maintain unity among the county's traditional rulers. As in Essex, there were worries over the activities of known royalists, like the courtier Sir Thomas Jermyn, and doubts over the allegiances of others.[44] On the 30 July at the Assizes at Bury St Edmunds two rival petitions were drawn up in response to the royal charge. Unfortunately, since we have little more than the petitions themselves, it is difficult to reconstruct the immediate political context in which they appeared. Nevertheless, the

---

[41] BL, Harleian MS 163, fol. 272 v; *CJ*/11/682; T. P. S. Woods, *Prelude to Civil War 1642: Mr Justice Malet and the Kentish Petitions* (Salisbury, 1980), pp. 97–9. In addition to the contacts he would have formed on his previous riding of the circuit, Sir Thomas Mallet knew at least one of the future royalists – Sir Humphrey Mildmay – as a neighbour on his Somerset estates: J. S. Cockburn, *A History of English Assizes 1558–1714* (Cambridge, 1972), p. 272; Lee Ralph, *Mildmay*, p. 136.

[42] BL, E202(23), *A Perfect Diurnal of the Passages in Parliament*, 18–25 July 1642, pp. 6–7; E202(24) *A Perfect Diurnal, or the Proceedings in Parliament*, 18–25 July 1642, pp. 6–7; BL, Egerton MS, 2651, fol. 118 r; Bodl. Lib., Rawlinson MS, Essex 10, fol. 79; BL, 669, f5(66); PRO, SP, 16/491/77, 90. Unfortunately, the only copy of the counter-petition, which survives in the Barrington papers, does not include a list of signatories: Egerton MS, 2651, fol. 119. Parliament's vulnerability is suggested by the fact that though it ordered that the original petitioners should desist from framing any such seditious petitions, it was forced to draw up a declaration to attempt to meet the original petitioners' concerns: BL, E202(23), *A Perfect declaration of the Passages in Parliament*, 18–25 July 1642, pp. 6–7.

[43] Parliament had agreed to order the Militia Ordinance to be executed in Suffolk (along with Cambridgeshire and Norfolk) at the beginning of July, but on 11 August, the Commons were still issuing an order to the Deputy Lieutenants of the county to put the militia in execution: *LJ*/v/172; *CJ*/ii/647–8, 714.

[44] BL, E114(36), *Special Passages*, p. 22. Compared to Essex, the absence of relevant sources makes it more difficult to recover the political contours of Suffolk in the period before the outbreak of civil war, but see Holmes, *Eastern Association*, pp. 48–51; A. Everitt, *Suffolk and the Great Rebellion* (Ipswich, 1961).

sharply contrasting nature of the petitions are themselves evidence of political division and of a royalist attempt to sway political opinion in the county. What makes them particularly interesting is the absence of any signatories from among the county's rulers. Both were from those groups below the level of the county gentry. The royalist petition was from the Grand Jury alone; that in support of Parliament was in the name of the chief constables and freeholders. If none of the rulers had a hand in the composition of the petitions, then the petitions, especially that in support of the Parliament, underline the political role of the middling sort and reflect a level of popular engagement that may help to explain the events of August 1642.

As in Essex, both petitions sought as much to mould, as to reflect, opinion in the county. The first petition to the king was in the name of the Grand Juries of the county. The lack of other evidence does not allow us to discover whether, as elsewhere, there had been an attempt to influence the composition of the Grand Jury,[45] but as we have seen there had been an attempt by the Crown to remodel the magistracy. The Grand Juries' petition echoed the Essex loyalist petition and, with its offer of lives and fortunes for the defence of his sacred person and kingdom, was intended to rally the county to his cause.[46] That the loyal petitioners carefully repeated each of the king's promises they had heard in the judge's charge at the Assizes – the safety and prosperity of all his people, the suppression of popery and seditious anabaptism, the defence of protestantism, and the maintenance of the law and the privileges of Parliament – suggests that its main audience was the county, not the Court. To that end, the petitioners added a pointed postscript calculated to appeal to all those worried by the county's experience of disorder. Thanking the king for his concern to maintain order, they added, 'of w[hi]ch yor Ma[jes]ties care we are the more sensible by reason of some Riots and seditious assemblyes of late risen amongst us, w[hi]ch by our obedience to yo[u]r Ma[jes]ties just directions & the wisdome of [your] Reverend Judges have been happily suppressed'.[47] Once again, suppor-

---

[45] This had been the case in Kent where Malet had persuaded members of the county gentry to serve on the jury: A. Everitt, *The Community of Kent and the Great Rebellion, 1640–60* (Leicester, 1966), pp. 95–6.

[46] Bodl. Lib., Tanner MS 63, fol. 110; Bankes MS 56/4, fols. 10–11. The petition was in the name of the 'grand Enquests' for Suffolk. It survives only in a copy which gives the names of the jurors for the two administrative divisions, the Geldable and the Franchise (for which divisions, see MacCulloch, *Suffolk*, pp. 20–23). That twenty-two signed for the former and only 10 for the latter suggests that not all jurors were prepared to sign. (Is it significant that there were fewer signatories from the area of the summer attacks?)

[47] To what incidents do the petitioners refer? The absence of the Quarter Sessions' records for the county for this period and the lack of any other reference leaves this an unanswered question. Had there been an earlier attack on catholics? This had been the

ters of the king reinforced the royalist theme of the threat to the social order.

On the same day, a counter-petition had been drawn up in the name of the chief constables, freeholders and inhabitants of Suffolk and offered to the Justices of the Peace. The language of this document is strikingly different in tone to its companion. 'The Cuntrie is full of greife and feare for his Ma[jes]ties longe absence from his Parlament and refusall to be informed and advised by there Councell ... And much affrighted by his Ma[jes]ties preparation for Warre', it declared. The petitioners called for the king to take the advice of his Parliament and to give his assent to their bills 'for the settlinge of the distempers in the Church'. They contrasted the putting out of the commission of peace gentlemen of known ability with the presence around the king 'of many persons odious through the Kingdome by the name of Cavalleers'. While their rival petitioners sought to play on fears of popular disorder, they stressed fear of a popish conspiracy. 'Our feares are much increased by the boldnesse of the Papists, and other p[er]sons ill affected to the publique peace', who are given places and powers of command. Again, we know little of the context of the drawing up of this petition. It is perhaps significant that the petitioners knowing the likely reception they would be given by the king's judges had presented the petition to the county's JPs at the Assizes. However, a note by one of the Assize judges, Chief Justice Banks on a surviving copy of the petition, indicates that the Justices refused to accept the petition. Does this offer confirmation that the petition with its denunciation of papists was the product of an initiative from below the ranks of the county's rulers? Shortly after, the petition was printed (along with a similarly pro-Parliamentary one from the Hampshire Grand Jury).[48]

The politicisation of the Assizes was clearly intended by the king and his supporters as a preliminary to the attempt to raise the royalist commission of array in the region. The neighbouring county of Norfolk had already witnessed an attempt to raise troops for the king in late July. On the 1 August the Commons were informed that several gentry had

fear of the Countess of Rivers' sister as early as January 1642: CUL, Hengrave Hall MS 88, 2, no. 150. Or were the petitioners referring to the earlier disorders by the troops and subsequent episodes of iconoclasm? The reference to the Assize judges might suggest that the episodes were more recent.

[48] Bodl. Lib., Bankes MS 52/30, fol. 60; BL, E112(9) *Two Petitions. The One to the* KINGS *most Excellent Majesty, The humble Petition of the Grand-Jury ...[at the Hampshire Assizes].* THE OTHER *To the Right Worshipfull the Justices of the Peace now assembled at the Assizes holden at Bury St Edmonds for the County of Suffolke. The humble Petition of the Chiefe-Constables, and Freeholders, Inhabitants in the said County attending the service there* (1642). We need to know more about the political and publishing process by which provincial petitions came to be selected for printing.

lately returned from the king to assist Lord Maltravers to execute the Commission of Array there, 'and that the papists there who lately expressed much fear began now again to grow confident'.[49] Other counties saw similar attempts, an attempt being reported to have been made in Essex's neighbouring county of Hertfordshire exactly a week before the attack on Lucas.[50] Two commissions had been issued for Suffolk, the second shortly before the August attacks, and we know that the Commission had been proclaimed from the pulpit in churches around Long Melford in mid-July.[51] In early August the Earl of Carlisle had been at Waltham Abbey in the south of the county to set up the Commission of Array in Essex, 'if he had not found that the Country would have opposed him'.[52]

Parliament was aware of, and anxious about, these developments. It had shown itself alert to the threat posed by the publication of royal proclamations and declarations – on the 21 July, it had passed an order to stay proclamations in the post from going into Norfolk, Suffolk and Essex – but it could not stop knowledge of them spreading. For example, the Commons' order prohibiting the publication of royal proclamations at Colchester itself became the subject of popular discussion within the town. Two days after the order two weavers passing others talking at the door and asking 'what news?' were told by one of the men, Richard Leues:[53]

> there was a proclamacion which came from the kinge to this towne which could not be published, but if hee the said Leues had brought it he would have spent his bloode but he would have had it published; & said why should not wee knowe the kinges minde as well as the Parliamentes mind, for the Kinge standes to mainteyne but one religion, & the Parliament stood to mainteyne all religions, Arminians, Brownistes, Anabaptistes & freewillers. And further said that the

---

[49] BL, 669 f6(54); Bodl. Lib., Tanner MS 63, fol. 111; Holmes, *Eastern Association*, pp. 56–7; J. T. Evans, *Seventeenth-Century Norwich: Politics, Religion and Government 1620–1690* (Oxford, 1979), pp. 122–3; R. W. Ketton-Cremer, *Norfolk in the Civil War* (1969), pp. 145–8; *PJ*, 3, pp. 274–5. The Commons ordered the execution of the militia to be expedited in Norfolk: *CJ*/ii/697.

[50] BL, E112 (15), *Some special and considerable passages from London, Westminster, Coventry*, 9–16 August 1642.

[51] Holmes, *Eastern Association*, pp. 52–5; Northamptonshire RO, Finch Hatton MS 133; Bodl. Lib., Dep. C, MS 165, no. 72. There is evidence that the king had been in correspondence with the Lord Lieutenant, the Earl of Suffolk (although he was not included on either of the commissions): *LJ*/v/297.

[52] *LJ*/v/280. A reference in the Waltham Holy Cross churchwardens' accounts reveals that Carlisle had some time before then entertained the king there: ERO, D/P 75/5/1, fol. 100. Predictably, the Essex Commission of Array represented a radical rejection of the Warwick-Barrington group: Northamptonshire RO, Finch-Hatton MS 133, unfol.

[53] CRO, D/B5, Sb2/7, fol. 298.

Parliament had done noe good since they did site, but sate for their owne endes to inrich themselves.

Leues, 'swore by the name of God that the Aldermen of this towne were some Annabaptistes, some brownistes, some Arminians & some free-willers, & that ... if anie combustion came that hypocrites should smarte for it and he would put his helpinge hand to it.' The glimpse afforded us by this cameo of what was being discussed on the streets of Colchester by a group of weavers reflects the politicisation of the people. It also suggests that the royalist message about the link between Parliament, popular disorder and sects was capable of attracting support from below the ranks of the gentry.

Politicisation of the pulpit was another important strand to the royalist campaign within the region. Control of the pulpit gave the king the means of publicising his declarations right at the heart of local society. If Parliament's supporters could use the pulpit (as was alleged to be the case in Essex in the elections to the Long Parliament), so too could the king's. While Parliament seems to have been able to prevent sympathetic county and urban authorities from reading the king's messages, the pulpit provided an alternative to courts and market places where the king might have his declarations read and proclamations publicised.[54] Ministers of patrons loyal to the king could be expected to preach up the king's cause and to preach down Parliament. The fact that some of the evidence for the political use of the pulpit comes from later accusations by their enemies before the committees for scandalous ministers, suggests the need for caution in the handling of the evidence. But enough is known to of the pre-histories of those accused to suggest that the general picture is correct. John Browning, Lord Maynard's minister and Prince Rupert's future chaplain, provides a typical example. Described as 'a notable Arminian and altar-adorer', he was said to have justified the king's attempt to arrest Parliament's leaders in January 1642 as 'a just act' since 'the members of the House of Commons lately accused of treason were justly so accused', and to have gone on to declare that 'there were forty more amongst them guilty of the same crime'. Edward Cherry, the Rivers' appointee at Great Holland, was reported to have said that he never knew any good the Parliament did unless it was to rob the country and pick purses, a favourite accusation with other ministers. In Suffolk,

---

[54] For examples, see J. White, *The First Century of Scandalous, Malignant PRIESTS, Made and admitted into Benefices by the PRELATES, in whose hands the Ordination of Ministers and government of the Church hath been. OR, A Narration of the Causes for which the PARLIAMENT hath Ordered the Sequestration of the benefices of severall Ministers*, pp. 8, 16, 18–19, 34, 37–8; Holmes, *Scandalous Ministers*, pp. 28–9, 32–3, 55, 79–80, 82–3, 117; BL, Additional MS 5829, fols. 9, 13–16.

the parson of Westhorpe had declared that the county had chosen such factious fellows for their knights, that the Parliament was not likely to hold.[55]

Ministers hostile to Parliament refused to co-operate in the publication of its policies. Robert Sugden, the vicar of Benhall, had refused to sign the petition 'for the removinge the popish Lords & Bishops out of the Parliament [January 1642], sayeing it came from a pack of puritans'. At High Ongar, the rector, Josiah Tomlinson, refused to allow Parliament's ordinances or the protestation to be read, and when he was persuaded at last to read it he said that he had no command to enjoin them to take it. At Stratford St Mary, the rector, Samuel Lindsell, had not only refused to take the protestation, but had also 'discouraged the people, saying hee, being our watchman, durst not but give us warning'. The rector of Little Cornard was reported to have said that, 'the Parliament & the whole kingdome ought to lay down their necks before the Kinge and submitt to performe whatsoever he should command them', declaring on another occasion, 'neither would he pray for the Parliament so longe as he lived'.[56]

By contrast, such ministers were eager propagandists for the king. When royalists in the region began preparations to raise the Commission of Array, several ministers proved valuable allies. On a Sunday in mid-July, the parson of Hartest and Boxted in Suffolk read the King's Declaration, presumably either that against the Militia Ordinance or for the Commission of Array. When a gentleman told him that Parliament forbade its publication, he answered that he would maintain it with his life and blood, and he went on to persuade ministers in neighbouring parishes to do the same, taking every opportunity to denounce 'Parl[ia-men]t's illeagal dealing in many acc[ti]ons'. In August 1642, the minister at Southwell in Essex, Edward Jeffrey, preaching on the text 'Servants obey yo[u]r Masters' (Colossians 3.22) was said to have declared that, 'the king hath not only power to command all your persons, but also power to take away your goods at his pleasure'. Jeffrey was accused of threatening to give the king a list of names of those contributing to the Parliament. At Purleigh, the rector Lawrence Washington, was reported to have published that those who assisted Parliament were traitors, a likely reference to the royal proclamation of 9 August 1642.[57]

---

[55] *PJ*, 1, 241, 304; *DNB*, *sub* Browning; White, *Century*, pp. 3, 49–50.
[56] Holmes, *Scandalous Ministers*, pp. 68–9; Bodl. Lib., Walker MS C5, fol. 106; Smith, *Ecclesiastical History*, p. 135.
[57] Bodl. Lib., Dep. C, MS. 165, nos. 72, 90; *CJ*/ii/684, 728; *PJ*, 3, 245; White, *Century*, pp. 3, 4, 8, 18, 22, 24–6, 49–50; Holmes, *Scandalous Ministers*, pp. 28–9, 37, 48–9, 63, 69; see also, pp. 32–3, 38–9, 41, 55, 79–80; *Stuart Royal Proclamations, 2*, pp. 790–4.

Worryingly for Parliament's supporters, it was not only Arminian or Laudian ministers who were involved. Ministers appalled by acts of popular reformation in their and others' churches and by the early emergence of separatist conventicles were increasingly inclined to see the king as the best protector of a reformed protestant church. Edward Symmonds, the rector of Rayne in Essex and erstwhile friend of Stephen Marshall, spent the months of June and July 1642 preaching against Parliament's actions. Symmonds was reported to have preached, 'that the Parliament would force the King to comply with those Laws that they shall make, and that they raise a Force against the King, and that they are not to be obeyed, though they command according to GOD, if it be not according to the King's Command. He, 'pressed his Auditory to believe whatsoever is set forth in the Declaration published in the King's Name, because a Divine Sentence in His Mouth, and He cannot err.' Here was a powerful exposition of the king's cause in the supposed heartland of the Puritan cause. As the London puritan Nehemiah Wallington noted, Symmonds was presented at the bar of the Commons, 'for preaching That we are bound to doe all yt his Maiestie commands and beleeve all his yt his Maiestie saith'.[58]

Control of the pulpit was used to amplify the key theme in royal pronouncements that Parliament's actions threatened order and hierarchy. The king was 'compelled by the Parliament & Parliament by the Rout', was the vicar of Ash Bocking's succinct comment. As early as November 1640, the minister of All Hallows, Barking in Essex had been presented to the Commons for saying, 'they are black Toads, spotted Toads and venomous Toads, like Jack Straw and Wat Tyler, that speak against the Ceremonies of the Church'. In Suffolk, William Keeble, the rector of Ringshall, who had stigmatised those who voted for the 'puritan' candidates in the county elections as 'leathercoats, scarecrows and squirrel hunters', was reported to have said in a sermon in 1641 in support of Bishop Wren's innovations, that 'Now … every man will deny the pope and yett be a pope himselfe to say & doe what he list'.[59] Dr Alexander Read, the minister at Fyfield in Essex was later presented

---

[58] *CJ*/ii/698; *LJ*/v/635–6; Edward Symmonds, *A Loyall Subjects Beliefe* (Oxford, 1643); *MR*, p. 12; BL, Additional MS 21,935, fol. 125.

[59] Holmes, *Scandalous Ministers*, pp. 41, 97–8; BL, E202(43) *A True and perfect Diurnall of the passages in Parliament, from Nottingham, Ashby and Leicester, and other parts*, p. 8; *CJ*/ii/3. Keeble was also alleged to have preached, 'we must not speake ag[ain]st o[u]r king although he be a pope or any Religion whatsoever'. It is not clear at what date the last alleged speech came but, like the information that when Keeble's study was searched there were found 'invective pamphlets against Parliament, it would tend to confirm that in the period before the summer of 1642, Keeble was a strong supporter of the King': Bodl. Lib., MS J. Walker, c. 7, fols. 163–4.

to Parliament, for saying that, 'it was utterly unlawful for a People to take up Arms for the defence of Religion, and that none but Brownists and Anabaptists are of another Opinion'. Multiplying tales of popular disorder offered confirmation of the message from the pulpit. As the soon-to-be sequestered minister of High Ongar was reported to have predicted, 'now the base must rule the Honourable'.[60]

Reports of statements hostile to Parliament suggested that royalist propaganda had hit home. An Essex man, and possibly a catholic, was reported to the Commons for saying, 'we might thank the Parliament for these troublesome times', a pithy echo of the message to be found in royal proclamations and pronouncements from the pulpit.[61] From Suffolk, Sir Simonds D'Ewes reported a rhyme recited by a gentleman's son in the course of a conversation which had taken place at Acton, home to the catholic Daniell family. This ran, 'one cuckold [Essex], two bastards [Warwick and Holland] and a pack of knaves/Strove to make subject[s] princes [Pym] and princes slaves'. This rhyme would seem to have been circulating more widely in the region; Edward Cherry, the Countess of Rivers' minister at Much Holland in Essex, was later accused of having published a scandalous libel against the earls of Essex, Warwick and Holland.[62] Without further evidence it would be ridiculous to regard these isolated fragments as representative of wider opinion. Such reports were rare, but given the imperfect means of communication and the sharp increase in political tensions, Parliament showed itself no better than its predecessor, the Privy Council, at judging the real nature of the threat such mutterings posed. Parliament's sensitivity to slights reflected its insecurity.

There was, then, within Essex and Suffolk and their neighbouring counties, a concerted campaign to raise support for the king. The accidents of record survival, as well as the eventual failure of that attempt, allow us only glimpses of what it has been argued here was a more organised attempt than has hitherto been allowed. Nor does the surviving evidence allow us to follow in detail the anxieties that this must have caused for Parliament and it supporters. The almost complete absence of political correspondence surviving for this period means that we are not able to track communications between the region and

---

[60] *LJ*/vi/37–8; Smith, *Ecclesiastical History*, p. 139.

[61] *PJ*, 2, p. 248. That the man, Henry Wilson, had gone on to say, 'that if Ireland were true to themselves, they could not be hurt from England', might suggest that he was a catholic. A family of the same name and living in the same area were presented for recusancy: J. M. Campbell, 'Estreat of fines imposed at Chelmsford Quarter Sessions 1641–1642', *ERec*, 1 (1959), pp. 25–32.

[62] *PJ*, 2, 207–8; White, *Century*, p. 3. Gentlemen at Chelmsford singing a song in derision of Parliament were made to appear before the courts: ERO Q/SR 318/69–70.

Parliament. Isolated fragments like the letter from Sir Thomas Barrington quoted at the start of this section suggest that such correspondence would have been much concerned with shifts of opinion within the county. But we must not allow hindsight to prevent a proper appreciation of the anxieties that would have been felt in the counties in the summer of 1642. Unable to gauge political opinion, Parliament's supporters within the region showed themselves very sensitive to expressions of dissent and were quick to report these to their MPs who in turn reported them to the House. Only a day after the original examination of the Colchester weavers who had questioned the banning of royal proclamations the Commons had been informed and had issued an order for their appearance before the House.[63]

The speed and sensitivity that Parliament and its supporters showed in their response to attempts to have read royal proclamations or in suppressing cases of dangerous talk tell their tale. Parliament and its supporters knew that they faced a co-ordinated attempt to claim political support in the region for a king who had begun to find it easier to represent himself as the defender of order. They could be neither certain of their own ability to carry opinion with them as they embarked on more radical measures, nor that royalist attempts would be stillborn. They knew that there were some whose political behaviour in the 1630s and since signalled that they would respond positively given the occasion, but what they did not, nor could not know, was what more general response this appeal would meet with. That Parliament was forced by the king's intransigence to introduce measures which could be seen as a radical rupture with the established polity and church, and as responsible for unprecedented levels of popular disorder, increased their uncertainty and the king's chances of success in raising support. The issue of who could claim authority to raise a military force sharpened these differences. When a group of Essex men were presented to Parliament for saying, 'that those Volunteers in the County of Essex that met to train, were Traitors', they added simply, 'that it was easy to prove it, it being against the King's Proclamation.'[64] While the elasticity of the accusation of malignancy – the label for royalists before the outbreak of civil war licensed the use of cavalier – was part of its appeal to Parliament and its supporters, it came at a cost. Its indeterminacy in a period of political instability meant a heightening of anxieties. Beyond the circle of known supporters of the king there lurked others, prominent among them

---

[63] *CJ*/ii/680. Prof. Hunt's dismissal of the royalist threat in Essex perhaps gives insufficient weight to the threat, and to perception of that threat, before the outbreak of armed conflict: *Puritan Moment*, pp. 298–9.

[64] *CJ*/ii/705.

catholics, whose numbers by virtue of their otherness could not be known and against whose unknown but, it suggested, increasing menace, Parliament's own propaganda cautioned.

The concerted attempt to raise royal support in the region in the summer of 1642 might have made the August action more welcome. Parliament itself had been grappling with the problems of how to prevent support reaching the king in advance of any declaration of war. Indeed, on the very day of the action at Colchester one gentleman wrote from London of 'the great care taken that the malignant party shall not be underhand assisted, neither with plate nor moneys, for both plate and moneys are stopped in the hands of carriers'.[65] In response to news of an attempt to raise the Array in Norfolk at the beginning of August, Parliament had ordered the county's MPs into the county to suppress any such attempt and to ensure that no catholic arms should be allowed to leave the county. At Norwich, where we have seen there were persistent anxieties about the popish threat, recusants were to be confined to their homes. On 17 August orders were given that the authorities at Cambridge should disarm all popish catholics and 'all other dangerous and ill-affected Persons'. On 18 August the Suffolk authorities were ordered to secure the county's magazine at Bury St Edmunds. On 19 August, as renewed attempts were made in the region to publicise the commission of array and the clash of arms seemed ever more likely,[66] the Lords ordered watches to be put in place in Cambridgeshire, Norfolk and Suffolk to apprehend all horse, arms, ammunition, money, plate and any persons attempting to execute the Commission of Array. On the same day, the Norfolk MP Sir John Potts wrote to Sir Simonds D'Ewes, 'I concur with y[o]u in ye fear of ungovernable numbers from whence my thoughts alwaies apprehended ye most remediless dangers, w[hi]ch God avert. My own endeavours heer have been for peace & hitherto wee are quiet, whensoever necessity shall enforce us to make use of ye multitude, I doe not promise my self safety.'[67] Given this context, the question to be asked here is did Parliament's leaders in Essex share Sir John Potts' concern or did they, as Clarendon's comment on the attack on Lucas suggests, 'make use of ye multitude'?

Since we lack direct evidence, there can be no simple answer to that question. However, a knowledge of the more immediate political context of Lucas's role in supporting the king and of his relations with Parlia-

[65] HMC, Cowper MSS, 2, pp. 321–2.
[66] LJ/v/251–2; Evans, *Norwich*, p. 123; CJ/ii/726; Raymond (ed.), *Making the News*, p. 64.
[67] LJ/v/306; BL, Harleian MS 386, fol. 233.

ment's leading supporters in the county might favour Clarendon's interpretation. Certainly there were scores to settle in 1642. The period of Personal Rule had created the possibility of a shift in power within the county which threatened the interest of the Earl of Warwick and his allies. When king and Parliament failed to secure an agreement and Lucas characteristically became active in support of the king, there were others, politically powerful, whose resentments need to be taken into account in order to comprehend fully Sir John's fate in 1642. The 'County' as well as the Corporation and commonalty of Colchester had good cause to welcome his fall.

Sir John Lucas's landed wealth easily qualified him for office within the county.[68] But he did not follow the usual *cursus honorum* of the landed gentleman wishing to assert his status within county society. Lucas appears never to have served as a Justice of the Peace.[69] All offices were the king's, but when Lucas exercised power he did so in offices that might be seen as more directly created to serve the royal interest – sheriff, deputy lieutenant, royal commissioner. His first tenure of office came in 1636 as sheriff of the county. That it coincided with a crisis in securing the co-operation of the county's rulers was probably not accidental. The delegation of the contentious collection of ship money to the shrievalty made the office in the second half of the 1630s very much that of the *king's* sheriff. Lucas's tenure of the shrievalty brought him both royal commendation and a potentially wide circle of enemies. He was an active enforcer of royal policy and in particular an aggressive (and highly successful) collector of ship money.[70] Lucas's particular exercise of the office of sheriff would seem to be echoed in that clause of the Grand Remonstrance which spoke of such sheriffs as 'were pricked out as would be instruments to execute whatsoever they would have to be done'.[71]

Lucas's predecessor, Sir Humphrey Mildmay, had found the collection of ship money difficult, and he had encountered exhausting disputes over assessment. 'There is noe penny p[ai]d that is not forced god helpe me amongeste the people', Mildmay complained. Mildmay, who was still collecting arrears in 1639, complained to the Privy Council of the

---

[68] Although Margaret's assessment (*True Relation*, p. 275) that 'there were few peers who had much greater estates, or lived more noble' owes something to daughterly devotion, the family were clearly among the wealthier gentry in the county: F. G. Emmison (ed.), *Feet of Fines for Essex 6: 1581–1603* (Oxford, 1993), p. 144.

[69] The name John Lucas appears only once in the Essex commission of peace, that for 1631/2, but against this name there is an (illegible) endorsement: PRO, SP, 16/212, p. 49.

[70] To judge by the exculpatory tone of one extant return to the Book of Orders it is possible that Lucas showed a similar unwelcome zeal in reminding the county's JPs of their duty, by then beginning to be neglected, of making regular returns: PRO, SP, 16/347/73.

[71] S. R. Gardiner (ed.), *The Constitutional Documents of the Puritan Revolution 1625–1660* 3rd edn (Oxford, 1968), p. 214.

obstruction he had experienced in collecting the tax from the chief constables, 'being Many of them, a generation of Discipliners, very zealous in all causes that concerne the hindrance of his Majesty's servise, and he may say ... kept on by such as [he] ... hopes the Board knows right well, and what their good wills are to the service'.[72] A list of those who had failed to pay ship money before Lucas's tenure and who were 'wilful hinderers' gives an idea of the strength of opposition Lucas had to overcome. The opposition included important county figures like Sir Thomas Barrington and Sir William Masham. At its head was the Earl of Warwick. Analysis of the pattern of opposition to the tax within the county confirms the leading role Warwick played. His officers and tenants were some of the most recalcitrant at agreeing a rate or paying the tax.

That Lucas inherited a situation in which the arrears for Essex were greater than in any other county reflected the strength of the opposition amongst some of the county's most important rulers.[73] But he seems to have cut through these problems by his active personal involvement in the collection of the tax. Something of the attention to detail he brought to the office is to be seen in the surviving assessment he drew up for every community in Essex with the names of all inhabitants liable for the tax.[74] Lucas's zeal was also reflected in accounts of his actions. The letter writer Edward Rossingham recounted the following story of Lucas. Having assessed the hundred near to him, Lucas sent to the high constables to apportion the assessment among the various communities. When they twice failed to act on their orders, 'he forthwith gets half a dozen of waggons. With these he goes in person to the houses of the aforesaid high constables, and distrains their goods ... Then he sells them, [and] so raiseth that sum of the money laid upon the whole hundred.' Lucas's imprisoning of a parish constable to get him to pay the ship money suggests that his zeal extended to ensuring enforcement at a lower level. In sharp contrast to his predecessor, John Lucas was able to raise the whole sum of £8,000 for which he was responsible, and to do so in little over a year.[75]

[72] PRO, SP, 16/301/95, /304/81; /327/7; /328/49; /375/67; 377/34; 415/76; *CSPD 1635*, p. 580; *1636–1637*, p. 229; V. A. Rowe, 'Robert second earl of Warwick and the payment of ship money in Essex', *TEAS*, 3rd ser., 1 (1963).

[73] PRO, SP, 16/344/71.

[74] This now forms PRO, SP, 16/358. Colchester as a borough is omitted from this list.

[75] R. F. Williams (ed.), *The Court and Times of Charles the First*, 2 vols. (1848), vol. 2, p. 273; ERO, Q/SBa, 2/30, unno. (petit. Rbt Miller, constable of Blakemore); PRO, SP, 16/344/71; 363/46 and 46.i, ii; /366/27; /371/74; /392/47; *CSPD 1637*, p. 394. By October 1637 only £400 was unpaid – since this was the sum demanded from the town does it represent Colchester's share? – and this was subsequently accounted for: SP, 16/370/74, /392/48.

Lucas's zeal in pushing through the collection of the tax was clearly unwelcome, not least to the Earl of Warwick. In January 1637, when Lucas was some months into his period of office, Warwick sought a meeting with the king. While Warwick stressed his own willingness to serve Charles, the Venetian ambassador reported that in the course of a long speech, 'he made no bones of telling the king frankly that his tenants were accustomed to the mild rule of Queen Elizabeth and King James, and could not bring themselves to consent to such notable prejudices'. The king's response to this showed an uncharacteristic degree of control, notes the ambassador; Charles merely observed that he hoped others would be as prompt in their support as Warwick. Despite this rebuff, Warwick and his allies attempted a more direct attack on Lucas, complaining in a petition of Lucas's overassessment of themselves. However, they were again unsuccessful. Charles himself was present at the meeting of the Privy Council in May 1637 to hear the complaints. Having heard that Lucas had assessed the 'abler sort ... somewhat more' to ease the poor, the king had had him called into his presence and had publicly and enthusiastically endorsed Lucas's actions.[76]

While the result of this pressure on Warwick was, it has been argued, the crushing of opposition to ship money in the county, it left a very different political legacy within the county. Ship money had given to the office of sheriff a political importance it had previously lost. In the case of John Lucas it had allowed an outsider to the county's ruling circles to best the Earl of Warwick and his leading ally, Sir Thomas Barrington, and to do so in a manner that paid scant heed to their status. Barrington (and possibly others) had had some of his goods distrained by Lucas in order to force payment of ship money.[77] Nor was it only at the level of the county's rulers that Lucas was likely to have stirred up antagonism. We do not know for certain whether Lucas' role in the collection of ship money provided a further occasion for conflict with Colchester's rulers, but it seems more than likely.[78] Elsewhere, Lucas's actions had left a

---

[76] *CSPV 1636–1639*, pp. 124–5; PRO, SP, 16/357/2.

[77] ERO, D/DBa, A2, fol. 33 v.

[78] Since the town had contested the amount it was required to pay from the first writ on maritime towns in the 1620s, and in 1636, having collected the reduced assessment, refused to hand it over to the sheriff as a breach of their privileges, there was clearly scope for further conflict with Lucas: PRO, SP, 16/61/79; 16/282/51; *CSPD 1635–1636*, p. 435; PRO, PCR, 2/46, pp. 176–8; Morant, *History*, vol. 1, p. 54 n.; PCR, 2/48, fol. 182. Later, the Mayor, none other than Henry Barrington, was in trouble with the Privy Council for failing to pay in any money, and despite threats Colchester had paid in only £100 by June 1638: PRO, SP, 16/389/127; /392/49. For an example of how urban factionalism in Colchester could get caught up with the issue of ship money, see the dispute between Barrington and William Lawrence: J. Hart, *Justice Upon Petition: The*

legacy of bitterness. The hundred of the county where Lucas had personally intervened to force through the collection of ship money was likely to have been one of the neighbouring hundreds, possibly Hinckford or Lexden, in which were found the clothing towns. Mildmay, Lucas's immediate predecessor, had found them 'very obstinate refusers of th[e]ir payem[en]t'. Some way into Lucas's shrievalty, Robert Aylett reported that Coggeshall had refused even to set a rate for either the first or second payment of ship money, a fact he sought to link to the presence there of puritan preaching, an association drawn also by Mildmay.[79] It was from these same areas that support for the attack on Lucas came.

Lucas's tenure of the shrievalty symbolised the potential of the period of Personal Rule to spawn a faction to oppose the hitherto dominance of the Earl of Warwick within Essex. Since coming into his inheritance in the early 1620s, Warwick had sought successfully to extend his power through the county.[80] The size and stability of his rent roll had laid the basis for his power within a county where the power of the only other peers was either compromised by their recusancy (as in the case of the Lord Petre and the Earl Rivers) or, as in the case of the Earl of Suffolk away on the border at Audley End, focused on adjoining counties. Ties of kinship and friendship with the gentry of Essex and other counties in the region extended his authority. Warwick's extensive patronage of godly lecturers and alliances with gentry families, who subscribed to his political and religious agenda, notably the godly Barringtons, long-time allies of the Rich family, strengthened his position. Royal office, most importantly as Lord Lieutenant and Vice-Admiral, reinforced Warwick's platform for power in the county, a power attested to by his early domination of Parliamentary representation in both county and boroughs.[81]

Warwick's ambitions had been furthered at first by favour at court. But opposition in Parliament to his erstwhile ally Buckingham had led to

---

House of Lords and the Reformation of Justice, p. 91 (where Barrington is wrongly rendered as Harrington).

[79] PRO, SP, 16/304/81; 335/67; /350/54; *CSPD 1636–1637*, p. 229. Aylett suggested a search of the minister's study and thought that 'no doubt many practises may be discove[re]d not ag[ain]st ye church alone'. At Dedham there was the same association between cloth, puritanism and a refusal to collect ship money: *CSPD 1635–1636*, p. 13.

[80] For much of what follows I am deeply indebted to the generosity of Christopher Thompson, whose study of the Earl of Warwick will provide the definitive study of county politics in this period. The analysis draws on a lecture he delivered to the 1987 summer school at the Local History Centre of the University of Essex, on an unpublished typescript, 'Court and country', and on many stimulating discussions.

[81] B. Donagan, 'The clerical patronage of Robert Rich, second earl of Warwick, 1619–1642', *Proceeding American Philosophical Society*, 120, no. 5 (1976), pp. 388–419; B. Quintrell, 'The government of the county of Essex, 1603–1642' (Ph.D. thesis, University of London, 1965), p. 33.

his loss of the Lord Lieutenancy in 1626 and to the purging of his allies from the ranks of the deputy lieutenants.[82] While Warwick was careful to try to preserve, at least publicly, those links with the Court upon which his own patronage and prosperity in part rested, political differences made even this show of harmony difficult. Warwick had refused to pay or to help collect the Forced Loan of 1626, and he took the lead in opposing both the extension of forest law and the imposition of ship money.[83] Warwick's power base in the county still made him a formidable figure and one whose support in administering the county could not easily be dispensed with, hence his restoration to the Lieutenancy. But, to his great annoyance, he held this in tandem with others until the death of Lord Maynard at the end of 1640.

In the 1630s Warwick and his allies, out of favour at court and in opposition to policies in both church and state, faced the emergence of a rival nexus for power in the county. In 1635 Lord Maynard had been appointed to share the Lord Lieutenancy with Warwick. This was a considerable snub to the earl and one he deeply resented.[84] Warwick and Maynard were clear opposites in both religion and politics. Maynard, a client of Buckingham, had played an active role in collecting the Forced Loan. Warwick sought to defend godly ministers and offer protection to silenced lecturers. Maynard was a committed Arminian and anti-puritan who counted Archbishop Laud a good friend.[85] While opposition from the Warwick–Barrington connection to the policies of the 1630s led to further loss of office, Maynard co-operated with and promoted those whose attitudes to royal power were rather different. The Earl Rivers was another associate of Buckingham, to whom he owed his title. He had proved a willing ally in the collection of the Forced Loan, using his power to ensure compliance in the areas where his estates lay.[86] Maynard was joined in a remodelled Lieutenancy by a group of deputies, of whom at least one, Sir Thomas Fanshawe, had been previously blocked from office by the Earl of Warwick. This group of men were also allies of Buckingham and their assumption of increasing power in the county rested heavily on favour at Court. As such, the Warwick–Barrington connection, had earlier been able to undercut their power and, as in the

---

[82] Quintrell, 'Government', p. 43.
[83] Cust, *Forced Loan*, pp. 102, 145, 260–84; W. R. Fisher, *The Forest of Essex: Its History, Laws, Administration and Ancient Customs* (1887), pp. 38–44; Rowe, 'Ship money', pp. 160–3.
[84] PRO, SP, 16/298/10.
[85] Cust, *Forced Loan*, p. 200; Tyacke, *Anti-Calvinist*, pp. 192–4. For evidence of Maynard's attitude to puritan preachers, see *The Eagle* (Cambridge, 1902), pp. 18–19.
[86] Quintrell, 'Government', p. 43; Cust, *Forced Loan*, pp. 200, 260–3.

1628 elections, to scotch attempts to capture representation of the shire for the Court canditates.[87]

However, Lucas' assumption of the shrievalty, and with it responsibility for collecting ship money, demonstrated the potential strength of the Maynard group, when a magistracy active in the implementation of royal fiscal demands, received consistent royal support. After his success at collecting ship money, Lucas, now knighted, became a deputy lieutenant, presumably an appointment he owed to Lord Maynard, rather than the Earl of Warwick. When the Scottish rebellion broke out, it was Maynard and his allies, among them Lucas, who busied themselves raising the troops and money to support the king. It may be the activities of this group that explain in 1639 the singling out of Essex, with Cambridge (of which it should be noted Maynard was also Lord Lieutenant) as counties 'where our officers found most respect from the Lord Lieutenant and deputies'.[88] The failure of opposition to ship money in the county and, with it, the retreat of the Earl of Warwick as a result of the royal threat to his own position and profit, underlined the real danger that these political shifts represented.[89] At the same time, Warwick and Barrington, were unable to prevent the silencing of godly ministers in the county or the implementation of the Laudian programme in the county's churches. As might be expected, Maynard welcomed these changes. Some of his associates were important allies to church officials like John Aylett who were attempting to root out opposition and to suppress nonconformity. Henry Nevill, the Court candidate in the county election for the Short Parliament, was another ally of Maynard. Aylett described him as 'a forward and active man' in the silencing of the godly preachers in the 1630s. A hostile newsbook report called him, 'a man formerly inclined to the late innovations introduced into the Church, and much in favour with the Bishops'. While Warwick and Barrington had helped to promote emigration to the New World, Nevill and Maynard had worked in tandem to obstruct it, acting as the eyes and ears of Charles' Council and bishops.[90]

For Warwick, then, Lucas's rapid rise through the ranks of the

---

[87] Cust, *Forced Loan*, pp. 200–1; Quintrell, 'Government', pp. 140–1; Thompson, 'Court and country', pp. 26–7.

[88] Bodl. Lib., MS Firth c. 4, pp. 597–9, 620; K. Sharpe, *The Personal Rule of Charles I* (New Haven and London, 1992), p. 802 and n. Does Lucas's service as deputy lieutenant, but not JP, reflect his preference for a post that offered a quintessential expression of the chivalric status of a gentleman: F. Heal and C. Holmes, *The Gentry in England and Wales, 1500–1700* (1994), p. 172.

[89] Rowe, 'Ship money', pp. 160–3. Warwick's appointees continued to hinder the collection of ship money even after the collapse of the main opposition in the county.

[90] *The Eagle* (Cambridge, 1915), p. 30; PRO, SP, 16/350/54; BL, E202(42) *An exact and True Diurnall of the Proceedings in Parliament*, 29 August–5 September 1642, *sub* 3

county's rulers symbolised the threat to his personal position and to those policies he favoured in church and state. While Lucas found it possible to advance his honour in service to Charles, Warwick found his honour slighted by the rebuffs the king had inflicted. For Warwick and his allies, Lucas represented the emergence of a grouping around Maynard that might be characterised, only somewhat anachronistically, as authoritarian royalists. While the Warwick–Barrington connection favoured a political order in which the king should rule through Parliament and the common law, Maynard and Lucas were more prepared to promote prerogative rule. While Warwick and his allies sought to ensure godly preaching and godly discipline, Maynard and Lucas, the protégé of Archbishop Harsnet, favoured Arminians and ceremonialists. Perhaps most worryingly, others in their group like Thomas Wiseman, Sir Richard Weston and Henry Nevill were suspected (with good cause) of popery, while yet others, notably Earl Rivers and the Petres, were open catholics who were to be very active in the catholic enterprise to raise money to support Charles in his war with the Scots. In 1638, the year in which Lucas was made a gentleman of Prince Charles' Privy Chamber, the progress of Marie de Medici, Charles I's mother-in-law, as she passed through the county from Harwich to London, marked out both physically and symbolically the shifts in power within Essex. It was Sir John Lucas who made provisions for her week-long stay at Harwich and who went to greet and escort her to his house where she stayed overnight 'pour y faire le matin ses devotions' and afterwards to admire Sir John's gardens. (What the godly of Colchester made of this can only be guessed at, as can the reactions of the Mayor, the future Quaker John Furley, at having to greet officially the mother of Charles' catholic queen. That she was not met at the boundaries to the liberties of the town as was customary with other royal visitors may give some clue to local feelings).[91] As she made her way through the county over the next few days, noticeable by their absence were visits to any of the houses of those associated with the Warwick–Barrington nexus.

It has been argued recently that 'the re-establishment of authority in the localities in the hands of the most important local families, was a

---

September PRO, CO, 1/9, fol. 214 v (my thanks to Christopher Thompson for bringing this document to my attention).

[91] [Jean Puget de la Serre], *Histoire de l'entrée de la regne mere du roy tres-chrestien dans la Grande-Bretagne* (1639), B2 v–D1 v; W. G. Benham, 'Marie de Medici in Essex, 1638', *ER*, 10 (1901), pp. 200–8; Countess of Denbigh, *Royalist Father and Roundhead Son: being the Memoirs of the First and Second Earls of Denbigh 1600–1675* (1915), pp. 148–9; J. Cooper, 'Civic ceremonial in Tudor and Stuart Colchester', *EJ*, 23 (1988), pp. 66, 67. I owe the information on the date of Lucas's appointment to the Prince's Privy Chamber to Christopher Thompson.

central beam' in Charles I's period of Personal Rule.[92] The example of Essex suggests the need for some modification of this judgement. We should not exaggerate the divisions that the 1630s created in the ranks of Essex's rulers. They could still co-operate in the face of unruly clothworkers or soldiers. However, Personal Rule in Essex had seen the county's rulers, previously notable for their lack of serious division, increasingly polarised around two groupings, and the experience had sown seeds of bitterness. When Parliament was recalled, Sir John Bramston informs us that in Essex, 'severall countrie gentlemen that had binn deputy lieutenants, and had been active in arrayinge or pressing soldiers were articled against, and the rest frightened into compliance with the mutinous partie.'[93] Was Sir John Lucas was one of those articled against?

Sir John Lucas's unswerving royalism made it certain that he would answer the king's call to arms. He had already given earlier (perhaps much earlier)[94] evidence of his intentions. Hitherto not noticed by those who have written about the August attack is the fact that Lucas had been trying to send support to the king since at least earlier in the year and that his attempts to do so were known by a wider circle than Colchester's rulers. On at least two earlier occasions in the summer of 1642 Lucas had attempted to offer support to the king and on both occasions Parliament had got wind of these attempts. In the second week of June the Commons had issued an order for Lucas to be summoned to attend the House. At the same time, they had written to the Mayor of Colchester, 'to be very diligent in making Stay of all Manner of Arms and Ammunition that shall be shipped in their Port'. The juxtaposition of the two items within the same entry makes it clear that Lucas had been attempting to send arms to the king. A little over two weeks before the August attack the House again found itself concerned with Sir John Lucas. On the 5 August the Commons had voted on the question, 'whether the Plate belonging to Sir Jo[hn] Lucas that was going to

---

[92] K. Sharpe, 'The Personal Rule of Charles I' in H. Tomlinson (ed.), *Before the English Civil War* (1983), p. 61.

[93] *The Autobiography of Sir John Bramston, K. B., of Skreens, in the Hundred of Chelmsford* (Camden Society, 32, 1845), pp. 74–5. For another example of the sense of division in the ranks of the county magistracy, see *ibid.*, pp. 75–6.

[94] It is possible that the Lucas family were caught up in the Army Plot. Daniel O'Neill was a friend of Sir Charles Lucas, who had served under his brother Thomas Lucas in Ireland, and Lucas's brother was examined before the Commons about their acquaintance: Staffordshire RO, Dartmouth MSS, D(W) 1778/I/i/28 (I owe this reference to the kindness of David Appleby); Coates, *Journal D'Ewes*, p. 158. In May 1641 Parliament had been worried about a correspondence between Colchester and Ireland and had ordered Colchester's authorities to intercept the mail: *ibid.*, p. 125.

Yorke, and is stayed by Order of this House, should be delivered unto him'.[95]

That Sir John Lucas's support for the king had already been brought to the attention of the House raises the possibility that others might have been involved in the action against Lucas. The network that linked the godly of towns within the region with powerful Parliamentary figures is brought out in a letter written by Robert Smith, one of the ministers of Sudbury, to Sir Simonds D'Ewes in 1641, in which he refers to the help the town expected from the lords Saye, Mandeville and Brook. When Colchester's rulers wished to inform Parliament of their discoveries they could, as was customary, communicate with their two MPs, Harbottle Grimston and Sir Thomas Barrington. The Mayor of Colchester described them as, 'two gentilmen who are oure neighboures, of whom the Country and the towne have a long tyme had greate experience off [sic] for theire abilityes and integretys'.[96] Grimston was well known since he was also Recorder to the Corporation and in that capacity alone would have kept up a regular correspondence with the town. Barrington was equally well known. As Colchester's MP he communicated frequently with the Mayor and others in the town, signing himself in his letters to the Corporation as 'yo[u]r very affectionate friende'. Connections between Barrington, for whom the town waits had played at his election at Chelmsford, and the rulers of the town were reinforced both by a shared membership of the godly and by personal ties.[97] Colchester's rulers' relationship with Barrington brought them very close to the leaders of Parliament. Through his membership of the Providence Island Company Barrington was linked closely to the leaders of the 'opposition' to Charles I.[98] Within the Commons, he was a leading ally of John Pym, with whom he was linked by marriage; within Essex, he was the Earl of Warwick's most important ally.

Warwick himself had direct links with Colchester. In a letter to the earl, Henry Barrington had told Warwick of 'how great a power you have in that towne'. As part of a general policy of extending his control over the Parliamentary representation of the Essex boroughs, Warwick had captured Colchester at the election of 1628, when his ally, Sir

---

[95] *CJ*/ii/615, 705.

[96] BL, Harleian MS 160, fol. 153; CRO, D/Y, 2/4, pp. 35–9.

[97] CRO, D/Y, 2/7, p. 69. Barrington's household accounts reveal that in 1641 he was the recipient of a gift of '3 loaves of sugar' from the Mayor of Colchester: ERO, D/Dba, A17.

[98] J. H. Hexter, *The Reign of King Pym* (Cambridge, Mass., 1941), pp. 45–6, 89; D. Brunton and D. H. Pennington, *Members of the Long Parliament* (1954), pp. 123–4; K. Ordahl Kupperman, *Providence Island 1630–1641: The Other Puritan Company* (Cambridge, 1993), pp. 7–9.

William Masham, was returned as one of the borough's MPs. He may also have had ambitions to influence the town's lectureship.[99] Warwick was too powerful and too close a presence for the Corporation to resist, but a shared religious and political identity must have eased his control. Moreover, Warwick was careful not to treat Colchester's rulers as his inferiors. At least in his public dealings and correspondence with the local elite amongst the Corporation, the earl was careful to accord them the respect to which their status as public men entitled them. 'Gentlemen and my very good friends' was how Warwick addressed the Corporation when he sought their votes in the elections to the Long Parliament. His allies in the county like Sir William Masham and, most important of all, Sir Thomas Barrington observed a similar conduct in their relations with the town's rulers.[100] Barrington received presents from Henry Barrington, Mayor and alderman. It has not proved possible to trace whether the two men were linked by ties of kinship, but Sir Thomas in his correspondence presumed such a link, employing the powerful language of cousinage.[101] In contrast with Sir John Lucas's aggressive continuation of his family's jurisdictional conflicts with Colchester, the Earl of Warwick was careful to acknowledge the town's rights. For example, finding himself by the terms of the 1635 charter sharing Admiralty jurisdiction in the town with the Corporation, he wrote to the Mayor, as 'your assured loving friend', promising not to infringe the charter, 'w[hi]ch I shalbe as carefull to preserve as any of yo[u]r Corporation, having ever had a good respect from you'.[102] Men like Warwick and Barrington were careful to acknowledge the important social distinctions among groups others simply lumped together as the people, that is, non-gentry. In their electioneering and in their role as patrons and landlords, they were prepared to recognise the importance of those labelled the 'middling sort', indeed to accept that group's own definition of themselves as the 'better sort'. At the outset of civil war,

---

[99] CRO, D/Y, 2/9, p. 53; Gruenfelder, *Influence*, pp. 155–8, 191–2, 206–7; C. Thompson, 'The Earl of Warwick and the county community of Essex', unpub. paper to the University of Essex Local History Centre 1987 Summer School; CRO, D/Y, 2/4, p. 139. As has already been suggested, the borough's loss of exemption from direct Admiralty jurisdiction may indicate that Warwick had had some part to play in the creation of a new Charter. He may also have had a hand in appointing his brother, the Earl of Holland, as the town's Recorder in 1627, although Holland lost this office on or before the awarding of the 1635 charter.

[100] CRO, D/Y, 2/4, pp. 89–92.

[101] In a letter to the Mayor of Colchester he mentions 'hartye thanks to my Cos. Barrington for ye oysters he helpes me with, for w[hi]ch I am his debtor every way': CRO, D/Y, 2/7, p. 65.

[102] CRO, D/Y, 2/6, p. 33.

Warwick supported the appointment of men of lesser social status to positions of authority.[103]

These links, as well as Warwick's office of Lord Lieutenant, provided occasions for meetings between the earl and the men implicated in *Mercurius Rusticus*. The town, for example, provided dinner for the Earl of Warwick and others in September 1629, when Henry Barrington was then Bailiff. Langley and Warwick were also known to each other. In August 1640 Warwick had written as Lord Lieutenant to 'my very loving friend Captain Langley'. Henry Barrington had also corresponded with Warwick. There were almost certainly other contacts which went unrecorded.[104] The Venn–Langley connection provided another strand to the possible links between Colchester's godly and Warwick, since Venn collaborated closely with Warwick and the other Parliamentarian peers. Indeed, Warwick's willingness to work with the radicals like Venn in London in the early 1640s and in doing so to countenance popular disorder – in London's churches and the streets around Parliament – to secure reformation might be thought to provide suggestive evidence of his likely attitude to, and involvement in, the attack on his political opponent, Sir John Lucas.[105] Just as the crowds in London helped Pym and his supporters to cleanse the House of Lords of popish bishops and malignant lords, so the popular attacks of the summer of 1642 enabled Parliament's supporters to free the region of the threat posed by malignants and papists.

The general absence of surviving correspondence for the relevant period means that we have no firm evidence of the information that flowed along these lines of communication. But political events after 1640 suggest that Colchester's rulers would have maintained their connections and that Warwick and Barrington would have been anxious to have been kept informed by them. That Colchester's January petition was accompanied by some gentlemen of Colchester and presented by Harbottle Grimston doubtless gave them an opportunity for consultation.[106] This must have been especially the case through the difficult summer of 1642 when as we have seen there appears to have been a concerted royalist move afoot to raise support. In addition we know that there were occasions for face-to-face discussion. Sir Thomas Barrington

---

[103] Thompson, 'County community'.

[104] CRO, D/Y, 2/3, p. 89a; 2/9, pp. 53, 343; D/B5, Cb1/8, fol. 439; Galpin, 'Household expenses', p. 223; A. Searle, 'Sir Thomas Barrington in London', *ER*, 2 (1967), p. 67. Warwick had tried to have his choice appointed as Colchester's Lecturer in 1627 (and perhaps again in the 1630s): CRO, D/Y, 2/2, p. 118; *VCH Essex*, vol. 9, p. 131.

[105] Brenner, *Merchants*, pp. 35, 355.

[106] *PJ*, 1, pp. 122–6.

was in the county in the summer 'about Subscriptions' and in Colchester, probably as late as July or early August in 1642.[107] It seems most unlikely that either he or Colchester's godly rulers would have allowed the occasion to pass without some reference to Sir John Lucas, given that in June 1642 Lucas had been summoned to attend the Commons and Colchester's authorities ordered to prevent his shipping away of arms. If, as the Mayor's letter suggests, Colchester's rulers had learned of Sir John's intentions in August 1642 only a day or two before, there might have been time to send off letters to London where Barrington was at the House, if not to have received replies. Nevertheless, given Parliament's specific response to Sir John's earlier attempts and its general orders to prevent the supply reaching the king, Colchester's rulers would have been in little doubt as to what Parliament would have required of them.

There can be also little doubt that Warwick and Barrington would have welcomed action to prevent Lucas joining the king. But what remains in question is whether they would have welcomed popular violence as a means of thwarting his plans. There is no direct evidence to allow an answer to that question. We have seen that they had good cause to dislike Lucas for the active support he had given to the implementation of royal policies in the 1630s. Warwick in particular would have resented Lucas for the challenge his efficient assessment and collection of ship money represented to his domination of the county and for the very public snub that the king's support for Lucas had delivered. Nevertheless any argument presented here must necessarily remain conjectural and heavily dependent on inference.

Perhaps the most important evidence that can be made to bear upon this question is the attitude of Parliament after the event to Sir John and his attackers. From the outset, Parliament treated Sir John Lucas not as a victim who needed protection, but as the guilty party. The day after the attack the Lords declared Lucas's actions in amassing arms for the king high treason and ordered both him and Thomas Newcomen to be brought up in safe custody as delinquents to answer for their actions.[108] When they appeared before the Commons, they were committed to separate prisons, and a committee, with strong 'war party' representation, was set up to prepare an impeachment for treason against Lucas. Shortly after the attacks both the Countess of Rivers and Sir John

---

[107] ERO, D/DBa, A2, fols. 66v–8. The evidence for this visit is to be found in an entry in Barrington's accounts which is undated but comes between entries for the 16 and 29 July. The entry for the second visit mentions the payment of bills on 18 August 1642. Essex MPs who were deputy-lieutenants had been ordered into the county in mid-July to see the Propositions put into effect: *CJ*/ii/681.

[108] *LJ*/v/318,319; *CJ*/ii/732–3; BL, Harleian MS 163, fol. 297v.

Lucas's mother petitioned the Lords for their protection and restitution of their property. The countess received a sympathetic hearing, but Elizabeth Lucas's plea went unanswered. The omission seems a further significant signal of the dominant group in Parliament's hostility to Lucas.[109] When on 21 September Lucas petitioned to be allowed bail, the Commons instead ordered his impeachment to be expedited. Despite this he was released from imprisonment in the Tower at the end of September, but only 'after great debate' and a close vote and at a bail of £40,000. For our purposes, the most telling aspect of the vote was the fact that Sir Thomas Barrington and Sir William Masham, Warwick's brother-in-law, had acted as tellers for those voting against bail.[110]

Does this evidence of the continuing hostility of Essex's rulers towards Lucas throw light on their likely attitude to the attack? Although it comes from a hostile witness, at second-hand and at a date later than the August action, the reported outburst by the Earl of Warwick when Sir John Bramston refused to serve at the Assizes, that 'such as refuse to serve their countrie, it should spue them out', suggests what his attitude to the attack on Lucas might have been.[111] From Warwick's own hand comes a letter, written a little over two weeks after the attack on Lucas, which offers confirmation of the attitude to which Bramston's story points. Writing about a military set-back in the south-west, Warwick urges, 'I pray, stand well upon your guard both military and politic, for you will never get the like opportunity if you slip this, which God hath put into your hands, and loose not your business with civilities and compliments. Give the Cavaliers an inch, they will take an ell. Do the work thoroughly . . .'[112] Given the delicate situation in the country and county at the time of the attacks and Lucas's known royalism, Warwick may not have been too troubled by the incivilities of the Colchester crowds. That six of the catholic victims had acted as collectors for Queen Henrietta's contribution to the Scottish campaign may also have influenced Warwick's attitude to their fate.[113]

The Parliamentary authorities' treatment of those responsible for the attack contrasts sharply with their vendetta against Lucas. At the same

---

[109] HLRO, MP HL, 29 August 1642 (petit. Eliz., Countess of Rivers), [August] 1642 (petit. Eliz. Lucas); *LJ*/v/331.

[110] *CJ*/ii/742, 775; BL, Additional MS 18777, fol. 6b; *CJ*/ii/742, 788–9; BL, E240(17), *A Continuation of certain Speciall and Remarkable passages*, 29 September–1 October 1642, p. 7. Bruno Ryves states incorrectly that Newcomen was released on 24 September; he had to wait until Christmas Eve to be freed: *CJ*/ii/900.

[111] *Autobiography*, p. 88.

[112] HMC 8th Report, 'The Duke of Manchester's MSS', p. 59.

[113] W. Prynne, *Hidden Works of Darkness Brought to Publike Light, Or, A Necessary Introduction to the History of the Archbishop of Canterburies Trial* (1645), p. 192. All but one of the collectors Prynne named were attacked in 1642.

time as they gave orders for Lucas's detention, the Lords represented the actions against him as those of 'the honest Inhabitants of that Town, and the parts adjacent' and talked of 'their peaceable Intentions'. The House declared: 'that in seizing upon the Horse and Arms of Sir John Lucas, prepared for assisting in the war now levied against the Parliament they have done a very acceptable Service to the Commonwealth, and such a one as doth express a great Zeal to their Religion and Liberties.' Although Barrington and Grimston were dispatched to Colchester with powers to send up any who upon examination they thought necessary to do so, it seems that this was an order directed against Lucas's possible associates. Certainly, none of those involved in the attack were called to answer before Parliament for their actions. Indeed, when both the sheriffs of Essex and Suffolk began to send out warrants to raise force to suppress the attacks, Parliament ordered them to stop and 'to forbeare to trouble & execute Justice upon them until the Kingdom be setled & at quiett againe, least it make the cure more dangerous'.[114] While later royalists among the Essex magistracy used the traditional language of riot, tumult and rebellion in referring to the attack, Parliament itself spoke more neutrally (and passively) of people, 'that are in disorders'.[115] At the local level, the Mayor – doubtless in accordance with Parliament's order of protection – did eventually examine at the end of September a handful of those involved in the attack on the Countess of Rivers, but none of those who had attacked Lucas appeared in Colchester's courts. Indeed, the borough's records maintain a crushing silence about the whole affair that yet speaks volumes about attitudes among its rulers to the attack on Sir John Lucas.

Those who thought like Barrington and Warwick were prepared as we have seen to allow (and perhaps the emphasis should be on to allow) a more active role for those below the gentry. Both may have been not unhappy to see crowds pull rails and images down. Barrington took an active role in pursuing ceremonialist ministers like Richard Drake of Radwinter. Warwick, a patron of sermons against popish idolatry, may well have been one of the two lords rumoured to have paid the charges of those questioned for disturbances in the church at Halstead.[116] In contrast to the Maynards, Nevills and Lucases, this acceptance was undoubtedly made much easier by shared political and religious ideas.

---

[114] *LJ*/v/319; *CJ*/ii/732–3. The order was relayed in a letter from Sir Nathaniel Barnardiston to the Suffolk sheriff which observed that the raising of men might provide a screen for the execution of the royalist Commission of Array: Bodl. Lib., Tanner MS 63, fol. 146.

[115] *CJ*/ii/737.

[116] H. Smith, 'Troubles at radwinter', *ER*, 34 (1925), p. 95; CUL, MS Mm.i.45, p. 38.

The anti-popery that informed the attacks on catholics in 1642 was not restricted to the people. It defined the puritanism of the godly. Harbottle Grimston, whose moderate presbyterianism made him otherwise less sympathetic to popular actions, was renowned for his anti-catholicism even in the changed circumstances of Restoration England.[117] The dislike Warwick and Barrington had shown for some of the policies pursued by prerogative before and during the Personal Rule was shared by merchant, clothier, farmer and clothworker alike. Warwick and Barrington were no less concerned than Lucas and Maynard with the defence of their honour and reputation, but Charles' rule had shown that it was from royal policies, which threatened loss of office and an inability to protect the property and religion of their supporters, that the greatest threat to their honour and reputation came.[118] Where there also existed a common interest in the further reformation of the church, in the propagation of godly preaching and in the suppression of sin and superstition, then it was possible for them to acknowledge a shared identity as 'godly people' and to allow the people a more active role. The belief in providence that was a corollary of their puritanism may also have helped them to accept the outcome of the attacks. They too may have subscribed to the belief of their fellow puritan and Yorkshire JP, Thomas Stockdale, articulated in his comment on the London crowd actions: 'The insurrections of the apprentices (as all ungoverned multitudes) are of very dangerous consequence; but God who works miracles can, out of such violent actions, bring comfortable effects.'[119]

Sir John Lucas's unswerving royalism and the role he had played both in the period of Personal Rule and the incipient royalist movement determined his fate. Whatever their role in the attack itself, Warwick and Barnardiston and their allies would have welcomed its outcome. As John Rous noted in his diary, 'this insurrection scareth all the Malignant party'. A report in a Parliamentary newsbook, drawing on a letter from Sudbury, spoke of the victims who, 'to give them [their attackers] satisfaction (if not of realitie) speak well of the Parliament'. As Sir

---

[117] B. Duke Henning, *The House of Commons 1660–1690*, 3 vols. (1983), vol. 2, p. 446.

[118] Witness, for example, Warwick's reported reaction to having to share the Lieutenancy: *CSPD 1635*, p. 385.

[119] D. Rogerson, 'Popular politics in the West Riding during the English Civil War 1640–1648' (M.A. thesis, University of Warwick, 1991), p. 82. Were Parliament's landed supporters also able to draw on the idea that God 'punished unjust princes by unleashing a plebeian chaos against a misgoverned state'? See the stimulating discussion in James, 'Concept of honour', pp. 42–3.

Thomas Barrington reported from Essex, 'this miscarriage of the people proceeding from their zeale to the Parliament did yet wrought this good effect that divers persons who were esteemed malignant before and refused to contribute monie horse or plate to Parliament did now bring in some monie or plate and others horses'.[120]

In Suffolk the consequence was a rapid acceptance of the Militia Ordinance in a county that had previously shown some reluctance. Four days after attacks began, the Lord Lieutenant, the Earl of Suffolk, who only two months before had purchased a chest of arms, wrote to Parliament expressing his willingness to assist in the execution of the Militia Ordinance. That crowds in Essex were reported to have given out that they intended to march to his house at Audley End may well have played a part in helping him make up his mind. It may also explain his eagerness a month or so later to see a house of correction erected in his part of Essex, 'findinge the pressinge necessitie thereof by the greate inconveniencies their parts suffer by multitudes of lewd p[er]sons'. If, as has been argued, support for Parliament among the gentry of Suffolk was weaker in the west of the county where the attacks were concentrated, then this may have made their consequences more acceptable to Parliament's supporters. As Clive Holmes has argued, the 'critical event was the violence in the Stour Valley'. The gentry, 'maintained their class unity at the expense of their previous conscientious scruples', accepting Parliamentary authority as the only guarantor of their property and persons. Fear of popular disorder remained a potent factor thereafter in the politics of the county.[121] Support for royalism within the region collapsed and most catholics, not unsurprisingly, opted for neutrality.[122] Popular action had helped

---

[120] BL, Harleian MS 163, fol. 308 r; BL, Additional MS 22,959, fol. 86 r; BL, E114(36), *Special Passages*, 23–30 August 1642, p. 22; *CJ*/ii/760. Even Harbottle Grimston, who was described after the Restoration by Bishop Burnet as 'much sharpened against popery', may have welcomed the ends, if not the means: Henning, *Commons*, vol. 2, p. 446.

[121] Bodl. Lib., Dep. C.153, Nalson, 2, 57; ERO, Q/SBa 2/47; *CJ*/ii/639; B. G. Blackwood, 'The cavalier and roundhead gentry of Suffolk', *SR*, 5 (1985), p. 2; 'Parties and issues in the civil war in Lancashire and East Anglia', *Northern History*, 29 (1993), pp. 105–6, 117; Bodl. Lib., Tanner MS 164, fols. 102–4; *LJ*/v/506–7. There was an ambiguity over the source of threatened plundering that was repeatedly used as justification for the process of military consolidation by Parliament culminating in the setting up of the Eastern Association: PRO, SP, 16/491/128; ERO, Q/S Ba 2/47 (October 1642); Holmes, *Eastern Association*, pp. 50–9; BL, Additional MS 18777, fol. 45a; BL, E88(15), *A Declaration and Ordinance of the Lords and Commons Assembled in Parliament, For the Associating of the severall Counties* (3 February 1643).

[122] K. Lindley, 'The part played by the catholics' in B. Manning (ed.), *Politics, Religion and the English Civil War* (1973), pp. 147, 149–51. The Suffolk authorities reported in early October that the catholics were eager to lend to Parliament: BL, E240(35), *A Perfect Diurnall*, 3–10 October 1642.

to snuff out a potentially serious proto-royalist movement. Hereafter, the region would become a major reservoir from which Parliament drew support, both fiscal and military. Paradoxically then, popular disorder was both responsible for the growth of support for a royalist movement and, after August 1642, for its collapse.

Part 3

The confessional crowd

5. The attack on ministers

For many ages, as well in forraigne parts as here at home, it hath beene the honor of this towne to be famous for religion
> Harbottle Grimston, Speech, Election Day, Colchester, July 1642[1]

Providence hath placed mee in one of the worst places in the kingdome for opinions.
> Giles Firmin to John Winthrop, 1646[2]

In the spring of 1640 a conversation took place in an Essex churchyard. One of those present, Edward Neale, was reported to have said, 'that the Apprentices were upp in Armes in London and it may be, as I thinke, they will arise, aswell in the Country shortly, w[hi]ch if they doe, I will acquaint them w[i]th our Parson Mr Greene for taking the Lord Archbishop of Canterbury his parte soe much as he doeth'. Shortly before crowds in London had attacked the Archbishop of Canterbury, William Laud's house. Citing Jeremiah 22.6 and 7 – 'And I will prepare destroyers against thee' – Neale had gone on to predict that 'the first houses they would pull downe should be the houses of those that tooke part with the Bishopps'.[3] Edward Neale's words offer a prophetic analysis of the reasons why ministers were among those attacked in the summer of 1642. In Suffolk, as in Essex, the church hierarchy had found allies among ministers who owed their appointment to the clerical

---

[1] Hertfordshire RO, Gorhambury MSS ix. A. 9, unfol.
[2] *WP, 5: 1645–1649*, p. 89.
[3] PRO, SP, 16/454/37, /468/139. Neale may have been the man of the same name who in 1652 was said to have declared, 'there were a thousand lies in the canonical scriptures, and that all the apostles were drunken rascals, and are we to believe what they say?': H. Grieve, *The Sleepers and the Shadows. Chelmsford: a Town, its People and its Past 2: From Market Town to Chartered Borough, 1608–1888* (Chelmsford, 1994), pp. 75, 90. A George Neale was indicted for burning the Book of Common Prayer at Shelley, in September 1642: ERO, Q/SR, 318/29.

patronage of families like the Rivers. These ministers had played an active role in the implementation of the hierarchy's counter-revolution and in the silencing and flight of godly ministers. It was both these general and specific contexts that explain the attacks on ministers that occurred in the summer of 1642.

Colchester exemplified these tensions. 'This towne had beene long possest with the spirit of disobedience to the doctrine and discipline of the church', was the opinion of an Essex royalist at the time of the siege of 1648. Colchester had indeed had a lengthy affinity with reformed religion. The town had been a centre of support for Lollardy, and protestantism had found early important adherents among both townspeople and members of the Corporation. By the later sixteenth century the town's rulers were firm supporters of reformed religion, and by the seventeenth century Colchester had acquired a justified reputation as a godly centre. But reality was more complex than the judgement of 1648 would suggest. Despite descriptions of Colchester as a godly centre – 'a Cittie upon a hill' – in early hagiographical reformed literature, as well as in later historical writing, the reception of reformed religion had been partial and uneven.[4] An awareness of Colchester's chequered religious history helps to thicken yet further the analysis of events in the summer of 1642 and, in particular, to explain the attacks on local clergy, foremost among them Sir John Lucas's chaplain, Thomas Newcomen.

Colchester's rulers' aspirations were, as in other towns of the period, to build a 'godly civic commonwealth'.[5] To that end they had mounted a campaign to secure both godly preaching and behaviour. While the 1635 Charter had excluded from exercising their political rights those convicted of adultery, fornication, drunkenness or common swearing, the court records for the town both before and after that date reflect a familiar concern with both moral reformation and social order.[6] But the

---

[4] While there had been early and wide support for the Reformation among the middling sort and artisans of the town, protestantism was by no means firmly established, and until the later sixteenth century the town's rulers had nervously followed the switchback of reaction and reform: J. Ward, 'The Reformation in Colchester, 1528–1558', *EAH*, 15 (1983), pp. 84–95; M. S. Byford, 'The price of Protestantism: assessing the impact of religious change on Elizabethan Essex: the cases of Heydon and Colchester, 1558–1594' (D.Phil. thesis, University of Oxford, 1988).

[5] P. Clark, ' "The Ramoth-Gilead of the Good": urban change and political radicalism at Gloucester 1540–1640' in P. Clark, A. G. R. Smith and N. Tyacke (eds.), *The English Commonwealth 1547–1640* (Leicester, 1979), pp. 167–87; R. D. Smith, 'Social reform in an urban context: Colchester, Essex, 1570–1640' (Ph.D. thesis, University of Colorado, 1996) (I am grateful to Dr Smith for giving me a copy of his thesis).

[6] P. Morant, *The History and Antiquities of the most ancient Town and Borough of Colchester*, 2 vols. (1748), vol. 1, p. 94 n.; CRO, D/Y, 2/10, p. 46. William Mott, a

pursuit of reformation by sword and word had encountered opposition. In Elizabethan Colchester, the reformation of manners pursued by the godly rulers had provoked popular opposition. Into the seventeenth century there is less obvious evidence of such a struggle. However that opposition was not restricted to those outside the Corporation is suggested by the fact that failure to punish drunkenness and swearing was one of the charges brought by the godly party, many of whom were members of the pre-civil war ruling group, against those who sought to unseat them in the 1650s.[7] The desire to secure godly preaching had also encountered obstacles. Local ministers, over whose appointment the Corporation had little or no control, proved inadequate to the task. The town's attempt to remedy this deficiency by the creation of a town lectureship had brought clashes with the ecclesiastical hierarchy which had ended in defeat in the 1630s.

At the same time as Colchester's rulers faced the problem of resistance to godly rule, they had also to grapple with a religious enthusiasm that threatened separatism. The town's rulers had put such an emphasis on the disciplinary power of the Word, not only because of the need to carry forward the reformation of the ungodly multitude,[8] but also because of the challenge posed by separatists in the town. It is of course impossible to recover how many of the townsfolk were attracted to separatism, but that the Laudian counter-revolution of the 1630s pushed more towards that position seems highly likely. While godly preachers were being silenced in the town (and county), there were those like the Colchester baker, 'a greate holder of Conventicles and an assiduous preacher', who declared it 'impiety to hinder any man from preaching to whom god hath given extraordinary understanding, and the gift of utterance'.[9] Thomas Lambe, presented with his wife in the summer of 1636 for not attending church, was the future baptist who in 1638 was reported to have told the churchwardens of St Giles that, 'he did wish that all churches were layd in the dust'.[10] In the face of the Laudian counter-revolution even

---

member of the Corporation, was the author two essays on how to relieve poverty, both hostile to unregulated aleselling: Hertfordshire RO, Gorhambury MSS, ix. A. 249.

[7] Byford, 'Price of Protestantism', chs. 3, 5 and pp. 148–50, 391; PRO, SP, 18/98/22.

[8] HMS Salisbury MSS, 5, pp. 394–5. One of the duties of the Lecturer was to deliver a sermon at gaol deliveries: Smith, *Ecclesiastical History*, p. 23.

[9] For examples of conventicling during the 1630s, see ERO, D/ACA/49, fol. 162; /52, fol. 19; /54, fols. 50 v, 97 v; PRO, SP, 16/351/100.

[10] Lambe was frequently before the church courts, and in 1639 he was before the High Commission to answer for keeping a conventicle: ERO, D/ACA/51, fol. 122; /52, fols. 233, 17, 93; /47, fol. 38; PRO, SP, 16/434. fol. 37. For his subsequent career 'as the first of the great intinerant evangelists of the revolutionary period and ... a key figure in the radical political movement that sustained the Levellers', see M. Tolmie, 'Thomas Lambe, soapboiler, and Thomas Lambe, merchant, general baptists', *The Baptist Quarterly*, 27

members of the Corporation had begun to waver in their allegiance to a church in which the religion of protestants no longer seemed guaranteed. In 1636 the High Commission had accused Mr Aske, the town clerk, of encouraging 'schismaticall persons (of which faction you have nourished and patronized many within y[ou]r towne of Colchester'.[11] In part, this may have been no more than an example of the church hierarchy's self-serving tendency to conflate 'non-separating puritans' with separatists, but it did point to a real problem in the town that, not unsurprisingly, became more pronounced from 1640 onwards. A discussion among three weavers on the streets of the town in 1642 about the political and religious developments had led one to swear, 'by the name of God that the Aldermen of this towne were some Annabaptistes, some brownistes, some Arminians & some freewillers'. In his speech on Election Day 1642, Harbottle Grimston had told the assembled gathering, 'For many ages, as well in forraigne parts as here at home, it hath beene the honor of this towne to be famous for religion'. Four years later at the same gathering in a speech full of references to 'unhappy jarrs and differences here at home amongst your selves', he was forced to speak in a very different vein: 'Gentlemen, I am affrayd we here in this towne are sicke of the Corinthian disease'.[12] By 1652 the Calvinist leaders of the Colchester Dutch community described Colchester as a 'town consisting mostly of Independents, Anabaptists and Separatists ... [where] the Magistracy and its Ministers and most of the inhabitants are great Independents who hate and despise even the name of Presbyterian Government', while the diarist Evelyn on a visit to the town in 1656 described it as, 'a ragged and factious towne now swarming with Sectaries'.[13] For some at least of Colchester's rulers their

(1977–8), pp. 4–13. The local courts proved ineffective in checking separatism: for example, a group of three men and their wives in St James's parish were presented almost continuously from at least the 1620s until the collapse of the Archdeaconry court in 1641: ERO, D/ALV/5, fols. 123, 184; D/ACA/46–54, *passim.*

[11] Bodl. Lib., MS Tanner 70, fols. 107–11 r; P. Collinson, *Elizabethan Puritan Movement,* (1967), p. 227; C. Burrage, *The Early Dissenters in the Light of Recent Research,* 2 vols. (Cambridge, 1912), vol. 2, p. 269; Ogbu Uke Kalu, 'The Jacobean Church and Essex Puritans: a regional study of the enforcement of church discipline and of the survival of puritan nonconformity, 1603–1628' (Ph.D. thesis, University of Cambridge, 1972), pp. 193, 347.

[12] P. Collinson, 'The co-habitation of the faithful with the unfaithful' in O. P. Grell, J. I. Israel and N. Tyacke (eds.), *From Persecution to Toleration: The Glorious Revolution and Religion in England* (Oxford, 1991), pp. 54–62; CRO, D/B 5, Sb2/7, fol. 298; Hertfordshire RO, Gorhambury MSS ix. A (the almost complete failure of the presbyterian classes of 1648 to secure either ministers or elders in all but three Colchester parishes lends support to the analysis, however theologically untutored its maker: *The Division of the County of Essex into Severall CLASSES* (1648)). Grimston had been telling his fellow MPs of his concern about the increase of separatists in Colchester since at least 1641: BL, Harleian MS 164, fol. 7 v; *WP, 3: 1636–1637*, pp. 484–8.

[13] O. Grell, 'A friendship turned sour: Puritans and Dutch Calvinists in East Anglia,

failure in the 1630s to secure a godly preaching ministry which could co-operate with the magistrate in the enforcement of moral discipline and Calvinist orthodoxy was all the more to be deplored because of the encouragement it gave to separatism.

The Corporation did not control the right of presentment to any of the twelve parishes in the town and its liberties.[14] This situation had arisen from the control that pre-Reformation religious bodies – the abbeys of St John and St Botolph – had enjoyed over the rights of presentation to to all but three of the town's churches. The Corporation's failure to secure these rights had meant that they had passed along with the Abbeys' lands to local landed families. With little or no say over the choice of parochial appointments, Colchester's Elizabethan rulers had established a town lectureship to ensure godly preaching. However, from the outset this became the focus of a running battle between the Corporation and the Bishops of London, who suspended or harried into emigration men whose conformity they doubted. The ecclesiastical hierarchy wanted the lecturer to be a minister with a benefice in Colchester. This was resisted by the Corporation since it would have diminished their power to appoint and retain a minister whose preaching met their godly standards. When in 1631 the Corporation sought to have William Bridges licensed as their preacher, Laud was said to have retorted angrily, 'When you want one you must go first to Dr Gouge and to Dr Sibs [leading godly preachers] and then you come to me, I scorn to be so used. I'le never have him to lecture in my diocese that will spew in the pulpit'. Despite the Corporation's attempt to find a conformable candidate, John Knowles, appointed in 1635, was forced to flee to New England, leaving the town without a lecturer until 1640. At the same time, action by the ecclesiastical authorities to limit the number of Sunday sermons in Colchester's churches exacerbated the dearth of godly preaching.[15]

That the Corporation had little say in the choice of ministers within its

1603–1660' in E. S. Leedham-Green (ed.), *Religious Dissent in East Anglia* (Cambridge, 1991), p. 66; *Memoirs of John Evelyn, Esq., F.R.S. Comprising His Diary From 1641 to 1705–6*, ed. W. Bray (n.d.), p. 248.

[14] Colchester's godly would have been well aware that this situation compared very unfavourably with the control over its ministers enjoyed by the godly of Ipswich, at least until Bishop Wren's intervention: K. W. Shipps, 'Lay patronage of East Anglian Puritan clerics in pre-revolutionary England' (Ph.D. dissertation, Yale University, 1971), ch. 6, pp. 243–66; Grace, ' "Factious humours" '.

[15] Smith, *Ecclesiastical History*, pp. 23–4; Collinson, *Puritan Movement*, p. 246; T. W. Davids, *Annals of Evangelical Nonconformity in the County of Essex, From the Time of Wycliffe to the Restoration* (1863), p. 133; *WP, 3: 1636–1637*, p. 59; CRO, D/B5, Gb 3, fol. 109 v; Shipps, 'Lay patronage', pp. 321–2; Smith, *Ecclesiastical History*, p. 23. In accordance with Laud's concern to limit lecturing, the arrangement by which two sermons were preached at different hours on Sunday afternoon had been brought to an end: PRO, SP, 16/218/43.

parish churches was a serious problem. That choice was exercised by gentry families who by the 1620s did not share the town rulers' vision of godly reformation made it all the worse. By the period with which we are concerned the Audley family controlled the right to present the minister to five of the parishes and the Lucas family had rights to a further three within the town as well as to several others in neighbouring parishes. The complaint of the nearby parish of Layer de la Haye that their minister was 'fforced upon them by Sir Henry Ardley [Audley]' gives some idea of the resentment this situation could create.[16] It is the control exerted by these families over religious patronage in a town where there was a strong puritan element that explains the attacks launched on local ministers, verbal from the 1620s, physical in 1642. While Colchester's godly resented the actions of local clergy like Newcomen in implementing the Laudian counter-revolution, they also resented the fact that it was the control over ecclesiastical patronage in the town exercised by gentry families like the Lucases that both made this possible and thwarted their own aspirations for a thorough and disciplined reformation. By the 1630s gentry patronage had ensured that there was at the heart of this godly city a group of conforming ministers who were prepared to co-operate in implementing what appeared to contemporaries to be a religious counter-revolution. An understanding of the threat this represented to Colchester's incomplete reformation offers a further layer of explanation for the attack on Sir John Lucas and, in particular, for the marked hostility of the crowds towards his chaplain, Thomas Newcomen. According to *Mercurius Rusticus*, when Barrington and Grimston were preparing to take Lucas and Newcomen to London,

> The Coaches are come, and the prisoners called forth; only Mr *Newcomin* they dared not carry out as yet, because the people threatened to tear him in pieces, As assuredly they had done, had not Mr *Grimston's* care been very great, who placing a Court of Guard on each side of Sir *Thomas Barrington's* Coach from the Prison dore, brought him forth unexpectedly and put him into the Coach, the people then not daring to strike or stone him, least the mischief intended should lighten on Sir *Thomas Barrington*.[17]

In 1643 the *True Relation, or, Catalogue of The Gentry, and Persons of Estate in the County of Essex that are Malignants* described Sir John Lucas as 'a favourer of Popery'. Clearly, such a charge from so obviously biased a source should not be taken too seriously. However, seen as

[16] G. Martin, *The Story of Colchester from Roman Times to the Present Day* (Colchester, 1959), p. 32; Smith, *Ecclesiastical History*, pp. 318–9, 313.
[17] *MR*, week 1, p. 4.

evidence of how Lucas was perceived by his puritan neighbours in a period where the Laudian counter-revolution encouraged the elision of the differences between anglican and Arminian, Arminian and catholic, the charge should be taken more seriously. When the *True Relation* labelled Lucas 'a favourer of Popery', it did so immediately after describing him as 'the chiefest actor in that County in the entertainment of the Queene-mother when she came into England'.[18] We have no direct evidence as to the nature of Sir John Lucas's religious beliefs. Unlike his brothers Thomas and Charles who both went to Cambridge, he appears not to have gone to university, spending some time abroad in France instead.[19] However, a clue to his religious beliefs is provided by the role played in his upbringing by Samuel Harsnett, then Bishop of Norwich, shortly after Archbishop of York. Harsnett, who had early in his career served as the master of the town's free school, had been appointed to the Lucas living of Shenfield. John's father, Thomas Lucas, had described himself as 'a great friend' of Harsnett, and Harsnett reciprocated this compliment, calling Thomas Lucas in turn his greatest friend. When Thomas died, Harsnett (who was probably present at the death bed) had acted as a friend to the family, using his powerful connections on their behalf. After Lucas came to maturity, Harsnett continued to act as his adviser. We can only speculate on the exact influence of this close relationship with Harsnett. But a knowledge of Harsnett's position as an anti-Calvinist, one of those 'Arminians avant la lettre', deeply hostile to stipendary lectureships in corporate towns and a strong ceremonialist, may help to explain Lucas's antipathy to his puritan neighbours as well as the family's preferences in ecclesiastical patronage.[20] While there is no direct evidence for the precise nature of Lucas's own beliefs, such

---

[18] *A True Relation, or, Catalogue of The Gentry, and Persons of Estate in the County of Essex that are Malignants, and have not contributed towards the publike Charge of the Kingdome* ... (1643), A3. Because of the anti-catholic character of the attacks, it is sometimes assumed – wrongly – that Lucas was himself a catholic: J. Lee Malcom, *Caesar's Due: Loyalty and King Charles 1642–1646* (1983), p. 25. John Childerley, the rector at the Lucas living of Shenfield, declared in his 1645 will, 'I professe myself to have lived in the faith and unitie of the holy Catholique Church': *WR*, p. 44.

[19] J. and J. A. Venn, *Alumni Cantabrigrienses, Part 1*, 4 vols. (Cambridge, 1922–7), pp. 112–13. Lucas appears in neither Venn nor J. Foster (ed.), *Alumni Oxoniensis, being the matriculation register of the University 1500–1714*, 4 vols. (Oxford, 1891–2). He was in France when his father died: PRO, SP, 16/7/27; /521/42.

[20] *DNB*, *sub* Harsnett; A. Hill, 'Sam Harsnett (1561–1631). The Colchester baker's son who became Archbishop and the friend of kings', *ER*, 51 (1942), pp. 9–16; PRO, SP, 16/7/27;/521/42; ERO, D/DC, 20/9 (Harsnett witnesses 1628 agreement to provide portions for Lucas's sisters); P. Lake, 'Calvinism and the English Church 1570–1635', *P&P*, 114 (1987), p. 35; C. Russell, *The Causes of The English War* (Oxford, 1990), p. 75; P. Collinson, 'Lectures by combination' in his *Godly People: Essays on English Protestatism and Puritanism* (1983), pp. 477, 489, 490–1.

evidence as we have suggests strongly that Lucas supported the church's hierarchy against those labelled puritan. Lucas's choice of the anti-puritan Thomas Newcomen as his chaplain is surely evidence of Lucas's own religious preferences.

There is no direct evidence that religious differences prompted open conflict between Colchester and Lucas in the period before 1640. The only open action by Lucas in support of the church hierarchy for which we have evidence is his role in the collection for the repair of St Paul's. That this allowed him in 1634 to enter Colchester with his fellow commissioners would have done little to improve relations with a town whose rulers stood on their liberties to escape payment and in which the collection was generally unpopular. Nevertheless, the indirect evidence provided by the activities of Lucas's proxies, like Samuel Cocke of St Giles, in promoting Laudian reforms and prosecuting its opponents, suggests that religious differences contributed to the conflict between Lucas and Colchester.[21]

The Lucas family controlled the appointment of the minister in at least six livings in and around Colchester. The character of the incumbents they chose for these livings hardly suggests a devotion to those who sought either further reform or the defence of Calvinism as the doctrinal basis of the English church. A variety of evidence bears this out. In 1629 ministers from three of these livings (as well as Stephen Nettles from Lexden, appointed before the living came into Lucas control) signed the petition of conformable ministers against the puritan preacher Thomas Hooker. This petition, and the counter-petition in support of Hooker, proved something of a litmus test in establishing clerical allegiances within Essex. Later, ministers from four of the Lucas holdings were complained of before the Committee for Scandalous Ministers for being upholders of the Laudian reforms and for being either incapable or unwilling to preach. The incumbents of at least five of the Lucas livings were sequestered in the 1640s.[22]

The failure of Lucas-appointed ministers to meet either the moral or religious standards of their puritan neighbours and parishioners in Colchester is suggested by the fact that they featured prominently in libels circulating in the town in 1622–3 and again in 1636–7. Libels seem

---

[21] PRO, SP, 16/276/42; /369/51; PCR, 2/48, fol. 192 v. For Cocke's role in the promotion of innovation and excommunication of parishioners for refusing to receive at the rail, see BL, Additional MS 5829, fols. 72–3; ERO, D/ACA, 51–4, *passim*.

[22] R. Newcourt, *Repertorium Ecclesiasticum Parochiale Londinense: An Ecclesiastical Parochial History of the Diocese of London*, 2 vols. (1708–10), vol. 2, pp. 387–8; PRO, SP, 16/152/4; BL, Additional MS 5829, fols. 45, 68–9, 70–3; J. Walker, *An Attempt Towards Recovering an Account of the Numbers and Sufferings of the Clergy of the Church of England, Heads of Colleges, Fellows, Scholars, etc. who were Sequestered, Harass'd etc. in the late Times of the Grand Rebellion* (1714), pp. 218, 236, 318, 330.

to have been a not uncommon medium through which religious debate was conducted in early modern Colchester. In one Elizabethan outbreak at least fourteen separate libels were in circulation. The Colchester libels originated from within godly circles, rather than as was often the case being directed against puritans, and they offer a further example of the symbiosis between popular, and puritan religious, culture.[23]

During the Christmas celebrations of 1622 a libel found pinned to a shop window had become the subject of general conversation in the town. Some suspected that it was the work of one Samuel Burrows, whom they labelled 'a potchet puritan', while the young Thomas Newcomen was said to be in pursuit of the author who had traduced his father. We will meet Burrows and Newcomen as adults joined again in conflict. The 1622 libel attacked four local clergymen – William Eyres, Gabriel Honifold, Mr Hawes and Stephen Newcomen, father of Thomas. The text has not survived, but we know that two of the clergy were pictured taking tobacco with the Devil who, it was said, 'wo[u]ld smoake them into hell', while another, William Eyres, was depicted 'with a hogg by him'. Eyres was rector in the neighbouring parish of Gt Horkesley, Honifold the minister at St Mary Magdalene, and Newcomen the minister at St Peter's, a living in the control of the Audleys, but to which the family had allowed the Corporation to present.[24]

Although the text has not survived, it is possible to guess at the nature of the libel. Conflict between ministers and their puritan parishioners was a not uncommon feature of religious life in Jacobean Colchester.[25] Newcomen, Honifold and Eyres had all signed the 1629 petition of conformable ministers for uniformity in the church, in effect an attack on the godly preacher, Thomas Hooker.[26] William Eyres provides another clue to the context of the attack. Eyres was John Lucas's uncle and appears to have lived with the family at St John's.[27] It appears that Eyres held Horkesley with another living, that of St Botolph's within the

[23] Byford, 'Price of Protestantism', pp. 211–44; P. Collinson, 'Elizabethan and Jacobean puritanism as forms of popular religious culture' in C. Durston and J. Eales (eds.), *The Culture of English Puritanism 1560–1700* (1996), pp. 32–57.

[24] CRO, D/B5, Sb2/7, fols. 71, 73 v-4; Newcourt, *Repertorium*, vol. 2, pp. 177–9, 334, 419–20; ERO, T/A, 547/1.

[25] Kalu, 'Essex Puritans', pp. 88, 117, 124, 346. To judge from later evidence the parish of St James had a sizeable puritan presence: *The Compton Census of 1676: A Critical Edition*, ed. A. Whiteman with the assistance of M. Clapinson (Records of Social and Economic History, NS, 10, British Academy, 1986), p. 51.

[26] PRO, SP, 16/152/4. In signing the petition, Eyres had added the comment, 'I greatly fear that to be true which is informed'.

[27] PRO, SP, 16/7/27; /152/4; /229/123. In 1640 Mistress Eyres, John's aunt, was described as housekeeper to his mother at St John's: SP, 16/450/36. That it was Eyres who was sent to France to inform John Lucas of his father's death suggests the close link between uncle and nephew.

town.[28] The first living was in the gift of the Lucas family, the latter belonged to the Audleys. The hog that was his companion in the libel might have been chosen to symbolise the greed implied by this pluralism. Certainly it was Eyres' interference with the town's lectureship that helped to determine his inclusion. In addition to his parish ministry, Eyres had held the town's lectureship from 1610 to 1619. We do not know the reasons for the termination of his tenure, but it is most unlikely that Eyres' performance of his duties would have satisfied the godly of the town. The later description of Eyres in the 1630s libel, as one who 'if tymes of Pooperye [i.e. popery] should com / a dayntie ffryer he wood make', gives a reasonable indication of how his religious orthodoxy was interpreted amongst Colchester's godly (and, given popular protestant representations of the monastic orders as the bloated figures of carnival, a possible further reference to his greed?). Eyres' role as an informant on the activities of the godly within Colchester can only have exacerbated feelings against him. When the town had appointed Francis Liddell as the lecturer in 1622 Eyres had sought to prevent this, claiming that the lectureship remained his under 'an instrument of the Bishop of London'. A letter of 1627, written after Liddell's death and when Eyres was again trying to dspute the lectureship, predicted that if Eyres was not appointed all the ministers of the town 'would band themselves against [whoever was chosen] . . . and make his life uncomfortable as they did the life of the good man deceased [Liddell]'.[29] Some sense of the tensions that the activities of Eyres and his clerical brothers created in the town is suggested in a letter written by Robert Aylett, the Bishop's Commissary and official in the Colchester Archdeaconry, to the Corporation. Writing some months after the libel's circulation, Aylett referred to 'ye factious multitude (who will allow *no minister* but of their owne calling & choise'.[30]

The 1622 libel highlights the potential conflict in a town where puritanism claimed the allegiance of many and a gentry-appointed parish clergy commanded the respect of too few. The counter-revolution launched by the ecclesiastical hierarchy made that conflict explicit. It

---

[28] There is some possible confusion here. Walker, *Sufferings*, p. 236 refers to a Thomas Eyres holding the livings of Mile End and Great Horkesley. Smith, *Ecclesiastical History*, (followed by *VCH Essex*, 9, p. 128) talks about both a William and a Thomas Eyres, the former being rector at Great Horkesley and lecturer, the latter holding this living with Mile End. None of these authorities discuss what the relationship between these two men was. The 1633 Visitation gave Eyres as the rector at St Botolph's: ERO, D/ACV 5, fol. 22.

[29] Walker, *Sufferings*, p. 236; Kalu, 'Essex Puritans', pp. 419–20; CRO, D/Y, 2/10, pp. 119–20; 2/2, p. 118; 2/4, pp. 139, 183.

[30] CRO, D/Y, 2/7, p. 19.

was this that was the occasion of the second libel which, although undated, can be assigned to 1636 or soon thereafter.[31] It was an attack on several of Colchester's parish clergy for their failure to fulfil the role of godly minister. Two of the clergy attacked in 1622, William Eyres and Gabriel Honifold, were again the target of criticism. Joining them were Theophilus Roberts and, assuming his father's place, Thomas Newcomen. In place of the effective preaching crucial to coming to a knowledge of a state of election, these 'dumb dogs' offered infrequent sermons, too often repetitions of stale texts, while in their personal lives they failed to meet the moral standards of their godly parishioners. The text of this libel survives in the State Papers (suggesting that in the changed circumstances of the 1630s an attempt was made to bring in the force of the Privy Council to crush criticism). The libel with its idiosyncratic orthography is worth quoting in full:

A Gaynst The person [i.e. parson] ore prest of St Nichalasses[32] in Colchester

The Complaynt which I haue in hand/is of our perech Teutore [parish tutor]/because with Bonner he is turnd/To be a persiecutor[33] or else with Jewlieas he is turnd/To be A falce backslieder/which macks me fere with hime he shall/in hell for ever Lye ther

I doe not meane that he is fallen/from the trew grace of God/for sertenlye I doe beleue/That it he never had But I doe mene from that falce shaw/which once of loue he maed/but now of envie malles splene/he makes A Comon traed

The reson whi ys onlye this/his perech [parish] would not yeld/That he a foolech Rayle may not/About the Tabell build

---

[31] PRO, SP, 16/229/123. The libel is assigned to *c.*1632 by the editor of the *CSPD*, while Hunt (*Puritan Moment*, p. 260) dates it to the summer of 1631, citing Smith (*Ecclesiastical History*, p. 63) who, besides noting the *CSPD* dating, implies that it should be dated to before 1633 when Roberts was translated to Berechurch. *VCH Essex*, vol. 9, p. 128 suggests a date of c. 1635. However, since the verses refer to the erection of altar rails it is more likely to date from or shortly after 1636 when a general order was made for the erection of rails in Colchester. St Nicholas was among those parishes ordered to provide rails and later in the year several of its parishioners were cited for refusing to contribute to the cost of the rails: ERO, D/ACA 51, fols. 15 v, 27 v, 38, 50, 61, 149 v.

[32] The pun in this mispelling was doubtless intended.

[33] Does the reference to Bonner, Bishop of London under Mary I, suggest local memory of Bishop Bonner's persecution or a reading of Foxe's *Book of Martyrs*? In an Elizabethan Chancery case concerning the circulation of libels in Colchester, one of which was titled 'the Buryale of Clere or th'actes and monumentes of the Mayor of Colchester', a defendant had cited Foxe in defence of the accusations made in the libel: Byford, 'Price of Protestantism', pp. 225–6.

Thay Asked hime The reson whie/That he would needs haue this?/His
answer was becaus the doges/Against it should not pise

But to bring his intent to pase/he knew not whoe to get/tell A piner & A
greasye Cooke[34]/A last his minde ded sett
An built A pound yae owt of hand/ffor to fullfell his will/And som tyme
like an Asse he stands/ther in he Against our will

And now all those that will not paie/to building of the same/Then unto
Dockter Aielets Cort[35]/he will return ther name
And there Against them shall be brought/a bell of excomunicacieon/The
which doe macke me thenke A thought/twell increase his damnasion

And trewly I Could well Awecht [awished]/That more would him
withstood/for why by there exsample then/Thay mait A doon mouch
good
And here in two I Ame to praise/which doe withstand hime stell/And had
thay purses to ther cause/of him thaid haue there will[36]

And one thing more of him Ile spake/which is of his great games/when as
his workes too no efeakt/and much lese is his paines
for whie he is an Iedle drone/tis petye he is not cast out/ye[a] A dome dog
& but once A month/A letell he then barkes out

And then Alase to no efekt/he dooth not pleas my will/for mouch Adoe
he haeth even then/his owr Glase to fell
Y[e]a in A sircle he doeth goe/in a manner like the Sonn/And in A yere
with mouch Adoe/his Sircle he can run

And thus he gooeth from text to text/tell he coms too the latter/but choos
for him Another text/he wood mack but simple matter
ore Like A Cartwhele he goeth round/ore like the horse in mell [mill]/
And once A month Anouf he thinks/the yere upp for to fell

And thus with the false Steward hee/Will not imploy his tallent/But yet
Amongst the Courtlye knaues[37]/he is Counteed A great gallant
& thus I have of owr person [parson]/Spak nothing but that's trew/But as
I have A Soull to save/I not given him half his dew

---

[34] It has not proved possible to identify who is being referred to here.
[35] Robert Aylett, Bishop of London's Commissary in Essex and Hertfordshire: B. P.
Levack, *The Civil Lawyers in England 1603–1641: A Political Study* (Oxford, 1973),
pp. 178, 207; F. M. Padelford, 'Robert Aylett', *Huntingdon Library Bulletin*, 10 (1936),
pp. 1–48; J .H. Round, 'Dr. Robert Aylett', *TEAS*, 10 (1909), pp. 26–34.
[36] It is probable that Richard Freshfield, a parishioner at St Nicholas, was one of those
referred to here. He later petitioned the Lords about his imprisonment for refusal to go
up to, and kneel, at the rails: HMC 4th Report, House of Lords MSS, pp. 42, 87, 89, 90.
[37] Was this a reference to the Audleys, patrons of Roberts' Berechurch living?

And yet Alase others ther be/in towne as bad as he/And in ther devlech
praktissis/are equoll in degree
and now becaus I would not have/you Ignorant of thees/ther names I will
in nomber four/here unto you disclose

And now with Aieres [Eyres] I'le begin/ffor antikwity sake/And if tymes
of Pooperye should com/A dayntie ffryer he wood make

And next to him is honnifowld/Who in mens mouths is bout and sowld/
he allso her[e] shall be in vowld/And shall for A knave with the rest
betowld
ffor all though A skoller great he be/& all soe A devine/yet better he loves
A pretye wench/And all soe A Cup of wine

the third as here I doe suppose/is newcommon that man/I'll need not
much of him disclose/because his acsions Can
ffor he a Brother with the rest/is in that which is evell/And trewlye tack
him at the best/he is one as bad's the devell

The Last of all is he of [w]home/my book here is recorder/And as a knave
I'le set him downe/her[e] with the Rest in order

The context for this libel was the conflict between these gentry-appointed
ministers and their parishioners over the implementation of Laudian
policy, in particular the elevation and railing in of the communion table
as altar – as the attack on Theophilus Roberts, minister at St Nicholas,
makes clear. In 1635 Dr Robert Aylett, a man who disliked puritans in
general and Colchester's 'factious multitude' in particular,[38] had given
orders for the erection of rails throughout the Colchester archdeaconry.
The elevation of the sacrament (and with it the intercessory role of the
priest) over the sermon could have been expected to create trouble in a
town where so many both on the Corporation and amongst the townspeople set such store by preaching. The reference in the verses to Bishop
Bonner, the persecutor of the Colchester protestants under Mary I, may
well have reflected a collective local memory of the earlier persecution
Colchester had witnessed. It certainly gives a strong sense of how the
local enforcement of the Laudian reaction was interpreted in Colchester's
godly circles. The references to the popish tendencies of several of
Colchester's clergy might be taken as evidence of an unsophisticated
theology, but they and the harking back to earlier Marian persecution
suggest the mental framework within which men and women in Colchester made sense of the religious developments of the later 1620s and

---

[38] Padelford, 'Aylett'; CRO, D/Y, 2/7, p. 19.

1630s. The juxtaposition of parson or priest in the very title of the libel, the reference to 'if tymes of Pooperye should com', reflected the growing anxiety of the godly within the region that the suppression of preaching and the revival of ceremonialism did indeed threaten a return to popery.[39]

By January 1637 the harrying of the churchwardens in successive meetings of the church court had ensured that almost all of the town's parishes had provided rails. But as Robert Aylett wrote to Sir John Lambe, his cousin and an ally of Laud, success was only achieved 'w[i]th much opposition especially in great clothing Townes'. This was certainly the case in Colchester. Many of those summoned to appear before the Colchester archdeaconry court in the period after the rails were erected for failing to pay the parish rate or to take communion had done so because, in the words of one, 'his conscience will not permit him to kneele' (i.e. at the rails to receive communion).[40] Aylett's order had set off a series of disputes in many of the town's parishes. A few stubborn parishes resisted the order, and even in those parishes where rails had been erected the court still had to take further action.[41] Out of these conflicts emerged local martyrs whose sufferings became the subject of printed pamphlets and would later be retold to a larger audience when Parliaments resumed in 1640 and censorship collapsed.

The conflict within the parish of St Botolph's and the fate of its churchwardens may serve as an example of the troubles elsewhere in the town.[42] What gave the conflict here added importance was the fact that St Botolph's was the church used by the Corporation. The churchwarden James Wheeler had mounted a sustained campaign against the rails. When his first strategy of pleading the parish's poverty failed, he argued that the altar policy was against the law. This was a claim he subsequently defended in a lengthy, closely argued 'remonstrance', studded with citations to statutes including both the Henrician Submission of the

---

[39] *WP, 3: 1636–1637*, p. 486.
[40] PRO, SP, 16/327/101. For Lambe, see Levack, *Civil Lawyers*, pp. 246–7; ERO, D/ACA/ 53, fol. 123 v.
[41] Attempts to subvert the order involved placing forms for the parishioners to sit on within the rails, parishioners failing to pay the rate for the rail, and ministers coming out of the rails to administer communion: ERO, D/ACA, 51, fols. 15 v, 27 v, 38 r, 50 v–51 r, 52 r, 61 r, 62 v, 71 r, 72 r, 78 v, 79 r, 81 r, 86 v–87 v, 114, 142, 149 v, 161 r, 175, 178 v, 189 r, 224 r, 233, 241, 252 v. A more persistent problem was the failure to come to the rails and kneel to receive communion. Samuel Otway, the minister at St James, had to be ordered not to deliver the communion to those who refused to kneel.
[42] C. P. Tyack, 'The humbler puritans of East Anglia and the New England Movement: evidence from the court records of the 1630s', *The New England Historical and Genealogical Register*, 138 (1984), p. 93. See the cases of Abraham Hill and Richard Freshfield, both of whom were imprisoned for their opposition to the rails: HLRO, MP HL, 21 January, 23 February 1640/41; *LJ*/iv/171.

Clergy and Magna Carta, to show that without the king's permission the bishops and clergy lacked the right to order changes. Twice excommunicated and called before High Commission, Wheeler was imprisoned for three years and, finally, forced to go overseas where he died. His fellow churchwarden had also been forced into exile.[43]

As was suggested by the 1636 libel, the role of the local clergy, and of Thomas Newcomen in particular, in the persecution and creation of local martyrs was deeply resented. Roberts, the minister at St Nicholas, which he held in plurality after 1633 with the Audley living of Berechurch, also acted as Robert Aylett's surrogate, presiding over sessions of the local church court. Apart from his role in the conflict within his own parish satirised within the libel, it had been Roberts who had presided over the archdeacon's court which excommunicated James Wheeler. Together with Honifold and another Lucas appointee, Thomas Tailcott of Mile-End, he had carried out the 1633 Visitation of Colchester.[44] But of all these ministers it was to be Thomas Newcomen who attracted the most hostility. The author of the libel was right to believe by 1636, of 'that man/I'll need not much of him disclose/because his acsions Can'.

In 1660 John, now Lord Lucas, described Thomas Newcomen as 'a man unblameable in his life, Orthodoxe in his doctrine, conformable to the doctrine and discipline of the Church of England'. Newcomen described himself as 'a true sonne of the church'.[45] He was an ultra-conformist and an eager ally of the Laudian counter-revolution. In this he followed his father, the Colchester minister Stephen Newcomen, whose generally unwavering orthodoxy was reflected in his inclusion in the 1622 libel, as well as his signature on the conformable ministers' petition against Thomas Hooker, but not his brother.[46] Thomas' brother was Matthew Newcomen, godly preacher at Dedham and one of the leading presbyterians in the 1640s. The godly of Colchester, some of whom like Daniel

---

[43] Martin, *Colchester*, p. 53; PRO, SP, 16/314/130; ERO, D/ACA/51, fols. 28, 38 v, 73 v, 125 v, 243; /52, fols. 52, 68 v, 91; *LJ*/v/156–7. Excommunicated and summoned to appear before the High Court, Wheeler's fellow churchwarden fled the kingdom: ERO, D/ACA, 51, fols. 15 v, 27 v, 73 v; HMC, House of Lords MSS, 11, *Addenda 1514–1714*, p. 253; *LJ*/iv/156.

[44] Newcourt, *Repertorium*, vol. 2, pp. 53, 176–7, 181–2; ERO, D/ACV, 5, fol. 26; PRO, SP, 16/314/130; G. Rickword, 'The visitation of the Rural Deanery of Colchester in 1633', *TEAS*, ns. 11 (1911), p. 37. The dispute between Roberts and his parishioners over the election of the sexton at St Nicholas in 1636–7 may have been a spillover from the earlier dispute over the rails: ERO, D/ABA, 8, fols. 27 r, 76 v, 161 r.

[45] PRO, SP, 29/9/108. The description is Newcomen's own.

[46] PRO, SP, 16/152/4. However, in an obscure episode earlier in his career Stephen Newcomen had been accused of complicity in a libel attacking the town lecturer for his denunciation of those prepared to relieve local separatists: PRO, STAC, 8/177/5.

Cole retained connections with nearby Dedham and who would have been among those who flocked in large numbers to hear Matthew preach, must have felt that they had got very much the worst of the litter.

Thomas had been educated at Colchester Grammar School and at St John's College, Cambridge (ironically on a scholarship to which he had been elected by the Corporation) which by then was becoming an anti-Calvinist seminary. In 1628 Newcomen had been appointed the rector of Holy Trinity, a living in the gift of the Crown. He held this in plurality with the parish of St Runwald's. St Runwald's was a very poor living which his father had previously served, but it was also a parish where many of the richest merchants lived.[47] Ironically, the rectorship at Holy Trinity provided a link with the Rivers family. The countess's protestant mother who had retired to Colchester was one of his parishioners and it was doubtless through this connection that Newcomen became a friend and counsellor to the Rivers' family.[48]

Newcomen's character had much in common with that of his patron, Sir John Lucas. He displayed a similar assertiveness in defending his clerical rights. Some idea of this trait is provided by Newcomen's longish account in his own hand in the parish register of St Runwald's of his successful attempt to claim a mortuary fee when the body of Sir Robert Naunton was brought through Colchester, en route to burial in Suffolk, in 1635. Newcomen had stood at the church door, 'with the booke and bear [bier] ready (the bell ringing as they passed by)' in order to claim by default a fee of 6s 8d.[49] More importantly, Newcomen had also carried on an aggressive campaign against puritans in his parishes and in the town more generally. An early sign of this conflict is provided by the decision of the churchwardens of St Runwald's to absent themselves from the visitation of 1633. The visitation found much wanting in their church. The warden ordered to remedy these deficiencies was none other than John Furley, leading member of the Corporation and later non-conformist, with whom Newcomen was to clash again later. It was Newcomen's aggressive enforcement of Laudian policy within the town that most explains his unpopularity. The case studies provided by two

---

[47] C. Fell Smith, 'The Essex Newcomens', *ER*, 2 (1893), pp. 35–40; J. H. Round, *Register of the Scholars Admitted to Colchester School, 1637–1740* (Colchester, 1897), pp. 6–7, 10–11; N. Tyacke, *Anti-Calvinists: the Rise of English Arminianism c. 1590–1640* (Oxford, 1987), pp. 193–4; PRO, SP, 29/9/108; CRO, D/Y, 2/2, pp. 283–4; ERO, TA, 547/1; D/ACA/24, fol. 305, /39, fol. 112. Newcomen was in possession of St Runwald's by the time of the 1633 Visitation: *VCH Essex*, 9, p. 334: ERO, D/ACV 5, fol. 26.

[48] The Dowager Countess of Rivers left Newcomen a bequest of books in her will, while her catholic grandson sought his friendship and advice: CUL, Hengrave MSS 1, vol. 3, fol. 262; /88, vol. 2, no. 144.

[49] CRO, D/P, 177/1/1.

causes célèbres illustrate the hostility stirred up by his interventions into the religious politics of the town.

In March 1632 a maid servant examined before the town's justices had said, 'that she denieth not but she said Mr Newcomen was a madd p[er]sone and said that it is as people saye you are a mad p[er]sone and her Mr and M[ist]ris badd her saye soe unto him'. The woman's master was none other than John Bastwick who, with Prynne and Lilburne, was to form the triumvirate of puritan martyrs of Charles I's Personal Rule. It was Newcomen, Bastwick claimed, who had tricked him into speaking against the Church, the offence for which he suffered his 'martyrdom'. When Bastwick had come to live and practise medicine in Colchester, he and Newcomen had been drinking companions.[50] But such friendship as there was had turned into a deadly enmity. Newcomen had brought legal actions against Bastwick in both secular and church courts, which ended with Bastwick having to appear before the High Commission in 1635. The High Commission dismissed the depositions of Bastwick's witnesses against Newcomen as 'scandalous, frivolous & impertinent'.[51] However, something of the bitterness of the conflict between Newcomen and Bastwick can be recovered from Bastwick's subsequent writings which are full of invective against Newcomen for his part in his entrapment. Bastwick consistently depicted Newcomen as a drunkard, who was anxious for clerical preferment but whose standards fell below those of the godly preacher. He was,

a prophane Priest in their towne, who to my knowledge, never was able to make a peece of true Latin ... and for his preaching for whom amongst his pot companions he was esteemed, I can say thus much that I never heard him make a sermon, all the time that I dwell in the towne, that was worth the hearing: but I found it printed to his hand.[52]

Newcomen's very public conflict with Bastwick ended with Bastwick sentenced to have his ears mutilated and condemned to life imprisonment. This punishment, which was said to have excited popular anger in London, must also have stirred up hatred locally against Newcomen. When, after the trial, Bastwick became a name with which to smear other of Newcomen's opponents in Colchester, one man retorted, 'it were good

---

[50] CRO, D/B5, Sb1/4, fol. 1. The main source for what follows is: F. M. Condick, 'The life and works of Dr John Bastwick (1595–1694)' (Ph.D. thesis, University of London, 1982), pp. 51–63.

[51] W. Notestein (ed.), *The Journal of Sir Simonds D'Ewes from the Beginning of the Long Parliament to the Opening of the Trial of the Earl of Strafford* (New Haven and London, 1923), pp. 232–3; PRO, SP, 16/261, fols. 177 v–9 v.

[52] *The Letany of John Bastwick* (n.p. 1637), p. 7. Bastwick does not attack Newcomen by name here, as he did subsequently in his other writings, but it seems clear that he is the intended object of this attack.

or better for the Church if there were a thousand more such as Bastwick was'. Newcomen's role in the case also served to remind the Corporation of its vulnerability in matters religious. Bastwick had accused Newcomen of attempting to elevate the church's authority over that of the borough, attacking in particular his frequent use of the High Commission against the townsfolk of Colchester. If, as has been suggested, Sir John Lucas was the lord whom Bastwick believed to be behind the plot against him, then the episode also provided a further worrying example of Lucas's ability to interfere in the borough.[53]

Bastwick had portrayed Newcomen as a stooge of the Laudian episcopacy. As he wrote in one of his printed accounts of the dispute:

> as soone as my *apology* was *arrived* NEWCOMIN the Preist *reported* in the country, that *it should* cost mee my eares: *and the one I should lose in Colchester, and the other at London, and something* more was added of other punishments...And what that *preist* reports that ordinarily hap[p]ens: for he commonly speaketh nothing which commeth not from the *Prelats mouthes* ... and whatsoever besides he had foretold, all that was executed upon mee, as if he himselfe had given the verdict, and this that I now relate is notoriously known to the whole country.[54]

The other *cause célèbre* again saw Newcomen's aggressive pursuit of conformity in defence of the Laudian policies of the 1630s challenge the town's own sense of autonomy. This dispute involved that 'potchet puritan', Samuel Burrows. Burrows came from a family whose puritanism had made them prime suspects for authorship of the 1622 libel and which had already brought them before the church courts.[55] In 1636 Samuel, now an adult, found himself once again on opposite sides to Thomas Newcomen. Burrows' case neatly encapsulates the tensions in Colchester between gentry-appointed clergy and their godly parishioners.

When the order had gone out to rail in the altar in Colchester's parishes, Holy Trinity was not listed among those required to certify. This did not mean however that Newcomen did not encounter opposition in the parish. While a trickle of parishioners were presented to the church courts for a variety of offences reflecting opposition to Newcomen's enforcement of the Laudian innovations, there was some more spirited opposition. One man, presented to the church court in the summer of

---

[53] *WP, 3: 1636–1637*, p. 487; PRO, SP, 16/499/14; Condick, 'Bastwick', pp. 51–63.

[54] *The Answer of John Bastwick, Doctor of Phisicke, To the exceptions made against his Letany by A learned Gentleman* (n.p., 1637), p. 25.

[55] Samuel's brother Francis was presented by the churchwardens of St Peter's for failure to attend church and for not kneeling to receive communion, while Samuel himself appears to have been presented for living incontinently with one Mary Garret (does this reflect a rejection of the marriage ceremony?): ERO, D/ACA 50, fols. 9, 102 v, 114, 127, 147 v, 159.

1636 for refusing to receive the sacrament, was reported to have said, 'doe you thinke that he will receive the bread and the devell togither', declaring 'that he would be brained before he would receive the holy sacrament after this manner'. At St Runwald's Newcomen seems to have faced more organised opposition. We know from the church courts that the churchwardens had been reluctant to rail in the altar. We know also that the parish contained a number of families who found Newcomen's care of the cure not to their liking and who were later to be prominent amongst the separatists of the 1640s and active in the 1642 attacks. The churchwardens at St Runwald's were pronounced contumacious for their failure to certify that rails had been erected and were subsequently threatened with excommunication. Despite some tactical footdragging, one of the churchwardens was eventually forced to comply.[56] But this was only the beginning of an even more bitter conflict. Newcomen had instructed his churchwardens to present any of his parishioners who would not come to the rails to the church court. Opposition to this requirement was particularly marked in the Colchester archdeaconry, and opinions within the episcopacy were divided about the necessity of receiving at the rails. But Newcomen went a stage further, refusing to administer the communion to any who would not kneel at the rails. For the godly in Colchester this was a requirement that emphasised even more the threat of idolatry implicit in the revised act of receiving at the altar.[57]

Opposition to Newcomen within St Runwald's was led by Samuel Burrows. Once again Newcomen's actions became the subject of a hostile printed account of the dispute. That William Prynne, the noted puritan controversialist, made it the subject of his 1637 pamphlet, *A Quench-Coale*, ensured Newcomen an even wider notoriety.[58] In 1636 Burrows had presented himself four times in the chancel of St Runwald's to receive communion, 'in his usuall seat to receive the same', but on each occasion Newcomen had refused to administer the sacrament unless he came to the rails. That Newcomen was anticipating later instructions – Laud had specified that parishioners should be encouraged, not forced to

[56] ERO, D/ACA 51, fols. 15 v, 38 r, 50 r, 51 r, 62 r, 72 r, 79, 87 v, 119 v.
[57] J. Davies, *The Caroline Captivity of the Church: Charles I and the Remoulding of Anglicanism 1625–1641* (Oxford, 1992), p. 229.
[58] *A Quench-Coale. OR A briefe Disquisition and Inquirie, in what place of the Church or Chancell the Lords-Table ought to be situated, especially when the Sacrament is administered?* (n.p., 1637), pp. 351–8. The account that follows draws mainly on Burrows' own account of early 1644 (PRO, SP, 16/500/18), Prynne's pamphlet, the court records of the Colchester archdeaconry (ERO, D/ACA) and the articles drawn up against Burrows in the High Commission (Bodl. Lib., Tanner MS. 70, fols. 107 r–11 r.) Since Burrows' case formed part of the accusation against William Laud at his trial, I have tried to corroborate wherever possible Prynne's account.

receive at the rails[59] – again suggests that he was not afraid to court conflict with his parishioners. Burrows was cited to appear before the local church court. He appeared and, despite his claim that he had been present to receive communion, was subsequently excommunicated. His response was to indict Newcomen in the secular courts at the town's Easter 1636 Quarter Sessions. By doing so, he successfully re-opened old tensions about relations between the secular and ecclesiastical authorities and their courts and exposed the threat Newcomen represented to the town. In his own statement of the case, Burrows claimed that the jury had found against Newcomen and that as a consequence Laud had had the jury and Recorder for the town bound to appear before the High Commission. In his pamphlet account, Prynne claimed that because the bill was ill-drawn, a claim for which there is corroboration, it was turned down by a jury packed with Newcomen's friends.[60]

The following Sunday Burrows was present in church when Newcomen published the sentence of excommunication. He refused to leave the church, claiming that the sentence was forged by 'his enemy' Newcomen and that since it was not in the king's name he could not obey it. Newcomen ordered the churchwardens to carry Burrows out, but Burrows persisted in claiming that they had no such authority to do so. Newcomen was therefore forced to abandon the church to Burrows. The following day Burrows carried on the controversy, this time with Dr Aylett, the Bishop's official in the Colchester archdeaconry. According to one account Aylett finally rounded on him, saying, 'O Sir, you are you are an audatious fellow indeed, you will indite your minister for Innovations, we will take you down in time, and teach you how to indite Ministers. I will excommunicate you in all the Parishes round about and throughout England, and see who dares absolve you.'

Nothing daunted, in October Burrows was again present in St Runwald's, forcing Newcomen to abandon the service, a scene re-enacted in two other churches that same day.[61] The following day, aided it was claimed by the town clerk, Richard Aske, he again attempted to indict Newcomen at the town's Quarter Sessions for not administering holy communion according to the Book of Common Prayer. When Newcomen countered by reading the sentence of aggravation of excommunication against Burrows, it was reported that two guns were shot off close

---

[59] For the background to the issue of rails, see Davies, *Caroline Captivity*, pp. 205–50. It was not until the 1637 Visitation that parishioners were ordered to receive at the rails and ministers not to administer beyond them: *ibid.*, p. 227–9.

[60] ERO, D/ACA, 51, fol. 120. For a copy of the indictment with the opinion of Sir John Lambe as to its insufficiency, see PRO, SP, 16/375/109; /337/84. Unfortunately, the Colchester sessions rolls for 1636 do not survive.

[61] PRO, SP, 16/339/77 (Notes prepared by Aylett for Laud).

to the church. Despite an attempt to prevent the indictment by the Recorder and Mayor, Robert Buxton, who, as a possible Arminian in the midst of Colchester's godly rulers, had shown himself willing to co-operate with the church authorities in enforcing the Laudian changes,[62] the jury found that it was a true bill. According to Prynne, Newcomen had the Quarter Sessions adjourned and the case transferred to King's Bench to avoid indictment.

At this point, Newcomen went to seek Archbishop Laud's help, lending support to Bastwick's claim that he was the prelate's favourite. Aske, the town clerk, also travelled to see Laud and was told that if he proceeded against churchmen in the temporal courts, he must look for as strict proceedings before the High Commission. Newcomen's return to Colchester with a pursuivant to take Burrows to appear before Laud set 'the whole Towne in an uproare'. Burrows, summoned to appear before the High Commission, had claimed that the Mayor in obedience to the court's summons had broken into his house and had set an armed guard around it. While he was in prison, he was again excommunicated. Burrows' opponents claimed that he had himself contrived his imprisonment to avoid appearing before the High Commission. Burrows, however, claimed that the Mayor had refused to take bail for him or to obey a writ of *habeas corpus* in the king's name, saying he would obey Laud's writ since it had come first.[63]

At his trial before the High Commission Burrows was joined by others from Colchester whom Laud suspected of co-operating with him in the indictment of Newcomen. The most important of these was Richard Aske, town clerk of Colchester, of whom Laud said, 'I ever found him the great maintainer of all wilful opposition against the church ... his zeal would have set the rails on fire, so soon as ever he had come near them'. Predictably, the articles against this group tried to smear them with the charge of subversion: 'you ... very much mislike and oppose Mr Thomas Newcomen a Reverend minister and preacher within ye towne of Colchester meerly bycause he is a man conformable to ye orders of our church & will not be drawn to ioyne wth you in yor extravagant refractory and schismaticall course'. But the articles also yield valuable evidence of how Newcomen was perceived by those who did not share his Laudian leanings. His opponents, who were accused of only coming to church after prayers were ended and just before the sermon began,

---

[62] Buxton was one of the members of the Corporation purged after the 1648 siege: CRO, D/Y, 2/10, p. 74. He was regarded as a 'worthy friend' by the catholic Audleys: ERO, D/ACW 13/272.

[63] ERO, D/ACA, 51, fol. 192 v. Bodl. Lib., Tanner MS 70, fols. 107–11; *The Works of Archbishop Laud*, ed. J. Bliss (7 vols., Oxford, 1851–60), vol. 4, p. 118.

had conspired to indict Newcomen for administering communion in some 'popish or schismaticall fashion'. In the charged atmosphere of the Laudian counter-revolution Thomas Newcomen's role as a zealous local enforcer of Laudian policy was interpreted through the filter of anti-popery.[64]

Beyond the well-documented disputes with Bastwick and Burrows lay a host of other conflicts. Newcomen made active use of the local church courts to discipline his parishioners, and not only his own parishioners. His interference in a dispute over the rails in the neighbouring parish of St Nicholas, the locus for the 1636 libel, again reflects his aggressive interventions into the religious politics of the town. That the case of Richard Freshfield, the St Nicholas parishioner against whom Newcomen had secured a warrant for his appearance before High Commission, resurfaced in a hearing before the Long Parliament must have added to the depth of feeling within the town against Newcomen.[65] As well as being seen to threaten the Corporation's power, Newcomen's use of the church courts to harry individuals also alienated important figures within the ruling group of the town. In 1638 Newcomen himself had presented several of his parishioners for absenting themselves from church, for their refusal to kneel, and for their failure to receive communion. Among these were two aldermen of the town, John Furley and Daniel Cole, the same man whom Bruno Ryves' account implicated in the attack on Lucas. John Furley, father of the younger John said by Ryves also to be involved in the attack on Lucas, was the churchwarden who had failed to appear at the 1633 visitation. Following the erection of rails, he, his wife, their son and daughter-in-law had been among a group of parishioners who had been presented to the church court, again by Newcomen himself, for absenting themselves from church.[66] Furley was also called into the High Commission in 1636, probably as a result of information laid by Newcomen, and he was again presented to the church courts by Newcomen himself in the later 1630s for a range of offences, including failure to receive the sacrament for two years and refusal to kneel to receive.[67]

[64] Laud, *Works*, vol. 4, pp. 119–20 (Laud also claimed that Aske's wife was a separatist, for evidence in support of which, see ERO, D/ACA/51, fols. 203, 224); Bodl. Lib., Tanner MS 70, fols. 107 r–11 r.

[65] HLRO, MP HL, 25 March 1642 (petit. of Rich. Freshfield). If, as seems likely, Freshfield was the same man who was involved in litigation with the Corporation, then Newcomen had met a martyr well able to exploit his case: *ibid.*, 12 July, 21 July 1641, 30 April, 5 July 1642; *LJ*/v/182.

[66] Cole was presented with his wife for not receiving the sacrament 'above twice' for the last two years and for not kneeling 'at the confession of sins, litany and the Collects of the Church': ERO, D/ACV/5, fol. 26; D/ACD/7, fol. 26; D/ACA/53, fols. 17 r, 24 r, 25, 239.

[67] Simpson, 'Furley', pp. 62–70; ERO, D/ACA/49, fol. 72; /53, fols. 9, 17 v. Furley had

As the response of those cited suggested, what lay behind their non-attendance was a tussle over the proper use of the church. While the ceremonialist Newcomen sought to make compulsory attendance at a church sacralised by the presence of Christ on the altar, his parishioners saw the absence of saving sermons as justification for gadding to other churches. As one of Newcomen's parishioners, Joanne Parks, succinctly noted, 'she comes to Church at all tymes when the minister preaches'. Like other parishioners summoned, John Furley's response was to cite the lack of preaching on Sunday afternoons for his failure to attend and to claim that 'the whole parish do usually go to other churches'. By contrast, Newcomen saw worship at the altar, conducted with rites of deferential reverence, as the centrepiece of parish faith. Thus, in April 1640 he cited before the archdeacon's court the wife of Edward Firmin, a man who himself had been in trouble with Newcomen. While her alleged offence was failing to come to the altar rails to give thanks for the safe delivery of her child, she complained that she had sat in 'the usuall Churching seat expecting that the minister would there church her as he had done others before and since'.[68] A final example reveals Newcomen's taste for such conflict with his parishioners. When a child was brought to be baptised, Newcomen, 'not being suffred *to crosse it*', proceeded to pronounce: '*We doe not receive this Child into the Congregac[i]on of Christ's Flock, neither doe it with the Signe of the Crosse, in Token yt hereafter it shalbe ashamed to confesse the Faith of Christ crucified . . .*'.[69] That this was one of the charges later brought against Newcomen before the Committee for Scandalous Ministers suggests the depth of distress his aggressive behaviour could cause.

These fragments of evidence reveal that Newcomen's parish churches, like others in the region, had become arenas for a cultural conflict of gesture (bowing to the altar, signing with the cross) and counter-gesture (remaining seated, or standing if the congregation was sitting, refusing to remove hats or to kneel).[70] Behind the symbols of this conflict lay important differences in matters of faith that might after 1640 move men and women to physical violence. The hostility shown towards Newcomen in the August attack reflected the deep hostility his activities as an agent

---

become a member of the Corporation in 1622, an alderman in 1634 and Mayor in 1638 : CRO, D/B5, Cb 1/7, fol. 208 v; /8, fol. 194; /10, fols. 19, 546.

[68] ERO, D/ACA/50, fols. 25 r, 239 r; /54, fol. 97; /52, fol. 235. Firmin was later a witness against Newcomen before the Committee for Scandalous Ministers: BL, Additional MS 5829, fols. 71–2.

[69] BL, Additional MS 5829, fol. 71 (emphasis in the original).

[70] W. Cliftlands, 'The "Well-Affected" and the "Country": politics and religion in English provincial society *c*. 1640–*c*. 1654' (Ph.D. thesis, University of Essex, 1987), p. 156.

of Laudianism had bred in a town whose identity as both an independent and godly civic commonwealth those activities had challenged.

Bruno Ryves, as we have seen, might be thought to have had a particular interest in emphasising ministers as victims, given the aims behind his fashioning of a narrative of the attacks in 1642. But it is clear that ministers were not infrequent targets of the crowds. Indeed, there were more attacks than Ryves reported. In Colchester Gabriel Honifold was also attacked. Ministers in the nearby villages of Little Tey, Great Birch and Peldon were also targets. At Great Holland near St Osyth, it is probable that the Rivers' appointee, Edward Cherry was attacked, as was their minister at Long Melford, Robert Warren. Others like Edward Symmonds at Rayne or Thomas Stevens, the minister at South Hanning-field, had been intended victims in the summer of 1642, but they had managed to escape.[71] It may not now be possible to recover the personal politics and animosities that helped to determine the selection of each of these particular ministers, but it is possible to see the broader pattern that explains why ministers should have been targeted. Like Newcomen, they owed their fate to an association with the Laudian counter-revolution that for some led to accusations of popery.

What had happened in microcosm in Colchester's parishes had happened more generally throughout the counties of Essex and Suffolk. Godly ministers had been silenced, forced into conformity or flight. Godly parishioners had witnessed worrying changes in both the liturgy and architecture of worship. Episcopal visitations and presentments to the local church courts had harried those who sought to resist ceremonial and doctrinal innovation. Until his translation to Ely in 1638, the Bishop of Norwich, Matthew Wren, had effected an equally thorough reform in Suffolk. In his 1636 Visitation he had suppressed weekly lectures, silenced and suspended ministers, and he had given orders for the railing in and reverencing of the altar.[72] Wren's success was aided by his decision to live in the county, but the more resented among the godly of the Stour Valley communities because their interstitial position between the bishoprics of London and Norwich had previously offered some shelter from

---

[71] *MR*, pp. 12–14. There had been frequent complaints against Stevens for neglect of his clerical duties at both this and his previous living: Smith, *Ecclesiastical History*, pp. 58, 257.

[72] *WP 3: 1636–1637*, pp. 355–63; *Collections of the Massachusetts Historical Society*, 4th ser., 7 (Boston, 1865), p. 9; WSRO, 909/6 (Act Book Archdeaconry of Sudbury 1634–1638: I am grateful to Peter Northeast for lending me his transcript of this document); D. W. Boorman, 'The administrative and disciplinary problems of the church on the eve of the civil war in the light of the extant records of Norwich and Ely under Bishop Wren' (B.Litt. thesis, University of Oxford, 1959).

a too rigorous episcopal inquiry. His success in enforcing conformity was reflected in the unusually large numbers from the county driven to emigrate as well as in the strength of opposition among those who remained. Parishes like East Bergholt and towns such as Ipswich petitioned against his policies, libels were circulated in the county and the 'rude affrontes' of the mariners and other inhabitants of Ipswich caused Wren to forsake the town as his place of residence, but not (alas for the godly) the county.[73] At the Suffolk Quarter Sessions at the beginning of 1637, the justice giving the charge was reported to have said that any minister who refused to administer the communion to those not coming up to the rails and kneeeling should be indicted. In 1639 there were indeed moves in both Essex and Suffolk to indict ministers before the secular courts.[74] But such opposition had no success and Suffolk, like Essex, had its share of martyrs. Ipswich, described in 1635 as 'exceeding facc[ti]ous',[75] had seen its lecturer, Samuel Ward, called before the court of High Commission and silenced after he had preached that 'there was cause to feare an Alteracon of Religion in the kingdome'.[76] That the activities of the bishops were deeply resented among sections of the people is brought out by the report that at the Essex elections to the Long Parliament at Chelmsford, 'the country people cryed out they would have no Bb: [i.e. bishops] nor highe Comission'.[77]

Although they were not as common as attacks on altar rails and the other detested symbols of Laudian rule, there had been attacks on ministers from late 1639 on. For example, in a disturbance at the clothing township of Halstead in October 1640 a group of men and women had seized and destroyed the surplice and hood, and struck the Book of Common Prayer from the hands of the curate. They had also beaten the curate for making the sign of the cross when he was baptising a child. His attackers had then kicked the prayer book up and down the church, 'saying it was a popish book', before burning it in the market along with the surplice. They had also burnt the books of the officials in the church

[73] PRO, SP, 16/337/19; *WP 3: 1636–1637*, pp. 356–7; Bodl. Lib., Tanner MS 68, fol. 14; ESRO C2/18(2).
[74] *Court and Times of Charles I*, 2 vols. (1848), 2, pp. 277–8; PRO, SP, 16/427/30; *CSPD 1639–40*, p. 148.
[75] The words are Sir Nathaniell Brent's when, acting in Laud's stead in the metropolitan Visitation of 1635, he identified Ward as 'the chiefe author of their inconformity': PRO, SP, 16/293/128, fol. 3.
[76] PRO, SP, 16/261, fol. 304 v. Ward's earlier activities had brought him into trouble with Wren's predecessors: R. W. Ketton-Cremer, *Norfolk in the Civil War* (1969), pp. 53–4. At Sudbury John Wilson had been forced to fly to New England: C. Mather, *Magnalia Christi Americana: OR, The Ecclesiastical History of New England, From the First Planting in the Years 1620 unto the Year of Our Lord, 1698* (1702), vol. 3, pp. 43–4.
[77] BL, Additional MS 35,331, fol. 78 v (a reference I owe to Christopher Thompson).

court which met there, an act reflecting popular hostility to the activity of the court in enforcing Laudian ceremonialism.[78] While the parishioners resented the fact that its ministers were appointed by the Bishop of London as patron of the living, John Etteridge, the pluralist rector of Halstead, had particularly annoyed his attackers. Etteridge had been an informant against non-conformable ministers in the 1637 Visitation, witnessing, it should be noted, against several for their failure to use the sign of the cross in baptism.[79] Both he and his curate had been the subject of various libels. A similar pre-history explains the attack on the abrasive (and Arminian) Richard Drake, rector of Radwinter. Both he and his church had been the target of troops, assembled to fight the Scots but more eager to defend the faith against what they saw as a threatened return to popery. Within the parish, Drake had been subjected to continual harassment that stopped just short of violence against him. Services were interrupted with the enquiry 'are you at Mass again' and by attempts to confiscate the surplice and prayer books, baptisms by heated arguments over the use of the sign of the cross, and a burial by a group of women cutting off the chaplain's surplice. As the nature of these attacks make clear there was a significant section of the parish who objected to the changes introduced by the Arminian and ceremonialist Drake and suspected that his enthusiastic support for the innovations threatened creeping popery.[80] These were well-documented attacks. There were others. There were probably more for which now no evidence survives. For example, at the beginning of July 1642, Brian Walton, the minister at Sandon, an Essex parish where the rails had been pulled down by a group of female parishioners, wrote to Lord Chief Justice Bramston of 'the personall abuses whereby I have been in danger of my life'.[81] But the attacks in 1642 represented a more concerted campaign.

It has not been possible to recover evidence of either their doctrinal position or of their relations with their parishioners for all of the ministers attacked in 1642. For example, it is not possible to suggest why in particular William Collingwood, the minister at Great Birch, was

---

[78] It is likely that those involved had themselves been in trouble with the courts. The yeoman husband of one of the women involved was later indicted at the assizes for separatism and for denying the authority of the king in ecclesiastical matters: Cliftlands, ' "Well-Affected" ', pp. 154, 322 n.

[79] Smith, *Ecclesiastical History*, pp. 87–8, 126; PRO, SP, 16/339/53; HLRO MP HL, 10 December 1640.

[80] Smith, *Ecclesiastical History*, appx D, pp. 179–91; BL, Additional MS 21,935, fol. 88 v; HLRO, MP HL, 21 March 1642/3.

[81] For example, at Hallingbury Magna, the minister Edward Thurman, subsequently sequestered, was assaulted by a parishioner while trying to christen a child; at Chelmsford, the minister Dr Michaelson suffered several attacks: ERO, Q/CP 3, p. 130; Smith, *Ecclesiastical History*, p. 111; *MR*, week 3, pp. 18–19; ERO, D/DEb, 15.

chosen as a target by the roving crowds. That Collingwood was appointed by the Bishop of London and later suffered sequestration may suggest some possibilities.[82] Another intended victim, Thomas Stevens of the Petre living of South Hanningfield had been the subject of frequent complaints about the neglect of his clerical duties, both here and at his previous living.[83] Of Thomas Meighan, the rector attacked at Great Braxted, little is known. But that he was one of the signatories to the petition of conformable ministers against Thomas Hooker, gives some hint of the possible reasons for his selection.[84] Behind other incidents can be glimpsed histories similar to that of Thomas Newcomen. His fellow victim at Colchester, Gabriel Honifold had shared an equally difficult relationship with the town's godly. Honeyfold was a pluralist, having been simultaneously the minister of St Mary Magdalene in Colchester and vicar at the nearby parish of Ardleigh, where shortly before the attack he had been involved in a dispute over tithes. He had presided at meetings of the church court at Colchester and in the surrounding villages, and he had signed the petition of the conformable ministers against Thomas Hooker. As one of a group of conformist ministers within the town, Honifold had long been an object of derision among the godly. He had been attacked in both the libels of 1622–3 and 1636 for his failure to fulfill the role the godly sought from their minister. The author of the 1636 libel mocked Honifold as, 'A skoller great he be/& all soe A devine/yet better he loves A pretye wench/And all soe A Cup of wine'. While it is likely that Honifold was one of the group of ministers who had opposed the town lecturer, he himself had failed to offer his parishioners adequate preaching. As the articles against him before the Committee for Scandalous Ministers noted, 'having charge of the Parish 28 yeares, he preached seldom ... & unprofitably'. As was the case with Newcomen, the attack on him (as reported by Bruno Ryves) was marked by sharp expressions of popular hostility.[85] His house was stripped, he was stoned as he was pursued through the streets and, forced from his temporary sanctuary by threats to pull down the house, he was forced to seek sanctuary in the town gaol. According to Ryves, in the middle of these attacks Honifold had sought the protection of Colchester's magistrates, but he had been turned away. The comment reportedly made then by Daniel Cole, one of the members of the Corporation who had suffered

[82] Smith, *Ecclesiastical History*, pp. 169, 309 (but ERO, T/A 547/2, p. 436 gives the Earl of Warwick as patron).

[83] Smith, *Ecclesiastical History*, pp. 58, 257.

[84] Bodl. Lib., MS J Walker c. 2, fol. 102; PRO, SP, 16/152/4.

[85] ERO, D/ACV/5, fols. 10, 19 r, 25–30, 36–7; PRO, SP, 16/152/4, /229/123; BL, Additional MS 5829, fol. 67; ERO, Q/SR 318/57; Q/SMg6, fol. 3; *MR*, p. 10.

from Thomas Newcomen's attention, gives a clue to his selection by the crowd. Alderman Cole, 'wondered he would offer to come abroad being a man so much hated'.

The minister at Little Tey had his cattle driven off, his money taken and, according to *Mercurius Rusticus*, was left with only the clothes on his back. Ryves claimed that the minister was 'guilty ... of nothing but a good and honest name'. The minister at this living had the misfortune to be called Erasmus Laud and had been presented by his namesake William Laud, as patron of the living, in 1631. Given our knowledge of early modern crowds' readiness to manipulate the symbolism of substitution to articulate protest, the claim that he owed his fate to a shared name has a certain plausibility. However *Rusticus'* evident ideological hostility suggests the need for caution. His account notes that Laud's appeal to the Colchester authorities met with an unsympathetic hearing, with Daniel Cole turning him away. However, knowledge of Laud's reputation amongst the godly suggests other reasons for both his treatment by the Colchester authorities as well as the attack on him. Laud's behaviour had offended his godly parishioners. According to the charges leading to his sequestration, Laud was commonly drunk, even on Sundays, so that he was not able to officiate. On several Sundays and Fast Days he had set his servants to work and had worked with them while the church remained locked. He preached only once every five or six weeks. By contrast, he seems to have been a committed ceremonialist using 'frequent superstitious cringing to the Altar'.[86] This partisan view may not offer a rounded picture of Laud, but it does offer evidence of a cultural and doctrinal clash which helps to explain why he attracted the attention of the roving crowds. If his selection was in part determined by a surname which offered an occasion for displaced violence, then popular perception of his own behaviour made the choice doubly appropriate.

If the attack on Francis Wright, the minister at Witham, took place during the attack on catholics there then it is possible to suggest too why he should have been selected. As Dr Cliftlands has argued, his drunken behaviour and fathering of several illegitimate children (which later led to John Walker being advised not to include him in his *Sufferings*) clearly scandalised his godly parishioners and failed to offer them the leadership for the moral reformation that the disorders of their clothing community made more urgent. Leading parishioners gadded to sermons at the neighbouring godly centre of Terling and one of them, Dame Katherine Barnardiston, as a direct consequence pointedly left a generous bequest to a group of godly preachers. Wright's failings which led to his

[86] ERO, Q/SR 319/16; *MR*, pp. 9–10; ERO, T/A 547/2; White, *Century*, p. 31.

appearance at least twice before the High Commission and his present-ment by the Essex Grand Jury for violently denying communion to several of his parishioners had made him notorious. In 1641 he had been complained of to the Commons not only for his moral failings (which included getting drunk on the communion wine), but also for being full of superstitious and idolatrous observations which centred on his devotion to, and elevation of, the sacrament of the altar. Wright's excessive ceremonialism as 'a superstitious Innovator' could easily be misinterpreted by the godly of the parish. That the offences for which he had been presented to the High Commission in 1632 included his agreement to the statement that most bishops were catholics, and a claim that he intended to die in that faith, would have confirmed their worst fears. Despite his notoriety, several appearances before the High Commission and complaints by parishioners to the archdeacon's court, Wright had been allowed to continue in his cure while other godly ministers, including Thomas Weld at neighbouring Terling, had been harried into silence and emigration. Wright's failings would have been the talk of the wider region. The dislocations of the summer of 1642 offered a chance for retribution.[87]

Other ministers attacked, two in Essex parishes close to Colchester and one at Long Melford in Suffolk, were linked by the fact that they all held livings of which the Countess of Rivers was patron. The Rivers family appointed to some nine parishes in Essex and to at least another three in Suffolk.[88] In general, we know too little of the relationship between the wishes of the parish and patron in the appointment of ministers. In particular, we perhaps know even less of how catholic landowners exercised their ecclesiastical patronage and, given the legal restrictions on convicted recusants (but not it should be noted 'church papists'), how far this restrained their influence. But it may be significant that there were suspicions about the commitment to the protestant faith of at least two of the ministers attacked.

John Cornelius, rector at Peldon, seems unpopular enough to have attracted the attention of crowds on two successive days in the August attacks and to have been singled out for further attacks by crowds drawn

[87] Cliftlands, '"Well-Affected"', appx D, pp. 377–80; Smith, 'Ecclesiastical History', p. 129; *CSPD 1635*, p. 217; S. R. Gardiner (ed.), *Reports of Cases in the Courts of Star Chamber and High Commission* (Camden Society, 1886) (I am grateful to Janet Gyfford, whose knowledge of early modern Witham allowed her to identify 'Mr Wright' as Francis Wright, for bringing this to my attention); Notestein, *Journal D'Ewes*, p. 261; HLRO, MP HL, 1 May 1643; White, *Century*, p. 26.

[88] Smith, *Ecclesiastical History*, pp. 52, 313, 314, 316, 317; *The Registrum Vagum of Anthony Harison, 2* (Norfolk Record Society, 33, 1964), *sub* Alpheton, Long Melford, Stanstead.

from both Colchester and his own parish in late 1642/early 1643. According to *Mercurius Rusticus,* Cornelius was plundered of some £400 worth of goods in August; 'they spared not his Library, nor his Wives Child-bed Linnen'. Cornelius himself had been away from home. On the first day the crowd had carried his servant to Colchester; on the second his house was robbed by a small crowd of women, some of whom had been at the attack on the Countess of Rivers' house at St Osyth. Bruno Ryves claimed that Cornelius' appeals for help to the Colchester authorities were also rebuffed, the man he sent being himself imprisoned. That one of Cornelius's servants was subsequently in trouble for libelling the earls of Warwick and Essex gives some clue to his political allegiances. Cornelius had only been rector at Peldon since November 1640, a living which he held with the vicarage of Clavering. He had previously been rector at the Suffolk village of Bildeston where he had been appointed in 1637 by Bishop Wren, who had refused to institute the man chosen by the patron. Little is known of either his tenure at Bildeston or at Peldon, although links between both villages and Colchester would have ensured that his activities there would then have been known about, not least by men like John Langley who had family ties with Bildeston. At Peldon, one man, Henry Durrel, had been bound over four months before the attack for abusing Cornelius, but there is no record of what was said nor evidence – apart from the fact that several of the attackers on the second day were from Peldon itself – to determine whether he was articulating more general feeling in the parish.[89]

In a petition at the Restoration Edward Cherry, the second of Rivers' appointees attacked, complained that 'by the violence of the late Warre [he] was in the year 1642 Constrained to forsake his Rectory'. Cherry was rector at the Rivers' living of Great Holland, some five miles from St Osyth. He had close links with the family, having been tutor to the Countess of Rivers' son who offered him protection in Cheshire after his flight from Essex. The subsequent accusations against Cherry suggest that his excessive ceremonialism was viewed with deep distaste by his godly parishioners. Cherry was said rarely to preach more than once a month and in doing so to devote most of his sermon to upholding innovations. His was a religion centred on altar-worship. He was accused of making repeated bows to the east, and he had refused to deliver the

[89] *MR,* pp. 22–4; ERO, Q/SBa, 2/48; Q/SR, 319/14 and 101 (Cornelius's servant deposed that he had in fact been carried to Colchester by the crowd: ERO, Q/SBa, 2/48, 2 January 1642/3); CRO, D/Y, 2/8, pp. 23, 31; S. Andrews, *The Building of Bildeston Vestry* (Brett Valley Histories, no. 6), pp. 1–2 (I am grateful to Sue Andrews for sharing her knowledge of Bildeston with me); Bodl. Lib., Tanner MS 68, fols. 342–9 r; ERO, T/ A 18, 21; A. W. Gough, 'The rectors of Peldon', *TEAS,* 3rd ser., 7 (1975), pp. 61–70; ERO, Q/SR, 316/34; N. Salmon, *The History and Antiquities of Essex* (1740), p. 441.

sacrament to those who would not come to the rails. That in the summer of 1640 a group of local iconoclasts had pulled down and burnt the altar rails hints at the conflict this had produced. At the same time, by word and deed Cherry challenged the godly's moral code. He was alleged to have been often drunk and to have said that it was more lawful to play, game and drink in the alehouse on Sunday than on any other day. Cherry's known hostility to Parliament at a time when the county was worried about the threat of an incipient indigenous royalist movement would also have marked him out. But perhaps most important was the suspicion of popery that his Arminianism brought. Cherry's doctrinal utterances clearly offended Calvinists in his congregation. He had taught that baptism washed away original sin and that all might be saved by the exercise of their free will. Apart from his association with the Rivers family and his view of his priestly role, there were other grounds that had caused the Essex authorities to suspect Cherry. The chance discovery of a letter he and his wife had written to her uncle then serving in the army had led to his examination about the meaning of their wishing him 'good success in that moste piouse and religious service you are in'. Since the uncle, Robert Appleton, then attending the king, was about to be sent to Ireland and was probably related to the family of the same name sequestered for their recusancy, it is not difficult to see why an otherwise innocuous letter – it was mainly taken up with a cold cure – should have aroused the authorities' suspicions sufficiently for it to be brought to the Earl of Warwick's attention.[90]

Ambiguity over confessional identity was certainly also an issue in the case of the third Rivers' minister (and the only one known to have been attacked by the crowds in Suffolk), Robert Warren, rector of Long Melford. If Warren was the only Suffolk minister attacked, it easy to see why. His career suggests many striking parallels with Thomas Newcomen in Colchester. Like Newcomen, Warren was a pluralist. When he was appointed to Long Melford in 1618, he was already rector of the Essex parish of Borley across the Stour.[91] In his aggressive support of the church hierarchy and active anti-puritanism, Warren seems a close cousin to Newcomen. But in Warren's case the fact that he was both a JP and an agent of Bishop Wren's in the county gave him a larger stage on which to operate (and, of course, to attract hostility).

---

[90] HLRO, MP HL, 21 June 1660; Bodl. Lib., MS J. Walker c. 3, fol. 178; ERO, Q/SR, 311/ 50 and 51; White, *Century*, p. 3; BL, Egerton MS 34,253, fols. 7–12. A John Appleton with property at Mundon in Essex had been sequestered as a recusant, but none of the other Essex returns of catholics for the period include any Appletons: *CCC*, p. 2746; Campbell, 'Estreat of fines', pp. 25–32; J. Mary and M. Nicholas, 'Essex recusants in an Exchequer document 1585–1642', *ERec*, 6 (1964), pp. 90–5.
[91] *WR*, p. 167; R. Freeman Bullen, 'Sequestrations in Suffolk', *PSIA*, 19 (1927), p. 163.

Warren's actions can be seen in microcosm in the case of the nearby town of Sudbury, a godly centre in whose affairs he had plenty of occasions to interfere both as a JP and as an agent of Wren.[92] The challenge his actions posed to the town's independence as a chartered borough raises parallels with the relationship between Newcomen and Colchester. Warren had become involved in the attempt of two local men to replace two of the town's ministers. The Andrewes brothers had purchased the impropriation of St Gregory's, one of the two parishes in the town, and wanted to remove the minister Robert Smith and John Harrison, who officiated at St Peter's chapel. The litigation to which this gave rise provides revealing evidence of how Warren was perceived by the godly.[93] Earlier, in 1633, Warren had been a member of a clerical commission to investigate ('molest' the godly called it) the conformity of Harrison, minister at the chapel of St Peter's.[94] Harrison had managed to retain his position, only to be later evicted. Thereafter, the Andrewes brothers had served the chapel with young men, whose services they acquired 'beast Cheape' and who were variously described as 'Alehouse haunters' and 'chanters' who took 'noe care or paynes to preach, to the great distast & discomfort of the people'. The high standards demanded by the godly were brought out in the comments on one of these replacements. The young scholar Robert Rash did preach on Sunday, but only in the mornings and not in the afternoons despite requests by the Mayor, 'whereby', it was claimed, 'profanenences & disorders happen in the afternoon'. The dispute mushroomed, with the town's rulers seeking to use their jurisdiction to hit back at the brothers. In their turn, the brothers used the church courts to harass the townsmen, citing them to Norwich over trifling matters and calling on the support of their ally Robert Warren. Warren was no friend to the town. At a meeting between him, another JP and two aldermen of the town called to settle a dispute over the over-rating, Warren called them 'threidbare Aldermen & reviled the officers with many grosse termes'.[95]

In the midst of this dispute a meeting of the clergy at Sudbury provided the occasion for further conflict between Warren and the town. The

---

[92] For an example of Warren's activity as a JP in the town, see *WP 1: 1498–1628*, p. 317.

[93] The main source for what follows is the legal papers drawn up for the town and which survive among Sir Simonds D'Ewes' papers: BL, Harleian MS 589, fols. 137–9. These are undated, but since D'Ewes was MP for the town in the Long Parliament they are likely to date from then. Smith, one of the ministers involved, was writing to D'Ewes about the case in May 1641: MS 160, fol. 153. Cases of refusals to pay tithes to the impropriators may also relate to this dispute: WSRO, 909/6, fols. 86 v, 226.

[94] *WP 3: 1636–1637*, p. 62.

[95] For later evidence of a significant godly presence in the town, critical of the choice of ministers, see M. Storey, ed., *Two East Anglian Diaries 1641–1729: Isaac Archer and William Coe* (Suffolk Record Society, 36, 1994), p. 16.

arrival of the Bishop's commissary's deputy was greeted by a libel set on the church and his meeting was disrupted mid-sermon by a large crowd of weavers and apprentices who proceeded to pull down the altar rails in St Peter's Chapel. A royal messenger sent to the town was placed in the town cage, and when Dr Warren secured his release a large crowd gathered and vented their anger in a burst of stone-throwing.[96] The aftermath of these episodes made it clear that it was not just Warren's intervention, but the religious differences informing his actions that created resentment in the town. Robert Smith, the minister at St Gregory's whom the Andrewes sought to remove with Warren's help, was one of the godly, writing to the town's MP, Sir Simonds D'Ewes in 1641 of his hope for, 'a purer worshippe & governement among us & yt [that] without any rite or rag of whoorish Rome remayninge.'[97] Warren made his own religious preferences clear when he sat in the town as a JP to inquire into the episode of the altar rails. He told the jury that 'they ought without farther inquirey or adoe, to find it a sacriligious Riot because it was god's house where men ought to praie & noe where els[e], for praieinge in theire families breeds conventicles & for meetinge together under Color of religion thay plaie the whores and Rogues togeather'. Finding the jury unwilling to find the crowd's action a riot, he was reported to have called them (amongst other names) 'puritannical' and to have threatened them with King's Bench, Star Chamber and imprisonment. Thus at one and the same time Warren's actions challenged both the town's religious and political identity.

Warren's zeal helps to explain why he was only one of two ministers in the Sudbury archdeaconry picked out as most able to help Wren in his 1636 Visitation. As the fallout from the Sudbury dispute made clear, Warren's active support for the church hierarchy had earned him the enmity of the godly in the town. They described him as 'a great stickler about the late innovac[i]ons as well in the churches in this towne as other places & very eager & bitter ag[ains]t many learned, grave and conformable men w[i]thout cause.' Like Newcomen, Warren had supported a religion centred on altar-worship and he had sought to deny the

---

[96] PRO, SP, 16/470/55; 16/439/41. This is undated, but assigned by the editors of the *CSPD* to 1639. The Privy Council had issued a warrant to another messenger for the arrest of the innkeeper in October 1640: *The Privy Council Register Preserved in the PRO*, 12 (1968), p. 38.

[97] BL, Harleian MS 160, fol. 153. Smith appears to offer another link between the events in the summer of 1642 and the Parliamentary leadership. His letter made it clear that he expected the help of Lords Say, Mandeville and Brook in securing a hearing in the town's case in the Lords. The Barrington family also had an earlier connection with the town through the minister John Wilson, who had been forced to migrate to New England: C. Thompson, 'New light on the Suffolk elections to the Parliament of 1628', *SR*, NS 10 (1988), pp. 218–24.

godly access to the regular preaching which for them constituted the centre of their religious activity. He had threatened one man for gadding to sermons and reportedly told him, 'that hee hoped ere longe there would be a lawe to punish such inordinate walkers'. Warren's role as an active ally of Bishop Wren in his attempt to suppress puritan preaching and to impose uniformity brought him wider notoriety. It made him an object of comment in the letters that passed among the godly of the region and New England.[98] Such was the contrast between Warren's zeal as a magistrate and indifference as a preacher that it had even made him the butt of a joke which circulated in the region and ended up in the jestbook of one Norfolk gentleman, Sir Nicholas Le Strange, who had the story from Dr Garnons, rector of Glemsford and Warren's near neighbour:

> One Doctor Warren, A Devine in Degree and profession, yet seldome in the pulpitt or church; but a Justice of the Peace, and very pragmaticall in secular businesse; having a fellow before him good refractorie and stubborne, well sirrha, sayes he, goe your wayes, I'le teach you Law, I'le warrant you: Sir sayes he I had rather your worshippe would teach us some Gospell.[99]

This was doubtless a sentiment shared by Warren's godly parishioners. Although it has not been possible to reconstruct Warren's pastoral relationship with the parish of Long Melford, it is not difficult to imagine what it might have been.[100] Melford was a prosperous living and to judge from fiscal records it made him one of the wealthiest men there. He had been involved in disputes with neighbouring manors over tithes, one of the inhabitants accusing him of behaving 'very cruelly'. If the troubled experience of Warren's successor is an accurate guide, the tithe in such a populous parish provided plenty of scope for conflict. That a manor was attached to the rectory offered a further area for conflict. According to Warren's successor after the Restoration, the 'evidences' of both Warren and his predecessors were 'sayd to be lost, and destroyed through ye rudeness, and fury of the then enraged, misguided multitude'. That the crowd seems systematically to have destroyed both the recent manorial

---

[98] Bodl. Lib., Tanner MS 68, fol. 78 r; *WP 1: 1498–1628*, p. 317, *3: 1636–1637*, pp. 62, 388.

[99] *"Merry Passages and Jests"*: *A Manuscript Jestbook of Sir Nicholas Le Strange*, ed. H. F. Lippincott (Elizabethan and Renaissance Studies, 29, Salzburg, 1974), p. 93. The editor's suggested identification of Warren with an earlier Norfolk clergyman is mistaken.

[100] Does the fact that the iconoclast William Dowsing did not mention Melford among the list of places he visited offer indirect evidence of earlier iconoclasm and of the strength of opposition to Warren's ceremonialism?: C. H. Evelyn White (ed.), *The Journal of William Dowsing of Stratford* (Ipswich, 1885).

court rolls, as well as the records of Warren and his predecessors relating to the tithe, suggests that the potential for conflict in these areas had been realised under Warren's lordship.[101]

Given this evidence of conflict with the godly of towns like Sudbury and the reputation it had brought him in the region, it is easy to see why the crowds in August 1642 should have attacked Warren. If, as was suggested earlier, the weavers of Sudbury made up a large part of the crowd active at Melford then 1642 represented an opportunity to revenge themselves on a man described as 'a continuall medler in the ... towne'. At Ipswich Warren had been a member of the commission sent by Bishop Wren whose purpose had been to curtail the freedom the town enjoyed in the appointment of its ministers and whose arrival had been the occasion for open protest in the town. If, as seems the case, some of the crowds in 1642 were drawn from Ipswich then they too would have relished the opportunity to secure revenge against Warren.[102]

All this helps to explain the severity of the attack on Warren. It also explains the symbolism of the shape the attack took. The Suffolk minister John Rous recorded of the attack on Warren, that 'him they huffed and shuffed about, but (as is said) hurt not otherwise'. Recollections of the attack, gathered in the early eighteenth century from old men then in their seventies, reveal that Rous's reference to Warren's having been 'huffed and shuffed' conceals a more purposeful action. A near-neighbour of Warren remembered that Warren was interrupted 'in ye midst of Divine Service, Call'd a false prophet & compelled to come out of ye pulpit whilst in ye midst of his Sermon, & returning home one ... beat a frying pan before him in derision, saying this is your Saint's bell'.[103] This has overtones of rough music and charivari, common forms of shaming sanction often derived from actions by authority and deployed against those who offended communal norms, in the latter case women (and men) whose behaviour threatened a gender order grounded on male

---

[101] PRO, E179/183/489a; V. B. Redstone (ed.), *The Ship Money Returns For the County of Suffolk 1639–40* (Ipswich, 1904), pp. 186–8; BL, Harleian MS 388, fol. 199; *The Chorography of Suffolk*, ed. D. MacCulloch (Suffolk Records Society, 19, 1976), p. 55; WSRO, 909/6 (a reference I owe to the kindness of Peter Northeast). Warren's successor after the Restoration, Nathaniel Bisby, complained bitterly of the destruction of the records and had a hard fight to restore the collection of the tithe: WSRO, FL 509/3/15, pp. 1, 5, 15 and fols. 620–1, 632 (I am grateful to Lyn Boothman for this last reference); C. Deedes, 'Dr Bisbie's manuscript collection for Long Melford', *PSIA*, 7 (1891), pp. 78–90.

[102] W. E. Leyton, 'Ecclesiastical disturbances in Ipswich during the reign of Charles I', *The East Anglian, or Notes and Queries*, NS 2 (Ipswich, 1887–8), pp. 209–10, 257–9, 315–7, 373–4, 405–6.

[103] *Diary of John Rous* ed. M. A. Green (Camden Society, 1856), vol. 66, p. 122; Bodl. Lib., MS, J. Walker, c. 1, fol. 309.

patriarchal authority. Since Warren's suspected popery offered an inversionary challenge to the confessional identity of the protestant church, this was an appropriate form of ritualised behaviour for the crowd to appropriate. A world turned upside down by Warren's suspected popery could be righted by the counter-inversion of rough music and mockery. Warren's house was also attacked. According to one account the house was 'rifled for his Gods, and a great many set about the market crosse, [and] termed young ministers'. These 'Gods' may well have been the images of saints which had been stripped from the church of Holy Trinity in Long Melford, but which we know were retained in the neighbourhood for some time after the Reformations of the sixteenth century. Christening inanimate objects 'young ministers' may have been an example of plebeian humour intended to attack Warren and his like for their failure to preach effectively. The market cross provided an obvious public space for this display, but the fact that the cross was a pre-Reformation structure and may itself have been subjected to an iconoclastic attack, would have made this choice even more appropriate. By echoing earlier episodes of iconoclasm, this public display was doubtless also designed to stigmatise Warren as an idolater for upholding the ceremonialism of the 1630s. Troops at Chigwell in Essex in the summer of 1640 had nailed the images they had pulled down to a post in the local market place and had written underneath them, 'This is the God of Dr Neutton', Newton being the name of a local minister. Elsewhere, troops who had confiscated 'wooden Gods' and crucifixes from a catholic household had tied them by their heels and had drawn them through the town before burning them, actions echoing the punishments inflicted upon catholic traitors.[104]

But this public display may also have been a deliberate attempt to symbolise suspicions about Warren's confessional identity, for what were these 'gods' doing in Warren's house? At Sudbury, Warren's actions had led to suspicions about his faith, 'for soe hee did expound the place of the apostle whereby he put a feare in the minds of divers the King's subiects that here was a change of Religion towards.' As we have seen in the case of the Essex ministers, an excessive ceremonialism could be interpreted by the godly as evidence of popery. But in

---

[104] D. Dymond and C. Paine, *The Spoils of Melford Church: The Reformation in a Suffolk Parish* (Ipswich, 1992), pp. 24–5, 39; E. Duffy, *The Stripping of the Altars: Traditional Religion in England 1400–1580*, (1992), pp. 489–90; E. Wigmore, 'Long Melford Market Cross', *Long Melford Historical and Archaeological Society Newsletter* (December 1995), p. 5; BL, Additional MS 21,935, fol. 89. The 1613 Melford Hall Estate Map, in the possession of Sir Richard Hyde Parker and reproduced by the Long Melford Historical and Archaeological Society (*Occasional Publications*, no. 4, 1995), clearly shows the market cross on Melford Green.

Warren's case the godly had even stronger grounds for their suspicion. In 1628 Warren had been reported to the Privy Council as being 'justly suspected of Popery'. When he died, he bequeathed his soul 'into the hands of Almighty God, trusting (notwithstanding my manifold sins and transgressions to finde acceptance with him unto Saveing mercy) through the charitie and passive obedience of a blessed Saviour satisfieing his ffathers iustice for mee'.[105]

At Ipswich Henry Dade, the man threatened with plunder by a local shoemaker, had a similar record to Warren and the other ministers. Dade's activities there as an official within the Court of the Admiralty had made him enemies which – if his meddling in the issue of a new charter was known – would have included members of the Corporation. As commissary for the Archdeaconry of Suffolk, Dade had played an active role in the enforcement of Bishop Wren's crusade against the godly. He had taken it upon himself to keep Archbishop Laud informed about emigrants to the New World and their backers among the godly clergy in the region. At Ipswich itself, Dade had become involved in a dispute with the town's godly that paralleled Newcomen's actions at Colchester and which also featured in a pamphlet by the puritan controversialist William Prynne. It was Dade who had excommunicated a local churchwarden for his failure to remove the verses he had caused to be inscribed from the New Testament: 'It is written, My house shall be called an house of prayer, but ye have made it a den of Theeves' (Mark 11.17). It was Dade also who had sought to bring Samuel Ward, Ipswich's godly preacher, into the High Commission, recognising that if his role became known he would, 'thereby incurre & indure the hatred of his adherents'. Although Dade escaped the fate of the other ministers, his intended plundering would seem to have a similar cause.[106]

In Colchester in the 1630s an aggressive episcopacy intent on enforcing uniformity in belief and conformity in behaviour was aided by zealous allies among the town's clergy. The activities of this fifth column served further to remind the town of the near-monopoly of clerical patronage exercised by a gentry whose own religious preferences were not those of the Corporation. It may well have been that in Essex the ecclesiastical 'enforcement machinery was like a blunt scalpel',[107] but when in the

[105] HMC Portland MSS, vol. 1, p. 2; PRO PROB, 11/307, fol. 241.
[106] M. White [W. Prynne], *NEWES FROM IPSWICH*, p. A4r PRO, SP, 16/250/54; /260/17; / 289/46; /302/140; /308/23; /326/46; /346/26; /474/50, 78; Bodl. Lib., Tanner MS 89, fols. 172–4; *CSPD 1629–1631*, pp. 531, 537; *CSPD 1633–1634*, p. 125; *CSPD 1636–1637*, p. 423; HMC Cowper MSS, vol. 1 (1888), p. 429.
[107] O. Kalu, 'Continuity in change: bishops of London and religious dissent in early Stuart England', *JBS*, 18 (1978), p. 45.

1630s Crown and church worked to support active local ministers then, as the case of Colchester showed, individuals could indeed be harried and persecuted. Critics of the religious changes were presented to the local church court and, where necessary, summoned to London to appear before the court of High Commission. The town clerk was forced to flee to the Netherlands, the town's lecturer to New England. Colchester was forced to bow to the enforcement of Laudian reform literally in the form of the church rails, by 1637 a powerful and ubiquitous symbol in each of its parish churches of the elevation of the sacrament over the sermon. As Thomas Seaward, a linen-draper in the town who was questioned for his opposition to the railing of the altar, told his inquisitors, 'nowe Justice was lockt up in this Land and there was no justice to be had in the kingdome'.[108] Moreover, as we have seen, Colchester tended to make sense of these changes in terms of a polarized discourse that conflated threats to the Calvinist faith with a return to popery. As a marginal note to the churchwarden James Wheeler's 'remonstrance' pithily observed, 'Turninge co[mmun]ian tables into Altars, & placeinge them altarwise is a popish practise & backslideinge to popery'.[109]

Central to this process was the role of Thomas Newcomen. Newcomen's zealous defence of the discipline and doctrine of the Laudian church deeply offended Colchester's godly and, in all probability, his actions excited a wider anti-clericalism. Newcomen's parishes experienced a revolution in their religious practices and beliefs which the parishioners, many of whom were important members of the Corporation, were unable to check. Moreover, the manner of its enforcement, calling in the support of outside agencies – both royal and episcopal – also challenged the authority of the town's rulers in a way that paralleled the actions of Sir John Lucas. Central to Bastwick's attack on Newcomen, as well as to that of Burrows, was the charge that Newcomen had attempted to elevate the church's authority over that of the town.[110] That the town clerk, Robert Aske, was forced to flee to Holland as a direct result of Newcomen's actions offered a potent

---

[108] PRO, SP, 16/497/14. Seaward, who had been previously before the church courts, seems to have copied Burrows in carrying his protest into at least two Colchester parishes. His protest, echoed elsewhere in the county, consisted of sitting with his hat on in church while the first and second lessons were read and refusing to take communion: ERO, D/ACA/48, fol. 201 v; /52, fols. 50, 69, 115.

[109] PRO, SP, 16/314/130.

[110] Newcomen was accused of trying to force the Mayor and one of the town's JPs to act as his parish officers and of calling the JP into the High Commission. His frequent use of the High Commisision against the town's inhabitants was also highlighted by Bastwick: Letany, pp. 7–8. Compare the role of the conformist minister Matthew Brooks in the politics of Great Yarmouth: Cust, 'Anti-puritanism', pp. 1–26

symbol of Newcomen's challenge to the town's cherished sense of autonomy.[111]

When Parliament was recalled in 1640 and the victims of the 1630s began to petition for relief, John Bastwick and Samuel Burrows were among them, their petitions highlighting the role Newcomen had played. At the same time, the collapse of censorship allowed the republication of the printed accounts of his conflict with his parishioners which we know to have circulated earlier in the region in the 1630s.[112] Locally, there was no need for such reminders. When in January 1642 Colchester petitioned the Long Parliament, the town had called for the reform of 'Idle, Double-Beneficed, Scandalous and ignorant Ministers, who have not onely bin carelesse of the duty required of them, but also in their places, very troublesome and vexatious'. We have already seen that the drawing up of the petition was a topic for discussion on the streets of Colchester, and there can be little doubt whom most in Colchester would have named when hearing this clause. Newcomen's active support for the religious changes of the 1630s made him, even though he did not hold a Lucas living, an ideal choice to be chaplain to Sir John Lucas. His royalism, evident in his preaching, made him an obvious ally in the plan to take support to the king.[113] But these qualities also marked him out as a target for the crowds in the summer of 1642. The depth of hatred they displayed reflected the hostility he had stirred up within the town. Bruno Ryves had no need to invent or exaggerate the intended violence towards Thomas Newcomen. As Sir Thomas Barrington reported to Parliament, he had been forced to take him into his care 'to free the towne of Colchester from innocent bloud'.[114]

The attacks on ministers in the summer of 1642 represented a reaction to the religious counter-revolution of the 1630s. Given that this was a more general development across the region, there may well have been further attacks for which evidence has not survived. Those ministers who we know to have been attacked owed their fate in part to their proximity to, and notoriety in, godly towns like Colchester or Sudbury. But their selection was also to be explained by the pre-history of marked conflict with their parishioners. The communities in which clergymen like New-

---

[111] Bodl. Lib., MS Tanner 70, fol. 109; *The History and Tryal of William Laud* (1695), p. 261.

[112] Notestein, ed., *Journal D'Ewes*, p. 233; HMC 4th Report, House of Lords MSS, p. 41. Copies of Prynne's *NEWES FROM IPSWICH*, reprinted in 1641, which also recounts the Newcomen-Burrrow conflict, had been circulating in the 1630s: Tyack, 'Humbler puritans', p. 98.

[113] He used the pulpit to denounce the king's enemies as traitors, preaching that 'the *Scots were damnable* Rebells for invading the Kingdome': BL, Additional MS 5829, fol. 71.

[114] *MR*, p. 4; BL, Harleian MS 163, fol. 307 v.

comen and Warren lived would have subscribed to the complaint in the Root and Branch petition against 'the encouragement of ministers to despise the temporal magistracy ... and live contentiously with their neighbours, knowing that they, being the bishops' creatures shall be supported'.[115] The attacks were the outcome of the religious and cultural divide between the godly of the region and ministers closely identified with, and active in implementing, the Arminian and Laudian programme of the 1630s. Aggressive men like Warren and Newcomen challenged a whole set of interests and represented in marked form the 'clerical pride' that brought in its train widespread anti-clericalism.[116] Although the godly were in the forefront of the attacks, it is probable that they were able to call upon others whose mobilisation was to be explained by popular anti-clericalism. But it is also possible that they were able to command wider support because of the popular perception that the religious counter-revolution of the 1630s threatened a return to popery. The language of anti-popery that was used to criticise clergy like Newcomen and Honeyfold in the Colchester libel and its symbols, evident in the charivari-like attack on Warren, align the attacks on ministers with the attacks on catholics that became the hallmark of the crowd actions after the attack on Sir John Lucas.

[115] S. R. Gardiner, *The Constitutional Documents of the Puritan Revolution 1625–1660*, 3rd edn (Oxford, 1968), p. 138.
[116] K. Sharpe, *The Personal Rule of Charles I* (New Haven and London, 1992), p. 401.

6. The attack on catholics

The Papists were the most popular common-place, and the butt against whom all the arrows were directed; and so ... an order was made by both Houses for disarming all the Papists in England: upon which and the like orders though seldom any thing was after done or no matter of moment, yet it served to keep up the fears and apprehensions in the people of dangers and designs ...

Edward Hyde, Earl of Clarendon[1]

ourselves togeather with you and the whole Kingdome ... be in great danger from ye Papists and other ill affected persons whoe are everie where very insolent and ready to act the parts of those savage bloud-suckers in Ireland if they bee not speedily prevented. By meanes whereof our Tradings especiallie of clothing and farming grow a pace to soe great a Damp as many Thowsands are like to growe to suddaine want, Nor can Wee expect any redresse thereof Unlesse the Bishopps and Popish Lords be removed out of the house of Peers.

The humble petic[i]on of the Knights, Gentlemen, Mynisters and other Inhabitants of the County of Essex, 20 January 1641/2[2]

On 26 May 1640, three sets of examinations were entered in Colchester's book of examinations and recognizances. The first, that of a 56-year-old Irishman taken by the Mayor, breaks off before being completed. For the second and third examinations, the Mayor was joined, unusually, by five of his fellow aldermen. The second examination was of two young girls, aged ten and eleven, about an incident which they had witnessed

---

[1] Edward Hyde, Earl of Clarendon, *The History of the Rebellion and Civil Wars in England Begun in the year 1641*, ed. W. D. Macray, 6 vols. (Oxford, 1888), vol. 1, p. 380.
[2] HLRO, MP HL, 20 January 1641/2.

late the previous night while playing in the streets. They told this extraordinary gathering of the town's magistrates a story of seeing two strangers, cudgels in hand, acting suspiciously. They had seen the men peer through a window, push rags into the house and then hasten away. The third set of examinations was about an incident which had taken place earlier that day and which involved a group of the young men of the town. According to one of those examined, John Oddey, he had been walking down East Street when he had become caught up with a group of the youth of the town. Joining them, he went along with them to All Saints' church where they had met Thomas Johnson, his master's son. Johnson had been asked by them to beat 'a litle boye's drume', and they had persuaded another very young boy to go along with the drum and to proclaim that all 'gentleman apprentices' should resort to *Mr* Lucas's fields.[3] According to another who had been called out of bed to join them, their supposed purpose was 'to play a match at foote ball'.

Football in early modern society with its large crowds and disrespect for the boundaries of property and proper behaviour often supplied both pretext and text for organised protest. Clearly, some such idea lay behind this incident. According to John Oddey, their real purpose was to have gone on to Mistress Audley's and Mr Barker's, there 'to see the horses which they had heard was there'. Inserted into this statement was the addition that the horses had arrived last Sunday, 'laden with armer [for] about 140'. Both the Barker and Audley families were catholics. Rumours of the arrival of the horses and armour clearly had provoked speculation among the young men of the town. Johnson the drummer deposed that he had heard several of the crowd say, 'that they heard yt [that] Byshippe Wren & many other horsemen and footmen were come to Mrs Audleyes & Mr Barkers and they would goe & see whether it were so or noe'. According to the others examined, they 'had noe intent to doe anie hurte; but if it were so as they heard then they intended to returne & to acquainte the towne with it'. Given the levels of violence associated with football play, this answer might be regarded as more than a little disingenuous.

There is nothing else in Colchester's records to throw light on these seemingly discrete episodes. However, there survives another account which not only shows that they were linked, but which also gives a very much better sense of what was really going on in the town. This was a report, by an unnamed 'discreet and understanding Gentleman who came into Colchester on Whitsun Tuesday in the morning and stayed

---

[3] CRO, D/B5, Sb2/7, fols. 277 v–8 (my emphasis). Assuming that this was St John's Field, a green just beyond the town walls, does the repeated use of *Mr* by the apprentices to refer to Sir John Lucas suggest a deliberate slighting of his status?

there that night', which was sent to the Privy Council.[4] His account came, he claimed, from honest men who had told him, 'that they dare not appeare in it, for feare of mischief, which may befall them from ye licentious multitude, soe animated as they are'. He reported that the Mayor – none other than John Langley – had raised the town's trained bands from their beds around eleven o'clock in the evening of Whit Monday on the report that two Irishmen had been seen walking about the town. According to our 'understanding gentleman':

> This suddayn alarm att yt time of night raysed (almost) the whole Towne, men, woemen, and children, and putt them into a verie great amazement, and fright ... The next morning, the people still re-mayning in much feare and perplexity, many Rumors were soon spread about ye Towne, some saying that a great number of Papists were assembled at Beerechurch (the house of ye Lady Audley, a Recusant) neer Colchester, to bring the Queene's Mother thither: Others sayd That ye Lord Archb[isho]p of Canterbury was come thither; others that it was ye Bishop of Ely. But some added, that they were not att Beerechurch, butt att Mr Barkers (another Recusant) at Monkquick [sc. Monkwick], neare ye said Towne of Colchester.

'These reports were all ye forenoone talke on Whitson Tuesday'. At one o'clock a drum was beaten through the streets, 'to which many loose people soon resorted', and proclamation was made to call all apprentices to meet at St John's Field and from there to go to Berechurch and Monkwick, 'to see what company was there'. Only after the drum had been beaten through the streets for an hour or so did the Mayor send for the drummer and commit him to prison. One hour later, a drumbeat again put the town in fear. But this time the drum was being used at the Mayor's order to summon the pressed men then in the town – Colchester was a rendezvous for the troops being assembled to fight the Scots – to assemble at the Town Hall.[5] The presence of some hundreds of troops in the town must have added to tensions there (as well as being an occasion for the town's inhabitants to reflect on the extraordinary political events through which they were living). At the time of the gentleman's stay in Colchester nobody was sure whether the apprentices had gone on to Berechurch and Monkwick, but he had learnt later that 'this Riotous Assembly, though they wanted their Drum, yet they did goe unto both those places in a verie disorderly manner'.

The tone of this report leaves little doubt that its author was no friend to either Colchester's Mayor or apprentices. As the conclusion to his

[4] PRO, SP, 16/458/13.
[5] Seven-hundred troops had been ordered to be brought to Colchester by late May: PRO, SP, 16/451/74; /454/45–6.

report makes clear, the purpose of its writing was to question both the motives and the actions of the Mayor, 'a man not long since in question before his M[a]ties Commissioners for Causes Ecclesiastical'. As to any action taken by Colchester's authorities:

> Some report, That ye Mayor or Recorder of ye Towne did make enquiry afterwards, and committed some of them for the fact. Others say, that they all make butt a jest of it. One of the Towne officers lately in London slighted it, saying it was butt a boye's Drum, and none butt few children and boyes followed it. And it is very likely that this will be made ye answer of them all unto it.

It is a pity that we do not know the identity of the author of this report, nor that of his informants. He seems to have succeeded in his purpose, for a month later John Langley found himself having to answer for his actions to the Privy Council, a situation he must have resented, not least for the slight offered to his mayoral authority and to that of the town.[6] Langley's *examination* provides further evidence of events in Whit week. According to Langley, two men had come to him and told him of the Irishmen, 'of whom it was suspected that they had some designe upon the Towne to fire it'. Although he claimed not to have believed the reports about the Bishop of Ely and the store of arms, he had summoned as many aldermen as he could, strengthened the watch at the gates, and had ordered about forty of the trained bands to march up and down the town for most of the night. The calling out of the pressed men was in response to an order for their training he claimed. When he heard that some people had set off to the Audley and Barker households, he sent after them. Several were arrested and these he claimed to have imprisoned for two weeks, only releasing them after they had been cautioned to appear at the next Quarter Sessions. Hearing later that some boys had managed to reach the houses, he went himself to Berechurch and sent two constables to the other household, where the crowd they found there obediently dispersed at their command and with no damage done. As predicted, Langley made light of the incident, 'since they were all little Children and had no weapons but sticks in their hands ... [and] ... their Drumme that was beaten was a little Drumme, like a Tabor'.[7] But as readers will have noted, what happened in Colchester in Whit week looks very much like a dry run for the attacks two years later (with of course the significant exception that, despite the rendezvous close to St John's, no attack appears to have been planned against Sir John Lucas).

---

[6] PRO, SP, 16/458/12: a document headed 'the *examination* of John Langley'.
[7] Since Colchester's judicial records do not survive for this period it is impossible to check Langley's claims, but examinations were taken of only three of the company, all of whom were in their early twenties.

Urban panics, prompted by the fear of catholics firing the town, were not uncommon. Elsewhere in the region, Norwich experienced a number of such episodes, and at Cambridge in July 1642 there were rumours of firing elsewhere 'by Papists'.[8] That fears about the activities of catholics should frequently take the form of fears of firing reflected the legacy of 5 November and the heavy threat, not least psychological, that fire posed to early modern urban communities. In Colchester's case this fear seems to have been fed by rumours circulating that catholics were massing at the homes of local gentry families, where arms were reportedly being stockpiled.[9] That the appearance of two Irishmen – to judge from the little girls' account intent on burglary, not arson – had been sufficient to set Colchester in uproar is eloquent testimony to the level of political tension in the region. It also hints at the high level of anti-popery that was a concomitant, some would say defining, characteristic of the high level of puritanism within the town. Firm commitment to Puritanism meant a greater sensitivity to the popish threat. Of the two men who had reported the suspicious sighting of the Irishmen to the Mayor, one was a man who might be expected to be particularly hostile to what he saw as the threat of popery. This was Thomas Lambe who had been frequently before the local church courts and who was later to play an important role as a Baptist in the world of radical politics and sectarian religion in London.[10] Intriguingly, Henry Barrington, one of the Colchester aldermen, later became involved in another panic in a very similar situation – a catholic gentleman living close to, but separate from, a godly town. That this was at Rye in Sussex suggests an eagerness on Barrington's part to help hunt out catholics wherever they might be.[11]

The Colchester incident offers vivid evidence of how political events at the centre were understood within the region. Both its timing and form reflect the proximity of the region to the capital and therefore the ease with which news and rumour of events there passed quickly into the

[8] In August 1640 Norwich was put in turmoil by rumours that twelve-thousand catholics were coming to fire the city: R. Clifton, 'The popular fear of catholics during the English Revolution', *P&P*, 52, p. 29; PRO, SP, 16/468/44; PCR, 2/52, pp. 728–9; Bodl. Lib., Tanner MS 63, fol. 89. Robin Clifton, 'The fear of catholics in England 1637 to 1645, principally from central sources' (D.Phil. thesis, University of Oxford, 1967), offers the most sustained account of these panics.
[9] K. Thomas, *Religion and the Decline of Magic: Studies in Popular Beliefs in Sixteenth- and Seventeenth-Century England* (Harmondsworth, 1973), pp. 17–20; E. L. Jones, S. Porter and M. Turner, *A Gazetteer of English Urban Fire Disasters, 1500–1900* (Historical Geography Research Series, no. 13, 1984).
[10] ERO, D/ACA/47, fol. 38; /51, fol. 122 v; /52, fols. 17, 233. For Lambe's later career, see M. Tolmie, 'Thomas Lambe, soapboiler, and Thomas Lambe, merchant, general baptists', *The Baptist Quarterly*, 27 (1977–8), pp. 4–13.
[11] PRO, SP, 16/467/104.ii; A. Fletcher, *A County Community in Peace and War: Sussex 1600–1660* (1975), pp. 102–3.

country. In 1640 news from London was full of anxieties about the popish threat. On 21 May, a letter from London into Suffolk carried the information, 'heare is a great deale of feares and tumults, fears of papis[ts] Risinge'. Another, written a week later, warned, 'the papists increas[e] in abundance, and ther[e] is great fear in the citty and a strong watch keept every wher[e] and a great search mad[e]'. If, then, Colchester's Mayor and apprentices feared what local catholics might be preparing to do, this was in part because such fears had gripped the capital. The timing of the crowd's assembly in Colchester was determined by the immediate panic over the Irish 'incendiaries', but its shape – action by the apprentices – was undoubtedly a deliberate echo of the actions of their London counterparts a fortnight earlier. We have already seen how talk in an Essex churchyard of the apprentices' rising had led to predictions that 'they would shortly rise in the Countrie'. The London apprentices had threatened action against the Queen Mother and Archbishop Laud; they too had marched with a drummer at their head.[12] While the activities of Wren when Bishop of Norwich and Laud when Bishop of London had rendered them notorious among the region's godly, the rumoured presence of Marie de Medici, suggests that rumours current in London that it was the Queen Mother who was the mastermind behind a popish conspiracy had reached Colchester, a town that had earlier been forced to welcome her when she had stayed as a guest of Sir John Lucas.[13] Like their London compatriots, the young men of Colchester saw themselves as having a particular role in the enforcement of the moral and confessional boundaries of the community. Their choice of St John's Green as the place of assembly seemed to confirm this, since this was where the youth of the town did their military training. According to one of those examined, they hoped that by their inspection of the Audley household that 'happily they might see some things there w[hi]ch might doe the towne [good].[14]

The reality of catholicism in Essex and Suffolk was not that suggested by anxieties then current of a large and growing cancer. In Essex, it has been

---

[12] BL, Harleian MS 386, fol. 71 (I am grateful to Lyn Boothman for bringing this letter to my attention); *Winthrop Papers 4: 1638–1644*, pp. 248–9. Pearl, *London*, pp. 39, 107–8; S. R. Gardiner, *History of England from the Accession of James I to the Outbreak of the Civil War 1603–1642*, 10 vols. (1901), vol. 9, pp. 132–4. Apart from other lines of communication, the apprentices' actions had been the subject of a royal proclamation of the 15 May which had been sent out into the counties: *Stuart Royal Proclamations 2, Royal Proclamations of King Charles I, 1625–46*, ed. J. F. Larkin (Oxford, 1983), no. 339, pp. 710–12.

[13] For details of these rumours, see C. M. Hibbard, *Charles I and the Popish Plot* (Chapel Hill, 1983), p. 156.

[14] PRO, SP, 16/454/37; /468/139; CRO, D/B5 Sb2/7, fols. 119 v–20, 277 v.

suggested that there were at the beginning of Charles I's reign some 600 'determined adult Roman Catholics', and that in a population perhaps of the order of 85,000. In Suffolk in 1641 there were only some 460 catholics convicted of recusancy.[15] However, such figures were not how those within the region judged the potential threat from catholics, even had they had access to them (which of course they did not). They understood the threat of catholicism partly in terms of the observable character of the local catholic community (which gave them cause for concern), partly in terms of their cultural inheritance of anti-popery (which was given a resonant local inflection within the region), and partly in the light of a powerful belief in a popish plot to subvert both church and state. Fears about popery were not related to the known size of the recusant population precisely because it was widely believed that there were far more secretly practising catholics.

Catholicism in the region clustered around the seigneurial household.[16] While the historian of Essex catholicism might note that only five per cent of armigerous families had strong catholic associations, it was precisely the fact that it was among the region's gentry that catholicism was upheld, and that several of the leading landowners and peers were among its strongest adherents, that most impressed (and alarmed) contemporaries. One such family in Essex was the prolific Petres. With their main seat at Ingatestone, the family and its many cadet branches had extensive estates in the centre and south of the county. Aristocratic households like the Petres continued to function as mini-courts for catholics in the region.[17] It had been the second Lord Petre who in 1633 had founded the Jesuit College of the Holy Apostles whose priests served the needs of the faithful in the four counties of Essex, Suffolk, Cambridge and Norfolk. When the protestant dowager Countess of Rivers was

---

[15] N. C. Elliott, 'The Roman Catholic community in Essex 1625–1701' (B.Litt. thesis, University of Oxford, 1976), repr. as issues *ERec*, 25–7 (1983–85), 25, p. 7; F. Hull, 'Agriculture and rural society in Essex, 1560–1640' (Ph.D. thesis, University of London, 1950), p. 122 (population estimate based on 1636–7 ship money assessment); K. J. Lindley, 'The Lay catholics of England in the reign of Charles I', *Journal of Ecclesiastical History*, 22 (1971), p. 202. The history of catholicism has not been as well served for Suffolk as for Essex, but see MacCulloch, *Suffolk*, and 'Catholic and puritan in Elizabethan Suffolk: a county community polarises', *Archiv für Reformationgeschicte*, 72 (1981), pp. 232–89; J. Rowe, 'Roman Catholic Recusancy' in Dymond and Martin, *Historical Atlas*, p. 88; G. H. Ryan and L. J. Redstone, *Timperley of Hintelsham: a Study of a Suffolk Family* (London, 1931), pp. 108–9.

[16] This has been argued to be more generally the case for post-Reformation catholicism: C. Haigh, 'From monopoly to minority: Catholicism in early modern England', *TRHS*, 31 (1981), pp. 129–47.

[17] The inventory of Robert, Lord Petre at his death in 1638 throws light on the links this forged; among those owing him money were familiar catholic names like the Whites, Southcotts and Waldegraves: ERO, D/P, F224, m. 4.

reported to be considering giving an estate not to her daughter Lady Penelope Gage, sister of Elizabeth, Countess of Rivers, but instead to Lady Gage's son-in-law, Francis Petre, a correspondent warned against it, saying, 'he is knowne to be most pervers[e] in his Religion, and wholly governed by iesuits as my L[ord] Rivers was.'[18]

Seigneurial catholicism could, as at Long Melford, produce large concentrations of catholics. Moreover, the network of connections between these households could increase the unease to which they gave rise. A confessional pattern of endogenous marriage between the faithful of the region created strong kinship networks. For example, Richard Martin of the Long Melford family married three times before his death in 1624–5. His wives came from the Mannocks of Giffords Hall, the Daniels of Acton (both fellow victims in 1642) and the Smith family of Tuddenham in Suffolk. In turn, the Daniels exchanged sons and daughters with the Martins of Melford Place. A daughter of the Daniels was to become the second wife of Robert Audley of Berechurch, whose own daughter married into the other neighbouring catholic family, the Barkers of Monkwick, fellow victims in 1642. The head of the Barkers at the time of the August attack was married into the Suffolk family of the Timperleys of Hintlesham, a family also related by marriage to the Greenes of Little Sampford who, in turn, were related to the Mannocks. Marriage had also formed links between the Audleys and the Darcys, the family of the Countess of Rivers.[19] The Rivers family were related by marriage to the Petre, Southcott (of Witham) and Waldegrave families. The White family, also victims in 1642 were related both to the Waldegrave family and to Richard Weston, Earl of Portland, another Essex landowner whose mother and estates were to suffer in 1642.[20] Marriage also created links with families in other counties in the region. The Bedingfields, Southwells and Waldegraves of Norfolk were related

---

[18] Quintrell, 'Government', p. 18; Elliot, 'Catholic Community', *ERec*, 27, p. 4; CUL, Hengrave MSS 88, vol. 2, p. 145. Many of the Petre family themselves became Jesuits: J. Jackson Howard and H. Farnham Burke, *Genealogical Collections of the Roman Catholic families of England* (n.p., 1887), pp. 39–40.

[19] W. C. Metcalfe (ed.), *The Visitations of Suffolk Made by Hervey, Clarenceux, 1561, Cooke, Clarenceux, 1577, and Raven, Richmond Herald, 1612* (Exeter, 1882), pp. 24–5, 52, 132, 152; M. J. Hartharn, 'The Audleys of Berechurch', *ERec*, 12 (1970), p. 44; Ryan and Redstone, *Timperley*, table 2, facing p. 50; Metcalfe, *Visitations Suffolk*, p. 151; Metcalfe, *Visitations Essex*, vol. 1, pp. 44–6, 140.

[20] CUL, Hengrave MSS, 2, fol. 123; E. Lauriston Conder, *Church of the Holy Trinity, Long Melford, Suffolk* (1887), pp. 72–3; A. Page, *A Supplement to the Suffolk Traveller* (Ipswich and London, 1844), p. 914; G. Dawson, 'The Jacobite Southcotes of Witham', *ER*, 63 (1954), p. 145; Howard and Burke, *Genealogical Collections*, p. 39. For evidence of the hospitality between the Rivers and Daniels family, see Howell, *Familiar Letters*, p. 111; D. Shanahan, 'The White family of Hutton', *ERec*, 8 (1966), pp. 33–7, 55–71, 78–8.

through marriage to Essex and Suffolk families, among them the Audleys, Martins, Daniels and Smiths of Cressing Temple.[21] There were many marriages which brought links with catholic families further afield. The Sulyard family of Haughley in Suffolk, victims in 1642, were related by marriage to noted and at times notorious catholic families like the Throckmortons of Worcestershire and the Treshams of Northampton-shire. Marriage also tied them to the Sheldons of the West Midlands, another family who were to become victims of crowd and troop action. The marriage of the second Lord Petre had brought links between the family and the Earls of Worcester, a family also the focus of godly anxieties in the run-up to civil war and a target for crowd action.[22] The Audley family demonstrates these wider ties. Henry, the victim of the 1642 riots, had married into the Packingtons of Chaddesley Corbet in Worcestershire (his mother's county), while his sister had married into the Thatchers of Sussex, one of the gentry households around which Sussex catholics concentrated.[23] The Countess of Rivers' family also had connections with Sussex catholicism. Her sister, Lady Penelope, in wedding Sir John Gage of Firle, had married into one of the leading catholic families in the county and one which had been the occasion of earlier rumours and scares. The Gages were also related to the Petres of Essex.[24] Such well-developed kinship links and the movements between catholic households that they occasioned, as part of the usual round of gentle sociability, might be seen to be threatening in another context. For example, rumours in 1627 that there was a conference of great papists at the Petre's house at Ingatestone caused anxiety in London. This perhaps had been a gathering to celebrate a familial rite of passage, but for the godly, given their belief in the conspiratorial character of popery, there

---

[21] The formidable Katherine Audley was the daughter of Sir Robert Southwell (Metcalfe, *Visitations Essex*, vol. 1, p. 140), while the Daniels and Martins were related by marriage to the Bedingfields and Waldegraves of Norfolk: Metcalfe, *Visitations Suffolk*, pp. 24–5; J. J. Howard (ed.), *The Visitation of Suffolke, Made by William Hervey ... 1561*, 2 vols. (Lowestoft, 1864–76), vol. 1, pp. 228–9, 242–3; Leicestershire RO, DE221/13/2/7.

[22] G. W. Marshall (ed.), *The Genealogist*, 4 (1880), pp. 231–2; E. A. W. Barnard, *The Sheldons, Being Some Account of the Sheldon Family of Worcestershire and Warwickshire* (Cambridge, 1936), pp. 49–50, 56; Howard and Burke, *Genealogical Collections*, p. 38; Clifton, 'Popular fear', p. 27.

[23] Hartharn, 'Audleys', p. 44; *VCH Worcestershire*, vol. 3, p. 39. The Packington household also formed a small island of catholicism: J. Willis Bund, *Worcestershire County Records, Division 1. Documents Relating to Quarter Sessions. Calendar of the Quarter Sessions, vol. 1, 1598–1643* (Worcester, 1900), pp. cxcviii, 644; W. Brace Bannerman (ed.), *The Visitations of the County of Sussex ... 1530 ... & 1633–4* (Harleian Society, 110, 1905), p. 54; Fletcher, *Sussex*, p. 99.

[24] A. W. H. Clarke (ed.), *The Visitation of Sussex AD 1662* (Harleian Society, 139, 1937), p. 51; Fletcher, *Sussex*, pp. 98, 100, 102; R. B. Manning, *Religion and Society in Elizabethan Sussex: A Study of the Enforcement of the Religious Settlement 1558–1603* (Leicester, 1969), pp. 155–6.

was always the possibility of a deeper and darker purpose to such covens.[25]

The geography of catholicism within the region added to the sense of menace. It was not simply the presence of large catholic households, but the fact that such households were to be found crowded into particular areas of the region that gave cause for alarm. The Petres and related families in south-central Essex represented one such concentration. There was another concentration to the west of the county around the small town of Saffron Walden. The cluster in the Stour Valley was particularly pronounced. Surrounding the cloth town of Sudbury with its godly and fiercely anti-catholic ministers and congregation were the catholic families of the Waldegrave, Daniel, Martin, Carey and Rivers families with large households at Long Melford, Acton, Borley and Bulmer.[26] Catholicism in the region might have been the faith of a minority, but seen from an encircled town like Sudbury their numbers could appear threatening.

Moreover, it was the otherness of catholicism to which these spatial arrangements gave rise that added to the sense of threat. Local catholic gentry families lived too close for their godly neighbours not to be aware of them, but just far enough away from these urban centres to make activities in their households the subject of speculation rather than informed observation. Colchester's inhabitants found themselves with close catholic neighbours who did not however live in the town, a situation identified by the historian of catholic panics as most conducive to the genesis of rumour and anxiety. The Rivers family lived in a little sea of what the historian of English catholicism in this period has called 'seigneurial catholicism' at St Osyth on the coast, some six miles from Colchester.[27] In September 1625 a conversation between a sailor and a shoemaker in the yard of the White Lion, one of the town's major taverns, turned on the issue of whether Viscount Colchester, the future Earl Rivers, was a catholic. Panic over the threat of catholic invasion had seen activities at their house become the occasion of gossip on the streets of Colchester leading to rumours that the family were shipping food to the Spanish enemy.[28] At Ipswich, the propinquity of the catholic Forster

[25] N. Briggs, 'William, second Lord Petre (1595–1637)', *ERec*, 10 (1968), p. 57; C. Z. Wiener, 'The beleagured isle. A study of Elizabethan and early Jacobean anti-catholicism', *P&P*, 51 (1971), pp. 27–62.

[26] Norfolk RO, VIS/4–6 (I am grateful to Peter Northeast for lending me his transcript of these visitation records).

[27] Clifton, 'Popular fear', p. 49; J. Bossy, *The English Catholic Community, 1570–1850* (1975), p. 177. Although Bossy argues that seigneurial catholicism was weaker in the south, households like the Petres also served as centres for their catholic tenantry.

[28] CRO, D/B5 Sb2/7, fols. 106 v–7r, D/Y, 2/7, pp. 271, 277.

family, some three miles away at Copdock, made them also the subject of wild rumours in the town.

The Audley family, the object of rumour in the Whitsuntide scare, provides an example of the tensions and conflict this could create. This large household lived sufficiently close to Colchester at Berechurch to prompt jurisdictional disputes with the Corporation. In the 1570s under Mistress Katherine Audley, the daughter of the Norfolk recusant Sir Robert Southey, the Berechurch household's reputation as a meeting place for large gatherings of catholics had brought it to the attention of the central government. Friction between catholic household and godly townsmen seems to have been inevitable. One London catholic living there had rebuked poor men for going to lectures, while in 1584 Colchester's authorities had imprisoned one of the servants for dangerous speech.[29] Not surprisingly, the heightened anxieties of the mid-1620s saw inquiries being made as to whether Sir Henry Audley went to church and they brought renewed conflict between townsmen and household. In the summer of 1626, Colchester's watch was summoned to stop fighting at the fair on St John's Green. They were met with a fusillade of oaths from Robert Ffrebarne, one of Sir Henry Audley's men. Told that each oath would cost him a twelvepence fine, he swore again and began to assault the watch. Ordered to stop in the king's name, Ffrebarne countered provocatively, 'in the Kinge of Spayne's name' and threatened that 'before the next fayer there would be another co[u]rse taken for watchmen'. This may have been no more than drunken bravado, but Ffrebarne had managed in a few words to summarise the fears of the godly about a group whose allegiance was uncertain and actions always potentially alarming. The exchange captures the fears of inhabitants of a town like Colchester of the latent threat posed by the presence of nearby large catholic households. As one of the watch told Ffrebarne, 'we are to feare there are to[o] many such as you are'.[30]

This was a further factor that contributed to the heightening of anxieties about the catholic presence in the region – the godly's sense of the dynamic of popery. While the catholic community in Essex had been growing from the low point of the 1580s, growth had come to an end in the 1620s.[31] However, this would not have been a perception likely to have been shared by the godly of the county. There was a long established pattern of administrative action designed to identify and

---

[29] PRO, SP, 16/120/26; *VCH Essex*, vol. 9, p. 126. The servant's crime was to have pointed out that Mary, Queen of Scots was next in line to the throne.

[30] Kalu, 'Essex Puritans', p. 172 n.; PRO, SP, 16/120/26; CRO, D/B5, Sb2/7, fols. 119 v–121 v.

[31] Elliott, 'Roman Catholic community', *ERec*, 27 (1985), p. 44.

neutralise the threat posed by catholic recusants. In addition to the regular presentment of catholics in local secular and church courts for offences under the recusancy laws, there were measures for disarming them whenever the international situation warranted. Thus, in the crisis of 1625–6, articles were drawn up in Suffolk for the presentment of catholics to monthly meetings of the justices and, as in Essex, orders were given for the searching and disarming of named catholic households. However, problems of defining exactly who were recusant had impaired the effectiveness of this policy of disarmament. Occasional conformity and the presence of church papists had ensured evasion of the recusant penal legislation. For example, Sir Henry Audley of Berechurch had flitted between conformity and recusancy. Even for known recusants, there is evidence that constables in parishes where there was a sizeable catholic presence failed to present them.[32] Thus, contemporaries could draw little confidence from the fact that catholics were a minority since the failure to enforce the penal legislation against them meant that they had little faith that all catholics had been identified. This failure fed the godly's fear that there were a large number of covert papists whose numbers could only be guessed at. For the godly, catholicism was as much an invisible, as visible, threat.

Robbed of accurate information, the godly's sense of the dynamics of popery were more likely to have been formed, within the broader context of the successes of the counter-reformation abroad, by their perception of developments in both Court and church. The presence of the king's French catholic wife and the well-publicised conversions of courtiers was linked to the belief, right or wrong, that Charles I was failing to enforce the penal legislation against catholics in the country. Within the region significant recent conversions, like that of the Countess of Rivers' family in 1625, could be read in the same way.[33] The greater opportunities that Jesuit missionaries were afforded for proselytising by Charles' protection from punishment of leading local families and by his more general laxity over enforcing anti-catholic legislation could only heighten fears. Jesuit priests, retained as chaplains in gentry households, were active in the region in the 1630s. The presence of these agents, the focus of exaggerated godly fears, provided

---

[32] BL, Additional MS 39,245, fol. 92 v; *APC 1625–1626*, pp. 228–9. For earlier searches in Suffolk, see HMC 14, MSS Wodehouse, appx 4, p. 435; ESRO, JC, 1/36 (microfilm of the Helmingham Hall Deputy Lieutenancy Book), fol. 11 v; B. W. Quintrell, 'The practice and problems of recusant disarming, 1585–1641', *RecHist*, 17 (1985), pp. 208–22; Webster, 'Pakingtons of Havington', *RecHist*, 12 (1974), pp. 203–15; Elliott, 'Roman Catholic community', *ERec*, 25–6 (1983–4), p. 43.

[33] Elliott, 'Roman Catholic community', *ERec*, 25–6, (1983–4), p. 11.

a link between the continental repression of protestantism and fears for England's future.[34]

Perhaps even more important in creating the sense of a growing catholic threat was the belief that what Laud and Wren really sought, with their silencing of godly preaching and insistence on ceremonial conformity, was a rapprochement with Rome. Hence the rumours that spread through the counties in 1640 that Laud had 'turned papist'. As early as 1632 Francis Wright, the minister at Witham, 'in his cupps', had told a tale of Laud having been present when 'Doctor Price' received the final sacrament from a priest and died in the catholic faith. When his companion, the son of Sir Thomas Wiseman, a family which had been presented for their catholicism, said that 'he thought most of the Bishops were in their judgements Roman catholiques', Wright swore 'yea, that they were, and most of the cleargie too'.[35] Locally, comment like that from Daniel Whitby, the minister of Theydon-Mount in Essex, who was reported to have said, 'that the Roman Church is a true Church, in respect of Fundamentall Points of the Religion' and that it was lawful for any Christian to join any nation in outward worship, seemed to threaten a more sinister and immediate agenda. A pamphlet attack on two Suffolk ministers, whom it was claimed were the prime focus of the Suffolk petition against scandalous ministers, constructed its accusation in terms of their association with known catholics.[36] This perception of a confessional shift was reflected in the frequency with which the innovations of the 1630s were decried in a critical discourse in which popery was the key term of abuse and which became more pronounced into the 1640s. From Essex, as early as 1629, it had been reported that the godly were clamouring against Laud, 'as a man endeavouring to suppress good

---

[34] The Jesuit College of the Holy Apostles covering Essex and Suffolk was founded in the early 1630s by the second Lord Petre: Foley, *Society*, vol. 2, pp. 391–613; Rowe, 'Roman catholic recusancy', p. 88; Dawson, 'Southcotes of Witham', p. 145; T. B. Trappes-Lomax, 'The Southcotes of Witham Place and their contribution to the survival of catholicism in Essex', *ERec*, 3 (1961), p. 109. The histories of individual families provide plenty of examples of the education of children at the Jesuit college of St Omer in the Spanish Flanders: G. Holt, *St Omers and Bruges Colleges, 1593–1730: A Biographical Dictionary* (1979), p. 105.

[35] D. Freist, 'The formation of opinion and the communication network in London 1637 to c. 1645' (Ph.D. dissertation, University of Cambridge, 1992), pp. 215–21; S. R. Gardiner, *Reports of Cases in the Courts of Star Chamber and High Commission* (London, 1886), p. 296.

[36] A. Milton, *Catholic and Reformed: the Roman and Protestant Churches in English Protestant Thought, 1600–1640* (Cambridge, 1995); D. Whitby, *The Vindication of a true PROTESTANT and faithfull Servant to his Church, Daniel Whitby, Rector of Theydon-Mount in Essex From Articles exhibited against him in the Exchequer-Chamber at Westminster, By a few Schismaticall, tempestuous, illiterate heedlesse People* (Oxford, 1644), p. 5; BL, E301(3): *A MAGAZINE OF SCANDALL. OR, A heape of wickedness of two infamous Ministers . . .* (1642), sigs. A3 v–4 r, B3 v.

preaching and advance popery'. Among the godly of the region Wren himself was given the nickname of 'Pope Regulus'. At Norwich the citizens petitioned in 1636 that Wren's actions were encouraging papists, citing the more than five-fold increase in presentments of recusants to Quarter Sessions as evidence. At Ipswich the opponents of Bishop Wren's commissioners declared that they feared that, 'they would have all [his] Majestie's subjects to be the Queene's subiects'. At Bures, a local gentleman asked by the churchwardens whether they should obey the order to rail in the communion table, answered, 'It's no matter, it's but a dance before Popery. The King hath a wife, and he loves her well, and she is a papist and we must all be of her religion, and that's the thing the Bishops aime at'. In the Colchester panic the popular naming of those being given shelter there also seems significant. The Queen Mother, Marie de Medici, Matthew Wren, the Bishop of Ely (who in August 1642 would be rumoured to be threatening to fire other communities in Essex), and William Laud, the Archbishop of Canterbury were all names unpopular among Colchester's godly, but they were also names suggesting the popular identification of Laudianism and Arminianism with popery, an identification by the early summer of 1642 being depicted pictorially in print. A similar conflation may well have led to the Arminian Lord Maynard being smeared with the accusation of popish leanings.[37]

Within the region of the attacks, the control exercised over church livings by catholic families provided pointed local evidence of this blurring of Laudian ceremonialism, Arminianism and popery. While convicted recusants should not have been able to exercise their right to present to the living, no such obstacle faced covert or church-papists.[38] The suggestion that they would have found Arminian and ceremonialist ministers more to their liking seems plausible.[39] Edward Cherry pre-

---

[37] K. Sharpe, *The Personal Rule of Charles I* (New Haven and London, 1992), p. 341; D. W. Boorman, 'The administrative and disciplinary problems of the church on the eve of the civil war in the light of the extant records of Norwich and Ely under Bishop Wren' (B.Litt. thesis, University of Oxford, 1959), pp. 130–2; W. E. Layton, 'Ecclesiatical disturbances in Ipswich during the reign of Charles I', *The East Anglian, or Notes and Queries*, NS, vol. 2 (1887–8), p. 259; *Collections of the Massachusetts Historical Society*, 5th ser., 1 (1871), p. 236; PRO, SP, 16/142/113, /314/130; BL, 202(42), *An exact and True Diurnall of the Proceedings in Parliament, from the 29 of August to the 3 of September 1642*, p. 2; J. Miller, *Religion in the Popular Prints 1600–1832* (Cambridge, 1986), plate 7. For Maynard, see above, p. 119.

[38] The whole issue of how the gentry in general, and catholics in particular, exercised their clerical patronage needs further investigation. According to the statute 4 James I c. 5, livings in the gift of convicted recusants in Essex and Suffolk were to be presented to by the University of Cambridge.

[39] For the suggestion that conforming catholics might provide a sympathetic group for Arminian ceremonialism, see A. Walsham, *Church Papists: Catholicism, Conformity and*

sented to the living of Great Holland by the Countess of Rivers, whose family controlled some thirteen parishes in Essex as well as several around their Suffolk estates, was an Arminian and ceremonialist. In January 1642 the discovery of a letter from him seems to have aroused the suspicions of the Essex authorities as to his religious allegiances. We have already seen that at the Rivers' living of Long Melford Robert Warren had been suspected of popery and had been accused by the godly of Sudbury of expounding 'the place of the apostle whereby he put a feare in the minds of Divers the Kings subiects that here was a change of Religion'. At Acton where the Daniels were patrons of the living, the minister Samuel Alsop was accused of setting up in the chancel 'the Jesuits' Badge in gold in divers place'. At Stoke by Nayland, the Mannocks' control of the right to present to the living doubtless played a part in their conflict with a group of godly parishioners.[40]

All these changes meant that central to fears about the popish threat was the belief that known recusants, catholics prosecuted for their religion, might be only the tip of an iceberg. If the argument that there has been an over-emphasis on the history of post-Reformation catholicism as the history of recusant separatism and a corresponding neglect of the evidence for catholic conformity proves correct, then contemporaries close to the ground had good cause to fear the presence of many 'church papists'. Earl Rivers, the husband of Elizabeth, Countess of Rivers, was later attacked as a church-papist, while his successor was denounced by the House of Lords in July 1642 as, 'lately a notorious professed Papist, and still suspected to be a Papist although he now come to the Church, as many other dangerous Papists do, with Purpose (as is conceived) to make themselves capable of Employment'.[41] Gentlemen like Thomas Bayles attacked at Witham had catholic connections that raised doubts about their own religious faith and may explain their selection by the crowd.[42]

Confessional Polemic in Early Modern England (Woodbridge, 1993), p. 98. For the Savage family's support of prominent anti-puritans, see Milton, *Catholic*, pp. 53–4.

[40] HMC Portland MSS, 1, p. 2; J. White, *The First Century of Scandalous, Malignant PRIESTS, Made and admitted into Benefices by the PRELATES, in whose hands the Ordination of Ministers and government of the Church hath been. OR, A Narration of the Causes for which the PARLIAMENT hath Ordered the Sequestration of the benefices of severall Ministers* (1643), pp. 3, 34; BL, Egerton MS 34,253, fol. 7; BL, Harleian MS 589, fol. 138; *Registrum Vagum of Anthony Harison*, pt II, pp. 310–12; *WP 3: 1631–1637*, pp. 380–1.

[41] M. B. Rowlands, 'Recusant women 1560–1640' in M. Prior (ed.), *Women in English Society 1500–1800* (1985), pp. 149–80. For the argument about the importance of conforming catholics, see Walsham, *Church Papists*; *A True Relation*, sig. A2 v; *LJ*/v/202.

[42] Bayles probably came from the Witham family prosecuted for their catholicism in the early seventeenth century and had both professional and close personal ties with the neighbouring catholic Sir John Southcott, who acted as godfather to his son: P. R.

The example of Henry Nevill provides powerful evidence of how these developments were perceived at grass-root level. Nevill, whose house at Cressing Temple was a target in September 1642, was popularly suspected of popery. When Nevill was a candidate at the county elections to the Long Parliament, Thomas Hownell, an artisan and member of the godly of nearby Terling, the parish of the silenced minister and New England emigrant Thomas Weld, had claimed that Henry Nevill 'was a Pope and kept twentie Popes in his howse'.[43] Nevill had not been presented for recusancy and in the 1630s he had been seen as a dependable ally – 'so forward and active man' – by the church authorities to whom he reported on the activities of 'puritan' ministers. Since this was the case, Hownell's claim might be taken as a jaundiced comment on his role as an active ally of the bishops and on his strident antipuritanism. In the summer of 1642 he was described as 'a man formerly inclined to the late innovations introduced into the Church, & much in favour with the Bishops delinquents'. Nevertheless, the godly of Terling, where Nevill held a manor, knew their man. Nevill's family history and associations make it clear that he was that particular bogey of the godly, a 'church papist'.[44] His grandfather had been a church papist; his father had made the Countess of Rivers' father and husband his trustees, and Henry himself was a good friend of the Countess. His uncle had married a daughter of the recusant Greene family of Sampford, his own daughter married into the catholic Mannocks of Stoke by Nayland, and his sons openly embraced catholicism. But even more relevant is the fact that Henry Nevill had a second household at Holt in Leicestershire where there had been a resident Jesuit priest since the 1620s and where mass was said regularly. In Leicestershire Nevill had links with catholic families of the region and on the death of his first wife he married into the prominent Nottinghamshire catholic family of the Markhams. Not

---

Knell, 'Essex recusants sequestered during the civil war and Interregnum: part 4', *ERec*, 12 (1970), pp. 17, 19. I am grateful to Janet Gyford for sharing her knowledge of Bayles with me.

43   ERO, Q/SR 309/31; K. Wrightson and D. Levine, *Poverty and Piety in an English Village: Terling, 1525–1700* (Oxford, 1995), p. 222. This outburst seems to have resulted from a heated political argument which ended in the binding over of the leading protagonists on either side: *ibid.*, 229–30. Hownell's sureties were both members of the Terling godly, information I owe to the kindness of Keith Wrightson.

44   Smith, *Ecclesiastical History*, p. 53, 55; PRO, SP, 16/350/54; W. A. Copinger (ed.), *The History and Records of the Smith-Carrington Family* (1907), pp. 199, 227–30, 522. Nevill's sister married into the Mannocks of Gifford Hall, his uncle into the recusant Greenes. Nevill himself married into the catholic family of the Nevills of Holt in Leicestershire, was guardian to the children of several catholic families, and remarried into the catholic Markhams of Nottinghamshire. His son, on his death, openly embraced catholicism: B. Elliott, 'A Leicestershire recusant family: the Nevills of Nevill Holt', *RecHist*, 17 (1984), pp. 173–80.

surprisingly, the historian of the family in Leicestershire labels Henry Nevill a church papist. Since the 1620s the family had received permission to hold services in their family chapel at Cressing Temple; was the accusation from neighbouring Terling based on observation or rumour of what went on there?[45] The ability of a man like Nevill not only to pursue his faith without detection or persecution, but also to act as an informant and ally to the bishops in their harrying of the godly, provided alarming evidence of the blurring of confessional boundaries the Laudian counter-revolution had permitted.

Perceptions of the threat of popery in the region drew as much on the past as on the present. Last, but not least, among the factors encouraging a belief in the popish threat was a retelling of England's history in which the 'black legend' of popish persecution loomed large, notably in the pages of the protestant martyrologist John Foxe.[46] Copies of Foxe's *Acts and Monuments* (more popularly known as the *Book of Martyrs*) were by law to be provided in each parish church. At one Suffolk parish in 1633 three separate reading desks had been built for each of the three volumes of Foxe. Among the godly of the region, like the iconoclast William Dowsing (who had as many as three well-thumbed copies), volumes of Foxe were much valued and lovingly bequeathed to their children. Its iconic status can be seen in the case of a Coggeshall clothier's widow who left a bequest to buy the *Book of Martyrs*, 'to remain to the use of all people for ever'.[47] Foxe's history was one in which men and women from the region had played an heroic part. An area that had offered an early

---

[45] BL, E202(42), *An exact and true Diurnall of the Proceedings in Parliament*, 29 August–5 September 1642; Copinger, *Smith-Carrington Family*, pp. 199, 227–32; Elliott, 'Nevills', pp. 173–80; Foley, *Society*, vol. 2, pp. 306–7; Clarke Library, Hastings Correspondence, box 11, HA 9579 (I am grateful to Mike Braddick for his help in obtaining a transcript of this document); P. Ryan, 'The history of Cressing Temple from the documentary sources' in D. D. Andrews (ed.), *Cressing Temple: A Templar and Hospitaller Manor in Essex* (Chelmsford, 1993), pp. 11–24.

[46] J. Ward, 'The Reformation in Colchester, 1528–1558', *EAH*, 15 (1983), pp. 84–95; Byford, 'Price of protestantism', pp. 113–23; *VCH Essex*, 2, pp. 32–4; *ER*, 50, p. 159; P. Collinson, 'The English conventicle' in W. J. Sheils and D. Woo (eds.), *Voluntary Religion* (1986), p. 240 and n.; J. Morrill, 'William Dowsing, the bureaucratic puritan', in Morrill, P. Slack and D. Woolf (eds.), *Public Duty and Private Conscience in Seventeenth-Century England: Essays Presented to Gerald Aylmer* (Oxford, 1993), pp 181–203.

[47] A. Eljenham Nicholas, 'Broken up or restored way: iconoclasm in a Suffolk parish' in C. Davidson and A. E. Nicholas (eds.), *Iconoclasm vs Art and Drama* (Medieval Institute Publication, Early Drama, Art and Music, monograph 11, 1989), p. 180 (I am grateful to Lynn Botelho for bringing this article to my attention; F. G. Emmison (ed.), *Essex Wills: The Archdeaconry Courts 1591–1597* (Chelmsford, 1991), pp. 158, 187. Patrick Collinson cites the example of a yeomen in the Suffolk clothing area whose copy of Foxe, valued at 14s., represented some four per cent of his estate. (I am grateful to Prof. Collinson for letting me see his unpublished paper on Thomas Carew.)

reception for heretical and reformed ideas had had considerable experience of repression under Mary I. In Colchester, a series of burnings had given a gruesome literalness to its description, bestowed upon it in early reformation panegyrics for its preaching, as a candle upon a hill. Memories of the Marian reaction and burnings were still alive in the region in the period before the attacks. The 1636 Colchester libel against Theophilus Roberts and his fellow ceremonialist ministers had compared Roberts to Bishop Bonner, Mary's catholic bishop entrusted with the persecution of protestants in Essex. Earlier in the town an Elizabethan libel had drawn evidence of its charges from a reading of Foxe and had deliberately echoed the *Book of Martyrs* in its title: 'the Buryall of Clere or th'actes and monumentes of the Mayor of Colchester'. At Coggeshall in the 1630s listeners to a christening sermon by a suspended minister were reminded of 'ye blood shed in Queen Maries dayes'. At Ipswich, the efforts of Bishop Wren to suppress the town's unconforming lecturer and ministers was said to have prompted the comparison, 'that they were never at their [this?] pass since Queene Maries dayes'. In a sermon in the summer of 1640 one Essex minister who spoke of his fear of the suppression of godly preaching was said to have recommended Foxe's *Book of Martyrs* to his congregation.[48]

Local knowledge reflected the customary practices within the region by which social memory of the 'black legend' was maintained. Central to both legend and memory was the Gunpowder Plot. The annual commemoration of this event in church service and sermon provided an opportunity for the regular recital of the popish threat. At Colchester itself the shock of 1605 had led one parish (of which Thomas Newcomen would later become minister) to record in its register, 'Let it alwaies be w[i]th all true thankfulnes remembred yt [that] God in his great mercye pr[e]s[er]ved o[u]r kinge & his whole familye, the whole state of this land & his gospell ... from an horrible treason by certeyne papists intended by blast of gunpowder.' The town had heeded the injunction. On what was popularly referred to as 'Gunpowder treason daie', there was an annual sermon, to which the Corporation processed in full regalia, 'to give thanks for his [God's] greate deliv[er]ance from the dampnable conspiracie of the gunpowder treason'.[49] At Ipswich the fiercely anti-papist Samuel Ward had, until his suspension from lecturing in 1635, been

---

[48] See above. Byford, 'Price of Protestantism', pp. 211–24; Layton, 'Ecclesiastical disturbances', p. 316; PRO, SP, 16/350/54; W. Hunt, *The Puritan Moment, the Coming of Revolution in an English County* (Cambridge, Mass., 1983), p. 283.

[49] CRO, D/P, 777/1/1. (I am grateful to Jane Bedford of the Essex Record Office for bringing this to my attention.) This annual sermon had been given since at least 1614, when the first reference to it occurs in the town's Assembly Book: CRO, D/B5, Gb2, fol. 137v.

urging the godly of Ipswich, 'to beware of relapse into Popery & sup[er]-stition, there wanting not endeavourrers as endevored to reduce it into this kingdome, meaneing Preists, popish Seminaries or Jesuits'. Ward seems to have used the occasion of 5 November regularly to warn 'his Auditory, that there was cause to feare an Alteracon of Religion in the kingdome'.[50] Godly gentry, including the Earl of Warwick, Sir Thomas Barrington and Sir Simonds D'Ewes, took care to see the occasion marked by an appropriate sermon in their parishes. At Hatfield Broad Oak, Barrington's practice of distributing money to both the ringers and the poor of the parish on that day, a practice followed in other communities in the region, offered a powerful combination of charity and commemoration.[51]

These acts of remembering were the same as those to be found elsewhere in the country, but in an area marked by the active presence of the godly they were perhaps more carefully observed. Indeed the evidence suggests that in response to changes in church and court they were more aggressively observed in the 1630s. In those circumstances the politics of memory became an even more important cultural resource. At Braintree in 1638 the local godly clothier family of Mott had left a bequest to buy land, the profits of the purchase to be distributed to the poor every 5 November so that Guy Fawkes' treason should never be forgot. In several Ipswich parishes the railing in of the communion table seems to have been the signal for a more marked celebration of 'Gunpowder Treason Day'.[52] While the purchase of service books for 5 November was a requirement laid on all parishes, the timing of these purchases, at Ipswich as well as elsewhere in the region, appears significant. The

[50] PRO, SP, 16/261, fols. 304 v–5 r; /278/65; T. Birch, *The Court and Times of James I*, 2 vols. (London, 1848), vol. 2, p. 232. Ward took his hostility to the extent of systematically obliterating the word 'pope' from books in the town library at Ipswich: Morrill, 'Dowsing', p. 201.

[51] T. Webster, 'The godly of Goshen Scattered: an Essex clerical conference in the 1620s and its diaspora' (Ph.D. thesis, University of Cambridge, 1993), p. 246; J. O. Halliwell (ed.), *The Autobiography and Correspondence of Sir Simonds D'Ewes During the reign of James I and Charles I*, 2 vols. (1845), vol. 2, p. 235; ERO, D/DB, A2, fols. 34 v, 68 v. Great Bromley, a village to the west of Colchester which appears in the 1630s to have offered some resistance to the order to rail in the communion table, also made such payments: CRO, D/P, 103/5/4. If it is not a function of erratic record-keeping, then the fact that it was only in 1640 that these payments, as well as the usual ringing, were recorded may be significant. The catholic Mannock family of Stoke by Nayland lived also at Great Bromley Hall (information I owe to Joy Rowe).

[52] Davids, *Annals*, p. 290. At St Stephen's the parish purchased a service book for 5 November in 1636–7, the same year that the rails were erected. At St Mary's Tower, a parish that had such a service book since at least 1628, ringing seems to have begun in 1637. At St Clement's, the parish purchased a book for the 5th November in 1635 and ringing on the 5th was recorded from 1637: ESRO, FB, 107/A1/1, fol. 24 v (from back); *ibid.*, FB A91/E1/1, pp. 75, 124; *ibid.*, FB 98/E3/1, fols. 25, 27.

service book for 5 November contained plenty of reminders of the threat posed by papists – and it included a prayer 'to root them out of the confines and limits of the kingdome'. Thus the godly were able to turn obedience to episcopal articles into an act of opposition, in effect appropriating the text of the 'official transcript' of anti-popery to express their anxieties about changes within the English church.[53] There may have been other responses. Only a chance reference in the course of an examination about the theft of a ring reveals that at Colchester in 1636, 5 November may also have come to be marked by some form of popular processional drama. Those examined were all at their doors 'to see the showe of the traitors w[hi]ch then came by'. It may well be that this was an innovation of that year. If so, its timing in a year in which an unwilling town had seen the railing in of altars successfully enforced is highly suggestive.[54]

The ringing of bells that marked the celebration of 5 November provided another popular mnemonic. The 1630s, it has been suggested, were marked by a 'rising intensity of ringing' on the fifth (and a neglect or perfunctory acknowledgement of ringing on the 'crownation' day of Charles I) in response to what was seen as the recrudescence of popery.[55] At Ipswich, whose inhabitants' puritanism was sufficiently well known to allow it to be satirized in the tale of a maid who modelled her sweetmeats 'from the Actes and Monumentes of John Foxe', 5 November was regularly marked by the ringing of the bells. Parishes which were later to

[53] BL, E238(1), *Articles to be Inquired of within the Diocese of Norwich in the first visitation of the Right Reverend Father in God, Matthew [Wren], Lord Bishop of Norwich* (1636), A2v; e.g. *PRAYERS AND THANKSGIVING To be used by the all the Kings majesties loving subjects, For the happy deliverance of His MAJESTIE, the QUEEN, PRINCE and STATES of the PARLIAMENT, From the most Traiterous and Bloody intended Massacre by Gunpowder, the fifth of November 1605* (1638). Chelmsford, where 5 November in 1641 was to witness serious iconoclasm, had also purchased 'a service book for god's great deliverance from the Gunpowder treason', probably in 1635 when the first reference to it appears in the overseers' accounts. Saffron Walden, where the bells had also been rung annually on this and other anniversaries, purchased two 5 November service books in October 1640 (but in this case at the same time as the purchase of two books for 27 March, the date of Charles I's accession): ERO, D/P, 94/5/1, *passim*.

[54] CRO, D/B, 5, Sb2/7, fols. 226r–v. The description suggests that this was something other than the procession of the Corporation to the sermon on 5 November.

[55] D. Cressy, 'The Protestant calendar and the vocabulary of celebration in early modern England', *JBS*, 29 (1990), pp. 41–7; Cressy, *Bonfires and Bells: National Memory and the Protestant Calendar in Elizabethan and Stuart England* (1989), pp. 61, 141–59. Only a systematic search would establish whether this was the case in this region, but in 1632 a group of parishes bordering on Colchester were presented for failing to hold a special service for the king's coronation day. It may also be significant that in 1640 the parishioners of one Colchester parish chose as the occasion for presenting several to the church court for their absence from church the previous 17 November (the accession day of the godly Elizabeth I, by then more enthusiastically celebrated than Charles' own, it has been argued): ERO, D/ACA 48, fols. 154v, 50v–51.

be at the centre of the crowd actions of the summer of 1642 also marked 5 November. At Long Melford the ringers were paid 6s. for ringing on 5 November in 1641, a payment seemingly significantly larger than on other occasions. In 1641 they also introduced ringing on 7 September, that godly prince Queen Elizabeth I's birthday. At Chelmsford, where the bells were rung on 5 November, the day had provided an appropriate occasion for large-scale popular iconoclasm in 1641. Both the timing and shape of this crowd action reflected anxieties in the region about a return to popery.[56]

Crises, triggered by news of events abroad, offered periodic reinforcement of the 'black legend'. In 1625, Charles' break with Spain had seemed to threaten an invasion, to which the eastern counties were thought to be particularly vulnerable. The crisis that followed allows us to see how quickly international developments focussed local fears on the threat from within. In early September, the Privy Council received information from Essex of 'a rumour in ye County of ye great Concourse of people to papests houses both hear and adiacent counties and of their preparations'. From Suffolk, there were similar reports of the bold and impudent speeches of the catholics, of their arming, and of their practices to raise stirs and tumults. The authorities there were ordered to investigate the rumoured assembly close to Ipswich of 200 catholics, some of whom it was said had just returned from serving the Archduke in the Thirty Years War. As a result of these anxieties, leading catholics in the region had had their arms inventoried and confiscated. As the example of 1625 shows, such fears were by no means to be found only at a popular level. The Earl of Warwick, writing to the Privy Council, referred to 'the greate Jealosies (not w[i]thout probable grounds) of some secret practise of the Papists'.[57] In such circumstances the celebration of the deliverance of 5 November doubtless took on an added meaning and gave occasion for godly preachers, as Thomas Hooker did at Chelmsford in 1626, to renew memories of earlier popish plots.[58] Later scares of foreign invasion helped to keep alive these fears.

Aggressive exchanges with local catholics able to draw comfort from catholic victories abroad also served to reinforce stereotypes within the

---

[56] PRO, SP, 16/261, fols. 304 v–5r; ESRO, C/9/2 (2), fol. 447; L. J. Redstone, *Ipswich through the Ages* (Ipswich, 1948, repr. 1969), p. 90; 'Extracts from the churchwardens' books of St Clement's, Ipswich AD 1574–1652, no. V', *East Anglian, or Notes and Queries*, NS 4 (Ipswich, 1891–2), pp. 6–7; WSRO, FL, 509/5/1 (loose churchwardens' accounts 1641–2); FL, 645/1/2, [unfol.] 1640–1641; PRO, ASSI, 35/84/10/23–4.

[57] PRO, SP, 16/6/41, 44, 60; 16/6/57.i; HMC 13, MSS Wodehouse, appx iv, p. 445; BL, Additional MS 39,245, fol. 92 v.; *CSPD 1625–1626*, pp. 181, 184.

[58] G. H. Williams (ed.), *Thomas Hooker: Writings in England and Holland, 1626–1633* (Harvard, 1975), pp. 53–88.

black legend of popery.[59] There were probably more instances of seditious statements than those traces that survive, all of which the surviving evidence suggests would have been the subject of much discussion among their protestant neighbours. From the Suffolk cloth district in 1637 came news of an alehouse brag by Thomas Skinner, the eldest son of a Lavenham landed family with recusant connections. It was reported among the godly that he had said, 'I will goe to Romm[e] but I would doo sommwhat that I mought be spocke of after we are de[a]d'. This, it transpired, was no less than a desire to kill the king.[60] In the same year the godly learnt that a member of the Rivers' family household at Long Melford who, having been observed to 'followe the courte', had been committed to the Tower 'for dyvers evil woords and purposes to the K[ing]'. The following year another Essex catholic was examined before the Attorney General. Mistress Cole, a member of the household at Cranham Hall whose head, Francis Petre, was said to be under the influence of the Jesuits, was interrogated about her reported claim that if she were queen she would kill the king for his persecution of catholics and, ominously, about conversations with other members of the household about 'the Gunpowder treason'.[61] In the crisis of 1625, one of a group of catholics committed to Colchester gaol for sedition, had said on observing the trained bands marching to the port of Harwich, that 'they were best to take heed of the back winge'. It is hard to imagine a pithier expression of local fears about the threat of a fifth column posed by the popish presence in the region.[62]

When Matthew Newcomen, the minister whose sermons at Dedham and elsewhere in the region attracted large audiences from towns and villages in the Stour Valley,[63] preached on 5 November 1642, he took as the text for his sermon, Nehemiah 4.11: 'And our adversaries said they shall not know nor see till wee come in the midst among them and slay them ...'

---

[59] For example, in 1633 suspicions arising from a conversation in a Witham alehouse about the late execution of a Jesuit in London led to information being laid against a seaman and letter carrier: PRO, SP, 16/252/67 i and ii.

[60] *WP 3: 1631–1637*, pp. 386–8; Bodl. Lib., Bankes MS 18, nos. 7, 18, 25; MS, 43, no. 36. The wife of Sir George Skinner of Lavenham Park had been presented for recusancy and he for non-attendance for seven years: *Registrum Vagum of Anthony Harison, pt 1*, p. 182, NRO, VIS/4, Lavenham (a reference I owe to Peter Northeast). Their son's earlier travels to Rome and elsewhere on the Continent had led to his detention in 1616: PRO, SP, 14/86/72–3.

[61] PRO, SP, 16/331/69; 356/55; /392/61; /393/2 and 24; *WP 3: 1631–1637*, pp. 355–6.

[62] PRO, SP, 16/12/70.

[63] One sermon preached in Suffolk by Newcomen just after the outbreak of the Irish rebellion brought 'abundance of ministers': A. G. Hollingsworth, *A History of Stowmarket, the ancient county town of Suffolk, with notices of the Hundred of Stow* (Ipswich, 1844), p. 145.

Skilfully repeating this text throughout his sermon, he drew a picture of a group whose religion absolved them from recognition of either law or oath and who were necessarily committed to the extermination of protestants. Recounting the history of catholic plots against Elizabeth and James I, Newcomen placed these episodes in the context of the wider popish plot and persecution which was threatening the godly on the Continent. He went on to construct a history of the 1630s which saw changes in Church and State at home as a plot to reintroduce popery under Charles, a king whom the popish party had seduced: 'First, bring in *Arminian doctrines*, then the *popish* will easily follow.' 'Doe you not thinke, there are as many *Papists* in *England now*, as there were at the *time of the powder Treason?*', Newcomen asked, leaving no one in doubt as to what he thought the answer to this question was.[64]

The belief in a popish plot to capture the counsels of Charles I and return England to subordination to the Pope was to become a major explicandum of the failure of king and Parliament to come to an agreement.[65] Catholic courtiers at the centre and a catholic nobility in the provinces were seen as a potential fifth column, ready to rise and aid a catholic invasion which it was feared would descend from Ireland or from the Continent.[66] Many developments fed these fears. Rightly or wrongly (mostly rightly in the case of Essex), English catholics were seen as natural supporters of Charles' authoritarian rule, contributing enthusiastically to royal finances and to the war against the Scots. The considerable presence of catholics in the king's army mustered to fight the Scots excited much comment. Preferment of catholics at the Court and protection of catholics in the country from penal legislation led to fears that both State and Church were threatened. These changes were interpreted against the wider background of a Europe in which the suppression of political liberties and of protestantism seemed to go hand in hand. The godly prince in whom had been placed hopes for the further purification of the religion of protestants had married a French catholic, entertained emissaries from the Pope, intrigued with catholic states and failed to defend protestants abroad.

---

[64] *The Craft And Cruelty Of The Churches Adversaries, Discovered in a sermon preached at St Margarets in Westminster, before the Honourable House of Commons Assembled in Parliament. Novemb. 5, 1642* (1643).

[65] For a discussion of the political background, see Hibbard, *Popish Plot*; for popular reactions to these developments, see Clifton, 'Fear of Catholics'. See also B. Magee, 'Popish plots in the seventeenth century: the great panic of 1641', *The Month*, 175 (1941), pp. 348–57; J. Miller, *Popery and Politics in England 1660–1688* (Cambridge, 1973), pp. 67–84.

[66] In September 1639, Essex had been put on alert because of the presence of a large Spanish fleet carrying troops: *CSPD 1638–1639*, p. 494.

At home, Charles had silenced Calvinist preachers and promoted an Arminianism whose doctrine on salvation many failed to distinguish from, and which local preachers attacked as a stalking horse for popery. Episcopal prohibitions on preaching and Laudian innovation in liturgy and architecture provided graphic evidence of these changes in every parish and, at the popular level, encouraged the tendency to perceive these changes as portending the return to popery.[67] Perception of these changes in a culture which tended to organise its thinking around binary oppositions slipped easily into seeing them as signalling the return of popery. It had been the 'polarity between popery at home and purity abroad' that had driven men and women from the eastern counties, and in particular in large numbers from the Stour Valley, to emigration.[68] Many thought, in Sir Simonds D'Ewes' words, that Laud and Wren were enemies of popery 'in word onlie' – an assumption for which the Colchester Whitsuntide rumours of their presence in a local catholic household provides evidence of popular acceptance.[69]

The history of the early 1640s was one of a growing anxiety about the popish threat and of frustrated attempts to secure effective legislation against catholics. Parliament proved better able to publicise the popish plot than to take effective action to defeat it. The apparent lack of actions against the threat local catholics represented, set against the fears raised internally by the developing political conflict and externally by the Irish rebellion and possible foreign intervention, seems to have sharpened local feeling against catholics. The movement (usual) of Irish migrants and (shocking) of protestant refugees from Ireland through the region served as a pointed reminder of the popish threat.[70] Harbottle Grimston was probably responding both to local anxieties raised by news of the outbreak of the Irish Rebellion and by local celebrations of 5 November when in early November 1641 he secured an order from the Commons for the Colchester authorities to search the house of Mrs Payne, a catholic, for arms and to intercept such letters as were to be sent from there to Ireland.[71] That the House had heard read on the same day the

[67] PRO, SP, 16/142/113; Milton, *Catholic*, pp. 43, 44–5, 72, 530.
[68] P. Lake, 'Anti-popery: the structure of a prejudice' in R. Cust and A. Hughes, *Conflict in Early Stuart England: Studies in Religion and Politics 1603–1642* (1989), pp. 72–106; S. Hardman Moore, 'Popery, purity and providence: deciphering the New England experiment' in A. Fletcher and A. Roberts (eds.), *Religion, Culture and Society in Early Modern Britain: Essays in Honour of Patrick Collinson* (Cambridge, 1994), pp. 257–89, quotation from p. 270; Thompson, *Mobility and Migration*.
[69] S. P. Salt, 'Sir Simonds D'Ewes and the legacy of ship money, 1635–1640', *Historical Journal*, 37 (1994), p. 259.
[70] ESRO, HD 53/2786, p. 7; WSRO, FL 668/5/9/67.
[71] W. H. Coates (ed.), *The Journal of Sir Simonds D'Ewes from the Beginning of the Long Parliament to the Opening of the Trial of the Earl of Strafford* (New Haven and London,

examination of Sir John Lucas's brother about his relationship with the Army Plotter, Daniel O'Neale, suggests another possible reason for the order.[72] Suspicious statements merited rigorous investigation, suspicious behaviour immediate action.[73] Thus, when a letter written by Edward Cherry, the minister of the Rivers' living at St Osyth (and victim in August 1642) with his wife and her brother, to Captain Robert Appleton was found on the highway, it was immediately referred to the Earl of Warwick. Clearly, it was the reference in the letter to the 'moste piouse & religiouse service you are in' and Appleton's position as attendant on the king at Windsor (and possible catholicism) that prompted such action. In April 1642 words spoken by one Henry Wilson, probably a member of a local catholic family living in the Ingatestone parish of the Petres, provoked similar alarm Wilson had said, 'we might thank the Parliament for these troublesome times, and that if Ireland were true to themselves, they could not be hurt from England'. Suspicions even broached the boundaries of respect for the proprieties of the social hierarchy. Letters from Lady Gilbiard to Sir James Simmons found on a drunken traveller were opened by the mayor of Sudbury and, 'beeing very obscure', were sent on to the town's MP, Sir Simonds D'Ewes.[74]

There is evidence to suggest that fears about the activities of local catholics were increasing on the eve of petitions heavily inflected with anti-popery being circulated in the region and sent to Parliament. On 14 January 1641–2, the Commons received information about Hengrave Hall in Suffolk, home to Lady Penelope Gage, the sister of Elizabeth, Countess of Rivers, 'where weere an 100 armes & soe great a resort of papists as the countrie about it weere much troubled at it'. Ten days later several Suffolk JPs with carts and a crowd of thirty arrived at the Hall without warning, broke down a door and carted away the arms. It is unlikely that the local inhabitants had been reassured by the protestations of Lady Gage that 'the armes had been 100 yeare in catholikes hands & never yet hurt a finger of any body & I wished they never

---

1923), p. 158; *CJ*/ii/312. I have not been able to find a reference to a Mrs Payne among the Colchester records, nor is she to be found among the lists of Essex recusants. There was however a Mrs Payne living in 1640 at Stoke by Nayland, home of the catholic Mannocks family: V. B. Redstone (ed.), *The Ship-Money Returns For the County of Suffolk 1639–40* (Ipswich, 1904), p. 194.

[72] *CJ*/ii/318. Sir Charles Lucas may well have served with O'Neale in the Low Countries: J. T. Gilbert, *A Contemporary History of Affairs in Ireland from 1641 to 1652*, 3 vols. (Dublin, 1879–80), vol. 1, pt 2, p. 799.

[73] *CCC*, p. 2746; BL Egerton MS, 34,253, fol. 7; *PJ*, 2, p. 248. For the Wilsons, see Campbell, 'Estreat of fines', *ERec*, 1 (1959), pp. 25–32.

[74] BL, Egerton MS 34,253, fol. 7; Harleian MS 383, fol. 189 r. It may be that Robert Appleton was related to John Appleton of Mundon in Essex who was sequestered for his catholicism: *CCC*, p. 2746.

might'. In a postscript to a letter to the Dowager Countess of Rivers, Lady Penelope had told her mother, 'we are dayly thre[a]tned by the comon sort of people & for our defence have nothing left us'. At about the same time the Daniells' house in Acton was ordered to be searched for 'popish arms'. This search seems to have been triggered by the interception at Sudbury of arms intended for the house.[75] In Essex, at least one catholic gentry household had been attacked in the earlier 1640 troop disorders at the instigation of a yeoman from Stephen Marshall's neighbouring parish of Finchingfield, who had told them that 'they should doe theire Country good service to teare him in pieces'. January 1642 had seen further popular violence against another catholic gentleman. At Maldon, the barn of Edmund Church was smashed and two stacks of unthreshed rye carried away by a crowd over a hundred strong. Since the crowd was drawn from a wide area and Church was a catholic, a strong supporter of Charles I's Personal Rule and a victim of the riots in the summer of 1642, the incident would seem to have more to do with the politics of anti-popery than a dispute over property and it may have been triggered by the anti-catholic petition being circulated from parish to parish shortly before.[76] That catholics felt threatened helps to explain why they should be seeking arms, but it can be imagined what effect such discoveries had upon local opinion.[77] The repeated demands from Colchester and the other towns in the region that they be fortified was clearly linked to fears of a possible catholic invasion backed by a rising of local catholics.[78]

Within the region growing anxiety over the catholic threat was reflected in a return to the more regular presentment of catholics to the local courts. There had already been a tightening of action against them in the later 1630s. For example, in 1638 the Essex JPs had been ordered at their monthly meetings 'to examine ye abuses for not collecting ye 12d on Sunday on recusants', a reflection perhaps of fears that a more

---

[75] BL, Harleian MS 162, fol. 324v; CUL, Hengrave MSS, 88, vol. 2, no. 150; *CJ*/ii/378; *CJ*/ii/396; *PJ*, 2, p. 178. This seems to be the implication in the Commons' order that 'such of those Arms as are already brought to Sudbury, shall be stayed there'.

[76] PRO, PCR 2/52, p. 634; ERO, Q/SR 316/24.

[77] In February 1642, the House of Commons ordered the Cambridgeshire JPs to search for arms in the house of Mr Tempest, a catholic, following reports that five cartloads of arms had been taken into the house three years ago, and that Tempest had been heard to say, 'Fear not, cousin, we have arms enough to destroy the county of Cambridge': *CJ*/ii/431; *PJ*, 2, p. 375. Tempest was the lord of the manor at Whaddon, a village where there is some evidence to suggest that there was also a godly presence: *VCH Cambridgeshire and Isle of Ely*, vol. 8 (Oxford, 1982), p. 142; W. M. Palmer and H. W. Saunders (eds.), *Cambridgeshire Village Documents*, 4, pt 2, p. 73.

[78] *PJ*, 1, pp. 123, 126; BL, E200(14), *Mr Grimston His Speech in Parliament: On Wednesday the 19th of January, Upon the Preferring of the Essex Petition*, AD 1641–2, p. 5.

permissive regime was weakening the controls on catholics.[79] From at least early 1639 there appears to have been more regular presentments of catholic recusants by hundredal juries to both Quarter Sessions and Assizes within the county.[80] The county's response to the Commons' order of December 1640 calling for the return of all recusants was swift and thorough, producing in effect a census of catholics, parish by parish.[81] Suffolk, as well as neighbouring counties, took similar action.[82]

Heightened tensions produced higher levels of presentment and indictment. Although such action resulted in the imposition of fines, they did nothing to remove the threat posed by the continued presence of catholics in local communities. A much longer history of fining and persecution had failed to suppress catholicism, and the same family names had occurred again and again. By contrast, other known recusants were not presented. The recusancy legislation did not offer an effective solution to the problem of 'church papists', nor to the frightening possibilities that there were many more catholics undetected and unpresented assembling in gentry households.[83] The response to Bishop Wren's attempt in 1636 to have both recusant papists *and* separatists presented had provided telling evidence of the county's religious anxieties, the extant returns recording for the most part only catholic recusants.[84] But it also provides evidence of the weaknesses in the system of detection and punishment. From Long Melford two Anabaptists were

---

[79] ERO, Q/SBa, 2/30, unno. (9 January 1638). This order may well be related to the entries in the parish register of Great Bromley from 1638 onwards of charges for presenting recusants: CRO, D/P, 177/1/1.

[80] ERO, Q/SR, 295/9; /304/75, 78–9; /305/25–7, 29; /306/39, 41–3; /307/35, 38–9; /309/ 11–13, 15; /310/64, 66; /311/9, 11–12, 17–18; /312/23–4, 26, 30, 124; /313/32, 35, 37–9, 42; /314/62–4; /315/77–8; /316/23, 26, 28–31, 92; /317/32–6. For the Assizes, see Mary and Nicholas, 'Essex recusants in an Exchequer document, 1585–1642', *ERec*, 6 (1964), pp. 90–5, 7 (1965), pp. 36–9.

[81] *CJ*/ii/46; PRO, SP, 16/426/67 (note of presentments for recusancy at a private session included in returns to the Book of Orders). The returns of catholics in response to the order of December 1640 can be found in ERO, Q/SBa 5.

[82] Suffolk's Quarter Session records have not survived, but we know that in response to the Commons' order directives were issued that 'recusants must all be endicted the next sessions': *Diary of John Rous*, ed. M. A. Green (Camden Society, 1856), vol. 66, p. 104. For Norfolk, see B. Schofield, *The Knyvet Letters 1620–1644* (1949), p. 99.

[83] ERO, Q/S Pe 1/4–8; Campbell, 'Estreats of Fines', pp. 25–32; Mary and Nicholas, 'Essex recusants', pp. 90–5; C. M. Hibbard, 'Early Stuart catholicism: revisions and re-revisions', *Journal Modern History*, 52 (1980), p. 31. Ironically, the disorders in the capital may have encouraged catholics to move to the counties: PRO, SP, 16/484/32.

[84] PRO, SP, 16/337/19; Bodl. Lib., Tanner MS 314, fols. 124r–5v. Ironically, Wren's efforts may have increased fears about the catholic threat, since they failed to produce any positive action to quell those fears. According to Laud, the grand jury refused to accept the bishop's certificate because he had also inserted 'recusant separatists, as well as recusant Romanists': *The Works of William Laud, Archbishop of Canterbury*, ed. W. Scott and J. Bliss, 7 vols. (Oxford, 1847–60), vol. 5, p. 341.

returned against the trend, but none of the large catholic households were presented. In the summer of 1641, Sir Thomas Barrington, writing from Essex, had talked 'of a strange tepidity, full of needless scruples, in the execution of that brave ordinance of both Houses for the disarming of Papists' which, worryingly, he attributed to 'a comixture of malcontents severely disaffected'. Significantly, it was not until the Quarter Sessions held in the summer of 1642 that Sir Henry Audley was presented for recusancy in Essex.[85]

On the eve of the August attacks the godly in the region found themselves facing a known threat of unknown proportions. While the developments of the 1630s seemed to suggest that there was a potentially greater threat from a catholic fifth column, policies in Church and State seemed rather to offer protection to catholics and to put obstacles in the way of attempts to punish them. Legal action in 1639 revealed that leading catholics within the region, among them some who were to be targets of the crowds in 1642, had been given royal protection against prosecution. At the end of 1640 the Essex Quarter Sessions received copies of the orders of the House of Lords extending privilege against prosecution for recusancy to peers and to their families and servants.[86] Increased presentment of recusant catholics to the local courts had made people more aware of the threat in their midst. The searches of 1639 had led to claims appearing in print that they had uncovered the names of above 200,000 families of papists.[87] But local action had not succeeded in securing effective measures to neutralise the popish threat.

Thus, reports from the localities of local scares and panics contributed to heightened tensions at the centre, while at the same time Parliament's harping on the catholic threat and orders to search catholic houses in the region proved mutually reinforcing in ratcheting up fears yet further. The increasing publicity given to the popish threat by a Parliament still unable to pass legislation to secure the disarming and neutralising of catholics greatly contributed to this heightening of tension. Parliament had identified the threat and proposed a solution, but it had shown itself unable to implement it. The conditions of political instability and

---

[85] Beinecke Library, Yale University, Osborne Collection, Sir Thomas Barrington to Lord Howard of Escrick, 24 July 1641. (I am grateful to Christopher Thompson for making available to me his transcript of this letter); Bodl. Lib., Tanner MS 314, fol. 124 v; ERO, Q/SR, 317/34. The churchwardens' accounts for Long Melford reveal that by 1641 they were presenting recusants, but not who was presented: WSRO, FL, 509/5/1/45.

[86] The Petres, Rivers, Southcotts and Mannocks all pleaded a royal letter of grace as a bar to prosecution under the recusancy laws: PRO, SP, 16/406/120, 122; /426/85; Elliott, 'Roman Catholic community', ERec, 25–6 (1983–5), p. 42; P. R. P. Knell, 'The Southcott family in Essex, 1575–1642', ERec, 14 (1972), p. 16; ERO, Q/S, Ba 2/43.

[87] Collections of the Massachusetts Historical Society, 4th ser., 6 (Boston, 1863), p. 160.

heightened tension produced by the failure of king and Parliament to arrive at a political settlement proved a fertile ground for the generation of panics and alarums. As the historian of these panics, Robin Clifton, has observed, there was a 'parallelism' between particular political events and heightened panics. Rumour was both an index of anxieties and, in its focus on the supposed role of catholics, an attempt to find an explanation which would provide a closure for fears. The Whitsun Colchester scare had identified the threat at Colchester. Other victims were also the subject of panics. There were panics on three successive nights at Ipswich about the rumoured activities at the house of the nearby Forsters. Stories circulated of a hidden army ready to cut the townsmens' throats. Rumour, it has been argued, not only expresses a consensus on the causes of anxieties; it also validates collective action to remove them.[88] Measures to seize recusants' arms were still being introduced into the Commons when the Colchester Plunderers took matters into their own hands. In August 1642 the Colchester crowds were at last able to put into effect action first canvassed in the 1640 Whitsuntide scare.

Popular anxieties and Parliamentary pressure help to explain why, after Sir John Lucas, the attacks should come to focus on catholic targets. Fear of popery made the catholics an unwelcome presence. Parliament's denunciation of them offered legitimation for an attack upon them. Thickening the description of the attack upon Sir John Lucas revealed several layers of conflict. Did anti-popery provide a cloak for the settling of scores that cannot be traced to confessional differences and which are only recoverable from similar micro-histories? Certainly, the Lucases were not the only gentry family to encounter difficulties in their relationships with the Corporation and commons of Colchester. Other families attacked may also have provoked more immediate conflicts within their own neighbourhood.

Like the Lucas family, the Audleys of Berechurch, had experienced conflicts with the town, not all of which can be traced to confessional differences. The Audleys owed their emergence as landowning gentry to the profits of the law and the spoils of the Dissolution. Thomas Audley had trained in the law, become town clerk of Colchester and gone on to a more spectacular career in the service of Henry VIII which had ended with him as Chancellor in the Court of Augmentations. Well-placed to profit from the pickings of confiscated monastic lands, he had acquired, among other lands, St Botolph's Abbey and the house of the Crouched

---

[88] R. L. Rosnow and G. A. Fine, *Rumour and Gossip: The Social Psychology of Hearsay* (New York, Oxford, Amsterdam, 1976); Clifton, 'Fear of Catholics', p. 211.

Friars in Colchester. With these purchases the family acquired both patronage in its parish churches and property within the liberties of the town, and with them the grounds for conflict.[89] Berechurch, the family's principal manor and place of residence was less than a mile from Colchester and, as with the Lucases at St John's, fell within that area of the town's liberties over which the Corporation claimed jurisdiction. Thus, the preconditions for conflict between family and borough were identical to those between the Lucases and Colchester. As was the case with the Lucases, the major area of dispute involved issues of jurisdiction, setting a borough jealous of its power and privileges under its charter against a landed family whose rank did not suggest easy acceptance of being ruled over by merchants and craftsmen.[90] More persistent trouble between the town and the Audleys seems to have flared up in the 1580s when the combative Katherine, widow of Robert Audley, headed the family.[91] That this was at the same time and over the same issues as the conflict between Sir Thomas Lucas and the town may be more than coincidental, since at least one other gentleman, Francis Jobson (for whom Thomas Lucas, described in Jobson's will as his friend, acted as executor) had also decided to challenge the Corporation's claim to exercise jurisdiction. At the same time, the Corporation and Mistress Audley were involved in a dispute over the muster. Like Sir Thomas Lucas, Katherine Audley refused to allow the Corporation to muster the inhabitants of Berechurch.[92]

Thereafter, there is less evidence of open conflict between the Audleys and the Corporation. There may be several reasons for this. Firstly, tension over the family's control of so many livings in the town would have been eased by an agreement in 1619–20 which gave the Corporation

---

[89]   S. E. Lehmbreg, 'Sir Thomas Audley: a soul as black as marble?' in A. J. Slavin (ed.), *Tudor Men and Institutions: Studies in English Law and Government* (Baton Rouge, 1972), pp. 3–31; P. Morant, *The History and Antiquities of the most ancient Town and Borough of Colchester*, 2 vols. (1748), vol. 2, pp. 30–1; Hartharn, 'Audleys', pp. 39–46; Smith, *Ecclesiastical History*, pp. 311, 313, 314, 318–319.

[90]   For example in 1565 when Thomas Audley had tried to exclude the town's officers from Berechurch: *VCH Essex*, 9, p. 110.

[91]   An attempt by the family to get themselves and the inhabitants of the parish rated for the subsidy with the county rather than the town led to open conflict. A riot and consequent suit in Star Chamber against the Audleys ended with the Privy Council finding for the Corporation: CRO, Sb2/4, fols. 4 v–5 v; D/B5 Gb 1(unfol.), 8 November 23 Eliz. I; D/B5 R7, fols. 184 v–5 v; D/Y, 2/10, pp. 77, 103, 163, 178; D/DRg 1/117; *APC 1581–1582*, pp. 78, 110, 124, 262–3.

[92]   CRO, D/Y, 2/10, fol. 178; F. G. Emmison, *Elizabethan Life 4: Wills Essex Gentry and Merchants* (Chelmsford, 1978), pp. 21–2. Shortly before 1581, Katherine Audley had been involved in a dispute with one of the leading families of Colchester over property which had resulted in legal action in Star Chamber: Byford, 'Price of Protestantism', pp. 257–8; *APC 1580–1581*, pp. 51, 126–7, 131.

the right to present the ministers in St James and St Peter's. In contrast to the relationship between Lucas and the town, both the Audley family and the Corporation were careful to maintain reciprocal exchanges of food – gentle deer for mercantile sugar – the last recorded gift of the latter coming in the year before the riots of 1642.[93] More importantly, the family's recusancy must have encouraged it to avoid conflict – the Corporation had been quick to wrongfoot Katherine Audley during the earlier disputes by introducing the issue of her catholicism.

The attack on the catholic gentleman, Edmund Church, also offers parallels with the attack on Sir John Lucas. For much of the sixteenth century John Church, a lawyer and a servant of the Earl of Oxford, then the dominant aristocratic figure within Essex, had been a bailiff within the borough of Maldon. He had managed the temporalities of Beeley Abbey as well as acting as agent on the De Veres' estates in eastern Essex. His catholicism had brought him into conflict with some townsmen, but he had played an important role in securing the town's charter of incorporation. Like the Earl's other agent, the Harlakendens at Earls Colne, the Churches may have benefited from the De Veres' descent into debt. In the seventeenth century Edmund Church had become a gentleman and a landowner with holdings not only in the vicinity of Maldon, but elsewhere in the county – including Colchester – as well as in other counties. Like Lucas, his activities at enclosing, though on a lesser scale, had brought him into conflict with the borough of Maldon and had led to legal action against him. It is not clear whether this lay at the root of his other conflicts with the town, but in 1629 he had been indicted in the borough's courts for speaking 'opprobrious words' against a member of the Corporation, and in the following year the town had petitioned the Privy Council about his unlawful and violent courses which, they claimed, had disrupted their commerce. Church, a convicted recusant, was also the impropriator of the rectory of St Mary's at Maldon. His politics too may have made him unpopular with others in the county. Some idea of what these were can be gleaned from the fact that at a meeting in Bedfordshire called to levy the Forced Loan of 1626, Church, who held land in the county, was the only one to offer payment. Like Lucas's malignancy, Church's recusancy offered his local opponents a chance to strike back at him even before the August attack, hence the first attack on him at the time of the anti-catholic January petition.[94]

[93] CRO, D/B5, Aa 1/4; CRO, D/B5, Aa 1/12; *ibid.*, Ab 1/8, rot. 20.
[94] W. J. Petchey, *A Prospect of Maldon 1500–1689* (Chelmsford, 1991), pp. 137, 125–6, 161–2, 195; *CCC*, 4, pp. 2402–3; PRO, KB, 790/1/112; Cliftlands, '"Well-affected"', p. 308 n.; *APC 1630–1631*, p. 122; *1599–1600*, p. 53; *1615–1616*, p. 87; *1616–1617*, p. 327; Smith, *Ecclesiastical History*, p. 205; G. D. Gilmore, 'The papers of Richard

The Rivers too had points of conflict with their neighbours in north Essex and Suffolk. The evidence of conflict is necessarily more fragmentary since on neither of their rural estates attacked did the family have as near neighbours a powerful (and record conscious) corporation like Colchester. Nevertheless, neither estate was more than a handful of miles from a borough – St Osyth from Colchester, Melford Hall from Sudbury – and there is evidence to confirm that the family lived close enough to be the subject of speculation and gossip among the townsfolk. On both of its manors in Essex and Suffolk the evidence suggests that the Rivers family pursued an estate policy that created the potential for conflict. There is some evidence of dispute with neighbouring lords of the manor, something perhaps hard to avoid since there were seven manors within Long Melford. At Long Melford the manorial records appear not to have survived, but the quick succession of a series of estate maps there – the manor was surveyed in 1580 and again in 1613 – might suggest that the family were committed to a policy of improving its estate income.[95] Immediately after the riot the Countess faced a rent strike on her manors. Some tenants she claimed were frightened by retaliation, but that others were 'happily well contented to take yt occasion to withould ... what they ought to pay' might confirm the suggestion of conflict between the family and its tenants.[96] Within recent times at both Melford and St Osyth the family had pursued enclosure to create deer parks. There were two parks well stocked with deer at St Osyth. What happened there might give some clue to how the Rivers regarded their estates more generally. In 1637, the earl had successfully petitioned the king to be allowed to demolish the tenements adjoining his parks and to annex the thirty acres of land to his Great Park, because he was annoyed 'by the ill neighbourhood of some poor inhabitants of tenements adjoining'. The manner of the creation of the Rivers' parks may have contributed to the attack in the summer of 1642. The 'dainty park' at Melford may have won the admiration of the essayist James Howell, but emparkment representing as it did a form of unproductive land use celebrating aristocratic status, was popularly detested and frequently the occasion of

Taylor of Clapham (c. 1579–1641)', (Bedfordshire Historical Records Society, 25/5 1947), p. 108; Bedfordshire RO, ABCV 96.

[95] BL, Harleian MS 97, fol. 94; D. MacCulloch (ed.), *Chorography of Suffolk* (Suffolk Records Society, 19, 1976), p. 55. Both maps remain in the possession of Sir Richard Hyde Parker at Melford Hall. A copy of the 1580 map and details of the 1613 map have been published by the Long Melford Historical and Archaeological Society, Occasional Publications, nos. 1 and 4 (n.d. and 1995).

[96] HLRO, MP HL, 29 August 1642 (petit. Countess of Rivers). In a later petition the Countess complained of 'her Tennants taking notice of some generall Ordinances for seising of estates doe ... refuse to pay her rents': HLRO, MP HL, 9 September 1642.

popular protest, with aristocratic parks a prime target of the crowds in the early stages of the English Revolution.[97] Other conflicts created scores that could also be settled in the August attack. In the autumn of 1641 there had been another neighbourhood conflict at Melford with the Countess complaining about the disorderly behaviour of the inhabitants of the nearby almshouse. Similarly, her husband's role as an arbitrator appointed by the Privy Council in the dispute with the Lucas family over Colchester's water supply may have won him few friends among Colchester townsfolk.[98]

In addition to these sources of local conflict, there is evidence, again paralleling the Lucas history, of potential conflict with Parliament's supporters among the county governors. Earl Rivers, father of the Countess, had been active in the collection of the Forced Loan in 1626. His role therein as an ally of Buckingham would have strained his relationship with the Earl of Warwick, who was active locally in the opposition to the Loan and who had fallen out with Buckingham. Excluded from local office after the popish panic of 1625/6 because of their catholicism, the Rivers nevertheless maintained close ties with the Court. The Countess's husband, Sir Thomas Savage, was also a friend of Buckingham, and he held office as chancellor in Henrietta Maria's court.[99] The couple named one of their daughters after the queen, to whose court the Countess was herself attached, Henrietta Maria bracketing her with the Countess of Buckingham as a special friend. As Rivers wrote to the king in 1637, 'my Daughter, the Lady Savage ... hath the honour to serve your Ma[jes]tie and I trust shall do when I am gon[e], with the same fidelity and devotion I ever carried toward your Crowne and person'. Such language, while conventional, suggests that, as with Lucas, the Rivers' attachment to the court and regime of Charles I might have earned them the hostility of Parliament's supporters among the county elites. In serving the king as a member of the county magistracy in Lancashire the Countess's husband' displayed an antipathy to those he regarded as puritan opponents of the regime.[100] Despite the fragmentary

[97] PRO, SP16/322, p. 57; W. A. Copinger (ed.), *County of Suffolk: its History Disclosed by Existing Records and Other Documents, being Materials for the History of Suffolk*, 5 vols. (1904–5) vol. 4, p. 115; J. Howell, *Familiar Letters or Epistola Ho-Elianne*, 10th edn (Aberdeen, 1753), p. 76.

[98] W. Parker, *The History of Long Melford* (1873), p. 210; PRO, PCR, 2/43, pp. 285–7.

[99] Cust, *Forced Loan*, p. 10; D. Mathew, *The Social Structure of Caroline England* (Oxford, 1948), p. 35 n. Rivers was one of the commissioners for Buckingham's estate and was sent for by the king after Buckingham's death: *CSPD 1627–28*, pp. 264, 342; CUL, Hengrave MSS, 88, 2, no. 13.

[100] CUL, Hengrave MSS 88, 2, no. 133; M. J. Havran, *The Catholics in Caroline England* (Stanford, 1962), pp. 54–5; C. M. Hibbard, 'The role of a queen consort: the household of Henrietta Maria 1625–1642' in R. G. Asch and A. M. Birke (eds.), *Princes,*

nature of the evidence there is sufficient to show that there were sources of conflict which doubtless prompted some of the Rivers' neighbours to join in the attack on their houses.

What of the other gentry families attacked? Here the evidence is even sparser for an assessment of the possibility of pre-existing conflicts with the communities in which they lived. In the case of major landowners like the Petre family there was certainly plenty of scope for friction. The Petre estates were amongst the largest in Essex. In the half-century before the attacks they had registered a significant increase in rental income. But whether this had been achieved at the cost of greater friction between landlord and tenants is not known. The historian of the family's estates suggests that this increase was made possible as much by competition among their tenantry as by any deliberate estate policy. Nevertheless, both the Petres' parks and ponds had been the site of some popular disorder before the civil war and after its outbreak there were far more sustained outbreaks of mass poaching. However, the nature of the surviving evidence does not permit a judgement as to how far this was opportunistic theft and how far conscious protest against aristocratic property.[101]

Clearly whatever the size of their landholding there was scope for conflict between gentry families and their neighbours and tenants. An exhaustive search might yield similar scraps of evidence for other families. But even given such evidence it is clear that the attacks did not flow along lines laid down by pre-civil war conflict, since by no means all gentry known to have been in dispute with their tenants or local communities were attacked. A search for inner histories to parallel that of the relationship between Lucas and Colchester is in danger of missing the most striking fact that with the exception of the Lucases all the other gentry families attacked were, or were suspected of being, catholics. Local disputes, where they existed, doubtless encouraged local support for the attackers. But it was the catholicism of the victims that was more important in explaining attacks involving crowds numbered in their thousands and drawn from a wide area. Plebeian as well as gentle catholic families were attacked. Faith, not fortune, determined their fate.

Patronage and the Nobility: the Court at the beginning of the Modern Age c. 1450–1650 (Oxford, 1991), pp. 405–6; *CSPD 1619–1623*, p. 346; *CSPD 1639–40*, p. 486; PRO, SP, 16/352/50; *CSPD 1627–1628*, p. 45.

[101] W. R. Emerson, 'The economic development of the estates of the Petre family in Essex in the sixteenth and seventeenth centuries' (D.Phil. thesis, Oxford, 1951), pp. 223–313; C. Clay, 'The misfortunes of William, fourth Lord Petre (1638–1655)', *RecHist*, 11 (1971), pp. 87–11; ERO, Q/SR, 287/19, 290/22, 319/22, 77, 83–4, 95, 103; Q/SBa, 2/48, /49; D/DP L36/26; BL, Egerton MS 2646, fol. 303.

Part 4

Reading the crowd

7. *Cloth and class*

And there is no doubt but that all right and propertie all *meum* and *tuum* must cease in civill wars: and wee know not what advantage the meaner sort alsoe may take to divide the spoiles of the rich and noble amongst them, who beginn alreadie to alledge, that all being of one mould ther is no reason that some should have so much & others soe little. And we see what former effects these civill broiles have produced amongst the Swiszers & in Germanie.

Sir Simonds D'Ewes, 8 June 1642[1]

Whereas Right honourable and Worshipful we Combers have petition'd unto Mr Smyth's Worship last fryday for worke & he told us that our townsmen had p[ro]mised him that we should have worke but it proufe noe such matter for I have asked both the townsmen & the Overseers & they regard not my complaint & [I] have not have had half worke Enough sinc[e] Witsentide & my Charg[e] is soe great that I can make shift noe longer for I have 5 Cheldren to keep & I had much adoue to keep them when I had worke Enough & I have made all the Shift that I can. For my owne part I never chardgd the towne for a penny, not soe I desire now but Crave work of them to mayntaine my Charg. I never took noe lewed course for to rong any man nor yet Rune about the Country as others have done as it is well knowne that some went for Corne to the sea sid[e] & tooke it by violen[ce]. Some again ran up to London beagging. I never stand but kept my worke & it is nothing els which now I crave to maintaine my Charg[e] that I may not take noe unlawfull co[u]rse for it is hard to starve Job saieth, since for skin & all that a man hath he will give for his life.

Richard Hammond, Essex clothworker, *c.* 1636/7.[2]

---

[1] BL, Harleian MS 163, fol. 153 v.   [2] ERO, D/DEb, 7/4.

Identifying the faces in the crowds of the summer of 1642 is difficult. Contemporary comment employed the traditional language of the 'many-headed monster' when discussing the social identity of the attackers. Those in authority described them variously and interchangeably as 'riotous people', 'riotous & disordered p[er]sons', 'rogues & other wicked desperate people', 'unruly people', 'tumultuo[u]s People'.[3] The original report from the Mayor of Colchester, while talking of a crowd of 5,000 men, women and children, referred otherwise to those who carried out the attack only as 'rude people'. A Colchester observer of the attack on the Audleys described the attackers as being drawn from 'the Com[m]on rude people'; in her petition to the House of Lords the Countess of Rivers, for example, blamed 'the rude multitude'. Since this was the language of 'the many-headed monster' such descriptions may reflect contemporary assumptions rather than contemporary witness. They were the commonplace of elite comment on their inferiors.[4] As is now well recognised they tell us much about elite attitudes and rather less about the identity of the crowds. It is perhaps less well recognised that such descriptions, especially in the political context of the 1640s, were partisan attempts to construct the crowd in such a way as to serve differing representations of the event. For example, the description by one catholic of the attackers as drawn from 'the whole country rout' might be taken to reflect an undiscriminating blindness bred by social distance. But this, and the general catholic preference for describing their attackers as the 'rude people', almost certainly represented an attempt to downplay the significance of the attack by attributing it to a group that most propertied contemporaries would have thought of as 'naturally' given to disorder. Given our knowledge of the inner-history of conflict between Sir John Lucas and the Corporation of Colchester, the Mayor's identification of the attackers as 'rude people' may have been intended to serve a similar purpose, distancing the town's rulers from any involvement in the attack by attributing it to plebeian dissidence.[5] Thus, without supporting evidence, such generalised descriptions tell us almost nothing about the reality of the social identity of the crowds.

Where such reports as we have do not automatically trumpet assumptions about the social bases of disorder in early modern England, they

---

[3] ESRO, FB, 19/I2/2, [nos. 12, 18]; BL, Harleian MS 365, fol. 209; Warwickshire RO, CR, 2017/C9/2.

[4] HLRO, Braye-Teeling MSS (22 August 1642); HLRO, MP HL, 29 August 1642; PRO, SP, 19A/95, fol. 85; PRO, SP, 16/491/128; Stoneyhurst College, Stoneyhurst MSS, MSS Angliae, 7, fols. 122–3. Foley, *Society*, 2, p. 426 mistranscribes 'country rout' as the more innocuous 'country round'.

[5] For a broader discussion of this political stratagem, see M. James, 'English politics and the concept of honour 1485–1642' (*P&P* supplement 3, 1978), pp. 42–3.

suggest that those responsible were drawn from the lower ranks of society. For example, the orders sent out to the parish constables in Suffolk after the initial attacks instructed them to ensure that 'noe poore people or p[er]sons of meane Condic[i]on be allowed to go forth' of the parish without good cause. Local observers sometimes employed a more neutral language. For example, those who attacked Edmund Church's property in Maldon were described by one of those present as 'ye poore people of ye neighbourhead [*sic*]'. This was a description that echoed the Earls Colne minister Ralph Josselin's reference to 'our poore people'.[6]

Who did in fact commit the attacks? This is not a question easy to answer. The civil war collapse of key courts in the prosecution of disorder means that there are serious gaps in the legal record for both Essex and Suffolk.[7] The complete lack of any extant criminal records for Suffolk for this period means that we know the names of none of the thousands said to be involved in the attack on the Countess of Rivers. It is clear from a letter of the Suffolk JPs that they did arrest some of the attackers. But the solitary name that we do have – William Bowyer – comes from Parliamentary records.[8] It was not only the collapse of authority that prevented the detection and punishment of the perpetrators. For a variety of reasons the Parliamentary authorities were not eager to see prosecutions brought. Even where they do survive criminal records are not without their problems. In particular, they cannot be assumed to capture a random sample of those allegedly involved since sometimes those prosecuted and convicted were pre-selected to match the assumptions of the authorities. All this makes it more than usually difficult to identify the faces in the crowd. We do have some evidence from the records of the criminal courts for Essex, but the legal record for the attacks amounts to no more than scraps of evidence – a couple of examinations in the Colchester and county records, the indictments of couple of men in the Essex Quarter Sessions and Assizes, and a handful of names from the gaol calendars.[9]

[6] ESRO, FB 19/I2 [no. 18]; PRO, SP, 23/113, pp. 125–6; *Diary of John Rous*, ed. M. A. Green (Camden Society, 1856), vol. 66, p. 13.

[7] The Essex Quarter Sessions did not meet for most of 1643 and the Assizes for the county did not meet after the attacks until the autumn of 1644. Although the Michaelmas and Hilary 1642 courts of Quarter Sessions appear to have met in Suffolk only the order book survives and the courts were suspended thereafter until 1644: ESRO, B105/2/1. There are no extant Assize records for Suffolk for this period.

[8] BL, Harleian MS 163, fol. 325; MS 385, fol. 209; *CJ*/ii/789. Nothing else is known about Bowyer, but he may have come from the local family of that name living at Stradishall some eight miles from Melford: C. E. Banks, *Able Men of Suffolk 1638* (Boston, Mass., 1931), p. 345.

[9] CRO, D/B, 5, Sb2 7, fol. 300; ERO, Q/SBa, 2/48 [2 January 1642/3]; Q/SR, 319/12, 16, 109; PRO, ASSI, 35/85/5, 58. There are a handful of other names in the Assize and

The inability or unwillingness of the authorities to arrest or prosecute the attackers means that it has been possible to recover only fifteen names from the legal record with confidence that they were involved in the attacks. Five – four men and one woman, Anne Seamer – were accused of taking part in the attack on the house of the catholic Daniel family in Bulmer. The legal record gives no more than their names. Further research suggests that one, Thomas Mayes, was a husbandman from Bulmer itself; another, George Ingham, may have come from the next parish of Little Yeldham where a man of the same name was described as a farmer in 1650. It has not been possible to find out anything at all about the other three.[10] Of the remaining ten attackers for whom we have names, two were described as labourers: Thomas Campion from the village of Stanway to the west of Colchester, indicted for the attack on the houses of the clergy at Great Birch and Little Tey, and John Egland from Tolleshunt Bushes, indicted for the attack on the Countess of Rivers' house at St Osyth. Four others were Colchester men – three weavers and a tailor – examined for their part in the attack at St Osyth. Of the women who were said to have been active in the attacks, we have the names of only three. In addition to Anne Seamer at Bulmer, we know of Sara Mann and Mary Hoy who were suspected to be part of a group of women who had attacked the house of the minister at Peldon. Mann was the wife of a Peldon labourer, presented for unlicensed victualling in the 1650s, while Hoy was a young woman from the hamlet of Bures in the Stour Valley, living out of service, who was probably the woman of the same name from there who had been presented to the local church court in 1637 for fornication with an Earls Colne man. Mary Hoy, whose (unnamed) brother was also said by one of Cornelius's servants to have taken part in the attack, mentions the name of another man – George Carter – for whom we have no further evidence.[11]

The names of only fifteen out of the thousands that were said to have taken part in the attacks scarcely provide an acceptable basis for generalisation. Taken at face value, these shards of evidence offer some confirmation of contemporaries' identification of the attacks as the work of the lower orders (but, if the attributions of farmer and husbandman are correct, some challenge too.) The relative invisibility of those whose names we do know – a search across a wide range of records yielded little additional information – might be taken to point towards their relative

Quarter Session records that might have been involved in the summer attacks, but in the absence of any evidence confirming a connection I have had to exclude them.
[10] ERO, Q/SR, 247/39–40, 346/53.
[11] ERO, Q/SBa, 2/48 (2 January 1642/3); PRO, ASSI, 35/95/2/26; /98/2. A Peldon fisherman was later bound over to keep the peace against Mary Hoy: ERO, Q/SR, 319/51.

poverty.[12] Limited as it is, the criminal record also suggests both that the attacks after Colchester were the work of roving crowds and that they were joined at each site by some of the local inhabitants. However, caution should be exercised since the legal record provides no evidence of how these unlucky individuals came to find themselves before the courts. Where, as is the case of those at Peldon, it was as a result of action by the victim then local faces may have been the only ones to be recognised. Where, as at St Osyth, those before the court were accused of theft it may be necessary, as in the case of the early modern food riot, to distinguish between the core of the crowd and those opportunists who subsequently took advantage of the disorder to steal. In all cases, we need to be alert to the fact that those prosecuted may have owed their selection primarily to their fitting the identikit image of the stereotypical rioter held by those in authority.[13] Perhaps the most important piece of evidence provided by the criminal records is the deafening silence about the attack on Sir John Lucas. We know the name of only one of the thousands alleged to have taken part in the riot against Lucas, a 'Mr' Cater, and that we owe to a political gibe made much later in the 1680s.[14]

Historians' discussions of the episode have identified the crowds, implicitly or explicitly, with the clothworkers of the region. However, there is no direct contemporary comment in support of this widespread supposition, and clearly the only reference in the criminal records to the presence of clothworkers is somewhat inconclusive.[15] The identification of the crowd with the cloth trade rests on the indirect evidence of a reading of the social geography of the area and a knowledge of the problems workers in the trade faced in the early 1640s. The domination of the textile industry at the centre of the area of the attacks suggests that crowds numbered in their thousands would almost inevitably have had

---

[12] For example, it has been possible to find the will of only one of those named, Leonard Searles, a Colchester weaver who died in the plague of 1666. From his will it is possible only to establish that Searles owned the house in which he lived: ERO, D/ABR, 7/274.

[13] For an excellent discussion of the selective nature of prosecution by the authorities, see R. Cobb, *The People and the Police: French Popular Protest 1789–1820* (Oxford, 1972), pt 1.

[14] Bodl. Lib., MS Top. Essex 1, fol. 121. This was probably William Cater, a baymaker, who was assessed on three hearths in the 1662 hearth tax for St Giles, the parish next to the Lucas house. Testamentary evidence suggests that Cater, later a member of the Corporation, came from the town's middling sort: CRO, D/B5, Cb2/27, fol. 284; ERO, D/ACW, 17/184; D/ABW 73/198; Q/SR 412/24; 413/58; 417/54.

[15] Thus Prof. Hunt's statement that 'depositions surviving from this affray [the attack on the Countess of Rivers at St Osyth] indicate that most of the rioters were weavers' is based on the fact that three out of the four men named were weavers. Depositions following in the manuscript Hunt cites yield the names of a further six weavers, but these were involved in the *December* attack on the minister of Peldon: CRO, D/B5, Sb2/7, fols. 300–3.

clothworkers in their midst. The scale of the crisis affecting the clothworkers suggests that they may well have comprised the core. At Colchester,
the epicentre of the August attacks, three thousand or more males were
directly involved in the cloth trade in the seventeenth century, a figure
that would need to be increased to take account of the heavy female
involvement in the trade. The proportion of the population directly
dependent on the cloth industry may have been even higher in the less
complex economies of the surrounding villages and townships. It was
from precisely these areas – Coggeshall, Bocking, Braintree and Halstead
– that *Mercurius Rusticus* identified support as coming for the attack on
Lucas. Many of the 'poore people' from Ralph Josselin's Earls Colne
were involved in cloth production. Other sites of the attacks, for example
Witham, were also important areas of production. In Suffolk, the
situation of the Rivers at Long Melford was similar to that of the
Lucases at Colchester. Melford, itself a large and populous centre of
cloth production, was embedded in the Suffolk cloth district. Three miles
to the south was the borough of Sudbury, the regional centre of the
industry, with a population perhaps approaching 2,000; four miles to the
south-west was the cloth centre of Lavenham with a similar size of
population.[16]

None the less, the identification of the crowds with clothing communities and workers needs some qualification. The wider geography of the
attacks, stretching beyond the cloth districts, of itself suggests the
involvement of other groups. This is borne out by contemporary
comment. Several accounts highlight the presence of seamen in the
crowds. They were said to have been active both at St Osyth and in the
actions originating from Maldon, and again at Colchester in December
1642.[17] Nor should the assumption that the attacks were the work of
only the poorer sort be allowed to go unchallenged. We have seen that
members of the middling sort were implicated in the attack on Sir John
Lucas. Their involvement was repeated elsewhere. The handful of names
we do have include both a farmer and baymaker (and the middling sort
in this as in other forms of crowd action may have found it easier to
avoid detection and detention). Arthur Wilson recounting his ride
through the areas of the attacks noted that 'many of the bett[e]r sort,

---

[16] N. Goose, 'Economic and social aspects of provincial towns: a comparative study of
Cambridge, Colchester and Reading, *c.* 1500–1700' (Ph.D. thesis, University of
Cambridge, 1984), p. 95 (table 3.1), pp. 160–9; J. Patten, 'Population distribution in
Norfolk and Suffolk during the sixteenth and seventeenth centuries', *Transactions of the
Institute of British Geographers*, 65 (1975), p. 49. D. Dymond and A. Betterton,
Lavenham: 700 Years of Textile Making (Woodbridge, 1982), p. 63.

[17] BL, Harleian MS 163, fol. 307 v; Stoneyhurst College, Stoneyhurst MSS, MSS Angliae,
7, fols. 122–3; CRO, D/B5, Sb2/7, fol. 301 v.

behav'd themselves as if there had been a disolution of all gover[n]-ment'.[18] We need to recognise therefore that the crowds in 1642 had a broader occupational (and geographical) spread and greater social depth than most contemporary commentators or later historical accounts suggest. We will return to the significance of the presence of these other groups in a later chapter.

Despite these qualifications, the coincidence of cloth and crowds was important for explaining events in August 1642. It was the presence of the cloth industry and the consequences for the communities where it was located that help to explain what seems most distinctive about the attacks seen within the broader context of seventeenth-century protest – the very large and mobile crowds more usually associated with the rebellions of the sixteenth century. The cloth industry created dense concentrations of workers and its spatial divisions of labour tied communities together in ways that made possible the assembly of such large crowds. The crises the industry faced, growing increasingly frequent from the 1620s on, had brought the clothworkers a reputation for disorder. More controversially, the problems and poverty that the clothworkers experienced *as a class* have been held to explain both the shape of the attacks and the choice of targets. An appreciation of the impact of the volatile cloth trade on the communities of south Suffolk and north-east Essex is therefore essential to understanding the morphology of the attacks.

The cloth industry in Essex and Suffolk was divided between two major forms of production, the heavy broadcloth of the 'Old Draperies' and the lighter cloths of the 'New Draperies'. By the eve of the attacks the former was largely restricted (save for the villages of Dedham and Langham in Essex) to the Suffolk side of the River Stour and was, after a succession of damaging crises in the early seventeenth century, in terminal decline. By contrast, the 'New Draperies' introduced in the mid- to later sixteenth century had promoted considerable growth within north-east Essex and, by the mid-seventeenth century, were being adopted in some Suffolk centres.[19] Despite some differences in technique, production within the

---

[18] CUL, Additional MS 33, fol. 20.

[19] Given its importance in both the history of the region and in economic history, it is surprising that there has been no full study of the industry. The valuable pioneering study is J. E. Pilgrim, 'The cloth industry in Essex and Suffolk 1558–1640' (MA thesis University of London, 1938), whose main findings appeared in Pilgrim, 'The rise of the "New Draperies" in Essex', *University of Birmingham Historical Journal*, 7 (1959), pp. 36–59. For a slightly later period, see K. H. Burley, 'The economic development of Essex in the later seventeenth and early eighteenth century' (Ph.D. thesis, University of London, 1957) and 'An Essex clothier of the eighteenth century', *Economic History*

Old and New Draperies was broadly comparable. It was co-ordinated within the system of putting out controlled by clothiers, who articulated production through both a sexual and spatial division of labour. They organised the purchase and preparation of the raw material, putting the wool out to be spun into yarn by spinners, usually women working in their own households. Between the spinning of the wool and the finishing of the cloth, production was artisanal (and, in theory, masculine) with weaving being carried out in the homes of formally (but, increasingly, formerly) independent weavers. The clothiers organised the finishing and sale of the cloth. In reality, production was more complex, involving a greater number of intermediate processes, from the sorting, combing or carding of the wool, its dyeing in the yarn or piece to the fulling, pressing and other processes involved in finishing the cloth.

Cloth production was therefore very labour intensive. As such it had created sizeable urban communities that, like Colchester, dominated not only the region's urban network, but also achieved a high ranking in the national urban hierarchy. Since this was predominantly a rural industry it had also created a whole series of swollen villages, of which Braintree and Witham in Essex with populations of a thousand or more and Long Melford and Lavenham in Suffolk with populations close to two thousand are good examples.[20] Whatever the reasons for the industry's location (access to raw materials and water power and to an agricultural region with underemployed labour were both important) the industry had come to dominate a wide area over both north-east Essex and south Suffolk. Within this region, the fortunes of the trade determined in large part the well-being or otherwise of most communities. In addition, the demand for yarn meant that spinning made an important contribution to the economies of families and communities spread far beyond this heartland and, of course, much of the agricultural production over a wider region was devoted to satisfying the needs of the industry's predominantly landless labour force. Beyond this, the need for both raw materials and markets for sales ensured that cloth production bound Essex and Suffolk communities into wider national and international trading net-

Review, 2nd ser., 11 (1958–9), pp. 289–301. For Suffolk, see G. C. Unwin, 'Industries: woollen cloth in the Old Draperies', VCH Suffolk, vol. 2, pp. 254–66; Dymond and Betterton, Lavenham. The recent general study by E. Kerridge, Textile Manufactures in Early Modern England (Manchester, 1985) confirms that there is considerable potential for a more detailed regional study.

20 J. Gyford, Witham 1500–1700: Making a Living (Witham, 1996), p. 4; Dymond and Betterton, Lavenham, pp. 42, 61n.; J. Patten, 'Village and town: an occupational study', Agricultural History Review, 20 (1972), pp. 6–7; L. Boothman, 'Long Melford 1604 – a plague examined' (Certificate in Local History thesis, University of Cambridge, 1992), appx. 9 (I am grateful to Lyn Boothman for letting me see a copy of this).

works. Central to this wider articulation was London, from which came much of the wool and to which was sent most of the finished cloth for sale and export. The umbilical cord woven of wool that bound the region to the capital was itself central in explaining events in 1642.

It is already possible to see that there were aspects of the structure of the trade that helped to fashion the attacks in 1642. The division of labour across space that the putting-out system represented created dense interrelationships between producers and between communities that helped to create the infrastructure for the attacks. The everyday movement of people and material in rhythm with the demands of the trade ensured regular communications. Wool went out from centres like Colchester along lengthening lines of supply – up to forty miles away – to be spun and brought back as yarn; in turn, yarn was sent out to be woven into cloth; cloth was then moved on to be fulled and finished. Apprentices seeking training and weavers seeking work moved easily between centres of production within a region that ignored political boundaries. The ease of population mobility doubtless ensured that familial and kinship networks re-inforced the economic links that had brought them about.[21] As was the case with other industrial workers local occupational solidarities created the basis for collective action, forging ties between, as well as within, communities. Weavers in a later dispute at Colchester threatened with military repression replied, 'theie did not care for they were strong enough & ... could have more in the Town & a thousand owt of the Countrye'.[22] But it was not simply the fact of large concentrations of clothworkers and the interrelationships between their communities that linked the clothworkers to the attacks. The dependence on a volatile industry subject to periodic crisis rendered those communities particularly unstable. This instability was exacerbated by changes within the social relationships of production which meant that poverty was for many of those employed within the industry a structural as well as a conjunctural problem.

Weavers were at the heart of the industry. As the weavers of Suffolk and Essex had declared in 1539, 'weyving ... is the hede and mooste pure poynt of Clothing'.[23] From quite early on in the history of the Essex and Suffolk cloth industry there had been tension between independent artisanal production and the ability of clothiers to control the trade. By

---

[21] Kerridge, *Textile Manufactures*, p. 160; S. Andrews, *At Work in Bildeston's Textile Industry* (Brett Valley Histories, no. 13, Bildeston, n.d.), p. 15; *VCH Essex*, vol. 9, p. 94. For examples of these potential networks, see CRO, 'Freemans' Books'; *ibid.*, D/B 5 Sb2/7, fols. 106 v–7 r, 193 v–4.

[22] CRO, D/B5, Sb2/9, fol. 223 v.

[23] *Tudor Economic Documents*, ed. R. H. Tawney and E. Power, 3 vols. (1924), vol. 1, p. 177.

the beginning of the sixteenth century, mercantile capital had come to play an increasingly dominant role in an industry where much production was for continental European markets and where its raw material (wool) had to be brought from increasingly distant suppliers. The clothiers exploited their ability to supply raw materials and to dispose of the finished product to acquire a dependent labour force. At Colchester, the growing importance of capital within the industry had produced a corresponding growth in wage labour by the later fifteenth century, a situation paralleled in the smaller Essex centres. In Suffolk, the creation of a class of dependent weavers had been even more marked.[24]

In an industry where most production was carried out in the households of the workers and where, accordingly, investment in fixed capital played a minimal role, labour supply was the key to increased production. This encouraged clothiers to multiply apprentices. The weavers of Bocking and Braintree complained to the Essex magistrates in 1629 that 'many Clothiers themselves take many apprentices which is still against us to breede workemen'.[25] Clothiers also employed unskilled or non-apprenticed workers. Looms were relatively cheap and clothiers anxious to expand production could either distribute looms or hire them out to those wishing to weave. To become a weaver required skills which could be learnt in less than the usual seven-year apprenticeship and, it seems, without even formal apprenticeship. In the crisis of 1622 a committee of Essex JPs reported to the Privy Council that the clothiers claimed that the New Draperies did not fall within any statute, that apprenticeship itself was not a legal requirement, and that therefore they were free to take any number of apprentices. In the same year Suffolk JPs responding to a proposal to make apprenticeship a prerequisite for participation in the New Draperies, told the Privy Council, 'we holde it very dangerous to putt down those that at this time doe use the said Trade, haveing not byn bound appr[e]ntice, they being two parts, of Three, that at this pr[e]sente do use the niew

---

[24] Britnell, *Growth*, pp. 183–4; J. A. Galloway, 'Colchester and its region, 1310–1560: wealth, industry and rural-urban mobility in a medieval society' (D.Phil. thesis, University of Edinburgh, 1986), pp. 200, 217; C. Johnson, 'A proto-industrial community study: Coggeshall in Essex *c*. 1500–*c*. 1750' (Ph.D. thesis, University of Essex, 1990), pp. 27, 120. An example of the loss of independence can be glimpsed in the vignette of one Colchester household where the wife spun and the husband wove, but both for one of the large clothiers: PRO, SP, 16/355/162.i; J. Pound (ed.), *The Military Survey of 1522 for Babergh Hundred* (Suffolk Records Society, xxvii, 1986); Dymond and Betterton, *Lavenham*, p. 13; J. C. K. Cornwall, *Wealth and Society in Early Sixteenth Century England* (1988) (but note Cornwall's argument for the relative prosperity of at least some clothworkers in the early sixteenth century: pp. 72, 200–1, 205).

[25] *Tudor Economic Documents*, vol. 1, p. 177; Bodl. Lib., MS Firth c. 4, p. 505.

drap[er]ie, and most of them able men, for by that meanes thear woulde be manye Thowsands, turned out of Worke, w[hi]ch could never come worse, then at this time, yt being our daylie labour, to keepe poore on work, through the Crye of them that would starve, if by other meanes they ware not helped'. At Colchester, even the poorer weavers were said to set boys, girls and 'wenches' to weave.[26] If the authorities were unable to regulate the over-supply of labour,[27] the weavers lacked proper guild structures by which they might have done so.[28] According to the Essex magistrates, the clothiers claimed that they were not tied to keeping journeymen by the year, with the result that those who had served a seven-year apprenticeship – many it was suggested were turned off before the completion of their term – were forced to work for the clothier 'by the piece'.[29]

A ready supply of labour and the loss of independence by the weavers combined to produce a poorly paid workforce. Poor wages were particularly a problem in the declining Old Draperies. At the beginning of the seventeenth century the Suffolk minister Thomas Carew in a bitter attack on clothiers complained that weavers in the declining Old Draperies in Suffolk earned 4d. a day at worst and 8d. at best.[30] In 1622 the workfolk of the Suffolk clothiers were described as 'being many in number & most of them of the poorest sorte'. Wages may have been little better in the New Draperies. The weavers of Bocking and Braintree had complained in the 1620s that their wages were 'but small in the best tymes'.[31] Many weavers were coming increasingly to depend on payment

---

[26] PRO, SP, 14/130/65; /129/59; Bodl. Lib., MS Firth c. 4, p. 51; CRO, D/B, 5, Gb3, fols. 179 v–80 v. There had been several unsuccessful attempts to bring the New Draperies within the scope of earlier statutes regulating the woollen industry: for example, PRO, SP, 14/140/8.

[27] The frequent repetition of such orders in Colchester shows their ineffectiveness: CRO, D/B5, Gb 2, fols. 82 r–3 r [1609]; PRO, SP, 14/104/97 [?1618]; 14/130/65 and /140/82 [1622–3]; Bodl. Lib., MS Firth c. 4, pp. 508–9 [1629]; CRO, D/B5, Gb 3, fols. 179 v–80 v [1636, 1638]; ERO, Q/S Ba 2/27 [1637]; *VCH Essex*, vol. 2, p. 267.

[28] That, as at Colchester, the 'guilds' were the creation of urban authorities suggests that the textile industry lacked a strong guild structure and that it was magisterial concerns with poverty and order that lay behind the decision to set up some organisation among the weavers.

[29] The 1661 wage assessment assessed the best journeyman weaver at £3 a year with an allowance of 10s. for livery: D. H. Allen (ed.), *Essex Quarter Sessions Order Book 1652–1660*, p. 189. This may help to explain why clothiers preferred to take on more apprentices and why the authorities had to stipulate a set ratio between journeymen and the much cheaper apprentices: CRO, D/B5, Gb 2, fols. 82–3; WSRO, Sudbury Borough Records, Liber Sextus, unfol., 31 October 1648.

[30] T. Carew, *A caveat for craftesmen and Clothiers, in Certaine godly and necessarie Sermons* (1603), sig. U2 r–v. (I am grateful to Patrick Collinson for bringing Thomas Carew's sermon to my attention.)

[31] Bodl. Lib., MS Firth c. 4, pp. 494–5.

by the clothier which, while it might be calculated by the piece, was for a growing number a wage, paid weekly, even nightly and, if evidence arising from a dispute in the trade can be believed, in advance. Colchester's bay and say makers referred to the poorer weavers 'whose wants are so greate, that they cannot be w[i]thout worke one weeke'.[32] As a report drawn up in Essex in a crisis in the cloth trade in 1629 reported:

> Lamentable is the beinge of all this Multitude of people which live by these Manufactures, few or none that Can subsist unlesse they bee paied theire wages once a weeke, and many of them that Cannot live unlesse they bee paied every night, many hundreds of them havinge noe bedds to lye in, nor foode, but from hand to mouth to mainteyne themselves, theire wives and Children.[33]

Problems of under- and un-employment were inscribed in the structure of the industry and its markets. In 1636 the Essex clothiers had claimed that the 'industrious weaver' could earn 10 to 12d. a day and a spinner 5 to 6d. per day, but this claim makes assumptions about regularity of work and employment which were unrealistic in the troubled 1620s and 1630s.[34] As the Essex magistrates declared, the clothiers 'indeede care not how many workmen there bee of weavers and Keamers [combers], etc. for by that means they can have theire worke done better cheape'. There were complaints from Colchester in the early seventeenth century against those who 'kepe soe manie Lo[o]mes & sett soe manie Lo[o]se jornymen on work in their houses that the porer sorte of the inhabitants w[i]thin this Town and lib[er]ties thereof cannot in the tyme of scarcetie of work gett sufficient work to mayntaine themselves and familye'.[35] Where periodic trade depression did not lead to unemployment, the weaver still faced a cut in his pay. As local wage assessments make clear magistrates did not regard themselves as having the responsibility to regulate rates of remuneration for those householders who had served their apprenticeship and wove 'by the piece'. They left the rate to be negotiated between weaver and clothier. Tied to the prices of finished cloth, the piece rate was very sensitive to market fluctuations.[36] Thus, in the crisis in the trade in 1636 the Essex justices

---

[32] BL, Additional MS 39,245, fol. 53 v; PRO, SP, 16/355/162.3; ERO, D/DEb, 7/2.

[33] Leicestershire RO, DE 220/209; Bodl. Lib., MS Firth c. 4, pp. 488–91.

[34] ERO, D/DEb, 7/7.

[35] Bodl. Lib., MS. Firth c. 4, p. 511; CRO, D/B5, Gb2, fol. 75 r. Orders were introduced to impose limits on the numbers of looms that masters might keep, to remove any journeyman from those who kept more than four looms, and to give their work to poor independent weavers.

[36] While the Essex wage assessment of 1661 fixed payments for journeymen weavers, it stipulated that the price for 'a weaver, being an householder, weaveing by the peece in great, as he can agree with the Clothyer': Allen, *Order Book*, p. 189. At Colchester the authorities did on occasion seek to regulate payment in response to pleas from the

reported, against the claim of the clothiers cited above, that the best weaver could not earn more than 4s. a week and others no more than 2 or 3s. As they concluded, this was 'smale wages to mainteyne a familie, paie house rent, and buy fire wood'. Low rates of pay meant that many weavers had few capital reserves with which to ride out the unemployment that quickly followed any slump in demand. The poverty of this large and growing group was summarised in a report by the Essex justices in 1629 that, 'there were more alreadie of the Weavers trade then Could live one by the other, for when tradinge is anything deade, as often in the yeare itt is, there is not worke to bee had for a number of them, and being used to no other labour, they imediatly fall into a miserable estate.'[37]

The clothworkers' vulnerability to poverty was exacerbated by the location and nature of the industry's markets. The expansion of the cloth industry had tied the fortunes of the region to markets (often overseas) which war, currency manipulation or harvest failure might (and did) disrupt. Suffolk's broadcloth industry was in terminal decline. From the early 1620s the New Draperies had undergone a series of crises as dislocations in the trade's continental markets and periodic harvest failure had produced slumps in demand. Of these, the latter had a particularly severe and double-edged impact. Since demand for cloth was highly elastic, food prices were a major determinant of the demand for cloth. High levels of landlessness meant also that most clothworkers were dependent on the market for food as well as work. Poor harvests therefore brought the threat of both unemployment and hunger. As the Essex magistrates informed the Privy Council in the dearth of 1631:

> although the poore doe suffer much in respect of the high prices of Corne, yet they are in farr greater misery in the most populous p[ar]tes of the Cuntrey whose trades consists in the makeinge of Bayes by reason that the Clothiers do forbeare to sett the poore weavers on worke, alleadging that they have already disbursed more then they are able and that their clothes lye upon their hands and they cannot sell them to the Merchants.[38]

weavers, for example setting piece rates tied to the price at which bays sold, with a minimum of ten, and maximum of twelve, shillings a week in 1635: CRO, D/B5, Cb 1/10, fol. 84 v. However, later figures suggest that 7s. 6d. a week was closer to what was paid: Burley, 'Economic development', p. 136; Burley, 'An Essex clothier', pp. 293–4; PRO, SP, 16/189/40 and 40.I; Andrews, *Bildeston's Industry*, p. 11.

[37] Bodl. Lib., MS Firth c. 4, p. 510.

[38] PRO, SP, 16/188/92. The particular vulnerability of the clothworkers to harvest failure that their double dependence on the market for both food and employment created helps to explain the regularity with which clothing townships in the region attempted to provide grain in years of dearth: *APC 1597–1598*, pp. 69, 230–1; PRO, SP, 14/142/14.ii; 16/185/2, /529/117; CRO, D/B5, Gb1, fol. 44 (1586), fols. 105 v–6 r, 110 r (1594–1595),

While it has been argued that the production of New Draperies in the towns was controlled by larger clothiers, there were many small clothiers, even in Colchester, the industry's centre, and small clothiers dominated the Suffolk 'Old Draperies'.[39] The limited fixed capital that clothiers needed to invest in an industry where much of the production was carried out in the households of the producers meant that to become a clothier required relatively little capital. The result was that many clothiers operated in a small way and depended heavily on credit and a quick turnover of finished cloth. In addition, they may have had to extend credit to the merchant purchasers.[40] This meant that many clothworkers were dependent for employment upon a group with a limited ability themselves to withstand adverse trading connections. Clothiers at Bocking in the depression of 1636–7 referred to 'divers of the meaner sort of clothiars [sic] of our towne their bee, which have lately (some one of them) sett 10 or 20 p[er]sons on worke in Combing Spineing and weaving, which nowe are not able to Suplye their owne families with worke, by Reson that there stooke [stock] lyeth dead by them in ware'. Since all clothiers, whatever the scale of their enterprise, had little fixed capital from which to worry about getting a return and sold cloth on credit, their response to any downturn in demand was to lay off workers.

Thus while increased demand – in contemporary parlance, 'a quick tyme' – had promoted growth, it had also produced an industry highly vulnerable to any downturn in demand. Poverty was therefore closely associated with the cloth industry. 'It is by common experience tried, upon what reason I know nott, that in those parts of this shire, where the clothiers doe dwell or have dwelled, there are found the greatest number of the poor', observed Robert Reyce in his early seventeenth-century description of Suffolk.[41] The structure of the cloth trade and its pattern of economic boom and slump in the century or so before 1640 marked the social and economic structure of those towns and villages in which

fol. 107 r (appointment of baker to bake loaves for distribution to poor), Gb2, fol. 84 (1609/10); Gb3, fol. 98 (1630), Gb4, fol. 3 (1647); *APC 1597–1598*, pp. 230–1; ; ERO, D/ P, 264/8/3, fol. 164; WSRO, FL, 509/5/1/49; T. F. Paterson, *East Bergholt in Suffolk* (Cambridge, 1923), pp. 118–21, 125.

[39] Pilgrim, 'Rise', pp. 50, 58; Pilgrim, 'Cloth Industry', pp. 105, 143, 145–9. It has been calculated that in Dedham, which formed part of the Suffolk 'Old Draperies' region, each clothier provided work for six to eight households (although this calculation ignores those whom the clothiers claimed to employ outside Dedham: PRO, SP, 16/529/117): A. R. Pennie, 'The evolution of Puritan mentality in an Essex cloth town: Dedham and the Stour Valley, 1560–1640' (Ph.D. thesis, University of Sheffield, 1989), pp. 26–7.

[40] For an example of Suffolk clothiers being paid in instalments over a year and even longer, see J. Webb, 'An Ipswich merchant's cloth accounts, 1623–24', *PSIA*, 37 (1990), p. 127.

[41] ERO, D/DEb/7/; F. Harvey (ed.), *Suffolk in the Seventeenth Century: The Breviary of Suffolk By Robert Reyce, 1618* (1902), p. 57.

production was located. Colchester had long been the largest single centre of cloth production. Its earliest growth had been based on production of broadcloth – the Colchester 'greys' – but depression in the mid-sixteenth century had given a warning of the problems dependence on the cloth trade would bring for the maintenance of order in the town. Weavers who in 1566 had plotted to raise their fellows in Essex and Suffolk had declared, the 'weavers' occupation is a dead science nowadays, and it will never be better before we make a rising'. The situation had improved little by the 1590s when Colchester's rulers referred to 'our town, abounding with so great multitude of poor people'.[42] Thereafter, the New Draperies brought renewed and rapid growth. Exports of cloth from the town increased some fourfold in the seventeenth century, with the first three decades seeing some of the most rapid growth. But growth exacerbated the problems of poverty. The detailed fiscal records of the early sixteenth century suggest that almost fifty per cent of those taxed were assessed on wages alone, over forty per cent on wages of only a pound a year. Just under fifty per cent of those assessed accounted for less than ten per cent of taxable wealth. By the 1670s, levels of exemption from payment of the hearth tax in parishes where there was a concentration of clothworkers registered extraordinary levels of up to seventy per cent. Depression in the cloth industry periodically exposed the underlying weakness in this pattern of growth. For example, in the crisis of 1637 some two thousand of Colchester's inhabitants (if accurate, about a quarter of Colchester's entire population) complained to the central government that they were 'reduced to exceedinge greate povertie by the smalnes of Wages'.[43]

For Colchester's rulers the association between the cloth industry and the threat of poverty in their town was axiomatic. Within the town's records orders relating to the regulation of poverty incorporated almost automatically measures relating to the regulation of the cloth industry.[44] The town's relative precocity in establishing measures for the relief of the

---

[42] Britnell, *Growth*, esp. pp. 75–83; M. Geevers, 'The textile trade in the late twelfth and thirteenth centuries: a study based on occupational names in charter sources', *EAH*, 20 (1989), pp. 34–73; F. G. Emmison, *Elizabethan Life: Disorder* (Chelmsford, 1970), pp. 62–4; HMC Salisbury MSS, 7, p. 526.

[43] Goose, 'Comparative study', pp. 63, 68, 178; Pilgrim, 'New draperies', pp. 54–5; Glines, 'Politics', p. 15; PRO, PCR, 2/47, p. 389. Local evidence confirms the reality suggested by these figures. It was said of the small Colchester parish of All Saints that, 'for the most parte [it] consistes of pore weavers' with not above twelve parishioners able to pay a rate of halfpence a week: CRO, D/DRe, Z9/7.

[44] For example, measures in 1613 to set up a workhouse to employ the able-bodied poor also incorporated orders regulating the number of looms and weavers anyone could set on work in their house and policing the employment of 'loose' journeymen: CRO, D/B5, Gb2, fols. 119 v–21 v.

poor – the town instituted a compulsory poor rate as early as 1557 – was directly related to the troubles experienced in the cloth industry. But the existence of a rate was in itself no guarantee that the town could cope in times of depression. In the 1620s the Corporation informed the Privy Council, 'the Towne of Colchester cheifly consists in making new Draperies w[hi]ch is altogeather decayed by the last great sicknes [the plague of 1625–6] and [has] soe much increased their poore, that the rate of Collection being trebled, will not now mayntaine them'.[45] Unable to meet the periodic crises through even an increase in the parish rate, Colchester was forced to adopt policies to restrict the problem – repeatedly seeking to restrict in-migration and privileging its own residents' access to scarce employment – while trying a range of expedients to increase poor relief funds, assigning fines and rents and raising lotteries with which to buy grain in years of dearth.[46]

Colchester's experience was replicated in the other Suffolk and Essex textile centres. There too intensified production swelled the numbers dependent on the vagaries of the trade for their subsistence. But there limited economic diversification meant that these centres were even more exposed to the problems that unregulated growth brought. For example, it was said of Witham in the later 1620s that, 'ye greatest nomb[e]r of the inhabitants … are very poore, occacio[n]ed by want of work in these deade times, ye s[ai]d towne being a baymakeinge Towne'.[47] Dedham, which continued to produce the coloured cloth of the Old Draperies, was said by 1628 to consist 'onlie of a nomber of Clothyers and a great Company of poore people w[hi]ch are by them sett on worke'. In Suffolk the problem was made more acute by the collapse in markets for the traditional coloured cloths of the Old Draperies. Important centres of production like Hadleigh had experienced increasing problems of poverty and disorder from at least the 1570s. Lavenham was described in 1627 as 'a greate and populous towne, subiecte to moche disorder'. By

[45] CRO, D/Y, 2/2, pp. 37–8; PRO, SP, 16/458/83. This undated petition is assigned to June 1640 by the *CSPD*, but since it refers to the bailiffs (who were replaced by a Mayor in the 1635 charter) it must be before that date. An entry in *APC 1627–1628*, pp. 316–7 suggests that it should be dated to early 1627.

[46] For examples of controls on in-migration, see CRO, D/B5, Gb1, fol. 78 r-v, Gb3, fols. 14, 83 r–v; D/B5, Sr, 14/19; Sb2/7, fol. 59. For examples of instructions to put off migrants from work and replace them with Colchester-born poor, Gb1, fol. 78; for increase in the poor rate, Gb3, fol. 31; fines and rents, Gb1, fols. 14–16 v; lotteries, Gb2, fol. 163, Gb3, fol. 22. In the 1590s the Corporation used a bequest of £100 to set up two clothiers as 'workmasters' to set the poor on work (although this appears to refer to spinning): Gb1, fol. 78; cf. fols. 133 v–4 r; see also Gb3, fol. 14 (an elaborate 1622 scheme for the putting out and overseeing of work by the Corporation).

[47] PRO, SP, 16/529/117; Leicestershire RO, DE 220/207. For the developing association between the Essex rural cloth industry and poverty in the Middle Ages, see L. R. Poos, *A Rural Society after the Black Death: Essex 1350–1525* (Cambridge, 1991), pp. 58–72.

1654 the cloth area of Suffolk was described as having many poor towns.[48] The depth of poverty cloth brought to communities in both Essex and Suffolk meant that by the 1670s at least forty per cent, and in the larger communities a worrying sixty per cent or more, were exempt from paying the hearth tax.[49] A few centres in the Suffolk 'woodland' did adopt the New Draperies. But while this meant that towns like Sudbury escaped the general collapse in traditional Suffolk cloth, it also meant that they too experienced the problems of poverty and disorder exacerbated by the introduction of the New Draperies. Attempts there to regulate the consequences of dependence on cloth paralleled those of Colchester.[50] Records for the smaller centres suggest that they were even less well equipped to cope. Long Melford did have a well-developed system of parochial poor relief but the records of its administration suggest that this can have done little to alleviate the problems of sudden and large-scale poverty among the clothworkers that any crisis in the trade brought.[51] In the depression of 1636, the only solution the Essex JPs could come up with to help the unemployed weavers in smaller centres like Bocking was to order the clothiers to provide them with work as spinners and to instruct the overseers to make up their wages by raising a rate to which clothiers would be expected to contribute more. Predictably this was a scheme that ran rapidly into trouble.[52]

The authorities' inability to remedy the causes or consequences of industrial depression was a further cause of instability in the region. Given the geographical concentration of poverty the cloth industry produced, the normal structures for relieving the poor quickly proved

---

[48] Kerridge, *Textile Manufactures*, p. 29; B. E. Supple, *Commercial Crisis and Change in England 1600–1642* (Cambridge, 1970), esp. pp. 41, 55–6, 82; Pilgrim, 'Rise', p. 5; W. A. B. Jones, *Hadleigh through the Ages* (Ipswich, 1977), pp. 32–3, 35; Dymond and Betterton, *Lavenham*, p. 41; A. Simpson, *The Wealth of the Gentry, 1540–1640: East Anglian Studies* (Chicago, 1961), p. 202.

[49] Johnson, 'Proto-industrial community study', pp. 215–7; H. R. French, 'Chief inhabitants and their areas of influence: local ruling groups in Essex and Suffolk parishes, 1630–1720' (Ph.D. thesis, University of Cambridge, 1993), pp. 61, 70–1. Recent work on the hearth tax suggests that these figures need to be used with caution, but they do provide valuable evidence of a trend that was already marked by the 1640s: C. Husbands, 'The hearth tax and the structure of the English economy' (Ph.D. thesis, University of Cambridge, 1986).

[50] WSRO, Sudbury Borough Records, Liber Quinto, p. 560; Liber Sextus [unfol.], 31 October 1648 (a restatement of orders regulating clothmaking since 1609); *APC 1630–1631*, pp. 230–1; PRO, SP, 16/190/54.

[51] Poor law records, which survive for the difficult harvest years of the 1580s and 1590s, record provision of relief for some 144 inhabitants, but the predominance of women (many presumably widows) and the fact that this represented only some ten per cent of the population gives little sign that local poor relief could do much to aid the clothworkers: WSRO, FL, 509/5/1/51,/52,/53,/54.

[52] ERO, D/DEb, 7/10, 13.

alarmingly inadequate whenever there was a crisis in the trade. As the JPs for the cloth district reported in 1629:

> when we fell into the examinac[i]on of the abilities of those p[ar]ishes w[i]thin the hundreds where the Clothworkers dwell, wee finde all soe equally interess[t]ed in that trade, as that wee know not any one p[ar]ish ... which are able to sett theire owne poore on worke and if wee should now goe aboute to force the neighbouringe parishes to Contribute to those townes, insteade of appeasinge the disorders now on foote, in some few of the great clothinge townes, wee should thereby infinitely encrease the Complaintes in all the p[ar]ishes.[53]

Periodic peaks and troughs had always been a characteristic of the industry, but the experience of the trade throughout the 1630s was one of underlying crisis caused both by problems in its markets and a structure that had permitted the too easy flow of labour into the industry.[54] The coincidence of dearth and depression in the crises of 1622–3 and 1629–30 led to widespread unemployment, distress and disorder, and the crisis of 1636–7 had brought further widespread unemployment and the threat of renewed disorder, a problem compounded by the plague which interrupted production in several textile centres between 1637 and 1641.[55]

With little or no land, few savings and no hope of other employment, it was the clothworkers who felt to the full the impact of these crises. Doubtless the 'ffiftie or sixtie families which have not soe much as a poore flock bedd to lye upon but are forced to lye only upon strawe, & can hardly gett that', reported from Bocking in the crisis of 1629 were the poorest group, but their plight provides a stark example of the vulnerability of workers within the trade.[56] Dependence on a textile industry in

---

[53] Bodl. Lib., MS Firth *c.* 4, pp. 493–4.

[54] Supple, *Commercial Crisis*, pp. 41, 55–7, 82, 103, 121; J. K. Fedorowicz, *England's Baltic Trade in the Early Seventeenth Century: a Study in Anglo-Commercial Diplomacy* (Cambridge, 1980), esp. pp. 91–7; H. Zins, *England and the Baltic in the Elizabethan era* (trans. H. C. Stevens, Manchester, 1972), pp. 166–7; W. B. Stephens, 'The cloth exports of provincial ports, 1600–1640', *Economic History Review*, 2nd ser., XXII (1969), pp. 238–40; Goose, 'Comparative Study', table 3.13, pp. 176, 181; Pilgrim, 'Cloth industry', p. 192. Pilgrim, 'Rise', pp. 51, 55, argues that the 1630s was a period of uncertainty rather than a genuine slump, but acknowledges that trade fluctuations were worse outside Colchester.

[55] Walter, 'Crisis of 1629'; ERO, Q/SBa, 2/43 (petit. of Witham), /45 (petits. of Witham, Bocking, Chelmsford); PRO, SP, 16/357/119 (1637, Hadleigh, Suffolk); Slack, *The Impact of Plague in Tudor and Stuart England* (1985), pp. 102–5. The records for Braintree which unfortunately break off in 1638–9 indicate that expenditure increased in 1630–1 and for most years remained high thereafter: L. Blewett, 'A duty to God and nature? Poverty and the poor law in Essex 1590–1700' (B.A. dissertation, University of Essex, 1986), appx, p. 41. Coggeshall's records, which unfortunately do not run up to 1640, indicate a very sharp increase in poor relief expenditure in the first three decades of the seventeenth century: Johnson, 'Proto-industrial community', pp. 235, 262.

[56] Bodl. Lib., MS Firth c. 4, p. 510.

which wages, 'but smale in the best tymes', had been cut in response to successive crises and kept low by the fresh supply of (unapprenticed) labour drafted in during spasms of renewed growth, had produced an alarming collision between structural and conjunctural poverty which was concentrated both locally and regionally. The report from the Essex JPs in 1629 gave a vivid account of the problems this created:

> wee Can hardly finde any one p[ar]ish ... in which the principall meanes for the maintenance of theire poore doth not depend upon the trade ... in soe much as in all the greate and populous p[ar]ishes not only in that parte but alsoe in all other parts of the Country where the trade of Clothinge is used the Inhabitants there doe extreamely Complaine of want of meanes of releiving the poore in theire owne p[ar]ishes, and of their disorder for wante of worke, and in the lesse p[ar]ishes ... greate Complaintes, for that the poore doe now want that worke which they formerly had from the Clothinge townes ...[57]

The poverty and vulnerability of those who depended upon the vagaries of the cloth industry help to explain the clothworkers' reputation for disorder. As the report from a neighbouring county warned, poverty bred a 'dangerous desperacy'. Within the region this had been reflected in the sixteenth century in both rebellion and riot. The conjuncture of trade crisis and the war-driven fiscal demands of the Tudor state had produced the Amicable Grant rebellion in which thousands of clothworkers had protested under the leadership of their captains 'Poverty' and 'Necessity'. Thereafter, periodic trade crisis or harvest failure had prompted projected attempts at a rising or riot. In 1566 discussions among a group of discontented weavers at Colchester had led one to say, 'I will get a horse and ride into a town in Suffolk and so come from thence to Bocking and Braintree and Coggeshall, and so straight through Colchester, and cry "They are up! They are up!".' His mental map reflects the unity of the economic region and his intended itinerary echoes the geography of 1642.[58] In 1622 clothworkers from Essex and Suffolk had staged protests over food, demonstrating once more the capacity of the cloth industry to sponsor combined action across county boundaries. This pattern had been repeated in Essex in 1629. Successive crises in the first half of the seventeenth century had produced a threat of disorder whose scale reflected the extent of poverty in the region.

---

[57] Bodl. Lib., MS Firth c. 4, pp. 495–6.
[58] PRO, SP, 14/138/3; G. W. Bernard, *War, Taxation and Rebellion in early Tudor England: Henry VIII, Wolsey and the Amicable Grant of 1525* (Brighton, 1986); Emmison, *Disorder*, pp. 62–4. In 1556 an attempted rising among the Essex clothworkers had intended to link up with their counterparts even further afield in Hampshire: Byford, 'Price of Protestantism', pp. 172–3.

Witham was described in 1628 as a town, 'standing most upon Clothing, wherein tradeing is soe bad and theire number of poore so greate and unruly, that they are not able to relieve or governe them'. In the wider crisis of 1629 it was reported from Coggeshall – 'a very poore towne and unruly' – as 'certaine the multitudes of the poorer sort must starve, or use unlawfull meanes to support themselves'. Of Bocking it was said, 'that towne abound[s] with poore, whereof many are very unrulie, and havinge noe employment will make the place verie hazardous for men of better Ranke to live amongst them'. In 1636 Colchester's rulers had informed the Lord Chief Justice that if the clothmakers had to give up their trade '(though it were but for a shorte tyme) we know the issue of it will be wofull, our towne consisting of many thousands of poore householders & workmen, w[hi]ch have not wherew[i]th to eate, but by the weekely paiem[en]t w[hi]ch they rece[i]ve from our baie & saye-makers'.[59] Then the crisis had been averted, but 1642 was to prove different.

In the early 1640s political crisis triggered an economic crisis. This was to hit the cloth industry particularly hard. As a petition from the Suffolk and Essex clothiers in early 1642 declared, London was 'the very fountain of our Trades'. The dependence of the cloth trade on London mercantile capital for its market added a final element of potential instability. This had been apparent when the plague epidemic of 1625 had created a general disruption of commercial links between counties and capital. The widespread unemployment that the failure of even individual London merchants quickly brought – and in the difficult trading conditions of the twenties and thirties such failures were more common – also revealed the dangers of dependence on London mercantile capital. Thus, anything that caused a crisis within London trading circles would have serious and immediate consequences for the region. As petitioners from Ipswich informed the Commons, 'being a populous and Port Town, subsisting chiefly by Clothing and Shipping ... we do quickly feel and suffer deeply in the disturbances and decay of Trading and Merchant affairs in London and elsewhere'.[60] When the failure of king and Parliament to reach a settlement prompted a commercial crisis in the capital in 1640–2,

---

[59]   Bodl. Lib., MS Firth c. 4, pp. 488–91; ERO, D/DEb, 7/14.
[60]   CRO, Acc. C32, box 11/14: *TO THE HONOURABLE THE HOUSE OF COMMONS, NOW ASSEMBLED IN PARLIAMENT The humble Petition of the Clothiers and other Inhabitants of the Countie of Suffolk, now attending this Honourable House, and of the Townes of Dedham and Langham in Essex* (1642); Pilgrim, 'Cloth industry', pp. 143, 145–51, 164; Supple, *Commercial Crisis*, p. 158; PRO, SP, 16/22/63, /538/64; W. S. Appleton, *Memorials of the Cranes of Chilton* (Cambridge, Mass., 1868), p. 71; BL, E135(35), *The Humble Petitions of the Bailifes Port-Men, And Other Inhabitants of Ipswich, in the County of Suffolke* (1641[/2]), pp. 4–5.

its consequences quickly ran back into the Colchester-Stour Valley region. This crisis was unlike the earlier crises. Its origins were political. Political uncertainty had created a 'crisis of mercantile confidence'. Merchants, their anxieties further aroused by talk of forced loans and debasement, were reluctant to tie up their capital in purchasing cloth, exhibiting instead 'an increased liquidity preference'.[61] In May 1641 Suffolk was one of a number of counties from which clothiers were complaining that they were neither able to sell cloth for money nor to get the moneys they were owed. The merchants had told them, 'this is noe time to pay monie, neither will they pay anie.' A letter of June 1642 to a merchant from his factor gives a good illustration of the merchants' response to political instability. The writer recommended no further purchases. 'I doubt at this Time Money is not so rife in that Country, and men so forward to buy, that I think little fear but that, if he turns off or leaves buying, his Workmen would be glad to come again at more settled Times, and it may be better cheap'. Besides, 'if things go badly ... and come to Pillaging or Destruction, you should have all the Cloth he had in the House to be reckoned to be your cloth'. Little wonder then that merchants showed a reluctance to tie up their capital in stock inventories or that this reluctance should increase as political uncertainty grew. As the clothiers of the West Riding of Yorkshire complained, 'Merchants, fearing what evill event may ensue upon these distractions, doe not take up our Cloath'.[62]

The impact of the withdrawal of circulating capital, first by the merchants and then by the clothiers, was especially pronounced on the textile districts of Essex and Suffolk. The industry was already in difficulty. The collision between structural economic problems and the increased range of fiscal demands necessitated by the war with the Scots at the end of the decade seems to have been the starting point for more serious difficulties. At the end of 1639, the Corporation of Colchester had decided to petition against the ship money levy of £400, primarily 'in regard of the deadnes of tradinge wthin this towne'. Less than two weeks later, the Mayor of Sudbury wrote to Sir Simonds D'Ewes, sheriff for the county, thanking him for his gift of 40s. to the town's poor and asking him not to overrate them for ship money, 'for the povertie of our towne

---

[61] Supple, *Commercial Crisis*, pp. 125–31 provides the best discussion of a period of economic difficulty still awaiting full exploration.

[62] HLRO, MP HL, 6 May 1641 (petit. of the clothiers of Berkshire, Wiltshire, Kent, Somerset, Worcestershire, Gloucester, Hampshire and Suffolk); *LJ*/v/126; BL, E144(6), *The Humble Petition of the Clothiers Inhabitinge in the Parish of Leeds, Vicarilage of Hallifax and other parts adjoyning in the County of Yorke* (1642).

is not unknowne to anie that dwell neere us'. In June 1640 D'Ewes himself had informed the Privy Council that 'deadnes of tradinge, low prices of all Comodities raised from the plough and paile, scarcitie and want of monie, great military charges of the last passed Summer, etc., accompanied with innumerable groanes and sighes are the daylie retornes ... received instead of payment.' Presenting petitions from Essex complaining of the depression in the cloth industry, Harbottle Grimston told his fellow MPs in early 1642 that taxes and customs had forced clothiers to abandon their trade and had brought many workers in the trade 'to beg for their bread, and the rest to live upon the Parishes' charge'.[63]

The context for all these comments might suggest an element of special-pleading, but figures for cloth production confirm the gloomy picture they paint. By February 1642, the clothiers engaged in the production of Suffolk shortcloths claimed that they had almost the entire production of the last eighteen months still on their hands. From the evidence of the customs returns it would appear that these same years saw the near-total collapse of the Suffolk short cloth industry.[64] At Colchester, the heart of the New Draperies, there was a sharp drop in production in the period immediately preceding the August attacks. Fines on cloth registered in the Dutch Bay Hall in Colchester provide a rough surrogate for levels of production. They registered a fall of over sixty per cent between 1641 and 1642 and remained low for the following year.[65] Judged thus, production in 1642 was at the lowest level recorded between 1636, when the series begins, and the end of the century. In a region where as we have seen many clothiers operated on a relatively small scale and were heavily dependent on a ready, often weekly, sale to finance their operations, the lack of buyers was very threatening. For clothworkers in an industry characterised by the easy mobility of factors of production and suffering the consequences of over-supply of labour and over-production, the slump was catastrophic. As the clothiers and workmasters of Essex had warned in 1629, the clothworkers were not able 'to subsist unlesse they bee Continually sett on worke, and weekly

---

[63] CRO, D/B5, Gb3, fol. 200; BL, Harleian MS 165, fol. 46, MS 160, fol. 186; MS 365, fols. 120 r-v (the date of the letter is supplied by PRO, SP, 16/456/41); BL, E200(14), *Mr Grimstone His Speech In Parliament: On Wednesday the 19th of January, Upon the Preferring of the Essex Petition, AD 1641/2*, pp. 3–4.

[64] HLRO, MP HL, 6 May 1641; *PJ*, 2, pp. 331–2; BL, Harleian MS 480, fol. 125; R. W. K. Hinton, *The Eastland Trade and the Common Weal in the Seventeenth Century* (Cambridge, 1959), appx d, pp. 227–9.

[65] Goose, 'Comparative study', table 3.13, p. 176: 1636, £33; 1638, £39; 1640, £48; 1642, £25; 1637, £34; 1639, £39; 1641, £41; 1643, £34. If it continued to be the case that the months immediately preceding the August attacks were the busiest period for cloth sales, then the impact of the slump must have been even more disastrous: Bodl. Lib., MS Firth c. 4, p. 489; Britnell, *Growth*, p. 181.

paied, And many of them Cannot support themselves & theire miserable families unlesse they receive theire wages everie night, which w[i]thout a weekly sale very few of ye workmasters are able without greate difficultie to p[er]forme.' Thus in 1642 the clothworkers were, in Professor Supple's words, the 'unfortunate residuary legatees' of the crisis.[66]

In the course of a speech in late January 1642, occasioned by petitions from the counties – among them Essex and Suffolk – complaining of poverty and threatened disorder, John Pym had told his fellow MPs:

> A third danger is of Tumults and Insurrections of the meaner sort of people by reason of their ill vent of cloth, and other Manufactures, whereby great multitudes are set on work, who live for the most part by their daily gettings and will in short time be brought to great extremitie, if not imployed, Nothing is more sharp and pressing than necessity and want: what they cannot buy they will take ... and if they once grow into a body, it will be much more difficult to reduce them into order againe, because necessity and want, which are the causes of this disturbance will still increase as the effects doe increase.[67]

Pym was doubtless seeking to play on the fears of popular disorder, but the August attacks could be seen as a fulfilment of this prophecy. The cloth trade had created industrial communities with dense concentrations of workers. Its markets and mode of production produced periodic slump and widespread impoverishment which the authorities were unable to control or relieve. The high mobility of both capital and labour within the industry had made it easy to expand production in response to increased demand. But it had also made possible a rapid response to any downturn in trade. Common dependence on the fortunes of the trade produced a synchronicity of response, and it did so over a wide area.

Previous crises had been marked by popular disorder. That association was renewed in 1642. In February 1642 the clothiers in the region had reported that, 'the cryes of the poor for work and their curses and threats come daily to our ears, and tell us of sadder consequences at the very door, and we [are] disheartened, and disabled, and our stocks wasted, and necessitated to give over our Tradings and ... to open the door to a most hideous confusion'. From Sudbury in the same month had come a report of large crowds of clothworkers assembling outside the houses of clothiers. Such reports had led Henry Oxinden to write to an unknown correspondent in the first week of February that, 'the poore handycraftsmen are alreadie driven to miserable want in all countries and

---

[66] ERO, D/DEb/ 7/1; Bodl. Lib., MS Firth c. 4, p. 486; Supple, *Commercial Crisis*, p. 1.
[67] *The Parliament's Vindication of John Pym Esquire*, 25 January 1641–2. (The Lords' Journal – *LJ*/v/535 – gives the date as 26 January.)

especiallie in this cittie; itt is say[d] that they are risen in Essex'.[68] Oxinden was wrong in his timing, but right in his analysis. Necessity and want on such a scale clearly helps to explain why the contours of the crowd action should model so closely the contours of the cloth trade.

But necessity and want, even on the scale to be found in the eastern clothing regions, are not in themselves a sufficient explanation of the August events. An argument that emphasises economic causation for the attacks in 1642 shares something of the weaknesses that can be found more generally in this (regretably) remarkably resilient mode of analysing popular protest. In particular, it shows a disregard for explaining the distinctive shape of the protest. Why should economic distress drive clothworkers to attack catholics and proto-royalists? In 1629 the clothworkers' protests had been mobilised by a politics of subsistence which dictated that the high price of grain and the machinations of middlemen were taken to be appropriate targets for crowd action. Neither the persons nor the property of the landed classes, catholic or otherwise, had been attacked. One man had attempted to capitalise on the widespread suffering of that year by 'animating of poore people to the nomber of sixe or seaven score to the earle of Rivers house, sayinge there was gold & silver enough'. His appeal had fallen on deaf ears.[69] Previous actions by the clothworkers had been paralleled by appeals to, not attacks upon, the local landed class. They had been expected in their capacity as magistrates to remedy popular grievances. Distress clearly played a part in the events in the summer of 1642, but poverty alone is not a sufficient explanation for the shape of events. What needs explaining is the selective choice of targets by the crowd.

Some historians have turned to the agency of class and class hostility to explain why it should have been the local landed class who were attacked in 1642. In doing so, they have echoed contemporary comment. Towards the end of 1642, Sir Simonds D'Ewes warned his fellow MPs that,

[the] storme that threatens us proceedes from the great and incredible number of poore amongst us who being scarce able to provide bread

---

[68] *PJ*, 2, p. 328; CRO, Acc. C32, Box 11/14 *The humble Petition of the Clothiers and other Inhabitants of the Countie of Suffolk, now attending this Honourable House, and of the Townes of Dedham and Langham in Essex*; D. Gardiner (ed.), *The Oxinden Letters, 1607–1642* (1933), i, p. 285.

[69] Robert Cousens, a husbandman of St Osyth, was committed to the house of correction (but only for one week). That a note of his offence also included 'stayinge of Corne by the waterside' suggests that he may have made his appeal at the scene of the 1629 crowd action over food. The following year Cousens was tried and branded for stealing from two rather more humble houses at St Osyth: PRO, ASSI, 35/71/3/97; /73/1/70; ERO, Q/SR, 273/76; Walter, 'Crisis of 1629'.

for themselves and families before, now these warres began are now like to be reduced to extreame want and misery as they will bee enforced to take some violent course for the releife of themselves and to spoile the richer and abler sort. I heare of some of them already that being told by Clothiers and others who sett them on worke that they shall shortly bee disabled for want of mony to imploy them any longer, they answered that they did not care for they hoped to live better then ever they had done, the meaning of which words I shall not need to expound for I thinke every man heare will easily understand them. This was once attempted by George Skekelus in Hungary to have made a parity of all men and by John Leyden in Germany, though they were both prevented by a higher providence, but the same was a few yeares before their attempts accomplished by the Swissers who extirpated all the Nobility and gentry amongst themselves, and wee had lately a sad example of the violence and insolency of this kinde of people in the County of Essex ... And therefore wee may iustly looke that in a short time every man that hath anything to loose shall bee accounted an offender and it will be a ruine to bee rich as it was during the Triumvirate at Rome and though some of us perhapps here may flatter ourselves to bee very popular yett I am afraid wee shall finde in the issue that they will deale with us [as] Polifemus promised Ulisses that they would devoure him last.[70]

Sir Simonds D'Ewes' reaction to events in the Stour Valley was one widely shared among his contemporaries. It is this essentially class-based analysis of popular involvement in the attacks that is shared by some later historians of the English Revolution. (Indeed, this reading could surface in the most unusual places. The author of a 1901 article on Melford Hall in *Country Life* compared events there in 1642 to the attacks made by French peasants on seigneurial chateaux in the French Revolution, and concluded that, 'East Anglian Roundheads showed far more animus and class feeling than other parts of England'.) A historical consensus, shared intriguingly by both Marxist and revisionist historians, has seen the role of the people in the attacks as one best explained by the deeper logic of class conflict. Historians have spoken variously of a 'latent hostility to the ruling class', 'an underlying rebelliousness against the ruling order' or, more strongly, of 'a bitter vein of class hostility'. It is this consensus that explains use of the August attacks as *the* example of

---

[70] BL, Harleian MS 164, fols. 271–2 v. Gygory Szekely led a rural revolt in 1514 against seigneurial oppression which saw the destruction and pillage of manor houses and castles: P. F. Sugar, P. Hanak and T. Frank (eds.), *A History of Hungary* (Bloomington and Indianapolis, 1990), pp. 78–80. I am grateful to my colleague Joan Davies for identifying Szekely.

'hostility to the gentry as a class' in David Underdown's general discussion of the determinants of popular politics in the English Revolution. Hence the episode's current status as the textbook example of class conflict within the Revolution.[71]

Class is now very much a contested category.[72] To the traditional reluctance of many early modern historians to accept its relevance for the period, has been added the more recent scepticism evident in recent trends in social theory. Within the tradition of class analysis, there continues to be a division between those who follow Marx in emphasising the fundamental structuring by relationship to the dominant means of production and Weberians who continue to argue for the more complex determinings of market, status and power. Within the Marxist tradition itself there are divisions between those who continue to adhere to an emphasis on the determination of structures and those who argue for the importance of seeing classes in terms of a consciousness which cannot simply be read off from relationship to the means of production.[73] Of the latter, the work of Edward Thompson has been especially important in emphasising the importance of cultural factors in creating the link between social being and social consciousness and, therefore, the need to see classes as formed through the medium of time and with the active agency of those who come to recognise themselves a class. More recently, work associated with what has come to be called 'the linguistic turn', has offered a more fundamental challenge to the assumptions of these theoretical discourses. In particular it has called into question the

---

[71] B. Manning, 'The outbreak of the English civil war' in R. Parry, ed., *The English Civil War and After 1642–1658* (1970), p. 16; Manning, *English People*, p. 180; Fletcher, *Outbreak*, p. 378; *Country Life*, 10, 19 October 1901, p. 502; Hirst, *Authority*, pp. 51, 230; D. Underdown, *Revel*, p. 169 (citing Manning, *English People* and Holmes, *Eastern Association*); J. Sharpe, *Crime in Seventeenth-Century England: A county study* (Cambridge, 1983), p. 43.

[72] Among the large body of literature in this field, see R. Crompton, *Class and Stratification: an Introduction to Current Debates* (Oxford, 1993); S. G. McNall, R. E. Levine, R. Fantasia (eds.), *Bringing Class Back In: Contemporary and Historical Perspectives* (Boulder, 1991); L. R. Berlanstein (ed.), *Rethinking Labour History: Essays on Discourse and Class Analysis* (Urbana and Chicago, 1993); B. D. Palmer, *Descent into Discourse: The Reification of Language and the Writing of Social History* (Philadelphia, 1990); P. Joyce (ed.), *Class* (Oxford, 1995); G. M. Sider, *Culture and Class in Anthropology and History: A Newfoundland Example* (Cambridge, 1986); W. H. Sewell, 'How classes are made: critical reflections on E. P. Thompson's theory of working-class formation' in H. J. Kaye and K. McClelland (eds.), *E. P. Thompson: Critical Perspectives* (Oxford, 1990).

[73] For a forthright emphasis on structuring – the 'collective social expression of the fact of exploitation, the way in which exploitation is embodied in a social structure' – see G. E. M. De Ste Croix, *The Class Struggle in the Ancient Greek World from the Archaic Age to the Arab Conquests* (1981), pp. 31–9 (quotation from p. 43). See also J. Krikler, 'Agrarian class struggle and the South African War', *Social History*, 14 (1989).

essentialist assumptions that social identities are created primarily in the sphere of production and that there is an automatic association between social structure, social consciousness and social action. Some have wished to see those relationships as contingent rather than determined, while others have stressed against the universalising assumptions of class the array of alternative identities. Within the linguistic turn, it has been argued that language does not merely reflect, but actively constitutes, the social order. Thus class in this reading becomes a discursive formation. Class is now seen to be the result of a cultural process in which new meanings are given to material realities and out of which are forged collective identities. This renewed emphasis on language in society raises afresh the problem of trying to relate categories of analysis which derive their force from a theoretical discourse to the categories with which contemporaries sought to make sense of their own societies.

The category of class has always been thought to pose difficulties for those studying early modern societies, since it is held that the theoretical discourses out of which it arose were developed in, and seemed more immediately relevant to, later social formations. Indeed, the unresolved tensions in sociological analysis between status and class as determinants of social identity have been seen as particularly relevant to understanding early modern forms of social stratification. Accordingly, some historians have denied altogether the validity of class in early modern society. Ironically, recent developments in critical theory which emphasise the multiplicity of potential identities might be taken to strengthen this denial. Some early modern historians do employ the language of class, but they use it more as a descriptive term, rather than an analytical category, to denote relations within a socio-economic hierarchy, but not the reality of a class-based society and class conflict. Others are prepared to talk of the structuring of early modern society in terms of class, but reserve this appellation for only one group, the landed class, and refer somewhat provocatively (and problematically, since class is surely a relational term) to early modern England as a 'one-class society'.[74] The early modern historians most comfortable in employing the language of class are those like Christopher Hill and Brian Manning whose historical work has been most deeply informed by a dialogue with Marxist analysis. Nevertheless, their work has been subjected to considerable criticism.

[74] See the contributions to M. L. Bush (ed.), *Social Orders and Social Classes in Europe since 1500: Studies in Social Stratification* (1992); S. D. Amussen, 'Gender, family and the social order, 1560–1725' in A. Fletcher and J. Stevenson (eds.), *Order and Disorder in Early Modern England* (Cambridge, 1985), p. 206 n.; cf. M. Fulbrook, 'The English Revolution and the revisionist revolt', *Social History*, 7 (1982), p. 256n.; P. Laslett, *The World we have lost* (1965), ch. 2.

For example, the attempt to discern a divide in the period between a feudal and bourgeois ruling class has been questioned, given the early reception of agrarian capitalism. Both this and Brian Manning's shuffling and re-shuffling of groups into classes in his writings suggest something of the problems of containing early modern society within the categories of *Capital* (rather than say the Marx of *Eighteenth Brumaire*). Most recently, Keith Wrightson has sought to rescue the validity of the language of class analysis for the early modern period. He has done so by showing how contemporary and theoretical categories might be reconciled by employing the contemporary 'language of sorts' to discern (for him, neo-Weberian) classes bound by similarities of economic position, status and power and by shared cultural characteristics and bonds of interest.[75]

For the most part, those historians who have employed the language of class in discussing the Stour Valley attacks have done so in a rather loose and unspecific way to draw attention to the element of social conflict within the attacks. As such, they have not elaborated on what they see as the class structure generating conflict. Most implicitly assume that the relationship is one between a landed elite and 'the people'. This use of an undifferentiated 'people' mirrors the conventions of early modern social taxonomists who also saw the fault line in their society running between gentry and commons, and it has interesting antecedents in a late-nineteenth/earlier twentieth-century historiography's emphasis on 'people's history'.[76] But such a conceptualisation poses problems. Use of 'the people' in this way runs the danger of ignoring the fact that in contemporary usage the term was as often prescriptive as descriptive. As such, it was context and rhetorical strategy that determined precisely which groups the term was held to comprehend – for example, republicans and popular radicals within the English Revolution envisaged very different memberships in their use of term 'the people'. The category of the 'people' has been challenged by recent discussion of the nature of the early modern social structure. Both the dichotomous view of society

---

[75] K. Wrightson, 'The social order of early modern England: three approaches' in L. Bonfield, R. M. Smith and K. Wrightson (eds.), *The World we have gained: Histories of Population and Social Structure* (Oxford, 1986), pp. 177–202; *ibid.*, 'Estates, degrees, and sorts: changing perceptions of society in Tudor and Stuart England' in P. Corfield (ed.), *Language, History and Class* (Oxford, 1991), pp. 30–52; *ibid.*, '"Sorts of people" in Tudor and Stuart England' in J. Barry and C. Brooks (eds.), *The Middling Sort of People: Culture, Society and Politics in England, 1550–1800* (1994), pp. 28–51.

[76] For the politics behind an emphasis on the common people and people's history, see R. Samuel, 'British Marxist historians, 1880–1980: part one', *New Left Review*, 120 (1980), pp. 41–2; B. Schwarz, 'The people in history: the Communist Party Historians Group, 1945–56' in R. Johnson, G. McLennan, B. Schwarz, D. Sutton (eds.), *Making Histories: Studies in History-Writing and Politics*, (1982), pp. 80–1.

implied by such usage and its assumption of a lack of significant social differentiation below the level of the gentry have been questioned. An argument has been made for the need to deconstruct 'the people', since the term's indiscriminatory lumping together of groups occupying very different positions and experiences within the social structure is primarily to be explained by its origins in elite-penned, top-down depictions of the social order. By contrast, emphasis has been given in the most recent analyses of early modern social change, to a significant process of dissociation and differentiation within those groups comprising 'the people'. In particular, attention has been drawn to the emergence of the middling sort. This is a group over whose composition there is some disagreement, but at whose core were substantial farmers, merchants and prosperous artisans.[77] Much of the most important recent histories of the period have charted their growing economic, social, religious and political importance in the period. The active presence of at least some of the middling sort in the crowds itself suggests the need for a more complex reading of the sociology of the attacks.

As we have already seen, most contemporary comment on the attacks were couched in the language of the 'many-headed monster' and spoke of the people in a way – 'rude people', an 'unruly Multitude', 'the rabble' – that implied that those responsible came from the lowest levels of society. Historians have for the most part identified 'the people' of these comments with the clothworkers.[78] The clothworkers' presumed participation in these and other forms of crowd action within the region has led one historian to argue that there existed among the clothworkers 'a nascent class-consciousness' and to locate the origins of this in the structure of the cloth industry and the social relationships and experience to which it gave rise. Similarly, a study of protests by seventeenth-century clothworkers in the West Country has argued that 'a bold historian' might label these 'artisans' a class.[79] It is the identification of the attackers with the clothworkers as a class that is held to explain the attack on the landed class. In assessing claims that the attacks reflected class hostility on the part of the clothworkers, we need to return to the

---

[77] G. Burgess, 'The impact on political thought: rhetorics for troubled times' in J. Morrill (ed.), *The Impact of the English Civil War* (1991), p. 72; D. Underdown, *Revel*, p. 3. For an argument that the term 'the people' in usual seventeenth-century usage meant artisans, independent craftsmen, yeomen and better-off husbandmen, see D. Underdown, *A Free-Born People: Politics and the Nation in Seventeenth Century England* (Oxford, 1996), p. 7.

[78] Holmes, *Eastern Association*, pp. 43–5; Hirst, *Authority*, p. 51; Fletcher, *Outbreak*, pp. 377–8.

[79] Sharpe, *County Study*, pp. 86–7, 208–9; *Crime in Early Modern England*, pp. 138–9; *In Contempt*, p. 257.

cloth industry and to an analysis of the social relationships of production within the cloth industry.

In a general discussion of popular politics in the English Revolution, David Underdown has suggested that the 'Marxist model' is most valid in places in which industrial and commercial development produced something resembling a class society.[80] There was, as we have seen, throughout the Essex–Suffolk textile region an undoubted trend towards the decline of independent weavers well before the 1640s. This is a process that some historians have been tempted to label proletarianisation. Inasmuch as this captures the dependency that landlessness and employment by the clothier brought it has some value. Indeed, the earlier loss of independence in the Suffolk and Essex Old Draperies had led the weavers of the leading centres (Colchester included) to complain in the sixteenth century that the clothiers' power to lower piece rates was leading to some of them becoming 'other men's servants'. Nevertheless, labelling this process proletarianisation and anachronistic talk of a working class overlook the complexity of the social relationships of production within the textile industry.[81]

These relationships continued to reflect the uneven penetration of mercantile capital. Positions and identities within the trade were determined partly by longer-term changes, partly by short-term cycles. There was no simple divide between rich clothier and poor weaver. Clothier might itself describe either a small producer working on his own account (its earliest usage) or, increasingly, the controller of circulating capital who set weavers directly on work and co-ordinated the division of labour.[82] Within the ranks of the weavers there was a gap developing between the poorer weaver with only one loom and the larger master weavers, whose growth in numbers has been seen as a concomitant feature of the increasing role of mercantile capital and against whom orders restricting the number of looms worked were directed in both Essex and Suffolk.[83] But the picture was frequently upset by changes of

---

[80] D. Underdown, 'Community and class: theories of local politics in the English Revolution', B. C. Malament (ed.), *After the Reformation: Essays in Honour of J. H. Hexter* (Manchester, 1980), p. 158.

[81] *Letters and Papers Henry VIII*, 14(1), 87; N. Carlin, 'Marxism and the English Civil War', *International Socialism*, 2 ser., no. 10 (Winter 1980–1). For a discussion of the problems in the use of the category artisan to describe social relationships of production in the cloth industry for a later period, see J. Rule, 'The property of skill in the period of manufacture' in P. Joyce (ed.), *The Historical Meaning of Work* (Cambridge, 1987), pp. 99–118.

[82] Burley, 'Economic development', pp. 121–2, 127; Dymond and Betterton, *Lavenham*, p. 12.

[83] Kerridge, *Textile Manufactures*, pp. 193, 195; CRO, D/B, 5, Gb2, fols. 74, 119 v–21 v, *ibid.*, Gb3, fols. 179 v–80 v; WSRO, Sextus Book, unfol. 31 October 1648.

status, from independent and possibly employing weaver-producer to dependent employee, changes dictated by fluctuating levels of demand for cloth. When times were good more weavers might hope to weave on their own account and even to put work out to others; when demand was low, it was the larger producers who were better placed to withstand conditions. Thus references to clothworkers suggest a homogeneity and unity that misrepresents the reality of social relationships of production within the cloth industry and the potential they carried for producing or deflecting conflict within the trade. The blurred lines between smaller clothiers and independent weavers who themselves sometimes set others on work may have worked against the open articulation of antagonisms between clothier and weaver. The shifts of status from dependent to independent weaver according to fluctuating demand may have worked against an acceptance of identity as waged labour, an identity otherwise suggested by the loss of independence in the longer term. Much of course would have depended on the relative proportion of those occupying these liminal and changing statuses. This is something that cannot be known for certain given our still limited knowledge about the reality of social relations of production within the trade.

These occupational ambiguities worked against a straightforward acceptance of an identity based on waged labour. While, as we have seen, the loss of independence was associated with a greater vulnerability to poverty, care needs to be exercised in converting estimates derived from assessments on waged income in fiscal records into an index of proletarianisation. Such a conversion not only flattens the clothworkers' experience of both relative prosperity and poverty; it also ignores their own experience of the organisation of work and the workplace. The weavers' relationship to the means of production, controlling if not owning it and being paid by the piece, meant that it was still possible for them to see themselves as selling the product of their labour, and not just the labour. If there is not the evidence to suggest, as has been done for eighteenth-century West Country clothworkers, that the weavers valued the putting-out system for the independence it gave them, the degree of independence many weavers continued to feel in their experience of work through their continuing control over the means of production and their work rhythms was important.[84] In 1631 clothworkers in Suffolk petitioned the Privy

---

[84] J. Walter, 'The social economy of dearth in early modern England' in J. Walter and R. Schofield (eds.), *Famine, Disease and the Social Order in Early Modern Society* (Cambridge, 1989), pp. 85–6; A. Randall, *Before the Luddites: Custom, Community and Machinery in the English Woollen Industry, 1776–1809* (Cambridge, 1991), pp. 31–9; E. P. Thompson, 'Eighteenth-century English society: class struggle without class?', *Social History*, 3 (1978), p. 158.

Council for reasonable wages, 'that they may be encouradged to followe their lawfull Callings without craveing Almes'.[85] Clothworkers in the region appear to have lacked the sort of guild structure that historically was important for the articulation of status.[86] Colchester's weavers did have their own wardens, as did weavers in some of the smaller Essex centres.[87] Little is known of their role, but it is surely significant that it was Colchester's rulers (paralleling the role played by urban authorities in Suffolk) that played the leading part in the regulation of the trade.[88] But despite this and the fact that formal apprenticeship was under threat in the New Draperies, those who worked in the cloth industry still distinguished themselves by their possession of a skill in their trade. Craft, trade, art and mystery were all terms were to be found in Colchester's records used to describe the clothworkers. Weavers accused of sedition in 1566 had referred to their occupations as a 'science'. The 'property of skill' then, as later, played an important part in the self-definition of the clothworkers.[89]

[85] BL, Additional MS 39,245, fol. 152. The struggle over enclosure and common rights at Colchester may well reflect the weavers' concern for their independence as much as the poverty that gave common rights additional value.

[86] Colchester did have some form of association for regulating the trade, but its title suggests this was not a craft guild and there are indications that it was dominated by employers. In July 1618 'The Masters, Wardens, and Commonalty of the Arts, Trades, or Misteries of the Clothiers, Cloth-Workers, Bay and Say-Makers, Woollen-weavers, Fullers, Tuckers, Kembers and Taylors of Colchester' received a formal royal grant of incorporation: *VCH Essex*, vol. 2, p. 393. Little is known of this company. It had masters, wardens and assistants and in 1634 was recorded as holding a capital messuage within the town, presumably as their hall: CRO, D/B5, Cb2/7, fol. 24; CRO, Acc. C104 (unsorted estate and family papers, 1425–1893). But this (and its possible predecessor) have otherwise a shadowy existence in extant records: PRO, SP, 14/129/70.I and II; 16/206/58, 59; /377/39, 40, 41; *APC 1623–1625*, p. 179, *1630–1631*, p. 12. The fact that in 1622 'the Company' had indicated its willingness to pay higher wages to weavers in response to a recommendation from royal commissioners suggests that it was dominated by the clothiers: PRO, SP, 14/129/70, 71

[87] CRO, D/B, 5, Gb2, fols. 23 r–4 v, 74 r–5 r. There is little in surviving records to indicate that the clothing townships had anything approaching formal guild structures, but incidental references suggest that the larger centres had some form of organisation, but give no indication of their purpose, effectiveness or continuity: Bodl. Lib., MS Firth c. 4, pp. 495, 504–5; *CSPD 1651–1652*, pp. 480–1; G. F. Beaumont, *A History of Coggeshall* (1890), pp. 174–5, 190, 257–8; Johnson, 'Community study', pp. 233–4, 276.

[88] At both Ipswich and Bury St Edmunds election of officials was with the consent of the urban authorities, to the extent that at Bury the company was 'entirely subordinated to the municipal authorities': G. Unwin, 'Industries: woollen cloth in the old draperies', *VCH Suffolk*, vol. 2, pp. 262–3. At Colchester it was the borough authorities that established the weavers' meeting, reserving to themselves the annual appointment of one of the two wardens, and prescribing the authority of the town's courts, not guild, to punish offences against the trade: CRO, D/B5, Gb2, fols. 23 r–4 v, fols. 82–3 r. Significantly, these orders were taken for the good government of the borough, general suppression of idleness 'and many other disorders', as well as the better maintenance of the freeburgesses.

[89] CRO, D/B5, Gb2, fol. 230; *ibid.*, Acc. C 10. For helpful discussions for a later period of how artisans saw their own identity, see R. W. Malcomson, 'Workers' combinations in

The differential relationship of clothier and workers to the means of production structured conflict within the trade. The limited control exercised by clothiers over the actual process of production gave scope for individual action by spinners and weavers within the opacity of the workplace.[90] Collective action took place around the issues of the terms of employment and payment. Clothiers had a vested interest in expanding the labour supply, weavers in its regulation. As the combers of Bocking complained in the crisis of 1636–7, 'rich men in a quick tyme they trade soe much that they waxe weary of their own neighbours & so sett strang[e]rs aworke'. Crises in the industry regularly exposed tensions between weavers and clothiers. Trade depression or harvest failure led to clothiers withdrawing their capital, abating wages to their workers, ceasing to put out work or restricting it to their immediate family or workfolk.[91] In the dearth of 1631 the Privy Council was the recipient of a petition, 'in the behalfe of 300 poore people inhabitinge in the Towne of Colchester, who are much distressd for the abatement of their usuall wage in theise tymes of scarcity and dearth'.[92] The petition has not survived, but it took as its reference a similar petition from the Suffolk New Draperies' centre of Sudbury. This had complained that,

> of late yeares most of the clothiers who by the labors of such poore Artizans have gotten g[rea]te estates out of a Covetous disposicon have abridged their wages … wherof div[er]s of them for wante of meanes have byn of late constreyned to sell their Bedds wheeles loomes and other their working tools to buy bread for them their wives and children and doe now live in a Lamentable Condicon, many of them redie to p[er]ishe for wante of ffoode.

In the next depression of 1636–7 the Privy Council received a petition from the poor weavers in Colchester complaining that 2,000 families who worked for the clothiers in Colchester were 'reduced to exceeding great want, poverty and misery by the smallness of wages or allowances for their work … that many of them are … not able to susteyne them w[i]th their labours in their said callings'. In a striking phrase, the weavers claimed that one of the larger Colchester clothiers, Thomas Reynolds,

---

eighteenth-century England' in M. C. Jacob and J. R. Jacob (eds.), *The Origins of Anglo-American Radicalism* (New Jersey and London, 1991); Rule, 'Property of skill'.

[90] This was labelled embezzlement by the clothiers who sought statutory controls to prevent such practices by use of the criminal law: ERO, Q/SR, 130/42 and 42a; PRO, SP, 16/355/162.i; J. Styles, 'Embezzlement, industry and the law in England, 1500–1800' in M. Berg, P. Hudson and M. Sonnescher (eds.), *Manufacture in Town and Country before the Factory* (Cambridge, 1983), pp. 173–210.

[91] ERO, D/DEb, 7/3; Q/SR, 266/121; Bodl. Lib., MS Firth c. 4, pp. 484–5, 494–5, 504–5; PRO, SP, 16/189/40; /188/92; BL, Additional MSS 39,245, fol. 65.

[92] *APC 1630–1631*, pp. 358–9.

was 'making merchandize of yor pet[ione]rs Labors'.[93] Despite evidence of structural conflict within the trade, clothiers would appear not to have been the target of *collective* actions by the clothworkers before the later seventeenth century, by which date their oppressions had become the subject of the balladeers.[94] Although the evidence of the 1631 Suffolk petition (if composed by the clothworkers themselves)[95] with its talk of the 'covetous disposicon' of clothiers suggests a proto-'labour conscious-ness', there was a recognition by the clothworkers that the cause of their problems lay elsewhere. As the weavers of Bocking and Braintree acknowledged, 'yet their masters are unable to help them by reason theire tradinge is taken from them, for the Marchants will not buy theire Bayes, soe that these stocks lying deade in theire handes are hardly able to helpe themselves'.[96] The symbiotic relationship between dearth and depression encouraged the clothworkers to blame another species of merchants for their plight – middlemen in the grain supply who were active in a region heavily implicated in supplying rapidly growing London with food. This was a form of action also rendered appropriate, it has been argued, by their own self-image as independent producers whose economic well-being was determined as much by the prices they paid as consumers as by the return they received as producers.[97]

[93] BL, Additional MS 39,245, fol. 152, SP, 16/197/72 (*APC 1630–1631*, p. 230 supplies the date of the petition); PRO, SP, 16/354/153 and 153.I; /355/92, 93, 162. Reynolds had been operating an early form of the truck system, hence the reference to 'merchandize', paying his weavers in cloth and undervaluing it when they tried to sell it back to him. He may also have paid his weavers in the tokens which he issued: G. C. Williamson, *Trade Tokens Issued in the Seventeenth Century in England, Wales and Ireland By Corporations, Merchants, Tradesmen, etc.*, 2 vols. (1889), vol. 1, p. 218. Reynolds claimed to set on work 400 households of spinners, 52 households of weavers and 33 households involved in the finishing processes. Compare the Suffolk clothier Samuel Salmon who in 1622 was said to employ about 200 men and women: PRO, SP, 14/131/95.

[94] CRO, D/B5, Sb2/9, fol. 245; *ibid.*, Sr 95, rot. 12; K. H. Burley, 'A note on a labour dispute in early eighteenth-century Colchester', *Bulletin Institute Historical Research*, 29 (1956), pp. 220–30; Bodl. Lib., Rawlinson MSS C151, fols. 214, 219v–20; J. Rule, *The Experience of Labour in the Eighteenth Century* (1981), pp. 126–7; STC 4734a, *The Clothiers Delight: Or, The Rich Mens Joy And The Poor Mens Sorrow. Wherein is exprest the craftiness and subtility of Many Clothiers in England, by beating down their Workmen's Wages* (1682).

[95] Subsequent legal action suggested that a local gentleman might have become involved in the drawing up of the petition in pursuit of a private feud: PRO, SP, 16/197/72.

[96] Bodl. Lib., MS. Firth c. 4, pp. 486–7. See also the comment about the situation in Bockinge: 'That towne abound with poore, whereof many are very unrulie, and havinge noe employment will make the place verie hazardous for men of better Ranke to live amongst them': *ibid.*, pp. 474–5.

[97] This was a response that continued to parallel the later, more specific trade disputes until late into the eighteenth century. Walter, 'Crisis of 1629'; CRO, D/B5, Sb2/9, fols. 223v, 226. For a suggestive treatment of parallel shifts in the politics of French textile workers linked to their (changing) perceptions of their status, see W. M. Reddy, 'The textile trade and the language of the crowd at Rouen 1752–1871', *P&P* 74 (1977), pp. 62–89.

For all the evidence of patterns of potential or actual conflict within the cloth trade, this has little to say about how class feelings might explain the clothworkers' participation in the attack on members of the landed class. If the clothworkers found their lives structured by the relationships of production and their status increasingly challenged, the conflict to which this gave rise occurred within the industry. Nor does the analysis provide evidence of the possibility of alliances with other groups taken to comprise 'the people'. Did the artisans constitute a separate class or did their changing situation make possible a recognition of common interests with others outside the trade? Weavers as 'semi-autonomous employees' who retained some control over their labour power and even the means of production might be said to occupy what has been called in contemporary sociological analysis a contradictory class location. It is this that helps to explain historians' difficulties in determining their position within early modern society. Within the Marxist tradition of writing on early modern England one historian, Brian Manning, has argued that artisans and smaller farmers, squeezed between rich and poor, sought to maintain a separate identity, while another, Norah Carlin, has seen the clothworkers in losing their independence become part of what she terms the working class.[98] Did clothworkers in Essex and Suffolk see their skill as setting them apart? Or did easy recruitment into a trade unable to police entrance break down the boundaries between them and other groups? We have little evidence as to how clothworkers regarded other urban and rural groups with whom they might be thought to have had similar interests.[99] The nature of the putting-out industry meant that although there was a degree of regional specialisation there was no social segregation. Moreover, the fact that the cloth industry was a major determinant of the general economic well-being of the wider region suggests that the clothworkers' grievances would have been more widely shared.

It is possible then to see how class played a part in the August attacks. Those who worked in the cloth industry found their lives structured in

[98] Crompton, *Class*, p. 71; B. Manning, 'Parliament, "party" and "community" during the English civil war' in A. Cosgrove and J. I. McGuire (eds.), *Parliament and Community* (Historical Studies, 14, Belfast, 1983), p. 115; Carlin, 'Marxism'. It is perhaps not clear whether Prof. Manning means to include clothworkers within this group.

[99] Clothworkers in the larger towns might have shared something of the suspicion of the town for the country. For example, there were signs that urban weavers resented their rural counterparts, and in boroughs like Colchester or Sudbury there was much to divide a weaver who was a freeburgess from a recent immigrant to town and trade: CRO, D/B5, Gb1, fol. 72 r; Gb2, fols. 23 r–4 v. Of course, in the smaller centres those who worked in agriculture would have been the clothworkers' neighbours.

ways that made collective action both possible and, perhaps, probable. Common dependence on a single industry was associated with long-term growth in economic vulnerability and a sensitivity to periodic and unpredictable short-term crises. Common dependence also introduced a synchronicity of response when crises occurred within the trade. It forged the solidarities of the trade. In a later dispute weavers processed around Colchester in 1675 soliciting support from their fellow artisans with the cry of 'stande up for the trade for the company is up'.[100] The extensive division of labour made possible the assembling of large crowds over an extensive area. The relative freedom from seigneurial supervision that came from living and working in a clothing community gave the clothworkers a tactical freedom with which to express hostility towards their superiors that those caught in the ties of landlord and tenant found harder to achieve.[101] William Cecil's famous observation that, 'the people [that] depend uppon the makyng of cloth ar warss condition to be quyetly governed than the husband men' was echoed by contemporaries in the seventeenth century. Among them was John Aubrey who believed that the poor rates of pay for workers in the trade meant that they were 'trained up as nurseries of sedition and rebellion', an observation based upon his experience of the cloth trade in the south-west.[102] In the eastern counties, a succession of comments – from clothiers, local communities and magistrates – underlined the association between the 'dangerous desperacy' of the clothworkers and the challenge to the social order. This was an association reflected in the central role the clothworkers played under the leadership of Captain Poverty in the 'risings' against the Amicable Grant in 1525 and irregularly renewed thereafter, most recently in the food riots in the decades preceding the August attacks.[103] The social and spatial divisions of labour that underwrote these forms of collective action help to explain why it should have been clothworkers who were at the heart of the August attacks.

If the crowds' actions were conditioned by class, then can we go further and say that the attacks were mobilised by 'hostility to the gentry

---

[100] CRO, D/B5, Sb2/9, fols. 223 v–6 v; PRO, SP, 29/374/57, /378/91.

[101] For some within the trade there may have been an even greater freedom from the usual constraints; young men were a prominent part of most early modern crowds, and in Colchester for example there were complaints that putting out cloth at piece rates 'is a great occasion that young men oftentymes live ydle, frequenting alehouses, and com[m]it many disorders': PRO, SP, 14/130/65.

[102] J. Pound, *Poverty and Vagrancy in Tudor England* (1971), p. 7; E. Kerridge, 'The revolts in Wiltshire against Charles I', *Wiltshire Archaeological and Natural History Magazine*, 57 (1958), p. 71.

[103] PRO, SP, 14/138/35; Bernard, *War*; MacCulloch, *Suffolk*, ch. 10; *Calendar of Letters and State Papers relating to English Affairs preserved principally in the archives of Simancas, 1, Elizabeth 1558–1567*, pp. 570–1; Walter, 'Crisis of 1629'.

as a class'? Here the evidence is less clear. To make class an effective explanatory category requires both a sense of an identification of interests within the class and a sense of differentiation from, and conflict with, other classes. While some historians put an emphasis on the process of structuring which creates a shared economic and social experience as the determinant of class formation and action, others argue that both action and consciousness cannot simply be read off from that position. If class is a contentious category, then that of class consciousness is even more divisive. But the question of consciousness is important since it raises the issue of agency, the ability of classes to function as real entities with capacities to act upon identifiable interests held to be in opposition to those of other groups. Take, for example, the position of peasantries within early modern societies. The major fault line between the peasantry and the seigneurial class gave a common structuring to their lives, and the relationship of power and domination to which this gave rise helps to explain the frequency of peasant actions against their seigneurs in this period. But without an appreciation of peasant consciousness – the peasants' own understanding of their own society – then it would be impossible to make sense of a pattern of actions in which peasant protests against individual seigneurs (or, in times of crisis, a wider group), frequently operated within the framework of an acceptance of the seigneurial system and sought to reform, not to abolish its relation-ships. As this example suggests, the formation of class consciousness is not given by social structure alone, since there is a complex and contingent relationship between structure and formation. Structuration presents a range of possible interests from which to forge a common identity, but those interests are dependant upon people's perceptions of their social identity for realization in action. In other words, class is not simply created by a common relationship to the social relations of production, but also by a common understanding of that relationship through a shared interpretation of lived experience. There is an obvious convergence here with work emphasising the importance of discourse and language in the construction of collective identities.

In 1642 we have no direct evidence of expressions of hostility towards the landed classes from *within* the crowds themselves, only the evidence of the stark fact of the attacks. Historians have sought to subvert the silences imposed on subordinate groups by the inequalities in the creation (and preservation) of texts by reading the ideas informing the repertoire of the crowd's actions. At their best such readings pay close attention to the statements, verbal and symbolic, made by the crowds themselves. However the argument that it was hostility towards the gentry as a class that mobilised the crowds in the summer of 1642 rests heavily on reports by the elite of what the people intended by their actions. Thus, the reading of the motives of the attackers in 1642 is in effect the reading given events by commentators drawn almost exclusively from the landed class. Where such accounts did not largely reflect the fears of the elite, they were as we have seen a deliberate exercise in propaganda intended to manipulate those same fears to force political allegiance for the king. In such tranquillity of hindsight as the continuing social turmoil of the 1650s afforded, the Earl of Warwick's steward recalled in his auto-biography that 'there was so great a Confusion at Melford that no man appeared like a Gentleman but was made a prey to that ravenous Crewe'. This was not however a state of affairs witnessed by him, but 'heard from all hands'. Sir Simonds D'Ewes may have earlier viewed with some sympathy crowd actions (albeit in France),[104] but his comments on the attacks reflected an underlying anxiety about the threat to the social and religious order posed by the political impasse and military conflict between king and Parliament. In the comparisons he draws between the August attacks and examples of popular radicalism stretching back to classical times he reveals his subscription to the view widespread among the landed classes of the people as the 'many-headed monster'. If then D'Ewes' report is to be taken as evidence of early modern class consciousness, it should more properly be taken as evidence of that of the rulers, not the ruled.

The indirect nature of the evidence for popular beliefs and behaviour is of course a larger problem in writing the history of the popular role within the English Revolution. Some historians have been content to exploit the evidence provided by elite comment, suppressing issues of provenance and context. The problems this presents can be seen in the following example. The incident at the elections to the Short Parliament in Essex already discussed would seem to lend support to the argument for the existence of hostility to the landed class. One man was reportedly applauded for saying 'that if Nevill had the day they would teare the gentlemen to peeces', claiming that 'there was a hundred more of his minde'. This episode was confirmed by Lord Maynard who reported that he found 'the rude vulgar people to grow to that insolency of from striking of private men to fall to menacing of us all to pull us in peeces'. But since both accounts come from the disappointed party at the

---

[104] BL, Harleian MS 163, fol. 325 (D'Ewes was clearly following a letter from a group of Suffolk JPs to the Speaker of the Commons); CUL, Additional MS 33, fol. 20 v; S. P. Salt, 'Sir Simonds D'Ewes and the levying of ship money, 1635–1640', *Historical Journal*, 37 (1994), p. 283. I have not found evidence of attacks on protestant gentry in Suffolk, besides the reported hostility towards Sir Robert Crane, one of the JPs making the report.

elections – Henry Nevill, the defeated court candidate, is the author of the first account – and from men whose correspondence make clear their strong dislike for even the legitimate popular role in the elections, we would be right to exercise some caution in accepting their account. Maynard's elision in collapsing an individual utterance into a generic statement of the 'the rude vulgar people' is itself revealing. In fact, the reported statement cannot be taken as straightforward evidence of *class* hostility since, as the context makes clear, it needs to be read as a threat to the 'court' party and the threat was accompanied by popular acclamation of those gentlemen supporting Parliament.[105]

Keith Wrightson has noted in the contemporary use of 'richer' and 'poorer' sorts the emergence of 'a language of radical differentiation ... a language pregnant with conflict'.[106] He makes the fruitful suggestion that the reception and use of a 'language of sorts' might be related to local social and economic structures and to the particular patterns of social relationships to which they gave rise.[107] Periods of crisis within the cloth trade had witnessed the articulation of more general resentment by clothworkers against their betters. A crisis in the Old Draperies in 1566 had prompted an attempt at a rising by a group of Colchester weavers, one of whose number had summarised their predicament: 'We can get no work nor we have no money, and if we should steal we should be hanged, and if we should ask no man would give us, but we will have a remedy one of these days, or else we will lose all, for the commons will rise ... Then will up two or three thousand in Colchester and about Colchester ... for ye shall see the hottest harvest that ever was in England'. In the dearth years of the 1590s another weaver was reported to have told a large crowd, that 'it would never be better until men did rise & seeke thereby an amendment and wished in his heart a hundred men would rise and he would be their captain to cut the throates of the rich Churles & the Rich Cornmongers'. In 1595 a Colchester alehouse run by a weaver's wife was the scene of a debate among its customers, occasioned by the demand for the repayment of a debt, which ended with one saying, 'thys ys no yeare to paye no moneye for I thinck if thys hold o[u]r wyffes & children wyll starve but by god's blood beffore we wyll starve we wyll not goe to the worst fyrst but we wyll goe to the best & pull the bayliffs out by [the] earrs ... yf all wyll consent to me you shall see a wholt [hot]

---

[105] PRO, SP, 16/449/48; BL, Egerton MS 2646, fol. 142.
[106] Wrightson, 'Social order', pp. 189–91; 'Estates', pp. 44–7. Wrightson does not specifically mention clothworkers in his discussion of the various 'sorts'.
[107] Wrightson, 'Social order', pp. 198–9. This is a point given some importance in contemporary sociological analysis; David Lockwood for example, argues that the perception of the larger society varies according to the structural locations within which lives are lived and from which the larger society is visualised: Crompton, *Class*, p. 41.

Colchester afor next Satterdaye.' Again, in the difficult winter of 1623–4 a conversation over pots of beer between two more Colchester clothworkers had led to one obseving, 'if this hard weather continue their [sic] are many poore in St Maries, St Marie Magdalene, St James & St Anns that will rise and we of St Peters will not stande and looke on and their [sic] be more pore then Riche and yf they doe rise we will begyn first wth the Bailiffs'.[108]

It is precisely this evidence that has led one historian to argue that, 'the pre-industrial poor did have a perception of the society in which they lived which, however imperfectly and temporarily, and however clouded by notions of deference or respect, was basically a perception based on notions of class'.[109] But interpretation of the evidence provided by sedition poses many problems in early modern society where, on the one hand, the absence of a police force meant that it was the 'community' which presented such cases to the authorities and where, on the other, there was an awareness that too public an expression of ideas labelled seditious might invite savage retaliation. Does the relatively small number of cases of sedition presented to the courts reflect the infrequency of such utterances and, as such, the shock they caused? Or were the handful of individuals so accused the unfortunate victims of neighbourly spite in a society where such views were more generally held?

The fragments of sedition we have for the clothworkers pose in an acute form the problems raised in James Scott's notions of the hidden transcript, the secretive and subversive discourse of subordinate groups. The scraps of evidence provided by the problematic evidence of earlier and isolated sedition cases are no substitute for the close observation in the anthropological or sociological present that enabled James Scott to grasp the concrete experience of class 'as it is lived' and to suggest the link between everyday understandings of class and the role of class consciousness in major acts of protest.[110] It may indeed be the case that, as Scott argues, subordinate groups are less constrained at the level of thought and ideology and more constrained at the level of political action where the daily exercise of power acts as a sharp constraint. But since Scott's 'sequestered social sites' of subversive discourse are in this case hidden from the historian, we cannot know how generally held the ideas expressed in sedition were. Nor is the evidence rich enough to allow

---

[108] Emmison, *Disorder*, pp. 62–4; CRO, D/B5, Sb2/5, fols. 186 v, 197 v–8 r; ERO, Q/SR, 136/11; CRO, D/B5, Sb2/5, fol. 186 v (cf. fols. 197 v–8 r); Sb2/7, fol. 88.

[109] Sharpe, *Crime*, p. 136.

[110] J. C. Scott, *Weapons of the Weak: Everyday Forms of Peasant Resistance* (New Haven and London, 1985); *Domination and the Arts of Resistance: Hidden Transcripts* (New Haven and London, 1990).

us to recover the informal discourses by which the clothworkers organised their daily understandings of their social world.

The rich attacked in these examples of sedition by clothworkers were for the most part members an urban plutocracy. Unlike other industries, for example mining, the social relationships of production within the cloth industry did not bring the producers into direct conflict with a landed class. In the rural centres clothworkers, if they held a cottage or small piece of land, would have come under the jurisdiction of manorial lords. In the larger urban centres, this was less likely. As a group, clothworkers did come under the power exercised by the gentry as the local rulers of the region. It was the gentry as JPs who were entrusted by the king's government with the regulation of the cloth industry. But while this might on occasion cause resentment among the clothworkers, the magistrates were seen in general as allies in struggles with the clothiers and as protectors in their role in policing the grain market.[111] Indeed, the leading role played by the Earl of Warwick in listening to the weavers' grievances in the crises during the period of Personal Rule may help to explain the level of popular support he was able to attract in the 1640s.

The relative absence of the gentry from the everyday lives of the clothworkers does not of course preclude the possibility that the clothworkers did display a hostility towards them. The attack on Sir John Lucas suggests that where a gentleman lived close enough to urban society to offer a provocative example of wealth and power then he could excite the hostility of the clothworkers. In the destruction of the Lucas enclosures in 1641 some of the crowd were said to have called out for 'Jack Lucas'. The derogatory use of Jack in current proverbs – one of which ran 'Jack would be a gentleman' – makes clear that this was a very deliberate slighting of Sir John Lucas's gentle status. This use of Jack had its parallel in those episodes where individuals deliberately taunted their betters with scatological claims that they too were in thrall to their bodily functions. This was a claim for a basic equality given greater resonance by a political culture in which discourses of the body were used to justify inequality and where, it has been argued, there was a deliberate attempt by elites to use control of the body as an expression of their social superiority.[112]

---

[111] See for example their role in the commission to examine the clothworkers' complaints in both 1629 and 1636/7: Bodl. Lib., MS Firth c. 4, pp. 484–509; ERO, D/DEb, 7/1–17. In 1617 one Colchester weaver claimed that various gentlemen had been sent commissions to investigate the weavers' complaints but had put them in their pockets (i.e. had done nothing): CRO, D/B5, Sb2/6, fol. 270

[112] HLRO, MP HL, 5 August 1641; G. L. Apperson, *English Proverbs and Proverbial Phrases: A Historical Dictionary* (1927), pp. 330–1; Tilley, *A Dictionary of the Proberbs*

Whether the clothworkers had first-hand and everyday experience of gentry wealth and power, the social hierarchy which underwrote the dominance of the landed class and which demanded acknowledgement of their superiority – not least through public rituals of deference – could excite hostility from both poorer *and* middling sort within the cloth industry. The shifting boundaries between independence and dependence and the vulnerability of (especially the poorer) clothiers to the commercial crisis of the early 1640s might have meant that it was not only the poorer sort who were involved in the attacks.[113] Clarendon referred to the West Riding cloth towns as 'very populous and rich towns (which depending wholly upon clothiers naturally maligned the gentry)'. This was a theme echoed by other accounts of allegiance in the Revolution. In Essex a local royalist later complained that the clothiers, 'were generallie sordid men whose passion for their profitt gave them such a continuall jealousie of the decay of trade, that the Parliament – whose constant stile was tenderness of commerce – found them allwayes disposed to receive their impressions, and to derive them to their workmen'. This in turn echoes a judgement from the Parliamentarian side in John Corbet's description of those in Gloucestershire who lived, 'not at the will of the gentry, but observed those men by whom those manufactures were maintained that kept them alive'.[114] We should be careful about generalising too freely from contemporary comment since there are plenty of examples in the region and elsewhere of a mutual respect between gentry and urban middling sort, though this was founded on common religious and political sympathies. But the middling sort in the clothing communities of Essex and Suffolk probably shared a similarity of outlook with that of their peers in Gloucestershire, of whom it was said that they were 'a generation of men truly laborious, jealous of their properties, whose

---

in England in the Sixteenth and Seventeenth Centuries (Ann Arbor, 1950); N. Elias, *The Civilizing Process 1: The History of Manners* (Oxford, 1978). For another example of the use of Jack to slight a member of the gentry, see M. Stoyle, *Loyalty and Locality: Popular Allegiance in Devon during the English Civil War* (Exeter, 1994), p. 143.

113 In the crisis of 1637 the clothiers of Bocking had distinguished between the 'better' and 'meaner' clothiers. All had been badly affected by the lack of sale, but of the latter some had laid down their trade, others were unable to employ their own families and, they observed, 'their bee divers Clothiars in our Towne, quite decayed in their estate, soe that whereas they weare of late masters, and did sett divers poore people on worke, they are nowe themselves become workemen, and take in worke from others': ERO, D/DEb, 7/1. For examples of the vulnerability of the clothiers in earlier crises, see *APC 1619–1621*, pp. 79–80; PRO, SP, 14/128/67, /282/130.

114 Edward Hyde, Earl of Clarendon. *The History of the Rebellion And Civil Wars in England Begun in the Year 1641*, ed. W. D. Macray, 6 vols. (Oxford, 1888), vol. 2, p. 464; HMC, MSS Duke of Beaufort, p.23; C. Hill, 'Lord Clarendon and the puritan revolution' in his *Puritanism and Revolution* (1958), pp. 202–5; Rollison, *Local Origins*, p. 131.

principall aime is lierty and plenty, and whilst in an equal rank with their neighbours they desire only not to be oppressed'. If so, then they might have brought their own animus to the attacks. Certainly the evidence of relations with the overbearing Sir John Lucas or the hostile comments of Henry Nevill (or the anonymous Essex royalist quoted above) suggest that the attacks could also have reflected the conflict between what a Suffolk contemporary called the scarlet and the blue – the gentry and the clothiers (the latter description taken from the colour of Suffolk cloth).[115]

Despite the absence of the gentry as targets of hostility, the surviving examples of sedition by the clothworkers do show how individual clothworkers could employ the dichotomous language of rich and poor in a way that both reveals potential enemies and possible alliances. The language of rich and poor might lack the specificities that would encourage us to talk of the language of class, but in the context of early modern society its very imprecision gave it a menacing inclusiveness. The more general evidence of early modern sedition suggests that it was in terms of this dichotomy that many saw their society. The term 'the poor' had the attraction (for some, the alarm) of offering a collective identity that could be remarkably inclusive. As the Colchester weaver had noted, 'their be more pore then Riche'. To the extent that the clothworkers chose to emphasise their poverty, rather than their artisan status, then this could have created the potential for a much wider alliance with those whose poverty and powerlessness they shared. Certainly, the vulnerability to poverty that was the increasing lot of many clothworkers might have encouraged this development (though here perception probably continued to lag behind the pace of economic change).

If, as recent work suggests, class as a political (and cultural) postulate is as important in the process of class formation as class as social fact, then the political action the attacks represented may have carried within them the potential for a sharper construction of class identities.[116] Political and religious divisions among the elite in the early 1640s had begun to open up a discourse that offered subordinate groups a language

---

[115] Rollison, *Local Origins*, pp. 13, 150; P. Collinson, 'Christian socialism in Elizabethan Suffolk: Thomas Carew and his *Caveat for Clothiers*' in C. Rawcliffe, R. Virgoe, R. Wilson (eds.), *Counties and Communities: Essays on East Anglian History Presented to Hassell Smith* (Centre for East Anglian Studies, 1996), p. 168. Rollison's chapter, ' "Small Thinges And Grande Designes": a revolutionary's history of the English Revolution' attempts a stimulating analysis of the political mentality of the Parliamentarian middling sort through the contemporary writings of John Corbet, from whom this quotation comes. It should be pointed out that Corbet's statement may also have been an attempt to constitute that identity he claimed to describe.

[116] G. Eley, 'All the world a text? From social history to the history of society two decades later' in T. J. McDonald (ed.), *The Historic Turn in the Human Sciences* (Ann Arbor, 1996), pp. 218–20.

with which to articulate a more conscious opposition to their superiors. The collapse of censorship and the public condemnation of the supporters of the king had produced a vocabulary of stigmatisation which, shorn of its immediate context, might have been deployed more generally against all superiors. Preaching before the House of Commons in December 1641, the Essex minister Stephen Marshall had told his listeners that 'the *vox populi* is: that many of the Nobles, Magistrates, Knights and Gentlemen, and persons of great Quality are arrand Traytors and Rebells against God taking part with wicked men, and wicked causes against the Truth'.[117] Some indication of the possibilities that the appropriation of this discourse and the elision of its qualifiers might open up is provided by a report of what was being preached amongst the sects in Chelmsford, the county town of Essex, within a year of the attacks:

> *That the Relation of Master and Servant hath no ground or warrant in the new Testament: but rather the contrary, for there we read, In Christ Iesus there is neither bond nor free, and,* we are all one in Christ.
>
> ... *That the Honours and Titles of* Dukes, Marquesses, Earles, Viscounts, Lords, Knights, *and* Gentlemen *are but Ethnicall and Heathenish distinctions not to be retained among Christians.*
>
> ... *That one man should have a Thousand pounds a yeare, and another not one pound, perhaps not so much, but must live by the sweat of his browes, and must labour before he eate, hath no ground in Nature or in Scripture.*
>
> ... *That the common People heretofore kept under blindnesse and Ignorance have a long time yeelded themselves Servants, nay slaves to the Noblity and Gentry: but God hath now opened their eyes and discovered unto them their Christian Liberty; and therefore it is now fit that the Nobility and Gentry should serve their Servants, or at least worke for their own maintenance, and if they will not worke they ought not to eate.*[118]

The source for this is none other than Bruno Ryves. But before we dismiss it out of hand as the product of either polemic or paranoia, we should note that it has been shown recently that Ryves received information about developments in Chelmsford from a member of the town's ruling group and that there is also independent evidence of the active presence of Brownists and others within the town.[119] If Ryves'

---

[117] S. Marshall, *Reformation and Desolation: or, A Sermon tending to the Discovery of a People to whom God will by no meanes be reconciled* (1642), pp. 45–6.

[118] *MR*, pp. 21–2.

[119] H. Grieve, *The Sleepers and the Shadows. Chelmsford: a Town, its People and its Past 2: From Market Town to Chartered Borough* (Chelmsford, 1994), vol. 2, pp. 17–18, 60, 62.

account was fashioned, rather than fictionalised, then it points to the potential for a more radical critique of the social order. Tensions in Christianity and its texts had led to ideas of spiritual equality being translated into claims for greater social equality in popular movements in the European past, a translation that would be repeated later in the English Revolution. To the extent that the oft-cited association between clothworkers and puritanism reflected reality, then there may well have been particular potential for some such ideas to have informed the August attacks. The remarkable spiritual confession of one Colchester woman, Rose Thurgood, might be taken as evidence of the circulation of such ideas. In her *Lecture of Repentance* she complained, 'how many rich worldlings even conspire against the poore man, who harms them not' and observed 'that rich and poore, all is one to God'. (But the conclusion she drew reminds us that religious critiques of society might have a very different agenda from those later read out from them. For Rose Thurgood, it was God who would punish the rich for their arrogance and covetousness.)[120] The radicalisation of popular political culture was only to come later in the decade with the emergence of radical groups like the Levellers. Had the attacks occurred later in the Revolution then they might have been able to draw on a language with which to articulate a more fundamental challenge to the landed classes. Ironically, the success of the attacks in neutralising the region made easier the restoration of political order by the region's rulers and probably helped to inhibit any such development in local society in the early 1640s.

Political division and the breakdown of order may then have given the clothworkers an opportunity to express their resentment at the inequalities of wealth and power, a contrast heightened by the economic crisis they found themselves facing and symbolised in the houses of the landed classes. If this was the case then the attacks on the houses paralleled those attacks on the chateaux of a continental nobility that have been taken as evidence of class hostility.[121] The August attacks represented one of those moments of high 'classness' of which groups exhibiting otherwise low-levels of class identity were capable. But to say that class may have played some part in mobilising the crowd is not to say that the crowds exhibited a class consciousness which informed their objectives and dictated collective action in pursuit of class interests. Nor that the

---

[120] R. Thurgood, A Lecture of Repentance (*c.* 1636), John Rylands Library, Eng MS 875, fol. 219 r. (I am grateful to Dr Jeremy Maule for the loan of a transcript of, and discussions about, this document.)

[121] For example, H. Heller, *Iron and Blood: Civil Wars in Sixteenth Century France* (Montreal, 1991) makes a strong, but not entirely convincing, argument along these lines.

attacks were on the gentry as a class. Why this should have been so takes us to the heart of the interpretive problem confronting the attempt to recover evidence of popular consciousness in the early modern period. Was the lack of support for an attack on the landed class to be explained by lack of agreement with such an aim, by fears of punishment, or by the constraints of the powerful cultural hegemony exercised by early modern elites in the public transcript of early modern society which asserted the naturalness of social hierarchy and the sinfulness of rebellion? Here the evidence does not suggest a parallel with those exceptional (and non-English) anti-seigneurial movements intent on fundamental social transformation that came so readily to D'Ewes' mind. Writing of the eighteenth century Edward Thompson has argued that the plebeian crowd lacked both consistency of self-definition in consciousness and clarity of objectives. Despite his emphasis upon the increasing employment of a language of sorts, Keith Wrightson too suggests that group identities below the level of the gentry rather than expressing a broader, more enduring, conscious collective interest, seem often to have been quickened into temporary existence by a common enemy or grievances.

If class hostility was a component of the attacks then it would appear to have been in that negative form apparent in earlier episodes of rebellion.[122] A preceding tradition of protest had exhibited what has been called for a later period 'spurious radicalism'.[123] Paradoxically, members of the gentry were attacked for not acting as gentlemen. This was a tradition that attacked both parvenue landowners for their disregard of the obligations gentlemen were expected to recognize in their relations with their tenants, and members of the 'old' landed classes for their abandonment of the supposed duties of 'good lordship' in the pursuit of estate improvement. Within this tradition crowds demonstrated an ability to secure the legitimation for their actions that a culture of obedience proscribing 'riot' made advisable by appropriating the official transcript of the gentry's publicly proclaimed self-definition. In 1642 stigmatisation of a section of the landed class by Parliament offered a licence for the August attacks, allowing some to settle private scores and others to express their hostility towards the privilege and power of the landed classes. But they were allowed to do so only within the dominant discourse that confined attacks to those – proto-royalists and papists – that Parliamentary policy and puritan preaching rendered legitimate targets.

[122] Thompson, 'English society', pp. 133–65; Wrightson, 'Social order', pp. 198; R. Hilton, *Bond Men Made Free: Medieval Peasant Movements and the English Rising of 1381* (1973), pp. 96, 220.
[123] H. Newby, *The Deferential Worker* (Harmondsworth, 1979), p. 398.

A little over two weeks after the original attacks, D'Ewes was writing of 'the rude multitude in divers counties [who] tooke advantage by these civill and intestine broils to plunder & pillage the Houses of the Nobilitie, gentrie & others who weere either knowen Papists or being protestants had sent or provided horses, monie or plate to send to the King, or such as being rich they would make malignant that soe they might have some couler to robb & spoile them.' Those who have argued for the reality of class conflict have made much of the fact that the crowds, as reported by D'Ewes, attacked 'both protestants and Papists'. These reports of attacks across the confessional spectrum perhaps lie behind historians' use of the Stour Valley episode as the example of 'hostility to the gentry as a class'. Drawing on the account by Arthur Wilson, Dr Sharpe writes that, 'rioting in 1642 showed ugly signs of developing from an attack on leading royalists to an attack on their social superiors in general'.[124] But ministers aside (and the crowds clearly doubted their devotion to the protestant faith), the only protestants for whom we have any evidence of their being attacked are Sir John Lucas, his brother and Sir Robert Crane (though in the case of the latter all we have is a report – again from Arthur Wilson – of his needing to retain a trained band in his house to protect him from threats made against him for helping the Countess of Rivers to escape.) D'Ewes's claim that the crowds attacked 'such as being rich they would make malignant that soe they might have some couler to robb & spoile them' finds little support in the evidence of those attacked.

Where accounts of the role of class conflict in the August attacks do not depend on the evidence provided by the fears (some might say fantasies) of elite commentators, there is a danger that they run the risk of offering an economically reductionist and essentialist reading of the determinants of the crowds' consciousness and actions. At their crudest they see the poverty of the clothworkers as sufficient evidence of those interests and reason for their actions or they assume, rather than demonstrate, that those caught up in the attacks were pursuing their class interests. While the pattern of collective political action in which clothworkers engaged before 1642 might be largely driven by crisis, the clothworkers' actions in 1642 can be neither adequately explained by patterns of conflict *within* the trade nor, despite their relative poverty, can they be reduced to those of economic automata.

If we are to attempt to read events to recover the meaning of, and

---

[124] BL, Harleian MS 163, fols. 324–5; Underdown, *Revel*, p. 169; Sharpe, *Crime*, p. 208. See also Robin Clifton's judgement: 'as the disturbances spread however they broadened in character into a general onslaught upon all gentry, protestant or catholic, Parliament or royalist': 'Fear of catholics', p. 229.

motives for, the crowds' actions then we need to pay more attention to the specificity of the crowds' targets in 1642. That the crowds attacked only proto-royalists and papists might be taken as yet another example of the plebeian crowd's opportunistic ability to exploit the divisions of high politics and the agenda of the 'official transcript' to license a settling of their own scores. But this would seem unduly reductionist. Early modern crowds were capable of articulating a more complex political consciousness. That the clothworkers' tradition of collective action frequently asserted a claim to take direct action in spheres outside the trade to remedy their distress has obvious parallels with 1642. From 1640 to 1642 a region defined by the presence of the cloth industry had experienced a double and interrelated crisis. The failure of Crown and Parliament to secure political settlement had created political instability. In turn, political instability had led to economic crisis. That the causes of political and economic crisis came to be seen at a popular level as identical is central to explaining the events of the summer of 1642. We need to take more seriously the crowds' own report of their actions and what a reading of the shape of those actions has to say in support of such statements. The dominant discourse informing the crowds' actions was that of anti-popery. Anti-popery provided a clear analysis of popular grievances in the region and a programme of action for their remedy. For the clothworkers and others of the poorer sort the structurings of class may have conditioned their understanding of the discourse, but the political significance of the actions of the crowds in 1642 should not be reduced to that alone. August 1642 at last saw the 'hot summer' that had been predicted in the earlier sedition, but it was a rise in the political temperature that brought it about. In 1642 the enemies of the people were the enemies of the state.

8. *Anti-popery and popular Parliamentarianism*

Amid these events the trade of this City and the kingdom is stopping altogether. The ordinary course of all trade has been interrupted and those who obtain their daily food by the work of their hands alone are reduced to the limits of despair. *These ignorant people, persuaded by those who profit from trouble, that these calamities proceed from the presence of the bishops and catholic lords in Parliament, have appeared more than once at the Houses of Parliament this week, and tumultuously demanded the exclusion of the bishops and of the catholic lords also, and that the goods of both shall be distributed for the relief of their present needs, otherwise they threaten orally and in writing that necessity will compel them to take more violent measures ...*

The Venetian Ambassador to the Doge and Senate, 14 February 1641/[2][1]

The Eastern Counties, Suffolk, Norfolk, and *Cambridgeshire* ... were happily kept from the beginning without any great combustion, though it were certain that many of the chief Gentry in those counties, bended in their affections to the King's Commission of *Array*: but they were not a part strong enough to engage their Countries in a War: For the Free-holders and Yeomen in general adhered to the Parliament: and those Gentlemen who attempted to raise men, or draw Forces together, or provide Arms for the King were soon curbed, and all their endeavours crushed at the beginning by those of the other side.

Thomas May, *The History of the Parliament of England which began on November the 3rd MDCXL* (1647)[2]

---

[1] *CSPV 1640–1642*, p. 291 (text in italics originally in cypher).
[2] Bk 2, ch. 6, p. 108.

1. The Command of the Parliament. 2. The Example of all Godly
and powerful Ministers. 3. The Motion of God's spirit in all God's
people, provoking them with one minde, to undertake the same
businesse.

A group of Parliament's soldiers in answer to the
question of what justified their taking up arms.[3]

When Arthur Wilson came to reflect on his experiences in the August of
1642, he concluded of the attack on the Countess of Rivers, 'she being a
recusant they made that their pretence but spoile and plunder was their
ayme'. His account, written some years later in the midst of a world
turned upside down by the unwelcome, and by then radical, intervention
of the people into politics, reflected the contempt of the seventeenth-
century gentleman for his plebeian inferiors – 'the Mouth' as Wilson
revealingly termed them. As we have seen, historians' later accounts of
the event share something of this interpretation. Thus Norah Carlin
writes, 'there were anxious moments, however, especially in Essex when
the Colchester mob acquired a taste for ransacking country houses and
seemed disinclined to draw the line at royalist country houses.'[4] In part,
this coincidence is not surprising given that the main sources that many
later accounts have drawn on are precisely the 'narratives' of Arthur
Wilson and *Mercurius Rusticus*.

But there is a deeper level of convergence. Consciously or unconsciously, most see the popular role to be explained by external pressures
determining their behaviour. Few allow an active agency to the crowds in
terms of a political role – hence, perhaps, Carlin's surprising use of the
pejorative 'mob'. As a general survey of popular protest in the seventeenth century by Buchanan Sharp could pronounce, the riots 'had much
more to do with the depressed state of the New Drapery and the chronic
poverty of the clothworkers than it did with what one historian argues
was a popular, pro-Parliamentarian sentiment'. This is (regrettably) still
a popular mode of analysing crowd actions which does not see the need
for an explanation beyond economic distress. While Clive Holmes
recognises that some of the attackers claimed to have acted in support of
Parliament, he writes of 'the element of class conflict in the August riots
... [being] partly concealed by the political and religious motivation
claimed by some of the participants ... But those present during the
riots, even Parliamentary supporters, had no illusions about "honest

---

[3] E. Simmons, *SCRIPTURE VINDICATED from the Mis-apprehensions, and Mis-applica-
tions of Mr Stephen Marshall In his Sermon Preached before the Commons House Of
Parliament* (Oxford, 1645), p. A3 v.
[4] CUL, Additional MS 33, fol. 20; Carlin, 'Marxism', p. 115.

inhabitants" with "peaceable intentions".'[5] Thus whatever the crowds themselves may have claimed, class provided the real explicandum of events. This tension within existing accounts is reflected in the ambiguity with which Brian Manning has handled the episode in his various writings on the period. Manning is the historian who has drawn most frequently on the episode and he is also the historian who is the butt of Sharp's disagreement quoted above. Writing in 1970 of the episode Manning emphasised that 'fear of papists fusing with anger over the trade depression released latent hostility to the ruling class.' In his 1976 account, where he too talks of 'mobs', the attacks were portrayed as spontaneous acts of popular resistance specifically against royalists which also revealed an underlying class edge. In his most recent account (1996) Manning, while continuing to emphasise the element of underlying class hostility, seems prepared to give more emphasis to the popular support for Parliament the attacks displayed.[6] Crowds are complex social phenomena and the tensions within existing accounts at least have the advantage of recognising this, albeit for the most part unconsciously. But in this chapter an attempt will be made to offer a reading of the crowd actions which emphasises both an active role for popular agency and which seeks to explain that role in terms of a popular Parliamentary political culture. As we have seen both the politics of distress and class had a part to play in the August attacks, but in place of the language of the riot and mob this chapter will advance – with deliberate anachronism – the idea of an active citizenry, mobilised by the politics of anti-popery and popular Parliamentarianism.

On 25 August 1642, Harbottle Grimston wrote from Colchester to Lord Viscount Fielding, that the 'unruly people' 'excuse themselves uppon a mistake'. Frustratingly, the letter ends by informing Fielding that its bearer will tell him more about this. To what does Grimston refer? It seems likely that this was a reference to a claim by the attackers to have Parliamentary authority for their actions. According to *Mercurius Rusticus*, 'some of the agents in that work, produced a printed Order of

---

[5] B. Sharp, 'Popular protest in seventeenth century England' in B. Reay (ed.), *Popular Culture in Seventeenth-Century England* (1985), p. 298; C. Holmes, *The Eastern Association in the English Civil War* (Cambridge, 1974), p. 43. Anthony Fletcher talks of the countrymen of the Stour Valley's 'unbridled enthusiasm for the cause', though he says this was mixed with 'anti-papist hysteria and political panic': 'Debate: Parliament and people in seventeenth century England', *P&P*, 98 (1983), p. 155.

[6] B. Manning, 'The outbreak of the English civil war' in R. Parry (ed.), *The English Civil War and After 1642–1658* (1970), pp. 12–16; Manning, *The English People and the English Revolution* (1976), pp. 171–80; Manning, *Aristocrats, Plebeians and Revolution in England 1640–1660* (1996), pp. 44–50.

Parliament ... by which they justified what they had done', but Sir Thomas Barrington had dismissed it as 'a false and faigned order, contrived by the malignant party to render the house [of Commons] odious'.[7] We should of course be wary of accepting Bruno Ryves' claim, since this incident provided a perfect illustration of the larger thesis structuring his narrative – that Parliament that was responsible for letting slip the 'many-headed monster'. However there is independent evidence to suggest that this incident was not an invention of Ryves' imagination. When Sir Thomas Barrington returned from Essex, he reported to the Commons that those he had met at Colchester had informed him that their actions 'had been grounded upon an order of Parliament'. Indeed, the first crowds he and Grimston had come across in the Stour Valley, had claimed 'that what they had done they did with an intent to serve the Parliament'.[8]

Events between 1640 and 1642 had certainly provided ample justi-fication for this claim. From the recall of Parliament to the outbreak of civil war represented an extraordinary period of politicisation. The proximity of Essex and Suffolk to the capital meant that their experience of this process of politicisation was more immediate and more intense. A whole network of exchanges tied Colchester and the region to London. There were weekly shipments of cloth from Colchester by sea or road to London, and as one of the major provisioners of the capital, the region sent grain, cheese and butter to London, some shipped through Col-chester, while livestock was moved on the hoof to London. The cloth trade necessitated travel to the capital by the cloth merchants controlling the trade whose regular trips made them informal letter carriers. The cloth trade, whose distribution and collection network enjoyed a formal symbiosis with the book trade, also provided a ready-made network for the distribution of the newsbooks and pamphlets pouring from the presses after 1640. The weekly movement of the carriers through the county provided an informal postal service which brought letters with news of events in London.[9] Carriers from Colchester and the other clothing towns went weekly to London on a Thursday, staying in the

---

[7] Warwickshire RO, CR 2017/C9/2; *MR*, p. 4.

[8] BL, Harleian MS 163, fols. 307 v–8. Barrington too had an interest in imposing his own reading of the motives of the attackers, in this case to calm, rather than to inflame, gentry anxieties. Both he and Grimston emphasised that the crowds had stopped immediately when told that their actions were unwelcome to Parliament and some had returned goods they had taken.

[9] For examples, see J. Thirsk (ed.), *Agrarian History of England and Wales*, iv (Cambridge, 1967), p. 572; *WP, 3, 1631–1637*, pp. 66–7; Ramsay, *English Woollen Industry*, p. 33; PRO, SP, 16/464/79; A. Searle, 'Sir Thomas Barrington in London', *ER*, 2 (1967), pt 2, p. 67. For a stimulating general discussion of the patterns of communication and the personal ties underpinning them, see A. Everitt, *Change in the Provinces: the Seventeenth*

same inns and street, and travelled back on Friday. By horse, the capital could be reached easily within less than a day. 'What news?' was the question commonly asked of those met with on the road into Colchester. Close links with London meant that what was talked about on the streets of the capital quickly became the talk of the region. For example, at Pattiswick in the cloth district of Essex, the attendance of the chief women of the parish at 'the childbed' of the wife of a local gentleman, Edward Thursbye, had been the occasion for Thursbye to pass on rumours he had heard while in London of the 'flight' of Archbishop Laud. When questioned subsequently about his source of information, he passed it off as 'what was spoken about the Towne'.[10]

The many ties between London and the communities and individuals within the region ensured that what was published, printed, said (or rumoured) in the capital quickly became known about in the region. At Colchester, Thomas Cotton, brother-in-law of Bastwick, was reported to have kept, 'some pe[e]vish intelligence in London weekly to send him the newes of the time which he usually readeth in the streets every markett daye ... about whom the zealouts thronge, as people use where Ballets are sunge'. It was a Suffolk clothier returning from the capital who had distributed pro-Scottish pamphlets among the Essex troops in the summer of 1640.[11] Litigation in the king's courts had always necessitated travel to and from London, but a trickle became a torrent as the injustices of the period of Personal Rule began to be investigated by Parliament. In the month before the attacks one particular case required 'a multitude of witnesses' drawn from the Corporation and freeburgesses of Colchester to be present for several days in the capital.[12] Super-imposed on these enduring patterns of communication were develop-ments brought about by the political crisis. The massing of troops and

Century (Occasional Papers, 2nd ser., no. 1, Dept of Local History, University of Leicester, 1972).

[10] *WP, 2, 1629–1630*, pp. 86–7, 345–6; *VCH Essex*, vol. 2, p. 284; T. S. Willan, *The English Coastal Trade 1600–1750* (Manchester, 1938), appx 2; J. Taylor, 'The Carriers' Cosmography' in A. Lang, *Social England Illustrated: A Collection of XVII Century Tracts* (Westminster, 1903), pp. 339–62; *APC 1625–1626*, p. 162; PRO, SP, 16/421/21. By 1638, Colchester had its own postmaster and the county a recognised series of stages for posthorses: *CSPD 1638–9*, pp. 137–8, 362–3.

[11] PRO, SP, 16/276/42; P. Lee Ralph, *Sir Humphrey Mildmay: Royalist Gentleman. Glimpses of the English Scene 1633–1652* (New Brunswick, 1947), p. 68; Searle, 'Barrington', p. 67; *WP, 2, 1629–1630*, pp. 86–7, 345–6; ESRO, C1/1/4; G. D. Ramsay, *The English Woollen Industry 1500–1750* (1982), p. 33; PRO, SP, 16/464/79 and 79.i; /465/4. The establishment of the post house in towns like Chelmsford and Colchester facilitated private as well as royal correspondence: *APC 1625–1626*, p. 162.

[12] HLRO, MP HL, 14 July, 28 August 1641, 30 June, 5 July 1642. Sudbury was to keep two men permanently in London in order to further its suits in Parliament: BL, Harleian MS 160, fol. 153.

the presentation of mass petitions to Parliament were but two of these that helped to accelerate the circulation of news. Less visible, but no less important, was the correspondence between the godly – like that of the puritan woodturner Nehemiah Wallington with his Essex friends or, presumably, committed Parliamentarians like John Langley with his brother-in-law, John Venn. That deponents to the destruction of Sir John Lucas's enclosures dated the action by reference to the execution of the Earl of Strafford provides a telling example of the penetration of a knowledge of political events into popular consciousness.[13]

Central to this process of politicisation was Parliament's publicisation of its actions in defence of political and religious liberties and its denunciation of those that threatened them. A Parliament seeking to call in support from below to counter the threat from above by a would-be absolutist monarchy employed a wide-range of public declarations and sought by a variety of means to disseminate these down to the level of the local community. The liberation of the printing press facilitated this, giving access to others who wished to convey a similar political message. A Parliament seeking to play up its representative role appeared to accord the people a greater role within the polity. This was paralleled by godly preaching which emphasised the role of God's people in the developing religious and political conflict.[14] From early 1642, the national public fast, ordered by Parliament to be held on the last Wednesday of each month, provided a highly charged occasion for prayers and preaching in each parish. Neither Parliament nor puritan preachers, as yet, gave a precise (or restrictive) definition to 'the people'. In the provinces, the clash of Parliamentary and royal orders inevitably prompted and promoted critical discussion. From the Parliamentary elections on, the various meetings and assemblies that response to Parliament's orders required provided the occasion for political assemblies at a local and regional level at which those gathered together might exchange news and opinions. The Essex freeholders' petition, one of a number presented to the Short Parliament in April 1640 condemning the policies of Personal Rule in Church and State and probably drawn up at the April Quarter Sessions, provided one moment of politicisation. By

---

[13] P. Seaver, *Wallington's World: A Puritan Artisan in Seventeenth-Century London* (1985), p. 191; HLRO, MP HL, 5 August 1641.

[14] *CJ*/ii/604; *Bibliotheca Lindesiana: A Bibliography of the Royal Proclamations of the Tudor and Stuart Sovereigns and Others Published Under Authority*, ed. R. R. Steele, 2 vols. (Oxford, 1910), no. 2171; Manning, *Aristocrats*, p. 74. For a rare study of preaching at the provincial level, see W. Sheils, 'Provincial preaching on the eve of the civil war: some West Riding fast sermons' in A. Fletcher and A. Roberts, *Religion, Culture and Society in Early Modern Britain: Essays in Honour of Patrick Collinson* (Cambridge, 1994), pp. 290–312.

1642 the meeting at Colchester to raise contributions on the Propositions for Parliament, which Ralph Josselin attended at the very beginning of August, was just one of a number which had taken place in the region, and probably resulted in yet another public statement of support. According to the newsbooks, Parliament in early August received letters from Colchester and other Essex towns affirming, 'that they continue resolv'd to the loss of lives and fortunes to defend the King and Parliament from all that shall endeavour to resist their lawfull proceeding'.[15] An understanding of the role this politicisation played in creating both a popular Parliamentarian political culture and a new political space for popular agency offers a deeper understanding of the politics of the crowds in the summer of 1642.

The interaction between events at the centre and the region promoted the belief that the people had a direct role to play in scotching the political threat represented by papists and, by 1642, by malignants (proto-royalists). In this, Parliamentary measures to mobilise popular support played a major role. With the approach of civil war, Parliament had moved to secure military support in the region. In Essex the execution of the Militia Ordinance was the occasion of large musters and declarations of support for Parliament. One of these, 'The humble Repromission and Resolution of the Captains and Soldiers, and other Inhabitants of the County of *Essex*', declared: 'with our Hands upon our Swords, we stand ready at your Command to perform our Vows to God, and Oaths of Fidelity to His Majesty ... and to spend our dearest blood in the Defence of the Lives and Liberties of our Countrymen'. While renewing the call for the return of the county's arms, the declaration denounced as traitors those who would support the king in a war against Parliament. This too was circulated around the county and attracted thousands of signatures (among them that of John Langley of Colchester). The surviving document makes it clear that, as in the case of the earlier January petition from the county, many parishes had had their own copies. These returns, the signatures of parishioners headed by that of the minister, hint at the process of reading and swearing to the declaration that took place locally throughout the county.[16]

[15] E. S. Cope and W. H. Coates (eds.), *Proceedings of the Short Parliament* (Camden Society, 4th ser., 19, 1977), pp. 275–6: ERO, Q/SR, 309; *Diary of John Rous*, ed. M. A. Green (Camden Society, 1856), vol. 66, pp. 12–13; ERO, Q/SBa, 2/46; *LJ*/v/290; BL, E202(33,38), *An exact and True Diurnall Of the Proceedings in Parliament, 8–15* August 1642, p. 4, 15–22 August 1642, p. 5; C. Durston, '"For The Better Humiliation of the People": public days of fasting and thanksgiving during the English Revolution', *The Seventeenth Century*, 7 (1992), pp. 129–149.

[16] *LJ*/v/141–3; 116–117; *CJ*/ii/629; HLRO, MP HL, 17 June 1642.

'The humble Repromission' contained a promise 'to stand or fall, live or die, together with you, according to our Protestation'. This was a reference to the Commons' Protestation of May 1641. The Protestation played a major role in promoting popular Parliamentarianism that has yet to be acknowledged. The same process of oath-taking at the level of the parish was central to the taking of the Protestation in the region. Originally taken by members of both Houses, subscription to the Protestation came to be required of all males over 18 years. Some 11,000 copies were printed and sent out to the parishes.[17] Taking the Protestation had begun in the region in the summer of 1641, and by February 1642 there were more organised efforts to get all men over 18 to subscribe.[18] Still too little is known of the impact of taking the Protestation.[19] But it is clear from scattered evidence that it was of major significance in fashioning a pro-Parliamentary popular political culture.

The swearing of oaths in early modern society was an act carrying with it onerous obligations. The author of *The nationall Covenant*, a pamphlet first delivered as sermons in the summer of 1641, emphasised the obligations of keeping an oath – a covenant – sworn before God and warned repeatedly that God himself would punish those who failed to honour their oath. As a printed declaration appearing at the beginning of August and appealing for support for Parliament declared, 'wee are bound by Our Protestation to defend, and woe to us if We do it not, at least to Our utmost endeavors in it, for the discharge of Our Duties, and the saving of our Soules'. That swearing the Protestation by the men of the parish (and sometimes in Essex, women and youths) took place in the parish church, that it was preceded by a sermon in which the minister was to acquaint the parish with the 'nature of the business', and that it was in places accompanied by the celebration of communion must have given an added charge to the swearing of an oath before God.[20] At the

---

[17] Gardiner (ed.), *The Constitutional Documents of the Puritan Revolution 1625–1660*, 3rd edn (Oxford, 1968), pp. 155–6; *CJ*/ii/132, 135; Steele (ed.), *Bibliotecha*, no. 1964; S. Lambert (ed.), *Printing for Parliament, 1641–1700* (List and Indexes, special ser., 20, 1984), p. 7.

[18] ESRO, FB, 19/12/2 [2]; FB, 107/A1/1, fol. 26; FB, 98/E3/1, fol. 34 v (St Clement's, 'for wrighting faire of 700 names of them that tooke the Protestation'); FBA, 213/D/1, [p. 1]; FC, 124/D2/1; FC, 130/D1/1; CRO, D/P, 171/1/1; D/P, 185/1/2; ERO, D/P, 218/1/1; D/P, 388/1/1; D/P, 296/1/1; *ER*, 25 (1916), pp. 92–4; *ibid.*, 26 (1917), p. 57. The Essex returns for Hinckford Hundred are to be found in HLRO, MP HL.

[19] D. M. Jones, 'Authority and allegiance in seventeenth-century England: the political significance of oaths and engagements' (Ph.D. diss., University of London, 1984), pp. 56–8 provides a useful starting point. I am grateful to Dr John Spurr for this reference. I am currently working on the politics of the reception and appropriation of the Protestation.

[20] C. Hill, 'From oaths to interest' in his *Society and Puritanism in Pre-revolutionary England* (1966), pp. 328–419; HLRO, MP HL, 20 February 1641/2 (certificate of taking

heart of this ceremony was the oath itself. A lengthy preamble to the oath (which was included in some of the printed versions) offered a concise reading of the recent past and the present dominated by a popish plot to undermine the protestant religion and to introduce tyrannical government. This was certainly central to the oath:

I, A. B., do in the presence of God, promise, vow and protest to maintain and defend, as far as lawfully I may with my life, power and estate, the true reformed protestant religion expressed in the doctrine of the Church of England, against all Popery and popish innovation within this realm, contrary to the said doctrine, and according to the duty of my allegiance, I will maintain and defend His Majesty's royal person and estate, as also the power and privilege of Parliaments, the lawful rights and liberties of the subjects, and every person that shall make this Protestation in what soever he shall do, in the lawful pursuance of the same; and to my power, as afar as lawfully I may, I will oppose, and by all good ways and means endeavour to bring to condign punishment all such as shall by force, practice, counsels, plots, conspiracies or otherwise do anything to the contrary in this present Protestation contained: and further, that I shall in all just and honorable ways endeavour to preserve the union and peace betwixt the three kingdoms of England, Scotland and Ireland, and neither for hope, fear or any other respects, shall relinquish this promise, vow and protestation.[21]

For Parliament itself, the Protestation came to supply 'their title to be in arms'. In the context of the early 1640s it became also an important justification for active popular participation in the work of reformation. William Bridges in sermons preached to Parliamentary volunteers at both Norwich and Yarmouth cited the Protestation as a reason for their engagement in defence of Parliament, an argument apparently repeated by Hugh Peter in his preaching. For members of the godly, like

---

Protestation at Birdbrook, Essex 'by there joyntly receiving of the Sacrament of the Lords Supper together and by the subscription of there hands'); *ibid.*, 21 February 1641/2 (Middleton, Essex); BL, E2211, *The Protestation made by The PARLIAMENT*, p. 8; BL, E170(8) *Judah's Joy at the Oath Layd Out in a Sermon on 2 Chro: 15, 15 for England's example in embracing the Parliamentary Covenant with readinesse and rejoycing* (1641); E113(3), T. Mocket, *The Nationall Covenant. Or, A Discourse on the Covenant Wherein Also the severall parts of the late PROTESTATION are proved to be grounded on Religion and Reason: With sundry Motives and Directions, tending to further our keeping Covenant with God* (1642), A1 v, pp. 1, 8, 20–22, 38; Whitby, *The Vindication of a true PROTESTANT and faithfull Servant to his Church, Daniel Whitby, Rector of Theydon-Mount in Essex from Articles exhibited against him in the Exchequer-Chamber at Westminster, By a few Schismaticall, tempestuous, illiterate needlesse People* (Oxford, 1644), pp. 8–9.

[21] Gardiner, *Documents*, pp. 155–6.

Nehemiah Wallington, the Protestation represented a covenant, a touch-stone by which to judge events in the Revolution. As the example of the man who warned Parliament about the notorious Kentish petition showed, 'being bound thereto by virtue of the Protestation', it was also a call to duty.[22] Ministers urged their parishioners, 'to have and set up a Copy of the Protestation in his owne house to minde himself so often as he goes in and out of his solemne vow and Covenant'. Thomas Mockett in his sermons on the Protestation emphasised that taking it imposed an obligation not only to reject popery but also actively to bring to justice those who opposed its terms. A document that, as in the manner of taking the Protestation prescribed for London, was to be held in the hand when swearing the oath itself became a talisman. Copies of the Protestation had been thrown into the king's coach when he had gone into the City to arrest his Parliamentary opponents; citizens who later came to Westminster Hall to protect Parliament wore copies of the Protestation or fixed them to their ensign, musket or the top of their pikes, 'hanging like a little square banner'; petitioners from Kent rode through the streets of London with copies in their hats and belts.[23]

As these examples suggest, an oath to defend Church, King and Parliament 'against all Popery and popish innovation' was popularly used to justify popular interventions in the political process. The pamphlet ENGLAND'S OATHS *Taken by all men of Quallity in the Church and Common-wealth of* ENGLAND, published by a minister 'for the Satisfaction of his Parishioners' provocatively printed the Protestation with the (equally anti-catholic) oaths of Allegiance and Supremacy. Pamphlets and sermons recognised the promise and problems in this reading of the oath. While in the hands of a Henry Burton it could become a charter for radical change, others struggled to reconcile the enthusiasm the oath could provoke with a culture of obedience in which reform should be left to the godly magistrate.[24] 'This *Protestation* gives

---

[22] C. Russell, *The Fall of the British Monarchies 1637–1642* (Oxford, 1991), pp. 295, 451; BL, E89(7), W. Bridge, *A SERMON Preached unto the Volunteers of the City of NORWICH and also to the Voluntiers of Great YARMOUTH in NORFOLK* (1643), p. 12; Brenner, *Merchants and Revolution: Commercial Change, Political Conflict, and London Overseas Trade, 1550–1653*, pp. 444–5; Seaver, *Wallington's World*, p. 147; LJ/iv/675.

[23] BL, E2211 *The Protestation*, p. 8; *PJ*, 1, pp. 17, 39; Seaver, *Wallington's World*, p. 151; Mocket, *Nationall Covenant*, pp. 22–3.

[24] Mocket, *Nationall Covenant*, pp. 17, 18, 19; BL, E127(36), *ENGLANDS OATHS Taken by all men of Quallity in the Church and Common-wealth of ENGLAND. The Oath of Supremacie. The Oath of Allegiance AND The late Protestation*; BL, E158(14), *The Protestation Protested: OR, A short Remonstrance, shewing what is principally required of all those that have or doe take the last Parliamentary PROTESTATION* (1641); BL, E164(4), *A Survay of That Foolish, Seditious, Scandalous, Prophane LIBELL, THE PROTESTATION PROTESTED* (1641); BL, E170(9), J. Geree, *Vindiciae Voti. Or a*

men no leave to breake their Ranks, it puts not a sword of authority into every private man's hand', declared the minister John Geree, an opinion echoed by Thomas Mocket in his sermons. But that is precisely what it was taken to do. The potential of the oath with its charge against popish innovation to legitimise independent popular action is brought out in the example of popular iconoclasts. At one London church a parishioner on the day of taking the Protestation told his fellow parishioners, 'Gentlemen we have heare made a protestation before Almighty god against all popery and popish Inovac[i]ons, and these railes ... are popish Inovac[i]ons, and therefore it is fitt they be pulled downe'. Thereafter, some youths 'w[hi]ch had taken the p[ro]testac[i]on' pulled down the rails. Similarly, at Norwich one of the apprentices who in February 1642 threatened to pull down the rails and organ in the cathedral, told the Dean and Chapter that, 'the Rayles, and Pipes, and other Innovations, was against the Protestation, and he had sworne against all Innovations and he would pull them downe where-ever he saw them, for so he was bound to doe by the Protestation that he had taken'. John Geree's exposition of the Protestation was written precisely to combat those who cited the oath in justification of their iconoclasm. Indeed, the appropriation of the Protestation was widespread enough to be listed by the author of the pamphlet, *Certaine Affirmations in defence of the pulling down of Communion Rails, by divers rash and misguided people, judiciously and religiously answered*, as one of the iconoclasts' prime justifications: 'Wee are bound by the last Protestation against Innovations'.[25]

There is evidence that such appropriations took place in the area of the attacks. Thomas Harvey, a weaver from Ralph Josselin's parish of Earls Colne, was accused of stealing and mutilating the Book of Common Prayer. Brought to court, he declared 'that it did not repent him that he had so done ffor since he had taken the protestac[i]on he could not sleep quietly till he had done the same'. According to *Mercurius Rusticus* those of Dr Michaelson's parishioners at Chelmsford who had tried to strip him of the surplice he was wearing had cried out against him, 'as a Perjurd Person that had violated his faith ingaged in the Protestation, to abolish Popery, of which (in their opinion) wearing the Surplesse was a part'. At Radwinter, there was disorder in the church when parishioners

Vindication of the True Sense of the Nationall Covenant, in a brief and moderate Answere to the Protestation Protested (1641).
[25] HLRO, MP HL, 30 June 1641; BL, E140(17), T. L., *True News from Norwich, being a certaine Relation that the Cathedrall Blades of Norwich (on the 22. of February. 1641 being Shrove-tuesday, did put them into a posture of defence, because that the Apprentices of Norwich (as they imagined) would have pulled down their organs*, p. 6; Geree, *Vindiciae Voti*, sig. A2r, B3, C3r, D2; BL, E164(4), pp. 4, 12; Mocket, *Nationall Covenant*, pp. 19–20; BL, E171[1], p. 4.

attempted to have the sign of the cross omitted at baptism on the basis of their subscription to the Protestation. The example of John Browning, Lord Maynard's Arminian minister at Much Easton who found himself summoned to the Commons to answer for saying *inter alia* that the canons of the church were as good as the Protestation suggest that he too may have faced parishioners who sought to use the oath to legitimise their opposition to innovations. In Suffolk, a man who laid information against a neighbouring villager for seditious utterances against Parliament did so in the belief that he was bound 'in conscience' by the Protestation so to do.[26]

Appropriation of the Protestation in these ways was not just the result of popular initiative. It was almost a natural outgrowth from the uses to which Parliament and preachers had sought to put the oath. Less than three weeks before the August attacks the Lords and Commons had issued a declaration which appeared in several printed forms. In justifying Parliament's call to arms to defend king, Parliament, liberties and true religion, this concluded: 'all which every honest man is bound to defend; especially those who have taken the late Protestation, By which they are more particularly tyed unto it and the more answerable before God, should they neglect it.' Printed copies of this declaration must have been reaching the region even closer to the period of the attacks.[27] Parliamentary declarations, godly preaching and individual conscience combined to underwrite the duties the Protestation imposed. It may be more than coincidence that the sermon Stephen Marshall preached before the Commons at the very time the Protestation was being taken in the region took as its text Judges 5.23: 'Curse ye Meroz', a curse delivered by the Angel of the Lord against those who, in Marshall's words, *came not out to the helpe of the Lord*. Clearly, an oath which required the swearer to 'oppose, and by all good ways and means endeavour to bring condign punishment all such as shall by force, practice, counsels, plots, conspiracies or otherwise do anything to the contrary in this present Protestation contained' could legitimise attacks on individuals as well as on idols.

By the summer of 1642 Parliament was devoting much effort to countering the threat posed by 'malignants' and 'delinquents', as supporters of the king were labelled. In July it had condemned as traitors and

---

[26] ERO, Q/SBa, 2/43, unfol. (Exam. Thos. Harvey, 3 Sept. 1641); *MR*, p. 19; Bodl. Lib., Rawlinson MS D158, fol. 43 v; Steele (ed.), *Bibliotheca*, no. 1964, p. 238; *CJ*/ii/408; *PJ*, 1, pp. 241, 304; Bodl. Lib., MS Walker C5, fol. 106; BL, Additional MS 5829, fol. 57; Harleian MS 160, fol. 153; HLRO, MP HL, 6 October 1642 (Info. Sam. Crossman). Harvey's act of defiance so shocked the king's supporters among the JPs that they made his case the centrepiece of their petition to the king: Leicestershire RO, DE 221/13/2/21.

[27] BL, E1451.

disturbers of the peace those who sought to raise forces under the king's Commission of Array, it had ordered its declarations against the commission printed and read at the Assizes, and had called upon local authorities to use the power of the county to apprehend and disarm those who sought to raise forces under the commission. These developments had reached a peak in August 1642. Less than a week before the attacks Parliament had once again condemned those who sought to assist the king with his military preparations as traitors, had ordered their apprehension and disarming – again with the assistance of the power of the county – and had called for them to be sent up to Parliament for punishment. Printed as a single sheet, the London bookseller George Thomason dated receipt of his copy as 19 August.[28] This order with its declaration that those who sought to 'assist his majesty in this War with Horse, Arms, Plate, or Money, are Traitors' and its demand that they should be brought before Parliament could be taken as a direct invitation for the attack on Sir John Lucas, a man who as we have seen had been suspected as early as June of trying to send arms and ammunition to the king and whose plate, intended for the king at York, had been stayed in early July. It is most likely that this was the 'printed Order of Parliament ... by which they [the attackers] justified what they had done' – in Grimston's words (but scarcely theirs, surely) 'excused themselves'. But as we have seen there were other candidates. As the attacks began in the region the House of Commons was drawing up an order promising 'that all such well-affected Persons as shall employ themselves in putting this Ordinance [to apprehend those acting in support of the Commission of Array] in Execution, should do an acceptable Service to the State, and shall be defended and protected therein by the Authority of both Houses'.[29] As the Venetian Ambassador reported (on the day after the attack on Lucas), Parliament:

> has given permission by proclamation to any official, constable or other private person to collect men, to arm and to attack those whom they know to be followers of the king's commands and who do not co-operate in the designs of the Parliament, which has left it perfectly open to any one to vent their private grudges under this pretext ... Even now many houses in the country and in this city have been

---

[28] Bodl. Lib., Tanner MS 63, fol. 101; CUL, Additional MS 90, fol. 138 r; BL, E238(20), *A Declaration of the Lords and Commons assembled in Parliament upon the Statute of 5 H.4, whereby the Commission of Array is supposed to be warranted* (1642); *CJ*/ii/681, 682, 711, 719; *LJ*/v/297, 303–4; Steele (ed.), *Bibliotheca*, no. 2247, p. 271; *CJ*/ii/615, 705; BL, 669, f5(70).

[29] *CJ*/ii/732.

violated, sacked and destroyed all together, and murmurings and outcries are heard in every direction.[30]

It was not just that Parliament's orders might be taken to licence popular initiative. Parliamentary propaganda deliberately sought to mobilise popular action against royalists. According to a newsbook published a week before the attack on Sir John Lucas, MPs had been ordered to send into the country to require the return of the names of all those who dared to publish royal proclamations, an action prompted by an attempt to read the Commission of Array in Essex's neighbouring county of Hertfordshire. As the king complained, Parliament had sought 'to raise an implacable hatred between the Gentry and Commonalty ... by infusing into them that there was an intention by the Commission of Array to take away part of their Estates from them'.[31] This had clearly been the intention of a pamphlet, dated 23 August 1642, whose title page declared *A MEMENTO For Yeomen, Merchants, Citizens, And all the COMMONS in ENGLAND: Who, if the Lo. PAULET (according to his unchristianlike Speeches at Wells, with his faction) gain a cruell Victory, are like to suffer from the high trade of Merchandise, to the humble estate of Manuall Labour.* This short pamphlet ended by informing its readers:

> That it shall be lawfull for any of his Majesties Subjects to disarme all Popish recusants, to seize upon the persons of all such as shall Execute the Illegal Commission of Array, or shall be actors and assistants in any of the aforementioned oppressions and violences, or shall furnish any Horse, Arms, Money or other Aids or Contribution for the Maintenance of this unnaturall War Raised by his Majestie against His Parliament: And to seize upon the Horses, Arms, Money, and other Provisions whereby they might be enabled to disturbe the Peace of the Kingdom.[32]

According to the Countess of Rivers, some of her tenants justified their refusal to pay rents to her after the attack by reference to 'some generall Ordinances for seising of estates'. In the spring of 1642 printed copies had been published of the Commons' order against catholic landlords who exploited their protestant tenants.[33]

Parliament's orders were given widespread circulation. They were printed for circulation, reported in the newsbooks, and published from the pulpit and judicial bench. Within the region of the attacks, the Suffolk minister, John Rous, provides a good example of how quickly

---

[30] *CSPV 1642–1643*, pp. 130–1.
[31] J. Raymond, *Making the News: An Anthology of Newsbooks of Revolutionary England* (Moreton-in-the-Marsh, 1993), p. 64; Husbands, *Exact Collection* (1643), p. 649.
[32] BL, E113(13), p. 8.
[33] HLRO, MP HL, 9 September 1642; Clifton, 'Fear of Catholics', p. 325.

knowledge could be gained of them, Rous noting in his diary the orders against those who supported the king.[34] Two episodes during the attacks in Essex suggest how these orders might be popularly perceived. Since the first comes from the pen of Bruno Ryves it needs to be read with caution. Erasmus Laud, one of the victims of the Colchester crowds, indicted several of his attackers, but the trial jury refused to find them guilty of felony. Challenged over their verdict by the justices, they answered that they did not think 'plundering ... to be felony by the Law', two particularly obstinate jurors insisting, 'that they were a malignant's goods, and the Parliament had given power to plunder such'. The words may be Ryves, but the sentiments they express seem sufficiently close to what we know was happening to command credibility. Again, when John Wenlock, who was rumoured to have a 'great store of Armes', was threatened with having his house pulled down and his goods taken away, he recorded his would-be 'Riflers' telling him, 'they had an order so to do, because I would lend no money to the Parliament.'[35] A similar process of popular licence derived from Parliamentary pronouncements may help to explain the attacks in the region on the clergy. Parliament's denunciation of those clergy whom it labelled scandalous and malignant may have constituted an act of delegitimisation that helped to legitimise the attacks. Edward Symmons, the minister at Rayne in Essex, who had been summoned to appear before the Commons and who was released only just before the start of the attacks, was to have been one of the crowds' victims. 'Behold what it is to be voted a Delinquent, or a scandalous Minister by the Committee; it is to be put out of the protection of the Law, and exposed to the fury of the people', was Bruno Ryves' comment. Symmons was not in the end attacked and Ryves' comment clearly served his purpose of fixing Parliament with the blame for the disorders, but the episode offers a glimpse of the process of labelling that could license attacks on individual ministers.[36]

There is evidence from elsewhere at about the time of the attacks of Parliament's pronouncements being seized upon to license popular actions. Earlier in August attempts had been made to enter Lord Cottington's house (and to plunder it, his servants alleged) at Hanworth in Middlesex by a crowd armed with a warrant from the Speaker of the Commons to prevent arms going to the king at York. The Earl of Dorset

---

[34] *Diary*, p. 120.
[35] *MR*, p. 23; *Humble declaration of John Wenlock*, p. 24. In October the Commons had declared that those who would not contribute to the defence of the commonwealth should be disarmed and secured: *CJ*/ii/808.
[36] *MR*, p. 14.

may have suffered a similar fate.[37] On 19 August Sir Simonds D'Ewes reported the Speaker as informing the Commons that the general warrants to search for arms (of which he had granted upwards of a hundred):

> were soe abused as noe man almost could bee in safety, for they searched what houses they listed under colour to search for armes or mony ... and afterwards if they saw a house well furnished though it were of never soe honest a protestant and a well wisher to the Parliament they would say hee was a malignant p[er]son and soe gett his house to bee rifled.[38]

It is surely significant that before the August attacks Parliament had been expressing similar anxieties about such a situation occurring in Essex. On 17 August the Commons had instructed the Essex MPs to write to the county's JPs 'to punish such as have or shall pillage any House of any Inhabitant in that county'.[39]

If then, as Barrington and Grimston reported, those who attacked Lucas did so in the belief that Parliamentary declarations legitimised their initiative, they could have been forgiven for so thinking.[40] A string of Parliamentary pronouncements stigmatising as malignants those who sought to support the king in civil war and calling for their detection and apprehension had been intended to secure support. The gatherings of the well-affected in Essex in June 1642 had condemned those who supported the Commission of Array as traitors and had promised, hands upon swords, to defend Parliament against them. Thus, when news leaked out that Sir John Lucas was proposing to carry support to the king at Nottingham, the crowds knew what to do – and believed they had Parliament's authority for so doing. It may have helped to confirm them in the rightness of their actions that the same newsbooks that carried reports of Parliament's declarations against malignants also carried reports of popular actions in other parts of the country against those seeking to implement the Commission of Array.[41] Sir Thomas Barrington clearly had a vested interest in representing the attackers in a favourable

---

[37] HLRO, MP HL, 15 August 1642; HMC Cowper MSS, vol. 2, pp. 321–2.

[38] BL, Harleian MS 163, fol. 295 v.

[39] CJ/ii/725. The context of this order suggests that it was disorder by the troops in the county that here concerned Parliament.

[40] Prof. Hunt's reference to the 'myth of a licence to rebel from some higher authority' and to the '*pretence* of legitimacy' (my emphasis) in the attacks seems insufficiently sensitive to the politics of early modern crowd actions. The claim of pretence relies on his reading of the hostile testimony of a victim of the December attacks: *Puritan Moment*, p. 304.

[41] BL, E113(18), *Special Passages from divers parts of the kingdom*, 16–23 August 1642, p. 12. If, as seems likely, *Mercurius Rusticus* was right about the Colchester crowds producing a printed order of Parliament, then it may have been a copy of the order to prevent arms going to the king.

light, but his report that the crowds returned the plundered goods on learning that they did not have Parliamentary authority might be taken to add weight to the argument for a strand of political motivation in the attacks. A similar belief in the legitimacy of popular action was to be found on the other side of the Stour Valley. From Sudbury a letter writer was reported as having said that the crowds plundered the houses of 'not onely Papists, but protestants, alleadging them to be persons disaffected to the Parliament'. If true, the identity of those 'protestants' remains unknown. Sir Robert Crane was said to have been menaced for his attempt to aid the Countess of Rivers, but the appearance of his name on not one, but two Commissions of Array for Suffolk might suggest that if he did attract the attention of the crowds there were grounds to entertain doubts about the strength of his allegiance to Parliament.[42]

It was not surprising that after dealing with Lucas the crowds should go on to attack catholic families. Nor that they should feel legitimised in so doing. The discourse of a popish plot was central to Parliamentary political culture. This represented the period of the 1630s to the present as a plot to capture the king, corrupt his Court, cancel Parliament and catholicise the church. In its key documents, Parliament had given considerable publicity to the reality of this subversive popish plot. The Protestation directly attributed the threat to protestantism and to Parliament to the designs of priests, Jesuits and other adherents of Rome. The Grand Remonstrance of December, 1641 contained an even more richly detailed exposition of the ambitions of the popish party. It constructed a history of the Personal Rule of the 1630s and more recent times which must have been familiar to many in Essex and Suffolk, attributing as it did the threat to religious and political liberties to a conspiracy of catholics aided and abetted by the Arminian party.[43] (Ironically, royal proclamations which sought to gain support by demonstrating that the king was equally concerned to see the laws put into effect against catholics lent weight to the belief that popery was on the increase and that the authorities had been 'too remisse' in failing to put laws into effect. A royal proclamation issued less than two weeks before the attacks began with a reminder that the king had ordered that the laws

---

[42] BL, E114(36), *SPECIAL PASSAGES And Certain Informations from severall places, collected for the use of all that desire to be truely informed*, 23–30 August 1642, p. 22; Northamptonshire RO, Hatton-Finch MS 133 (I am grateful to Christopher Thompson for providing me with a copy of this.)

[43] Clifton, 'Fear of Catholics', pp. 201–8; Gardiner, *Documents*, pp. 202–32; D. L. Smith, 'The root and branch petition and the Grand Remonstrance: from petition to remonstrance, in D. L. Smith, R. Strier, D. Bevington (eds.), *The Theatrical City: Culture, Theatre and Politics in London 1576–1649* (Cambridge, 1995), pp. 209–32.

against popish recusants be enforced and was issued in a version which reprinted an earlier proclamation against popish recusants.)[44] Beyond official declarations there was a constant harping on the popish conspiracy in the newsbooks and pamphlets by then appearing in large numbers. For example, the Scottish tract *Information from the Scottish Nation to all those true English*, which we know to have been distributed among the troops raised in Essex, repeatedly attacked 'Papists, Prelats and other fire-brands'. Between the Protestation and the Remonstrance the bloody outbreak of the Irish Rebellion in November 1641 offered confirmation of protestant fears. Lurid accounts of the bloody massacres of protestants by papists quickly appeared in print in large numbers. If we take the books and pamphlets collected by the London bookseller, George Thomason as representative, then by April 1642 over one-third of the output of the presses dealt with the Irish rebellion, often in highly sensationalist ways. Not surprisingly, many came to believe with Nehemiah Wallington that 'all these plots in Ireland are but one plot against England'. Beyond print culture, the circulation of libels which linked moral deviance at Court to the religious deviance of creeping popery represented a further way in which existing cultural conventions facilitated ready acceptance of the reality of a popish plot.[45]

If Parliament was successful in publicising its belief in a popish plot, it had been less successful in neutralising that threat. The period before 1640 had seen the failure of penal legislation to wipe out catholicism. Indeed developments in the 1630s, especially at Court, had encouraged the belief that toleration had permitted an increase in the catholic presence, a belief fed by the perceived confessional ambiguities of the English church in the 1630s. There were therefore repeated attempts in the Long Parliament, with MPs from the region of the attacks playing an active part,[46] to secure laws against the popish threat. There were bills to disarm catholics, to take into custody and hold hostage 'Persons of such papists, as are the Men of chiefest and greatest Quality in all Counties', and to prevent 'the Dangers that may happen by Popish

---

[44] *Stuart Royal Proclamations, 2, Royal Proclamations of King Charles I, 1625–46*, ed. J. F. Larkin (Oxford, 1983), pp. 736–7, 739–42, 763–4, 795; BL, E112(22).

[45] PRO, SP, 16/464/79.i; K. Lindley, 'The impact of the 1641 rebellion upon England and Wales, 1641–5', *Irish Historical Studies*, 18 (1972), pp. 143–76; Seaver, *Wallington's World*, p. 166; A. Bellany, '"Raylinge Rymes and Vaunting Verse": libellous politics in early Stuart England' in K. Sharpe and P. Lake (eds.), *Culture and Politics in Early Stuart England* (1994), pp. 285–310.

[46] The Essex MPs in the Commons were active in the business of trying to secure this legislation: see, for example, *CJ*/ii/24. The Earl of Warwick played a similar role in the Lords; he had been active against catholics in 1625/6 and was one of the twelve peers to present a petition against 'the great increase of popery': *CSPD 1640*, pp. 639–41, *CSPV 1640–1642*, pp. 78–9.

Recusants'[47] The Commons also sent out a stream of orders. Some were general – for catholics to leave London, for lists of catholics to be returned from the counties. Others were more specific, naming individual catholics who were to be investigated or to have their arms seized. The actions the projected legislation envisaged against catholics was well publicised, the newsbooks playing their part in giving wider publicity to the Commons' concerns to counter the catholic threat.[48] They have an obvious resonance with the shape of the crowds' actions in 1642.

Agreement as to the nature of the threat had not brought effective action by authority. A detailed list of those catholics that the Commons had wanted secured as dangerous persons in late November 1641 had included only one name for Suffolk – Sir Robert Rookewood – and none at all for Essex. In January and February action had been ordered against individual catholics in the region. But the number of houses searched – less than a handful – were insufficient to represent a serious attempt to deal with the problem. They were however sufficient to spread alarm – and perhaps to offer a model for later, popular action. That at Hengrave, home to the Countess of Rivers' sister, Lady Penelope Gage, had involved a large crowd, the breaking open of the armoury and the seizing of carts on the highway to take away the arms. Similarly, the search of the Daniells' house at Acton must have been the occasion of talk at Sudbury since it was to there that the arms seized were taken, and the search may well have been triggered in the first place by the interception in Sudbury of arms being sent to the Daniells.[49] Knowledge

[47] For the frequency of such efforts, see Clifton, 'Fear of catholics', pp. 163–88; *CJ*/ii/24, 38, 41–2, 46, 58, 85, 91, 99, 104–6, 111, 113, 115, 123, 131, 135–7, 144, 153, 157–8, 161–2, 165, 168, 171, 182–3, 193, 199, 216, 219, 223, 234, 236, 261, 263, 270–1, 273, 277–78, 302, 305, 318–9, 321, 324, 325, 327, 330–1, 333, 343, 349–50, 355, 357, 384, 387, 394, 402–4, 407, 414–5, 422, 447, 470, 472, 479, 490, 523, 526, 538, 546, 566–7, 580, 600, 606, 608, 625, 647, 718, 723, 726, 730, 733, 891; *LJ*/iv/167, 187, 197, 270, 316, 369–70, 384, 429, 445–6, 449–50; /v/307, 310, 318.

[48] For example, BL, E201(14), *Diurnal Occurrences, OR The Heads of all the Proceedings in PARLIAMENT, 7–14 February 1641* includes in the same issue a reference to a bill to disarm catholics and notice of an order to search the house of Lord Petre in Essex for arms and set a strong guard over him and his house. Cf. E201(14), *The True Diurnall Occurrances, OR The heads of the Proceedings of both HOUSES IN PARLIAMENT*, 31 January–7 February 1642; E202(38), *An Exact and True Diurnall of the Proceedings in PARLIAMENT*, 15–22 August 1642, p. 1.

[49] *LJ*/iv/449; W. H. Coates (ed.), *The Journal of Sir Simonds D'Ewes from the Beginning of the Long Parliament to the Opening of the Trial of the Earl of Stafford* (New Haven and London, 1923), p. 175n.; BL, E201(14), *Diurnall Occurrences, OR The Heads of all the Proceedings in PARLIAMENT, 7–14 Feb 1641 ... With Some Remarkable passages touching the Lord Peters*; *CJ*/ii/378, 396; CUL, Hengrave MS 88, vol. 2, nos. 149–50; BL, Harleian MS 162, fol. 324 v; *PJ*, 1, pp. 178, 328.

of Parliament's attempts to neutralise the catholic threat when set against its failure to provide effective action could only heighten anxieties.[50]

The January 1642 petition from the inhabitants of Suffolk calling, *inter alia*, for the execution of the laws against catholics had justified their petitioning with the claim, 'most of us [have] solemnly protested to maintaine the protestant Religion against all Popery'.[51] As this reference to the Protestation and Parliament's subsequent exegesis suggests, the oath to protect Church and State against the threat of popery could be taken to justify action against papists. The many parishes that took the Protestation on the fast day in February 1642, set aside to assist their protestant brethren in Ireland, experienced in the conjunction of oath and fast a provocative example of the threat that popery posed.[52] As Thomas Mocket told his listeners in a sermon preached on the occasion of taking the Protestation, 'You may be assured that whatsoever the papist and their adherents and abettours here, do or may pretend, they have the same spirit and principles, and will doe as their brethren and confederates in *Ireland* have done, if, and so soon as they have the power and opportunity.'[53] The very act of taking the Protestation had itself been an act of both inclusion and exclusion, defining membership of the local religious and moral community. Parishes which, in compliance with Parliament's orders, made a point of including in their lists of subscribers the names of catholics who had not taken the oath marked their exclusion from the community. It is perhaps not surprising that at Bulmer in Essex those so marked out ended up as victims of the crowds in the summer of 1642.[54] For some catholics their inability to take the Protestation oath rendered it a shibboleth.

Parliamentary pronouncements in the period before the attacks could be taken to offer a more precise endorsement of popular agency in action against catholics. Catholics were to be identified, seized, and disarmed. At the end of August 1641 Parliament had issued an order, subsequently printed, for 'the speedy disarming of Popish Recusants'. This had

---

[50] Clifton, 'Fear of catholics', pp. 163–88, 206–8.
[51] Bodl. Lib., Arch. G. C5, no. 59, *To the Honourable, The Knights, Citizens And Burgesses In the House of Commons in Parliament. The humble Petition of sundry of the Knights, Gentlemen, Free-holders, and other of the Inhabitants of the County of Suffolk, to the number of above 13000 presented Jan 31 1641[/2]*. I am grateful to Helen Weinstein for securing a copy of this document for me.
[52] ESRO, FBA, 213/D/1, [p.1]; J. Wilson (ed.), *Buckinghamshire Contributions for Ireland* (Bucks. Record Soc., 21, 1983), p. xii.
[53] Mocket, *Nationall Covenant*, p. 14. For a call to explore the significance of fast days as 'symbolic political ceremonies', see J. F. Wilson, *Pulpit in Parliament: Puritanism during the English Civil Wars, 1640–1648* (Princeton, 1969), p. 63.
[54] BL, E2211, *The Protestation made*; HLRO, MP HL, Protestation returns: Bulmer, Borley 20 February, Liston 23 February, Stebbing 24 February, 1641–2.

publicly acknowledged the failure of previous legislation, had attributed this to the wiles of the catholics in avoiding detection, and had broadcast the fact that 'Popish recusants have always had, and still have, and do practise, most dangerous and pernicious Designs against the Church and State'. Only a week before the attacks began, there had been yet further moves in Parliament against catholics, the newsbooks carrying reports of an order for the strict search of all recusant houses and seizure of any arms found – by force if necessary.[55]

In asserting a popular right to police the confessional boundaries of local society – a right that would be repeated in much later acts of protest[56] – the crowds might be seen only to be extending their customary role in the detection and presentation of popish recusants. In the enforcement of religious conformity, as in so many other areas of the early modern state, the courts depended upon policing from below, from the local community, for the presentation of catholics to the courts. From 1639 there had been, as we have seen, a notable quickening in the process of presentation of catholics to the courts in Essex and Suffolk, in part a response to Parliamentary directives. The steep rise in the numbers of catholics returned to the courts in Essex in the twelve months before the attacks must have both reflected and, in turn, fed fears about the menace of popery. As with the taking of the Protestation, the returns of large numbers of popish recusants to successive local courts highlighted both their presence and their partial exclusion from local society. The day after Parliament had condemned her son as 'a notorious papist' and called for his arrest, the Countess of Rivers was presented at the summer Essex Quarter Sessions as a popish recusant.[57]

Thus, in attacking catholic houses, the crowds were responding not only to fears prompted by belief in a popish plot – throughout August the notion that the king had put himself at the head of a papist army had been gaining ground – but also to the many cues that Parliament and preachers had given them. In the very week preceding the attacks orders had gone into the region to disarm catholics and confine them to their

---

[55] Stoneyhurst MSS, MSS Angliae, vo. 7, fols. 122–3; *LJ*/iv/384–7; BL, E171(14); *LJ*/v/ 307, 310, 313, 318; *CJ*/ii/729–30; BL, E239(10), *Certain speciall and remarkable passages from both Houses of Parliament*, 16–23 August 1642; E202(36), *A Perfect Diurnall of the Passages in Parliament*, 8–15 August 1642, p. 7; E202(38), *An Exact and TRUE DIURNALL of the Proceedings in PARLIAMENT*, 15–22 August 1642, p. 1; Clifton, 'Fear of catholics', p. 225.

[56] See, for example, T. Harris, *London Crowds in the Reign of Charles II: Propaganda and Politics from the Restoration until the Exclusion Crisis* (Cambridge, 1987), esp. ch. 4; G. Holmes, 'The Sacheverell Riots: the crowd and the church in early eighteenth century London', *P&P*, 72 (1976), pp. 55–85.

[57] Elliott, 'Roman catholic community', table 2, p. 48; *LJ*/v/201–2, *CJ*/ii/664; ERO, Q/SR, 317/34.

houses.[58] As the crowds were reported to have cried after the attack on Sir John Lucas, 'now they were met together, the Parliament and Country expected it of them to deale in the same manner with the Papists'. This interpretation of Parliament's stigmatising of papists was probably more widely shared. According to the well-informed catholic account of the attacks, the captains of trained bands to whom appeals were made to protect the catholic victims were reported to have said that they doubted whether Parliament would allow them to do so. Those Justices to whom the catholics made appeals for protection were said to have replied, 'it is a fearful thing to protect Papists'.[59]

If it is legitimate to read the actions of the crowds in the summer of 1642 not simply in terms of economic distress or class tensions but also in terms of the interaction between Parliamentary and popular political culture, then it remains to establish how far that political awareness penetrated. There is of course a danger in over-explaining crowd actions, in reifying crowds and their constituents as *the crowd*, and in attributing to them a common motive or single purpose. In crowds above a certain size, it may be important always to be aware of the distinction between what has been called the inner and outer crowd.[60] To this point we have been concerned with the inner crowd, that group or groups who were responsible for, and carried the ideas explaining, the crowd's initial formation and purpose. We need finally to consider how widely their motivation was shared. In these, as in other crowd actions, there were doubtless those who joined in the attacks for a variety of purposes, not all of which, and especially the personal, can be recovered by the historian. While some saw an opportunity for excitement or for revenge for personal slights, others may have been mobilised by the panic that rumour bred, though in this last case the force of rumour needs to be understood within the context of a pre-existing culture of anti-popery that gave rumour its credibility. Despite the complexity of motivation to be found within crowds, it is possible to suggest that there was a wider subscription to the politics informing the attacks.

We might begin with a reminder that the assumption that the crowds were socially homogeneous, composed only of 'rude people', needs questioning. Not the least of the problems with existing accounts of the attacks is a reductionist reading of the 'popular' that ignores important

---

[58] *LJ*/v/251–2; J. T. Evans, *Seventeenth-Century Norwich: Politics, Religion and Government 1620–1690* (Oxford, 1979), p. 123; *CJ*/ii/726.

[59] A. Fletcher, *The Outbreak of the English Civil War* (1985), p. 329; Stoneyhurst MSS, MSS Angliae, vol. 7, fols. 122–3.

[60] E. Canetti, *Crowds and Power* (Harmondsworth, 1973), pp. 16–18.

social differences (and political and religious experiences) below the level of the gentry. As we have already noted in discussing the social composition of the crowds, there is evidence that some of those involved in the attacks were drawn from those contemporaries labelled the middling sort. Thomas Wilson's reference to the presence of the better sort may be significant since this was the language by which local elites described themselves. This propertied group of farmers, traders and artisans had higher levels of literacy, were associated with the strength of puritanism in the region, and could draw on their experience of serving in the local offices of state, parish and manor. Their presence in the crowd would strengthen the argument for the interaction between Parliamentary and popular political culture. In the one case where a detailed study has been possible of the social dynamics of the conflict – the original attack on Sir John Lucas – there is plenty of evidence to support Wilson's observation that the middling sort were involved.[61] Given their numerical representation in regional society, the middling sort would always have represented but a small proportion of the crowds. But their role at Colchester suggests we should look critically at pejorative accounts of the social composition of the crowds as the 'ruder sort' which come, almost exclusively, from second-hand royalist and hostile sources.

In the absence of records identifying the attackers, we cannot know how commonly the experience of middling sort involvement at Colchester was repeated, nor exactly what proportion of the crowds were drawn from the middling sort. Nor can we be certain of the exact nature of their involvement. As the example of events at Colchester suggests it probably ran the spectrum from passive licence, through active encouragement to direct participation. Indeed, the assumption that there was a clear distinction between popular and official action needs challenging. At Sudbury, the Mayor had on his own initiative seized horse being sent between catholic households in Essex and Suffolk. In October 1642 the Commons seemingly had to authorise retrospectively the actions of a 'Mr Browne' who was operating in Essex, seizing horse and arms from local catholics.[62] Clearly, it would be a mistake to draw too clear a line between the crowds and the communities from which they were recruited, since there was a wider consensus about the nature of the threat that their victims posed. The petition to the 1642 summer Assizes in Suffolk

---

[61] CUL, Additional MS 33, fol. 20. Apart from the members of the Corporation in conflict with Lucas, there is information to suggest that the one alleged participant in the attack on Lucas for whom we have a name was from middling sort circles; this 'Mr Cater' was a member of the Corporation in the 1680s: BL, Stowe MS 835, fols. 37, 48 v.

[62] BL, Additional MS 18777, fol. 33b; *CJ*/ii/814, 833.

in the name of the chief constables, freeholders and inhabitants of Suffolk, complaining that 'our fears are much increased by the boldnesse of the Papists', originated from, and sought to represent, middling sort circles.[63] At Ipswich, where opposition to Bishop Wren's activities had produced a similar coalition between Corporation and crowd, rumours of happenings at the house of the local catholic family the Forsters had led 'the chief of Ipswich' to send men to investigate stories of a 'hidden army'. This had then been followed by crowd action. Members of the Corporation, men like Peter Fisher, Robert and Samuel Duncon, who had been active opponents of Wren and Laud (and suffered for it) and who were to be enthusiastic servants of the Parliament, would have shared the objectives of the crowds.[64] Activists like the iconoclast, anti-papist and signatory to the Essex January 1642 petition, William Dowsing, a member of the godly circle around Matthew Newcomen at Dedham, would have welcomed the defeat of the popish menace. Even members of the middling sort who disapproved in general of popular violence, may have been able to say as the London woodturner, Nehemiah Wallington, did of popular iconoclasm, 'I doe not iustifie or approve of them in this but I see a hand of providence shewing the evilnesse of our times with the neglect of Iustis.'[65]

Employing the simple polarities of middling and poorer sort runs the risk of obscuring the fact that there was no simple divide in the crowds between the propertied, literate and powerful and the property-less and illiterate. In reality, the social composition of the crowds probably reflected a more gentle gradation in levels of wealth, education and political and religious experience.

The earlier analysis of the social relations of production within the cloth industry suggests that crowds drawn from the cloth trade might reflect such a spectrum. The presence of the clothworkers offers evidence of the interrelationship between economic distress and political aware-ness in mobilising the crowds. A previous pattern of protest in which clothworkers had demonstrated the ability to combine crowd action over dearth with the presentation of petitions to the county's magistracy suggests a level of political ability that qualifies contemporary emphases on their disorder and unruliness. Indeed, it could be argued that the particular dependence of the industry on political protection and regula-

---

[63] BL, E112(9), *Two Petitions*.
[64] Foley, *Society*, vol. 2, p. 450; F. Grace, '"Schismaticall and Factious Humours": opposition in Ipswich to Laudian Church Government in the 1630s' in D. Chadd (ed.), *Religious Dissent in East Anglia 3: Proceedings of the Third Symposium* (University of East Anglia, 1996) pp. 107, 113–15; Boorman, 'Bishop Wren', pp. 34, 116; Morrill, 'Dowsing'.
[65] Morrill, 'Dowsing', pp. 175, 176–8, 183–4; BL, Additional MS 21,935, fol. 94 v.

tion would have made those involved in the cloth trade more politically aware. In the region, as in other cloth regions, the ability to protect the interests of the industry was an acknowledged factor in the selection of MPs. At the same time the greater independence of voters in 'semi-urbanised, semi-industrialised' areas was reflected both in the need to canvass their support and in their greater involvement in the electoral process.[66] The working relationship between clothiers and clothworkers would have provided the infrastructure for political discussion, economic crisis the occasion. A jaundiced Essex royalist claimed that Parliament found the clothiers, 'allwayes disposed to receive their impressions and to derive them to their workmen so that the clothiers throughout the whole kingdome were rebels by their trade'.[67] In the crisis in the trade at the end of the 1620s the clothiers had complained that 'many of them are afraid to repaire to their owne dwellings least they should bee oppressed with Multitudes of those poore people whose necessities make them very unrulie'. In the crisis of the early 1640s crowds of clothworkers again massed outside the houses of the clothiers, who reported 'the cryes of the poor for work and their curses and threats come daily to our ears'.[68] As the language of the Suffolk clothiers' petition of February 1642 makes clear, the clothiers fully subscribed to the thesis of the popish plot.

Recent work has shown that the interface between Crown patronage and the economic interests of particular industries played a prime role in determining the political allegiance of industrial workers. The royalism of the Devon tinners has been linked to the significant benefits their industry derived from the Crown's patronage and protection; the opposition of the free miners of Derbyshire and elsewhere to the royal cause has been traced to the Crown's threat to their customary rights.[69] For the cloth industry, the period of Personal Rule had been associated with a series of depressions. Its beginnings had coincided with a crisis, of which the conflict between Crown and merchants created by the contentious issue of the legality of customs impositions was a contribu-

---

[66] CRO, D/Y, 2/4, pp. 35–9; Appleton, *Cranes*, pp. 71, 75; M. Dean, *Law-Making and Society in Late Elizabethan England: The Parliament of England, 1584–1601* (Cambridge, 1996), p. 142. Cust, 'Politics' in R. Cust and A. Hughes, *Conflict in Early Stuart England: Studies in Religion and Politics 1603–1642* (1989), pp. 160–2 (clothiers featured significantly among the list of signatories on Sir Francis Barrington's election indenture); CRO, Acc. C32, Box 11/14.

[67] *TEAS*, 4, p. 210.

[68] Bodl. Lib., MS. Firth C. 4, pp. 486–7; CRO Acc. C32, Box 11/14 *Humble petition*.

[69] M. Stoyle, *Loyalty and Locality: Popular Allegiance in Devon during the English Civil War* (Exeter, 1994), pp. 156–8; A. Wood, 'Custom, identity and resistance: English free miners and their law c. 1550–1800' in P. Griffiths, A. Fox and S. Hindle (eds.), *The Experience of Authority in Early Modern England* (1996), pp. 249–85; A. Hughes, 'Local history and the origins of the civil war' in Cust and Hughes, *Conflict*, p. 242.

tory cause.[70] Successive crises had produced a series of complicated struggles over the definition of their causes and, accordingly, their solution. Clothiers blamed the merchants; merchants had blamed the trade for shoddy and fraudulent work. Clothworkers had sought to blame both merchants and the clothiers for attempts to alter conditions of employment. The Crown, frequently unable to effect positive measures and driven, Canute-like, to command clothiers and merchants to continue to purchase cloth for which there was no effective market, sought to parry local representations with the accusation that it was masterless men who pretended a lack of work who were the real instigators of disorder. The crisis of the early 1640s saw a similar struggle over definitions. Both king and Parliament sought to make political capital out of the problems in the cloth trade, both playing on the popular disorder that the political impasse threatened to coerce their opponents. Charles had sought to use the trade slump to reinforce the traditional image of the monarch as the protector of his people and – a message directed more at the gentry – the guarantor of social order. But his attempts brought no relief.[71] Neither did Parliament's. But Parliament was more successful in imposing its definition of the cause of crisis. As the Essex royalist quoted above noted in explaining the geography of support in the county, Parliament's 'constant stile was tenderness of commerce'.[72] The problems of the cloth trade had featured in some of the key Parliamentary documents of the early 1640s.[73] Parliament now

---

[70] Supple, *Commercial Crisis*, pp. 41, 55–7, 82, 103, 113–14, 121; Walter, 'Crisis of 1629'; *CSPV 1629–1632*, pp. 7–8.

[71] BL, Additional MS 39,245, fols. 53 v–4; Walter, 'Crisis of 1629', pp. 66–71. A 1638 royal commission to investigate problems in the cloth trade had reported in June 1640, but no action seems to have been taken on its recommendations which were probably lost in the midst of the developing political stalemate: *HMC, Portland MSS*, vol. 8, pp. 2–3; G. D. Ramsay, 'The Report of the Royal Commission on the Clothing Industry, 1640', *EHR*, 107 (1942), pp. 482–93; *Stuart Royal Proclamations, 2*, pp. 712–4; Supple, *Commercial Crisis*, p. 124; BL, 669f3(48), *The Clothiers Petition to his Majestie: With His Majesties gracious Answer*; *LJ*/iv/581.

[72] *TEAS*, 4, p. 210. Parliament was as unsuccessful as Charles in threatening the Merchant Adventurers' Company with the loss of their trading privileges if they failed to buy up the unsold cloth, a policy borrowed from earlier Crown practice: *LJ*/iv/237. The Commons' response to the later petitions was to set up a committee to examine the problems in the marketing of Suffolk cloths: *CJ*/ii/429.

[73] Among the grievances detailed in the Grand Remonstrance of December 1641 was the claim that religious persecution by Charles' bishops had led to clothworkers fleeing to Holland, taking with them their trade, 'which hath been a plentiful fountain of wealth and honour to this nation'. This repeated the charge of the Root and Branch petition of December 1640 which had blamed the Bishops' party for the lack of work in the cloth trade: Gardiner, *Documents*, pp. 143, 215. It was these claims that Bishop Wren sought to deny, arguing that it was the poor wages paid by the clothiers and the stop of trade that lay behind the emigration: C. Wren, *Parentalia: or, Memoirs of the Family of the Wrens* (1750), p. 101.

sought to use the economic crisis to mobilise political support. Papists, bishops and corrupt councils, it held, were responsible for the political impasse that had created economic distress and prevented the necessary measures for its relief.

This message was at the heart of the petitioning campaign in 1642. The City of London's petition of January 1642 had informed the Lords, 'there is such Decay of Trading, and such Scarcity of Money ... as it is likely in very short Time to cast innumerable Multitudes of poor Artificers into such a depth of Poverty and Extremity, as may enforce them upon some dangerous and desperate Attempts, not fit to be expressed, less to be justified ...'[74] Unless measures were put in place to reduce political tensions by disarming catholics, defeating the Irish rebellion and putting the strength of the kingdom into the hands of those trusted by Parliament, there could be no relief for 'the Miseries of so many Thousands of poor People, that otherwise threaten too plainly the Transgression of their Duties in such dangerous Ways, as may disturb the Public Peace and hazard the Honour and Safety of the King, Parliament and Kingdom.'

Petitions from the region echoed this analysis. The January 1642 petition from Essex included the ominous observation that lack of reform, 'cause[s] such decay of clothing and farming (the two trades of our County, whereby the multitudes of our people have lived) that wee tremble to thinke what may follow thereupon'. That from Colchester informed the Commons, 'we finde the trade of Clothing, and new Drapery, upon which the livelihoods of many Thousands, men, women, and children in this Towne doe depend, to be almost wholly decayed, and poverty abundantly to grow upon us'.[75] In February 1642, the clothiers of Suffolk and parts of Essex, petitioned the king that the fears of the City,

in whom the breadth of our Trade and Livelyhood consisteth, have so blasted their hopes, that the Merchants forbeare exportation; our cloths for the most part, for the space of this 18 moneths remaine upon our hands, our stocks lying dead therein, and we can maintaine our trading no longer: The cryes for food of many thousands of poore, who depend on this Trade, doe continually presse us, not w[i]thout threats, and some beginnings of mutinies: so that if some speedy reliefe doe not intervene, we can expect no lesse then confusion.[76]

---

[74] *LJ*/iv/538–9. Parliament too was concerned by the threat, setting up a committee to prevent the extraordinary concourse of people coming to Parliament: *PJ*, 2, pp. 285–8.

[75] BL, E134(13), *Three Petitions*.

[76] CRO, Acc. C32, box 11/14, *TO THE HONOURABLE THE HOUSE OF COMMONS, NOW ASSEMBLED IN PARLIAMENT The humble Petition of the Clothiers and other Inhabitants of the Countie of Suffolk, now attending this Honourable House, and of the Townes of Dedham and Langham in Essex* (1642).

What those fears were the Essex petition to the Lords made clear: 'ourselves, together with you and the whole Kingdom ... be in great Danger, from the Papists and other ill-affected Persons, who are every where very insolent, and ready to act the Parts of those savage blood-suckers in *Ireland*, if they be not speedily prevented'.[77] The petition from the county of Suffolk asked the Lords:

> to remove the Occasions of the general fears and Discontents of the Commons of this Kingdom, which your Petitioners conceive to be the principal Ground of the Stop of Trade, especially that of cloathing, upon which the Estates and Livelihoods of many Thousands do depend, who very lately, in regard of the Wants, by their Speeches and Gestures express sad Intentions of disturbing our public Peace if they be not speedily prevented.[78]

In earlier crises the clothworkers had threatened to march to the capital to make known their grievances, and some in 1629 had even flocked to Court to acquaint the king with their sufferings. So it was in 1642. In February Parliament had learned with alarm that the clothworkers were preparing to come to London in numbers – some sixteen- or seventeen-thousand it was reported from Suffolk – to petition.[79] Shortly before the August attacks, a petition from the neighbouring county of Norfolk declared that the failure to disarm and punish the catholics, 'dampeth our spirits, makes sad our hearts, takes away the life of our trading, breeds scarcenesse of money, [and] brings on such poverty as we can scarce keep the poore from mutiny'.[80]

Thus, in the first half of 1642 the clothing districts of Essex and Suffolk had found themselves facing serious economic problems, the most obvious sign of which was widespread unemployment. The region's dependence on, and proximity to, London meant that it was doubly sensitive to events in the capital. The reluctance of London merchants to take up cloths prompted by their fears of political instability quickly threatened distress in a region still recovering from earlier crises. At the same time, the region was politically open to the news and rumours originating in London. The same carts that brought back unsold cloths also brought news of the plotting of papists and their malignant allies. Those who had accompanied the petitions brought with them stories of the activities of catholics within the region and returned with tales of the

[77] *LJ*/iv/539.   [78] *LJ*/v/573.

[79] Bodl. Lib., MS Firth c4, p. 509. Parliament sent letters to towns 'where clothing was exercised to desire them not to repair to London with any numbers'. Nevertheless, the Suffolk petition was said to have been accompanied by a throng at least a thousand strong: *PJ*, 1, pp. 266, 272, 276; *CJ*, 2, 412.

[80] BL, 669f6(54), *The humble petition of many thousands of the Inhabitants of Norwich*. This was reprinted in late August of the same year: BL, E114(27).

political ferment in the capital. It was the machinations of the papists and their allies which prevented agreement between king and Parliament; the crisis of confidence produced by the lack of political settlement that explained the crisis in the cloth industry. Both politically and economically, the catholics and their allies could be seen as the cause of the nation's and the region's problems. If crowds in London 'tumultuously demanded the exclusion of the bishops and of the catholic lords also, and that the goods of both shall be distributed for the relief of their present needs', then so too could their provincial counterparts. Thus, when Sir Thomas Barrington reported from Colchester on the causes of the August attacks, he informed Parliament, that the crowds were, 'threatning to plunder all the Papists in that County, which (they conceived) was the causes of all these troubles and distractions in the Kingdome, and were the occasions that they, their wives and children were brought into great want and extremity, (by the great decay of trading) and for that they have plotted the ruine and destruction of this Kingdome.'[81] Barrington may have had his own reasons for amplifying this message, but it is clear that he reflected a deeply held popular view. When trouble flared up again in the region at the end of 1642, it was reported that:

> there are great number of unruly people that gather together, and are very hardly appeased, but would very faine plunder the Papists and malignants as being the cause of these present distractions, which stop all trading that the poorer people cannot be able to subsist, and therefore they begin to argue the case, whether in this great necessity it be not lawfull, for to take something from those that have bin the cause to deprive them of all manner of livelyhood as to perish for hunger.[82]

It is possible that clothiers confronted by angry clothworkers had a self-interested reason to encourage their workers to identify the machinations of malignants and papists as the *real* cause of their distress. John Corbet's observation that the clothworkers in Gloucestershire 'observed those men by whom those manufactures were maintained that kept them alive' suggests the potential power the clothiers had.[83] But the symbiosis thought to exist between puritanism and the cloth industry, reflected in the Essex and Suffolk clothiers' petition with its godly language or the strong support weavers as a group gave to the godly cause at Colchester,

[81] *CSPV 1640–1642*, p. 291; BL, E114(30), *A Message*, p. 2. It is of course possible that Barrington, a man whom we have seen earlier concerned about the relative inaction against catholics in Essex, used the occasion to amplify this message.

[82] BL, E242(31), *A Continuation of certaine Speciall and Remarkable Passages*, 24 November–1 December 1642, p. 6.

[83] Rollison, *Local Origins*, p. 131.

undoubtedly helped to fashion this convergence.[84] Richard Baxter emphasised that 'the middle sort of Men, especially in those Corporations and Countries which depend on clothing and such Manufactures' supported Parliament. This association was a commonplace in the contemporary political sociology of the Revolution offered by Clarendon and others.[85] Thus the clothworkers were not simply indulging their reputation for disorder in the August attacks. Their actions could be seen as an appropriate political response to the problems they faced. In 1642 the politics of the trade and Parliamentarianism coincided.

Although we know too little of individual faces in the crowd, the role of two other groups in the crowds make it possible to offer case studies which illustrate the possible social depth to political motivation. The first of these were the Parliamentary volunteers, being assembled in the region to fight for Parliament, the second the local seamen. The presence of these groups who, like the clothworkers, had a reputation for disorder provides further evidence of a strong strand of popular Parliamentarianism in the attacks.

Bruno Ryves emphasises the role played by volunteers – there were said to be some four or five hundred assembled in Colchester – in both the attacks on Lucas and on John Michaelson in Chelmsford. Confirmation of their presence comes from the well-informed account by a local catholic which specifically singles out the volunteers in both the attack on Lucas and on the Petre family. Many of the volunteers had been raised in Colchester for Lord Saye's regiment. Whilst we must be wary of Ryves' bias – 'fit souldiers for such a Leader' was his comment on the Colchester followers of Saye – the volunteers could have been expected to have had a strong leaven of politically conscious men, strongly committed to Parliament's cause. The presence of men like Roger Roberts or John Oddey, both of whom were known to have served from Colchester in Parliament's forces, would have given a stronger sense of direction to, and legitimation for, the crowds' actions. John Oddey had been among that group of young men who two

---

[84] The distinction Prof. Hunt draws between godly gentlemen and 'drunken weavers who blamed catholics for the crisis of the cloth trade' seems overdrawn: *Puritan Moment*, p. 309.

[85] R. Dean Smith, 'Social reform in an urban context: Colchester, Essex, 1570–1640' (Ph.D. thesis, University of Colorado, 1996), pp. 101, 116–7, 170–1; Byford, 'Price of Protestantism', p. 192; *Reliquiae Baxterianae*, p. 30; D. Underdown, *Revel Riot, and Rebellion: Popular Politics and Culture in England 1603–1660* (Oxford, 1985), pp. 168–70, 194–5, 203, 206–7, 276–8; Stoyle, *Loyalty and Locality*, p. 155–6, 160–1; Manning, *English People*, pp. 210–15. For a stimulating attempt to tease out the connections between clothiers, clothworkers, puritanism and Parliamentarianism, see Rollison, '"Small Thinges"'.

summers before had attempted to raise their fellows to march to the houses of nearby catholics. Roger Roberts had been involved in the earlier destruction of the Lucas enclosures. He enjoyed the nickname of Bishop Blaze. His sobriquet reflected the macabre (and analogical) humour of an early modern popular culture in which the combers had taken as their patron saint Blaze, whose martyrdom through flaying made him an apt choice for the group of workers charged with preparing the wool for spinning. But it also reflected that culture's punning creativity since Roberts, himself from a family of clothworkers, had been given his nickname 'for that not long before hee had made a speech touching Bishopps'.[86]

The role played by the second group, the seamen, in the attacks suggests that even those whom Clarendon and others might dismiss as the rabble were not necessarily divorced from participation in this political culture. Sailors were a prominent group within the economy of Colchester and other coastal towns in the region. Those involved in the attacks were variously described as sailors or mariners. The latter term, it has been suggested, usually denoted superior status, but it is doubtful whether those using these labels intended any such distinction here. Most of those who drew their living from the fishing and coastal carrying trades of the region would have been included by contemporaries among the poorer sort. Certainly, the one detailed study we have of this group for the region suggests that poverty was a very common experience. It may be important however in explaining their participation in the attacks that theirs was not the more stable poverty of the rural labouring poor. As was the case in the cloth trade, there might be both differing levels of wealth between groups within the trade and, at the same time, especially in the case of fishing, common vulnerability to violent seasonal and longer-term fluctuations bringing experience of both prosperity and poverty. Seamen in the Essex and Suffolk coastal trade were also likely to have been badly affected by the trade crisis of the early 1640s and consequent unemployment, about which their counterparts in and around London had petitioned the Lords.[87]

[86] Stoneyhurst MSS, MSS Angliae 7, fols. 122–3; *MR*, pp. 1, 20; HLRO, MP HL, 5 August 1641 (Deposition Phil. Dawson); CRO, D/Y, 2/7, p. 289; PRO, SP, 28/129, pt. 4, fols. 96 v, 105. A Robard Robards had been one of the signatories to the petition complaining of the practices of a Colchester clothier: PRO, SP, 16/354/116.

[87] Dean Smith, 'Social reform', table 1.2, p. 36; Goose, 'Tudor and Stuart Colchester: economic history', *VCH Essex*, vol. 9, pp. 84–7; K. R. Andrews, 'The Elizabethan seaman', *Mariner's Mirror*, 68 (1982), p. 256; A. R. Michell, 'The Port and town of Great Yarmouth and its economic and social relationships with its neighbours on both sides of the seas 1550–1714' (Ph.D. thesis, University of Cambridge, 1978), esp. pp. 27, 44, 52–8, 96, 114, 120, 130; *LJ*/iv/544; BL, E131(20), *The Two Petitions of the County of*

But again economic problems would provide only a partial explanation for their involvement in the attacks. For the sailors of the region also had a close association with anti-popery. In the struggles between the town of Ipswich and Bishop Wren it had been the sailors, a dominant group in the town's economy, who had played an important part in the opposition to the bishop. When Wren had sought to suspend the town's godly preachers, it had been the talk of the town that, 'the Saylers threatened [that] if Mr Scott & the rest of the minist[er]s w[hi]ch were suspended were not restored when they came home they would either knocke the Bishopps braynes out or pull his house down over his head'. According to reports circulating among the godly, it was the mariners' rude affronts that had forced Wren to give up his residence in Ipswich. Later, in the elections at Ipswich to the Long Parliament, there had been a confrontation between the sailors and the supporters of the likely Court candidate, Henry North. Significantly, the sailors were said to have been restrained only by one of the local ministers.[88]

Sailors in the period had a reputation for disorder.[89] But that the sailors' role was more than an acting-out of the disorderly reputation they enjoyed in the period, or merely an expression of the solidarities their work experience encouraged, is brought out in the statements made by them. During the 1636 disorders at Ipswich the crowd of apprentices, ship's carpenters and sailors that had besieged the bishop's house in protest against the silencing of their ministers had demanded, 'their heavenly foode in w[hi]ch Cause they would spend their blood'. More strikingly still, among the petitions the Long Parliament had received in the early months of 1642 was one from mariners and seamen of the coast of Suffolk, Norfolk and Essex. Their petition informed the Commons that, 'there is noe seamen that are papist and therefore [they] fear lest they shall suffer most by papists'. With some 2,800 signatures claimed for this petition, the very process of petitioning may have served to further the politicisation of this group.[90] Indeed, the opportunities for regular association that ports in general and the coastal trades in particular

---

Buckingham ... As also the humble Petition of the Mariners and Sea-men, Inhabitants in and about the ports of London, and the River Thames ... (1641–2).

[88] M. Reed, 'Economic structure and change in seventeenth-century Ipswich' in P. Clark (ed.), *Country Towns in Pre-Industrial England* (Leicester, 1981), pp. 102–3; ESRO, C2/18[6], fols. 17, 23; *WP, 3, 1631–1637*, p. 356; BL, Harleian MS 158, fols. 286–94 r.

[89] This was especially the case with those sailors recruited to serve in the King's Navy who faced arrears of pay, see R. Lockyer, *The Life and Political Career of George Villiers, First Duke of Buckingham 1592–1628* (1984), pp. 286, 340–4, 361–2, 420–1, 447–8, 452–3.

[90] ESRO, C2/18(2); *PJ*, 1, pp. 362, 365; *CJ*/ii/428; BL, Additional MS 21,935, fol. 173.

allowed may have permitted, as has been argued for a later period, a greater degree of political discussion.[91]

As the Ipswich petition suggests the sailors' particular vulnerability to foreign catholic powers helped to sharpen their anti-popery. A petition from their London counterparts had spoken of their 'sad experience by their Travels in Forreigne parts, [of] what evils and miseries, that religion ... [has] brought forth'. The sailors' anti-popery was doubtless also linked to their historic role in the defence of England against the popish threat of the Spanish Armada in 1588, something which was celebrated in popular ballads and which linked them to the anti-popery of the Parliamentary and later navies. Certainly, their identity as traditional defenders of the realm against popish powers encouraged an identification with the Parliamentary cause. As *The SEA-MAN'S PROTESTA-TION Renewed, Confirmed and Enlarged* declared, 'Wo be to England when there is no Parliament'. This little pamphlet was issued as a justification for the sailors' role in the defence of Parliament in the dark days of January 1642 ('to the terrour we hope of all Papists') and for their participation in a civil war against an army of 'atheists and papists'. Since the pamphlet is without an author, its provenance remains uncertain, its title page declaring only that it was ordered to be published by the Vice-Admiral. But even if it did not originate from among the sailors themselves, the image it seeks to fashion for the sailors confirms their anti-popery and asserts their godliness: 'although we have no Churches, we make our prayers as well as you, and the same God you have at shore is ours at sea'. Citing 1588, the seamen declare that, 'for our Religion, King, and Country, we do and will advance our Colours against the world'. Defence of the country at sea was advanced to justify their actions on land. Once again, as the title suggests, it was the Protestation from which the sailors drew justification for their actions. The text of the oath the pamphlet included, though closely modelled in form and content on the Protestation, employed its own language, promising 'before Almighty God to maintain with my dearest life and blood, the *protestant Religion* as it was established in the dayes of Queen *Elizabeth*, ... [to acknowledge the king] ... stand for the Privileges of *Parliament*: [and] urtely [utterly] from my heart to abhor all *Poperie* and Popish innovations. *So help me God.*'[92]

---

[91] Karel Davids, 'Seamen's organizations and social protest in Europe *c.* 1300–1825' in C. Lis, J. Lucassen and H. Soly (eds.), *Before the Unions: Wage Earners and Collective Action in Europe, 1300–1800* (*International Review of Social History*, Supplement 2, n.d.), p. 366.

[92] *The SEA-MAN'S PROTESTATION Renewed, Confirmed, and Enlarged. THE FIRST Concerning their Ebbing and Flowing to and from the Parliament House at Westminster,*

This image of the sailor as the godly defender of Parliament was likely to have found a sympathetic echo among the sailors of the east coast. Sailors from the region involved in the important coastal traffic of coal had a reputation for their godliness; the Mayor of Newcastle had complained in 1639 of 'the Ipswich puritans [who] have so wrought with the ship-men' that he had been unable to load coal for six weeks.[93] Their anti-popery owed a good deal to the godly preaching of preachers like Samuel Ward in Ipswich and William Bridges in Yarmouth, whom we have encountered preaching fiercely anti-popish sermons and appealing to the Protestation. By November 1642, if not earlier, three hundred mariners were serving as volunteers at Ipswich, offering a further example in support of the argument of Conrad Russell that preaching played a decisive role in assembling volunteers from towns for Parliament. It may be significant that it was two Ipswich sailors who stood surety for the shoemaker of that town accused of threatening to plunder Henry Dade, the hated agent there of Laud and Wren.[94] Thus the presence of sailors in the attacks can be explained in part by their role in protecting and policing confessional boundaries. As *The SEA-MAN'S PROTESTATION* proudly boasted, they had sworn to protect, 'that which *Rome* with all her curses shall not blast ... the firm establishing of our *protestant Religion*: in defence of which chiefly, we display our Colours on the seas, and expose each drop of bloud we have'.[95]

The example of the sailors suggests that anti-popery aligned to the support of Parliament could be found more generally at a popular level within the region. Anti-popery, with its protestant reading of England's past and its annual celebrations of deliverance, had come to be a major strand within a developing national political culture. Subscription to an anti-popish discourse was particularly marked among the godly, for whom it has been seen as a defining characteristic of their confessional

---

the 11th of January 1642 THE Latter, As the Cause and Matters, now stand (1643). Thomason dates his acquisition of a copy to 9 May.

[93] *CSPD 1639*, p. 157.

[94] C. Russell, *The Causes of the English Civil War* (Oxford, 1990), pp. 21–2; ESRO, C8/4/7 [3 March 1642–3].

[95] BL, E131(20), *Humble Petition of the Mariners*; *PJ*, 1, p. 362; *CJ*/ii/p. 428; *LJ*/iv/544; ESRO, C2/18, fols. 14, 23; BL, Additional MS 18777, fol. 73a; C. H. Firth (ed.), *Naval Songs and Ballads* (Publications of the Navy Records Society, 33, 1908), pp. xix–xx, 18–24, 34–6; B. Capp, *Cromwell's Navy: The Fleet and the English Revolution 1648–1660* (Oxford, 1989), pp. 286, 301; M. Rediker, *Between the Devil and the Deep Blue Sea* (Cambridge, 1987), p. 173. For links between Bridges' gathered congregation and the Parliamentary fleet, see Capp, *Cromwell's Navy*, p. 304. For the role of seamen in support of the Parliamentary cause in Devon and suggestions for this association, see Stoyle, *Loyalty and Locality*, pp. 89–91, 158.

identity. But the emphasis on the popish plot might also be expected to have appealed to a larger constituency than the 'godly' within the region since, as Robin Clifton has argued, anti-popery provided the basic language of political analysis in a popular political culture with, as we have seen in Colchester and elsewhere, regular reminders of the black legend of popery. The godly reputation of the region, the close association between puritanism and groups like the clothworkers (of which the Job-quoting comber cited at the head of chapter 7 may stand as an example), and the region's particular experience of the Arminian counter-revolution gave anti-popery here added purchase. Paul Seaver's masterly reconstruction of the political world of Nehemiah Wallington, a humble woodturner, offers rare detail of how popular belief in the reality of a popish plot could become the master key to deciphering political events. At the popular level, as well as at the level of godly minister and magistrate, developments in the 1630s had been interpreted through the political lens of popery.[96] The idiom of anti-popery had provided a popular vocabulary for the articulation of protest. Within the region altar rails had been derided as 'pillars of popery', the vestment as 'rags of Rome', the prayer book as 'a Popish book' and 'the invencion of the pope of Rome'. Services conducted by Arminian ceremonialists had been met with the taunt of 'are you at mass again', parishioners attending them with a scoffing inquiry as to whether they were going to say mass or a few paternosters, ministers with the accusation of 'Popish Priest'.[97]

There was a ready acceptance of the theory of a popish plot in a region which had a reputation for godliness and where, as we have seen, anti-popery was marked. Petitions originating in the region were heavily laced with the language of anti-popery. In January 1642 there were petitions to Parliament from both Essex and Suffolk and their leading towns. That from the county of Suffolk, said to be subscribed by some thirteen or fourteen thousand hands, called for the removal of popish lords and bishops from the House of Lords. The petitioners complained that their continuing presence in the Parliament was, with 'the not execution of Laws against the Papists', the reason for the crop of plots and conspiracies, of which they saw evidence in the Irish Rebellion. Petitions from Essex, two from the county and one from Colchester, also attacked the insolencies of papists and called for their disarming. One from the county told the Commons that we conceive 'ourselves togeather with you and the whole Kingdome to be in great danger from ye Papists and other ill affected persons whoe are everie where very insolent and ready to act the

---

[96] Clifton, 'Antipopery', p. 55; Seaver, *Wallington's World*, ch. 6, esp. pp. 165–8; Clifton, 'Fear of catholics', p. 55.
[97] See above. Whitby, *Vindication*, p. 1.

parts of those savage bloud-suckers in Ireland if they bee not speedily prevented.'[98] The petitions were part of a larger petitioning campaign whose purpose was to secure the enactment of measures to disarm catholics, punish malignants, put the kingdom in a state of defence and to expel from the Lords the bishops and popish lords whose continued presence there was thought to be the main obstacle to agreement between King and Parliament.[99] The synchronicity and similarity of the petitions might suggest that such petitions to Parliament originated not in the provinces, but at the centre.[100] If this was the case (and we need to know much more about the process of petitioning before accepting that it was), it does not mean that the Essex and Suffolk petitioners themselves did not readily subscribe to the position advanced. Anti-popish panics had continued to flare up in the region after the earlier scares at Colchester.[101]

If the petitioners were responding to cues, they were responding to cues with considerable local resonance, and in doing so they were continuing their own earlier campaign of petitioning.[102] The particular inflections of their petitions and their specific list of demands reflect how the godly of the region had experienced the period of Personal Rule. That from Suffolk recalled their former petitions against Bishop Wren and scandalous ministers, while that from Colchester expressed the desires of a godly city for further reformation of the church and attacked the Book of Common Prayer, something for which the petitioners found themselves strongly criticised by some MPs. The petition of the clothiers

---

[98] HLRO, MP HL, 20 January 1641/2; BL, E134(13), *Three Petitions, The One, Of the Inhabitants of the Towne of Colchester: The other Two, Of the County of Essex*; *CJ*/ii/ 387; *LJ*/iv/523.

[99] For this petitioning campaign, see the valuable analysis in Fletcher, *Outbreak*, pp. 191–227. For the expression of these demands see, for example, the London petitions: *PJ*, 1, 228–32, 235–6; HLRO, MP HL, 1 February 1642 ('The humble petition of many poore distressed women in and about London'); BL, 669f4(54), *The humble Petition of many thousand poore people, in and about the Citie of London*; BL, 669f4(55), *The humble Petition of 15000 poore labouring men, known by the name of Porters, and the lowest members of the Citie of London*; *LJ*/iv/575 (10 February 1642, Northamptonshire); G. W. Johnson, *Memorials of the Reign of Charles I*, 2 vols (1848), vol. 2, pp. 367–72 (February 1642, Yorkshire).

[100] This seems certainly to have been the case with the petitions of March and April 1640 from the Essex and Suffolk freeholders where the language of the petitions was almost totally identical: Cope and Coates (eds.), *Short Parliament*, pp. 275–6; Bodl. Lib., Tanner MS 67, no. 69, fol. 174.

[101] BL, Additional MS, 21,935, fol. 187; J. Nalson, *An Impartial Collection of the Great Affairs of State*, 2 vols (1683), vol. 2, pp. 661–2; BL, E179(10), *Bloody Newes from Norwich, OR a True Relation of a bloody attempt of the Papists in Norwich, to consume the whole City by fire* (1641), an account which yokes Norwich's experience with an account of the atrocities in the rebellion in Ireland.

[102] For earlier petitions originating from the region, the first in November 1640 coinciding with the calling of the Long Parliament, see: *CJ*/ii/25, 54–5; ESRO, C6/1/5; Notestein (ed.), *Journal D'Ewes*, pp. 249, 258, 283, 415 and n.

of Suffolk with those of Dedham and Langham in Essex, delivered in February 1642, expressed anger that 'the service of God and his day is prophaned, many souls endangered even to hell, by a multitude of ignorant idle Drunken, leud, and prophane Ministers'. It called upon Parliament 'to settle the worship of God in a purer way', to see the order against images in churches 'scandalous and offensive to the people' fully executed, and Monday markets, which caused the Lord's day to be much abused, 'inhibited'.[103] The ideological intensity and strong godly flavour make it clear that this was no petition drawn up in London. Indeed the reference to Dedham in the title suggests that someone like Matthew Newcomen, the godly preacher there and strong anti-papist, may have had a hand in its penning. Anti-popery lay at the heart of this petition too. The clothiers, having informed the House that they were 'still lying under a weight of pressing inconveniences', went on to identify the causes, which arose:

> principally from the great fears that do afflict the hearts of his Majesties subjects, especially in the Honourable City of *London*, the very fountain of our Trades, and livelyhood, by reason of the great distractions and distempers in matters of Religion and Church-government. The boldness of Jesuits, Priests, and other malicious Adversaries, out-daring the most severe Lawes, presuming upon the lenity of this State, which hitherto they have enjoyed to God's great dishonour, and danger of our Religion: Their hellish rage against our brethren in *Ireland*, their threats and daily plottings against our persons, religion, peace and liberties . . .[104]

Suggestions that the impetus for the petitioning campaign may have originated at the centre miss the point that, whatever their origin, the petitions both reflected and shaped political consciousness in the region, serving to educate and extend support. The drawing up of the petitions and their circulation for signature provided a further point of politicisation. This was certainly the case with the petition of January 1642 from the county of Essex, the signed copy of which still survives. On its presentation to Parliament, 30,000 were said to have signed the Essex petition. Signatures were sought parish by parish from communities assembled in church, and in a process in which both minister and pulpit were important it is not difficult to imagine to what use ministers like Stephen Marshall, whose signature heads the return from Finchingfield, would have put the occasion.[105] A similar process must have been

---

[103] Bodl. Lib., Arch. G. C5, no. 59; *PJ*, 1, pp. 122–6, 227–8, 230–1, 235–6; *CJ*/ii/404; BL, E132(20), *The Foure Petitions of Huntingdonshire, Norfolk, Suffolk and Essex*.

[104] *Humble Petition of the Clothiers*; *PJ*, 1, p. 333.

[105] T. Webster, *Stephen Marshall and Finchingfield* (Studies in Essex History, 6, Chelms-

necessary to secure signatures for the Suffolk county petition. Large crowds – 'mightie multitudes' – also accompanied the petitions to London. The Essex January petitions declared on their title page that the petitions had been 'brought by many Thousands of the County of Essex'. That from the Suffolk clothiers was delivered by a large crowd, 'a thousand and better comming with them'. As we have seen, it might easily have been more. Upon 'information that some 16,000 clothiers and others are coming out of Suffolk', the House had had to send letters via the Suffolk MPs to the towns 'where clothing was exercised to desire them not to repair to London with any numbers'.[106]

That the petitions might both express and shape popular perceptions is brought out by the incident that took place in Colchester around the time of the town's petition to Parliament of January 1642. When Robert Meawes, a weaver, recalled an exchange that took place on the town's streets between him and one George Rayment, he dated its occurrence by reference to the king's attempted arrest of the Five Members (perhaps the original subject of the exchange). In the course of the argument Rayment had declared that, 'none did partake with the Parliament but puritanly Rogues and round heads', to which Meawes the weaver had retorted in a direct echo of the language of the petition that it was not puritans and roundheads who troubled the kingdom, but 'the Byshopps and Papists'.[107]

While the evidence of the petitions confirms a widespread subscription to a belief in the existence of a popish plot, it also reflected anxiety that little had been done within the region to meet that threat. We have already encountered Sir Thomas Barrington complaining from Essex in

ford, 1994). The original petition is to be found in the House of Lords Record Office, HLRO, MP HL, 20 January 1641/2. There is brief discussion of the document in Holmes, *Eastern Association*, pp. 26 and 245 n. Later depositions against John Mow, curate at Great Bardfield and a strong supporter of the king, show that the petition was the subject of discussion in the parishes. Mow was alleged to have said, 'they were all forsworn which subscribed the Petition for voting the Popish Lords out of the House': Smith, *Ecclesiastical History*, p. 141.

[106] A. Kingston, *East Anglia and the Great Civil War* (1897), p. 31; BL, E134(13), *Three Petitions; The one of the inhabitants of the town of Colchester: the other two of the county of Essex* (1642); *PJ*, 1, p. 123; BL, E201(11), *The Diurnal Occurrances in PARLIA-MENT from the 17. of Jan. to the 24*, p. 3; E201(16), *Diurnal of Occurrences OR The Heads of the Proceedings in both Houses of PARLIAMENT*, 7–14 February 1641[/2], A3; E201(14), *Diurnal Occurrences, OR The Heads of all the Proceedings in PARLIA-MENT*, 7–14 February 1641[/2]; *PJ*, 1, pp. 266, 331–3; CJ/11/412, 423. The Commons were told that 'there came a 1000 horsemen' to deliver the Suffolk petition; if true, this would suggest, in a society where horse ownership was a mark of social status, a strong middling-sort presence.

[107] CRO, D/B5, Sb2/7, fol. 306. On examination, he dated the exchange from reference to the king's attempt to arrest the five members in the House of Commons (4 January 1641/2).

the summer of 1641, 'of a strange tepidity, full of needless scruples, in the execution of that brave ordinance of both Houses for the disarming of Papists'.[108] The petition from 'sundry of the Knights, Gentlemen, Free-holders, and other of the Inhabitants' of the county of Suffolk protested at,

> the not execution of Laws against the Papists (who notwithstanding through the providence of God, have been discovered in many of their treacherous plots against the King and State) they & their adherents are still emboldened in the mischievous plots and conspiracies, a lamentable experience of whose treasons and bloody cruelties we heare is daily presented to this Honourable Assembly from Ireland.[109]

Thus a constant theme in the petitions from early 1642 on was the continuing threat that the papists posed and the petitioners' consequent need to defend themselves. The Suffolk petitioners declared themselves, 'greatly distracted and full of fears of some sudden & cruell design to break out ... which puts us into an unsettled condition'. The petition from the Corporation and inhabitants of Ipswich, where rumours of local catholics arming had led the town's rulers to send men to investigate, highlighted the threat from Ireland 'and the encouragement from the Popish partie here, the number, libertie, power and boldnesse of the Papists and their partie'. Fearing rumours of great preparations abroad, they called for the kingdom to be put in a posture of defence and the 'Papists disabled from doing mischief, and the Laws put in execution against them'. Colchester called for the fortification of the town, the county of Essex for the strengthening of Languard fort which had been allowed to fall into decay, the clothiers of Essex and Suffolk for the repair of 'our Forts'. Even small communities were taking steps to arm themselves, the cloth township of Braintree purchasing six muskets for the defence of the town in early February 1642. Earlier panics about threatened invasions had shown the region's particular sense of vulner-ability. In the case of Essex the failure to return or make good the county's arms which had been taken for the Scottish war was a running grievance and left the county feeling even more vulnerable. A further petition from Colchester for its fortification was received by the Commons on the same day as the attack on Sir John Lucas.[110]

---

[108] Yale University, Beinecke Library, Osborne Collection, Barrington to Lord Howard, 24 July 1641; *LJ*/v/201–2; *CJ*/ii/664.

[109] Bodl. Lib., Bod. Arch. G. C5, no. 59: *Humble Petition Suffolke*.

[110] BL, E135(35), *The Humble Petitions of The Bailiffs, portmen and other the Inhabitants of Ipswich in the County of Suffolke* (1642); HLRO, MP HL, 20 January 1642; *PJ*, 1, p. 126; CRO, Acc. C32 Box 11/14; *The Maynard Lieutenancy Book, 1608–1639*, ed. B. W. Quintrell (Essex Record Office, Essex Historical Documents, no. 3, 2 vols., 1993), vol. 1, pp. 82–90; *CSPD 1638–1639*, p. 494; ERO, Q/SR, 313/34; *ibid.*, D/P, 264/8/3,

In response to Parliament's bidding and the orders of the county's magistracy, local communities had continued to return with growing frequency and in greater numbers the names of popish recusants. But the demands of the Suffolk petitioners, 'to disarm and confine Recusants, and that the Laws against them may be fully executed' remained unanswered. From Norfolk at the beginning of August it was reported 'that the papists there ... who lately expressed much fear began now again to grow confident'. Only a few weeks before the attacks petitions in both Essex and Suffolk to the summer Assizes continued to raise the spectre of the catholic menace. 'O[u]r ffeares are much increased by the bouldnesse of the Papists and other p[er]sons ill affected to the publique peace', declared the pro-Parliamentary petition presented at the Suffolk Assizes. Ironically, the charge with which the king required the judges to open proceedings (itself in print by late July) had also raised the spectre of popery, placing first the need 'to suppresse Popery ... by putting the Lawes made against them in due execution', a theme echoed in the 'loyal' petitions presented by the Suffolk Grand Jury and the proto-royalists among the Essex magistracy and Grand Jury.[111] Thus, in the very summer of the attacks the Assizes provided a further forum for politicisation. Indeed, what those present at these important meetings in the political and social life of the counties heard would have encouraged them to assume that there was political agreement on the need to do something about the catholic threat.

Godly preaching, to which Clarendon gave a direct role in causing popular attacks on the gentry, served as another point for the wider dissemination of anti-popery. It set the Laudian counter-revolution within the context of a broader conspiracy by a popish party to destroy both political and religious liberties. It too contributed to the fashioning of an active role for the people. Parishioners at Ipswich were reported to have heard preached, 'that they were to fighte for the puritie of the Gospell and the liberty of their Ministers, and that then was the tyme of fighting, now that Superstition and Idolatry were thrust upon them'. Throughout the 1630s the 5th of November had provided a point within the popular calendar for ministers to remind their parishioners of the popish threat. The service books for that day set out a service which reminded parishioners of the papists' 'blood-thirstie malice' and required

fol. 132 v; *LJ*/v/126, 141–3; *CJ*/ii/730. In presenting the Colchester petition, Harbottle Grimston, stressed the need to defend the exposed coast against the threat of foreign invasion of which there was much talk: BL, E200(14), *Mr Grimston His Speech in Parliament: On Wednesday the 19th of January, Upon the Preferring of the Essex Petition, AD 1641–2*, p. 5.

[111] *LJ*/v/573; *PJ*, 3, pp. 274–5; Bodl. Lib., Bankes MS 52, fol. 60; Bankes MS 56, fols. 10–11; MS Rawlinson Essex 10, fol. 79; Tanner MS 63, fols. 1–2; BL, E108(7).

them to pray to God, 'to root them out of the confines and limits of the kingdome'. By the later 1630s, they also provided for a sermon. After the recall of Parliament, 5 November continued to provide an occasion both for popular celebration and, as at Ipswich in 1641, godly sermons.[112]

Preachers intent on recruiting support for Parliament in the face of the coming conflict, like Ralph Josselin at Earls Colne, who for 'affection to god and his gospell ... endeavoured publike promoting' of the cause, or Stephen Marshall who was said to have preached often out of his own parish, necessarily offered an activist message. Godly preaching, like that of Thomas Hooker at Chelmsford in the 1620s, 'burdened each individual with the spiritual responsibility for the course of history'. Whatever his own intentions, Stephen Marshall's language in his sermon *Meroz Cursed*, first preached first before Parliament in February 1642 and thereafter on some sixty occasions, was capable of being taken to underwrite popular agency. That the Parliamentary soldiers quoted at the head of this chapter cited his sermon as one of the reasons why they took to arms confirms that it did. As Marshall preached, 'all people are cursed or blessed according as they doe or doe not joyne their strength and give their best assistance to the Lords people against their enemies'.

'It is no new thing to finde the Mighty in strength, the Mighty in authority, the Mighty in wealth, the Mighty in parts, in Learning, in Counsell, to engage all against the Lord, his Church and Cause. The Lambe's followers and servants are often the poore and off-scouring of the World ... when the mighty of the World do oppose the *Lord*, God's *meanest servants* must not be afraid to oppose the *Mighty*', Marshall had declared. As a libel set up at the entrance to Parliament had declared, 'the voice of God was the cry of the people'. It is easy to see how this might be taken in the anxious days of the summer of 1642. The London woodturner Nehemiah Wallington himself noting the text observed that its message was that God's curse was 'because they came not out to help the Lord, to help the Lord against the mighty'.[113] Such preaching

---

[112] Edward Hyde, Earl of Clarendon, *The History of the Rebellion And Civil Wars in England Begun in the year 1641*, ed. W. D. Macray, 6 vols. (Oxford, 1888), p. 319; ESRO, C2/18, fol. 14; *PRAYERS AND THANKSGIVING To be used by all the Kings Majesties Subjects, For the happy deliverance of His MAJESTIE, the QUEEN, PRINCE and STATES of the PARLIAMENT, From the most Traiterous and Bloody intended Massacre by Gun-powder, the fifth of November 1605* (1638). This appears to have been identical to earlier editions of the service book, but is it significant that the one earlier edition I have been able to examine, that for 1630 (CUL, Syn. 7.63.377) omits the provision for a sermon?

[113] G. H. Williams (ed.), *Thomas Hooker: Writings in England and Holland, 1626–1633* (Harvard, 1975), p. 51; BL, E133(19), S. Marshall, *Meroz Cursed, OR A SERMON PREACHED to the Honourable House of COMMONS* (1641[/2]), pp. 8, 9; Webster, *Marshall*, pp. 4, 5, 17, 18; P. Collinson, *The Birthpangs of Protestant England: Religious*

doubtless helped to encourage the godly of the region to believe, with their London counterpart Nehemiah Wallington, that since the struggle between God and Antichrist was conducted through human agency that they were 'under a special Covenant' (language that he and others used precisely to describe the Protestation) which demanded action of them. Wallington himself was convinced that this apocalyptic struggle had reached a new intensity by the summer of 1642, and it was precisely in the activities of papists and malignants that he saw evidence of this. To judge from the complaint of the Suffolk minister, Lionel Gatford, *Meroz Cursed* was a popular text among Parliamentarian preachers in the region. So too, he claimed, was David's words in 1 *Chronicles* 22.16: 'Arise and be doing'. This was a text that was even more appropriate for mobilising support for Parliament. That it was so used is suggested by Gatsford's retort: '*Arise and be doing*? What I beseech him? ... I am afraid *God's house* is not so well beloved of him; no, rather arise and be pulling down *God's house*, or arise and be plundering thy neighbour's house'.[114] The Shelley man who had predicted that 'they would rise in the Country' and pull down the houses of those 'that tooke part with the Bishopps' had cited *Jeremiah* 22.6–7, 'And I will prepare destroyers against thee ...' It was godly preaching, as Professor Hunt has argued, that helped to forge the 'puritan moment' out of which the attacks came.[115]

Where puritan providentialist preaching reflected aspects of the popular mentality it might command acceptance beyond the immediate ranks of the godly. There is a history of the 1630s, yet to be written, in terms of a providentialist politics. To unravel the conflict over the interpretation of the providential judgements of God plunges us into the semiotics of the weather, war and plague. This is unfamiliar territory within standard political histories of the decade. But for the godly, happenings within these spheres were 'sermons written in the daily events of human affairs'. For example, one sermon at a christening ceremony in Coggeshall pointed to the persistence of plague in the county and went on to argue that when judgements are in a land, 'we must search out ye

and Cultural Change in the Sixteenth and Seventeenth Centuries (1988), p. 127; Russell, *Fall British Monarchy*, p. 342; CRO, D/P 103/5/4, CRO, D/B5, GB 3, fol. 219 v; ESRO, FB, A91/E1/1; C9/2(2), fol. 447; Macfarlane (ed.), *Diary*, p. 12; *SCRIPTURE VINDICATED*, A3–A4 r, pp. 86; Seaver, *Wallington's World*, p. 166. The example of William Dowsing's reading suggests that printed copies of the sermons before Parliament were quickly received within the region: Morrill, 'Dowsing', p. 181.

114 Seaver, *Wallington's World*, pp. 175, 147, 166–77; BL, E113(3), Mocket, *National Covenant* (1642); Sheils, 'Provincial preaching'; BL, E94(1), L. Gatford, *An Exhortation to Peace: With an Intimation of the prime Enemies thereof* (1643), p. 23. For another example of the use of the Meroz text, see Smith, *Ecclesiastical History*, p. 177.

115 PRO, SP, 16/468/139; Hunt, *Puritan Moment*, pp. 279–310.

true cause, to witt o[u]r Altars and such superstitious Adorations and bowing at names and such Idolatrous mixtures of religion and ye treading downe of God's people & until these causes be removed ye Plague will not cease'. In another sermon there in early November 1635, the minister was reported to have said, that 'he thought in his Conscience yt ye plague of God was in ye land for ye new mixtures of religion yt is commanded in ye churches'. William Prynne in his pamphlet *Newes from Ipswich*, circulating in the region in the later 1630s, also attributed the plague to the suppression of godly preaching. Laud's order prescribing a weekly fast had ordered that where sermons were allowed they should last no longer than an hour. Writing to John Winthrop from Suffolk in 1637, Robert Reyce, who had earlier complained of the failure to order a fast in the face of the plague, informed him that the troubles brought the almanac makers by their too curious predictions had forced them silently to 'leave all presages to the evente of every season'. Nevertheless many had noted the 'sondry strange alterations this laste yeere now paste', something which Reyce himself linked to the incidence of plague and others to the threat to the harvest by unseasonable weather. Fasts were important occasions within the political culture of the godly. In 1636 the minister at Leigh was in trouble for holding a day-long fast for the cessation of pestilence and for seasonable rain. These examples probably provide glimpses of practices and beliefs that were more widespread through the region. According to the informant against the minister at Leighs such fasts were common throughout Rochford Hundred, which was the heartland of the Earl of Warwick's power within Essex.[116] It was precisely against this reading of the weather that Laud, as Bishop of London, had declared famously earlier in the decade that, 'this last year's famine was made by man and not by God'. Within Essex itself at least

---

[116] S. Hardman Moore, 'Popery, purity and providence: deciphering the New England experiment' in A. Fletcher and A. Roberts (eds.), *Religion, Culture and Society in Early Modern Britain: Essays in Honour of Patrick Collinson* (Cambridge, 1994), pp. 257–89; Seaver, *Wallington's World*, pp. 154, 157, 160; PRO, SP, 16/350/54; T. Webster, 'The godly of Goshen scattered: an Essex clerical conference in the 1620s and its diaspora' (Ph.D. thesis, University of Cambridge, 1993); *Collections of the Massachusetts Historical Society*, 4th ser., 6 (Boston, 1863), pp. 407–8, 410; *A Forme of Common Prayer Together with an order of fasting: for the averting of God's heavie Visitation upon many places of this Kingdome* (1636); *WP, 3, 1631–1637*, p. 401; Matthew White [William Prynne], *NEWES FROM IPSWICH*, A2 r–v; Williams (ed.), *Hooker: Writings*, p. 80; Whitby, *Vindication*, p. 34; *CSPD 1636–1637*, p. 29, *ibid.*, *1637*, p. 260; Durston, 'Public days of fasting'; P. Collinson, 'Elizabethan and Jacobean Puritanism as forms of popular religious culture' in C. Durston and J. Eales (eds.), *Culture of English Puritanism* (1996), pp. 50–56. For evidence of the potentialities of providentialist preaching in the context of the French Wars of Religion, see B. B. Diefendorf, *Beneath the Cross: Catholics and Huguenots in Sixteenth-Century Paris* (New York, 1991), pp. 150ff.

one conformist minister felt the need to combat this doctrine of judgements by attributing the plague to murmurings against the prayer book. Amongst the godly of the region then unseasonable weather was interpreted as an unfavourable judgement on policies and events in the 1630s. But the 'politics of weather' could have been expected to have resonances beyond the ranks of the godly in a popular culture in which reading the weather for its extra meteorological significance remained important and in an economy whose heartbeat was the harvest. Here perhaps was another example of what has been called, 'the rough and irregular interface between clerically prescribed Calvinist religiosity and the mentality of sections of lay society awkwardly, if not improperly, aligned with the godly elite'.[117] The logical action prescribed by this providentialist politics was of course the need to purify the community of the polluting presence of those persons and practices which offended God.

Finally, at a more basic level anti-popery and rumour in a region where the very name of the Pope appears to have taken on a sexual connotation could of itself mobilise even the least politically literate.[118] Local elites were perhaps not above using anti-popery to attract wider support. Where, as at Chelmsford in February 1642, the money collected for the fast was distributed among the poor, an echo of the practice in some Essex parishes of distributing money to the poor on 5 November, the occasion could be made to deliver a complex message of inclusion and exclusion around the themes of protestantism, poverty and anti-popery. A later, hostile, report claimed that when the Earl of Warwick and Sir Thomas Barrington had been 'sent into Essex to raise the Country, [they had] told the people in publick meetings, that the Queene was landed with an Army of 13000 Papists'.[119] But the power of anti-popery did not rest on elite patronage. Its force is brought out by the experiences of Henry Forster of Copdock, victim in 1642, whose family lived close – too close – to the godly centre of Ipswich.

What stories were not raised against him? of armies underground which he had trained up in his court by night; of I know not how many cooks, who after having dressed and served in a vast number of oxen,

[117] S. R. Gardiner (ed.), *Reports of Cases in the Court of Star Chamber and High Commission* (Camden Society, 1886), pp. 43–9; A. Walsham, '"The Fatall Vesper": providentialism and anti-popery in late Jacobean London', *P&P*, 144 (1994), pp. 36–87.

[118] See the case of an Essex man before the church courts for thrusting his hand beneath the sheets of a woman's bed and saying, 'he would not come to Rome but he would see the Pope': Bodl. Lib., MS Eng. Lang. e6, fol. 2.

[119] ERO, D/P, 94/5/1, fol. 327v; *Persecutio Undecima. The CHURCHES Eleventh Persecution* (1648). This may refer to June 1642, but Christopher Thompson in a personal communication has suggested a later date.

and not so much as a bone coming out again for them to pick, all quitted his house and service; and the maid of the parson of the next parish was said to have taken her oath that she saw a cart load of bright armour enter our great gate, which vain and false report gained even so much upon sober men, that three nights together our house was beset by men sent by the chief of Ipswich for to discover the hidden army, etc., but the rabble of Ipswich was so incensed thereby, that they could scarce be kept from gathering into a head to come and pull our house down over our heads, lest we should cut their throats with the hidden army ... [120]

This rare and vivid glimpse of the fears that were circulating in the region shortly before the attacks reveals the explosive nature of popular anti-popery. As Peter Lake has suggested, 'while the anti-popish spasm lasted, the most committed protestants were offered an opportunity to lead bodies of opinion far broader than those normally deemed Puritan'. The Essex royalist, Sir Humphrey Mildmay, who on 5 November 1642 recorded in his diary that all the household were at home '& in all fears', knew the threat that day posed. [121]

Robin Clifton, the historian of anti-popish panics in the first half of the seventeenth century, has argued that, 'the marked sense of legitimacy which informed their [officials'] actions – deriving from Statutes, Proclamations and Privy Council instructions – could also inspire direct action by the lower classes'. [122] Events in Essex and Suffolk in the summer of 1642 appear to provide a perfect illustration of the validity of his argument, if we add Parliamentary declarations to his list of legitimising documents. Instructions issued by Parliament to the Essex authorities a little over a month after the attacks began offered confirmation of the crowds' reading of Parliament's intent: the authorities were to suppress any attempt to raise the Commission of Array, search and seize horse, money and plate from any they suspected of being malignants, and disarm both popish recusants and clergy. [123]

Before the events of August 1642, Parliament's propaganda battle with

---

[120] Foley, *Society*, 2, p. 450.
[121] P. Lake, 'Anti-popery: the structure of a prejudice' in Cust and Hughes, *Conflict*, p. 83; BL, Harleian MS 454, fol. 54 v. According to a (possibly malicious) newsbook account the crowds who opposed the Marquis of Hertford's attempt to raise the Commission of Array did not know who they were to fight against, other than 'supposing they were Papists': J. Wroughton, *A Community at War: the Civil War in Bath and North Somerset 1642–1650* (Bath, 1992), p. 88.
[122] Clifton, 'Fear of catholics', pp. 50–1.
[123] BL, E121(1), *Instructions Agreed upon by the Lords & Commons assembled in Parliament* (5 October 1642), pp. 1–4, 8–9.

the king had seen the development of a critique that had identified papists and, increasingly, malignants (*scire* pro-royalist clergy and gentry) as the authors of a plot to prevent king and people reaching agreement and to subvert both law and religion, if necessary by force of arms. Intent on securing support, and increasingly nervous of their ability to do so given the radical measures to which the king's intransigence put them, Parliament had gone to great lengths to ensure the widest publicity for its pronouncements. To this end, they exploited both print and oral culture. The politicisation of the pulpit, of which we can catch only glimpses in the published sermons of preachers in the region like Stephen Marshall and Matthew Newcomen, offered a powerful reinforcement of the belief in the reality of the threat posed by the popish plot. It was this against which Clarendon complained when he wrote of those preachers, 'who under the notion of reformation and extirpating of Popery, infused seditious inclinations into the hearts of men against the present government of the Church, with many libellous invectives against the State too.'[124] Finally, propaganda, print and pulpit carried an invitation to the people to participate in the work of protecting and promoting the programme of reformation in Church and State. This had not been intended as an invitation to independent action. However, as popular appropriation of the Protestation shows it could be read to be. Parliament's Declaration of 2 August arguing the duties laid on its supporters by their taking of the Protestation oath had gone on to list the enemies of the programme of reformation who were threatening civil war. It had identified a coalition of 'Papists, an ambitious and discontented Clergy, Delinquents obnoxious to the Justice of Parliament, and some ill-affected Persons of the Nobility and Gentry'.[125] This reads like a hit list for the attacks that began less than three weeks later. In the light of all this it does not seem surprising that Sir Thomas Barrington and Harbottle Grimston should have 'found great Multitudes of People assembled together, upon ... a Declaration set forth by both Houses'.[126] Bruno Ryves' interpolation that the crowds' grounds for thinking themselves legitimised to take action were false offers a poor guide to the rich process of politicisation that had produced the popular belief in the legitimacy of their actions.

---

[124] Clarendon, *History*, vol. 2, pp. 319–20.
[125] BL, E145,1 *A declararation of the Lords and Commons ... setting forth the Grounds and Reasons, that necessitate them at this time to take up arms...*, p. 3.
[126] *CJ*/ii/741.

Conclusion

Coming to Colchester they there found a body of 5 or 6 thousand men, who upon their telling of them how displeasing the rifling and pillaging of Sir John Lucas his howse was to the Parliament they expressed much sorrow for what they had done, and said that they would bee willing to obey the Parliament, conceiving that what they had done had been grounded upon an order of Parliament and therefore if the Parliament were safe it was as much as they desired and that they did thereupon disperse themselves and made restitution of divers of those goods they had taken.

Sir Thomas Barrington's report to the House of Commons, 24 August 1642[1]

The Enemie being possest of the house [of Sir John Lucas], exercis'd their brutall rage upon the bare Walls for there was nothing else that remain'd, this being one of the first houses in England which suffred by that fatall libertie of the subiect, which the prophane Vulgar in the beginninge of these disorders soe passionately petition'd the Parliament to graunt them; who (intending to serve themselves of their blind furie, not only suffred, but applauded their violence to their neighbours, but like unskilful Conjurers they often raised those Spirits which they could [not] lay, for under cover of zeale to the cause the poor level'd the Riche of both parties.

Royalist account of the siege of Colchester 1648[2]

[1] BL, Harleian MS 163, fol. 307 v–8 r.
[2] Beaufort House, Gloucestershire, MS Duke of Gloucester. I am grateful to Margaret Richards, the archivist, for making it possible for me to see a copy of this document.

The political struggle to impose a definition on an action and to make it stick is frequently at least as important as the action *per se.*

James Scott[3]

Sir John Lucas survived to the Restoration and better days, but not before having his further share of troubles. Skipping bail, he joined the king at Oxford and fought for him in the civil war, rumours circulating in 1643 that he and his brother Sir Charles Lucas intended to bring royal troops into Essex.[4] In 1645 he had sought and secured a peerage since 'his Affection to his Majesty's service was notorious enough, and ... his Sufferings were so likewise', although Clarendon implied this was in fact the reward for a judicious bribe. Was it significant that Lucas preferred to take his title of Shenfield from another of his Essex manors? He appears not to have returned to St John's – subjected to further destruction during the siege of Colchester – dividing his time between the country and London. Nevertheless, his extensive estates at Colchester continued to bring him into conflict with the town. That his decision not to return to Colchester was motivated as much by concerns for safety as comfort is suggested by his reaction to the outbreak of the second civil war. While his brother Charles led the royal forces to his martyrdom at the siege of Colchester, Sir John – in marked contrast to his behaviour in 1642 – hightailed it up to London, 'the better to avoid all suspicion of engagement' and, according to Harbottle Grimston, he even 'did doe some good offices whilst he was in the Countrey to the Parliam[en]t's party'. Nevertheless, he was briefly in prison again in the 1650s on suspicion of conspiracy against the Cromwellian regime, finding himself on that occasion the butt of humorous verse.[5] Restoration brought Lucas revenge. His name was conspicuously absent from the list of those

---

[3] J. C. Scott, *Domination and the Arts of Resistance: Hidden Transcripts* (New Haven and London, 1990), p. 206.

[4] *CJ/ii/*742, 759, 775, 788–9; M. Keeler, *The Long Parliament, 1640–1641: a Biographical Study of its Members* (Philadelphia, 1954), pp. 246–6, 323; J. H. Hexter, *The Reign of King Pym* (Cambridge, Mass., 1941, repr. 1960), pp. 20 n., 38, 49, 322; BL, E240(17), *A Continuation of certain Speciall and Remarkable passages*, 29 September– Ocober 1642, p. 7; *MR*, p. 5; BL, Additional MS 18777, fol. 6b; *ibid.*, Egerton MS 2646, fol. 311 r.

[5] *The Life of Edward, Earl of Clarendon ... Written by Himself* (3 vols., Oxford, 1709), vol. 1, pp. 187–8; W. H. Black (ed.), *Documents of Letters Patent and other Instruments Passed under the Great Seal of King Charles I at Oxford* (1837), p. 247; London County Council, *Survey of London*, vol. 26 (1970), p. 96 (a reference I owe to the kindness of David Appleby); *LJ/*xii/255; PRO, SP, 21/9, pp. 148, 149; T. Birch (ed.), *A Collection of State Papers of John Thurloe, esq., secretary to the first council of state and afterwards to the two protectorates* (7 vols., 1742), vol. 3, pp. 574, 593; *Notes and Queries*, 7th ser., 10 (1890), pp. 41–2. The appointment to the family living of a minister earlier in trouble for his anti-Parliamentarian views may have added to the attractiveness of Shenfield over St John's: BL, Additional MS 18777, fol. 134.

who signed the 1660 *Declaration and Address of the Gentry of the County of Essex who have adhered to the KING, and suffered Imprisonment, or Sequestration, during the late Troubles* which renounced all thoughts of revenge. At Colchester Lucas had the undoubted satisfaction of having his erstwhile enemies in the Corporation attend the re-interment of his martyr brother at the family church of St Giles and of presiding over a number of suits in which some of his leading opponents were accused of misusing charitable funds. Less happily, his wife died a year later – on the very anniversary of the original attack on St John's. (Did Lucas himself mark the sad coincidence?) Ironically, this ultra-loyalist died in 1671 having opposed and offended his king. It was said that he died of the chagrin he felt when the printed copy of a speech he had made in the Lords when the king was present had been ordered to be burnt by the common hangman. Thus was it possible for a more forthright opponent of the later Stuarts to appropriate a spectral Lord Lucas and to place in the mouth of his ghost a scurrilous condemnation of the Stuart dynasty.[6] But it was for his 'perfect loyalty' that Lucas was longer remembered, securing for himself a place in the printed roll calls of martyrs for the loyal cause that in the later seventeenth century passed for histories of the English Revolution.[7]

What of the other victims? The effects of popular and Parliamentary plundering (the royalists' synonym for sequestration) combined to see the Countess of Rivers end her life in a debtor's gaol.[8] Sir Henry Audley spent three years in France, but returned to attempt to clear himself

---

[6] BL, E669, f25(1); CRO, D/B5, Gb4, fol. 240; D/Y 2/10, pp. 170–1; PRO, C91/8/1, 4, 15, C93/26/2PROB 11/338, fol. 37; *CSPV 1671–1672*, p. xxxvii; *My Lord Lucas His Speech in the House of Peers, Feb. the 22 1670/1 Upon The Reading of the Subsidy Bill the second Time, in the presence of his MAJESTY* (1670); Bodl. Lib., MS Rawlinson D924, fols. 315r–6.

[7] J. Wenlock, *To the most illustrious, High and Mighty Majesty of Charles II . . . the Humble Declaration of JOHN WENLOCK*, Langham (1662), p. 35; W. Dugdale, *The Baronage of England OR An Historical Account Of the Lives and most Memorable Actions of Our English Nobility* (2 vols., 1675–6), vol. 2, pp. 473–4; J. Heath, *A Chronicle of the Late Intestine War in the Three Kingdoms of England, Scotland and Ireland* (1676), p. 180; D. Lloyd, *Memoires of the Lives, Actions, Sufferings and Deaths of Those Noble, Reverend, And Excellent Personages that Suffered in . . . the late intestine Wars* (1668), p. 474; HMC MSS Earl of Portland, 2, p. 137. A less obvious record of his sufferings may find an echo in the writings of his sister Margaret Cavendish and her husband, the Duke of Newcastle: see the orations 'against Civil Warr' and 'against a Tumultuous Sedition', in her *Orations of Divers Sorts, Accomodated to Divers Places* (1662), esp. pp. 262–5. Hostility to citizens' wives, it has been argued, 'remain the focus of animosity throughout . . . [her] plays': S. Wiseman, 'Gender and status in dramatic discourse: Margaret Cavendish, Duchess of Newcastle' in I. Grundy and S. Wiseman (eds.), *Women, Writing, and History 1640–1740* (1992), pp. 176–7; BL, E83(1), *A Declaration Made by the Earl of Newcastle*, E92(17), *A Declaration of the Right Honourable the Earl of Newcastle*.

[8] ERO, Q/SR, 320/61; *LJ*/vi/19, 57, 89, 90; HLRO, HL MB, 10, 22 May, 12 June 1643; *CJ*/ iii/73, 75, 89, 125; *CCC*, p. 1857; Wall, *Long Melford*, p. 22; L. Dow, 'The Savage hatchment at Long Melford', *PSIA*, 26 (1955), p. 217.

(unsuccessfully – he was still under suspicion in the 1650s) of the charge of being a papist. By then he was, surprisingly, uncertain as to whether he had been attacked in 1641 or 1642.[9] What was left of his house was said to have became a farmhouse after further destruction at the siege of Colchester. When he died in 1667, his monument recorded that 'Mindful of his Mortality, he did not rebuild his house destroyed by the fury of the Civil War'.[10] Thomas Newcomen was released from imprisonment in London in December 1642, a decision that might perhaps have owed something to the good offices of his brother, the godly Matthew Newcomen. In 1660, supported by John Lucas, he petitioned the king as 'a long and great sufferer for his Loyalty to your Ma[jes]yie'.[11] Robert Warren survived just long enough to be restored to Long Melford at the Restoration – and to meet renewed opposition to paying tithes. He died in 1661, choosing, perhaps significantly, to be buried at his other living of Borley in Essex. Henry Nevill had been an active supporter of the king in the civil war and perhaps as a result of the costs of this and of sequestration he sold much of his Essex lands, transferring his political activities to the less hostile environment of Leicestershire where his other main estate lay and where he took as his second wife a known recusant. At the Restoration Nevill petitioned for financial compensation and was made a Knight of the Royal Oak.[12] The experiences of other victims were similar: a mixture of flight and sequestration, followed for the fortunate few by recompense at the Restoration.[13] By contrast, Bruno Ryves was well-rewarded for his services to the royal cause. A series of royal preferments culminted in his appointment as Dean of Windsor and Scribe to the Order of the Garter.[14]

[9] PRO, SP, 19A/95/85.

[10] PRO, C2/Chas I/L21/52; SP, 16/482/2, 40; SP, 19A/95/85; SP, 23/65/68, /224/69; L. H. Gant, *The History of Berechurch in the County of Essex* (Colchester, 1930), p. 5; Bodl. Lib., MS Rawlinson A34, fols. 569–71; K. Mabbitt, 'The Audley chapel in Berechurch Church', *TEAS*, 22 (1940), p. 93.

[11] HLRO, MP HL, 30 December 1642; *WR*, pp. 159–60; PRO, SP, 29/9/108 and 108.i. Newcomen had become chaplain to the Earl of Salisbury, who presented him to a living in Hertfordshire, from which another crowd temporarily dispossessed him after the Restoration: W. Le Hardy, ed., *Calendar to the Session Books, Session Minute Books and other Sessions Records, 1658–1700* (9 vols., Hertford, 1905–39), vol. 6, pp. 87–8.

[12] Copinger, *Smith-Carrington Family*, pp. 230–2; B. Elliott, 'A Leicestershire recusant family: the Nevills of Nevill Holt', *RecHist*, 17 (1984), pp. 174–7; PRO, SP, 29/17/51.

[13] P. R. Knell, 'Essex recusant sequestrations during the civil war', *ERec*, 9 (1967); PRO, SP, 23/79/194, /156, p. 17; ESRO, HD, 1538/294/2; *CSPD 1671–2*, p. 58; *CCC*, pp 2402–3; *WR*, pp. 148–9, 158–9, 163, 164; G. Holt, *St Omers and Bruges Colleges, 1593–1730: A Biographical Dictionary* (1979), pp. 105, 203–4; Bodl. Lib., Tanner MS 226, p. 53; Clay, 'Misfortunes of William, fourth Lord Petre'; ERO, Q/S, Ba2/49, 50; Q/SR 320/108, 163 ; BL, Egerton MS 2646, fol. 303; Dawson, 'The Jacobite Southcotes of Witham', *ER*, 63 (1954), p. 145; HLRO, MP HL, 23 June 1660 (petit. Fras Wright).

[14] Ryves continued his defence of the Crown after the Restoration, for example

On Parliament's side, there was some falling away from the cause in the region, despite the successful containment of the attacks, as events into the 1640s seemed to confirm the inversion of social and religious hierarchies which they could be taken to have presaged. In Essex, the Earl of Warwick and Sir Thomas Barrington, both presbyterians, exhibited some anxieties over the later turn of events.[15] At Colchester Harbottle Grimston – another presbyterian who, even before the summer of 1642 had moderated his attacks on the bishops in the face of evidence from there of the activities of religious separatists – had given up his residence in the town by early 1643. Having fallen out with the town, he was writing letters of complaint to the mayor about the threat to his 'reputac[i]on, honestie and Creditt' that could almost have been penned by Sir John Lucas. By the mid-1640s the annual speeches he delivered at the mayor's election with their talk of the looseness of men's lives and unhappy divisions echoed Sir Simonds D'Ewes. In 1649 Grimston resigned his Recordership and, having been imprisoned at Pride's Purge, went into temporary exile. Given this history it is less surprising to find him at the Restoration as Speaker of the Convention Parliament welcoming back Charles II as a deliverer of his people 'out of a Chaos of confusion and misery' or delivering the charge to the Hertfordshire Quarter Sessions in 1663 which reminded his audience of their deliverance 'from plund[e]rings and sequestrations'. But Grimston had not entirely forgotten the lessons of earlier events – only some three months after the Restoration he was urging upon the king the necessity for an act to regulate the cloth industry.[16] Even amongst Colchester's rulers the

appropriating a providentialist politics to preach that unseasonable weather was a sign of God's anger that the king's opponents had been insufficiently punished: *DNB, sub* Ryves.

[15] HMC 7th Report, Lowndes MSS, p. 557; C. Thompson, 'The Earl of Warwick and the county community of Essex', unpub. paper to the University of Essex Local History Centre 1987 Summer School; W. L. F. Nuttall, 'Sir Thomas Barrington and the puritan revolution', *TEAS*, 3rd ser., 2, (1966), pp. 60–82. By 1644 not even the Suffolk county committee was immune from these anxieties: BL, Harleian MS 163, fols. 324, 325; MS 164, fols. 271–2v; 'The papers of Sir Nicholas Bacon in the University of Chicago Library', *List and Indexes Special Series*, 25 (1989), p. 432.

[16] CRO, D/Y, 2/8, pp. 31, 67; Hertfordshire RO Gorhambury, MSS ix A.9, unfol. [1646, 1663]; BL, Harleian MS 164, fol. 816 v; J. T. Cliffe, *Puritans in Conflict: The Puritan Gentry during and after the Civil Wars* (1988), pp. 4–5; W. H. Coates, ed., *The Journal of Sir Simonds D'Ewes from the First Recess of the Long Parliament to the Withdrawal of King Charles from London* (New Haven and London, 1942), p. 150 and n.; D. Brunton and D. H. Pennington, *Members of the Long Parliament* (1954), p. 122; B. Duke Henning, *The House of Commons 1600–1690*, 3 vols. (1983), vol. 2, pp. 445–8; W. Corbett (ed.), *The Parliamentary History of England from the Earliest Period to the Year 1803* (36 vols., 1806–20), 4, 1660–1668 (1808), pp. 56–8; *The SPEECH which the SPEAKER of the House of Commons Made unto the KING In the House of Lords at His Passing of the BILLS 29 August 1660*, pp. 1, 6; *The Speech Which the SPEAKER of the*

fear of a re-enactment of the August events by 'our unruly multitude whoe are ready upon all occasions to worke mischeife, by plundering or otherwise' had shown itself in a marked reluctance to allow the town's trained bands to leave the town.[17] By 1648 troops had to be stationed in Colchester to scotch threats of plundering, now directed against 'the Roundheads and Independants'. During the siege of the town later that year Henry Barrington's house was attacked by royalist troops and known supporters of Parliament were threatened with plunder. The later 1650s even brought reports of an attempt within the town to gain support for a rising in support of a restored monarchy.[18] At the Restoration, it was the turn of Matthew Newcomen, Thomas's presbyterian brother, to be threatened. A Boxted weaver was reported to have said, 'he would never have to work or weave again for they would plunder Colchester ...[and] he would be one of the first to pull Mr Matthew Newcomen of Dedham out of the pulpit and roast him alive'.[19]

Colchester's notoriety meant that for the writer of one royalist newsbook Colchester came to be a title to bestow on other towns in recognition of their disorderly support for Parliament.[20] During the civil war the town had sought to profit from Sir John Lucas's disgrace. In 1650 the sequestration commissioners had written of their failure to establish details of his estate there, 'soe much obscured as the discovery we have made of it was thorow many Jorneyes and much difficulty, it being a service that all men declyne assisting us in ... [and] contracting the most odium upon us'.[21] But after the Restoration a collective amnesia about the attacks was evident within Colchester. In a town where public life continued to be marked by religious and political factionalism, the changed circumstances after 1660 meant that it was found expedient (and perhaps profitable) to allow the public memory of the 1640s to be the miracle of Lucas's brother's execution, over whose site (so early tourists were told) no grass would grow.[22] (Nevertheless,

---

House of LORDS Made unto the KING In the House of LORDS, at His Passing of the BILLS ... 13 September 1660, p. 6.

[17] *LJ*/v/102; *CJ*/iii/137, 184; BL, Egerton MSS 2646, fol. 275 v; 2647, fol. 361 r; HMC 7th Report, Lowndes MSS, p. 562.

[18] BL, Harleian MS 6244, fol. 8; CRO Acc. C32, Box11/14; M. Storey (ed.), *Two East Anglian Diaries, 1641–1729: Isaac Archer and William Coe* (Suffolk Record Society, 36, 1994), p. 46; *The Publick Intelligencer*, no. 207, 12–19 December 1659, sub. 17 December.

[19] CRO, D/B5, Sb2/9, fols. 17, 116 v.

[20] *Mercurius Aulicus* described Newbury as 'the very Colchester of Berkshire', quoted in C. G. Durston, '"Wild as Colts untamed": radicalism in the Newbury area during the early modern period', *Southern History*, 6 (1984), p. 40.

[21] PRO, SP, 23/252/21.

[22] PRO, SP, 23/252/21; E. L. Cutts, *Colchester* (1888), p. 202. As was noted in the early eighteenth century, the grass was kept from growing, 'by art ... for the sake of getting

the taunt of involvement in the attacks made against a political opponent during a dispute in the town in the later seventeenth century, confirms that local knowledge retained an intimate memory of events in 1642.)

After the Restoration, while the ruins of St John's continued to offer Colchester a brooding mnemonic of events in 1642, memory of the August attacks was to be confined to the domain of local history.[23] Nevertheless, the fact that crowd actions had erupted into the public transcript of events in the 1640s meant that they could be rediscovered by national histories in the later nineteenth century.[24]

In 1642 the narrative and meaning of crowd actions was written not by the crowds, but by those in authority. As James Scott has observed, 'the "official transcript" as a social fact presents enormous difficulties for the conduct of historical and contemporary research on subordinate groups. Short of actual rebellion, the great bulk of the archives is consecrated to the official transcript. And on those occasions when subordinate groups do put in an appearance, their presence, motives and behaviour are mediated by the interpretation of dominant elites.'[25] Throughout the early modern period and beyond authority was usually the first historian of crowd actions which it chose, in accordance with its prejudices and presumptions, to label disorder and to prosecute as riot. The problems this has produced in attempting to understand the actions of formally

money by shewing people this lying wonder': 'Further notes on the siege of Colchester', *ER*, 58 (1949), p. 54.

[23] Surprisingly, even those who perhaps had most to gain from keeping alive the memory of the attacks exhibited only partial recall. For example, the pamphlet *To All the ROYALISTS That Suffered for His MAJESTY and to the rest of the Good People of England. The Humble APOLOGY of the English CATHOLICS* (n.p., 1666), cites (p. 14) only the case of Edmund Church. Only a few years after the event, Sir Henry Audley could not remember whether the attacks had been 'in the yere 1641 or 1642': PRO, SP, 19A/95/85.

[24] J. H. Round, 'Colchester during the Commonwealth', *EHR*, 15 (1900), pp. 641–64; T. C. Glines, 'Politics and government in the borough of Colchester, 1600–1693' (Ph.D. thesis, University of Wisconsin, 1974); Dann, Rowland and Wright, 'Civil war and political strife, 1642–48' in D. Stephenson (ed.), *Three Studies in Turbulence* (Colchester, 1976), pp. 7–9. In the more rural locations memories may have lasted longer. John Walker in compiling his *Sufferings* was able at the beginning of the eighteenth century to obtain first-hand accounts from Long Melford of the attack on Robert Warren: Bodl. Lib., MS J. Walker, c1, fol. 309. Memories may have lasted even longer. The family of Sir Richard Hyde Parker, the present owner of Melford Hall, tell a story of the Countess of Rivers throwing the string of pearls which she is depicted wearing in her portrait there into a pond as she fled. When I spoke to the Long Melford Historical Society in 1992 a member of the audience informed me that a place name in the nearby village of Great Waldingfield is thought to derive from the events there in 1642; Waldingfield was in fact the rendezvous for the trained bands assembled to disperse the attackers: BL, Harleian MS 385, fol. 209.

[25] Scott, *Domination*, p. 87.

powerless groups in the past have come to be recognised – though not always acted upon.

If the attempt to read crowds in early modern society faces a general problem, analysis of the 1642 episodes faces particular problems of its own. There was an immediate struggle over the representation of events at Colchester. That authority on the very eve of civil war was fractured meant that the construction of the event was carried out not through the courts, but through competing political narratives. Those in authority in the region chose not to prosecute the crowds and so denied the historian even the lists of names that can provide a starting point for analysis. Stigmatisation as enemies of Parliament also denied the crowds' victims the voice that access to the protection of the courts would have given them. Parliament's first response was to gloss the actions as 'a very acceptable Service to the Commonwealth' by the 'honest Inhabitants' of Colchester and its surrounding area. But the attack on Sir John Lucas and the other victims handed royal propagandists an ideal opportunity to level an accusation of promoting social anarchy against Parliament. It provided a perfect illustration of what in a Declaration issued in October 1642, Charles I highlighted as 'the great pains and endeavours these great pretenders to peace and charity have taken, to raise an implacable hatred between the Gentry and Commonalty ... by rendring all persons of honour, courage, and reputation, odious to the common people, under the stile of Cavaliers ...'[26] Royalists claimed to see little difference between the actions of Parliament and the actions of the crowds. They deliberately conflated the two, later carrying over the language of plunder, itself a recent addition to the language, to describe the actions of the sequestrators with their 'Plund[e]ring warrants'.[27] Royalist narratives, while founded in part on testimony by some of the crowds' victims, clearly constructed their accounts to maximise fears of the 'many-headed monster'. Accounts by authority of the attacks were, in this sense, doubly partisan. These contrasting conspiracies – of silence on Parliament's side and of complaint on the royalists' – mean that writing the history of the attacks remains problematic despite their latter-day notoriety.

Confronted by these problems, an argument has been advanced for the

---

[26] *LJ*/v/319; Husbands, *Exact Collection of all Remonstrances* (1643), p. 649. By early 1643 there were accusations and counter-accusations between Parliament and the King that it was the other side who were encouraging popular plundering of their enemies: F. P. Verney *Memoirs of the Verney Family during the Civil War*, 2 vols. (1892), vol. 2, p. 151; BL, E126(26), *Special Passages and Certain Informations*, 1–8 November 1642.

[27] CUL, Additional MS 33, fol. 25 v; Cliftlands, ' "Well-affected" ', p. 36. 'Sir, my house was ransacked and (to use the new word) plundered': C. D. Gilbert, 'The catholics in Worcestershire 1642–1651', *RecHist*, 20 (3), 1991, p. 342; *The Compact Edition of the Oxford English Dictionary* (2 vols., Oxford, 1971), vol. 2, p. 1023, *sub* 'plunder'.

importance of contextualisation in reading the meaning of the social and political dramas expressed in crowd actions. The analysis has drawn on a triple, and interrelated, contextualisation. First, an interrogation of the immediate context of the construction of competing narratives of the 1642 attacks. Second, an understanding of the meaning of the crowd actions within the context of place and time: the complex local context of economic, social, religious and political structures and the impact upon them of changes, largely derived from the actions of Charles I's government in both church and state. A knowledge of the local context for the attacks makes possible a 'thick description' revealing the layers of conflict that help to explain the particular shape of the crowds' actions as well as the choice of target. Finally, it has been argued that a full understanding of the meaning of the attacks can only be recovered within the context of the process of politicisation in the early 1640s and development of a Parliamentary popular political culture. Thus the attack on Sir John Lucas and others needs to be read both within the context of the micro-politics of Colchester and the wider politics of a region where there was a strong puritan and Parliamentary identity and royalist attempts to raise the Commission of Array on the eve of civil war.

Seen in this light, events at Colchester were only one of a series around the kingdom in which attempts by the king's supporters amongst the aristocracy and gentry to raise the commission of array were prevented by crowd actions. These seem to have been particularly common in the south-west, a region with striking similarities with the Essex and Suffolk cloth districts. At Cirencester in Gloucestershire in August 1642 an attempt by Lord Chandos to raise support for the king was prevented by crowds which, as at Colchester, combined clothworkers and Parliamentary volunteers. In Devon the Earl of Bath's attempt to raise the Commission of Array at South Molton was defeated and he and his followers driven off by a crowd of men and women, said to number upwards of a thousand. In Wiltshire, a similar attempt by the Marquess of Hertford at Marlborough was prevented by popular seizure of the county's arms. The Marquess had met the same response in Somerset from crowds numbered in their thousands.[28]

There are some striking parallels here with events at Colchester. Towns were the sites of all these actions, and the crowds were drawn from regions characterised by the triumvirate of cloth, puritanism and Parlia-

---

[28] D. Rollison, *The Local Origins of Modern Society: Gloucestershire 1500–1800* (1992), pp. 155–8; D. Underdown, *Somerset in the Civil War and Interregnum* (Newton Abbot, 1973), pp. 31–40; J. Wroughton, *A Community at War: The Civil War in Bath and North Somerset 1642–1650* (Bath, 1992), pp. 78–88; Stoyle, *Loyalty and Locality*, pp. 39–40; Manning, *English People*, pp. 166–71.

mentarianism.[29] Moreover, there is evidence that the crowds comprised both poorer and middling sort and that, as in the Somerset episode, there was gentry involvement too. More detailed local work on these episodes might uncover other parallels. For example, events at Marlborough offered the Corporation an opportunity to escape the domination of the Marquess of Hertford, whose nearby house and main estate had made him an overpowerful neighbour. But even without detailed local research it is clear that the most obvious parallel is that actions at Colchester were also politically motivated and aimed at preventing the recruitment of support for the royal cause. All of these episodes can be seen as responses to the intensive political campaign of Parliament to secure support and to organise opposition to incipient royalism. It was Parliament's denunciations of its opponents and declarations calling for their detection and detention that provided an important context for, and legitimation of, these crowd actions.

Although threats of violence and destruction were reported from the other episodes, there appears to have been little to match what happened in Essex and Suffolk in terms of the level of destruction and length of action. What explains the difference? In some cases, notably Somerset, active gentry leadership in the organisation of opposition to the royalists probably prevented independent popular action. The actions there against the royalists were closer to the military skirmishes of the civil war. By contrast, the relative lack of a significant resident gentry in the area of the Stour Valley and the absence of gentry leadership probably afforded less opportunity to control the eastern crowds.[30] Nevertheless, it is difficult to judge whether there was a real collapse of authority in the region that permitted the attacks to spread. The evidence might suggest that there was at least a temporary collapse of authority after the attack on Lucas in the face of rumours about the popish threat. But as we have seen, there is also evidence to suggest that the consequences of the attacks were not unwelcome either to the local authorities, as at Colchester, or to the region's Parliamentarian rulers.

Several historians point to the levels of economic distress in explaining the extent of the attacks in the region. According to Buchanan Sharp,

---

[29] This perhaps lends greater weight to the argument over regional political cultures started by David Underdown's work that the key variable in explaining the distribution of popular Parliamentarianism was the presence of the cloth industry, rather than simply a wood-pasture ecology: Stoyle, *Loyalty and Locality*; M. Ingram, 'From Reformation to toleration: popular religious cultures in England, 1540–1690' in T. Harris (ed.), *Popular Culture in England, 1500–1850* (1995), p. 104.

[30] C. Holmes, 'The county community in Stuart historiography', *JBS*, 19 (1980), p. 73; J. Spratt, 'Agrarian conditions in Norfolk and Suffolk 1600–1650' (MA thesis, University of London, 1935), map facing p. 101.

'the riots in the Stour Valley of Essex ... had much more to do with the depressed state of the New Drapery and the chronic poverty of the clothworkers than it did with what one historian argues was a popular, pro-Parliament sentiment'. Clive Holmes too has argued that 'the motive, at least in the Stour Valley, was an economic crisis of serious dimensions'.[31] Depression in the cloth trade was not however confined to Essex and Suffolk. The problem with accounts that emphasise the role of economic distress is that they threaten to deny a role for an active popular agency. In this reading crowds are mobilised by external stimuli. But the responses of those affected by crises are never blind. Necessarily, they are shaped by the popular understanding and construction of the causes of the crisis.

For other historians the answer to the distinctiveness of the 1642 attacks in the eastern region is to be found in the relationship between economic distress and class hostility. Brian Manning, the historian referred to by Buchanan Sharp, suggests that it is the politics of class that provided a popular understanding of the causes of crisis. Writing in 1976 he argued that,

the well-to-do remained concerned primarily with political and religious issues, but amongst the lower classes bread-and-butter questions loomed larger. At the same time the economic distress caused the middling and poorer people to involve themselves in politics and to take part in demonstrations. They would not have become so involved if the crisis had been concerned purely with political and religious questions. But once they were involved, the nature of the crisis changed: economic questions advanced from the rear to the front of the stage, and the mere fact of the involvement of the people changed political conflicts and religious antagonisms into social conflicts and class antagonisms.[32]

In 1996 Manning's argument appeared to have shifted to allow a larger role for politics in the August attacks: 'these were not just food riots and were more than anti-popery riots, for they were politicised by the crisis between king and Parliament and motivated by support for Parliament'. (Even this statement is not without its problems since it seems to dismiss food riots as little more than reactions to economic distress and to ignore the evidence of the complex politics of subsistence that could inform such actions.)[33] Having acknowledged the role of popular support for Parlia-

---

[31] Sharp, 'Popular protest', p. 298; Holmes, *Eastern Association*, p. 44.

[32] Manning, *English People*, p. 102.

[33] E. P. Thompson, 'The moral economy of the English crowd in the eighteenth century', *P&P*, 50 (1971), pp. 76–136; J. Walter, 'Subsistence strategies, social economy and the politics of subsistence in early modern England' in A. Hakkinen (ed.), *Just a Sack of Potatoes? Crisis Experience in European Societies, Past and Present* (Helsinki, 1992).

ment, Manning goes on to argue however that, 'it was not quite as simple as that: it is true that the crowds were selective in their targets, however they did not confine themselves to searching for arms, and the violence of their assaults on the property of the wealthy landlords is indicative of underlying class hatred which cloaked itself in legitimacy by choosing to attack those aristocrats who could be identified by reference to Parliament's generalised denunciations of "papists" and "malignants".'[34] This later argument raises the possibility that the crowds, while following Parliament's policy for neutralising those who they were told threatened their livelihoods and liberties, could nevertheless have appropriated the legitimation it afforded to license an attack on their betters.

Clearly crowds are complex, polyphonic phenomena. Any crowd contains within it groups and individuals with varying motives. Crowds are events and their intentions may change over time. In this sense there can never be one correct reading of crowd action. Undoubtedly, the presence of some of those involved in the attacks was to be explained by the economic distress they faced; others would have welcomed the chance that collective anonymity offered to strike back at their betters. An expression of hostility towards their wealthier betters was a strand in later social protest concerned with confessional identities.[35] Yet others in the crowds must have been attracted by the excitement of the event and the opportunities it offered for opportunistic plunder. Nevertheless, for crowds to form out of diverse groups and diverse aims there needs to be a shared meaning to their actions. Moreover, the culture of obedience that lay at the heart of early modern political culture placed a particular premium on crowds developing a sense of legitimacy for their actions in order to mobilise successfully. The collapse of authority after 1640 might have rendered legitimation less necessary, the force of anti-popish rumour made it nugatory in 1642. But for individuals to become a crowd they need a language with which they can forge a unity.

In 1642 that language was both anti-popish and, for a time, pro-Parliamentarian, part of what for a slightly later period Bernard Capp has christened a 'new-model' popular culture.[36] Its use might help to

---

[34] B. Manning, *Aristocrats, Plebeians and Revolution in England 1640–1666* (1996), pp. 49–50.

[35] See, for example, T. Harris, *London Crowds in the Reign of Charles II: Propaganda and Politics from the Restoration until the Exclusion Crisis* (Cambridge, 1987), esp. ch. 4; Holmes, 'Sacheverell riots', pp. 55–85; N. Rogers, 'Popular protest in early Hanoverian London', *P&P*, 79 (1978), pp. 70–100; Rogers, 'The urban opposition to Whig oligarchy, 1720–60' in M. and J. Jacob (eds.), *The Origins of Anglo-American Radicalism* (1984), pp. 143–5; G. Rude, 'The Gordon riots: a study of the rioters and their victims' in his *Paris and London in the Eighteenth Century* (1970), pp. 268–92.

[36] B. Capp, 'Popular culture and the English civil war', *History of European Ideas*, 10 (1989), p. 32.

explain the presence of the godly and 'well-affected' who had already demonstrated their agency in the popular iconoclastic attacks on the Laudian church that had greeted the collapse of the period of Personal Rule. That it was also shared by the clothworkers is evidence of its wider reception. Sir Thomas Barrington informed the Commons that he had found the crowds, 'threatening to plunder all the Papists .., which (they conceived) were the causers of all these troubles and distractions in the Kingdome, and were the occasions that they, their wives and children were brought into great want and extremity (by the great decay of trading)', an identification of the causes of their problems repeated in the later, threatened winter wave of attacks.[37] The discipline that the crowds demonstrated in their selection of targets provides important evidence of the wider subscription to this belief. Historians have made some play of the reports originating from Suffolk of attacks on 'the houses aswell of protestants as Papists'. Clive Holmes, for example, draws on such evidence in support of his argument that the attacks were 'unpolitical incidents'.[38] But this is based on a misunderstanding. According to the account in the newsbook, apparently drawing on a letter from Sudbury which first notes such attacks, the crowds attacked protestants, 'alleadging them to be persons disaffected to the Parliament'.[39] For all the fears expressed, the crowds' victims were either vulnerable to the charge of being promoters of popery or opponents of Parliament.

In the case of the crisis of the early 1640s then the dominant discourses of anti-popery and Parliamentarianism helped both to construct and to articulate an understanding of events and, therefore, of appropriate responses. The clothworkers undoubtedly received this discourse in terms of a classed reading. It was the machinations of malignants and papists in preventing a settlement between king and Parliament that explained popular distress. But the clothworkers did not separate out the economic as a distinct sphere. Their reactions to the events of the 1640s were also shaped by the experiences and values of the communities in which they lived, communities in which the relationship between puritanism and cloth was often marked. For the clothworkers at the heart of the crowds the activities of papists explained the problems they faced in their industry and the challenge to their religion and liberties. Popery presented a potent threat to lives and liberties, as well as to livelihoods.

---

[37] BL, E114(30), *A Message*, p. 1; BL, E242(31), *A Continuation of Certaine Speciall and Remarkable Passages, from both Houses of PARLIAMENT, and other Parts of the Kingdome*, no. 21, 24 November–1 December 1642, p. 6. The repetition offers some check on the possibilities of Barringon having himself made interpolations into the reported speech for political purposes of his own.
[38] Holmes, *Eastern Association*, p. 44.   [39] BL, E114(36), *Special Passages*, p. 22.

In his most recent statement on class and popular political action within the English Revolution Brian Manning argues rightly that, 'it is a false dichotomy in conservative historiography to set an interpretation in terms of religion against one in terms of class, and to regard religious explanation of the conflict as an alternative to social explanation ...'[40] If *Mercurius Rusticus* is to be believed (and that must remain a large if) then the discourse of puritan preaching could have been appropriated by the people within the region to denounce their betters. This was the fear of Sir Simonds D'Ewes who had told his fellow MPs before the attacks that some of the 'meaner sort ... beginn alreadie to alledge, that all being of one mould ther is no reason that some should have so much and others soe little'.[41] The radical potential of both the strands of Christian egalitarianism and saintly zeal that could be read out of the Bible had been seen in earlier continental movements and they were to inform the politics of the radical groups that emerged in the later stages of the English Revolution.

But the attacks of 1642 were not followed by the outright attack on the gentry that D'Ewes had predicted and many feared. That legitimation then was provided by the discourses of anti-popery and popular Parliamentarianism meant that any centrifugal tendencies were more easily contained within that discourse. This might permit attacks against Parliament's opponents among the landed classes, but not its supporters.[42] When there was an attempt to revive the attacks towards the end of 1642 and it was reported out of Suffolk that the poorer sort 'begin to argue the case, whether in this great necessity it be not lawfull, for to take something from those that have bin the cause to deprive them of all manner of livelyhood as to perish for hunger', the report made clear that this threat continued to be directed against 'Papists and malignants'.[43] The move to open conflict that the civil war brought forced royalists in the region to abandon their estates if they wished to join the king. Parliament moved quickly to claim the estates of the king's supporters for itself, thus forestalling both the need and opportunity for further popular action. Sequestration gave Parliament's supporters among the office-holding middling sort legitimate grounds to interfere with the gentry's estates and, although this was not the intention, the poorer sort

---

[40] Manning, *Aristocrats, Plebeians*, p. 4.   [41] BL, Harleian MS 163, fol. 153 v.

[42] In Devon in late 1642 there were similar reports of threatened 'combustions' amongst the county's clothworkers, but the historian of civil war popular politics in the county notes, 'it is significant that – on the one or two occasions when gentlemen were attacked or abused ... it was because they were Royalists, rather than because they were gentlemen': Stoyle, *Loyalty and Locality*, pp. 145–6.

[43] BL, E242(31) *Continuation of Certaine Speciall and Remarkable Passages*, 24 November–1 December 1642, p. 6.

licence to trespass.[44] But the estates were to be for the use of the Commonwealth, not commoners. There may well have been those in the crowds who used the 'official transcript' of Parliamentarian rhetoric to legitimise an attack on their betters.[45] Nevertheless the legitimisation of protest within the framework of anti-popery and popular Parliamentarianism helped to ensure the restoration of order within the constraints of a dominant discourse of political, not social, conflict.

Recent work on class has re-emphasised the importance of political action in constructing, rather than confirming, class identities. In 1642 Parliament's successful restoration of order and re-statement of the official transcript of how the attacks should be read made impossible collective action based on the radical appropriations of puritan preaching. In this sense, we can only guess at the possibilities that 1642 might have unleashed. Had the attacks come later in the history of the Revolution there may have been other, more radical discourses which the attackers could have appropriated. But they did not. Even then the robustness of the structures of local rule – maintained by a middling sort which had secured its economic interests in the development of agrarian capitalism by an alliance with, rather than opposition to, the landed class – and the resilience of the cultural hegemony that the landed classes exercised might have made their successful radicalisation and generalisation unlikely.[46] Moreover, knowledge of the tradition of protest in the century before these attacks suggests that many of the crowd actions read as attacks on the landed class were in fact attacks on individual members of, or as in the example of Ket's rebellion, sections of, the gentry for their failure to act like true gentlemen. Gentlemen were attacked for what they were not, rather than for what they were. In 1642 gentlemen (and others) were attacked for what they were: papists and malignants. It was their confessional and political identities that determined their fate.

---

[44] BL, Additional MS 18777, fol. 10b; Clarendon, *History*, vol. 2, pp. 328–9; Cliftlands, ' "Well-affected" ', ch. 3; C. O' Riordan, 'Popular exploitation of enemy estates in the English Revolution', *History*, 78 (1993), pp. 183–200.

[45] For the notion of the 'official transcript' and its relationship to the organisation of resistance, see J. C. Scott, *Weapons of the Weak: Everyday Forms of Peasant Resistance* (New Haven and London, 1985); Scott, *Domination and the Arts of Resistance: Hidden Transcripts* (New Haven and London, 1990). That by 1648 troops were having to be stationed in Colchester to scotch threats of plundering now directed against 'the Roundheads and Independants' might argue for a more contingent relationship between the clothworkers' socio-economic position and political identity: BL, Harleian MS 6244, fol. 8.

[46] J. Walter, 'The impact on society: a world turned upside down' in J. Morrill (ed.), *The Impact of the English Civil War* (1991), pp. 104–22; J. Morrill and J. Walter, 'Order and disorder in the English Revolution' in Fletcher and Stevenson, *Order and Disorder in Early Modern England* (Cambridge, 1985), pp. 137–65.

One final strand of analysis has been employed to negotiate the difficulties posed by the 'official transcript'. A 'thick description' of the crowds' actions offers confirmation of this reading of the 1642 crowds. Early modern crowds were often heavily inscribed with ritualised forms of behaviour whose semiotics provide evidence of attitudes and intentions less contaminated by (literally) authoritative accounts. In the case of the events of 1642 most accounts are second-hand and general. They offer a stereotype of riotous crowds intent on plunder. We lack the detailed and occasionally fine-grained descriptions which depositions in legal records sometimes provide of the shape which other forms of early modern crowd actions took. The few depositions we do have record what was seen or done, but not what was said. Their structure is given them by the examining authorities' concern to investigate acts they construed as theft. Nevertheless, as we have seen, the evidence of the nature of the attack on Robert Warren at Melford shows how the crowd could draw on the symbols of an inversionary popular culture to express their suspicions and to define the nature of their confessional community. Even though we lack similarly detailed descriptions for most of the attacks, it is still possible to suggest how the symbolic statements made by the crowds' shaping of their actions offer evidence of the political nature of the attacks.

The crowds were very selective in their targets. They attacked those whose actions were thought to threaten their physical and spiritual security: malignants (proto-royalist), ministers whose aggressive support for the ceremonialism of the 1630s was taken as evidence of popery and, above all, catholics. That the crowds did not simply plunder the houses of their victims but, where we have evidence, wrought large-scale destruction offers further clues to the meanings behind their actions. This level of destruction may provide a parallel with the untiling and destruction of brothels in the sixteenth and seventeenth centuries and meeting houses in the seventeenth and eighteenth centuries by early modern crowds.[47] These were actions, with roots in officially prescribed policy, which asserted a popular claim to police the moral and confessional boundaries of their communities and sought literally to remove the sources of moral or religious pollution. An earlier example of crowd action by soldiers recruited for the Scottish campaign neatly brings out this association. A woman convicted as a reputed prostitute before a mock court staged by the soldiers had been ducked in a well. This was in

[47] K. J. Lindley, 'Riot prevention and control in early Stuart London', *TRHS*, 5th ser., 33 (1983), p. 109–26; Harris, *London Crowds*, p. 52; Harris, 'The bawdy house riots of 1688', *Historical Journal*, 29 (1986), pp. 537–56; Holmes, 'Sacheverell riots', pp. 64–7; J. Stevenson, *Popular Disturbances in England 1700–1870* (1979), pp. 20–1.

itself a popular appropriation of a gendered punishment used by local courts. But the soldiers' choice of a well from which the catholics had drawn their holy water and their reported taunt that 'when the papist come for holy watter instead of holy watter they shall have [w]hore's watter' suggests a popular ability to deliver complex messages about pollution, defilement and cleansing.[48]

Thus the level of destruction in the attacks of 1642 which excited contemporary comment and which was reported as plunder may also be read as an attempt to remove the polluting presence of popery which providentialist preaching and Parliamentary politics had identified as the cause of the country's present woes.[49] It was a case of confessional purging, examples of which abounded in post-Reformation Europe. Popery threatened society. It did so at one remove by provoking the punishments of a jealous Old Testament God for the country's failure to purify the church. Of this, the poor harvests and pestilence of the 1630s offered recent and painful evidence. The persistence of popery offered a more immediate threat in the form of a fifth column of papists intent on the slaughter of their godly neighbours. The belief that 'the towne was in jeopardie' and that the magistrates by their inactivity 'would suffer theire throats to be cutt' was behind another plebeian attempt 'at a disarming of Papists' by a cobbler and others in Southampton in early September 1642 that, had it been realised, might have offered direct parallels with events in Essex and Suffolk in 1642.[50] It is worth recalling that 'plebeian' catholics were also attacked in the summer of 1642 and that those who offered the victims refuge, were threatened with destruction of their houses, something which earlier analyses of the episode emphasising the class-specific nature of the attacks do not acknowledge.[51]

This reading of the shape of the crowd's actions prompts comparisons with other forms of crowd action and their legitimations. At Colchester the act of carrying the arms from the Lucas household and depositing them at the town hall doubtless reflected the crowds' concern over the threat that an armed and pro-royalist household posed.[52] But their

---

[48] BL, Additional MS 21,935, fol. 90 v. For the use of ducking by the courts, see J. W. Spargo, *Juridical Folklore in England Illustrated by the Cucking-School* (Durham, North Carolina, 1944).

[49] Cf. N. Z. Davis, 'The rites of violence: religious riot in sixteenth-century France', *P&P*, 59(1973), p. 59.

[50] R. C. Anderson (ed.), *The Book of Examinations and Depositions 1622–1644, vol. 4, 1639–1644* (Southampton, 1936), pp. 42–3.

[51] In the case of the attack upon the mother of the Earl of Portland 'the poore peoples houses who offer'd to receiue her [were also] threatned to be pulled downe': HLRO, MP HL, 6 September 1642 (petit. Earl of Portland); Stoneyhurst College, Stoneyhurst MSS, MSS Angliae, 7, fols. 122–3.

[52] HLRO, Braye-Terling MSS, no. 11.

actions and choice of destination suggest a parallel with the relationship between popular involvement in the policing of the grain market and the sense of legitimacy that was such a marked characteristic of participation in the crowd actions over food.[53] For example, crowds in the West Country in 1614 asserted a right to police the grain market by seizing grain being taken out of the region and depositing it at the houses of local officials.[54] Both this and the action at Colchester demonstrated a popular claim to participate in the regulation of the commonwealth. Whether the Colchester crowd's action implied a criticism of the inactivity of the authorities, as was certainly the case in the West Country actions, cannot be known.

Crowds who protested over food derived a sense of legitimation from, and often shaped their actions in accordance with, government policy. Similarly, the 1642 crowds could derive the right to police the confessional boundaries of local society from the role accorded them by authority. The legal responsibility of local communities to present local recusants to the courts, a responsibility frequently re-iterated and undertaken in the region in the two years before the attacks, underwrote this belief. As the 'souldiers, country clowns and women' were reported to have declared after the attack on Lucas, 'that now they were met together, the Parliament and Country expected it of them to deale in the same manner with Papists'.[55] Given the failure to neutralise the popish threat, crowds in Essex and Suffolk may also have felt that they were justified in acting in the absence of action by authority. According to a newsbook report, the seizure of money, plate and ammunition from catholic households by the Mayor, townsmen *and* people of Brackley in Northamptonshire in August 1642 had been met with thanks from Parliament for 'their diligent care to preserve the peace of the Weal publick in disarming of Papists'.[56] The belief that inactivity by authority justified activity by the crowd was certainly to be found in acts of religious violence in the French Wars of Religion. Indeed, there are striking parallels in particular between the events of 1642 and events in the St Bartholomew's Massacre. The catholic crowds drew legitimation from both ordinances of the Parlement and pulpit preaching and, as at Colchester, were mobilised by those whose service in the City militia and

---

[53] Thompson, 'Moral economy'; Walter, 'Grain riots and popular attitudes to law'. For the increased activity in the presentation of catholics see above, pp. 226–7.

[54] WRO, Q/S Gt Roll T 1614/161, 167–71.

[55] Stoneyhurst College, Stoneyhurst MSS, MSS Angliae, 7, fol. 122.

[56] BL, E202(43), *A True and Perfect Diurnall of the passages in Parliament, from Nottinghamshire, Ashby and Leicester and other parts* (my emphasis in text). It would be helpful to know more about this episode; the brief description in the newsbook of those involved in the action suggests a very close parallel with the action against Sir John Lucas.

government gave them authority to command. In early modern England, as in early modern France, crowds could derive the right to police confessional boundaries from the role accorded them by the State and from the incitement offered by zealous preaching. In seventeenth-century Colchester, as in later sixteenth-century Paris, religious violence 'was didactic and coercive as well as vindictive'.[57]

We have one final description of the shape of the crowds' actions. After the crowds had destroyed much of Lucas's property, 'to shew that their rage will know no bounds, and that nothing is sacred or venerable which they dare not to violate, they breake into *St Giles* his Church, open the vault where his ancestors were buryed and with Pistols, swords, and Halberts, transfix the Coffins of the dead.'[58] According to one historian, William Hunt, who draws on the episode, 'the corpses were dismembered, and the rioters paraded through the town with the hair of the dead in their caps.' According to the account from which Hunt draws this detail, the attackers:

broake open the tombe of their [Lucas] Ancestors, amongst whom the Lady Lucas and Lady Killigrew, the mother and Sister of the present Lord Lucas, were so lately buried, that their sinues and haire were unconsum'd. These Slaves tore asunder the[i]r ioynts, and threw them about the vaulte with prophane scoffs at the resurrection, and spightfull reproaches of the decencie, which they call'd the luxurie of their lives, (the inveterate scandall w[hi]ch the poore cast upon the rich). Then they cutt off their hayre, and wore it in their hatts in triumph.

These 'rituals of collective obscenity' might be read as representing the most outright challenge to the social hierarchy in the whole episode. Like the 'revolutionary exhumations' in the Spanish civil war in the twentieth century, they might be taken to signal the confrontation of old, and the celebration of new, values symbolised by the repudiation of even 'common decency'.[59] Since it has been argued for this period that the funeral monuments of the gentry served to express their status and to secure honour for, and the continuity of, the blood lineage, then these actions might indeed be read as a symbolic challenge to the gentry.[60] And

---

[57] Davis, 'Rites of violence', pp. 51–91; B. B. Diefendorf, *Beneath the Cross: Catholics and Huguenots in Sixteenth-Century Paris* (New York, 1991), esp. chs. 9 and 10 and pp. 65–6, 103. Of course, one major difference was that the English crowds did not kill their victims.

[58] *MR*, p. 3.

[59] B. Lincoln, 'Revolutionary exhumations in Spain, July 1936', *Comparative Studies in Society and History*, 27 (1985), pp. 241–60.

[60] N. Llewellyn, 'Claims to status through visual codes: heraldry on post-Reformation funeral monuments' in S. Anglo (ed.), *Chivalry in the Renaissance* (Woodbridge, 1990), pp. 145–60.

that indeed is how they were intended to be read – by Bruno Ryves from whose pen comes the only description of the attack on the vault in *1642*. We cannot discount the detail of 'rioters' wearing the corpses' hair as favours in their caps. But if this happened, it happened in 1648 during the siege of Colchester, from which the above account is taken, and not in 1642, as the reference to *Lord* Lucas's mother – very much alive in 1642 – should have made clear.[61] We cannot say that the attack on the family's vault did not happen in 1642. But that the same events were said to have occurred both in 1642 and in 1648 might raise a question mark over the veracity of Ryves' account. Like the transgressions of gender and social space represented by the 'rude' intrusion into the Lucas 'Ladies Chamber', 'violations of the Sepulchers of the dead' – also proscribed by the laws of war – offered Ryves' readers compelling evidence of the threat represented by Parliament's unleashing of the many-headed monster.[62]

Parliament's initial message to the attackers that 'they have done a very acceptable Service to the Commonwealth, and such a one as doth express a great Zeal to their Religion and Liberties' might equally be read as an attempt to represent the initial attacks as favourably as possible.[63] But an attentiveness to the selectivity that the crowds showed in their choice of targets and the fashioning of their actions suggests that the attacks were indeed informed by and reflected a political awareness that accounts emphasising the role of economic distress miss. There has been a growing recognition of the level of political awareness capable of being displayed by those below the level of the gentry. But in the case of the English Revolution there has been perhaps a danger that the exciting recent work on popular politics has encouraged a greater concern for the contours, rather than the content, of popular allegiances.[64] Events in the summer of 1642, set within the broader context of popular responses to the politics of the 1630s, provide evidence of a popular political culture that informed and legitimised the crowds' actions.[65]

At the core of this popular political culture were religion and history. The protestant legacy stretching back to the Reformation and the

---

[61] Neither of the sources cited by William Hunt – *MR* and the Mayor of Colchester's letter – provide any support for the claim: Hunt, *Puritan Moment*, p. 302. Hunt has clearly transposed 1648 for 1642, drawing on, but not citing, the account of the siege: HMC MSS Duke of Beaufort, pp. 19–30. The quotation above is taken from a xerox copy of the original manuscript at Badminton House.

[62] *MR*, A4 v; Donagan, 'Atrocity', p. 1142.   [63] *LJ/v/319*.

[64] D. Underdown, *Revel, Riot and Rebellion: Popular Politics and Culture in England 1603–1660* (Oxford, 1985); J. S. Morrill, 'The ecology of allegiance in the English civil wars' in his *The Nature of the English Revolution* (1993), pp. 224–41; Stoyle, *Loyalty and Locality*. But see now, Underdown, *Freeborn People*.

[65] Walter, 'Crown and crowd'.

corresponding history of popish persecution and plotting shaped popular reactions to events in a region noted for the level of support for the godly, puritan cause. The Bible, especially in the pages of the Old Testament, offered both justification for, and examples of, a people active in defence of their faith. The example of Edward Neale, that opened chapter five, citing Jeremiah – 'I will prepare destroyers against thee' – as justification for an attack on the local ceremonialist and Arminian clergy or of Stephen Marshall preaching on the text of 'Curse ye Meroz' suggests the uses to which these messages could be put.[66] Popular political culture was informed also by a tradition of popular political participation. There was popular participation in a double sense. The nature of the early modern English state with its lack of a formal bureaucracy, dependence on policing from below and rule through both the agency and institutions of the law gave the people an active role in governing the commonwealth. The monarchy's concern to translate power into authority by justifying its rule in terms of the needs of the commonwealth and its people, and the frequency with which this message was re-stated – publicly and in a variety of fora – to ensure popular co-operation meant that participation in governing afforded also an instruction in the codes of government. The widening franchise, product both of impersonal economic trends and of deliberate decisions by a Commons suspicious of the Crown's intentions towards it, meant that groups below the gentry had the vote and participated in the election (rather than witnessing the selection) of MPs in contests where from the 1620s on anti-popery provided a powerful political language.[67] The growth of print culture ensured the wider dissemination of information, the growth in popular literacy its wider reception.

Events in the English Revolution significantly enlarged the scope for an active popular political role. After 1640 the collapse of censorship meant that pulpit and pamphlet could inform a yet wider public.[68] The very fact of the fracturing of authority rendered allegiance a question of choice rather than of custom. Parliament, needing more active popular support and participation than anything envisaged in the monarchical

---

[66] C. Hill, *The English Bible and the Seventeenth-Century Revolution* (1993), esp. ch. 3.

[67] D. Hirst, 'Elections and the electorate 1603–1642' (Ph.D. thesis, University of Cambridge, 1973), pp. 198–9. For a suggestive analysis of the political significance of anti-popery, see R. Cust and P. G. Lake, 'Sir Richard Grosvenor and the rhetoric of magistracy', *Bulletin Institute Historical Research*, 54 (1981), pp. 42–4.

[68] Cust, 'Politics and the electorate' in Cust and Hughes, *Conflict*, pp. 134–67; D. Hirst, *The Representative of the People? Voters and Voting in England under the early Stuarts* (Cambridge, 1975); R. Cust, 'News and politics in early seventeenth-century England', *P&P*, 112 (1986), pp. 60–90. For a revealing example from Suffolk in October 1642 of the arrival of printed news in local society leading to a discussion in a shop as to whether Charles I was a tyrant, see Bodl. Lib., Bankes MS 52/31.

state, informed (and politicised) the people by a stream of printed declarations and devised the political oath of the Protestation to secure their allegiance. We have seen how popular reception and appropriation of the Protestation promoted an active political role for the people within the Revolution. Puritan preaching and its construction of a godly people reinforced the idea of an active citizenship that had always been part of puritan teaching. All these developments converged to open a space for a more active popular political culture. The attack on papists and malignants in the summer of 1642 was one consequence of these developments.

If this analysis is correct, it suggests that historians need to re-consider how they have analysed these and other civil war crowds. Arguments about the motivation behind popular actions in the English Revolution too often draw on the evidence of elite contemporaries, representing as straight reporting what should more properly be seen as evidence of elite perceptions or, more often, prejudices. Grand narratives which use particular episodes of crowd actions to support larger theses run the risk of misrepresenting or misunderstanding the event if they ignore or suppress the contexts within which those actions took place or fail to question the provenance of the evidence on which they draw. Earlier discussions of popular allegiances within the English Revolution have identified a quartet of categories – deference, localism, class and regional cultures – and sought to discriminate between them.[69] A study of the crowds of 1642 suggests that instead of seeking to disaggregate the causes of their creation and to give primacy to any one factor – in this case, economic distress or latent class hostility – as their motivation, we need to take seriously the politics behind the crowds' actions. Then we can begin to see how the language within which this politics was expressed could accommodate these other factors, not as a cloak, but as an integral part of the analysis it sponsored.[70] It would be a mistake to over-explain crowd actions. But the actions of the crowds in 1642 were informed by a politics of rights, not least the right of the people to take action in their defence.

---

[69] Underdown, *Revel*, chs. 1, 3–4.

[70] Compare Natalie Zemon Davis' plea that the real motivation in early modern French religious violence should not be reduced to the social: Davis, 'Rites of violence', p. 54, and in J. Estebe and N. Z. Davis, 'Debate. The rites of violence: religious riot in sixteenth-century France', *P&P*, 67 (1975), pp. 127–35.

Index

Past and Present Publications

General Editor: JOANNA INNES, *Somerville College, Oxford*

Land and Popular Politics in Ireland: County Mayo from the Plantation to the Land War, Donald E. Jordan Jr.*

The Castilian Crisis of the Seventeenth Century: New Perspectives on the Economic and Social History of Seventeenth Century Spain, I. A. A. Thompson and Bartolomé Yun Casalilla

The Culture of Clothing: Dress and Fashion in the Ancien Régime, Daniel Roche †*

The Sense of the People: Politics, Culture and Imperialism in England, 1715–1785, Kathleen Wilson*

Witchcraft in Early Modern Europe: Studies in Culture and Belief, edited by Jonathan Barry, Marianne Hester and Gareth Roberts*

Fair Shares for All: Jacobin Egalitarianism in Practice, Jean-Pierre Gross

The Wild and the Sown: Botany and Agriculture in Western Europe, 1350–1850, Mauro Ambrosoli

Witchcraft Persecutions in Bavaria: Popular Magic, Religious Zealotry and Reason of State in Early Modern Europe, Wolfgang Behringer

Understanding Popular Violence in the English Revolution: The Colchester Plunderers, John Walter

* Also published in paperback
† Co-published with the Maison des Sciences de l'Homme, Paris